POST-CRITICAL CRIMINOLOGY

Edited by
Thomas O'Reilly-Fleming
University of Windsor

Prentice Hall Canada Inc.
Scarborough, Ontario

Canadian Cataloguing in Publication Data

Main entry under title:

Post-critical criminology

ISBN 0–13–101395–5

1. Criminology. 2. Criminal justice, Administration of.
I. O'Reilly-Fleming, Thomas, 1951-

HV6025.P68 1996   364   C95–931742–2

© 1996 Prentice-Hall Canada Inc., Scarborough, Ontario
A Viacom Company

Prentice-Hall, Inc., Englewood Cliffs, New Jersey
Prentice-Hall International (UK) Limited, London
Prentice-Hall Hispanoamericana, S.A., Mexico City
Prentice-Hall of India Private Limited, New Delhi
Prentice-Hall of Japan, Inc., Tokyo
Simon & Schuster Asia Private Limited, Singapore
Editora Prentice-Hall do Brasil, Rio de Janeiro

ISBN: 0-13-101395-5

Acquisitions Editor: Marjorie Munroe
Developmental Editor: Shoshana Goldberg
Production Editor: Avivah Wargon
Production Coordinator: Deborah Starks
Cover Image: Olena Serbyn

1 2 3 4 5   RRD   99 98 97 96

Printed and bound in the USA

To my dear mother, Alice Fleming

Contents

Preface

Post-Critical Criminology represents the collective effort of a group of critical scholars across Canada to move beyond the structures of critical criminology that, by the end of the 1980s, had been exhausted at both theoretical and empirical levels.

While the promise of critical criminology had largely faded by this time the measured idealism of its advocates still flourished within the academy. Increasingly, critical criminologists have had to struggle to maintain the integrity of their discipline from attacks emanating both from within and without. Ensconced largely within departments of sociology in Canada, criminology programs experienced dramatic growth in the 1980s. While capitalizing on this increasing student demand, sociologists have increasingly intruded on the subject matter of criminology, trying to reshape it in their own image as cyclical fiscal crises cause a restructuring of institutions. Part of the *raison d'être* of this volume is to reassert the distinctness of at least one part of the criminological enterprise.

This book has been organized in the following way. First, the introductory chapter provides a synopsis of some recent waves of critical criminology, which leads to an overview of the remaining chapters. The chapters deal with a diversity of post-critical issues, which expand the boundaries of current theoretical forms. They include the social construction of delinquency, street crime, the use of the law as an instrument of reform, the social control of women, the historical development of policing, the consideration of progressive theoretical forms, the court process, and youth school violence. These initial chapters are followed by contributions on feminism/ethical issues and the criminalization of women; masculinities and criminal victimization; domestic violence and mandatory arrest; the impact of the Charter on aboriginal Canadians, racism, and women's rights; crime prevention; the penal system; law and colonialism; and the future of criminological theory. In selecting and ordering the chapters there has not been an attempt to artificially categorize these issues within subsections; rather, the chapters are bound together by a focus on pushing the cutting edge of critical criminological theory slightly further in the appropriate direction. While the issues do move from a consideration of wider societal patterns to issues of rights, gender, race, and theory, it is more instructive to conceive of the book as one that can provide a basis for students to be introduced to the direction of post-critical criminology.

The chapters have been written in a style that reflects the complexity of the questions with which they must deal but are highly accessible to student readers. I take it that the initial instruction of a new generation of critical scholars begins with this kind of volume. In embarking on this criminological journey we should not be surprised to find that the road remains long, winding, and particularly strewn with hazards.

Acknowledgments

The collecting and editing of a collection of mostly original articles in any field is an immense undertaking that can only be realized through the collective efforts of a number of people. In this context I would like to extend my deep thanks to those who were instrumental in seeing this project to its conclusion.

First, Mike Bickerstaff of Prentice Hall, who believed in the project and acted with utmost professionalism in the early stages of the project. Second, Avivah Wargon and Renate Walker, who provided editorial guidance in bringing the book to fruition. Shoshana Goldberg provided able and patient editorial assistance. Marjorie Munroe oversaw the project from the West Coast office.

Livy Visano, my criminological brother at York University, provided some constructive and not altogether unwelcome advice and criticism at key junctures, and I value his friendship. Ron Hinch pinch-hit in a tough situation and I appreciate his friendship. Ross Hastings and Tullio Caputo were more than helpful in providing names of contacts when I was putting the contributors' list together. Those who attended the 1991 Critical Criminology Roundtable at Kingston first provided the suggestion for a series of books to examine our own sense of malaise, and I thank all of those who contributed to the original idea, including Bob Ratner, Gail Kellough, Frank Pearce, Laureen Snider, Elizabeth Comack, and John McMullan. I also benefited from my recent discussions with Richard Quinney on his perspective of peacemaking. Elliot Leyton has provided solid advice and unfailing friendship throughout these past few years and I wish to wholeheartedly thank him for this. I also wish to thank Philip Jenkins and Eric Hickey for their work and friendship, which I value greatly. Finally, a nod of appreciation to my mentor, Terence Morris, a true Renaissance man.

This book would not have been possible without the very capable assistance of my wife, Patricia O'Reilly, and the patience of my three children, Kate, Patrick, and Tom. My brother Scott has kept me laughing with his late-night calls, and I appreciate his unflagging support.

Finally, my thanks to Perry, Andria, Carmen, and Sue, the wonderful support staff in the Department of Sociology and Anthropology at the University of Windsor.

Thomas O'Reilly-Fleming
Windsor and Galway, Ireland, 1996

LEFT REALISM AS THEORETICAL RETREATISM OR PARADIGM SHIFT: TOWARD POST-CRITICAL CRIMINOLOGY

Thomas O'Reilly-Fleming

INTRODUCTION: THE EMERGENCE OF CRITICAL CRIMINOLOGY IN CANADA

> The problem here is that such divisions might also lead to the all-too-familiar radical factionalism in which internecine wars among critical thinkers sap new life from each other's potential growth. (Henry and Milovanovic, 1991, 294)

The field of critical criminology remains in a self-induced malaise. The early cutting edge of theory generated by Taylor, Walton and Young's (1973) call for a recasting of the criminological enterprise has degenerated into a fractured present, which has been reluctant to draw upon its historical strengths to awaken from its self-induced coma. It is little wonder that by 1988, Cohen was moved to publish a collection of essays entitled *Against Criminology*, since his viewpoint reflected the ambivalence felt by the slowing of the first wave of critical theorizing that had rushed by in the 1970s through the mid-1980s. Before the advent of the "new" criminology of the 1970s, the interactionist perspective (Ericson, 1975), as well as the work of Goffman (1960) and Lemert (1951), had given rise to an increasing disenchantment with the focus of mainstream criminology. In concert with radical movements within society — the hippie movement of the late 1960s, the rebirth of feminism in the early 1970s, the counterrevolution in musical forms and art — criminology began to reinvent itself. That reinvention involved a recasting of generations of criminological theory, and its reinterpretation for modern society.

The "old" criminology was in part abandoned, in part reworked, in a mounting deconstructionist fervour. What emerged was a new "humanism," which recognized deviance as a natural phenomenon within the capitalist state, and linked itself with idealistic notions of the end of repressive state structures. Some twenty years later there has been radical change, but not that which might have been expected. The collapse of the Berlin Wall following the failure of the USSR's economic system dealt a body blow to much of the Marxist underpinnings of a significant stream of radical criminological thought. Similarly, in Britain, the United States, and Canada the late 1970s and early 1980s heralded the end of liberal/socialist governments and the emergence of right-wing politics that advocated strong anti-crime platforms with a focus on lengthy imprisonment as an appropriate response to crime.

It can be said that the first wave of critical theorizing in Canada emerged in the early 1980s (Fleming and Visano, 1983) followed by a second wave in the mid-1980s (Fleming, 1985; MacLean, 1986; Ratner and McMullan, 1987). During this period *The Journal of Human Justice*, which was viewed as a journal of praxis incorporating voices from the nonacademic community, was originally planned by Ratner, MacLean, McMullan, Caputo and Fleming at a 1986 meeting in Boise, Idaho, and continues to publish.

However, by the 1990s there was little to show for more than a decade of work in the area of critical criminology compared to the romantic notions that first fueled the critical revolution. Theoretical directions remained unexplored, left criminology had managed through internal power struggles to mortally wound itself, and new theoretical forms, including postmodernism and feminism, began to ascend, often at the cost of critical criminology, which seemed bound for the scrap heap of history. There were few works that could be used as exemplars of cooperative research endeavours within the Canadian criminological context. Large sections of the history of the development of Canadian legal institutions remained unwritten. Animosities between various academic programs in criminology, and between individuals, had trampled the romantic notions of the 1970s and earlier. Scholars of one school maligned the works of other scholars, based not on sound academic criteria but upon personal animosities. Criminology became, and remains widely viewed as a discipline divided. The losers, ultimately, have been all criminologists, whether they come from the radical left, the far right, or balance precariously in between.

The positivists and mainstream criminologists not surprisingly avoided the self-destructive debates that consumed the critical left in Canadian criminology during the 1980s. Rather, they spent much of their energy producing texts and government-funded research reports, which amount to little more than "liberal tinkering" enterprises at best, or the reinforcement and extension of dominant class interests at worst. Administrative criminology, which eschews explanations of the causes of crime and focuses instead on the control and correction of offenders, has emerged to wrest the reins of history from traditional positivistic criminology.

This chapter explores directions for a post-critical criminology that have emerged out of criminological inquiry in the late 1980s and early 1990s. I provide and draw upon several schools of criminological thought, including peace-making, socialist-feminism, post-modernism, justice studies (Havemann, 1992) and genesis forms of critical criminology in assessing left realism. I do not provide a complete review of these perspectives, which are available elsewhere (MacLean and Milovanovic, 1991). My argument is that critical criminology's decline reflects the strong divisions that have emerged within the field and that have produced a fractured discipline, which is in dire need of reconciliation in order to move beyond the current malaise. Critique is a method of inching toward renewal, of encouraging the paradigm shift. This implies more than endlessly rewriting histories of the "invention" of modern critical schools, or repeating attempts to reconcile existing schools of thought; it requires a reordering of the priorities of criminological work in terms of the realities of the modern state, global economies and the rapidly emerging communication revolution. Beginning with a critical appraisal of the legacy of left realism, progress toward a post-critical approach can be made.

LEFT REALISM: RENEWAL AND CRITIQUE IN CRITICAL CRIMINOLOGY

So criminology, even in its radical variants, may become less concerned with crime than with its own reproduction. (Ruggiero, 1992, 124)

Left realism emerged as a field of academic inquiry during the late 1970s in Britain. There have been an exhaustive (if not exhausting) number of attempts to write (and recast) the history of the development of this school of thought; therefore, I will not rehearse these events once more (DeKeseredy and Schwartz, 1991; Lea and Young, 1984; MacLean, 1989; Taylor, 1992; Young, 1987). However, I do take issue with several of the components of these largely self-serving histories that cavalierly junk the work of many critical criminologists while attempting to aggrandize the work of left realists. In its early development, left realism emerged as a response to the perceived rise of the neo-conservative right in post-war British politics. As the bloom of the new criminology faded following its relegation to the peripheries of major political, social, and economic debates within a rapidly changing British economy, critical, or radical, criminologists balanced perilously on the edge of irrelevancy (a theme I shall explore later in this chapter). In this hostile environment, Jock Young (1979) was foremost in attempting to forge a new vision of the place of criminology within the new Thatcher-dominated, free-enterprise, capitalist state, and he deserves high praise for attempting to develop a new stance that could jettison the failed dream of only a few years earlier. The work of Young and others, which tried to distance itself from the earlier work for which they had provided both catalyst and direction, was not entirely successful.

In their zeal to condemn the few idealist radicals they could find from Young's home bases in Notting Hill Gate and Middlesex Polytechnic, they were in essence self-destructing (Young, 1986, 1987, 1988) or seeking renewal. The idealists had argued for a Marxist-inspired transformatory revolution while society moved in a completely opposite direction. The dream was truly over. Now there had to be individuals to blame, and thus exoneration to be found in shaking off the cloth of youthful insight, now failed rhetoric.

Left realism emerged, according to some historical accounts, as a reaction to the left idealist nature of writings found predominantly in British left criminological scholarship, and because there was a need to accept street crime as "real." The difficulty with these reinterpretations of historical developments in this field is that they rely upon secondhand interpretations already constructed by proponents of left realism, and have been produced by academics who have no reliable cultural voice to offer in their characterization of the British cultural, political, and social developments that fueled left realism (DeKeseredy and Schwartz, 1991). Most disturbing perhaps is that the history and critiques of left realism arise predominantly from the ranks of left realists themselves. This kind of self-promotion and needless production of critique has to be distinguished from more objective stances. While radical approaches have traditionally suffered the fate of either being ignored or severely criticized, self-production is a dangerous path. What is surprising, and perhaps ultimately instructive, about these accounts is the lack of involvement of those most directly affected by such a criminological agenda. Such people are often trotted out to justify the research agenda of left realism, but somehow miss out on being part of the process. Here are the significant tenets of realism as stated and restated ad nauseum throughout numerous "accounts" of its development (see Lowman and MacLean, 1992; Young and Matthews, 1992; MacLean and Milovanovic, 1991, for examples):

1. Violent street crime is a significant problem for working-class people.

2. Working-class people predominate as the victims of all forms of crime in society; they are the casualties of state and corporate criminality as well as of street crimes.

3. Left realists strongly criticize the work of left idealists, mainstream criminologists and critical criminologists who do not identify themselves as realists. There is a sense that there is the world of left realists and the "rest" of criminology. Interestingly, as Taylor (1992) notes, left realism has had little impact outside of Britain, aside from scattered pockets of committed individuals in Canada, Britain, and the United States. In Canada, for example, a small number of people have clearly associated themselves with left realism, including Brian MacLean (a former colleague of Young), Walter DeKeseredy, Dawn Currie, Frank Pearce, and in his later works John Lowman.

4. Realists employ large-scale surveys as a means of providing more realistic, less state-controlled or manipulated data for the victimized in society.

Realists argue that victimization surveys, as constructed by the state, do not accurately reflect the true extent of the victimization of women (DeKeseredy and Hinch, 1991) and others in society. This requires wresting control of the production of crime statistics, measures of victimization, and police accountability from state-sponsored agencies.

5. They are supposedly engaged in the construction of crime control strategies directed at alleviating the victimization of the working class and in providing an alternative to the law and order campaigns waged by the "exceptional state" (Ratner and McMullan, 1985). This also includes involving the community in crime prevention, police accountability exercises, and in gaining more control over their own communities. Inherent also is a movement toward minimalism in policing and its removal from social service functions.

Given the foregoing accounts, what are the problems with left realism as a "theoretical approach"? First, left realism cannot lay claim to status as a theory any more than interactionism before it (Ericson, 1975). Left realism is, in reality, no more than an exercise in dubious politics and the cult of personality. Contrary to the accounts of scholars DeKeseredy and Schwartz (1991), left realism emerged in the British context as a response to Thatcher's complete dismantling of the faltering labour agenda, which had reduced Britain to a country incapable of functioning under continual rail, power, and other labour strikes. Given the stone wall of rejection of criminology as irrelevant, certain British academics of note — foremost among them Jock Young — struggled to reinvent, once again, the face of critical criminology for the British working class. Since the attempt to humanize societal treatment of deviance had been rejected by the time of the Conservatives' rise to power, critical criminologists were faced with the hard reality that their work had had little impact on governmental policy formation during the 1980s and would have even less relevance in the 1990s.

While acknowledging their substantial contribution to forcing criminological debate during a period of decline in the discipline generally, there is much to criticize following an examination of the realist agenda. First, the realists proceeded from an assumption that all those who came before them had not viewed working-class crime — whether intra-class in nature or victimization of members of the working class by society — as crime. In fact, this focus had been the subject of numerous British efforts from the critical school, and had emerged in positivistic studies and in the practice of psychiatric social work (Box, 1983; Cohen, 1972). The realists assumed too much in aggrandizing their own perceptions as somehow unique or innovative. In MacLean's (1991) analysis he argues that some critical criminologists engaged in the romanticization of criminals by shifting the focus of inquiry to the state, leaving street criminals as the victims, and viewed state-defined criminals as themselves victims of social processes that were beyond their control. MacLean argues that victims are denied their "experiences and suffering." The conclusion that street crime is simply "predatory," however, brings us squarely back to the realm of correctionalist criminology that critical thinkers have been scurrying from for some two decades. Who amongst the positivists — Sellin, Nettler, Wolfgang — would disagree that predatory crime is real crime and should be so punished?

The realists began to move away from the Marxist straitjacket of crime as socially constructed and focused on the predatory criminal and his or her actions. After all, can victims of crime live through their victimization secure in the knowledge that left realism recognizes the predatory nature of street crime in working-class districts as such? Can one imagine a left realist addressing a community hall meeting in the St. Francis Community Centre in South London to inform the residents of a housing project that the crime they experience is real? Do they really require such information and will left realist studies that tell them about more previously unreported forms of victimization provide them with the political and economic tools to transform their day-to-day living conditions? The answer is, unfortunately, obviously not.

The same can be said for the rest of criminological efforts aimed at empowering working and disenfranchised persons. The more we confront the reality of our failures to communicate, and to communicate something of use that can be translated into praxis, the more we may be able to construct a post-critical criminology of value outside of the academy. In my own struggles with this problem, I have some sense of the frustration realists must feel. Again, they must be congratulated for trying, through vehicles like the Islington Crime Survey and work on victimization, to make a difference. However, my own romantic notions of the prospects for the development of working-class criminology in Canada (Fleming, 1985) still lay largely unrealized. The Canadian academy, which was once hard on those who espouse radical notions of the direction of criminological inquiry, has now been linked with a very watered-down form of critical criminology. The membership of the Human Justice Collective represents well this movement into accommodation with previously liberal and mainstream criminologists. I first explored this inclusivity and the removal of artificial boundaries to collaboration in *The New Criminologies* at a time when there were few identified critical criminologists in Canada. Now there are very few whose work could not be characterized as in some ways critical in content. The expanding boundaries of critical criminology have moved toward inclusiveness, and have embraced liberal variants of critical scholarship.

One of the difficult junctures for left realists is that a theoretical perspective cannot simply be built upon broad-stroke attacks against other criminologists. Despite the claim of left realists, radical criminologists did produce work that looked at victimization within the working class both during the 1970s and 1980s. Left realists' focus on the "working class" is, on many levels, difficult to support. First, there is no suitable definition of this term offered in the writings of left realists that informs the term. Furthermore, if the term did have any validity in Britain, which I would argue it does not, then it is certainly not transferable to the Canadian context. Most of the "working class," by definition, are working. The crimes of working-class people are viewed by Young (1986, 12) as "an inevitable result of their poverty," and as an attempt to "redress" the balance caused by the "inequitable nature of present-day society." But this analysis amounts to little more than romanticizing criminals and imbuing them with a consciousness that is only demonstrable on a superficial level. It is excuse-making that cannot be reconciled with the reality of crime. How does Young explain to his colleagues the working-class criminal who rapes women? Is this just revenge on a society that denies the working-class male access to certain types of females? Outside of the realm of economic crime and select forms of victimization, realists have experienced difficulty in extending their theoretical perspective.

Young (1986, 12) also argues that the causes of working-class crime are "obvious and to blame the poor for their criminality is to blame the victim." Young presumes that the nature of such crime is economic. Still, he interchanges the terms "poor" and "working class." There is a world of economic difference between the poor of Young's Britain of the late 1970s and early 1980s and the working class, as my own residence and work in the areas of Lewisham and Horne Park clearly demonstrated. Again, the working class work (as often now do the poor, of course). In a startling contradictory article, DeKeseredy and Schwartz (1991) argue precisely the opposite of Young on these issues. They accuse idealists of "romanticizing the working-class criminal (and)...studying the crimes of the elite." Young, on the other hand, calls for a focus on "the ruling class: the police, the corporations and the state agencies." Young's approach would by its very nature include the various apparatuses of state control, including the media, which Schwartz and DeKeseredy reject in their denouncement of studies of moral panics as bogus phenomenon "created by elite opinion-makers such as the media." "Street crime is 'real'" they claim. Did anyone ever think otherwise? While we can agree that the police act in a manner consistent with the reproduction of the social order rather than through an interest in pure crime control, it is not readily apparent that the work of the police can be dismissed as solely of this type.

Left realists have far to go in demonstrating that police are not attentive to crime within working-class districts, if these can even be identified as distinct districts within our urban cores. It is difficult to reconcile the middle-class intellectual status of left realists with their championing of the less fortunate in society, particularly when their rhetoric sounds more like preaching than encouragement to empowerment. Likewise, the position of left realists that they "have been highly criticized by criminologists from both the right and the left...based upon an incomplete understanding of left realism" and despite this "have been extremely prolific researchers and writers" (MacLean, 1991b, 11) is not logical. This statement summarizes one of the main problems analysts have encountered in the writings of left realists (Ruggiero, 1992): the false logic that production in the face of criticism is a substitute for substance. I would contend that it is not others who have failed to understand left realism (Menzies, 1992;

Taylor, 1992) but that realists have been unable to convey variously the "realist project" (Lowman and MacLean, 1992, xi) or agenda with any degree of clarity.

While the basic politial tenets that underscore this approach at producing a criminology for and with "working people" are simplistic enough (in some ways too simplistic), how these translate into a theoretical imperative is less evident. Finally, one of the distinct clues that it is still difficult to separate left realists from their critical and radical colleagues (despite protestations to the contrary) is that they have to make declarations of this status in their writings before it is evident they are theoretically or empirically far removed from old critical stances. If the supposition is that they are more attuned to "real" solutions to present crime/policing problems than those who live and work in the community, or other critical criminologists, then there is little to support this contention. For all the disparaging of left idealists that has poured forth, it is evident that most of those who have been categorized thusly supported both immediate and long-range initiatives in their work, although left realists chose to interpret their work within a narrow theoretical band.

I think the argument that critical criminologists were not able to muster sufficient alternatives for crime control in 1970s Britain is supported. Equally supported is the evidence that criminologists, in general, have little impact on social control policies, policing, community responses to crime, and public perceptions of crime. It behooves us to remember that the only criminology work to make the best-seller list in the United States was James Q. Wilson's *Thinking About Crime* (1986). In the realm of criminology, books written about serial murderers and true crimes enjoy sales that dwarf those of academic criminologists. In a sense we have not accepted a simple truth: few people in wider society are interested in what criminologists have to say about anything!

In our own preoccupations with the limitations of the discipline, we have hit theoretical and empirical barriers yet largely ignored the one barrier of significance: the poverty of our work in terms of real social change and our inability to intervene in spite of the quality of our work.

There is no doubt that left realists have made a substantial contribution to criminology, one that is couched in forcing criminologists to contemplate the nature of the work that we do and its impact on wider society. As Young (1986, 8) noted, failure is not new to criminology, but neither should failure deter us from setting off in new theoretical directions.

Several other salient criticisms of left realism have been offered by Ruggiero (1992, 123–124), who views the proponents of this approach as having formed a new elite with much in common with the criminological impressarios of an earlier, positivistic era. The advocates of left realism tread precariously on a narrow ledge, which puts them "in danger of losing touch with everyday needs and aspirations and, in the words of Baudrillard, society becomes degraded, mortified and moralized" (1992, 123–124).

1. Left realists identify themselves with the leading edge of social struggles.

2. The efforts of these academics result in a politicization of criminology.

3. These foci result in certain marginalized and disenfranchised groups being shunted out of the realm of research and concern, since they do not "inhabit the legitimate political arena" (123).

4. Left realists thus view themselves as the "avant-garde" of the criminological enterprise.

5. While some minor attention is paid to qualitative issues, left realists largely espouse quantitative methodology, with some notable exceptions (see, for example, Lowman, 1986). The instrumentation of administrative criminology at the expense of the sociological imagination inherent in qualitative research has the effect of inadvertently reintroducing positivistic notions that have long been discarded in criminological circles.

Left realism as an approach is still bound tightly in the straitjacket of enduring criminological categories, according to a variety of critics. A common thread of discontent that emerges from the literature is the acceptance of realists of the ascendancy of the criminological enterprise. Rather than backing away from continued empirical investigation of phenomenon that are recognized to be significant crime problems, we find realists contentedly assuming the former place of the positivists as workers in the world of administrative criminology. It is convenient that some significant portions of the left realist agenda fit with state-sponsored interests in victimization. Ruggiero (1992), among others, questions this symbiotic relationship between left realism and the state. Some might argue that state sponsorship of a "people's criminology" amounts to little more than the co-opting of alternative visions. How can the left realist researcher who enjoys highly lucrative government research grants remain on the side of the people? Is the intellectual agenda one of reconciling one's position with self-assurances that eventually one's revelations on the more pervasive and predatory forms of "working-class" crime will impact on the state, local, or community level? The practical notions and aspirations of left realists should not be lightly discarded for, on one level, they represent what realists started out criticizing themselves: a misguided form of idealism that may yet yield results.

Feminists have not made a significant impact on the development of left realist theorizing, and a review of realist literature suggests that the central issue of patriarchy (Daly and Chesney-Lind, 1988) is ignored in the construction of paradigms meant to address victimization in its core form. Carrington (1994), in a review of the disconnected discourses of feminist criminology and postmodernism, argues that the general forms of solutions or answers suggested by left realism are not realistic. This reflects an understanding of the fluidity of human relations. She suggests, "We can no longer find comfort in explanations of social phenomenon based on essentialisms, grand narratives, secure foundations or fixed subjects" (Carrington, 1994, 271). Needless to say, one can also add that feminists have long debated the categories of law and women, for example, as being poorly constructed in terms of the manner in which criminology deals with its subjects and/or objects.

Another area of departure for feminists from the left realist agenda is their support for the curtailment of state powers in order to give local communities more control over their affairs (as in the movement to self-determination by aboriginal peoples). However, this is also accompanied by a movement by left realists that is contradictory in nature. Realists have argued for increased intervention by the state in crimes of violence, and in expanding categories of behaviours that might be viewed as abuse-crime (DeKeseredy and Hinch, 1991), they produce more potential for criminalization. The necessary corrective lies in attention to the issues of women's victimization throughout society that is informed by an analysis of power relations under capitalism.

In the realist vision of a severely downsized police presence within society there is some difficulty for feminists and others. While the realists view policing that involves more obvious social functions within society as necessary, it is difficult to imagine the creation of new agencies that could cope with these functions in a meaningful way on a 24-hour basis, given Canada's current fiscal crisis. Fear of crime — a major theme of feminist writings — and the need to alleviate this through a restructuring or reeducation process will hardly be hastened by a lessened police presence.

BEYOND LEFT REALISM AND TOWARD POST-CRITICAL CRIMINOLOGY

For left realists, crime is a square whose four vertices are identified as the offender, the victim, the state, and the community (Jones, MacLean, and Young, 1986). This square can be thought of as the framework that permits the construction of our ideas about crime. Realist work, thus far, has focused primarily on the victim and police as control workers. The work of the realists attempts to suggest that the focus of much victimology work in the past, and contemporarily, has been upon variables that are of little significance to actual victims of crime. Their work has attempted to expand the boundaries of definitions of acts that can be considered anti-social and in some cases criminal. The effect has been support for widening the net of social control (Cohen, 1985), which, while it may appease some feminist authors and victims' advocacy groups, amounts to little more than an embracing of increasing state powers. This may be a result of realists' attempts to have relevancy to a feminist movement that has largely been disenfranchised within the development of this British-conceived and male-dominated movement in criminology. Perhaps feminist scholars view the work of many realists with jaundiced eyes because their work presumes to give passing nods to the concerns of women without including their ideas in determining the path of theory, research, praxis, and empowerment. The appeal of victimization studies may lie in their potential to place left realist criminology at the centre of debates about the development of society through the pursuit of research that is politically correct, institutionally supported, and likely to have little more effect in policy decisions than the work of a previous generation of "liberal tinkerers" (Ratner, 1985). Ruggiero (1992, 128) has gone so far as to question whether, in the locally centred research of left realists, the capacity to construct the reality of crime actually exists. He argues that what may be produced is little different from the gathering of public opinion with little chance to control for the effects of the presence of the researcher in the field. Finally, in a similar vein, it can be suggested that in efforts to develop a "new" or "real" victimology we run the risk of making individuals "victims of victimology itself." It can also be suggested that on several levels there are victims who do not self-identify since they are unaware of their own victimization. Since these represent a significant, untapped source of concern (for example, the victims of environmental contamination, the homeless, etc.) there is a pressing need for criminology to seek out these forms and address them in research.

The realists have borrowed heavily from their critical past in their attention (at least theoretically) to issues of political economy and crime. The work of Barak (1992) on homelessness in the American context bears witness to the kind of research that is still required to find linkages between structural influences and individual life chances. Part of the agenda of new criminological discourses will have to be directed back toward the issues that inform and feed the development of criminogenic conditions.

Finally, the realist agenda often reads like lost Mertonian tablets when it comes to the issue of crime causation. In emphasizing social deprivation as a core issue, that is, the engendering of expectations with little expectation for many of the realization of social opportunity (Lea and Young, 1984, 262–265), they revive another ghost of the positivist era. While it may be useful to understand the disjuncture between heightened expectations and societal barriers to advancement, work that has been expressed most cogently in Shaver's work on the genesis of mass murderers and serial killers (1986), how does this work address this problem? The realists are unable to rise to the task of relating concepts of discontent and relative deprivation to the creation of crime in capitalist societies. Indeed, beyond this it is difficult to imagine how this would be accomplished in cross-cultural translation. The realists' ability to do so has been questioned: a class analysis cannot account for the shifting nature of social relations in working-class communities and the transposition of roles that people living in these areas experience, often on a daily basis, moving from criminal to victim to spectator (Pitch, 1986). Their analysis of the nature of the class relations, when combined with a retreat into Mertonian dialectics, severely weakens their arguments for the utility of the local survey.

CONCLUSIONS

In conclusion, I would concur with Ruggiero (1992) who has called for sociologists to examine the roots of scholarly agendas such as those displayed in the writings of left realists. This is to suggest that a fifth vertex, one that involves the examination of the sociologist, is integral to the evolution of left realism. Simply put, left realists, in concert with all critical criminologists, are unable to honestly assess the impact of their view of society, crime and crime control, particularly the ways in which it influences their theory and research.

Left realism has moved critical criminology away from the limitations of earlier radical forms, particularly an overreliance on Marxist visions of social change (Hinch, 1985). However, the perspective, while drawing in some ways on the legacy of earlier concentrations on the subjective, lived experience of crime, has not been able to capitalize on the lessons of earlier social researchers. It is laudable that realists have reattuned criminology to a concern with the interaction between institutions and individuals and away from paradigms that artificially straitjacket and separate interactive processes (Ericson, 1975). As Caputo and Hatt have argued in this volume, it is only by acknowledging and constantly reassessing our links with the past, no matter how politically untenable in contemporary society, that we will be able to move our discipline forward. We need to move toward considerations of the effects of rapidly changing global economies, the impact of transnational corporations, the degradation of our living environment, race/diversity issues, and a focus on gender. This movement toward local research with global implications, and the transformation of criminology into a truly public discourse and discipline will inexorably alter the nature of the post-critical approach. In many ways, the contributors in this book struggle to construct this new approach given the theoretical realities and failures of the past two decades.

The lessons of realism are that it is necessary to construct criminological agendas in concert with others who are not uniformly like-minded in their approach to the study of crime. Realism is a form of intellectual elitism, despite its aspirations to build a peoples' criminology, as if such an approach would ever reflect a uniform consensus by the people emancipated. There is a need to assess left realism's agenda and the ways in which it either deliberately or inadvertently constructs crime within our society, while ignoring other forms of explanation and criminality. It is an appropriate juncture for the restructuring of left realism and the consideration of emerging approaches in the post-critical era.

POST-CRITICAL APPROACHES

The subject matter of this book is the development of post-critical approaches to the explanation and understanding of crime. The authors represented in this volume are a diverse collection of scholars who are involved in criminological research across Canada. The subject matter of their papers is the exploration and elucidation of post-critical theoretical forms, both in the form of pure theory and empirical investigation.

In Chapter 2, Bernard Schissel provides an exploration of the construction of moral panics in modern society. Schissel, in expanding the forms developed by

Jenkins (1994) and Barak (1988) on social construction and newsmaking criminology respectively, examines the manufacture of youth-crime panics in the Canadian context. Schissel's analysis extends to the role of the mass media and the collaboration of social institutions of control. He argues that such crusades generate little in the form of reliable information that reaches the public, but rather play on ignorance as an inducement to allow social control agencies a free hand in "get tough" law and order campaigns. The movement of social control out of the family and into the hands of the police and courts increasingly creates an almost *parens patriae* society. As children are relinquished in ever increasing numbers to institutions of social control there has been little in the way of public critique (O'Reilly-Fleming and Clark, 1993).

Schissel ably traces the historical development of child control efforts and places these within a post-critical framework. He contends that a social constructionist approach must be informed by various existing paradigms, including Marxist criminology, left realism, feminist criminology, and the work of Foucault. Schissel presents a synthesis of these at times converging, at times opposing approaches in order to acknowledge the multiple realities of crime and the need to uncover classist and sexist agendas that underscore discourse in the public arena. This answers the criticism of some feminist authors concerning the need for criminologists to place these issues centrally in the search for truths. In examining youth crime, Schissel provides detailed accounts of the Bulger case and the murder of an 11-year-old boy in Chicago that was widely reported in the media, and an analysis of a special issue of *Maclean's* focusing on children who murder. Schissel points out the need to move to a theoretical schema that can take account of victimization at the structural level, rather than the immediate victimization found in morality tales in which youngsters become symbols of violent crime that owe more to myth than reality.

Chapter 3 concerns itself with the occupational health and safety of sex service workers, or prostitutes. Female prostitutes predominate in Canada according to the author, Fran Shaver, comprising some 67 to 90 percent of all street prostitutes. Much of the current societal debate on prostitution, and that which is generally repeated in criminology courses, involves the issues of decriminalization and the legal vagaries of solicitation and communication. Prostitutes are considered a health and social risk in our society and are targeted for research and ultimately control. Shaver argues that the protection of prostitutes is embedded in criminal law, a law which, I would argue, emerges from a patriarchal view of the sex trade. Shaver demonstrates that law and policy are far removed from the reality of the sex trade and its regulation. As with moral panics, there is little empirical information, which is nonetheless used to subjugate and control the actions of prostitutes. This allows personal and systemic prejudice to reign over grounded, empirical data.

Shaver's work brings sex-trade work out of the shadows of deviantization processes by demonstrating the direct parallels between the work prostitutes perform and the work performed by nonsex trade workers. In this she moves in the direction of humanizing deviance and brings it into the realm of the conventional in the wider public consciousness. The author accomplishes this by analyzing data on 80 street prostitutes working in Montreal. Her findings reveal that the reality of street crime includes violence, theft, and arrest; in other words, victimization from the street and from authorities. Despite media-generated notions of the lives of prostitutes, Shaver found that they practise safer sex and are less likely than their male counterparts to use nonmedical drugs. Shaver argues for the normalization of prostitution within research, which places it in the context of a connected sex-service industry (sex, pornography, sex shows) crossing gender barriers, and cognizant of the parallel nature of sexual and nonsexual service work. The implications for a post-critical criminology arise from the foregoing and an understanding that the deviance/crime barriers are thinly drawn in Canadian society, and subject to movement at any time. In recording street level data on crime and deviance, Shaver's work does much to address the issues of deconstructing patriarchy and the need to build accounts that arise from lived street experience.

Chapter 4 is E. Jane Ursel and Stephen Brickey's examination of the potential of law as an instrument of reform. Specifically, their chapter deals with Manitoba's zero-tolerance policy on family violence. Their chapter analyzes whether both Marxist and feminist critiques of the utility of law are borne out in the Manitoba experience in controlling domestic violence. Law as an instrument of reform has several notable limitations: it is a blunt instrument; legal reforms are rarely put into practice (they are instead modified by agents within the legal system); it is typically accompanied by inadequate enforcement; and if there is public resistance these efforts are likely to fail.

Drawing from substantive data sets culled from personal interviews with the public (*N*=533), 1,600 cases disposed of by the Family Violence Court, and arrest figures that explore dimensions of police use of discretion, they discovered that the setting up of a specialized court to deal with domestic violence addressed feminist concerns regarding the inequitable treatment of women and children before the law. The dynamic of increasing arrests led to increased public interest and awareness of domestic assault and pressure to reform court procedures to deal with an exponentially expanding caseload. The authors discovered that the increased use of police in what had previously been widely regarded as a personal affair had a transformative effect. Wife abuse was now a phenomenon that could be publicly observed and dealt with.

The net effect of the new courts was to produce substantially higher rates of conviction than companion courts. Legal reform and the use of the police as an instrument of social control escape their negative connotations in this dramatic model. The police and courts, the research demonstrates, are not the impenetrable institutions that many critical scholars have assumed them to be. Rather, they are open to radical change that can have direct positive consequences for dealing with the reality of crime.

In Chapter 5, Sylvie Frigon discusses how women are constituted as criminal subjects in contemporary social control systems. She asserts that the bodies of women lie at the heart of this designation, an extension of Foucault's (1975) work on the production of docile bodies in society. To accomplish this, she examines first the philosophical root of the making of the female subject in writing about crime and the association between women and their bodies. She then proceeds to develop sketches of the ways in which the deviance and criminality of women is presented within our society. She argues that, by its nature, the label "woman" is inherently "deviant," as construed within a male-dominated society and system of social control.

Frigon proceeds to provide a detailed analysis of the subjugation and torture of women during the search for witches in Europe during the fifteenth century. She interprets the focus of witch-hunts as "gender specific" in its primary orientation toward women. Frigon then turns her attention to premenstrual syndrome (PMS) and its construction in modern society. Her attention turns to the use of PMS as a defense in three cases of homicide, as well as a defense in the case of a battered woman and the ways in which the law interprets women's bodies. Frigon concludes that women's treatment under the law and courts, and indeed within wider society, corresponds to a specific and historical construction of femininity. Her work uncovers the relationship between women's attempts to achieve greater consciousness of inequalities and the threat this poses to male domination. Women, then, are seen as transgressors when they take their protests and bodies from the private domains in which they are deprived of power into the public forum.

Chapter 6 is criminologist John McMullan's writing on the historical development of policing in response to issues of lawlessness and disorder. McMullan focuses on policing in London, England and more pointedly on the interrelations between communal, state, and private dimensions of order. The chapter explores the character of communal coercion and social order, the question of collective self-policing, the interplay of various factors in the production of social order and disorder, and the nature of police organization during this period and the emergence of private forms of coercion in the city.

McMullan's analysis not only addresses the issue of producing informed historical analysis, but directs us to the importance of rejecting generalized visions of the development of social controls that are bound by preexisting categories. Both communal and private forms of policing are demonstrated to have lengthy histories that are rich in detail and complex in nature. The nature of early policing directs us to the consideration of groups and individuals who would not normally be considered forms of "police," but (which he has discovered) played a significant role in policing activities and the development of the idea of police in the popular conscience. McMullan finds strong links between current and previous forms of policing. Ignoring these kinds of factors limits our analysis of present-day policing since our historical imagination is cut short by this lack of attention to expansion of the boundaries of policing forms. The author's work directs us to consider policing not in isolation, but in the context of the wider social, economic, political, and legal spheres in which its various forms have developed.

Robynne Neugebauer-Visano's contribution in Chapter 7 discusses the possibilities of moving from liberally dominated discourses within criminological theory to more progressive forms which imply authentic liberation for marginalized groups and individuals in society. The 1990s, according to the author, have been characterized by divisive struggles inside and outside of criminology. Many of the common expressions of cultural exclusion, including anti-lesbianism, homophobia, racism, and class elitism, remain largely unexplored, and so the roots of criminalization evade description, analysis, systemization, and action. She argues that post-critical pedagogy must directly confront the challenges of capital and the fundamental betrayal of critical directions. She contends that critical criminology has undergone a fundamental transformation during the 1980s examining diverse institutions at both the local and global levels.

In order to escape from these limitations, critical criminologists must adopt the language of critical pedagogy in order to be liberated from dominant ideologies that inhibit critical appraisals of existing social relations. Criminology, for the author, is still caught within attempts to engage in legitimation performances in terms of scholarship, funding, publishing, and other efforts to gain professional privilege. She goes on to demonstrate the ineffectiveness of criminology in dealing with key issues that confront society. Despite numerous public inquiries into policing, little has been accomplished other than the reiteration of socially acceptable solutions that are conveniently never implemented. Critical criminology has cooperated with the transformation of women in subjects of social research and inquiry through numerous commissions and studies that have focused on reproductive technologies and violence. The author concludes that much of what passes for critical and mainstream criminology does more to pathologize and deviantize than to liberate, if we have the courage to examine criminology itself as an historic form in Canadian society.

In Chapter 8, Gail Kellough focuses on getting bail. From her research in 1992 and later, she examines the granting of bail in a Toronto court. Kellough's work probes the basis of court decisions in an effort to comprehend the major themes of the legal interchanges that occur in court and the behind-the-scenes negotiations and tactics that produce the final court product. Pretrial release is a significant issue before the Canadian courts and the author's work does much to illuminate the issues underscoring pretrial release. In this way it also provides valuable information on the considerable gap that exists between formal law and its day-to-day administration at points of power in the judicial spectrum.

Kellough examines a number of cases that are both typical and atypical of these forms of proceedings. What arises in the author's research is a distinct gap between the legal presumption of innocence required to be honoured in Canadian law and the practice of the court in depriving liberty to the accused on other than the strict grounds allowed by various forms of legislation. The costs to society of holding persons pending their trial can run into the thousands of dollars for the commission of a petty offense of shoplifting that netted the criminal a few dollars. Kellough argues against the use of pretrial detention because of its proven association with longer sentences at the time of trial. Since it is likely to be women, aboriginal, black, and immigrant individuals who are thus detained, Kellough views this as a major point in the continuum of control. Her research provides a beginning for what Foucault (1977) referred to as the "micropolitics of control." The collusive nature of the current judicial system leaves justices as silent witnesses to the recommendations of the Crown for detention, where Kellough notes, judges accept such recommendations without question. Even in contested cases, the Crown is free to pick out only those negative aspects of the accused's history that will support his or her case. The bail system, one must conclude, is simply another mechanism for ensuring social inequality and injustice. Kellough's work leads us further into the settings in which post-critical criminology must partly seek its future: in the recording of empirical evidence of social injustice and its relation to larger social institutions that perpetuate these injustices against the weak and vulnerable in Canada.

Chapter 9, written by noted expert on juvenile justice W. Gordon West, examines the nature of youth school violence in Canada and its interpretation by various interested constituencies, including professionals, police, victim's rights groups, and criminologists. West focuses his attention on the raging debate concerning youth violence in schools. He begins his analysis by indicating that public debate on these issues is difficult since major contributors do not agree on fundamental terms and definitions. In some instances this goes beyond mere disagreement to the deliberate bending and obfuscation of factual material in order to underscore the points being made in public debate on approaches.

West's analysis is constructed first by an examination of the historical origins of discursive practice within the Canadian context derived from the evolution of legislative practice and rhetoric during the past century. West questions the meaning of "violence" within the school context, since the various manifestations of violence (verbal, psychological, and physical) are not understood. The site of violence remains, West concludes, overwhelmingly in the residence. This does not mean that school violence can be trivialized. In studying data on youth crime in the Toronto area, we are struck by the substantial number of reports, particularly on crimes involving sexual violence, a weapon, and extortion. However, West is able to demonstrate that these figures are open to considerable interpretation, and have been manipulated by the police for the purpose of obtaining support for their increasing budgetary demands (Fleming, 1983), a not-unknown phenomenon. West argues that there has been little real increase in school crime in recent years, particularly in the use of violence. Most incidents remain "minor." Youth violence is a particularly volatile criminological topic with strong moral connotations that engender fear among parents and schoolchildren alike. Whether it is driven by zero tolerance or idealistic notions about the elimination of violence through the eradication of poverty, much of what is done on behalf of youth seems destined to accomplish little. West questions the utility of much of our criminological enterprise in the past two decades. He suggests that we begin with an examination of the social construction of phenomena such as youth violence to reassess the nature of what it is we are doing, and what we hope to accomplish through our efforts.

A similar theme continues in the work of Colette Parent and Françoise Digneffe in their examination of feminist contributions to ethical issues within the criminal justice system, particularly focused on the criminalization of women. The two Francophone scholars proceed to examine various feminist positions vis-à-vis such interventions. The authors explore various critical understandings of women, first as accused and then as defendants within our system of justice. They argue that law and criminal justice have little to offer concerning the needs and interests of women, and they assert that the level of this criticism is rapidly escalating. In their examination of victims of crime they note that voices of dissent have arisen from victims who view the nature of criminological work with derision, representing yet one more group with the power to produce labels.

The authors move on to an examination of the place of ethics in criminal justice debates. Women have been excluded from the ethical debates that inform our efforts at social control and criminalization as much as from similar efforts to assist them in the role of victims. They support a system of renewal based on "communicative ethics," which arrive at the construction of ethics through progressive discussion. This is in some ways dramatically similar to the type of consensus-building that was the centre of aboriginal negotiations in the Canada-Mohawk crisis (O'Reilly-Fleming, 1993). The search for *a priori* rules is abandoned in this model. They conclude that a progressive dialogue that recognizes the failures of the criminal justice system to combat continuing social problems is required, as well as sustained communication across and within gender lines.

Chapter 11 moves on from this debate to explore men, masculinities, and crime. Kathleen Burke and Brian Burtch consider the emerging concern with masculinities in the context of the nature of criminal victimization in its relation to men. The authors explore the ways in which new forms of masculinity may be developed that would counteract both criminal and noncriminal forms of violence perpetrated by males. This includes attempts at domination over both males and females. The authors review literature from the growing field of masculinity studies that supports images of men by connecting them to violence, as well as supporting the construction of masculine "traits" and contradictions in the male experience. The literature suggests men have "fragile" identities, are in crisis, or in need of liberation.

The authors argue the aim of post-critical interpretations must be to subvert notions of male omnipotence, focusing our attention on how gender is fractured. They argue for the restructuring of masculinities along lines of social class, disabilities, race, and ethnicity. The authors conclude that the inclusion of an understanding of masculine socialization processes and the influence of gender are essential to the construction of post-critical forms. In connecting our efforts toward social justice, we must reexamine the overwhelming involvement of men in crime and what can be done to move away from a society that promotes male socialization to violence and domination.

Chapter 12 returns us to the issue of domestic violence and the issue of mandatory arrest policies. The authors, Jacqueline Faubert and Ronald Hinch, argue that such policies are created within a specific context within which state resources are directed toward a problem without necessarily eliminating the problem. There arises then a contradiction between investment in policing a problem versus dealing with social conditions that give rise to the problem in the first place. The authors argue that the solutions offered give rise to new conflicts, which in turn require resolution. They go on to examine the genesis of this policy through an analysis of sociopolitical factors, the influence of social science research, and the effectiveness of the program. They conclude that the response of the state has been to focus concerns about spousal assault on police policy, which required little or no effort on its part. Thus, reform was acknowledged but effectively limited within the state apparatus of control. Another contradiction that arises is that such policies render women more dependent on the state for protection, leaving them in a new state of continued dependency.

Law professor Michael Mandel eloquently explores the impact of the Charter of Rights and Freedoms in Canada in producing inequality before the law. Mandel explores the manner in which Canadian society is structured for inequality in both power relations and living standards. While aboriginal peoples have not been the focus of significant scholarly work on the part of Canadian criminologists, Mandel brings the issue of their rights before the Charter to the forefront. He argues that the experience of aboriginal peoples offers irrefutable proof that legalized politics are useful in the face of massive social inequality. Indeed, aboriginal Canadians have found that, throughout history, lawmakers have attempted to deny natives their rights, either partially or entirely. The failure of aboriginal groups to secure entitlements under the Charter that should have been granted, due to government reluctance to acknowledge these claims, is instructive on the abuse of aboriginal Canadians in the legal forum.

Mandel goes on to discuss the treatment of racism under the Charter through an investigation of the Zundel and Keegstra cases. His analysis clearly demonstrates the reluctance of the state to become involved in cases of demonstrated racism, and the attempt of a private citizens' coalition to force the prosecution of Zundel. In the end, Zundel was acquitted by the Supreme Court of Canada in a decision that is appalling in its ramifications. The decision suggests that the rights of racists take precedence over those who have been victimized by racists and by the justice system that we trust to ensure that rights have reasonable limits. Finally, Mandel deals with some of the legal issues that have most affected Canadian women. His chapter suggests that close analysis of the behaviour of law and its social impact provides a clear avenue for the development of a more responsive, person-centred criminology. It also notes commonalities in struggles of disenfranchised groups and ordinary working people that can be united in bold challenges to the legal order.

Chapter 14 deals with an important issue that has often been overlooked in critical writings on crime: crime prevention. While much critical work focused on the outcome of various crime and crime control scenarios, little attention has been paid to crime prevention. Ross Hastings contends it is time to abandon punitive and rehabilitative approaches (which have fallen on hard times) and replace them with a comprehensive and integrated strategy. The focus would be on targeting the factors associated with crime and victimization in a proactive and preventative manner. Hastings notes that many of the promises of prevention have not been fulfilled, despite its appeal to a variety of academic and public constituencies. The way of the future lies in the resolution of underlying theoretical and political debates, which, while seemingly uniform in support of strategies, mask deeply held differences concerning approaches to crime prevention. Second, we have attempted to deliver on few of the devised programs of prevention that have been developed, and it is therefore premature to suggest that prevention is not effective. This argument is bolstered in the field of juvenile justice by the lack of alternative-measures programs in a system where 90 percent of every dollar is spent on institutional beds (O'Reilly-Fleming and Clark, 1993).

Hastings proceeds to deconstruct the arguments at the heart of the superficial consensus on crime prevention strategies. From this analysis he draws out common threads and composes a conceptual framework that specifies a range of options for implementation. Finally, the chapter ends with a consideration of this framework for the planning and implementation. This chapter suggests that, rather than revisiting old and tired strategies, it is time for a radical reorientation and rethinking of these approaches to more constructively attend to the issues of prevention.

Chapters 15 and 16 present the views of Kevin McCormick and Jean-Paul Brodeur respectively on the penal system. McCormick suggests that the technological revolution currently sweeping through American prison systems—both in the form of privatization and electrification of the carceral—has significant importance for the future development of the prison archipelago. The electronic prison may now move beyond the walls of the penitentiary to the walls of our domiciles. Punishment need no longer be centred in a fortress of control; now, in an Orwellian view of the future, both private and public spaces have the potential to become centres for control of deviance. Technology, in McCormick's view, now forms a carceral culture, and interaction is becoming increasingly technological. Rather than acting as liberator, technology is seen to possess a dark side that permits state intervention in our private worlds and the transfer of control to a multiplicity of sites in our society, fulfilling Foucault's (1975) ultimate concept of the carceral network. Technology is a convenience that is fast infiltrating our methods of restraining the "bad" of our society, yet while we do this we tighten the bonds of our own straitjackets.

Brodeur explores the question of postmodernism in penology in his intriguing and exhaustive analysis of the debates, raising two questions: (1) will future developments in penology be related to a program that has been developing over the past two centuries or is it discontinuous with what we have been experiencing? and (2) is the sociology of modernity equal to the task of considering the present developments in penology? He attempts to defend the position that we are in need of a radical transformation in conceptual apparatuses in order to comprehend an increasingly complex social reality.

Brodeur proceeds to provide a review of the history of the terms "postmodern" and "modern" and discovers that we are moving into the role of interpreters of reality in a way that corresponds to the vision propagated by the powerful. Like their contemporaries in sociology, criminologists have lost the power to legislate, and have been cast in a supportive role within the social control dialogue. Brodeur takes issue with the shifting goals of the penological enterprise and suggests a movement beyond legitimation. We are asked to move to a rational and consistent system in our efforts. The penal system, as research has consistently shown, is dealing with increasing numbers of persons under its control. Recently, American President Bill Clinton has supported a renewed building program for penal institutions and was instrumental in passing legislation that awards life sentences to thrice-convicted felons. In essence, the Democrats have stolen the law and order campaign of the right or else converged in their appreciation of the voter appeal of moral panic. Brodeur insists that community sanctions, alternatives, and intermediate forms of punishment lie at the heart of useful reform. He directs us to the issues of sex and ethnicity in our analysis of the modern penal enterprise. To move out of the penal "dead end" will require the development of community, accountability, and the overcoming of inertia. Brodeur concludes that a post-critical account of penal saturation will have to deal with the core issues of how to resolve the postmodern dilemmas, of which these developments are a culmination.

Chapter 17 concerns itself with the study of law and colonialism in the work of Russell Smandych and Gloria Lee. Their chapter is an attempt to understand the transformation of dominant mechanisms of social control in western Canada from 1670 to 1870. The authors present a theoretical framework derived from feminism, social control theories, the study of legal pluralism, and the study of colonization. The model they develop provides a tool for research on aboriginal peoples that connects the issues of legal change, colonization, gender, and resistance.

The final two chapters deal with the construction of new theoretical directions for a post-critical criminology. George Pavlich and R. S. Ratner explore the postmodernist attack on modern criminological theory. They try to establish the centrality of the "individual-society" exemplar and argue that postmodernism problematizes this exemplar. After a careful analysis they suggest a route for post-critical efforts that would develop a countermodern discourse.

Tullio Caputo and Ken Hatt appropriately end the book with a well-constructed review of the state of critical theorizing in Canada. They provide a reasoned review of the development of critical schools in Canada and their impact on the direction of criminological inquiry. They suggest a four-quadrant model of modern theorizing in criminology, drawing upon traditional theoretical strengths. Through a continuing synthesis of theoretical imperatives—micro-synchronic, macro-synchronic, micro-diachronic and macro-diachronic approaches—the development of critical criminology is placed within an understandable and useful context for the building of new theoretical forms. They review critiques of critical criminology from a variety of quarters and arrive at a series of suggestions for future theorizing in criminology. They suggest four core problems that must be addressed: the problems of conflation at both levels of analysis; nonassumption of natural evolution approaches or the automatic reproduction of social relations; the centrality of the relationship between the analyst and the subject of analysis; and the implications of these changes for a post-critical criminology and the very definition of crime. By taking a number of positive steps the authors believe "criminology could be reconceptualized as that set of discourses in which power is generated, mobilized, resisted and elaborated through expertise concerning harm and governance."

Throughout these collected chapters readers will be introduced to cutting-edge scholarship on the very nature of criminology as a discipline. It is obvious that criminology is undergoing an extended state of self-analysis and criticism in order to emerge (it is hoped) as a renewed field of inquiry that benefits from (but leaves behind in large measure) the failed theories of another era. While the dream of the new criminologists is over, their dream can fuel a new and dynamic field of inquiry, as the contributions to this book clearly demonstrate.

REFERENCES

Barak, Gregg.   1992. *Gimme Shelter*. New York: Praeger.

————.   1988. "Newsmaking Criminology: Reflections on the Media, Intellectuals and Crime," *Justice Quarterly*, 5:565–587.

————, and **Bob Bohm.**   1989. "The Crime of the Homeless or the Crime of Homelessness," *Contemporary Crisis*, 13:275–288.

Baudrillard, Jean.   1981. *For a Critique of the Political Economy of the Sign*. St. Louis: Telos Press.

Black, Donald.   1989. *Sociological Justice*. New York: Oxford University Press.

————.   1976. *The Behaviour of Law*. New York: Academic Press.

Bourdieu, Pierre.   1977. *Outline of a Theory of Practice*. New York: Cambridge University Press.

Box, S.   1987. *Power, Crime and Mystification*. London: Tavistock.

————.   1983. *Power, Crime and Mystification*. London: Tavistock.

Brasswell, Michael.   1990. "Peacemaking: A Missing Link in Criminology," *The Criminologist*, 15(1):3–5.

Brigham, John, and **Christine Harrington.** 1989. "Realism and Its Consequences: An Inquiry into Contemporary Sociological Research," *International Journal of the Sociology of Law*, 17:41–62.

Carrington, K. 1994. "Postmodernism and Feminist Criminologies: Disconnecting Discourses," *International Journal of the Sociology of Law*, 22:261–277.

Cohen, S. 1988. *Against Criminology.* New Brunswick, N.J.: Transaction Books.

———. 1985. *Visions of Social Control.* Oxford: Polity Press.

———. 1972. *Folk Devils and Moral Panics: The Creation of the Mods and Rockers.* London: Blackwell.

Daly, K., and **M. Chesney-Lind.** 1988. "Feminism and Criminology," *Justice Quarterly*, 5:497–538.

DeKeseredy, W., and **R. Hinch.** 1991. *Woman Abuse.* Toronto: Thompson.

———, and **M. Schwartz.** 1991. "British and Left Realism: A Critical Comparison," *International Journal of Offender Therapy and Comparative Criminology*, 35(3):248–262.

Ericson, R. 1975. *Criminal Reactions.* Aldershot: Gower.

Fleming, T., ed. (see also **O'Reilly-Fleming**). 1985. *The New Criminologies.* Toronto: Oxford University Press.

Fleming, T., and **L. Visano,** eds. 1983. *Deviant Designations.* Toronto: Butterworths.

Foucault, M. 1977. *Discipline and Punish.* New York: Pantheon.

Gelsthorpe, L., and **A. Morris,** eds. *Feminist Perspectives in Criminology.* Milton Keynes: Open University.

Goffman, E. 1960. *Asylums.* New York: Praeger.

Havemann, P. 1992. "Canadian Realist Criminology in the 1990s: Some Reflections on the Quest for Social Justice." In *Realist Criminology*, edited by J. Lowman and Brian MacLean, 101–114. Toronto: University of Toronto Press.

Henry, S., and **D. Milovanovic.** 1991. "Constitutive Criminology," *Criminology*, 29(2):293–316.

Hinch, R., ed. 1994. *Readings in Critical Criminology.* Toronto: Prentice Hall.

———. 1985. "Marxist Criminology in the 1970s." In *The New Criminologies in Canada*, ed. T. Fleming. Toronto: Oxford University Press.

Jenkins, Philip. 1994. *Using Murder: The Social Construction of Serial Murder.* New York: Aldine de Gruyter.

Jones, T., B. MacLean and **J. Young.** 1986. *The Islington Crime Survey: Crime, Policing and Victimization in Inner-city London.* Aldershot: Gower.

Kinsey, R., J. Lea and **J. Young.** 1986. *Losing the Fight Against Crime.* Oxford: Blackwell.

Lea, J. and **J. Young.** 1984. *What Is to Be Done About Law and Order?* London: Penguin.

Lemert, E.   1951. *Social Pathology*. New York: McGraw Hill.

Leyton, E.   1986. *Hunting Humans*. Toronto: McClelland & Stewart.

Lowman, J.   1986. "Street Prostitution in Vancouver: Some Notes on the Genesis of a Social Problem," *Canadian Journal of Criminology*, 28(1):1–16.

——, and **B. MacLean,** eds.   1992. *Realist Criminology: Crime Control and Policing in the 1990s*. Toronto: University of Toronto Press.

MacLean, B.   1991a. "In Partial Defense of Socialist Realism: Some Theoretical and Methodological Concerns of the Local Crime Survey," *Crime, Law and Social Change*, 15(3):213–254.

——.   1991b. "Introduction: The Origins of Left Realism." In *New Directions in Critical Criminology*, ed. B. MacLean and D. Milovanovic, 9–14. Vancouver: Collective Press.

——.   1986. *The Political Economy of Crime*. Toronto: Prentice Hall.

——, and **D. Milovanovic.**   1991. *New Directions in Critical Criminology*. Vancouver: Collective Press.

Matthews, R.   1987. "Taking Realist Criminology Seriously," *Contemporary Crises*, 11:371–401.

——, and **J. Young,** eds.   1990. *Issues in Realist Criminology*. London: Sage.

Menzies, R.   1992. "Beyond Realist Criminology." In *Realist Criminology*, edited by J. Lowman and Brian MacLean, 139–158. Toronto: University of Toronto Press.

O'Reilly-Fleming, Thomas and **B. Clark**, eds.   1993. *Youth Injustice*. Toronto: Canadian Scholars Press.

Pepinsky, H., and **R. Quinney.**   1991. *Criminology as Peacemaking*. Bloomington: Indiana University Press.

Pitch, T.   1986. "Viaggio attorno alla criminologia: discutendo con i realisti," *Dei Delittie delle Pene*, 3:469–89.

Ratner, R. S.   1985. "Inside the Liberal Boot." In *The New Criminologies in Canada*, ed. T. Fleming. Toronto: Oxford University Press.

——, and **J. McMullan,** eds.   1987. *State Control: Criminal Justice Politics in Canada*. Vancouver: University of British Columbia.

——.   1985. "Social Control and the Rise of the 'Exceptional State' in Britain, the United States, and Canada." In *The New Criminologies in Canada*, ed. T. Fleming. Toronto: Oxford University Press.

Ruggiero, V.   1992. "Realist Criminology: A Critique.": In *Rethinking Criminology: The Realist Debate*, edited by Jock Young and Roger Matthews, 123–140. London: Sage.

Schwartz, M., and **W. DeKeseredy.**   1991. "Left Realist Criminology: Strengths, Weaknesses and the Feminist Critique," *Crime, Law and Social Change*, 15(2):51–72.

Scraton, P. ed.   1987. *Law, Order and the Authoritarian State*. Milton Keynes: Open University.

Smart, C. 1976. *Women, Crime and Criminology: A Feminist Critique.* London: RKP.

Taylor, I. 1992. "Left Realist Criminology and the Free Market Experience in Britain." In *Rethinking Criminology*, edited by Jock Young and Roger Matthews, 95–122. London: Sage.

———. 1981. *Law and Order: Arguments for Socialism.* London: Macmillan.

———., **P. Walton,** and **J. Young.** 1975. *Critical Criminology.* London: RKP.

———. 1973. *The New Criminology.* London: RKP.

Wilson, J. 1986. *Thinking About Crime.* New York: Aldine.

Young, J. 1988. "Radical Criminology: The Emergence of a Competing Paradigm," *British Journal of Criminology*, 28:159–83.

———. 1987. "The Tasks Facing a Realist Criminology," *Contemporary Crises*, 11:337–356.

———. 1986. "The Failure of Criminology: The Need for Radical Realism." In *Confronting Crime*, edited by R. Matthews and J. Young, 4–30. London: Sage.

———. 1979. "Left Idealism, Reformism and Beyond: From New Criminology to Marxism." In *Capitalism and the Rule of Law*, edited by B. Fine et al., 13–28. London: Hutchinson.

——— and **R. Matthews.** 1992. *Rethinking Criminology: The Realist Debates.* London: Sage.

POST-CRITICAL CRIMINOLOGY AND MORAL PANICS: DECONSTRUCTING THE CONSPIRACY AGAINST YOUTH

Bernard Schissel

INTRODUCTION

The concept of the moral panic was used in critical criminological research in the late sixties and early seventies to study the phenomenon of putative crime waves and the origins of public panics about crime (Hall et al., 1978; Cohen, 1972). Much of the literature concentrated on (a) how atypical or rare events come to raise the collective ire to the point where the public demands law reform, (b) how official and popular culture accounts of criminality are based on overgeneralized, inaccurate and stereotypical descriptions of criminals and their associations, and (c) how the public panics that resulted were mostly directed at working-class or marginalized people. Much of the research, in addition, focused on moral panics over youth crime, especially in relation to alienated, organized, gang-based delinquents.

Many of the panics that typified the sixties and seventies appear today in similar form, if not content. And as described by a newly-developing body of current literature on moral panics (Kappeler, Blumberg and Potter, 1993; Painter, 1993; Jenkins, 1992), public perceptions of the degree and form of violent crime are largely inaccurate and exaggerated. The current research on moral panics differs in content from previous research in that current analyses concentrate on what might be labeled peripheral deviances: ritual abuse, serial killers, pedophilia, and child abuse. While not to diminish the seriousness of these crimes, it is important to note that, with the exception of child abuse, most of the phenomena under study are quite rare. And as typified by past moral panics, the rare occurrences nourish the debate and the panic.

Little attention has been paid, however, to the moral outrage that has greeted an apparent youth crime wave in Canada, or to the consequent moral attack on youth as a subculture. This is not to suggest that the moral panic surrounding youth crime is subtle or hidden. On the contrary, the attack on youth has been vocal, concerted, and politicized, fostered by the portrayal of idiosyncratic examples of youth crime as typical. In this chapter, I attempt to place the current panic on "out of control" youth in the context of both critical and post-critical research in criminology and law. The youth crime panic needs to be analyzed from both perspectives: from a critical perspective, we need to understand the role of political and economic forces in the construction of deviance and in the subsequent control of marginalized people; and from a post-critical deconstructionist position, we need to address the role of language and discourse and the power of discursive agents in legitimizing and stabilizing the moral panic debates. The existing public debates on youth crime, while largely uninformed, have the potency and the scientific legitimacy to direct public opinion and to effect social control policy that stigmatizes and controls those who are most disadvantaged and most victimized. Further, with specific reference to youth crime, I want to suggest that the primary effect of media and official accounts of youth crime is to decontextualize the act for public consumption, allowing those with direct access to discourse to direct and control public opinion. The portraits of youth criminals that public crime accountants paint are largely portraits of nihilistic, pathological criminals who act alone or as members of gangs, criminals devoid of ethical ballast. The decontextualization of youth crime, however, misses a fundamental consideration in understanding crime: most repeat young offenders and their families are victims of socioeconomic impoverishment and are more than likely to be repeatedly victimized as clients of the systems of law, social welfare, and education.

This chapter begins with a discussion of the workings of moral panics and then discusses these panics in the context of contemporary and historical Canada. I then introduce the theoretical orientation that melds critical criminology with the post-critical/postmodern perspective, which deconstructs discourses. Finally, I illustrate how discursive processes in media representations mould and shape public opinion, which, in turn, acts to legitimate the existing social order and to advocate public policy that controls the marginalized.

MORAL PANICS, POLITICS, AND PUBLIC POLICY

Moral panics are characterized by their affiliations with politics, with systems of information, and with various institutions of social control, including the legal system. The operation of the moral panic is both symbolic and practical, and functions within the confines of an already existing orthodox state machinery, which is closely tied to the mechanisms of production. And, most importantly for this chapter, moral panics are constituted within a discourse that has a profound effect on public opinion; as I discuss shortly, media presentations of decontextualized events are a powerful dimension of legitimating punitive discourse.

The Symbolic Crusade

Most youth-focused crime panics argue either to protect children or to condemn them. Warnings that children are constantly in danger lead to lobbies against child abuse, child pornography, prostitution, pedophilia, serial killers, smoking, and drunk driving. On the other hand, those who believe simply that all children are potentially dangerous have lobbied for the reform of the *Young Offenders Act* (YOA), implementation of dangerous-offender legislation, and the increased use of custodial dispositions for young offenders. This ambivalence between protecting and condemning children is embodied in our cultural approach to child rearing, which advocates both affection/protection and physical punishment. Further, it is ironic that we tend to punish those who are both most dear to us, in the form of our children, and those who are farthest removed from us, in the form of the hardened criminal.

The growing focus on criminogenic children seems to set the limits of social tolerance and seeks to change the moral and legal environment to reflect those limits. While harm to children is the threshold of tolerance, such child-centred symbolic lobbies reflect the belief that, as a subculture, children are also unpredictable and volatile. The attendant rhetoric invokes images of gangs and connections between nihilistic behaviour and music and dress styles (grunge is a typical example). The conception of the youth subculture is, in general, portrayed as aimless and calculating. The anti-youth lobby is a potent, symbolic mechanism for framing youth crime—and ultimately all conduct—in ambivalent yet moralistic terms.

The Interdependence of Panics

Moral panics are characterized by the reality that they emerge in groups and tend to foster one another. The current movements in Canada directed at gun control, the drug trade, gang violence, car theft, and dangerous offenders all arise from discussions about young offenders. Highly sensational incidences are interpreted as part of an overall social menace, and subsequent events are contextualized in this gestalt of fear and framed in the same kind of fear-provoking language. Further, the success of one panic lends credibility to another, and the result is a generalized lobby for increased social control at all levels.

The Role of the Mass Media

The Canadian newspaper industry has become monopolized by a few major media corporations. In effect, there is very little competition for the moral attention of Canadians. The newspaper industry's lust for selling news results in sensationalist, uncontested accounts that are often fictitious and largely removed from the social and economic context in which they occur. I discuss media presentations at length in a subsequent section, but at this point I wish to identify the primary functions of media portraits of crime: (a) the creation of a world of insiders and outsiders, acceptability and unacceptability in order to facilitate public consumption; (b) the connecting of images of deviance and crime with social characteristics; and (c) the decontextualization of crime in anecdotal evidence that is presented as omnipresent truth.

The Interdependence of Institutions

Moral crusades are often typified by the collaboration of various institutions of social control. On the issue of youth permissiveness, it is important to realize that institutions like medicine, education, social welfare, religion, and government are all involved in the work of understanding and controlling youth crime. It is not surprising, then, that public accounts of specific youth crimes or of the youth crime epidemic generally draw on experts from other institutions to lend credibility to their claims and to persuade audiences that the concern for growing youth crime is legitimate and widespread. The interdependent and the multi-institutional nature of moral panics is an important focus for the critical researcher in uncovering the claims to legitimacy and power that are made in public discourse.

YOUTH CRIME WAVES IN CANADA

Contemporary Debate

As mentioned in my introductory comments, for several years now Canada has been embroiled in a heated debate surrounding the nature, extent, and control of youth crime. Since the inception of the *Young Offenders Act* (1983), public opinion has concentrated on apparently increasing crime rates amongst youth and on the inability of the YOA to effectively curb youth crime. Feature articles in Canadian newspapers throughout the late eighties and early nineties have been consistent in their determination that youth violence is rapidly on the rise in Canada ("A Year of Youth Mayhem," *Vancouver Sun*, September 19, 1992), that "Youths Treat Crime as a Joke" (Saskatoon *Star Phoenix*, May 31, 1989) in defiance of the ineffective *Young Offenders Act*, and that kids literally have been "Getting Away with Murder" (*Montreal Gazette*, April 8, 1989). Much of the public panic has been fostered by official statistics that show quite clearly that official youth crime rates have increased in the past few years.

The public policy response to this growing public panic has been swift and pointed. New legislation regarding the YOA is intended to increase maximum sentences to 10 years, to transfer 16- and 17-year-old young offenders to adult court, and to abolish the confidentiality provision of the YOA, especially for repeat, violent offenders. It also aims to make mandatory the treatment of all young offenders. Furthermore, the Neighbourhood Watch lobby is advocating the lowering of the age for young offenders from 12 to 10; it has received considerable national support. At the provincial level, Manitoba has passed legislation to implement boot camps for young offenders of all stripes, and Alberta Premier Ralph Klein publicly advocates the execution of young offenders who commit murder. These dramatic public policy reactions emphasize the power of the law and order lobby in Canada regarding young offenders, and are stark reminders that public opinion is volatile and focused on the perceived dangerousness of young people in Canada.

As with most moral panics, however, public sentiment surrounding youth crime is poorly informed. While it is true that official crime rates have gone up rather dramatically from 1986 to 1993, the rise in the number of charges laid is primarily the result of society's increasing reliance on the courts and the police to deal with youth misconduct. Many schoolyard violations and domestic disputes among teenagers now end up in the court system; years ago such incidences were handled by the school or the extended family. Furthermore, the incidences of violent assaults by youth has purportedly remained relatively stable since 1986. In fact, the numbers of youth charged by police decreased by 7 percent in 1993, although there has been an increase in violent crime. Most of the increase, however, did not involve either injury or weapons, and most importantly, youth are responsible for less than 15 percent of all violent crimes in Canada.

The types of anecdotal evidence that are presented in the print and television media stand in contradistinction to the aforementioned data; they are clearly directed to the promotion of youth crime as an epidemic. And, as I will illustrate in this chapter, these singular depictions have tremendous political potency when framed in a certain type of rhetoric.

History of Canada's Youth Crime Panics

When we look at the history of youth crime in Canada, it becomes readily apparent that moral panics surrounding youth crime are not new, but are contingent upon or related to socioeconomic conditions. For example, late in the nineteenth century, refugees from the famine in Ireland and orphans from poverty-ravaged Britain were received by Canada. Between 1873 and 1903, more than 95,000 children came from Britain's slums and orphanages under the sponsorship of child immigration agencies (Carrigan, 1991). The demand for these children was high because they served as domestic servants and field workers, and yet many of these disaffiliated youths ended up on the street when their services were no longer needed. The term "street arab" came to be attached to homeless juveniles who lived in overcrowded urban areas, juveniles who were uneducated, without parents, or unsupervised. Many of these "street urchins" ended up in Kingston Penitentiary among the ranks of adult criminals.

As is the case with most youth crime of today, much of the juvenile crime in nineteenth-century Canada was minor, involving trespass, petty theft and truancy. While education was not compulsory, children who were not in school were targeted for being "on the street"; much of the policing of youths was the result of a social welfare/custodial approach to truant and wayward youths. The moral panic that drove public policy at this time was also the result of the public's perception about the connection between drugs, gang violence, and youth crime. Immigrant youths, upon suffering discrimination and intimidation from the nonimmigrant majority, formed gangs to provide security and social and economic opportunity. As is the current moral panic about youth crime, the rise in juvenile crime in early twentieth-century Canada was perceived by political officials as the result of immigrant gangs' involvement in interracial violence and drug trafficking and use. Carrigan points out that the linkage between drug use and juvenile delinquency reached a point at which, in Vancouver, the government asked the justice system to investigate the drug usage of all teenagers brought before the courts. In addition, the crime panic that ensued embraced a picture of young persons drawn into the dark web of criminal exploitation:

> Newspapers carried stories claiming that young girls were being lured into prostitution through drugs and that young boys were selling in the streets. Dope dealers, it was claimed, were offering free drugs to young people to get them addicted. (Carrigan, 1991, 221)

The public outcry in early twentieth-century Canada was driven by the political posturing of legal and political officials that youth crime was the result of the connection between race, immorality, and drugs. The "Child Saving Movement" (Platt, 1969), which presumably grew out of a deep social concern for child welfare, resulted in the Juvenile Delinquents Act of 1908, which gave the state absolute authority to intervene forcibly in family life, denying the family's right to due process. And, as it is with today's panic, responsibility for youth deviance fell squarely on the shoulders of poor families and their imputed social characteristics: deficient intelligence, uncaring parents, and poor home environments. It is evident that the history of youth crime is repeating itself in contemporary Canada.

The task for the critical criminologist, then, is to make sense of this modern-day moral panic in terms of content, origins, and influence. To do this, we require a post-critical orientation that is composed of several constructionist perspectives.

SOCIAL CONSTRUCTIONISM AND POST-CRITICAL CRIMINOLOGY

The social constructionist approach, which is generally unconcerned with the truth or validity of claims, focuses on how people come to accept the definitions of social problems, the claims regarding the origins of crime and criminality, and the effective and moral social policy responses. The social constructionist approach draws on critical criminologies in an attempt to understand the artificially constructed nature of crime panics and to identify the powerful players in creating moral messages. Obviously, the media has a significant role to play in the creation and communication of messages, but the task of the critical criminologist is to understand the rationale for one-sided or decontextualized versions of criminal incidents. And, of course, the role of the state and its affiliations with business and the media are necessary foci. An important avenue of analysis in the social construction paradigm is to focus on the plausability of truth claims made in support of a moral panic. Part of the deconstruction of truth claims is an understanding of how a problem is constructed, becomes part of public discourse, and shapes public policy.

The following theoretical orientations fall under the broad rubric of social constructionism, and are presented as necessary theories in the development of a post-critical criminological approach to moral panics that focuses on the latent messages in public discourse.

Marxist Criminology

The traditional Marxist perspective addresses the political context of moral panics, and, as a result, attempts to place the development of such panics in the context of economic crises and rising development (Hall et al., 1978). The basic argument is that during times of economic crises, governments use preemptive or proactive social control strategies to manage the volatile marginalized classes. Social fears, which are veiled in the public rhetoric of class dysfunction and family values, fuel police and state responses to underclass crime, while targeting underclass families for their deviance in everything from pornography to gambling to alcohol and drug abuse.

Despite trends away from Marxist analyses of moral panics—which include Weberian studies into interest-group influences and competition for moral control in a plural society—the Marxist tradition maintains an awareness that marginalized peoples tend to be the focus of law and order strategies and that manipulated public opinion is an oppressive and class-based phenomenon. Neo-Marxist theories, in the vein of Gramsci and Habermas, augment traditional Marxism by focusing on how ideology operates as a hegemonic mechanism in identifiable historical junctures and how truth, as a result, is inextricably tied to politics. Foucault, while not an avowed Marxist, further adds to the debates with his studies of the knowledge-based mechanisms through which moralities come to be universally accepted, even among the most marginalized. Overall, the Marxist tradition maintains our awareness that public opinion and professional knowledge claims are constructed at certain points in time and are the result of class-based politics.

Left Realism

The left-realist development in critical criminology has focused the debates on crime and justice in the context of "taking crime seriously." This maxim suggests that before society can deal with the structural inequalities that underpin disparities in criminal behaviour and judicial outcomes, it must understand and deal with the immediate needs of those most at risk to criminal victimization. This concentration on victimization is based on the assumptions that much criminal behaviour is intraclass; people are victimized by—and consequently fear—largely associates or people in the same social environment. As a result, the focus of research (and short-term public policy) is to meet the immediate needs of crime victims in terms of crime prevention and personal protection (see Lowman and MacLean, 1992 for left realism and crime control and MacLean and Milovanovic, 1991 for postmodern orientations in left realism).

While the left-realist movement has held to the basic tenets of political economy understandings of crime and punishment, it has pushed the debate into the post-critical arena by accounting for the needs and desires of victims, offenders, and the communities from which both are drawn. As a result, research and the ensuing social policy debates, focus on the multiple realities (including those based on race and gender) of criminal behaviour and the need for adaptable and effective criminal justice policies. The left-realist focus on victimization is central to the synthesized theoretical position I present later in this chapter, which argues for a discourse analysis of public panics that focuses on victimization as the core concept in construction and manipulation of public opinion.

Feminism and Criminality

One of the major contributions that feminism, as a general theoretical approach, has made to criminology is the conceptualization of crime, security, and justice as gendered phenomena (see Currie, 1991; Smart, 1990; Gelsthorpe and Morris, 1990 for post-critical insights into feminist theorizing). Women and men live in different worlds of criminality, fear, and victimization, and by studying crime as genderless, more traditional criminologies have hidden the reality for women that includes (relative to men) higher levels of fear, hidden victimization in the home and workplace, harsh treatment by the criminal justice system, and—most importantly for this chapter—veiled attacks by public officials and media sources.

Explanations of criminality have focused on nontraditional families, nontraditional motherhood, single parenthood, and poverty as causal factors in youth criminality. Feminism's concentration on the role of patriarchy in framing women's crime, and the imputed female role in criminogenesis, is insightful in that it provides a point of reference for understanding the contradictory claims in popular depictions of crime. Media presentations maintain that women are more susceptive to victimization and poverty than men, but they are also, through inadequate parenting, the producers of criminality and are, in essence, the inadvertent victimizers of children.

Foucault and Power and Knowledge

Foucault's work on power and knowledge is particularly important in understanding moral panics because it concentrates on how the scientific disciplines frame deviances in an objective, individualized manner, and analyzes the techniques by which power is deployed through the exclusive discourses of experts. As we will see in the media depictions of youth crime panics, public discourse is directed by the claims of experts who attempt to make sense of social problems through positivist eyes. Their legitimacy and their power stem from their claims to superiority as experts and their access to exclusive knowledge. Foucault's primary contribution to this debate, then, is that knowledge brokers, who are charged with understanding criminality, are powerful constructors of portraits of crime. Furthermore, this typically postmodern approach focuses on language as a source of power. Discourse, knowledge and power are inextricably connected in Foucault's paradigm, which awakens us to the need to deconstruct official and public opinion accounts. The identification of those who are responsible for directing public opinion, however, is left unstudied in a Foucauldian paradigm and that is when we need to turn to the Marxist- and feminist-based theories for guidance.

Theoretical Synthesis

I argue that these four general constructionist approaches can be synthesized in understanding the origins of the current moral attack on youth and the ensuing conservative law and order lobbies. The orientation of my approach is decidedly postmodern in the understanding of the multiple realities of crime and in the concern for the need to unveil the public discourse that hides classist and sexist agendas. A synthesis of idealist, realist, and feminist approaches with the postmodernist, deconstructionist position addresses the critiques of postmodernism as politically inert and localized (Hunt, 1991). The three critical theoretical positions reassert the importance of progressive politics in understanding a stratified world and in advocating structural change.

In the following section, I illustrate how media representations of the youth crime wave are constructed and presented in a manner that is both ideological and mythical. The postmodern, Foucauldian approach allows us to analyze how the language, and the signs and symbols of media discourse, frames social problems in seductive, yet ideological ways. The following media "stories" illustrate how the seduction works.

MEDIA REPRESENTATIONS AND THE DECONSTRUCTION OF CRIME MYTHS

I draw on three examples of media representations of youth crime to illustrate the power of decontextualized accounts and the ability of the media messages to represent the unusual as usual. The depictions of these incidents receive little or no public censure, other than in a limited amount of academic literature. What is interesting about all three depictions, however, is the politically correct, nonoffensive nature of the discourse. Importantly, when this discourse is unpacked, it becomes obvious that the subtle, politically palatable message is ideologically very directed and potentially powerful. The three depictions are very different, however, in how they manage the message. The message is the same, nonetheless, and it is simple: youth crime is endemic in society, it is somewhat inexplicable, and it requires dramatic and stern intervention.

Youth Crime and the Morality Play

The first example uses the unbelievable and the inexplicable to appeal to people's sense of despair by concentrating on the horror and the potentiality of violent behaviour and bystander apathy. In 1992, James Bulger, a 2-year-old British child, was abducted from a Liverpool shopping centre by two boys under the age of 13; he was dragged away along a railway track and beaten to death. This incident happened in plain view of passersby who failed to help, for reasons speculated on at great length by the media.

　　This case is noteworthy in part for the horrific nature of the crime and the fact that the convicted were so young, but it is most noteworthy in its evolution into a morality play. As Bradley (1994) argues, "This rarest of murders has been transformed into a symbol of everything that is wrong with Britain today" (12). The search for a rational explanation for the murders, the initial focus of the media, was replaced by a protracted campaign to understand this crime as only the result of the worst side of the human condition. The argument that evil incarnate is part of the human condition forewarns the potential in all citizens to become like the murderers of James Bulger. For if 10-year-olds, who in our estimation are too young to have had the chance to become corrupted, are capable of this behaviour then so are we all. But the class-based nature of this account becomes evident when newspapers such as the *London Sun* and the *Evening Standard* began speculating about the potential of certain kinds of families to persist outside of civilized society. It is at this point that state institutions (including the justice system and social services), along with conservative politicians and investigative reporters, engaged in a new type of class-oriented rhetoric surrounding the competency of parents in raising moral children. All three sources of opinion began to discuss the parents of the accused as somehow part of the flawed underclass with typical pejorative attributes, such as single motherhood and broken homes. The discourse centred on the classic cases of abuse and neglect that were deemed to be the result of privation; by extension, all children living in privation or in broken homes were at risk. This reactionary backlash harkens back to the turn-of-the-century justice system that was preoccupied with detecting predelinquency on the bases of social and cultural behaviour.

As Bradley points out, the resulting political debates about the Bulger murder called for more moral intervention, more classical punishment, and an attack on liberal politics. But what is most clear from this incident is that the drama that was played out after the crime created an audience response to portrayed nihilistic criminal behaviour, which described as being the result of the drift into immorality by the lower classes (with the attendant criminogens of pornography, alcohol, and promiscuity). And liberal social policies were blamed.

By fictionalizing and exploiting the tragedy of the victim, the media, in concert with conservative politicians, were able to nurture a public panic, which resulted in the call for more law and order and more intervention in the lives of marginalized families. Most noteworthy in this type of crime depiction is its ability to reconstruct and recontextualize the singular events of a case into a moralistic, societal framework in which moral breakdown, class privation, and the devolution of family values are indicted. The oppressive potential of a highly classed society and the immorality of blaming and punishing the victim of economic forces is disregarded. The mechanism of this disregard is illustrated in the following example.

The Decontextualization of Crime

The second example illustrates how media reporting tends to remove crime from its socioeconomic context and recast it in moralistic and emotional frames of reference that leave the reader with a sense of foreboding. In Chicago in September of 1994, an 11-year-old boy was murdered in a gangland-type slaying. The article in the news services (Saskatoon *Star Phoenix*, August 31, 1994) concentrated on the child's affiliations with gang members, the types of crimes he had committed in his young career (including the gang-related murder of a 14-year-old girl), and the lamentations of community leaders who blamed the system for failing the child. The article then changed abruptly to discuss a previous investigation by social services that revealed the boy had been scarred by systematic physical abuse in his family, and that social services had intervened unsuccessfully. The article then centred on the fact that he was taken from his mother and placed in the care of his grandmother, who eventually relinquished custody to welfare agencies. The final words in the article, supplied by a local police superintendent, were a message to all youths that the promises of gangs often have fatal consequences.

In summary, the article evoked sympathy for the child offender/victim and lamented the inability of the system to effectively care for him. But mostly the article discussed the family's pathology, the suggestions of a broken home headed by women, and the implications that gangs are at the core of the criminal world. While half-truths were present in the article, the major import occurred through omission. The article ignored the socioeconomic context in which the child and his family lived, the economic reality of social welfare agencies that are financially unable to carry out their mandates, and the reality of industrialized societies that discard people to make a profit.

The most striking sentiment expressed, however, is that this death and the crime that precipitated it are indicative of a generation of children out of control. The article leaves the reader with a sense of foreboding that nothing is to be done and that stricter crime control measures, while not solutions, are the only possible reactions. What is missing in this analysis, besides the context of the crime, is the reality of this child as a survivor. It is remarkable in one sense that an 11-year-old child can survive on the streets on his own for three years. It is understandable that the only context for such survival is gang affiliations, when legitimate avenues of support fail and the struggle to survive is neither pathological nor indicative of a degenerating society. It is more likely, in fact, a normal human response.

The reader is left with reason for panic. Apparently nihilistic behaviour at such a young age is an affront to our collective desire to care for the young, for when the young are corrupted, the society must be morally self-destructing. The sense of pessimism inherent in such accounts is a powerful indication that nothing is working and that something corrective must be put into place. While crime-control policy statements are absent, the insinuation is that the problems of youth are individual, family-based problems that need interventionist solutions.

The Exception as the Rule: The Invocation of Experts

The third example is from a 1994 issue of *Maclean's* magazine in which the cover story is entitled "Kids Who Kill: Special Report." The cover page shows a young man dressed in jeans, T-shirt, and an inverted ball cap holding a gun in a fashion that depicts his ability and familiarity with the weapon. Most striking about the depiction, however, is the ordinary and typical dress of the lethal youth, with the inverted ball cap as the icon of modern youth culture.

The article discusses three Canadian cases in which young offenders had committed murder. The individual cases are presented in temporal and graphic detail, and are accompanied by family photographs of the victims and their relatives, a grisly crime scene, and one of the young offenders in a prison garden. The articles concentrate on several dimensions of teenage criminality and imply that these levels of explanation are the most rationale and fundamental, and consequently offer the most hope for the control of deadly violence amongst youth. The first suggestion is that youth crime is erratic and unpredictable, and by implication, is threatening to everyone. The article invokes expert medical testimony to attest to the psychotic and inherent natures of these acts. Youths like these—and the article stresses the ordinariness of their communities and activities—can be found anywhere; psychopathic killers can be housed in the bodies of normal-appearing youths. The reader is left with the impression that a youth killer (and youth criminals in general) could be the boy—and the article is very gendered—next door.

The second suggestion that we see in the profiles of the three murders is part of the attempt to unpack and reconstruct the psychic lives of the young killers. The reports focus on elements of outside influence, such as exposure to pornography, the emulation of notorious movie criminals (the movie *Silence of the Lambs* is mentioned several times throughout the article), and the dysfunctionalities of family styles, including strict discipline, lax discipline, absentee fathers, single motherhood, and poverty. The ostensible markers of delinquency are introduced into the criminality equation as warning signs for pathological behaviour.

The preamble to the three case studies is quite telling in how it represents the "problem of youth crime" in language that is laden with sinister references to the unique predatory nature of the young killer. Further, the introduction offers a litany of inexplicable killings by children that have raised the public pressure to reform the *Young Offenders Act*. The last paragraph in the article, however, hypothesizes that what youth criminals have in common is a "stunning lack of empathy" for their victims. The article finally calls on the work of an eminent psychiatrist to make sense of the youth crime wave; his conclusion is that more adolescents are now borderline personality types "like the characters in the *Silence of the Lambs*" (Kaihla et al., 1994, 33) than in the past. His last warning is to the irresponsible parent for creating the young Hannibal Lechter. While the article attempts to be evenhanded in explaining the position of detractors who argue for the lenient handling of young offenders, the overall journalistic slant is that, somehow, the youth generation is nihilistic, and that the state's social control mechanisms are not doing enough to curb the increasing youth violence in our society.

The overall article does present a compelling case for the continual attempt to understand and deal with youth killers. It would be impossible for anyone not to feel and share the extreme tragedy and loss felt by the victims and their relatives and communities. And, of course, there is a continuing need to protect people from harm. What the article transmits, however, is a sense of helplessness, a sense that youth homicide is characteristic of a degenerating youth culture. By invoking experts and their discourse, the article presents youth violence as unexceptional and commonplace; by speculating on the origins of youth criminality, this type of discourse recirculates moral indictments against family types, social classes, and gendered environments. What we are left with, then, is a constructed world that is polarized into good and bad, where criminals are of a certain social caste, a world in which the answers to problems, once again, are to be found in law and order.

Media Commonalities

Three media depictions illustrate the different ways that public discourse frames youth crime. What is most important from an analytical, moral panic framework is how these accounts of criminal behaviour use individual examples as the norm, and how the criminal behaviour is decontextualized from the stuctured nature of the society. Furthermore, when crime problems are framed in the context of morality, parenting, and poverty, the problem of crime is individualized, the legitimacy of "normal," affluent lifestyles is reinforced as is the legitimacy of the social order. In essence, the moral panic draws on existing ideological beliefs about crime and criminality and reinforces this ideology by fomenting fear about the unpredictable and expandingly dangerous nature of youth activity. When we take such public culture depictions of youth crime and place them in a post-modern critical framework, it allows us to critique positivist/modernist claims regarding the nature and extent of youth crime, and to place this critique in the contexts of debates surrounding class and criminogenesis, gender and parenting, and offense and victimization.

VICTIMIZATION

A critical discourse analysis of the media presentations of crime and justice shows us that the concept of victimization is a recurrent focus in many of the public accounts of youth criminality. The language of victimization evokes both sympathetic and empathetic passions in the observer/reader.

Victimization is used as a discursive mechanism in two ways. First, textual and pictorial depictions of victims' experiences are intended to evoke very primal, passionate responses to fear of crime and potential victimization. The vicarious victim experience frames our understanding of the criminal event and serves to create empathy not only for the victim, but also for advocates of law and order. Second, explanations for youth deviance are made in the context of family and cultural victimization, and, indeed, the insinuations include gendered, class-based families as potential victimizers of their children.

We are left, then, with dual accounts of victimization, which establish that there is a need for panic and that innocent children are the victims of an uncaring, dangerous, poverty-stricken class. And, of course, one of the dilemmas that we encounter as critical analysts, which has been expressed by left realists, is that victimization is a real problem and it does impact on people's lives. Crime needs real solutions and this contention is difficult to refute or ignore. The importance, however, in understanding the concept of victimization is that it is a volatile, powerful discursive tool, which evokes collective passions and which feeds law and order politics.

What is missing, then, from these essentially popular cultural depictions of crime is a sense of larger victimization at the structural level. Certainly this is not a new understanding of the decontextualization of crime. But what is important here is how depictions are constituted in discourse that is, at once, believable, instructive, and policy-forming. This is where critical, postmodern insights are useful in unpacking the language of labeling, identifying the political and economic forces that drive the discourse, and analyzing the political and economic advantages that accrue from the denigration of marginalized, relatively powerless people.

CONCLUSION

It is becoming increasingly apparent that moral panics, typified by the current call for a more punitive and stricter *Young Offenders Act*, are generally poorly informed. This chapter argues for a revisiting of the concept of the moral panic in an attempt to understand the collective passions that drive conservative law and order strategies. The sociological question that remains then is whether public sentiment precedes the activities of discursive agents like politicians and media specialists, or whether these typical moral entrepreneurs direct public passions for political and economic benefits. A related and more basic question is whether we need even concern ourselves with the causal origins of socially constructed moral panics. We might simply take Foucault's phenomenological approach on the connections between power and knowledge; we need only understand the dynamics of power and not the origins. If we take this phenomenological approach, however, we accept a type of postmodern stance that is both noncritical and legislatively inert. It is at this point that we need to draw on feminist theory for its insights into the role of patriarchy in the linguistic and discursive construction of social problems, on theories of political economy for the analysis of the class-based nature of crime panics, and on left realism for its insistence that, despite the constructed and potentially oppressive nature of moral panics, crime is a problem of structural origins that must be confronted through both short-term, amelioratory policy as well as long-term structural reform.

Finally, I offer in this chapter the concept of victimization as a central focus for deconstructing moral panics and ensuing crime control policies. The theoretical and methodological synthesis proposed in this chapter also responds to some of the criticisms of postmodernism for discarding the important political economy concepts—the state, capitalism, class—and for failing to account for the gendered reality of crime and victimization.

REFERENCES

Bradley, Ann. 1994. "A Morality Play for Our Times," *Living Marxism*, January:10–13.

Carrigan, D. Owen. 1991. *Crime and Punishment in Canada: A History*. Toronto: McClelland & Stewart.

Cohen, Stanley. 1972. *Folk Devils and Moral Panics: The Creation of the Mods and Rockers.* Oxford: Blackwell.

Currie, Dawn. 1991. "Realist Criminology, Women and Social Transformation in Canada." In *New Directions in Critical Criminology,* edited by Brian MacLean and Dragan Milovanovic, 19–26. Vancouver: The Collective Press.

Gelsthorpe, Loraine, and **Allison Morris.** 1990. *Feminist Perspectives in Criminology.* Buckingham, UK: Open University Press.

Hall, Stuart, Chas Critcher, Tony Jefferson, John Clarke, and **Brian Roberts.** 1978. *Policing the Crisis: Mugging, the State and Law and Order.* London: Macmillan.

Hunt, Alan. 1991. "Postmodernism and Critical Criminology." In *New Directions in Critical Criminology,* edited by Brian MacLean and Dragan Milovanovic, 79–86. Vancouver: The Collective Press.

Jenkins, Philip. 1992. *Intimate Enemies: Moral Panics in Contemporary Great Britain.* New York: Adeline de Gruyter.

————. 1991. *Intimate Enemies: Moral Panics in Contemporary Britain.* New York: Aldine de Gruyter.

Kaihla, Paul, John DeMont, and **Chris Wood.** 1994. "Kids Who Kill: Special Report," *Maclean's* magazine, August, 32–39.

Kappeler, Victor E., Mark Blumberg, and **Gary W. Potter.** 1993. *The Mythology of Crime Delinquency.* Prospect Heights, Ill.: Waveland Press Inc.

Lowman, J., and **B. MacLean.** 1992. *Realist Criminology: Crime Control and Policing in the 1990s.* Toronto: University of Toronto Press.

MacLean, B., and **D. Milovanovic.** 1991. *New Directions in Critical Criminology.* Vancouver: The Collective Press.

Painter, Kate. 1993. "The Mythology of Delinquency: An Empirical Critique." Presented at the British Criminology Conference, Cardiff University.

Platt, Anthony. 1969. *The Child Savers: The Invention of Delinquency.* Chicago: University of Chicago Press.

Smart, Carol. 1990. "Feminist Approaches to Criminology or Postmodern Women Meets Atavistic Man." In *Feminist Perspectives in Criminology,* edited by Loraine Gelsthorpe and Allison Morris, 70–84. Buckingham, UK: Open University Press.

PROSTITUTION: ON THE DARK SIDE OF THE SERVICE INDUSTRY

Fran Shaver

INTRODUCTION

Prostitution is rarely considered to be a tenable occupation. Nevertheless, it provides a theoretically interesting context in which to examine occupational health and safety (OHS) issues for women. First, it is a female-dominated work activity (rough estimates indicate that 67 to 90 percent of the street prostitutes in Canada are female (Department of Justice, 1989)). Second, the workers are highly stigmatized, not only by the general public and citizen groups who periodically demand that their streets be "cleaned," but also within the legal and scientific discourse of legislators and academics. These two characteristics alone are sufficient to raise questions regarding the possibility of gender bias and the social order that supports it.

Historically, the health and safety policies regarding prostitution that have been put in place embrace the assumption that the workers themselves—especially the female workers—are a *threat to others*. The *Contagious Diseases Act* (enacted in 1865–1870), for example, was designed to protect military men from venereal diseases. The statute authorized the detention of diseased prostitutes for up to three months at certified hospitals (CACSW, 1984, 131). "Between 1918 and 1920 over 18,000 women who were believed to be infected with VD, or who were considered likely to become infected, were rounded up by the US government and committed to prison hospitals. [Female] prostitutes were the main target of this containment. Significantly, none of their customers were rounded up" (Brock, 1989, 13). Policies directed at the sanitary policing of prostitutes are still evident today, in spite of evidence demonstrating that the link between prostitutes and the spread of sexually transmitted diseases (STDs) and AIDS is exaggerated (Rosenberg et al., 1988; Shaver, 1985, 497).

Policies addressing the *risks to workers*—the more common way to address OHS issues—tend to have been established in the form of criminal law and tend to impact negatively on those they were designed to protect. Shortly after Confederation, the new federal government in Canada enacted provisions prohibiting the defilement of women under the age of 21, consolidated and expanded the vagrancy provisions to embrace males found to be living on the avails of prostitution, and adopted new statutes proscribing the procurement of women for unlawful carnal connection (McLaren, 1986, 131, 136). These statutes were designed to protect women and children from the wiles of the procurer, pimp, and brothel keeper. However, as McLaren (1986) clearly demonstrates, these statutes—and others that extended and strengthened the penalties—failed to provide the protections envisioned and, in many cases, increased the risks for women. Our current prostitution-related laws continue to impact negatively on women, often serving to place them in high-risk situations, rather than provide safer working conditions (Shaver, 1993, 164).

Both systems, whether set up to *contain the threat* or to *protect the workers* are woefully inadequate (McLaren, 1986; Walkowitz, 1981). This inadequacy is grounded in both systemic and personal prejudice, supported by a lack of accurate empirical information about the actual conditions of the sex trade, and the day-to-day experiences of the workers. This chapter redresses the balance by introducing data that more accurately reflect the circumstances of street prostitutes, and by demonstrating the way in which their OHS concerns parallel those of women in non-sex-work occupations.

I begin by locating sex work and sex workers within the OHS literature on Canadian women (Messing, 1991). Next, I present some data specific to the health and safety of street prostitutes. Finally, I identify several research strategies that will improve our knowledge about the health and safety of sex workers. In the process, the implications of this research for nonprostitute women will be considered.

STUDY POPULATION AND DATA COLLECTION

The evaluation of working conditions is based on two different samples of women and men practising street prostitution in Montreal. The interviews were conducted in the summers of 1991 and 1993 during three months of intensive field work. During these two periods, four student assistants and I spent many evenings and nights on streets frequented by prostitutes. We interviewed a sample of them (including 60 women and men in 1991 and 52 in 1993) regarding their working conditions, work activities, job history, and family situations.[1] Data regarding the job hazards experienced by female and male workers, and an evaluation of their general health problems and safer-sex practices will be the primary material used in this chapter.[2] Interviews lasted between 30 to 90 minutes and generally took place off the street over coffee. A small number were conducted in the home of the worker.

The mean age of the female sex workers in 1991 and 1993 was 22.4 and 21.8 respectively; that of the male sex workers was 24.7 and 23.1 respectively. All but three or four had been involved in prostitution activities for more than a year; 25 percent had been working for ten or more years. Over 50 percent of the women and men we interviewed had completed high school.

SEX WORK AND THE LITERATURE ON OHS

Fifty-five percent of Canadian women 15 years of age and over are in the labour force (Statistics Canada, 1988, 1). Unlike Canadian men in the labour force—who are distributed more evenly across all occupational groupings (Messing, 1991, 8)—most of these women are concentrated in the human-service industries, especially those at the lower level: 31 percent are in clerical and related occupations, 15 percent are in services, 10 percent are in sales, and 8 percent work in medicine and health occupations. This represents approximately 65 percent of the female labour force (Messing, 1991, 19). Further, in two of these groupings (clerical and related, and medicine and health) the vast majority of the workers (79 percent) are women. The gender distribution of those employed within services and sales is much more equitable (54 percent men to 46 percent women and 43 percent men to 57 percent women respectively (cf. Table 1)).

There are no estimates with respect to the proportion of women in the labour force who are involved in the sex trade. Nevertheless, there are estimates of the gender breakdown *within* the sex trade. Field studies conducted for the Justice Department in the late 1980s indicate that between 67 and 90 percent of street prostitutes were women. In Calgary, 82 percent of the prostitutes identified in head counts were female; in Toronto, 75 percent of those counted were female; in Halifax, 67 percent, in Vancouver, 90 percent, and in Montreal, just over 80 percent were female (Department of Justice, 1989, 42–44). These data most closely reflect the gender distribution in the clerical and health categories. The gender equity seen in services and sales does not carry over to the "dark side" of the service industry: 80 percent of those practising street prostitution are women and 20 percent are male (see Table 1).

TABLE 1 Major Occupational Groups Employing Women by Gender of Worker (Canada, 1986 and Montreal, 1988)

	Female (%)	Male (%)	Total (000's)[1]
Clerical and Related:[2]	79	21	2,260
Medicine and Health:[2]	79	21	599
Services:[2]	54	46	1,621
Sales:[2]	43	57	1,267
Street Prostitution:[3]	80	20	—[4]

1. Rounded to the nearest thousand.
2. Source: *Dimensions, Occupational Trends, 1961–1986*. Statistics Canada, Catalogue 93–151. Ottawa: 1988. These four occupational categories employ approximately 65 percent of the women in the labour force.
3. Based on head counts of street prostitutes in Montreal (Canada, 1989, 42–44).
4. Unknown.

Research in the occupational health and safety of women has been neglected, especially with respect to human-service occupations (where I would place sex work). According to Messing (1991, 8), "few, if any, studies have specifically examined the health and safety effects of jobs done by waitresses, child care workers, cleaners, sales clerks, receptionists or teachers—over a million Canadian workers". Nurses have been fairly well-researched but other hospital workers such as nurses' aides, aides, and orderlies have not (Dewar et al., 1992). Because the working conditions in these sites often pose risks to the employees, this lack of research is unacceptable. Hospitals especially have been identified as high-risk workplaces:

> Hospital workers are injured twice as often as other [human] service workers. They are exposed to at least 179 skin and eye irritants and 135 agents producing a risk of cancer or reproductive effects. In addition, they may suffer from shift work, emotional problems and, in psychiatric wards, aggression from patients. (Messing, 1991, 63)

The lack of research in the OHS of women is even more severe with respect to women in sex work. Furthermore, when sex work has been examined it has usually been from a deviance perspective, which tends to stigmatize those who perform the work, and has largely excluded concerns for OHS issues. This charge extends to research by feminist scholars as well, where the ambivalence toward prostitutes and prostitution has meant that OHS issues have been peripheral to the debate. This is an unfortunate oversight for there are many similarities between sex workers and those in other occupations.

Researchers have identified several factors that pose a risk to working women and men.[3] Many of these factors are *common* (but not specific) to many women's jobs.[4] *Stress* is a leading one. As Messing (1991, 41) suggests, "Workers often talk about how stressful their jobs are, and this usually refers to feelings of nervousness or anxiety that are connected with their work, induced by emotional pressures from clients, colleagues or superiors". Individuals may distinguish between physical and mental suffering but the body does not. "Technically, there is a stress reaction which can be induced by many types of stressors, physical, mental and emotional." Reactions include insomnia, digestive problems, anxiety, depression, heart problems, and malfunctioning of the immune system, and can be provoked by many workplace conditions, from noise to chemicals to sexual harassment. Messing (1991, 43) also notes that "'double disadvantaged' aboriginal, immigrant or disabled women may suffer from additional stressors such as isolation, discrimination or difficulties in communication." Similarly, the stigma attached to sex work represents a double disadvantage—and consequently additional stress—for sex workers. Stress is a common condition of the sex-work environment: 83 percent of the women we interviewed in 1993 described their work as stressful or very stressful.

Messing (1991) also provides a full list of additional characteristics common to many women's jobs that pose specific health and safety risks. Here,

I limit the discussion to those conditions most common to both sexual and asexual human-service workers: responding to the needs of others, repetitive work with the hands, standing, sexual harassment, shift work, and exposure to illness and infections. In almost all cases, the research in these areas is underdeveloped.

Most of the traditionally female occupations require *responding to the needs of others*, whether they are patients in hospitals, children in schools, customers in supermarkets, or "tricks" on the street. Regardless of the work situation—fast-paced with a low turnover, as in the case of hospital workers who would like to spend more time with patients, or slow-paced with a high turnover, as in the case of sex workers who would like to spend as little time as possible with clients—these exchanges can be rewarding. By their very nature, however, they are also demanding and difficult. Stress, exhaustion, and burnout are common occurrences among human-service workers regardless of the service provided, but very little research has related these risks to the specific aspects of working conditions (Messing, 1991, 46).

Boring, repetitive work is also common to both asexual and sexual service workers. Hospital laboratory technicians repeat the same procedures over and over; so do sex workers. Women factory workers tend to be concentrated in jobs where they make rapid, repetitive hand movements; so do sex workers. This type of work has been associated with anxiety attacks and musculoskeletal problems such as wrist pathologies (Messing, 1991, 47), yet little research has been conducted in this area. Female sex workers complain about both of these problems, and often complain about the boring, repetitive nature of their work; 88 percent strongly agreed that they do the same things over and over.

Standing is also characteristic of both sexual and asexual service workers. Street prostitutes, cashiers, store clerks, tellers, and factory and laboratory workers all stand for long periods of time. Messing cites studies demonstrating that this position exerts a demand on leg muscles—causing pain—and impedes blood circulation—causing swelling (Messing, 1991, 49). Prostitutes who stand outside, even during the cold Canadian winter, and who wear very high-heeled shoes as part of their "uniform" experience many of these symptoms: 76 percent of the women we interviewed in 1993 complained of sore feet.

Researchers are beginning to recognize *sexual harassment* as a stressor in women's jobs. Harassed women have reported digestive problems, insomnia, and tension (Messing, 1991, 53). It is common but not limited to situations where women are entering jobs previously reserved for men. A 1989 study commissioned by the Montreal Urban Community Police "found that over 30 percent of the 250 policewomen on staff had been victims of sexual harassment by their colleagues" (Colpron, 1989, cited in Messing, 1991, 53). Sexual harassment can be manifested in even more serious assaults: "In the U.S. it has been estimated that there are between 156 and 710 cases of rape in workplaces every year," and "an [other] American study reports that convenience store cashiers (who often work evenings and nights) run a high risk of sexual assault, as much as 20 times greater than that of other women" (Seligman et al., 1987, cited in Messing, 1991, 53, 73).

It remains to be seen whether women who practise street prostitution are at greater or lesser risk than policewomen and store cashiers, but sexual assault is definitely a reality of their working environment. Fourteen of the 30 female sex workers we interviewed in 1991 were sexually assaulted in the 12 months prior to the interview; 22 had been physically assaulted. Furthermore, prostitutes who are physically or sexually assaulted will have more difficulty than other women pursuing their case with the police (Shaver, 1985, 496). Assault is not the only risk: there have been 31 prostitute homicides in Canada during the period from June 1992 to December 1993.[5]

Shift work is another reality for many working women: large office buildings are cleaned at night and health-care institutions are staffed 24-hours a day, as are many factories. Many women simply work late hours in bars and restaurants. In the OHS literature, the harm in shift work is most often linked to disruptions to the hormones and chemicals that are produced cyclically in the human body, making it ideal for most people to sleep at night and work in the day. Messing (1991) reports higher-than-average numbers of sleep and stomach disorders, fatigue, irritation, and aggression have been found among Swedish shift workers. She also cites a Quebec study of hospital workers that showed a relationship between insomnia and more than four years of shift work (1991, 54). Shift work may also hurt family and social life. Prostitutes, as well as the researchers interviewing them, work a very late shift. We were generally in the field from nine o'clock at night until three or four o'clock in the morning. Since such scheduling played havoc with our family, leisure, and work lives, it more than likely created similar problems for the sex workers we interviewed.

I mentioned above that hospitals represent a high-risk work environment. *Illnesses and infections* are a substantial part of that risk. Workers are exposed to germs through contact with patients, blood, human waste, and soiled clothing. Hepatitis B infection is common and hospital workers are concerned about exposure to the HIV virus, although it is generally agreed that infection with the HIV virus is much less likely than hepatitis infection (Messing, 1991, 65). Our interviews indicate that these concerns are shared by sex workers: the vast majority (90 percent) are tested regularly for HIV and other sexually transmitted diseases.

A final feature common to many "women's jobs" is that women and men in these occupations are *treated differently and have different experiences*. This in turn means that their risks are different. Furthermore, as Messing argues (1991, 29), the failure to recognize that women and men are doing different jobs within the same occupational grouping serves to conceal important differences in the occupational health and safety risks they face. Gender patterns with respect to these factors are also evident in street prostitution. It is to these differences that we now turn.

WOMEN AND MEN SEX WORKERS ARE DOING DIFFERENT JOBS

In common with asexual-service workers, women and men doing sexual-service work have *separate job titles*. Women are most often called prostitutes, hookers, working girls, or whores. Men, on the other hand, are referred to as male hustlers or simply hustlers, terms that carry much less stigma than the labels given to the women.

Their occupational demographics are somewhat different as well (cf. Table 2). Women, in comparison to men, are less likely to work alone, more likely to have regular schedules and more likely to report that street prostitution is their only source of income. Surprisingly, we found that women's careers appeared to be shorter: the women had worked an average 5.1 years in the business compared to an average 7 years for the men. However, a closer look reveals that men drop in and out of prostitution work more often than do women—almost twice as often. Once we develop a measure sensitive to those periods we will likely find that women have longer careers than men.

TABLE 2 Selected Occupational Demographics of Street Prostitutes by Gender of Worker (Montreal, 1991 and 1993)

	1991		1993	
	Female (*N*=30)	**Male** (*N*=30)	**Female** (*N*=26)	**Male** (*N*=26)
% Yes, work alone[1]	27%	90%	—	—
% with regular work schedule[1]	77%	53%	—	—
Mean no. days work per week[2]	5.8	4.1	5.8	5.3
% reporting sex work as only source of income	80%	60%	50%	12%
Mean no. years in sex work[3]	5.1	7.0	4.8	6.5
Mean no. of periods when dropped out of sex work for month or more[1]	5	9	—	—

1. This question was not included in the 1993 Interview Guide.

2. The 1993 figures include reference to both full-time and part-time days; the 1991 figures refer to days in general.

3. These figures were calculated by subtracting the respondent's current age from the age s/he began working regularly. In 1993, however, we specifically asked the respondents to estimate the number of years in sex work: the mean figures for women and men were much closer together (4.3 years and 4.9 years respectively).

Our data also indicate that their work roles are somewhat different: the women point out that the sexual services they provide are very limited and are delivered in a short time (15–20 minutes) using a condom. Nongenital touches—kissing, hugging, hand-holding, prolonged eye contact, the touching and stroking of breasts—are rarely part of their repertoire. They service an average 28.5 clients per week. Hustlers, on the other hand (regardless of their sexual orientation), tend to engage in and enjoy a greater variety of services than do female prostitutes, are somewhat less likely to insist on using condoms, and on average negotiate lengthier time periods. They report spending an average of 40 minutes with each client (this is an average 20 minutes more with each client than the women). They service an average 14.5 clients per week.

GENDERED DIFFERENCES IN THE OHS OF STREET PROSTITUTES

In common with asexual-service workers, the dissimilar jobs done by women and men sexual-service workers are also paralleled by important differences in the occupational health and safety risks they face. As mentioned above, the data in our study permit several comparisons between the working conditions of women and men practising street prostitution in Montreal in 1991 and 1993. We have information from both data sets regarding the more traditional hazards associated with sex-work activities (sexual and physical assault, rape, theft, control by pimp, drug use, condom use and STDs). The interview guide used in 1993 was designed to be more sensitive to a wider variety of OHS concerns. As a consequence, the data also include information regarding general health problems such as sore feet, shortness of breath, back pain, insomnia, and the extent to which the work is regarded as generally stressful, boring, and repetitive. These data are presented in Table 3.

Although women and men are equally likely to conclude that their work is boring, women (88 percent) are more likely than men (54 percent) to consider it repetitive. They also assess it as more stressful than men (83 percent to 54 percent) and indeed it is much more risky and hazardous for them. In comparison to men, women report more rape and assault, are more likely to be robbed by their clients, and are more likely to be arrested. The data in Table 3 compare the mean number of hazardous incidents experienced in the last 12 months before the interview. With respect to all four types of incidents—rape, assault, theft by client, and prostitution-related arrest—the average number of incidents reported by women is substantially higher and significantly different than the average numbers reported by men. Women are also twice as likely to be working for someone else, usually identified as "my pimp" or "my man." While one cannot simply assume that this creates a situation that is directly harmful to the worker, it certainly increases the risk.

TABLE 3 Working Conditions in Street Prostitution by Gender of Worker (Montreal, 1991 and 1993)

	Female (N=30)[1]	Male (N=30)[1]
Boring: Percentage who find work very boring[2]	28%	28%
Repetitive: Percentage who strongly agree they do the same things over and over[2]	88%	54%
Stressful: Percentage who describe work as very or somewhat stressful[2]	83%	54%
Hazardous:[3]		
Rape	.83	.10
Assault	2.0	.40
Theft by Client	.80	.20
Prostitution-Related Arrest	1.37	.37
Percentage who work for another[4]	50%	0%

1. Unless otherwise stated, the data are taken from the 1991 sample.

2. Based on the 1993 sample: 25 females and 26 males.

3. The figures reflect the mean number of incidents experienced in the last 12 months.

4. Most often identified as "my pimp" or "my man."

There are also gender differences with respect to more traditional health problems. First, if seeing a doctor is an indication of taking better care of oneself, then women prostitutes are doing just that: 44 percent of the prostitute women we interviewed in 1993 visited a doctor or clinic more than nine times in the past year, compared to 15 percent of the male hustlers. These women were also slightly more likely to assess the state of their health as very good (44 percent to 32 percent).

Second, as Table 4 shows, women have somewhat different complaints than men: at least 40 percent of the women experience sore feet, shortness of breath, fatigue and general weakness, and insomnia at least once a week. Sore feet are the women's biggest complaint: 76 percent identify it as a problem. Given the very high heels most tend to wear while working, this does not come as a surprise. Men's complaints exceed women's only with respect to upset stomachs, headaches, leg cramps, and difficulty concentrating. It remains to be seen whether this is due to their more extensive use of hard drugs (see discussion below and Table 5).

High heels and drug use aside, it is constructive to recall that insomnia and upset stomachs have both been identified as reactions to stress and sexual harassment (Messing, 1991, 45, 54). Upset stomachs and general fatigue have also been identified by cashiers and hospital workers as reactions to shift work (Messing,

1991, 72). Although this suggests that many of the more traditional health concerns of sex workers parallel those of women and men in non-sex-work occupations, it is essential to remember that there are other health concerns that set them apart, particularly those related to safer-sex health practices while on the job. These concerns include client discretion, condom use, hard drug use, and tests for HIV and STDs. Nevertheless, while the nature of their concerns might set them apart from non-sex-service workers, gender differences are still evident.

TABLE 4 General Health Problems Experienced by Street Prostitutes at Least Once a Week by Gender of Worker (Montreal, 1993)

Symptom	Female (N=25)	Male (N=25)[1]
Sore feet	76%	48%
Shortness of breath	48	24
Fatigue/General weakness	48	40
Insomnia	40	32
Back pain	32	20
Upset stomach	32	42[2]
Headaches	32	40
Cramps (legs and stomach)	24	44
Difficulty concentrating	24	48
Diarrhea/Constipation	16	8[2]

1. N=25 unless otherwise stated.

2. N=24 due to missing data.

As can be seen in Table 5, both women and men use a great deal of discretion with respect to the clients they take on: all of the women and 83 percent of the men are in the habit of refusing clients on a regular basis. Both also practise safe sex while on the job. Nevertheless, it is clear that the women are much more consistent about it than the men (all but a few use condoms all the time during all sex acts). These figures are even more striking when compared to the condom use of a sample of college students with more than one partner in a six-month period. Only 48 percent of the women and 40 percent of the men in that sample reported using a condom all of the time.[6]

Both the male and female prostitutes were also cautious with respect to risks related to HIV and other STDs. They were regularly tested for AIDS/HIV (women only somewhat more often than men) and reported similar numbers of episodes with STDs over the last two years (0.77 and 0.70 episodes respectively). However, 63 percent of both women and men reported zero episodes in the last two years, suggesting that there is a very small number of sex workers who are chronically infected, as opposed to a large number of sex workers who are occasionally infected.

There are some striking differences with respect to drug use. Women are much less likely than men to be involved with hard drugs such as cocaine, crack, or heroine (7 percent compared to 50 percent) and much less likely to be high on drugs while working (10 percent compared to 60 percent). In 1993, of the men who used hard drugs, 80 percent stated that they injected them. Of the small number of women (7 percent) involved in hard-drug use, none injected and were thus, overall, at much less risk than the men.

TABLE 5 Safer-Sex Health Issues and Street Prostitution by Gender of Worker (Montreal, 1991)

	Female (N=30)	Male (N=30)
Percentage Having Refused Tricks:	100%	83%
Percentage Using Condoms Always During:		
Oral sex	97%	55%
Anal sex[1]	100%	90%
Vaginal sex[2]	100%	75%
Tests For AIDS/HIV:		
Yes, tested negative	90%	83%
No, never tested	10%	17%
Mean Number of STD Episodes in the Last Two Years:	.77	.70
Actual Number of STD Episodes in the Last Two Years:		
Percentage reporting zero	63%	63%
Percentage reporting one	20%	27%
Percentage reporting two or more	17%	10%
Percentage Using Hard Drugs at Least Once in the Last Week:	10%	60%
Percentage High on Drugs While Working:	10%	60%

1. Very few provide this service (four women and seven men).

2. Very few men (three to four) provide this service.

ISSUES TO BE EXPLORED

These data clearly indicate the utility of examining sex work and sex workers from an occupational health and safety perspective. Not only are there definite parallels between sexual-service and asexual-service work, there are also significant differences that are revealed when gender is taken into account. Nevertheless, much more work must be done in order to extend the work started here.

We can begin by rethinking our approach to the study of prostitution. First, treating it as legitimate work is not entirely outrageous: the sexual-service industry is expanding in size, an increasing number of people involved are involved willingly, and prostitutes' rights organizations are lobbying for this status (Jennes, 1990; McGinnis, 1994; Pheterson, 1989). Second, although it is currently a female-dominated industry, it is essential to acknowledge the role of men within the industry—not only as managers (pimps), but also as workers. Many contemporary studies examine prostitution by focusing only on female prostitutes. Making male sex workers more visible will facilitate gender comparisons crucial to our understanding of the industry. Third, recognizing that street prostitution represents only *one* aspect of a multifaceted industry, which includes many different forms of prostitution, pornographic production, and sexual spectacle (both audio and visual), will facilitate the selection of appropriate control groups. Once this is done, cross-occupational comparisons can be made both within the sex-work industry and between the sex work and other service-work industries. Such comparisons are required in order to assess the source of risks: is it the worker's gender, the job, the working hours, or the illegal status of sex work that creates the problem? Cross-occupational comparisons will also further our understanding of the OHS risks of sex workers. Finally, we also need to learn more about the interactions of workplace conditions with variables such as age, heredity, lifestyle, and socioeconomic status (including such factors as education and family background) and their effects on health.

Sex work is a theoretically interesting context in which to study OHS issues. Breaking down the barriers to the study of the OHS of sex workers is also highly practical. The findings, with respect to the gender differences in sex work and the cross-occupational differences and similarities, will help determine whether the risks involved in street prostitution are job based (i.e., linked to the commercialization of prostitution) or gender based and, therefore, linked to broader social issues. They will also serve to reinforce the work of others, such as Messing (1991) and Messing, Dumais, and Romito (1993) who are struggling to break down the barriers to the study of the occupational health and safety of women.

ENDNOTES

I would like to thank Bill Reimer for his comments on an earlier version of this chapter, which was presented at the CRIAW Annual Meeting, St. John's (November, 1993). The research for this chapter is supported by grants from SSHRC, FCAR, and Concordia University.

1   The 1991 database also includes interviews with 20 transgender prostitutes (10 transvestites and 10 transsexuals). These respondents are not included in the analysis conducted for this chapter.

2   We have information from both fieldwork periods regarding the more traditional hazards associated with sex-work activities (sexual and physical assault, rape, theft, control by pimps, drug use, condom use, and STDs). In addition, the 1993 guide contains a number of open-ended questions regarding job activities, client and coworker relations, and a series of questions about general health issues.

3   See Messing (1991) for a review of the literature in this area.

4   This discussion draws on the reviews of the literature by Messing (1991) and Messing, Dumais, and Romito. (1993).

5   Private conversation with John Fleishman, Director of Research Services, Department of Justice, Ottawa (December, 1993).

6   Data taken from a 1993 random sample of students at Concordia University coordinated by Taylor Buckner, Department of Sociology and Anthropology.

REFERENCES

Baruch, Modan et al.   1992. "Prevalence of HIV Antibodies in Transsexual and Female Prostitutes," *American Journal of Public Health*, 82(4):590–592.

Brock, Debi.   1989. "Prostitutes Are Scapegoats in the AIDS Panic," *Resources for Feminist Research*, 18(2):13–17.

Canadian Advisory Council on the Status of Women (CACSW).   1984. *Prostitution in Canada*. Ottawa: Canadian Advisory Council on the Status of Women.

Department of Justice.   1989. *Street Prostitution: Assessing the Law Synthesis Report*. Ottawa: Department of Justice.

Dewar, Belinda-Jane and **Jill Macleod Clark.**   1992. "The Role of the Paid Non-Professional Nurse Helper: A Review of the Literature," *Journal of Advanced Nursing*, 17:113–120.

Jennes, Valerie.   1990. "From Sex as Sin to Sex as Work," *Social Problems*, 37(3):403–420.

McGinnis, Janice Dickin.   1994. "Whores and Worthies: Feminism and Prostitution," *Canadian Journal of Law and Society*, 9(1):105–122.

McLaren, John P.S.   1986. "Chasing the Social Evil: Moral Fervour and the Evolution of Canada's Prostitution Laws, 1867–1917," *Canadian Journal of Law and Society*, 1:125–165.

Messing, Karen.   1991. *Occupational Safety and Health Concerns of Canadian Women— A Background Paper*. Ottawa: Labour Canada.

Messing Karen, Lucie Dumais, and **Partizia Romito.**   1993. "Prostitutes and Chimney Sweeps Both Have Problems: Towards Full Integration of Both Sexes in the Study of Occupational Health and Safety," *Social Science, Medicine and the Law*, 36(1):47–55.

Pheterson, Gail.   1989. *A Vindication of the Rights of Whores*. Seattle: The Seal Press.

Rosenberg, Michael J. and **Jodie M. Weiner.** 1988. "Prostitutes and AIDS: A Health Department Priority?," *American Journal of Public Health*, 78(4):418–423.

Shaver, Frances M. 1993. "Prostitution: A Female Crime?" In *In Conflict with the Law: Women and the Canadian Justice System*, edited by Ellen Adelberg and Claudia Currie, 153–173. Vancouver: Press Gang Publishers.

———. 1985. "Prostitution: A Critical Analysis of Three Policy Approaches," *Canadian Public Policy*, 11(3): 493–503.

Statistics Canada. 1988. *Dimensions, Occupational Trends 1961–1986*. No. 93-151 (November). Ottawa: Statistics Canada.

Walkowitz, Judith. 1981. *Prostitution and Victorian Society*. Ann Arbor: Cambridge University Press.

THE POTENTIAL OF LEGAL REFORM RECONSIDERED: AN EXAMINATION OF MANITOBA'S ZERO-TOLERANCE POLICY ON FAMILY VIOLENCE

E. Jane Ursel
Stephen Brickey

INTRODUCTION

If social activists were to base their strategies of legal reform on the literature from the sociology of law, the message would be clear: avoid the law as a vehicle to promote progressive change. Although there is no agreement on the best avenues to improve the conditions of people in relatively powerless positions, there is a consensus that the law is not one of these avenues. The sociology of law has come full circle in its view of law as an instrument of change. Early sociologists such as Sumner viewed law simply as a reflection of the strongly held values of the public and not as an institution capable of altering social practices. Then, in the 1960s and 1970s, a body of literature developed that suggested that, within limits, law could be used as an agent of change (cf. Evan, 1965).

More recently, some schools of Marxist and feminist academic work have taken the position that, with few exceptions, law is not an arena in which to engage in progressive struggles. While much of this debate has been in the area of feminist concerns (Comack, 1993; Snider, 1991; Sheptycki, 1991; Burstyn, 1985; Lacombe, 1988), others have addressed this issue when examining such diverse phenomena as corporate crime (Sargent, 1991), environmental crime (Schrecker, 1989), legal aid (Snider, 1986), and crime prevention (Hastings, 1991). Writing from feminist and Marxist perspectives, this literature takes a critical and often skeptical view of the possibility of "real change" through law reform.

Although there are variations in the arguments used to discredit the use of law as an agent of change, a common theme that runs through many of the arguments is that it is not possible to control how a specific legislative or policy initiative will be implemented within the legal system. Given the rigid structure of law, the constraints imposed by legal discourse, and the relative independence of those who work within the legal system, reform efforts will be incapable, with sufficient precision, to determine what effect, if any, a specific law or state policy will have.

Within this view, law is seen as a blunt instrument that is ineffective in implementing social reform. At best, the impact of the law simply fails to produce the intended effects; at worst, it produces unintended results that only worsen the conditions that were targeted for reform. The purpose of this chapter is to assess these issues through the examination of a legal reform that we define as a success: the treatment of family violence offences by the criminal justice system in Manitoba. After reviewing the literature on law and change, a description will be given of the efforts that have been made in Manitoba to restructure the way in which family violence is dealt with by the criminal justice system. Following this description, an account will be given of why this reform was worthwhile and the applicability of this case to the larger issue of law and social change.

LAW AS A BLUNT INSTRUMENT

Much of the literature devoted to law as an agent of change has attributed the failure of legal reform to the fact that law is a blunt instrument (Livingstone and Morison, 1990). Even when there appeared to be a victory through the passing of legislation or a policy initiative by the state, the absence of any substantive change was interpreted as the inability to influence how the reform was implemented within the legal system. The assumption that simply introducing a legislative or policy initiative would be sufficient to either eliminate the proscribed behaviour or, alternatively, ensure that prescribed behaviour would be complied with by the public proved to be incorrect. When social scientists empirically examined the effects of these legal reforms, they often found that the legal reforms had little, if any, impact. The explanations that have been given to account for these failures typically fall into one of the following categories.

Public Resistance

One of the axioms of legal reform is that substantial change is unlikely if that change is opposed by the general public, or at least a significant number of the public. Accounts of the failure of prohibition note the number of people who did not view consumption of alcohol as intrinsically bad and were willing to violate the law in order to obtain the proscribed beverage (Gusfield, 1963). This could also account for the failure of legal initiatives to control the use of various drugs.

It is typically in those instances of public resistance to legal reform that unanticipated consequences of the reform emerge, often resulting in conditions that are worse than the original problem. Thus, Massell's analysis (1973) of the early Soviet Union's attempt to implement revolutionary change in Central Asia by legally abolishing patriarchy revealed that the legislative changes worsened the position of women, both economically and in terms of their physical safety.

Smart (1989) refers to this phenomenon as the juridogenic nature of law. Juridogenesis refers to the potential of legal reform to produce effects that make conditions worse for those the reform was intended to assist. Since, according to Smart, it is not possible to know in advance which laws may by juridogenic, the wisest strategy is to avoid the law as a tool to implement social change.

Inadequate Enforcement

Even when there is public support for a legal reform, if the state does not provide adequate resources to enforce the law or ignores the way in which criminal justice personnel apply the law, the effect will be minimal. Literature on the subject is replete with examples of how inadequate resources in the areas of workplace, health and safety law (Reasons, Ross, and Patterson, 1981), environmental law (Schrecker, 1989), and corporate crime (McMullan, 1992; Snider, 1993) have resulted in these laws having minimal impact. The reticence of the state to allocate resources to enforce these laws is usually attributed to the fact that the violators represent powerful, economic interests aligned with the states and the laws are seen to be primarily for the purpose of appearance and not substance.

The other issue that arises in examining the law as a crude instrument of social change is the fact that law enforcement personnel are often free to ignore the law or apply it in a manner that suits their own purposes. In these instances, the state is either unable or unwilling to control how criminal justice personnel apply the law. This is not so much an issue of adequate resources as one of law enforcement and court personnel independently determining which laws to give priority to through selective enforcement by the police, lax prosecution by Crown attorneys and lenient sentencing by the judiciary. Again, it is not difficult to find examples where criminal justice personnel have applied the law in a style that negates the impact of the law. The traditional handling of sexual assault that led to the double victimization of rape victims by police and the courts (Clark and Lewis, 1977), the use of due process rules by the police to further their interests of crime control (Ericson, 1981; McBarnet, 1979), the reluctance of police to invoke the law in cases of wife abuse, and the traditionally minimal enforcement of drunk-driving laws illustrate the power of criminal justice personnel to determine the impact of law.

Legal Discourse

A more recent explanation for the ineffectiveness of legal reform is that the law's discourse will shape reforms into practice that bears little relationship to the original intent of the reform. Smart (1989) takes the position that the law's claims to truth—through the determination of what facts are relevant and irrelevant and the consequent disqualification of broader structural realities—serve to invalidate women's experiences and negate the impact of any legal reform that deals with women's concerns. Thus, when women use law to promote change they fall into a trap in which legal initiatives undergo a mutation whereby the new policy is transformed into an ineffective and sometimes harmful policy. Implicit within this view of law is the belief that it is not possible to have a significant influence on legal discourse or the determination of what is or is not relevant when an issue reaches the legal domain. Because the law is inherently androcentric, it is argued that women should resist the law's promise to solve their problems. This argument is reminiscent of earlier Marxist arguments that viewed legal reforms as futile because of inherent class biases within law (Balbus, 1977; Mandel, 1986).

While we acknowledge that the legal system, in both structure and operation, is embedded with assumptions and practices that are detrimental to women and the poor, it does not necessarily follow that these elements are immutable. To cite instances where legal reforms have failed is not sufficient evidence of this immutability, any more than reference to historical examples of unsuccessful attempts to lobby for political rights would be sufficient evidence that such struggles cannot be won. Instead, we would argue that past examinations of failed legal reforms are valuable in identifying areas—both within the legal system and in the larger society—that must be taken into account by social activists in order to increase their odds of success.

Recent changes in the Manitoba government's approach to family violence provide an opportunity to empirically examine how the legal reform was implemented within the criminal justice system and the impact of legal reform on a specific problem. The components of the criminal justice system, to be assessed are the changes in police protocol regarding how officers deal with family violence incidents and the creation of a specialized court devoted solely to criminal charges related to family violence. Specific focus will be given to those areas that have been previously identified as impediments to legal reform: the degree to which the public supports the reforms; traditional approaches to family violence taken by criminal justice personnel and the efforts to change these approaches; and the strategies and tactics used to modify those elements of the legal discourse that had the potential to diminish the impact of the legal reform.

METHOD

Several different data sources were used in the present research. Data on the public's views of wife abuse and its treatment by the criminal justice system were obtained from questions from personal interviews that were part of a 1991 survey conducted by the Winnipeg Area Study, a survey research institute at the University of Manitoba. The 533 respondents to the survey were selected from a systematic random sample of households in Winnipeg. The respondents were 18 years of age and older and were selected to ensure that a relatively equal number of males and females were included.

Data used to assess the police response to the initiative on family violence were the spousal charges laid by officers of the Winnipeg Police Department and the RCMP over an eight-year period beginning in 1983. These two police forces are responsible for policing more than 90 percent of the population in Manitoba.

The most extensive data component of the research is at the court stage of the criminal justice system The court analysis assesses the specialized Family Violence Court (FVC) and its outcomes in relation to nonspecialized courts in Winnipeg. To achieve this comparative analysis three court data sets are utilized: (1) the FVC data set, which consists of 1,600 cases disposed in the first year (1990–91) of the courts' operation; (2) the general court data set, which consists of 500 crimes against persons disposed of in general court over a period of one year (1991); (3) the "before" data set, which consists of 1,625 wife-abuse cases that were disposed of over a period of four years in general court prior to the introduction of the specialized court.

The sampling procedures utilized in each court data set differ and require a short explanation. The FVC data set involves a total population of cases heard and disposed within the study period rather than a sample. In the first year, 1,800 cases entered FVC, and 1,656 of these cases were disposed within 18 months (the study period). The FVC data set of 1,600 cases represents 97 percent of all cases disposed. The outstanding 56 cases were not recorded because 16 were at the Court of Appeal and 40 files were misplaced and did not come to the research unit in time to be recorded.

The general court data was based on a sample of cases involving crimes against persons taken from the nonspecialized provincial criminal court. The sample was determined by including all cases disposed within a particular study period. Because of the slow processing time in general court, there was a concern that few trial cases would be disposed within the limited study period. Therefore, two samples were collected. The first involved all cases set for trial that were disposed within the 10-month period of January to October 1991. In this period 187 cases set for trial were disposed. Not all of the trial sample were finally disposed through a full trial. Although originally set for trial, 28 percent of the trial sample was disposed through a guilty plea, and 32 percent were disposed through a stay of proceedings. As a result, only 76 of the 187 cases scheduled for trial actually proceeded through a full trial. In total 108 (or 21 percent) of the 500 cases were resolved through trial. This is comparable to the FVC data set in which 20 percent were resolved through trial. In addition to the trial sample, an intake period of six months (from July to December 1991) was designated to track all crimes against persons that entered provincial court. Within the six months, 997 cases entered the system; however, only 313 were disposed by the end of 1991. The two sampling procedures provided us with an overall sample of 500 cases in general court.

The "before" data set consists of a 53 percent sample of all spousal-abuse cases handled in the Winnipeg courts from 1983 to 1986. These cases were not randomly sampled. In 1983 and 1984, all cases in the first eight months of each year were recorded. This resulted in a sample of 59 percent of all cases in 1983 and a 61-percent sample of all cases in 1984. In 1985 and 1986, government staff working with domestic-abuse cases collected and coded cases as part of their job, collecting a 61-percent sample in 1985 and a 35-percent sample in 1986. Although a random sampling technique was not employed in any of the four years, the relatively large sample size (1,625 cases out of a total of 3,085 court cases) reassures us that these cases are reasonably representative of the spousal-abuse cases heard over the four-year period.

Data were collected from the same source in all three court data sets. Information was taken from the Crown attorney's case file upon disposition of the case. These files are very complete and include police reports as well as all particulars relating to the crime and the accused, including prior records The schedules used to record the data were identical for FVC and general court data sets; however, the schedule used for the "before" data set was much shorter and included fewer variables. Nevertheless, the variables used to measure court process, attrition, and sentencing are comparable for all three data sets (Ursel 1993).

CHANGING THE CRIMINAL JUSTICE SYSTEM

Despite academic cynicism about the merits of legal reform, women's groups have been lobbying the state over the past 15 years to recognize the crime of wife abuse and to treat it as a serious criminal offence. They demanded an end to the prevailing double standard: if a person struck a stranger it was considered assault, which activated a criminal prosecution procedure; if a person struck a family member or lover it was treated as a problem within the relationship and counseling was advised. Ending the double standard meant rigorous and consistent enforcement of the law. The stated goals of activists and reformers were: (1) police must charge in incidents of assault or abuse regardless of the relationship between the victim and the perpetrator; (2) Crown attorneys must take these cases seriously and pursue a prosecution; (3) sentencing must reflect the seriousness of the crime. These three expectations provide our measures of the impact of reform within the criminal justice system. Did social activism succeed in producing the desired effects, or did the impediments to reform undermine the policy changes designed to change police and court behaviour? Prior to examining these dimensions of Manitoba's zero-tolerance policy, it is first necessary to examine the public support for the state's initiatives.

Public Support

In addition to lobbying for political action on domestic violence, the women's movement has also been a significant catalyst in changing the public's perception of domestic violence as a private matter to that of a serious crime that merits state intervention. From its inception, the initiative taken by the provincial government received strong endorsement from the public. One of the first initiatives was a directive from the attorney general of Manitoba to instruct the police to lay charges in all instances of wife abuse where there were reasonable grounds to believe that a crime had been committed. A survey of Winnipeg residents one year after the mandatory charging policy was issued indicated that 85 percent agreed with the directive, 8 percent were undecided and 6 percent disagreed. A follow-up study in 1991 indicated further growth in support, with 87 percent agreeing with the directive to charge, 8 percent remaining undecided and only 4.5 percent disagreeing. Such immediate and overwhelming public support for such a significant change in criminal justice policy is virtually unprecedented and revealed the extent to which a policy of criminalizing family violence was, from the public's standpoint, long overdue.

Despite the strength of public support for the directive, the 1991 survey also revealed considerable suspicion among the public that the police were not always following the directive. When asked whether they believed the police followed the directive, only 6.6 percent of the respondents felt the police always did so; 37.7 percent of the respondents thought the police followed the directive in "most cases." The remaining 55.3 percent of the respondents indicated they thought the police followed the directive only "sometimes" or "rarely." While there was strong public support for criminalization there was also strong public suspicion that the system was not fully conforming to these new policies.

This suspicion about the nature of justice available to victims of family violence extended to the courts as well. The 1991 survey of Winnipeg residents revealed considerable concern that the courts did not sufficiently understand the needs of abuse victims. In fact, the public appeared to have less confidence in the judiciary than they did in the police. While 44 percent of the sample stated that the police followed the directive "always" or "most of the time," only 28 percent of the sample stated that the courts had an understanding of the needs of abuse victims "always" or "most of the time." This combination of strong public belief that criminal justice intervention is a proper response to family violence, along with a strong suspicion that not all members of the justice system adequately carry out their duties, put the criminal justice system under close public scrutiny.

The Media

In the last decade, the mass media have played a critical role in articulating public concern over family violence and in facilitating public scrutiny of the criminal justice system's response to this crime. From 1983 to 1992, there were 242 articles in the *Winnipeg Free Press*, the newspaper with the largest circulation in the province. These articles covered the entire range of issues surrounding the phenomenon of family violence and its treatment by the criminal justice system. In addition to reporting instances of particularly violent episodes of wife abuse and child abuse, and conveying the results of research and national reports related to family violence, the media also reported instances where the actions of the criminal system were deemed inadequate. These would include occasions when members of the judiciary made inappropriate comments at the time of sentencing, the inability of restraining orders to prevent abuse, and the failure of the police to respond quickly to an abusive incident.

The media's continuous reporting of issues related to family violence and their monitoring of the criminal justice system served to keep the public's attention focused on the issue of family violence and to further pressure the government to be accountable for its actions in dealing with the problem.

The Police

While the police have always had the legal mandate to treat family violence as a serious crime, it was common knowledge that the police typically exercised their discretion to not invoke the law in wife-abuse cases and encouraged the victim and offender to informally resolve the dispute. In their review of the literature on the police handling of wife abuse, DeKeseredy and Hinch (1991, 31) found that the reluctance of police to attend to these crimes was explained by a constellation of beliefs held by police officers. These beliefs included the idea that these incidents were private matters best dealt with by the parties involved, the perception that police intervention in domestic disputes presents a significant risk of physical injury to police officers, the belief that battered women sometimes deserve their fate as victims, and the belief that most women would not testify against their partners if the case did appear in court.

Given their view that wife abuse was a private matter and that some women were reluctant to testify against their partners, the police also traditionally took the position that it was the victim's responsibility to formally lay charges. By placing the onus on the victim to lay a charge, the police were also allowing the abuser to hold the victim responsible for any legal action taken.

Pressured by women's groups, Manitoba's attorney general issued a directive in 1983 to all police departments to lay charges when there were reasonable and probable grounds that an assault had taken place. Although full compliance with this directive did not take place immediately, the data over an eight-year period indicate that police began to treat wife abuse as a serious crime.

As Figure 1 illustrates, the number of charges laid by the RCMP and the Winnipeg Police Department increased from 1,136 to 2,779 over an eight-year period. This represents a 145-percent increase in spousal-assault charges from 1983 to 1990. The data on police charging suggest that police compliance with the mandatory charging policy was gradual and became more consistent over the years. Although we have no data on the actual number of spousal-assault cases that took place during this period, it is highly unlikely that the increase in the charges laid by the police forces in the province could be accounted for by such a dramatic increase in the actual number of incidents. The more plausible

FIGURE 1   **Number of Cases of Spousal Assault Where Charges Were
Laid, Winnipeg Police and RCMP From 1983 to 1990**

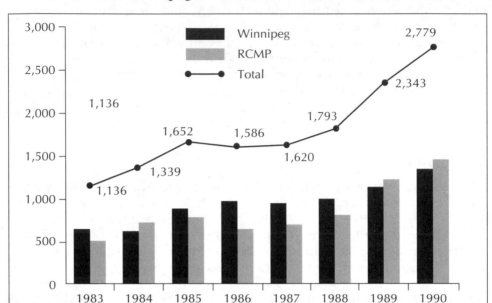

explanation is that the police have, over the years, been increasingly conforming
to the mandatory charging policy.

The increase in charges laid indicates a change in the police response to wife
abuse over time. There were, however, incidents that came to the public's attention
where the apparent inability of the police to effectively intervene led to the deaths
of three women at the hands of their partners in 1990. As a response to these concerns and others, the justice minister commissioned an independent review of the
treatment of wife-abuse cases by the criminal justice system (Pedlar, 1991). Known
as the Domestic Violence Review (DVR), the report was released in 1991.

While the report acknowledged that the police response to domestic violence had significantly improved since the charging directive of 1983, a number
of recommendations were made to further improve police response in domestic-
violence cases. The DVR made five major recommendations regarding police
procedures:

- extend the definition of spouse to include any intimate partner, past or
  present
- develop a dispatch protocol to ensure that all calls are relayed to police
  for attendance
- clearly communicate to all parties that it is not the victim who is laying
  the charge(s)

- offer the victim transportation to a place of safety
- ensure that the presence or absence of alcohol on the part of either of the parties is not a factor in the consideration of laying a charge

In response to the DVR, in 1993 the Winnipeg Police Department issued a new procedure manual on domestic violence to its police officers. The new manual was prepared in consultation with the Crown and women's groups over a period of one year, and includes all of the above recommendations. The opening section of the new policy document states: "It is a police duty and responsibility to lay a charge when there are reasonable grounds to believe that a domestic assault or some other offence has occurred. Charges shall be laid whether or not the victim wishes to proceed with the matter, and even in circumstances where there are not visible injuries or independent witnesses . . ." Although it is too early to systematically assess the impact of the new policy document, the expectations of the police department are that the number of arrests for domestic violence will "skyrocket" (*Winnipeg Free Press*, 1993).

An additional refinement of the system was the creation of a telephone hot line that enables police officers to have immediate access to the court history of every domestic-abuse offender in the province who has appeared in court. The data bank lists every person in the province who is currently on bail for domestic-violence crimes or who is subject to a restraining order, peace bond, nonmolestation order or probation order. The system was put in place in response to a well-publicized incident in which a man obtained a gun permit even though he was the subject of a peace bond. The man later obtained a firearm and killed the woman who was supposed to be protected by the peace bond.

THE COURTS: TWO RESPONSE MODELS

As reforms at the police level led to mounting arrest rates, the volume of family-violence cases entering the courts provoked a crisis. The combination of higher numbers, close press scrutiny and public skepticism about the wisdom of judicial decisions created a momentum for court reform. This confluence of events was not unique to Manitoba. With the increased charging of wife abusers by police, the courts could not easily dismiss the greater attention being given to this crime. Throughout the 1980s, most jurisdictions in Canada experienced the dual pressures of mounting arrest rates and increasing media and public demand for change in the criminal justice system. However, Manitoba's response has been and remains unique in Canada. The two types of responses that have emerged in Canada are

1. The Manitoba model, which combines mandatory arrest policies with a specialized criminal Family Violence Court.
2. The mainstream model, which combines mandatory arrest with "no drop" prosecutorial policies.

The mandatory arrest policy focuses on the police, greatly reducing their discretion in the pursuit of a higher charge rate. The "no drop" policy focuses on Crown attorneys and directs prosecution to proceed with a case in court regardless of the wishes or intent of the victim. The intent of the "no drop" policy is to encourage rigorous prosecution; the consequences for the Crown attorney is greatly reduced discretion.

The mainstream model speaks to the old double standard that minimized the criminal nature of assaults among family members and kept them out of criminal court. The mainstream model directs its personnel to treat family assaults like any other assault and prosecute rigorously. This results in more family-violence cases going to court. However, treating family-violence cases like any other assault does not address the unique problems that arise when the victim is highly bonded to and dependent on her assailant. The Manitoba model, in particular the Family Violence Court, is designed to respond to both concerns: end the historic double standard and consider the particular needs of vulnerable victims. The mainstream model is premised on the belief that all are equal before the law; the Manitoba model is premised on the understanding that victims of family violence are particularly vulnerable and a just intervention must take this into consideration.

The very creation of the FVC confronts two basic assertions made by critics of legal reform. The first assertion is that once a reform occurs the matter disappears into the bowels of bureaucracy, blocking the possibility of monitoring or measuring the implementation of the reform. The second assertion is that once an issue enters the legal domain it is not possible to have any significant influence on legal discourse or the determination of what is or is not relevant within the legal domain. Our observations suggest that a reform does not always render the issue invisible. In fact, the charging directive had quite the opposite effect. By responding to domestic violence through arrest, the police transformed what had previously been a private and socially invisible act into a crime that entered a public court and was recorded in official crime statistics. In short, wife abuse became publicly observable and calculable in its extent.

Once the charging directive was issued, the public's ability to observe the criminal justice response to wife abuse was substantial. Increasing media coverage of court cases and the public response to that coverage led to growing public criticism of the criminal justice system. Rather than co-optation and containment of reform at the police level, the charging directive set up a dynamic that demanded further reform of the courts.

Despite skeptics' belief in the impenetrability of legal discourse, the philosophy behind the adoption of the specialized court came from feminist discourse confronting and overriding one of the most fundamental premises of liberal legal discourse: "all are equal before the law." Essential to the idea and legitimacy of creating a separate court was acceptance of the feminist critique; women, children and elderly victims of violence are victims of systemic inequality and cannot confront their assailant in court as equals before the law.

The Family Violence Court

On September 17, 1990 the Family Violence Court in Winnipeg began operation. It handles first appearances, remands, guilty pleas, and trials for spouse abuse, child abuse and elder abuse cases. Cases eligible to be heard in the FVC involve crimes against persons in which the victim is or was in a relationship of trust, dependency and/or kinship with the accused. This broad definition encompasses a range of intimate relations, including homosexual and heterosexual, married and common law, boyfriend and girlfriend. All child-abuse cases are heard in the FVC on the assumption that all children are in a position of trust and dependency in relation to adults. More than 53 different Criminal Code charges have been recorded in this court, ranging from mischief to murder, possession of a weapon to uttering threats, with physical assaults being the most common charges in cases with adult victims and sexual assaults most common in the child-abuse cases.

The intent behind specialization was to create a court staffed with specialized personnel that would be sensitive to the difficulties that arise when the victim-witness is dependent on the accused. The goals of the court were: (1) to increase victim/witness information and cooperation to reduce case attrition, particularly at the prosecutorial level (through a reduction in stays of proceedings); (2) to process cases expeditiously, aiming for an average three-month processing time from first appearance to disposition; (3) to provide more consistent and appropriate sentencing to better protect the victim, to mandate treatment for the offender where suitable, and to increase monitoring of offenders (through probation services), all of which reinforce the policy of zero tolerance for family violence in Manitoba.

Components of Specialization

Specialization of the court was achieved in a number of ways. One of the first considerations was the allocation of courtrooms that would only hear FVC cases. In order to meet the goal of processing cases in three months (from entry to disposition), it was essential to avoid competing for court time in the over-burdened general court system. Dedicated courtrooms were essential for responding to the rapid and unanticipated increase in family-violence court cases associated with the opening of the specialized court. Based on volume in previous years it was initially estimated that 28 hours of court time per week could handle the anticipated work load. By the end of the first year this number had increased to 52 hours a week and by the end of the second year it had doubled to 102 hours per week.

The second component of specializing the FVC was the recruitment and training of specialized court personnel. This began with the creation of a team of specialist Crown attorneys who would only prosecute family-violence cases. The next step was the selective assignment of particular judges to hear FVC cases.

Judges were selected on the basis of self-identified interest in and support of the new court, as well as their experience in handling family-violence cases in the past. To assist the victim through the court process, two support services worked closely with the court, the Women's Advocacy Program, which provides support to women whose partners have been charged with abusing them, and the Child Abuse Victim Witness Program, which assists children required to give testimony regarding their abuse.

Policy changes became a part of the new court, and in October 1990 the Department of Justice issued a directive on prosecuting spousal-abuse cases. The policy outlined protocol and procedures to ensure that Crown attorneys would be guided by the dual mandate of rigorous prosecution and respect for the needs of the victim. The final component of the specialized court was the creation of an interdepartmental and interdisciplinary Court Implementation Committee that addressed policy and implementation issues related to the operation of the specialized court.

CONFRONTING PROCEDURAL IMPEDIMENTS

While outcomes are, in the final analysis, the best measure of a reform's success, process is also a critical factor, particularly in light of the fact that legal reform critics identify most of the impediments to real reform as lying in the presumed untouchable domain of implementation. The "blunt instrument" school of thought maintains that the state is either unable or unwilling to control how criminal justice personnel apply the law. Similarly, Smart (1989) suggests that the discourse and culture of law is so hegemonic that new laws and policies will mutate under the force of legal tradition to become at best ineffective and possibly harmful. How immutable is legal culture and tradition?

In the design of the FVC, considerable attention was paid to the attitudes and orientation of the criminal justice personnel. The architects of the new court were well aware of the "work culture" and concepts of success that prevailed in prosecutors' offices and operated as impediments to the successful prosecution of domestic-assault cases.

Prior to specialization, "domestics" were the "grunt" work of the prosecutors' office, one, or two steps above traffic court. Junior prosecutors with little experience were often called upon to handle these complex cases, which had no status among their peers. The combined effect of low status, reluctant witnesses and conviction as the sole measure of success was a severe structural disincentive for Crown attorneys to take on such cases or invest much energy in them. In short, the work structure and definition of success in the prosecutors' office militated against rigorous prosecution or sensitivity to the victim in spousal-abuse cases.

The introduction of the FVC raised the status of spousal-assault cases and consequently the status of the Crown attorneys working in the specialized court. The old view of the Crown attorney with a domestic caseload as a poor functionary stuck with "hopeless" cases was replaced with a public and peer image of specialist prosecutors with unique skills for handling important and complex criminal cases. The speed with which this new definition took hold was amazing and thoroughgoing in all important regards: defence demeanor, victim response, public and peer assessment. Thus, with specialization, Crown attorneys could and would receive acknowledgment for the extremely difficult work of handling spousal-assault cases.

The second structural barrier was the prevalent view of conviction as success. Under the old criteria, the Crown attorney would confront the reluctant victim as the single greatest problem with the case. Often the Crown would report feeling greater frustration and/or hostility toward the victim than toward the perpetrator. With the introduction of the dual mandate, rigorous prosecution and sensitivity to the victim, the definition of success underwent a dramatic transformation. The moderating effect of a victim-sensitive orientation encouraged the Crown to define success in terms of those interventions that would protect and/or assist the victim, protect the public and increase the possibility of treatment for the perpetrator. A number of Crown attorneys who dealt with spousal-assault cases in both the old system and the new FVC report a tremendous sense of relief that they no longer find themselves in an adversarial relationship with the victim.

The combined effect of improved working conditions, a broader definition of success, better status and acknowledgment of their work, and policies that are enabling rather than restrictive have all transformed the work and the attitudes of the Crown attorneys in the FVC. In response to these altered conditions, Crown attorneys in the Family Violence Prosecutorial Unit have demonstrated remarkable ingenuity in achieving high conviction rates, despite the perpetual challenge of reluctant witnesses. The emergence of a hybrid of the ever-present phenomenon of plea bargaining—testimony bargaining— is but one example.

There is no formal policy on plea bargaining in FVC or in any other court, and it is practised extensively in FVC and general court. Canadian studies suggest that plea bargaining occurs in 60 percent (Solomon, 1983, 37) to 70 percent (Ericson and Baranek, 1982, 117) of the cases that go through criminal court. The practice of plea bargaining is just as pervasive in FVC. Approximately 58 percent of the cases disposed in the first year entered a guilty plea, typically as a result of some "agreement" with the Crown. About 70 percent of these guilty pleas were entered in docket or screening court. In these early plea-bargain cases, the "bargain" is typically between the Crown and the defence and/or the accused.

There is, however, another form of bargaining that we have observed in FVC that may be unique to this specialized court. In such cases, the Crown "bargains" with the victim-witness. These cases of "testimony bargaining" typically occur when cases are scheduled for trial and the victim is reluctant to testify because of her fear that her partner will go to jail. The Crown will discuss the case with the reluctant witness and indicate a willingness to reduce the number of years to be served or the severity of the charges, and/or recommend probation and court-mandated counseling in return for the victim/witness's cooperation. Guilty pleas entered at trial (30 percent), when the accused and defence counsel observe the presence of the witness in court, are often a result of "testimony bargaining."

The characteristic feature of family-violence cases—victim dependence on and bonding with the accused—is probably the most important factor in explaining the high rate of plea bargaining and the unusual practice of testimony bargaining found in FVC. Successful plea bargaining meets the requirements of rigorous prosecution and achieves court intervention and sentencing, while sparing the victim the trauma of testifying and the Crown the uncertainty of relying on victim testimony. Through the process of traditional plea bargaining or the more innovative testimony bargaining, the Crown is able to meet the dual and potentially conflicting mandates of rigorous prosecution and sensitivity to the victim.

Opening the Doors to Justice

Departments of Justice have historically been among the most introverted of government offices, a pattern premised on the strongly held belief that matters of justice are the exclusive business of judges and lawyers. This tradition within legal culture has fueled the belief that legal institutions are impenetrable, which discourages and disparages attempts at legal reform. However, the development of the FVC, initiated and administered by an interdepartmental and interdisciplinary Court Implementation Committee, marks a significant departure from the "closed shop" phenomenon typical of justice departments. In addition to all the key decision-makers and actors within the provincial court system, the committee includes members from the Women's Directorate, the Department of Family Services, an outspoken feminist lawyer in private practice and a feminist academic experienced in court research. These members represent a broader community of interest and bring to the committee considerations of justice that extend beyond the court process.

While the Court Implementation Committee did not handle the day-to-day administration of the FVC, it was much more than an advisory committee. The committee was the architect for the specialized court and continues to play a key administrative function in the justice department. For example, the committee was the body responsible for negotiations with the ministers involved to relocate the Women's Advocacy Program from the Department of Family Services to the Department of Justice. Further, the committee initiated treasury board submissions for additional staff for the prosecutorial unit and arranged for the expansion of dedicated courtrooms from 28 hours per week to 102 hours per week.

Thus, the committee represents a substantial move toward the democratization of justice. This democratization was integral to the legitimation of the FVC as an alternative to the old general court model, which was perceived as insensitive to the needs of victims. Although the creation of the FVC was undertaken to empower victims, it also had the effect of empowering a much larger community. Other departments and disciplines and the community at large have much greater input in the operation of the FVC than in any other court.

There is considerable evidence that in both the design and implementation of the new court the legal system proved to be less impenetrable than critics of reform would suggest. Herein, perhaps, lies some room for cautious optimism. However, regardless of the evidence that the inner sanctums of legal culture can be penetrated, or that hallowed legal discourse can be challenged, none of this would amount to much if it didn't produce the desired effect. Thus, the next section will examine the outcome of the FVC in relation to the nonspecialized courts.

Comparative Analysis of Court Outcomes

Historic criticisms of court processing of wife-abuse cases have focused on the large number of cases that are stayed and do not proceed to court, and the lenient and inappropriate sentences that trivialize the seriousness of such crimes. If the criticisms of the courts' processing of wife-abuse and family-violence cases prior to specialization were accurate, and if the Family Violence Court has lived up to or approximated its goals, we would expect the following relationships between the three data sets. First, we would expect the "before" data set to exhibit the highest rate of stays and the highest attrition rate of the three courts. Second, we would expect the FVC to be equivalent to or better than general court in case attrition. Third, we would expect the "before" cases to have the most lenient sentences and the highest rate of conditional discharge of the three courts. Fourth, while we would expect the FVC and general courts to be equivalent in severity of sentencing, we would expect differences to emerge in terms of types of sentencing. We would expect the FVC to put greater emphasis on longer term monitoring (via probation) and court-mandated treatment than the sentencing in general court or in the "before" data set. Table 1 presents the case attrition rate for the three data sets.

TABLE 1 Case Attrition by Data Set

Case Outcome	Before (N = 1,625)	FVC (N = 1,600)	General (N = 500)
	%	%	%
Stay	31	22	32
DFWOP[1]	10	8	6
Discharged	—	3	3
Dismissed (not guilty)	6	4	2
Attrition	47	36	43
Proceed to Sentence	53	64	57

[1] DFWOP: Dismissed for want of prosecution

Table 1 indicates that there is not the expected difference between the stay rates in the "before" data set and the general court data. However, the "before" data does reveal a higher attrition rate overall, due to a higher rate of cases "dismissed for want of prosecution" (DFWOP) and cases found not guilty. Overall, case attrition in the "before" data is somewhat higher (5 percent) than in general court. The most significant difference that emerges is the difference between FVC and the other two courts. The FVC has a significantly lower stay rate: at 22 percent it is 10 percentage points lower than general court and 9 percentage points lower than the "before" data. The FVC also ha a marginally lower DFWOP rate and not-guilty percentage than the "before" data. The consequence of these differences is that the FVC has a significantly higher percentage of cases that proceed to sentencing: 11 percentage points higher than the "before" data and 7 percentage points higher than the general court data.

The fact that the FVC has the highest percentage of cases proceeding to sentence of the three courts indicates a dramatic change with the introduction of the specialized court. This data indicates a serious response to previous criticisms as well as a substantial prosecutorial benefit from specialization. However, getting to sentencing is only half the battle; the quality and appropriateness of the sentence is essential to meet the feminist demand for serious sanctioning of the crime of wife abuse. Based on past criticisms of the courts and the stated goals of the FVC, we anticipate that the "before" data set will demonstrate the most lenient sentencing pattern and that FVC outcomes will be comparable to or more severe than the general court outcomes. Table 2 presents the sentencing pattern by data set.

TABLE 2 Sentencing Pattern by Data Set

Case Outcome	Before (N = 1,625)		FVC (N = 1,600)		General (N = 500)	
	#	%	#	%	#	%
Total proceeding to sentence	813	53	1,015	64	270	57
Probation	181	11	789	49	137	27
Suspended sentence	225	14	307	19	45	9
Incarceration	93	6	252	16	93	19
Fine	198	12	196	12	92	18
Conditional discharge	229	14	102	6	44	9

Note: When the number of cases in the different sentencing categories are added up, the total is greater than the number of cases that proceeded to sentencing because each case may have more than one disposition. For the same reason, the percentage totals exceed 100.

Table 2 reveals the pattern we had anticipated. The "before" data set reveals the highest rate of conditional discharge of the three courts and the lowest rate of incarceration and probation. It appears that criticisms of past sentencing practices in wife-abuse cases were accurate. When we compare the FVC with the "before" data we find the combined effect of higher attrition rates and more lenient sentencing in the past produces dramatic numerical differences of great significance in outcome. The two data sets have amost identical numbers of cases ("before" 1,625 and FVC 1,600). However, given the same starting point only 181 persons from the "before" data set received probation while four times as many individuals, or 789 persons, received a probation sentence in FVC. Similarly, only 93 individuals were incarcerated in the "before" data set while three times as many individuals, or 252 persons, were incarcerated in the FVC data set.

It is not only the type of sentence but also the court orders or conditions attached to sentencing that indicate a new sentencing pattern in the FVC. Table 3 provides information on the use of sentencing in the three data sets.

The FVC stands out as the court that imposes the most labour-intensive conditions from the perspective of corrections. Not only does it sentence a higher proportion of individuals to probation but it requires these individuals to be supervised in a higher percentage of cases. The FVC also has the highest rate of court-mandated treatment relative to the other two courts. The FVC mandates one-third of all persons who enter the court into treatment, with the most frequently mandated treatment being for spousal abuse. The "before" data set and the general court data are similar in mandating approximately 10 percent of their population to treatment, with the most frequently mandated treatment being for alcohol abuse. The high incidence of supervised probation and the high percentage of court-mandated treatment are in response to community demands for greater supervision and victim requests for treatment for their partner.

TABLE 3 Conditions on Sentencing by Data Set

Case Outcome	Before (N = 1,252)[1] %	FVC (N = 1,600) %	General (N = 500) %
Supervised probation	N.A.	32	23
Court-mandated treatment	10	31	11
Batterers treatment	2	16	3
Alcohol treatment	5	12	5
Other treatment	3	3	3

[1] The sample size for the "before" data set is 1,252 because information was not available on court orders for the 1983 data.

One of the consequences of the above changes in court processing has been a massive increase in caseload at the corrections end of the criminal justice system. Just as reform of policing procedures provoked reform in the courts, the existence of the FVC has provoked a major restructuring of corrections. In 1993, Probation Services of Manitoba opened a Family Violence Unit in Probation that is providing supervision and treatment to approximately 1,000 offenders annually in Winnipeg alone.

These outcomes suggest a fundamental change in the criminal justice system's response to wife abuse. The zero-tolerance policy articulated by the Minister of Justice in 1990 has responded to community demands that wife abuse be treated like a crime and punished accordingly.

DISCUSSION

As the Manitoba experience illustrates, it is possible for a legal reform to have a profound impact in an area where victims have been traditionally ignored. The error made by some students of law is to either assume that the struggle is over when a new law or policy has been announced by the state, or to assume that it is not possible to influence how a specific legal reform will be implemented by practitioners within the legal system. Under these assumptions, it would be logical to infer that legal reform is a blunt instrument that may have no impact or may produce results that lead to conditions worse than the problems that led to the legal change.

We would argue, however, that these assumptions are false. Numerous studies have proven the first assumption to be incorrect: the simple declaration of a new law or policy, by itself, is unlikely to produce change, particularly in an area where the change either confronts existing class and patriarchal interests, lacks public support, or attempts to control behaviour such as victimless crimes, which are relatively immune from enforcement. The current findings suggest that the second assumption is also false. Just as active lobbying can, in some circumstances, influence decisions in the political arena, active monitoring and intervention within the legal system can affect how a legal reform is implemented. While it is no doubt true that many reforms have been short-circuited because of inadequate implementation, the present findings reveal that the police and courts are not impenetrable institutions.

Following the implementation of the mandatory charging policy in 1983, there were a number of strategic points in the criminal justice system where the responses of the key actors could have led to the failure of the state's attempt to take wife abuse seriously. First, the police could have ignored the directive and continued to exercise their discretion by not charging abusers. Second, the prosecutors, given their predisposition to define wife-abuse charges as nuisance cases, could have shown reluctance to diligently pursue the cases by staying those cases where the victim was reluctant or unwilling to testify against her partner. Third, the judiciary could have negated the impact of the initiative by meting out lenient and inappropriate sanctions to those convicted of abuse-related offences. Finally, the government could have muted the impact of the family-violence initiative by not allocating additional resources to the court and corrections.

The effects of the family-violence initiatives in Manitoba reveal that there has been a significant increase in the number of men being held accountable for assaulting their partners, a notable increase in the availability of women's shelters (Ursel, 1991) and the development of treatment programs that are attempting to reduce the incidence of abusers repeating their behaviour. While some feminists would argue that these initiatives are inconsequential because they do not address the patriarchal conditions that give rise to abuse (Smart, 1989; Barnsley, 1988), we would argue that this is an unrealistic measuring rod to gauge success. By this standard, minimum-wage laws and the unions' struggle to establish the 40-hour week were inconsequential because they did not erode the foundation of capitalism within Canada. We believe that a more fundamental criterion for measuring success is whether or not the reform produced an improvement in the day-to-day lives of the individuals affected. The fact that abused women now have recourse to the law when they are assaulted and receive support from all components of the criminal justice system indicates to us that these reforms have been successful.

Much of feminist theorizing on the role of law has produced a dilemma for those who seek to challenge the inequities within the legal system. While these theorists are justifiably critical of the law's treatment of women, their conceptualization of the law and the legal system is one that encourages inaction. Those feminists who take a structuralist view of the law see legal reform as incapable of creating any change that will produce significant benefits for women. Within this framework, any reform efforts, particularly in the area of criminal justice, will be co-opted by the state and will not only result in increasing women's oppression, but will also increase the power and legitimacy of the state (Snider, 1991; Barnsley, 1988). As Ursel (1991) points out, this overly deterministic conceptualization of the state is not only historically inaccurate, it precludes any efforts to directly challenge laws and legal practices that operate to the detriment of women.

The more recent postmodern feminist critique of legal reform is equally cynical on the possibility of women achieving gains through legal reform. From the postmodernist premise that general theories have little value in understanding the world, these writers take the position that it is not possible to develop general strategies that will allow women to use the law to their advantage. Smart, for example, argues that there are no general properties in law that will allow us to determine a specific legal reform's success or failure. Given this assumption, she states: "It also follows that we cannot predict the outcome of any individual law reform. Indeed the main dilemma for any feminist engagement with law is the certain knowledge that, once enacted, legislation is in the hands of individuals and agencies far removed from the values and politics of the women's movement" (Smart, 1989,164). The assumption is that while women may be effective in influencing politicians to create legal reforms, they will have little or no power in influencing those who are responsible for implementing the reforms.

While the above theoretical positions have little in common in their rationales for dismissing law reform, the message for women is the same: do not attempt to engage the law in your efforts to improve the position of women. We believe that the effect of this message can best be described as the *politics of disem-*

powerment. By dismissing political action in the area of legal reform as, at best, naive efforts to improve women's position and, at worst, action that strengthens the state and further subordinates women, the effect is to disempower groups seeking to bring about progressive changes in the law. Since the criteria these theorists use to identify politically viable strategies for change are so restrictive, to follow them would lead to a virtual political paralysis. If, for example, these theoretical positions had been used as the guide for political action by feminists in Manitoba, the family-violence initiatives undertaken within the criminal justice system would not have been tried. That these initiatives were implemented and have proved to be reasonably successful speaks volumes about the wisdom of dismissing legal reform as a strategy to promote women's interests.

REFERENCES

Balbus, Isaac D. 1977. "Commodity Form and Legal Form: An Essay on the 'Relative Autonomy' of the Law," *Law and Society Review*, 11: 571–588.

Barnsley, Jan. 1988. "Feminist Action, Institutional Reaction," *Resources for Feminist Research*, 17(3): 18–21.

Burstyn, Varda, ed. 1985. *Women Against Censorship*. Vancouver: Douglas and McIntyre.

Clark, Lorenne and **Deborah Lewis.** 1977. *Rape: The Price of Coercive Sexuality*. Toronto: The Women's Press.

Comack, Elizabeth. 1993. *Feminist Engagement with the Law: The Legal Recognition of the Battered Woman Syndrome*. Ottawa: Canadian Research Institute for the Advancement of Women.

DeKeseredy, Walter and **Ronald Hinch.** 1991. *Woman Abuse: Sociological Perspectives*. Toronto: Thompson Educational Publishing.

Ericson, Richard. 1981. *Making Crime: A Study of Detective Work*. Toronto: Butterworths.

——, and **Patricia Baranek.** 1982. *The Ordering of Justice*. Toronto: University of Toronto Press.

Evan, William M. 1965. "Law as an Instrument of Social Change." In *The Sociology of Law: A Social Structural Perspective*, edited by William Evan, 554–562. New York: Free Press.

Gusfield, Joseph. 1963. *Symbolic Crusade: Status Politics and the American Temperance Movement*. Urbana: University of Illinois Press.

Hastings, Ross. 1991. "An Ounce of Prevention . . ," *The Journal of Human Justice*, 3(1): 85–95.

Lacombe, Dany. 1988. *Ideology and Public Policy: The Case Against Pornography*. Toronto: Garamond Press.

Livingstone, Stephen and **John Morison,** eds. 1990. *Law, Society and Change*. Aldershot: Dartmouth.

Mandel, Michael. 1986. "Democracy, Class and Canadian Sentencing Law." In *The Social Basis of Law: Critical Readings in the Sociology of Law*, edited by S. Brickey and E. Comack, 137–156. Toronto: Garamond Press.

Massell, Gregory. 1973. "Revolutionary Law in Soviet Central Asia." In *The Social Organization of Law*, edited by D. Black and M. Mileski, 226–261. New York: Seminar Press.

McBarnet, D. 1979. "Arrest: The Legal Context of Policing." In *The British Police*, edited by S. Holdaway. London: Edward Arnold.

McMullan, John. 1992. *Beyond the Limits of the Law*. Toronto: Garamond Press.

Pedlar, Dorothy. 1991. *The Domestic Violence Review Into the Administration of Justice in Manitoba*. Winnipeg: Manitoba Department of Justice.

Reasons, Charles, Lois Ross and **Craig Patterson.** 1981. *Assault on the Worker: Occupational Health and Safety in Canada*. Toronto: Butterworths.

Sargent, Neil. 1991. "Law, Ideology and Social Change: An Analysis of the Role of Law in the Construction of Corporate Crime." In *The Social Basis of Law: Critical Readings in the Sociology of Law*, (2d ed.), edited by E. Comack and S. Brickey, 289–309. Toronto: Garamond Press.

Schrecker, Ted. 1989. "The Political Context and Content of Environmental Law." In *Law and Society: A Critical Perspective*, edited by T. Caputo et al., 173–204. Toronto: Harcourt Brace Jovanovich, Canada.

Sheptycki, J.W.E. 1991. "Using the State to Change Society: The Example of 'Domestic Violence'," *The Journal of Human Justice*, 3(1): 47–66.

Smart, Carol. 1989. *Feminism and the Power of Law*. London: Routledge.

Snider, Laureen. 1993. *Bad Business: Corporate Crime in Canada*. Scarborough: Nelson Canada.

———. 1991. "The Potential of the Criminal Justice System to Promote Feminist Concerns." In *The Social Basis of Law: Critical Readings in the Sociology of Law*, (2d ed.), edited by E. Comack and S. Brickey, 238–260. Toronto: Garamond Press.

———. 1986. "Legal Aid, Reform and the Welfare State." In *The Social Basis of Law: Critical Readings in the Sociology of Law*, edited by S. Brickey and E. Comack, 169–195. Toronto: Garamond Press.

Solomon, P.H. 1983. *Criminal Justice Policy, From Research to Reform*. Toronto: Butterworths.

Ursel, E. Jane. 1993. *Final Report: On the First Year of the Family Violence Court*. Ottawa: Department of Justice.

———. 1991. "Considering the Impact of the Battered Women's Movement on the State: The Example of Manitoba." In *The Social Basis of Law: Critical Readings in the Sociology of Law*, (2d ed.), edited by E. Comack and S. Brickey, 261–288. Toronto: Garamond Press.

Winnipeg Free Press. 1993. "Domestic Violence Attacked: 'Serious Numbers' of Arrests Predicted Under Police Policy." 121(221): A1.

A GALLERY OF PORTRAITS: WOMEN AND THE EMBODIMENT OF DIFFERENCE, DEVIANCE, AND RESISTANCE

Sylvie Frigon

[I]f a woman have an issue, and her issue in her flesh be blood, she shall be put apart seven days: and whosoever toucheth her shall be unclean until the even. And every thing that she lieth upon in her separation shall be unclean: every thing also that she sitteth upon shall be unclean. And whosoever toucheth her bed shall wash his clothes, and bathe himself in water, and be unclean until the even.

(Lev. 15:19–21).

The criminal woman is ... a monster. *Her normal sister is kept in the paths of virtue by many causes, such as maternity, piety, weakness, and when these counter influences fail, and a woman commits a crime, we may conclude that her wickedness must have been enormous before it could triumph over many obstacles.*
(Lombroso and Ferrero, [1895] 1980, 152; emphasis added)

I was very curious to meet the Greenham women, *for the press had decorated them with such loathsome and frightening adjectives ... They'd been accused of being* 'sex-starved' *which sounded a lot more deadly because it made them sound* so dangerous. *... the Greenham women smelt of 'fish paste and bad oysters' also haunted me for it had such distressing sexual associations ... As these women had been attributed with almost every unsavoury characteristic,* I had become very curious to see why they aroused such violent hatred and to discover how evil-smelling and odious the Greenham women could be.
(Blackwood, 1984,1–2; emphasis added)

Mad, bad or pre-menstrual?

(Edwards, 1988)

The body may be the home of the soul and the pathway of the spirit, but it is also the perversity, the stubborn resistance, the malign contagion of the material world. Having a body, being in the body, is like being roped to a sick cat.

(Atwood, 1994)

INTRODUCTION

As the above vignettes indicate, this chapter is a discussion of how women are constituted as criminal subjects and how their bodies are at the core of this construction. The question of the body is an important one in criminological and penal practices but has rarely been theorized.[1] In history, different techniques have been used to punish offenders, including torture, humiliation, various rituals of degradation and the death penalty as a real "theatre of horror"[2] (decapitation, guillotine, public hangings, electric chair and more recently lethal injections). The creation and management of "docile bodies" (Foucault, 1975) are still very present in our criminal system by way of therapies and, even more recently, electronic monitoring.

Women have not escaped the regulation of bodies and minds, and I will attempt to explore how some examples of the social and penal controls of women's bodies have emerged. To undertake this task, this presentation will be divided in two sections: (1) the marking of differences in the philosophical constitution of the female (embodied) subject and the association between woman and body; and (2) a gallery of portraits of the deviance and criminality of women. In the second section, I chose to examine the representations of some *disorderly* women. Disorderly because of their evilness, such as in the case of witches in the Middle Ages. Disorderly because criminal women deviate from appropriate gender norms. Disorderly because of their horrible deeds, such as in cases of homicide and conjugal homicide. Disorderly because they suffer from a syndrome, the premenstrual syndrome or the battered woman syndrome. Disorderly because of their political protests, as in the cases of the suffragettes and the Greenham Common Women in England. But also the entry of these disorderly women defines what constitutes being a good woman. This good woman is, however, never quite "ordinary" or "normal." In fact, being a woman is forever being deviant (Hutter and Williams, 1981; Schur, 1984).

Other examples of the regulation of women's bodies and minds can be found in criminological literature. For example, criminal women's biological constitution was viewed as pathological, a view that helped develop typologies of offenders (both men and women) as well as penal institutions for women. According to Dobash, R.E., Dobash, R.P., and Gutteridge, (1986), Maudsley appears to be the first British doctor to identify the "normal functionings of women's bodies as a cause of insanity and deviance, arguing that normal menstruation, pregnancy and lactation could form part of a pathological condition" (113–114). He then concluded that sexual deviations in women were the product of the "...irritation of the ovaries or uterus—a disease by which the chaste and modest woman is transformed into a raging fury of lust" (114). Havelock Ellis (1890), for his part, argued that women found guilty of infanticide were "endowed with excessive down in their faces, that female thieves went grey more quickly, were uglier, and exhibited more signs of degeneracy (especially of the sexual organs) than ordinary women" (Zedner, 1992,337).

Early twentieth-century views of female crime were that of the "eugenics" movement (Dobash, R.E., Dobash R.P., and Gutteridge, 1986,111). The "degenerate woman" was born. As a result, it appears that "the basis of crime no longer lay in sin or in faulty reasoning but in an aberration or abnormality of the individual's constitution" (Garland, 1985,111). However, in the case of female criminality, this new medical and psychiatric interpretation was more intricately bound to moral reasoning (Zedner, 1991). The female offenders, of course, were the antithesis of ideal femininity. In order to achieve this "ideal femininity," women will, in some way or another, suffer the regulation of their bodies and minds (Schur, 1984).

In order to understand and situate contemporary debates about the representations of women as unruly and disorderly, historical analyses of how women are constructed are necessary.[3] This will permit us to trace the continuities and discontinuities of the modern meaning of the embodiment of femininity and its transgression in diverse cultural and socio-political spaces and times. In this chapter, I will examine different images of women who are considered transgressors of moral, cultural, and legal boundaries. I will now explore images related to "women" and examine how their representations work in creating, reflecting, and perpetuating what it is to be a "woman" and, by extension, what it is to be "out of place." As Gallop suggests, "re-presentation, replication, the substitutability of one woman for another" (1982, 132) will be highlighted.

In tracing some of the dominant themes of the representations of women, the symbolic order, I hope, will unfold. Women are located in *lacunae*. "Unruly women" point to major cracks in this symbolic order, the masculine order. The dominant themes discussed in this chapter display the "fascination for and fear of the *female body*" (Young, 1990, 45). Woman is already other and deviant. In fact, "she ... is making a spectacle of herself" (Russo, 1986, 213). Bakhtin's concept of "grotesque" is embodied in a series "...of taboos around the female body as grotesque (the pregnant body, the aging body, the irregular body) and as unruly when set loose in the public sphere." Following that argument, we can tentatively suggest that women and their bodies *seem* to be "always already transgressive—dangerous, and in danger" (Bakhtin, quoted in Russo, 1986, 214).

ON THE MAKING OF DIFFERENCE AND DEVIANCE

A central issue that seems to underlie the various discussions of the studies on women and crime is how they are seen and theorized as embodying deviance. The embodiment of this deviance stems, in part, from the definitions of difference, equality, morality, and reason, which have been problematized in some philosophical works.

Since I want to argue that criminology is embedded with those philosophical conceptions, I need to start by examining some of the philosophical foundations of Western political thought. I will thus suggest a way of looking at how some ideas were incorporated in the frameworks of analyses of studies on women's deviance and crime.

It has been widely argued that, in liberal philosophy, concepts such as rights, reason, morality, and equality are of central importance. I will try to make the argument that the "male person" is taken, in Western political thought, to be the norm. This is important because it may be argued that criminology, as other academic disciplines, has also taken the man as the norm, as associated with the aforementioned concepts (Scraton, 1990). In fact, in the particular case of criminology, the "deviant, criminal" man is the "deviant, criminal" norm. Male deviance is considered to be "normal" deviance. This leaves women or the "deviant, criminal" women in a difficult position. Does the male category include the female? Or is the female category *exclusive*? How do women fit in the established framework? How does the construction and criminalization of femininity operate? This also presses us into the difference/equality nexus.

The Philosophical Constitution of the Female (Embodied) Subject

Through the examination of the philosophical constitution of the female subject, we will see how the issues of difference, equality, and rationality have been made problematic in Western political thought, and have been central in presenting and representing women's bodies as transgressive. This endeavour might lead us to further understand the historical construction of the subject "woman" and how these conceptions impact on the construction of criminological (embodied) subject.[4]

It can be argued that Western political thought has been constructed through the application of dualisms (Coole, 1988). These dualisms will be my starting point because, in my view, they have shaped debates not only in philosophy but in other fields of knowledge as well. They are also relevant in this overview because they affect our concept of gender. The following basic oppositions are believed to "lead a subterranean existence, structuring Western thought in general and its political tradition in particular" (Coole, 1988, 2): mind/body; subject/object; reason/passion; culture/nature; and, associated more directly to politics, state/individual; public/private; universal/particular. And indeed, the polarity male/female serves to give meaning to the rest and to reinforce the dichotomies. Lloyd argues that the origin of these dualisms can be traced back to the Pythagorean table of opposites, developed in the sixth century B.C.:

> There were ten such contrasts in the table: limited/unlimited, odd/even, one/many, right/left, male/female, rest/motion, straight/curved, light/dark, good/bad, square/oblong ... "Male," like the other terms on its side of the table, was constructed as superior to its opposite ... (1984, 3).

In fact, women have not simply been excluded from Western thinking, but rather the very understanding of femininity has been premised on this exclusion. Coole (1988) argues that there is an apparent egalitarian treatment of women in Plato, but underneath these principles, there is a belief that women are less rational, less capable of virtue, and less ready to learn than their male counterparts. Although he discusses opportunities for women's equality in *The Republic*, Plato's reasoning is based on the elimination of "feminine" qualities. However, Coole suggests that Aristotle's claims were at the forefront of the natural sexual divisions up until the eighteenth century: "To this extent, it would be correct to see Plato as a progenitor of radical sexual politics and Aristotle as the harbinger of women's oppression"(1988, 30). However, it could be argued that in both Plato and Aristotle, there is a normative notion of humanness that is not separable from masculinity. As Coole shows, these ideas were imported in the Middle Ages and served as transmitters from ancient to modern times; they presented women without judgment, reason, and also "as vain, duplicitous, capricious, seductive, weak-minded, generally inferior and, often, as downright evil" (1988, 70).

Despite the rational form of thinking prevailing in liberalism, these beliefs endured. For example, Hobbes (1588–1679) and Locke (1632–1704) both believed in abstract freedom and equal rights, but women—due to their biological weakness and not so much their teleological inferiority—could not have freedom. The problems with the contractarian tradition (Hobbes, Locke, Rousseau, and more recently Rawls) can briefly be highlighted by examining Locke's view, as it has been celebrated as the origin of modern liberalism.

Although Locke stresses the idea of natural equality, there is an ambivalence in regard to women. For example, he denies that husbands have a God-given right to rule their wives but allows for the natural basis for the subordination of wives to husbands. Wives have to obey their husbands because they are "abler and stronger" (*Second Treatise*, II, par. 82). Hence, for Locke, women had to compromise their natural rights. Liberal ideas were thus exported in order to assign women with a specific role and place in society. Wollstonecraft's works (1759–1797; see, for example, Wollstonecraft, 1982) refuted the idea that women were not able to reason by simultaneously focusing on the equality and the recognition of difference in/of women (Pateman, 1991). *Vindication of the Rights of Woman* (1792) was pioneer in terms of its focus on women and the application of egalitarian reform principles to this group, a focus that had been almost omitted and silenced before her writings. At that time, it was innovative to even recognize women as an oppressed group, since writers such as Locke and Rousseau did not do so. Wollstonecraft's most powerful argument for the socialization and education of women is their innate capacity to reason. Reasoning was seen as progress in the eighteenth century, and it was believed that the fruits provided by reason would be of the greatest hopes.[5] Moreover, Wollstonecraft argued that women should be considered as rational subjects "instead of being educated like a fanciful kind of *half* being—one of Rousseau's wild chimeras"(44). Her analysis can be divided in two parts. The first is based on the argument that if women are given full citizenship they will be good wives, mothers, and daughters, while the second focuses on the fact that, if society fails to do this, social disintegration will result.[6]

However, Wollstonecraft is fundamentally trapped in the problems of Enlightenment for her work assumes the unproblematic nature of the concepts of reason and rights. She argues that women should have the same rights as men, using the man as "norm." Nevertheless, there is no doubt that despite its shortcomings, Wollstonecraft's work creates a space for women. Nineteenth-century feminists pursued Wollstonecraft's goals as described in *Vindication*. Seventy-nine years later, John Stuart Mill and Harriet Taylor embraced the ideas developed in the *Vindication*.

The works of Mill and Taylor also celebrate rationality, but fundamentally their views, as well as those of Wollstonecraft, imply the suppression of the feminine.

> ...while the suppression of the flesh which it implies, only continues that distaste for the body and hence for reproductive activities...which had traditionally granted to things female an aura of baseness...there lurks Platonic and Christian opinion that the truly equal woman is she who eliminates all traces of femaleness. (Coole, 1988, 153)

Wollstonecraft, Mill, and Taylor have been very influential in the history of liberal feminist thinking. Since then, feminists have demanded that liberal ideas and ideals be applied to women. Eighteenth-century feminists, such as Wollstonecraft, argued that women as well as men had natural rights. Nineteenth-century feminists such as Mill and Taylor applied utilitarian arguments in their demands for equal rights for women under the law. Twentieth-century feminists, in light of the development of liberal theory of the welfare state, advocated social reforms and equal opportunities for women.

With the benefit of hindsight, however, it is possible to argue that this project was misguided. It is problematic to deny differences between men and women. In fact, it may be suggested that in liberal conceptions of human nature, women represent negativity. The "female" is essential to philosophy as its internal negation, the "other." The problem posed by the "other" category is even clearer in Simone de Beauvoir's *The Second Sex*. Rationality, together with concepts such as difference, equality, and morality are central to our understanding even in more recent discussions of women, as I will demonstrate in the following discussion of de Beauvoir and Gilligan.[7]

De Beauvoir's *The Second Sex* is important in showing how the representations of woman as "other" are articulated and also to see philosophy's constitution of the female subject. However, de Beauvoir's stance is problematic in the sense that, while expanding on the conceptual frameworks of Sartrean and Hegelian dualistic phenomenology to analyze "woman's experience," it remains trapped in these prescribed analytical tools. For example, de Beauvoir presents and exposes the "scandal" of women's situation through an exposition of women's lived experiences in the framework of dualistic phenomenology of Sartre and Hegel. This, in turn, posits these terms in opposition: subject/object;

immanence/transcendence; responsibility/bad faith; in-itself/for-itself; and essential One/inessential Other. Of course, women are "object" and "inessential other," only capable of transcendence and bad faith, and thus doomed to immanence (de Beauvoir, 1972, 29). Mackenzie argues that her discourse of the female body is, in fact, two discourses of the female body (1986, 147). The first is a *constructivist* account of woman's body, reflecting her description of its social construction and the construction of femininity. On the other hand, the female body is presented as inherently passive, immanent, and fleshy. This seems to locate woman's oppression in her *oppressive* body.

Hence, woman needs to escape from her body in order to become a subject capable of transcendence. Drawing from Mackenzie, we can suggest that both descriptions adopted by de Beauvoir are flawed. In remaining within the philosophical framework of Sartre and Hegel, de Beauvoir is prey to the danger of accepting the categories and conceptions (e.g., subjectivity and rationality) that are defined in opposition to the feminine. In this discussion of rationality, the norm of reason is masculine, while the other side of reason has been attributed to (white bourgeois) women (of Western countries). The notions of "equality" and "difference" are also implied throughout this discussion. However, there is a major shift in thinking in how rationality, rights, difference, morality, and equality are viewed in radical feminism.

For radical feminists, rationality and morality are masculine constructs. This is what needs to be challenged if women are to be given a voice—a different voice. Within this perspective, the debate over the question of difference dominates and not equality, as was the case in liberalism. The difference/equality debate is very important in theorizing women's unruly bodies, and thus is related to the concept of morality, as discussed by Gilligan (1982). This view, which is rooted in radical feminism, is that the man is not the norm and that women's experiences should be taken as legitimate sources of knowledge. Until the emergence of radical feminist theory, women had to be like men—it was not desirable to be different because being labeled different meant that you did not fit the norm. Increasingly, though, radical feminists made the point that women were different and this difference was celebrated. It was argued that there were different values, ways of seeing, knowing, and being in the world, which were gendered. In fact, Gilligan's work validated the feminine and gave meaning to what was defined as irrational, illogical, and inconsistent. Despite its shortcomings, Gilligan's work recently gained importance in criminology for its focus on justice for women (Heidensohn, 1986; Daly, 1989).

To conclude this first section, let me simply say that women's place in theory rests on a major paradox, that of their concurrent exclusion and inclusion. As I have tried to show, Plato and Aristotle insisted on difference as one of the foundations of the politics of dominance. Within the contractarian tradition, thinkers such as Locke, Rousseau, and more recently Rawls believed in a different rationality between men and women. Hobbes and Locke, nonetheless, believed in abstract freedom and equal rights. For her part, Wollstonecraft argued simultaneously for equality and the recognition of difference and nearly eighty years later, Mill and Taylor celebrated rationality and sexual equality for women. For Simone de Beauvoir, women's "otherness" impacted on her rationality.

For all these authors, it seems that, to be rational, women need to eliminate all traces of their femaleness. With the emergence of radical feminism, this view shifted completely. For example, Carol Gilligan's work shifted the debate because she argued that "morality" and "rationality" are masculine constructs and women should not be compared to the masculine norm but should be viewed through women's own experiences. In fact, what becomes important is that women do not need to eliminate their femaleness, their flesh or their body to be capable of rational acts. And the debate, as I have attempted to show, continues to oscillate between difference and equality. This is what I will try to explore in the illustrations provided in the gallery of portraits.

A GALLERY OF PORTRAITS

The body represents a theoretical gap and void at the heart of the criminological enterprise and this is the result, in part, of the Cartesian divide between mind and body (Currie and Raoul, 1992). The mere acknowledgment of the body casts a shadow on the pursuit of rationality and objectivity of both the social theorist and the conditions of the production of knowledge. In fact, Smart (1989, 91) argues, "It has been essential for the acceptance of the claim of objectivity and scientificity that there be a clear dissociation from supposedly natural elements like the functions of the body."

Feminists have been involved in exploring the body as well as contesting the ways it has been traditionally problematized. The fact that women have been associated with the body means that they have been posited on the other side of reason. The portraits that I propose in the next section are not exhaustive but are attempts to show how women's protests, resistance, and "criminality" have been disqualified by portraying them as "heretics," "mad," at the "mercy of their hormones," or suffering from a "syndrome." As these portraits will suggest, women's bodies and minds are, simultaneously, *in danger* and *dangerous*.

Witches: The Embodiment of Difference, Deviance, and Resistance

To begin this gallery of portraits, I will discuss and analyze the image, meaning, and consequences of the "witch," a very powerful representation in the portrayals of certain (deviant) women, even in the twentieth century. As Heidensohn suggests:

> Women are no longer hunted as witches in Scotland, nor indeed anywhere in the British Isles. The witch image, however, does remain, at least as a folk memory. It sits on top of a pyramid of related images of deviant women as especially evil, depraved and monstrous. (1985, 92)

In this section, I will provide a background for the relevance of this iconography for the representation of women as deviant by presenting the social and political context of witchcraft (particularly in the contexts of English, Scottish, and French witch-hunts). I will also focus on four theories of witchcraft in order to illustrate how and why the witch craze occurred and why women were the main targets. In order to understand the witch craze more fully, I will discuss three questions: (1) why did the witch craze start in the fifteenth century?; (2) why were women the main victims of the witch craze?; and (3) was the witch craze gender-related or gender-specific (Hester, 1992)?

According to conservative estimates (MacFarlane, 1970; Ben-Yehuda, 1985), from the early decades of the fifteenth century until 1650, between 200,000 and 500,000 witches were executed in continental Europe, of whom more than 85 percent were women.[8] It is often suggested that the witch craze started in the fifteenth century because medieval society was eroding just as a new social, political, economic, scientific and religious order was being established. Although there were very positive reactions to these new social arrangements, there were also very violent, negative ones. Thus, the witch-hunt, aimed at reestablishing the old social order, was rooted in a search for collective identity. It is interesting that the "century of genius" and some famous people of the time believed in the reality of witchcraft, demonology, and witches. As Ben-Yehuda (1985) notes, Newton, Bacon, Boyle, Locke, and Hobbes all believed in demonology. Even at these times of great philosophical, artistic, and political enlightenment, "[t]ens of thousands of [witchcraft] trials continued throughout Europe generation after generation, while Leonardo painted, Palestrina composed and Shakespeare wrote" (Russell, 1977, 79).

But why were *women* the victims of this witch craze? It has often been argued from the empirical evidence that certain types of women were the targets of this witch-hunt. The view that predominantly older and "deviant" women were the targets is supported by the British cases, yet not by the Continental witch craze. However, as many scholars suggest, the major factor in the prosecution was the fact that they were women. Ben-Yehuda writes:

> At the beginning of the witchcraze, we often find that accused witches were widows, spinsters, or "strange" old women. Later on, married women and young girls were persecuted as well. Various historical sources reveal that neither social status nor age made any difference as the most crucial variable was the fact that most victims were women. (1985, 38–39)

Moreover, we are also in a position to ask, after Hester (1992), if the witch craze was, in fact, gender-related or gender-specific? The first perspective has been adopted by an important number of scholars, including Larner (1981) and Szasz (1971). For them, the fact that the majority of the victims of this witch craze were women is only *one* aspect and/or an indirect consequence of the craze. Despite this, Larner admits that, "witch-hunting is woman-hunting or at least it is the hunting of women who do not fulfill the male view of how women ought to conduct themselves" (1981, 100).

My reading of the witch craze reflects that it was gender-specific. In fact, the witch craze is significant because it primarily attacked women. Ehrenreich and English (1976) take such a view. For them, it was a way of eliminating women from medical practice. For Daly (1979), it was also a more general attempt to control women who were transgressing a masculine order by rejecting marriage (spinsters) or surviving it (widows). Despite the various reasons suggested for the emergence of the witch craze, women seem to have been viewed as a threat one way or another. This threat is translated, for our purposes, in the following four theories.

Theories of Witchcraft

In order to grasp the significance of the witch craze, I will discuss three theories of witchcraft provided by Szasz (1971): the witch as mental patient, the witch as healer, and the witch as scapegoat. I will then offer a fourth theory, the witch as sexually deviant.[9] These theories will be presented in order to show and discuss their relevance to gender.

Witch as Mental Patient   In *The Manufacture of Madness*, Szasz parallels the practices of the Inquisition and those of modern institutional psychiatry.[10] He tries to show that the social controls of institutional psychiatry and its underlying concepts, rhetorical devices, and applications resemble those of the Inquisition. Like the Inquisition, psychiatry as a modern method of manufacturing madness "fulfills a basic human need—to validate the Self as good (normal), by invalidating the Other as evil (mentally ill)"(xxvii). Zilboorg argues that "the *Malleus Maleficarum* might with a little editing serve as an excellent modern textbook of descriptive clinical psychiatry of the fifteenth century, if the word *witch* were substituted by the word *patient*, and the devil eliminated" (Zilboorg, quoted in Szasz, 1971, 68).

A series of authors associated witchcraft with mental illness (Philippe Pinel, 1745–1826; Jean Etienne-Dominique Esquirol, 1772–1840; Jean-Martin Charcot, 1825–1893). The results of the psychiatric interpretation of witchcraft were twofold. First, witches were objects of psychological interest and "their behavior was regarded as proof of the transhistorical and transcultural 'reality' of mental illness" (Szasz, 1971, 81). Second, the behaviour of prosecutors, inquisitors and judges was ignored. Szasz argues that although the psychiatric theory of witchcraft may not help us understand witchcraft itself, it is valuable in regard to our understanding of psychiatry and its pivotal concept of mental illness. In conclusion, the politics of witchcraft are evident in Szasz's point that "what is called 'mental illness' (or 'psychopathology') emerges as the name of the product of a particular kind of relationship between oppressor and oppressed"(81).

More importantly, however, is the well-documented fact that women were the ones seen as witches and as mad, and the label "mad" became associated with women. Ussher (1991) suggests that "Madness, hysteria or insanity came to replace the catch-all description of "witch" as a label applied to women who were in some way deviant, in some way different: women who did not fit" (60).

Witch as Healer   To understand the second theory of witchcraft, it is important to note that during the Middle Ages, medicine and other knowledges were not constituted as "scientific" forms of knowledge. The sorceress, the good witch, or the Wise Woman was the only one to use magic rites to heal and control disease (Ehrenreich and English, 1976). She was a physician, an astrologer, a necromancer, a prophet, and a sorceress. Hence, she was a challenge to the Roman Catholic Church because of her methods and popularity. Witchcraft was viewed as a "revolt against the authority of the Church" (86). As Michelet remarks:

> Is there one science you can name that was not originally a revolt against authority? Medicine above all was truly and indeed Satanic, a revolt against disease, the merited scourge of an offended God. Plainly a sinful act to stay the soul on its road toward heaven and replunge it in the life of this World! (Michelet quoted in Ehrenreich and English, 1976, 86)

The censure of healing was directed not only at witches but also at physicians. This was based on the premise that man was created by God and that man belonged to God. The accusation was not that they could not heal but that their healing was evil. Interestingly, Szasz notes that no modern male psychiatric historian acknowledges the "witch as healer and therapist, the true mother of the modern, privately practicing physician and psychotherapist." Instead, "[m]an (the Masculine Physician) robs Woman (the White Witch) of her discovery: he declares her mad, and himself the enlightened healer" (1971, 92).[11]

Witch as Scapegoat   While psychiatrists advocate the psychopathological theory of witchcraft, historians tend to support the scapegoat theory of witchcraft. They hold the view that witches were offered as sacrifices in a society rooted in symbolism and Christian theology. The belief in witches and their persecution "represent an expression of man's search for an explanation and mastery of various human problems, especially bodily diseases and social conflicts" (95). They provided a scapegoat for the difficulties and troubles of society, as the Jews had provided during certain periods. The parallels are obvious: "economic and emotional uncertainty, the apprehensions about physical security, and metaphysical fears for the salvation of the soul; deflection of turbulent antisocial impulses against a single defenseless group" (97).

Hence, whereas the psychiatric interpretation of witchcraft locates the problem in mental diseases of certain individuals, the scapegoat theory relates it to certain social conditions that permitted these beliefs and practices.

Witch as Sexual Deviant   Finally, the description of witches as sexually deviant is particularly important in making the connection between the Inquisition and gender (sexual) roles. The sexuality of women, which was most noticeable in witches, was both "terrible and terrifying" (Ussher, 1991, 49). I argue that they were seen as *dangerous* and *in danger*. In fact, the *Malleus Maleficarum* dictated "all witch craft comes from carnal lust which in some women is insatiable" (Sprenger and Kraemer, 1487 quoted in Ussher, 1991, 49). Hence, it is because women are viewed as insatiable that they are more often accused of witchcraft. Ussher and others argue that women who are more openly and actively sexual are also more often accused of witchcraft. Additionally, the fecundity of women and particularly menstruation were some of the most central foundations of the link between women and witchcraft. Scot (1584) writes:

> Women are also monthly filled full of superfluous humours, and with them the melancholic blood boils; whereof spring vapours, and are carried up, and conveyed through the nostrils and mouth, etc., to the bewitching of whatsoever it meets ... And of all other women, lean, hollow-eyed, old beetle-browed women are the most infectious. (quoted in Ussher, 1991, 49)

Hence, the fears associated with witchcraft seem also associated with reproduction and menstruation. The fear of witchcraft might seem to be related to the fear of woman, her body, her fecundity, her blood. The *Malleus Maleficarum* endorsed and perpetuated such a view and reinforced the view that women, as the weaker sex, could not resist having sex with Satan. This fourth theory of witchcraft served also as a powerful transmitter of an ideology that equated women with demonology.

Given the evidence provided, women seem to have been effective symbols of a new ideology and became symbols of fear. It is also argued that the social position of medieval women was a subject of constant debate between the Church and the aristocracy; however, their subordination seemed to be accepted. On the one hand, women were regarded as superior beings (e.g. the Virgin Mary cult), and on the other they were viewed as dangerous and seductive (Eve). Of course, women from different social positions were seen differently. Lemay (1978) argues that in the thirteenth and fourteenth centuries, universities presented women as inferior and dangerous. In fact, Ben-Yehuda continues that "[t]he lecturers emphasized that menstruating women kill little children, that women insert chemicals in the vagina in order to wound the penis of a sexual partner, that they feign virginity and conceal pregnancy" (1985, 61). As we can see, scientific and medical discourses provided the ideological basis for the persecution of certain women.

Similarly, Brown (1969) and Colin (1972) argue that the Renaissance and Reformation were characterized by economic, monetary, commercial, and urban revolution, which gave rise to individualism and egoism. Thus, the limiting of offspring, the prevention of pregnancy, and infanticide that resulted from this period provoked serious demographic changes in the fifteenth and sixteenth centuries. This situation was also denounced by the Church as evil and thus linked to witchcraft. Trexler notes that

> child-killing has been regarded almost exclusively as a female crime, the result of women's inherent tendency to lechery, passion and lack of responsibility...Infanticide was...the most common social crime imputed to...witches...by the demonologists. (1973, 98, 103)

Wet nurses (midwives) were thus sought to prevent this, but they were soon chief suspects of witchcraft as the Dominicans suspected that they had knowledge and expertise (which they had) of birth control and cooperated in infanticide.[12] This is how the phenomenon of women as victims of witch-hunts may be understood.

The witch trials show how women and their bodies have been seen, simultaneously, as in danger and dangerous. Hence, they needed to be controlled, regulated, and even exterminated. The body of woman has also been controlled because of its mysterious functions: menstruation, pregnancy, maternity, and others. This control continues today, and its manifestation can be seen in the discussion of premenstrual syndrome (PMS). Given the legal ramifications of PMS, I now turn to an exploration of the construction of menstruating women's bodies as needing explanation, control, and treatment.

Menstruating Women: Taboos of Exclusion

> my blood leaves me
> each month to flow
> into the earth becoming
> once again the power of
> the universe without which
> no man can be (...)
> when riddled or burned my body
> is found by my sisters of Sappha's
> genes and they follow me (...)
> from the witch hunts and massacres
> of me in my innocence that still curse
> the men in medical, religious and political places;
> those men who try to hide from my swollen tongue
> on the days that I was hanged in england;
> trying to hide from the charcoaled bones (...)
> my blood has flowed without mercy
> to be scorned and defiled
> in the man-made courts of the land.
> now, tired of my body being bled dry
> I come back from places
> that men cannot see
> to claim this blood
>   that is me (Stafford, 1994, 9)[13]

Blood. Historically, and even today, menstruating women have been considered in danger and dangerous. For this reason, they have been excluded from everyday activities and sometimes relegated, in some societies, to a small hut, usually with other menstruating women (Delaney, Lupton, and Toth, 1988). They were quarantined because they were believed to emit a *mana*, or threatening super-natural power. As an example, Delaney, Lupton, and Toth suggest that the fear of menstrual blood and its powers probably led a "New Guinea Mae Enga tribesman known to the anthropologist M.J. Meggit [to] divorce his wife because she had slept on his blanket while menstruating and, still feeling not quite safe from her evil influence, later killed her with an ax" (7).

The existence of taboos in past cultures and societies means that menstruating women were considered unclean and contaminated. Hence, it was necessary to restrict their contact with society because of their so-called impurity. For example, they were not allowed to prepare meals for men and could not have sex with them because men could suffer castration. The Maori of New Zealand believed that the blood could do extreme harm to men. The Mae Enga believed that contact with menstruating women would "sicken a man and cause persistent vomiting, 'kill' his blood so that it turns black, corrupt his vital juices so that his skin darkens and hangs in folds as his flesh wastes, permanently dull his wits, and eventually lead to a slow decline and death" (Meggit quoted in Delaney, Lupton, and Toth, 8–9).

There were, however, positive aspects to menstrual blood. It was thought to be a remedy for leprosy, warts, birthmarks, and prevent the inception of evil spirits. But, by and large, menstrual blood was considered a "curse" (de Beauvoir, 1972, 24).

Similarly, Brown explores women's writings during the Quiet Revolution in Quebec in the 1960s where many focus on women's experiences of their bodies. These experiences of the body are seen as an "oppressive regime based on Catholic conceptions of woman as responsible for Original Sin, and the flesh—particularly that of women—as evil" (Brown, 1992, 222). Hence, in one of Marie-Claire Blais's most popular novels, *Manuscrits de Pauline Archange* (1968), the young heroine sees, and is taught by nuns, that her genitalia embody "le lieu du péché" (the site of sin). It is also "a symbol of Divine punishment which they must bear in shame, for in the eyes of God they are, as Marie-Claire Blais's (1970, 100) heroine says, 'des animaux inférieurs' [inferior animals]" (Brown, 1992, 227). In three novels in particular, *Une forêt pour Zoé* by Louise Maheux-Forcier (1969), *La nuit si longue* by Nellie Maillard (1960), and *Les Apparences* by Marie-Claire Blais (1970), the ficti-tious women all share hatred of the body. This hatred is

> captured in their belief that the menstrual flow is the indisputable sign of women's infamy. In their minds, this blood is cursed blood, a defiled and defiling liquid ... Descendants of Eve, whose sin of disobedience all women have been condemned to expiate, these protagonists are equally convinced that their salvation, and that of their daughters, rests on their ability to imprint in the latter's minds the mythi-cal belief that menstruation is first and foremost the physical proof of their sex's unworthiness, uncleanliness, and inferiority. (Brown, 1992, 227)

The above myths and taboos rested on the assumption that men were the norm and women diseased because men have been historically associated with the mind and reason, and women have been associated with the body and lack of reason. This idea gained currency in the medical practice where women have been treated as nonrational beings at the mercy of their "raging" hormones.

The Construction of Premenstrual Syndrome (PMS)

> The heay pain beforehand makes the woman feel bloated, weighted down with the engorged pelvic mass. The gripping pains at the onset may severely incapacitate her. Almost worse than all this is the preceding week's depression, seemingly miraculously lifted with the onset of the flow. Women vary in how they view these ordeals....(Ashurst and Hall quoted in Stoppard, 1992, 119)

PMS is a medical construct. The existence of premenstrual syndrome was first defined by gynecologist Robert T. Frank in 1929, but it was not until the 1970s that it gained widespread recognition with the work of Dr. Katherina Dalton, a British doctor.[14] Dalton was to become the world's leading expert on PMS and served as an expert witness in the three British murder cases which I will discuss shortly.

The 1993 Diagnostic and Statistical Manual of Mental Disorders (DSM-III-Revised) published by the American Psychiatric Association (the leading authority on diagnostic decisions in North America) included the diagnosis late luteal phase dysphoric disorder (LLPDD), which is equivalent to PMS. This nonspecific classification was described as a mental disorder in clinical research and is consistent with the medicalization of women's bodies (Kendall, 1992; Stoppard, 1992). In 1994, the fourth edition (DSM-IV-TM) refers to a specific disorder called the premenstrual dysphoric disorder, which "differs from the 'premenstrual syndrome' in its characteristic patterns of symptoms, their severity, and the resulting impairment" (DSM-IV-TM, 716). In fact, "it is estimated that at least 75% of women report minor or isolated premenstrual changes. *Limited* studies suggest an occurrence of "premenstrual syndrome" (*variably defined*) of 20% to 50%, and that 3% to 5% of women experience symptoms that may meet the criteria of this proposed disorder" (716; emphasis added).

The symptoms include markedly depressed mood, anxiety, affective lability, anger, decreased interest in usual activities, lethargy, and other physical symptoms. This medical evidence finds its way into courtrooms.

PMS as a Defence

The principles underlying law assume that an autonomous being is capable of moral judgment and rationality and is responsible for his or her actions; but law also accepts the idea that mental illness or defect can sometimes defeat free will.

The PMS defence surfaced in England when PMS gained acceptance as an identifiable medical problem with a possible medical cure. However, historically, such a defence based on PMS had been used. In 1833, in England, a 16-year-old girl was charged with setting fire to her master's house. The defence claimed that she was not responsible since she was acting as a result of an illness and the non-appearance of catemenia. She was acquitted (Edwards, 1988, 456). In 1845, a servant girl to a respectable family killed the infant child of her master and it was thought that she had laboured under disordered menstruation probably caused by "obstructed menstruation." The defence claimed she was undergoing treatment for amenorrhea and because of this disease she was not responsible for her actions. She was found not guilty on the grounds of insanity (456). In 1851, Amelia Snoswell murdered her baby niece and was acquitted on the grounds of disordered menstruation. Lizzie Borden, a "famous" murderess in the early twentieth century, killed her father (30 wounds) and her stepmother (20 wounds) with an ax. It was determined that she committed the murders—at least her stepmother's—during a seizure. At the trial—she was asked why she had blood on her skirt; she answered that she had her period. It was said that she suffered from peculiar spells during menstruation and she was acquitted of both murders.

Some contemporary cases in the 1980s in Britain reintroduced the debate. Women charged with murder were finally accused of manslaughter because they were thought not to be responsible for their actions because premenstrual syndrome had reduced their responsibility.

A Ms. English, a 37-year-old mother of two from Colchester, killed Barry Kitson, her live-in lover for three years. The relationship was strained for several reasons, including the fact that he was an alcoholic, violent, and abusive (Benn, 1993, 162). On the night of the murder, he had been taunting her, saying he had another lover. They fought and Kitson stormed off to go to the pub. When English went to pick him up they fought again, this time about his drinking. He "lashed out" at her with his fists and stormed out of the car saying, "I hate you and never want to see you again." While English was driving off, she raced toward him in a "paroxysm of fury." Kitson was crushed against a telephone pole, his leg almost severed; English got out of the car in a state of disbelief. Kitson died in hospital 15 days later (Benn, 1993, 161). English pleaded guilty to manslaughter on grounds of diminished responsibility.[15] She was tried and received a conditional discharge and a 12-month driving disqualification. It was accepted that premenstrual syndrome is in fact a disease of the mind. Katherina Dalton provided evidence as an expert witness and said that English was "suffering from an aggravated form of what is known as premenstrual syndrome" (Laws, Hey, and Eagan, 1985, 69). Dalton testified that English had been suffering from PMS since 1966, which made her very temperamental and unpredictable. The defence lawyer's argument, which showed how much her lover destroyed her and their relationship by drinking, was seen as less crucial to the defence than Dalton's PMS argument.

Sandie Craddock, 29, was tried for manslaughter for stabbing a fellow barmaid to death (Benn, 1993, 156). She had a history of violent behaviour: 45 previous convictions (Edwards, 1988, 456). She was also on progesterone, a treatment for PMS. She apparently did not remember the act, which appeared to be random, and had been repeatedly committed by the courts to mental hospitals. Craddock pleaded guilty to manslaughter. It was accepted due to diminished responsibility and she received a three-year probation order with the condition she continue hormonal therapy treatment (Benn, 1993, 157). It was again accepted that premenstrual syndrome is a disease of the mind as defined in the *Homicide Act*, 1957. Dalton examined Craddock's diaries and claimed that she was suffering from PMS. Dalton argued that PMS was a disease of the body and therefore a disease of the mind in that the bodily metabolism is upset, which in turn upsets the mental processes. On another occasion, Craddock (now named Smith) came into conflict with the law for having threatened to kill a police officer and for possessing an offensive weapon. Again, Dalton testified that her violent conduct was due to a reduction in her progesterone therapy. Craddock received a three-year probation order with provision of medical treatment.

Anne Reynolds was an only child and was frequently lonely, if not unloved.[16] Her father died when she was 11-years-old shortly after they had an argument; she has often blamed herself for his death. As a teenager, she attempted suicide twice, spent time in a mental hospital, and suffered from severe depression (Benn, 1993, 167–68). Her relationship with her mother was very strained. Reynolds was able to successfully conceal her pregnancy from her mother, whom she lived with (Benn, 1993, 168), then gave her child up for adoption (Edwards, 1988, 456). On the night of the murder, Reynolds came home after work, had an argument with her mother and went to bed. She felt disturbed that night and decided to sleep in the same room with her mother on a camp bed. Plagued by a "funny feeling," she got up, saw a hammer, and repeatedly struck her mother on the head with it. She made a "half-hearted" attempt to arrange the room to make it look like a burglary, but abandoned this story soon after she got to the police station. The jury concluded that she was not suffering from an illness that night and convicted her of murder. On appeal, Katherina Dalton provided evidence that Reynolds was suffering from a combination of premenstrual tension and postnatal depression (Benn, 1993, 165–166). The conviction was changed to manslaughter on the grounds of diminished responsibility. She received a probation order on the condition she follow psychiatric treatment (Edwards, 1988, 456).

The PMS defence has also been used in Canada (Sheehey, 1987; Kendall, 1992; Faith, 1993).[17] For example, the *Babcock* v. *Babcock* (Kendall, 1992) case, a noncriminal case, shows the extent of the possible use of PMS in the social control of women. In this case, a British Columbia Supreme Court judge "considered a woman's PMS condition to be an important factor in denying her custody" (Kendall, 1992, 132).

Hence, the alarm over women's violence produces "a particular meaning of women as possessors of pathologically suspect bodies" (Laws, Hey, and Eagan, 1985, 68) and as yet another example of "all women's reduction to their unruly bodies and irrational emotions" (Faith, 1993, 45). Moreover, the legal recognition of PMS as a disease "may deflect attention from other social and economic causes of crime and could, more generally, invalidate women's actual and legitimate feelings of anger" (Kendall, 1992, 132), as was the case for English.

Despite the fact that the analysis supporting the premenstrual syndrome is biological and medical and that the analysis underlying the battered woman syndrome (BWS) is psychological and sociological, the next section will explore how the question of the regulation of the unruly bodies and minds of women is always central. It seems relevant and necessary to see how some of the ideas encapsulated in the discourse underlying the PMS defence are also echoed in the BWS defence in cases of women who kill their abusive partners. As Ann Jones, writer of *When Women Kill,* suggests in the 1994 National Film Board documentary of the same title:

> The courts have never been able to deal with women who kill, particularly women who kill men; that is a very bad thing in the view of most men, so the courts have bent over backwards to try and find ways to explain that in terms of the particular psychological aberration of the woman. In the 19th century, the talking about a delicate lady, a flower of womanhood, then the courts would acknowledge that indeed she must have been insane at this moment and perhaps she would be acquitted of the crime. That's the pattern that has continued right up until the present. The courts still entertain pleas of insanity from women, only nowadays we do it in a more sophisticated way, so that in England the PMS defence, the premenstrual syndrome defence was popular to explain why a woman committed the irrational act of killing the husband. In the U.S. and now in Canada we have turned to the battered woman syndrome. (Verbatim from NFB documentary, *When Women Kill,* 1994)

Female Conjugal Homicide and the Battered Woman Syndrome

I am concerned here with the issue of spousal homicide—more particularly women who kill their abusive partners[18]—and the relevance of the battered woman syndrome defence used in these cases as an indicator of how women's disruptive bodies and minds are important in the construction of these cases.

To briefly highlight some of the elements I consider important in relation to the battered woman syndrome, I will focus on one landmark case in Canada. For the purpose of this exposé, I will not focus on the importance of this landmark case for the legal recognition of violence against women, but rather on the possible implications of the translation of women's actions as irrational and women as suffering from a syndrome.[19]

Angélique Lyn Lavallée was in an abusive relationship with her partner, Kevin Rust, for three years. One night in 1989, during a party, Rust told Lavallée that he would kill her after the party. She later said she believed that her life was threatened. In her statement to the police she said:

> I ran in the house after Kevin pushed me. I was scared. I was so scared. I locked the door ... I went upstairs and hid in my closet from Kevin. I was so scared ... He came into my bedroom and said "Wench, where are you?" OK then he

turned and saw me in the closet. He wanted me to come out but I didn't want to come out because I was scared. I was so scared ... He grabbed me by the arm right there. There's a bruise on my face also where he slapped me ... The rest is a blank, all I remember is he gave me the gun and a shot was fired through my screen. This is all so fast. And then the guns were in another room and he loaded it the second shot and gave it to me. And I was going to shoot myself. I pointed it to myself, I was so upset. OK and then he went and I was sitting on the bed ... and said something like "You're my old lady and you do as you're told" or something like that. He said "wait till everybody leaves, you'll get it then" and he said something to the effect of "either you kill me or I'll get you" that was what it was. He kind of smiled and then he turned around. I shot him but I aimed out. I thought I aimed above and a piece of his head went that way. (*R.v. Lavallée* at 329. [1990])

She was charged with murder but she pleaded self-defence and she was acquitted with the help of the expert evidence provided by a psychiatrist on the issue of the battered woman syndrome. There was an appeal made by the Crown but the Supreme Court of Canada reinstated the acquittal. This judgment was seen as a feminist victory. The judgment, given by Madam Bertha Wilson, argued that the court needed to allow for women's perspectives to be heard and considered, for the traditional doctrinal issues (such as the "reasonable person" or "reasonable man") did not accommodate women's experiences of battering. On this point, the court made the following remark:

> The respondent was entitled to have the jury consider her actions in the light of her own perceptions of the situation, including those perceptions which were the product of our nation's "long and unfortunate history of sex discrimination." Until such time as the effects of that history are eradicated, care must be taken to assure that our self-defense instructions afford women the right to have their conduct judged in light of the individual handicaps which are the product of sex discrimination. To fail to do so is to deny the right of the individual woman involved to trial by the same rules which are applicable to male defendants. (559)

Did the Canadian court take into account the structural inequalities of men and women and the asymmetric relation of violence? Of course, it is a good thing that Lavallée's experiences of violence were taken into account and that standard legal doctrine was questioned. However, let us see how the rationale of the decision was constructed.

The expert evidence on the battered woman syndrome was an important aspect in this case. This expert evidence was provided by a psychiatrist who relied on Dr. Lenore Walker's 1984 book *Battered Woman Syndrome*. It is important to note two things. First, Lavallée did not testify; a psychiatrist gave expert testimony about Lavallée's experiences of violence, which was then translated into psychiatric and legal language.[20] Second, the BWS defence was used, which reconstructed the homicide as a psychological disorder in opposition to wider social issues such as gender inequality and power differentials in intimate relationships. BWS is catalogued as a mental disorder in the 1994 *Diagnostic and*

Statistical Manual of Mental Disorders under the post-traumatic stress disorder category. Even if the BWS, as expert evidence, should help explain Walker's three-stage cycle of violence, describe how the defendant "fits" within the category of the battered woman, and substantiate the defendant's claim that she honestly believed she was justified in using deadly force, it reiterates the power of the psychiatric categories (such as BWS and PMS), in that they translate women's behaviour as an individual disorder/pathology. Even if in the *Lavallée* decision the actions of the defendant were seen as justified, the battered woman syndrome will possibly lead to the construction of women's action as abnormal. As the first part of this chapter documents, reason—when applied to women, and here to Angélique Lyn Lavallée—does not refer to the traditional and masculine construction of reason. Consequently, Lavallée's rationality, and by extension women's rationality, is understood as a pathological state, namely the battered woman syndrome. In fact, the case of *Lavallée* represents the "negation" and erasure of the Woman of Reason in legal discourse, as she is propelled in the universe of unreason (see also Young, 1992).

There have been positive implications of *Lavallée* but also negative ones. Sheehey (1993) discusses a series of cases since *Lavallée* in which BWS has not secured acquittals for women because they did not "fit" the BWS criteria, and BWS was not admissable. She suggests, for example, that in three cases, *Howard* (1992),[21] *Catholique* (1990),[22] and *Eyapaise* (1993),[23] the racism of the criminal justice system in the construction of aboriginal women was one of the reasons why BWS could not be used as a defence:

> While the violence of white women is pathologized as unwomanly, and rendered explicable through the BWS and the re-characterization of the women as stuck in the cycle of violence, paralyzed, and helpless, the violence of Aboriginal women in Canada may be seen, through the lens of racism, as consistent with stereotypes of Aboriginal women, and thus not requiring rationalization through syndromization. (Sheehey, 1993, 13)

To conclude this section, we can ask ourselves if there is a continuity between PMS and BWS. Is there continuity of the medicalization and criminalization of women's bodies and minds? The process of medicalization refers "to the process and product of defining and treating human experiences as medical problems" (Bell, quoted in Stoppard, 1992, 126). PMS is pathologized by the way it has been seen as deviant from the (masculine) norm. In fact, Stoppard argues:

> The medical view of women's bodies implicitly takes male biology as the norm of human health. Against the male-biased standard, female reproductive biology, with its inherent cyclicity, is seen as deviant. Women's biological differences from men are recast in terms of illness or disease. In effect, the medical model reproduces women as deficient or dysfunctional men. (1992, 126)

Similarly, BWS is also confronted with this norm. This norm is not biological but psychological and social. This is consistent with a study by Broverman and his colleagues done in 1972 that dealt with the perceptions of mental health professionals and concluded that the healthy (sane) adult was in fact the healthy (sane) adult man. The convergence of many traits between the sane adult and the sane adult man led them to this conclusion: higher independence, more aggressive, more competitive, less emotional, and more objective. On the other hand, even the sane woman deviated from these characteristics; she is more passive, more dependent, less aggressive, less competitive, more emotional, and less objective. Hence, the "normal" woman is sick and deviant and cannot be a mentally healthy (sane) adult.

As is the case with PMS, BWS points to the fact that traditional defences (provocation, self-defence) are not open to women and that, as Jones suggests in *When Women Kill,* the courts "have bent over backwards to try and find ways to explain that in terms of the particular psychological aberration of the woman." Moreover, PMS and BWS are being catalogued as mental disorders (by Dr. Dalton in PMS cases in England and by Dr. Shane in BWS cases in Canada). The only viable experts are doctors and psychiatrists, which means that women's actions are potentially translated in medical/psychiatric discourses.[24]

Another area of convergence between the two syndromes and the construction of women as witches is that women are seen as *dangerous* (killing) and *in danger* (violence against women), which blurs the boundary between *victimization* and *criminalization*. When women transgress society's understanding of gender, they offend. In the case of women who kill their violent partners, they have committed a serious offence against marriage and they have deviated from appropriate gender roles. Similarly, women's political protests are interpreted as deviance from womanhood, motherhood, and the discursive meanings of women. Again, women's actions and/or protests are seen as "unreasonable." Keeping this in mind, I now turn to women's political protests to examine the representations of women, and I again highlight the construction of women's bodies and minds as unruly and disruptive.

Women's Political Protests: Instances of Similarity

As I mentioned earlier, women who transgress penal norms are often transgressing or seen as transgressing appropriate gender roles and norms of femininity. As an illustration of this, we can see how women defined as "terrorists" have broken with the codes of womanhood and femininity. Four dimensions can be identified in relation to women terrorists (Jaccoub, 1989). The first is the physical dimension, where women are viewed as either beautiful or ugly. The second is the gender dimension, which is linked to women's nature and role. Women are often viewed as being masculine, cruel, nonfeminine, as rejecting appropriate female roles, and sometimes of being lesbians. The psychological dimension is the third and the sociopolitical dimension is the fourth. Hence, even if terrorism is defined as a strategy of violence of individual, collective, or institutional force with the goal of changing social, political and economic structures, women's activities are reinterpreted in an analysis linked to their sexual roles.

The meaning of their actions is individualized and pathologized and loses its political character.[25]

There are many ways of neutralizing the political aspect of women's political protests. In the case of the Greenham Common women and the suffragettes, three main techniques and processes can be identified: (1) the criminalization of women's demands; (2) the sexualization of women's protests; and (3) the medicalization of women's voices as hysterical.[26] The disciplinary matrix criminalization/sexualization/medicalization is therefore an important way of disqualifying women's resistance and defiance to masculine hegemonic order.

I will briefly explore the discursive meanings of Greenham women as "other" and unrepresentable. The Greenham Common peace camp is a protest by women outside a cruise-missile base in Berkshire, England. It began in 1981 and still continues today, albeit in a different way. However, their protest is attacked and censured.

As referred to in the vignettes at the beginning of this chapter, Blackwood (1984) testifies to this violence when writing that the Greenham women were portrayed as dirty, communists, Russian spies, lesbians, sex-starved, and bad mothers, to name a few. Their disqualification proceeded by a disqualification of their bodies and sexualities. The consequences of these associations led to negative attitudes about their demands.

Additionally, the Greenham Common women as objects of analysis are simultaneously products of a specific historical period and a recent display of the representation of women's "civil disobedience" (Doggett, 1990) in censuring ways (Young, 1990). The censure was operated under the disciplinary practices of the master-narratives of the law, sexuality, and medicine (Young, 1990).

Other instances similar to the Greenham Common women include the suffragettes, the Women's Peace Crusade, the Women's International League for Peace and Freedom, and the Women's Caravan of Peace (Young, 1990). In fact, it would be possible to envisage that the future use of the name "Greenham women" could be taken as a means of condemnation as the members of the Women's Social and Political Union were named "suffragettes" in 1906 by the *Daily Mail* (150). Similarly, the Women's International League for Peace and Freedom was described as "... 'women peace fanatics' (*Evening Standard*), 'folly in petticoats' (*Sunday Pictorial*), 'shipload of hysterical women' (*The Globe*), 'the Peacettes' (*Daily Express)* (note the reappearance of the suffix '-ette')"(150). However, the resemblances and similarities between the aforementioned epithets and descriptions of women's protests show that the censure of the Greenham women was *"already written"* (Grimshaw, 1986, 27). Before the press coverage began, there was a long history of representation.

The disciplinary matrix criminalization/sexualization/medicalization is clearly in operation in the process of disqualification of women's political campaigns. As I will show, the demand for the right to vote is evacuated from the descriptions and representations of women. Their resistance and defiance to masculine hegemonic order is reinterpreted in different censuring ways. With this in mind, I will examine the disciplinary matrix of regulation, control and censure in the case of the suffragette movement by briefly exposing the discursive practices of law and medicine.[28]

The censure of these women points to wider conceptualizations of womanhood. It is a specific historical moment in which precise normative prescriptions about woman's role and place were in operation. Ideal/typical norms about women were not constructed at the particular moment of this group's campaign; rather, norms had been constructed from the Victorian era into the "votes for women" campaign. Hence, it could be argued that women's demand for the right to vote was surrounded by a certain kind of regime of meanings that precluded as well as framed their demands. This led to their demands being evacuated and dismissed.

The protest of women reached a significant phase when, in 1910, the British House of Commons announced that a bill for the enfranchisement of women was to be abandoned. On this day, called "Black Friday," groups of women marched to the House of Commons. Scores of women were injured by policemen; 135 statements of brutality reported by women were recorded. What is striking about those injuries is that they were often of a sexual nature. One member of the Women's Social and Political Union (WSPU) recalled later:

> One policeman...put his arm round me and seized my left breast, nipping it and wringing it very painfully, saying as he did so, "You have been wanting this for a long time, haven't you?" (Brailsford and Murray, 1911, quoted in Young, 1988, 281)

Black Friday was portrayed as disorder—disorder stemming from women themselves. Additionally, comparisons between the women's protests and situations under communist regimes were drawn. The *us* and *them* were created from various media images. Moreover, the images and metaphors used to describe women's protests were woven together to suggest the idea of a battlefield in which a war between reason, democracy and order (the police, government, and us), and unreason, communism, and disorder (women) was fought. As a result, the mad cannot make legitimate protests and demands. This irrationality was epitomized in *The Times*:

> Mrs. Pankhurst and her *maenads* have produced their answer...It takes the now stereotyped form of broken glass...None of its previous follies have been so thoroughly calculated to discredit the suffragist cause...No one can surely have imagined destruction on this scale in London as the work of a few unbalanced women whose only grievance lies in an insignificant point of Parliamentary procedure...For whatever may be thought of the...agitation its immediate evidence is simply *infantile*...An act of *wanton and hysterical self-advertisement*. (March 3, 1912, quoted in Young, 1988, 283; emphasis added)

The first control mechanism of this protest that I now want to turn to is the discourses of criminality and law and order. This was an important moment in the process of criminalizing militancy. Techniques of neutralization emerged to confront this disorder, and included the tightening of the law of public assembly, sentences of hard labour, and the enactment of the "Cat and Mouse" Act, which broadened the legal powers of detention (285). Tightening the laws of public assembly had the effect of driving the women's campaign further underground, making it illegal. Nonetheless, these disciplinary powers were met with resistance.

Also, the suffragettes were sexualized. Their behaviour was not considered proper, ladylike, or acceptable. The militancy was degrading to womanhood. They were inversions of the ideal type of woman and the good mother. They were described as either oversexed, undersexed, unattractive or in need of a man. These discursive strategies converge with the social control of the Greenham Common women.

The third explanation of women's behaviour was rooted in a medical/psychiatric model. These women were disorderly, unruly, and hysterical. *The Times* writes:

> the hysterical, the neurotic, the idle, the habitual imbiters of excitement...Some of them are out with their hammers and their bags full of stones because of dreary empty lives and high-strung, over-excitable natures: they are regrettable by-products of our civilisation. (March 16, 1913, quoted in Young, 1988, 288)

Their militancy is mixed with the bad consequences of the women's movement and mental disorder. Of course, these ideas were also used in controlling Victorian women. A condemnation of women was thus operated and their demands evacuated. Hence, criminalizing, sexualizing and medicalizing the suffragettes disqualified not only the suffragettes themselves, but also the discursive category of woman.

CONCLUSION

The various examples provided in this gallery of portraits illustrate how women have been constituted as "criminal" subjects and how this is done through the criminalization of women's bodies. The process of criminalization, defined as "the application of the criminal label to a particular social category" (Hall and Scraton, 1981), when applied to women corresponds, I would argue, to a specific and historical construction of femininity.

As I discussed in the first part of this chapter, women have been historically constructed as embodying difference, unreason, and otherness. For thinkers such as Plato, Aristotle, Locke, Wollstonecraft, and even de Beauvoir, women needed to eliminate all traces of their femaleness to be considered rational. Women had to be the same as men, to some extent. With radical feminism, this idea shifted completely. They argued women were different but were also capable of reasoning, of making moral judgments and so on. However, the idea that women were different and thus embodied deviance continued.

As a consequence, the criminalization of the witch, the Greenham Common women, and the suffragettes, used as illustrations in this chapter, operates through the sexualized, embodied construction of their deviance. The witch is seen as a threat to an established order. This order is social, sexual and medical. The Greenham Common women are a threat to "patriarchal relations and the control enjoyed by men" (Chadwick and Little, 1987, 269). Similarly, the suffragettes were posited on the side of unreason and disorder. By their protests, the suffragettes were a threat to a masculine "democratic" order. In an attempt to disqualify their political protests, they were (re)presented as being out of place and as being inversions of accepted femininity. All these examples show that when women contest the *private* space by entering the *public* space, they offend—they transgress.

On the other hand, the criminalization of certain women is premised on the "syndromization" of their actions, which can be located in their biological processes (PMS) and their psychological processes (BWS). This is, however, also echoed in the process of criminalization of political protesters. By doing so, women's bodies and minds are seen as the result of the "unstable workings of the ever-mysterious female body" (Benn, 1993, 171) and potentially dangerous. This requires control and treatment.

However, in order to shift away from this understanding of "femininity in transgression," feminists must go beyond a model of justice that focuses either on a "sameness" or a "difference" model because of their limitations (Kendall, 1992). Moreover, we must go beyond the confines of law and criminology. For example, in order to understand how women are constituted as embodied "criminal" subjects, we must "de-centre" law (Smart, 1989). By doing so, we will be able to expose the claim to "truth" of law and validate women's experiences of law and order by shifting the question from "more law? more order?" to "whose law? whose order?"

This question is acute in the success of the battered woman syndrome, which should, nonetheless, be supported on a number of levels and which might provide some tools for subsequent feminist interventions in law. First, it seems that the gender bias in law has been recognized. Second, woman's viewpoint (in contrast to the "reasonable man") has been heard. However, the justice system readily embraces the discourses of the "psy" profession, which are more compatible with the dominant legal discourse. And as Smart (1989) and others warn us, feminists must be cautious about their reliance on law because of its power to define and disqualify women's experiences. In the use of BWS, for example, the focus is on the irrationality of the woman's response or the rationality of the battered woman. Hence, she is not a "reasonable man" but she is not a "reasonable woman." Again, we are going full circle. Women's actions are forever unreasonable and embody difference and deviance.

The process of deconstruction that I have sketched here is a modest attempt at theorizing the "body" of law and order and the "body" of women that might suggest ways of going beyond the impasse. More research about the multiple voices of women must be done to further explore the embodiment of difference, deviance, and resistance, for the universal category of woman does not exist.

ENDNOTES

1   For a notable exception, see Feinman (1992) *The Criminalization of a Woman's Body*, which discusses the criminalization of motherhood (abortion, pregnancy, contract motherhood, and maternity).

2   See on this subject: Van Dülmen (1990), *Theatre of Horror*.

3   In an attempt to show that women's political protests have been disqualified, I provided an exploration of this through a genealogy of women's madness (see Frigon, forthcoming).

4   This journey is, however, not without problems. Clearly, re-readings of the origins of Western political thought enter into a hermeneutic circle, whereby our interpretation is imbued by contemporary interests.

5   This view is reiterated by Condorcet (1976).

6   This analysis is elaborated by John Stuart Mill, to whom I will refer shortly.

7   Given the limited space, I will not discuss the Marxist's views of rationality, which differ in many respects from those of liberals. However, suffice it to say that praxis rather than pure, rational thought is considered as the characteristic of human activity, seeing rationality as inseparable from praxis. Hence, in my view, Marx and Engels introduce a promising alternative to the liberal approach to politics. This view, however, falls short with regard to women because Marx, like Mill, appoints a certain group with political rationality and this group excludes women. It takes as central work that is more likely to be done by men. For example, giving birth, raising children, and working in the domestic sphere are not considered "productive" work.

8   *The Burning Times* (1990), a documentary produced by the National Film Board of Canada, suggests that nine million women were, in fact, executed in Europe within a period of 300 years. They consider the witch craze as a genocide of women.

9   A more detailed discussion of the contemporary representations of women as witches or as evil has been provided elsewhere (Frigon, 1994a).

10   Szasz contrasts institutional psychiatry and contractual psychiatry. The former is imposed on the individual through private or public institutions whereas the latter is a contract negotiated between an individual and a therapist.

11   When we examine the exclusion of women's knowledge of medicine during the witch craze we can see how this has a contemporary resonance with the debates surrounding midwifery.

12   It is perhaps interesting to note that there was a new statute to regulate and criminalize infanticide, which thus became a crime in 1623 in England (see Smart, 1992).

13   Through poetry, Norma Stafford expresses her experiences of incarceration in the *Journal of Prisoners on Prisons* (see Stafford, 1994). Reproduced with the kind permission of the editor of this issue, Robert Gaucher.

14   As early as 1953, she published with Raymond Greene an article entitled "The Premenstrual Syndrome" in the *British Medical Journal* (see Greene and Dalton, 1953).

15   "Diminished responsibility" is available in England as a defence but not in Canada.

16   Anne Reynolds wrote an autobiography, *Tightrope* (1991).

17   The controversy of the PMS defence has received considerable media attention in the Canadian press in the 1980s and 1990s as the following headlines attest: "Raging Female Hormones in the Courts," *Maclean's*, June 15, 1981; "Pre-menstrual Stress a Legal Defence," *The Toronto Star*, January 22, 1982; "Treatment for PMS Ordered as Stabber Put on Probation," *The Globe and Mail*, February 10, 1987; "All-Woman Jury Rejects PMS Claim," *The Gazette* (Montreal), December 18, 1988; "Les règles de la folie," *Le Devoir*, April 15, 1993; "Is PMS a Mental Illness?," *The Gazette* (Montreal), August 2, 1993; "The PMS Controversy: Is It Hormonal, or Legitimate Anger? And Should It Be Classified as a Psychiatric Illness?" *The Gazette* (Montreal), May 10, 1993. See in relation to this Chrisler and Levy (1990) "The Media Construct a Menstrual Monster: A Content Analysis of PMS Articles in the Popular Press."

18   In the United States, it is estimated that only 1 percent of battered women kill their partners. However, 30 percent of victims of murder have been women at the hands of their partner, compared to 6 percent of men killed by their spouse (Boisvert, 1991, 192). According to an Ontario study, women constitute 75 percent of victims of conjugal homicide (femicide). Between 1974 and 1990, 417 women and 141 men have been killed by their partner (Ontario, 1992).

19   *R. c. Lavallée* (1990), 76 C.R. (3d) 329 (S.C.C.). Elsewhere, I have discussed this more at length (see bibliography). Nonetheless, many studies exist on the legal relevance of BWS in Canada, including Boisvert (1991), Comack (1993), Croker (1985), Noonan (1993), Sheehey (1993).

20   See Comack (1993) for a discussion of this issue. On the similar issue of the disqualification of women with regard to rape, see Smart (1989).

21   *R. v. Howard* (1992), 8 B.C.A.C. 241 (C.A.).

22   *R. v. Catholique* (1990), N.W.T.J. No.164 (N.W.T. Sup. Ct.).

23   *R. v. Eyapaise* (1993), 20 C.R. (4th) 246 (Alta. Q.B.).

24   To confront this problem some feminists have suggested that women working in shelters, for example, could be called as experts in those cases (Sheehey, 1993).

25   Various examples across time and space could be examined. For example, during the French Revolution in 1789, Théroigne de Méricourt is involved in the Revolution and is thus seen as transgressing appropriate gender norms. She is viewed as mad and is confined. In contrast with other political protesters, her head is not cut off; thus, her actions are not given the status of political activities. (see Roudinesco, 1989).

26   See Young, 1988 for a discussion of these techniques in relation to the suffragettes.

27   For Sumner (1983), the function of censure is to "mark off the deviant, the pathological, the dangerous and the criminal from the normal and the good. As such they are clearly moral and political in character"(195–6).

28 I will focus mainly on the Women's Social and Political Union (WSPU), a group of women who campaigned for the enfranchisement of women in the early twentieth century (see also Young, 1988).

BIBLIOGRAPHY

American Psychiatric Association. 1994. *Diagnostic and Statistical Manual of Mental Disorders*, 4th ed., rev. Washington, DC: American Psychiatric Press.

————. 1993. *Diagnostic and Statistical Manual of Mental Disorders.* Washington, DC: American Psychiatric Press.

————. 1987. *Diagnostic and Statistical Manual of Mental Disorders*, 3d ed., rev. Washington, DC: American Psychiatric Press.

Ashurst, P., and Z. Hall. 1989. *Understanding Women in Distress.* London: Tavistock/Routledge.

Atwood, M. 1994. *The Robber Bride.* Toronto: McClelland & Stewart/Seal Books.

Benn, M. 1993. "Body Talk: The Sexual Politics of PMS." In *Moving Targets: Women, Murder and Representation,* edited by H. Birch, 152–171. London: Virago Press.

Ben-Yehuda, N. 1985. *Deviance and Moral Boundaries.* Chicago: University of Chicago Press.

Blackwood, C. 1984. *On the Perimeter.* London: Fontana.

Blais, Marie-Claire. 1970. *Les Apparences.* Montréal: Editions du Jour.

————. 1968. *Manuscrits de Pauline Archange.* Montréal: Editions du Jour.

Boisvert, A.-M. 1991. "Légitime défense et le "syndrome de la femme battue: *R. c. Lavallée," Revue de droit de McGill,* 36: 191–215.

Broverman, I., S. Vogel, D. Broverman, F. Clarkson, and **P. Rosenkrantz.** 1972. "Sex-Roles Stereotypes: A Current Appraisal," *Journal of Social Issues,* 28: 59–78.

Brown, A. 1992. "Unhiding the Hidden: Writing during the Quiet Revolution." In *The Anatomy of Gender,* edited by D. Currie and V. Raoul, 222–231. Ottawa: Carleton University Press.

Brown, P. 1969. "Society and the Supernatural: A Medieval Change," *Daedalus,* 104: 133–51.

Burning Times, The. 1990. Ottawa: National Film Board.

Chadwick, K. and **C. Little.** 1987. "The Criminalization of Women." In *Law, Order and the Authoritarian State,* edited by P. Scraton, 254–278. Milton Keynes: Open University Press.

Chrisler, J., and K. Levy. 1990. "The Media Construct a Menstrual Monster: A Content Analysis of PMS Articles in the Popular Press," *Women & Health,* 16 (2): 89–104.

Colin, M.   1972, *The Discovery of the Individual, 1050–1200*. London: SPCK for the Church Historical Society.

Comack, E.   1993. "Feminist Engagement with the Law: The Legal Recognition of the 'Battered Woman Syndrome'," Canadian Institute for the Advancement of Women Papers, no. 31, 62 pages.

Condorcet, J.   1976. *Condorcet: Selected Writings*. Indianapolis: Bobbs Merill.

Coole, D.   1988. *Women and Political Theory*. Hertfordshire: Wheatsheaf Books Limited.

Crawford, M. and **R. Gartner.**   1992. *Woman Killing: Intimate Femicide in Ontario, 1974–1990*. The Women We Honour Action Committee. Toronto.

Croker, P.   1985. "The Meaning of Equality for Battered Women Who Kill in Self-Defense," *Harvard Women's Law Journal*, 8: 121–153.

Currie, C. and **V. Raoul.**   1992. *The Anatomy of Gender*. Ottawa: Carleton University Press.

Dalton, K.   1978. *Once a Month*. Great Britain: Fontana.

Daly, K.   1989. "Criminal Justice Ideologies and Practices in Different Voices: Some Feminist Questions about Justice," *International Journal of the Sociology of Law*, 17: 1–18.

Daly, M.   1979. *Gyn/ecology: The Metaethics of Radical Feminism*. London: The Women's Press.

De Beauvoir, S.   [1949] 1972. *The Second Sex*. Reprint, Harmondsworth: Penguin.

Delaney, J., M.-J. Lupton, and **E. Toth.**   1988. *The Curse: A Cultural History of Menstruation*. Urbana and Chicago: University of Illinois Press.

Dobash, R.E., R.P. Dobash, and **S. Gutteridge.**   1986. *The Imprisonment of Women*. Oxford: Basic Blackwell.

Doggett, M.E.   1990. "Greenham Common and Civil Disobedience: Making New Meanings for Women," *Canadian Journal of Women and the Law*, 3, 2: 395–419.

Edwards, S.   1988. "Mad, Bad or Pre-menstrual?," *New Law Journal*, July 1.

Ehrenreich, B., and **D. English.**   1976. *Witches, Midwives and Nurses*. London: Writers and Readers.

Faith, K.   1993. *Unruly Women: The Politics of Confinement & Resistance*. Vancouver: Press Gang Publishers.

Feinman, C., ed. 1992. *The Criminalization of a Woman's Body*. New York: The Haworth Press.

Foucault, M.   1975. *Surveiller et Punir*. Paris: Gallimard.

Frigon, S.   1994a. "Femmes, hérésies et contrôle social: Des sages-femmes et au-delà," *Revue femmes et droit (Canadian Journal of Women and the Law)*, 7, 1: 133–155.

Frigon, S.   1994b. "Le syndrôme de la femme battue: Stratégie de disqualification ou de résistance des femmes en droit," Congrès de l'*ACFAS*, Section: Création et application de la loi pénale, May 16–20, UQAM, Montréal.

Frigon, S. 1994c. "Corps, féminité et dangerosité: La construction d'un discours normatif," *Congrès de l'ACFAS*, Section: Etudes féministes, May 16–20, UQAM, Montréal.

Frigon, S. Forthcoming. "A Genealogy of Women's Madness," *British Criminology Conference Papers*.

Frigon, S. Forthcoming. "Descalificación de la Protesta de las Mujeres a Través del Discurso de la Locura" (On the Disqualification of Women's Protests Through the Discourse of Madness), *Travesìas—Temas Del Debate Feminista Contemporáneo*, Buenos Aires, Argentina.

Frigon, S. Forthcoming. "Locas por Matar: Una Radiografia del Discurso de las Mujeres que Matan a sus Maridos Violentos y la Utilización del Sindrome de la Mujer Maltratada en Canadá," (Folles à tuer: Une radiographie des discours sur les femmes qui tuent leur conjoint violent et l'utilisation du syndrôme de la femme battue au Canada), *Travesìas—Temas Del Debate Feminista Contemporáneo*, Buenos Aires, Argentina.

Gallop, J. 1982. *Feminism and Psychoanalysis*. London: Macmillan.

Garland, D. 1985. *Punishment and Welfare*. London: Heinemann.

Gilligan, C. 1982. *In a Different Voice—Psychological Theory and Women's Development*. Cambridge: Harvard University Press.

Greene, R., and **K. Dalton.** 1953. "The Premenstrual Syndrome," *British Medical Journal*, May 9: 1007–1014.

Grimshaw, J. 1986. *Feminist Philosophers: Women's Perspectives on Philosophical Traditions*, London: Harvester Wheatsheaf.

Hall, S., and **P. Scraton.** 1981. "Law, Class and Control." In *Crime and Society*, edited by M. Fitzgerald et al. Milton Keynes: Open University Press.

Heidensohn, F. 1986. "Models of Justice: Portia or Persephone? Some Thoughts on Equality, Fairness and Gender in the Field of Criminal Justice," *International Journal of the Sociology of Law*, 14: 287–298.

———. 1985. *Women and Crime*. New York: New York University Press.

Hester, M. 1992. *Lewd Women and Wicked Witches: A Study of the Dynamics of Male Domination*. London: Routledge.

Hutter, B., and **G. Williams.** 1981. *Controlling Women: The Normal and the Pathological*. London: Croom Helm.

Jaccoub, M. 1988. "Les femmes et le terrorisme," *Revue Beccaria*, 1(1): 31–45.

Kendall, K. 1992. "Sexual Difference and the Law: Premenstrual Syndrome as Legal Defense." In *The Anatomy of Gender*, edited by D. Currie and V. Raoul, 130–146.

Larner, C. 1981. *Enemies of God*. London: Chatto & Windus.

Laws, S., V. Hey, and **A. Eagan.** 1985. *Seeing Red: The Politics of Pre-Menstrual Tension*. London: Hutchinson and Co. (Publishers) Ltd.

Lemay, R. H. 1978. "Some Thirteenth and Fourteenth Century Lectures on Female Sexuality," *International Journal of Women's Studies*, 1: 391–400.

Lloyd, G. 1984. *The Man of Reason: 'Male' and 'Female' in Western Philosophy*. London: Methuen.

Locke, J. 1970. *Two Treatises on Government*. Edited by P. Laslett. Cambridge: Cambridge University Press.

Lombroso, C., and **E. Ferrero.** [1895] 1980. *The Female Offender*. Reprint, New York: Fisher Unwin.

MacFarlane, A. 1970. *Witchcraft in Tudor and Stuart England: A Regional and Comparative Study*. London : Routledge and Kegan Paul.

Maheux-Forcier, Louise. 1969. *Une forêt pour Zoé*. Ottawa: Le Cercle du Livre de France.

Mailhot, M. 1967. *Le Portique*. Ottawa: Le Cercle du Livre de France.

Maillard, Anne-Marie [Nellie Maillard]. 1960. *La nuit si longue*. Ottawa: Le Cercle du Livre de France.

Michelet, Jules. [1862] 1965. *Satanism and Witchcraft: A Study in Medieval Superstition*. Translated by A.R. Allinson. Reprint, New York: Citadel.

Mill, J.S. [1869] 1906. *The Subjection of Women*. Reprint, London: Longmans, Green and Co.

Noonan, S. 1993. "Strategies of Survival: Moving Beyond the Battered Woman Syndrome." In *In Conflict with the Law: Women and the Canadian Justice System*, edited by E. Adelberg and C. Currie, 247–270. Vancouver: Press Gang Publishers.

Pateman, C. 1991. *Feminist Interpretations and Political Theory*. University Park: Pennsylvania State Press.

———. 1988. *The Sexual Contract*. Cambridge: Polity Press.

R. c. Lavallée (1990), 76 C.R. (3d) 329 (S.C.C.).

Reynolds, A. 1991. *Tightrope*. London: Sidgwick & Jackson.

Roudinesco, E. 1991. *Madness and Revolution: The Lives and Legends of Théroigne de Méricourt*. Translated by Martin Thom. London: Verso.

Russell, J.B. 1977. *The Devil*. Ithaca: Cornell University Press.

Russo, Mary 1986. "Female Grotesque: Carnival and Theory." In *Feminist Studies/Critical Studies*, edited by T. de Laurentis, 213–229. Bloomington: Indiana University Press.

Schur, E. 1984. *Labeling Women Deviant: Gender, Stigma and Social Control*. New York: Random House.

Scraton, P. 1990. "Scientific Knowledge or Masculine Discourses? Challenging Patriarchy in Criminology." In *Feminist Perspectives in Criminology*, edited by L. Gelsthorpe and A. Morris, 10–25. Milton Keynes: Open University Press.

Sheehey, E.   1993. Developments in Canadian Law After *R. c. Lavallée*. Unpublished paper.

Smart, C.   1992. "The Woman of Legal Discourse," *Social & Legal Studies*, 1: 29–44.

———.   1989. *Feminism and the Power of Law*. London: Routledge.

Sommer, B.   1984. "PMS in the Courts: Are All Women on Trial?," *Psychology Today*, August, 36–38.

Sprenger, J., and **H. Kraemer.**   [1487] 1973. *Malleus Maleficarum, Le Marteau des Sorcières*. Translated by A. Sanet. Reprint, Paris: Plon.

Stafford, N.   1994. "my blood," *Journal of Prisoners on Prisons*, 5(2): 9.

Stoppard, J.   1992. "A Suitable Case for Treatment? Premenstrual Syndrome and the Medicalization of Women's Bodies." In *The Anatomy of Gender*, edited by D. Currie and V. Raoul, 119–129.

Sumner, C.   1983. "Rethinking Deviance: Towards A Sociology of Censures." In *Research in Law, Deviance and Control*, edited by S. Spitzer. London: JAI Press.

Szasz, T.   1971. *The Manufacture of Madness*. London: Routledge and Kegan Paul.

3/M.   1987. *Personal Autonomy and the Criminal Law: Emerging Issues for Women*. Ottawa: Canadian Advisory Council on the Status of Women.

3/M.   1988. "Wild Women: The Censure of the Suffragette Movement," *International Journal of the Sociology of Law*, 16(3): 279–293.

3/M.   1990. *Femininity in Dissent*. London: Routledge.

Trexler, R.C.   1973, "Infanticide in Florence: New Sources and Firsts Results," *History of Childhood Quarterly*, 1: 98–116.

Ussher, Jane.   1989. *The Psychology of the Female Body*. London: Routledge.

Ussher, Jane.   1991. *Women's Madness: Misogyny or Mental Illness*. Amherst: The University of Massachusetts.

Van Dülmen, R.   1990. *Theatre of Horror*. Cambridge and Oxford University Press: Basil Blackwell and Polity Press.

Walker, Lenore.   1984. *Battered Woman Syndrome*. New York: Springer.

When Women Kill. 1994. Barbara Doran. National Film Board of Canada. Ottawa.

Wollstonecraft, Mary.   1982. *Critical Edition of Mary Wollstonecraft's A Vindication of The Rights of Woman: With Strictures on Political and Moral Subjects*. Troy, NY: Whitston Publishing Co.

———.   1792. *A Vindication of The Rights of Woman*. London: Printed for J. Johnson.

Young, A.   1992. "Representations of Femininity and Violence in Legal Discourse." Paper presented at the Second World Congress on Violence and Human Coexistence, Montreal, July 12–17.

Zedner, Lucia.   1992. *Child Victims: Crime, Impact, and Criminal Justice.* Oxford: Clarendon Press.

Zilboorg, G.   1935. *The Medical Man and the Witch During the Renaissance.* Baltimore: Johns Hopkins University Press.

CHAPTER 6

POLICING, LAWLESSNESS, AND DISORDER IN HISTORICAL PERSPECTIVE

John L. McMullan

INTRODUCTION

An important feature of the social history of policing is that the old and the new, the formal and the informal, the public and the private and the local and the national overlap, intersect, and interact with each other, in complex and contradictory ways. Understanding the development of policing requires a sensitivity to its emergence, variability, and uniqueness, as well as to the discrete and tentative nature of historical explanation (Styles 1987; Brogden 1982, 1987; Spitzer 1987; Reiner 1985). Many studies of policing are marred by the tendency to substitute all transforming concepts like "industrial revolution" or "urbanization" for a detailed analysis of power, economy, custom, and law when it is clear that these unmediated assumptions cannot bear the explanatory demands placed on them (Innes and Styles 1986, 430–431; Johnston 1992, 212). This said, however, we need not abandon all general structural explanation. Too much focus on unique, diverse, incremental, and uneven developments may obscure the extent to which underlying structuring trends in policing follow the same continuous direction (Abrams 1982; McMullan 1987a; Spitzer 1981, 1987; Carson and Idzikowska 1989). Diversity and local change need not be "proof of a lack of system change, but the evidence from which it must be historically reconstructed" (Hay and Snyder 1989, 15).

This chapter seeks to provide an understanding of policing in London that takes the dynamic interplay between local conditions and general development as the primary locus of explanation (Carson and Idzikowska 1989, 270; Swift 1988, 236; Styles 1987). The sociologically interesting problems relate as much to the *interrelations* between communal, state, and private dimensions of order as to the dimensions themselves. What follows examines the multiplicity of policing forms, and demonstrates that they are not distinct places with inherent properties, but rather are "strategic fields" where political, economic, and customary interests emerge, coalesce and collide, and where diverse visions of social order intersect, conflict, and reform (Foucault 1980, 1991).

I focus on London during the early modern period because it was the great metropolis of England and one of the larger business centres of Europe. It experienced profoundly the shock waves of commercial capitalism in the seventeenth century and was the epicentre of social experimentation concerning problems of social disorder and policing (Beier 1978, 1985; Beier and Findlay 1986). The decline of communitarian control, the rise of commodified schemes of order and the socialization of legal control occurred most comprehensively in London, and the reforms provided a general model for similar innovations in England and in the world (Brogden, 1982, 1987; Spitzer and Scull 1977; Palmer 1988; Ascoli 1979). Not much happened in the metropolis that did not have an impact in changing English demography, society, and economy (Wrigley 1967; Beier and Findlay 1986).

The chapter begins with a discussion of the character of communal coercion and social order. It then explores why collective self-policing was transformed. I study the interplay between economy, geography, custom, and political authority in the production of order and social disorder. Next, I analyze the watch, the constabulary, the city marshalcy, Privy Council measures, the militias and trained bands, and the army, and examine their relative capacities to monitor and manage crime and social disorder. Finally, I look at the emergence of private forms of coercion—informing for profit, spying, and thief-taking, and explore how entrepreneurial policing intersected with communal and state-based forms of crime control. I conclude by drawing out some lessons for rethinking the early social history of policing.

SELF-HELP, COLLECTIVE SECURITY, AND SOCIAL ORDER

Late medieval and early modern London was governed by the principle of social obligation, or collective security. The ancient Saxon and Norman institutions of hue and cry, posse comitatus (the sheriff's power to call out every man between 15 and 50 years of age), collective fines, bans, and outlawry were predicated on the feasibility of collective, informal, local, and voluntaristic reactions to crime and disorder (Weisser 1979; Sharpe 1984; Emsley 1983). These arrangements amounted to a system of collective liability whereby all members of a community accepted an obligation for the good behaviour of each other. Entire villages, parishes, and town wards were thus charged with the duty of policing themselves. Tithings, and then more substantially hundreds, shire reeves, and sheriffs had the administrative responsibilities for overseeing the king's peace and ensuring the collective obligation of active pursuit, arrest, and presentment by means of the hue and cry (Critchley 1972, 2; Lee 1901, 5; Hart 1951, 23; Hewitt 1965, 5). The hue and cry enjoined entire communities to exchange information, chase, and ultimately bring to justice all law-breakers upon pain of punishment. It "depended upon the watchfullness of private citizens who would set off the alarm" (Weisser 1979, 56).

By the beginning of the fourteenth century the office of constable had eclipsed that of the sheriff. Sheriff's turns gave poor recompense for presenting alehouse offenders at legal sessions and ensuring for the maintenance of bastard children (Shoemaker 1991, 218). Like the constabulary, the watch was unpaid and part-time.

Justices of the peace also rose to a position of prominence in local government. Statutes were passed adding to their duties and powers, "perhaps 300 of them between the mid-fourteenth and late sixteenth centuries" (Sharpe, 1984, 28). They came to possess considerable civil powers and quickly superseded officers of parochial origin. Their position was filled in rotation "from among qualified citizens of sufficient wealth and local standing to command the respect due of the office" (Sharpe 1984, 29). Justices of the peace were empowered to conduct the preliminary examination of suspects and witnesses in cases of felony, take recognizances, commit suspected felons to prison, ensure witnesses and prosecutors appeared in the relevant courts, and bind over the unruly to be of good behaviour (Moir 1968; Gleason 1969; Sharpe 1984). As Shoemaker (1991, 35) observes, the number of statutes authorizing "summary conviction by justices" increased significantly during the seventeenth century, and on-the-spot justice involving fining, whipping, and commitment to a house of correction were used as alternatives to the more traditional legal procedures. Their office became "an instrument through which national power could be exerted over traditional, local authority" (Weisser 1979, 93).

The role of the early modern law-enforcement agent was largely undifferentiated from neighbourhood ward, parish, or village roles and their territorially based bonds and relationships (Kent 1981, 31-39, 46; 1986; Sharpe 1980, 108). Because the job was temporary, the distinction between official public authority and unofficial private power was somewhat arbitrary. Often, the result was that formal control over the lawlessness of local communities was balanced by parochial customs, community traditions, and informal folk justice (Herrup 1985, 1989; Kent 1983; Wrightson 1982). The recognizance, for example, was a widely used legal instrument designed to prevent violence and crime and to regulate "undesirable" and "dangerous" outsiders. Its purpose was not trial and conviction but the management of peace and security (Samaha 1981, 204; Shoemaker, 1991, 25–27; Sharpe, 1980, 108; 1988, 254–255). Henry Norris of Hackney, the most urban justice for whom a detailed notebook survives, settled informally 38 percent of the criminal business brought before him (Shoemaker 1991, 43–46). Even the condemned were convinced to make a penitent end in a theatre of punishment, which offered grand spectacle and a last dying commitment to communal values (Sharpe 1985, 156).

This form of indirect rule amounted to two concepts of order: the local and the state (Knafla 1983; Kent 1986, 286; Wrightson, 1982, 158–159; Emsley 1987, 11–12). As King puts it, "individuals and communities were highly selective in their approach to the law and its institutions, taking advantage of assenting to or reversing certain parts while attempting to ignore, flout or oppose others" (1984, 33–34). This pragmatic and personalized approach meant that law enforcement and administration was in the end a shared communal obligation (Sharpe 1984; Kent 1986; Weisser 1979, 54–55). As Herrup notes, "by the time a felon was finally hanged as many as three dozen men had participated in the decision-making process" (1985, 107). The workings of the citizen judiciary and of the criminal law was a "multiple-use right" within which the various groups "conflicted with, and cooperated with and gained concessions from each other" (King 1984, 58; Brewer and Styles 1980, 19). It was the most important way in which the people at large, "the custodians of the 'little tradition' participated in the 'great tradition' of their social superiors" (Sharpe, 1988, 248).

The enforcement of law and order throughout the seventeenth century was also a process that depended on "multilateral assent to the policies of government" (Wrightson 1982, 153). Localism was seen to be generally compatible with the king's rule. With crown-appointed justices of the peace exercising authority over the parish constables, "the whole stemmed ultimately from the sovereign, and the periphery derived authority from the centre" (Critchley 1972, 16). The prosecution of felonies belonged to both the commonwealth and the monarch. The harm caused by crime was greater than the loss of any single individual. "It was the King who stood as the symbolic victim, and who had to be revenged" (Herrup 1989, 3).

Early modern governments distinguished themselves by exhorting, encouraging, ordering, and coercing local officials to play their parts effectively (Wrightson 1980, 41–46; Kent 1986, 290; Sharpe 1980, 103–117; 1988, 255–256). The activities of these governments were "great administrative achievements," which produced closer connections between the responsibilities of local communities, the needs of central government for the enforcement of policy and law, and the grievances of both gentry and commoner (Corrigan and Sayer 1985; Wrightson 1982, 154, 170). Nowhere was this more evident than in the enforcement and administration of vagrancy laws where the policies of the government led to a very real increase in state authority. Here the new powers of summary arrest, judgment, and punishment were extended to parish constables, as well as to chartered bodies (such as bridewell) and they were eagerly taken up by "officials in every parish in the land" (Beier 1985, 169, 158). No matter how flexible they were in relation to specific local circumstances, the constable and the justices of the peace were essentially "of the gentry and, at one or two removes, of the state" (Sharpe 1984, 93).

In London, responsibility for policing rested with the lord mayor who issued precepts to ward aldermen or to relevant captains of the city's trained bands. Behind the lord mayor stood the king and the Privy Council ready to intervene and to call the municipal authorities, the sheriffs, the provost marshals, the watch and ward, and the constables to account. The city suburbs were the responsibility of the justices of the peace, and if military aid was needed, the lords lieutenant of the adjoining courts of Middlesex and Surrey (Emsley 1983, 25; 1991; Lindley 1983).

Taken together, civil as well as military authorities formed a loose structure for the prevention and suppression of crime and social disorder. Yet, the great bulk of policing, even in London, depended on the direct participation of the community. Law officers were not usually in command of legal *force majeure*. The occasional muster of a posse or use of troops were *in extremis* measures. Far more often, legal officials were expected to call on the public. In this sense, "authority was not something separate from or exercised upon the citizenry; it was not 'other' but emanated from the people themselves" (Brewer 1980, 24).

Fine-grained surveillance and rule, however, was not the norm. The state had limited technical ability and superintending resources to monitor the day-to-day lives of urban populations. There were remarkable discrepancies in levels of law enforcement by class and by district. Officials in one ward rigorously enforced laws that were broken with impunity in another. One or two energetic justices or constables could have considerable impact on a city ward. Contrarily, constables, marshals, or magistrates who disliked a new piece of legislation could go far to prevent its implementation or nullify its effect in a particular city suburb. Those in control of a city parish or ward often allowed considerable latitude to the known local offender while conversely treating vagrant outsiders by means of judicious regulation, prosecution, and strong punishment (Sharpe 1984, 82; Samaha 1981, 201–204; Brewer 1980, 24; Wrightson 1982, 157; Emsley 1991, 10–13; Linebaugh 1991). Among Londoners, it was "the unemployed, the unconnected, the newly arrived migrant, and young, single women who were particularly liable to be brought before justices of the peace" (Shoemaker 1991, 313).

The subordination of local communities to the rule of central administration and a national code of law was not always easy to accomplish. The enforcement of legal discipline was resisted by a fraction of the populace and the fabric of order woven by Tudor and Stuart local government frayed at the edges (Hunt 1983). There were whole communities in which "social relations were characterized not by control and deference [but] by dissociation and mutual wariness" (Wrightson 1982, 182). For example, the colliers of Kingswood Forest, near Bristol, were an ungovernable people. "Satisfactory evidence was sometimes hard to obtain, arrest warrants could seldom be executed and witnesses and jurymen might be encouraged to think better of the colliers' supposed 'offences' after suitable forms of intimidation" (Malcolmson 1980). Local enforcement officers, in addition, were reluctant to work with state officials in the suppression of some popular gatherings or festivities. And in matters of taxation and military impressment, constables were under "considerable pressure to withdraw their support of the state's demands and to side with local opinion" (Kent 1986).

In cases of victimless crime (i.e., suppression of alehouses, church attendance and the like), "the populace at large was reluctant either to accept the law's definition of an offence...or to enforce the law" (Kent 1986, 294). Even when victims could be found they had to pay the costs of private prosecution or arrange for payments in kind. Loss of time and court costs had to be weighed against injury incurred, monies gained, and enmities caused (Samaha 1981, 192; King 1984, 57–58; Hay 1980; Sharpe 1980, 110–111; Hay and Snyder 1989; Weisser 1979). There were even limits in the treatment of vagrants. Local authorities sometimes acted alone, refusing to obey royal commands, especially where costs were incurred. In such cases, justices of the peace "put their own pockets first, their country second and the interests of the Crown third" (Beier 1985, 147). Not surprisingly, we find constables in legal trouble, "bound over for allowing an escape; indicted for lodging vagrants and wandering persons; reprimanded for failing to execute warrants....and reported for failing or refusing to report religious conventicles" (Sharpe 1984, 76).

The general reliance on unpaid amateur officials seems to have led to a flexible and minimally intrusive form of coercion when compared to eighteenth- or nineteenth-century counterparts (Giddens 1987). Yet, despite its diversity and legitimacy it was liable to collapse from within and to radical change from without. The frankpledge, the hue and cry, the posse comitatus, and the use of communal fines were best applied with success in "small and settled communities where most inhabitants knew one another and where communal customs and obligations were widely accepted" (Kent 1986, 308–309). Such conditions were not always the case or found everywhere in early modern England. As Beier notes communal control "was useless when it came to dealing with itinerant strangers" (1985, 146) and it was most uncertain in London where large, open, commercial, densely populated communities made regulation, detection, apprehension, and prosecution highly problematic (Wrightson 1982, 171; Sharpe 1984, 74; Shoemaker 1987; 1991).

URBAN ECONOMY AND SOCIAL DISORDER

In London, the transformation of communal policing was swift. Compliance was a problem because the principles of gratuitous community service and collective security were modified by profound economic and political changes (Critchley 1972, 22; Hart 1951, 24). Throughout much of the sixteenth and seventeenth centuries, serfdom was in decline. New sets of class relations asserted themselves in the countryside. A gradual transition from feudalism to capitalism was enhanced by the spectacular extension of overseas trade and the widespread seizure of colonial markets. Emerging overseas trading cartels restructured the English economy, undermined the prominence of provincial towns, and made London *the* economic centre of the country (Fisher 1976, 205; Hobsbawm 1967, 50–51; Wrigley 1967, 48–50). In turn, the growth of London as the economic engine of England heightened the size and pace of capitalist expansion into the countryside. As Chartres notes, London's importance as a "consumer was greater by a factor of at least two than that of the rest of the country" (1986, 191). This led to a range of agricultural effects, which, together with the spectacular growth of exports under bounty, generated enormous productivity and profound structural changes.

A cyclical movement occurred between the increase in capital accumulation and the growth in a landless population. The first was possible, in part, because of seizures of overseas markets, changes in the organization of production, and rising food and consumer prices resulting from the expanding populations of towns and cities (Hill 1969). But as well the populations of towns were being pulled from the growing numbers of dispossessed people forced to sell their labour power. Peasants were being cut off from the land, and arable land was increasingly being converted from tillage to pasture (James 1967; Kitch 1986; Tawney 1941). The peasants and small landowners became the "free aristocracy," which shifted into wage-labour and industry. Capitalist development thus "penetrated and transformed much of the countryside long before the Civil War" (Moore 1967, 19).

London's population growth in particular was remarkable. It evolved from a middling city of 120,000 in 1550 to 200,000 in 1600; in 1650 the population was 375,000, and 490,000 in 1700 (Findlay and Shearer 1986, 39). Whereas the population of England almost doubled from 3 million to 5.1 million between 1550 and 1700, that of London quadrupled from 120,000 to 490,000. In 1550, only 4 percent of the national population were Londoners, but by 1700 London could claim almost 10 percent of the population (Findlay and Shearer 1986, 38).

London, then, was the flashpoint for capital-labour push and pulls. Economic centralization, especially in the woolen-cloth export trade, stimulated investment in manufacturing and in new craft guild production. In turn, new industrial development (especially in the city suburbs) attracted migration. A minimum of 8,000 to 10,500 new immigrants yearly came to London in the period between 1650 to 1700. Thousands came to take up apprenticeships. In the early 1550s, the annual number of apprentices was around 1,500; by 1600 it was approximately 5,000 and that level remained constant to 1700 (Beier and Findlay 1986, 15, 9–10; Kitch 1986).

The profits of trade also flowed into financing conspicuous consumption and large government projects. This buttressed London's relative importance and size. The liaison between merchant and monarch was particulary close in the period 1550 to 1700, with royal governments relying heavily on "London merchants for loans, who in turn received profitable jobs as revenue farmers, patentees and monopolists" (Beier and Findlay 1986, 16). "The state's cash worth to the London economy around 1630 was 600,000 pounds a year to the holders of high offices and privileges" and a further "£300,00 a year under Charles I for such items as household and wardrobe costs." The payout to office-holders alone was £340,000 to £360,000 per annum or nearly 15 times more than in Henry VII's day and far surpassing the rate of price inflation" (Beier and Findlay 1986, 13–14). Increasing centralization of the nation's political life in London meant not only an increase in the state civil service but substantial increases in the numbers of peers, Members of Parliament, court personnel, gentry, and their families, servants, and entourages. Legal affairs, land market transactions, commerce, industry, and the pursuit of profitable office caused the landed classes to invade London as never before. This incursion inspired a great rebuilding in London as well as a considerable demand for consumer goods and services (Brett-James 1935; Fisher 1961, 1976).

The concentration of political and economic life in London also made it a preferred centre of labour migration. Jobs, higher wages, relaxed rules of apprenticeship in the city suburbs, reliable food supplies, and poor relief combined to attract and hold the multitude of migrants to London (Pound 1971; Chartres 1986; Kitch 1986; MacFarlane 1986). By no means, however, were the benefits of growth distributed equitably among city dwellers. Grinding poverty and a volatile casual labour market meant social dislocation and demoralization for many. Climactic crises, foreign wars, and plague epidemics affected the recent immigrant populations and reflected the appalling conditions of housing and sanitation for the poor (Slack 1986, 62). Social problems abounded: vagrancy, alcoholism, prostitution, youth deviance, violence, crime, and rioting, to name the major ones (Beier 1978, 1985; Lindley 1983; Burke 1985; McMullan 1982, 1984; Harris 1986; Sharpe 1984; Shoemaker 1991; Wrightson 1982).

The growing possibilities for disorder and crime were accompanied by features of the coercive capacity of the absolutist state. The state possessed neither central control over the means of violence nor the infrastructure to coordinate effective power. State power was a delicate artifice of political compromise and intrigue. Networks of powerful cliques were woven into a rudimentary system ordered by access to court favours, positions, and influence. Loyalty was largely commercialized, purchased with services and material benefits (Williams 1979; Hurstfield 1967; 1973; Stone 1965; MacCaffrey 1969, 97). As Hurstfield observes, the fiscal needs of the state prompted "putting up for auction the machinery of government itself" (1973, 312). The procurement and sale of public position at all levels of bureaucracy, city, county, and crown was the "white noise of English administration" (Brewer 1989, 17), but it lacked safeguards and led to the widespread farming of offices for personal profit (Hurstfield 1973, 304–305).

The sale of offices had important implications for the mediation of law and lawlessness. First, patronage predicated on arrangements with powerful patrons produced a population with effective immunity from the very laws they were supposed to enforce. The political influence of patrons was normally sufficient to guarantee selective law enforcement, the neutralization of definitions, processes, and agencies of legal order, obvious and widespread bargaining, and frequent abrogation of specific regulations (Shoemaker 1991; Samaha 1974; Wrightson 1980; Plumb 1967).

Second, the direct manipulation of law by private principals affected the formal organization of the state. Patrimonial bureaucracy was liable to much abuse. The prizes were small, the offices poorly paid, the terms of appointment ill-defined, and the fees and profits attached to offices only hazily known. The private exploitation of political advantage created a vast "black market" in which incumbents speculated on their offices with impunity (MacCaffrey 1969, 125). Justices of the peace, prison keepers, and city marshals, for example, frequently acquired their posts through sponsorship, and a system of tutelage linked under-keepers to keepers and to prison overseers, much to the detriment of both crown and subject (Dobb 1953; Gleason 1969; Moir 1969; Howson 1970; Salgado 1977; Ascoli 1979, 27).

Third, the centrality of the sale of offices to social control processes and its abuse made the meaning of legal censure unsure. The absence of both a professional army and a paid bureaucracy meant that legal coercion was achieved more and more by a combination of the state (ie., reprieves and rewards). The administrative scope of the state was radically circumscribed, even within the city of London where state power was most concentrated. As Lindley notes, "the civil and military resources available...were found to be largely inadequate and unreliable; they left the King without any effective control over events in the streets of his capital" (1983, 126).

By the mid-seventeenth century there were major fissures in the structure of communal control. What was everybody's business became nobody's duty. Social problems in the city abounded (Beier 1978, 1985; McMullan 1984, 1987; Sharpe 1984; Lindley 1983). The records of the central government confirm that rioting was on the increase. Food riots — around 40 in the years between 1585 and 1660 — and enclosure riots were more frequent because bad harvests and the parcelling of former common fields into private, consolidated holdings had increased (Thomas 1976; Wrightson 1982, 174). Infused with a sense of folk justice about prices, wages, and common rights, rioters challenged patrimonial authority with force (Rude 1959; Sharp 1988; Clark 1976; Fletcher and Stevenson 1985; Lindley 1982).

Traditional holidays and festivals such as Shrove Tuesday, May Day, and Bartholomew Fair were also known causes of social worry (Lindley 1983, 109). Shrove Tuesday riots occurred "on at least twenty-four of the thirty-nine years" between 1601 and 1640 (Lindley 1983). Popular xenophobia, combined with a strong anti-Catholicism made foreign embassies and their staffs liable to many assaults. Returning and unpaid sailors and soldiers were a frequent source of tumult in the capital as they defied proclamations, smashed windows, attacked houses, snatched food, and scuffled in the streets for overdue pay. Gentlemen at the Inns of Court and their servants contributed to disorder by an overzealous defence of their immunities and privileges. This frequently took the form of resisting law officers, violently mishandling constables, sheriffs, watchmen, and marshals, and rioting against officials when citizens rescued their servants from custody (Burke 1985; Ashton 1983).

The numbers involved in such actions were substantial, varying from two or three dozen rioters in the more modest incidents to crowds numbered in the thousands in their more spectacular protests. The Shrove Tuesday riots of 1617, the Chancery Lane disturbances of 1618, the protests of sailors and soldiers threatening retribution for unpaid wages in 1627, the riots over the pursuit and eventual murder of Dr. Lambe in 1628, the confrontation between army officers and the city sheriff's officers one year later, the bawdy house riots of 1668, and the weavers' riot of 1675 all comprised crowds numbering from 1,000 to 5,000 (Lindley 1983, 110–115; Pearl 1961, chap. 4; Harris 1986; Dunn 1973).

The prisons too erupted into revolt and riot. The Kings' Bench and Marshalsea jail in Southwark faced rebellions against prison conditions and corruption, as well as outright mutinies in 1620, 1639, and 1640 in which the trained bands were needed to restore order (Pearl 1961, chap 4). Problems of disorder did not suddenly cease in 1640. At the outbreak of the English Revolution, London witnessed disorder on an unprecedented scale. Economic crisis, political instability, and plague contributed to a crisis of authority whereby "the population of the cities of London and Westminster, the suburbs and the south bank of the Thames took to the streets in their thousands to demonstrate or take direct action" (Lindley 1983, 115–116). Rioting continued throughout the Restoration period as well, and included economic, political, sexual, religious, and moral motives (Harris 1986; Dunn 1973; Holmes 1976; Rogers 1978). A study of prosecutions by indictment at the Middlesex Quarter Sessions for the period 1663 to 1721 concludes that the number of riots increased fivefold (Shoemaker 1987, 276).

Vagrancy was also a pressing social problem in early modern London. The evidence of Bridewell Court Books suggest there was a twelvefold increase in numbers, from 60 in 1560 to 815 in 1625, outpacing the population's growth rate. Most importantly, these migrants "*became* vagrants in London because of conditions there" (Beier 1978, 208). Mainly young and male, and drawn from the ranks of apprentices and servants, they were especially prone to the vicissitudes of economic underemployment, often ending up homeless and jobless. Idle and masterless, vagrants "begged, sold ballads, brooms, and pamphlets; shined shoes; and hung around the streets, ships and market stalls, they were caught stealing and [picking] the purses and pockets of passers-by" (Beier 1978, 210). For women, conflicts between masters and their menials led to sexual exploitation, unwanted pregnancy, and prostitution. What the records of crime make clear is that there "existed a whole strata at the bottom of society which were potentially criminal for the simple reason that occasional pilfering when the opportunity arose was part and parcel of their means of survival" (Wrightson 1982, 163).

Vagrants included the persistently criminal as well as the opportunist and the puzzling. Contemporary observers and city officials were aware of a world of crime. While they undoubtedly constructed the image of the vagrant as *the* criminal stereotype, those in authority had grounds for some of their fears (Curtis and Hale 1981, 111–126). In London, the sheer mass of the population made control more difficult than in the countryside. The concentration of wealth gave the thief, burglar, and prostitute infinitely more targets. The size of the metropolis made for anonymity and concealment, and the organization of city geography afforded a territorial base that fostered a routinization of criminal activities (Cressey 1970, 53–60; Power 1972, 1986; Findlay and Shearer 1986). Many city areas were notorious as "nurseries of the begging poor" and "base tenements of lewdness, evil, licentiousness that do harbour thieves, rogues and vagabonds" (Power 1972, 258–259). Any official, for example, who ventured into the precincts of "the Mint," an ancient debtors' sanctuary, did so at their peril. They were ducked in tubs of urine, covered with every sort of filth and dumped in the open sewers that ran down the streets. In 1705, it took 21 constables and four justices of the peace "to fight a pitched battle with 'shelterers' before they could seize a bankrupt and his wares" (Brewer 1980, 24). Confidence cheats were Londoners almost to a man, and gambling, thieving, and prostitution in the metropolis reached considerable levels of organization and maturation (Beier 1985, 129, 135). The focal unit was the canting crew, the small criminal work team (two or three members), craft-specific, and confederated, in which informal patterns of authority prevailed (McMullan 1982, 1984, 1987a; Sharpe 1984; Rock 1977). Crime lacked a large gang-style organization, but "those very qualities made it more difficult to suppress" (Beier 1985, 144).

How then did coercive institutions in London respond to riot, vagrancy, and crime? How did they maintain social order in the absence of effective means of direct surveillance and punitive certainty? What new strategies of policing were developed in the laboratories of power in London?

TRANSFORMATIONS IN POLICING AND STATE COERCION

The prevention of popular disturbances, vagrancy-related disorder, and crime was liable to amelioration through positive steps (such as poor relief), through careful legal manipulation of public events and timetables (so as to preserve order by not courting disorder), and through the promotion of "sequestration policies" that demarcated the idle, the masterless, and the infirm and segregated them in hospitals, bridewells, and workhouses (Foucault 1967, 1977; Pearl 1981, 123–131; MacFarlane 1986, 252–277; Beier 1985, 149–169; Slack 1984; Innes 1987, 42–122; Giddens 1987, 182). But ultimately the prevention of disorder came to rest on the quality of formal coercive institutions.

By the mid-seventeenth century, the offices of the constable and the watch were fragmented. Their already heavy workloads were compounded by increased and sometimes contradictory orders, edicts, charters, and privileges, and by restrictions on the powers of arrest of law-enforcement agents. In some ward precincts, constables had no jurisdiction, and could not enter, pursue, or arrest. In others they needed official approval, and seldom could leave the boundaries of their wards except by agreement of the neighbouring constabulary (Rumbelow 1971).

Occupational hazards also limited their activities. Constables were liable for wrongful arrests and for loss of prisoners in their custody, and were penalized by having their property repossessed or by having their business forfeited to pay off court debts (Brewer 1980, 22–23). They had to patrol hostile areas, cope with more numerous gangs of thieves and robbers, investigate the multitudes of base tenements, patrol the hidden and concealed lanes, alleys, and courtyards, control riots, and manage the severances of growing numbers of vagrants. Volunteer constables and watch were at considerable physical risk, particularly in policing the areas where sanctuaries and traditions of defiance and force prevailed, and where the physical terrain made detection and apprehension difficult (Brindenbaugh 1968, 390–392; Brewer 1980; McMullan 1987a). "Office-holders and freemen were few in these lawless parts" (Beier and Findlay 1986, 21).

The onerous workload of the watch and constables was further complicated by divided responsibilities to more than one authority. Constables and the watch were at the disposal not only of their local officials but also of the Privy Council, and were further obliged to obey the orders of provost marshals and city marshals. This overlap of authorities produced considerable confusion, conflict, and hostility. Attention to duty was not always applauded by the citizenry, and informal and conciliatory approaches to rioting were sometimes mistaken by central governments as complicity with law breakers (Lindley 1983, 118).

Economic considerations also acted against holding office and serving watch. Commercial interests cut across public office. The compulsory tasks of serving as constables or on the watch were unpaid, and directed valuable energy and time away from income-earning ventures. Financially-able citizens found methods to exempt themselves from policing functions. They deputized their apprentices or domestics as replacements, hired substitute labour, or paid a fine to the parish to be released from service (Critchley 1972, 18; Hart 1951, 24; Tobias 1979, 31). They secured certificates of exemption (such as the Tyburn Ticket), which were awarded to some for conviction of others for certain serious criminal offences (Emsley 1983, 25; Beattie 1986, 52). These in turn were often sold by the person who earned them, "and in some parishes they commanded a high price as a means of getting out of irksome duties" (Tobias 1979, 32; Samaha 1974; Rumbelow 1971). The original obligation of community service was quickly replaced "by the payment of assessments to hire men to perform those duties" (Lindley 1983, 119).

The duties of the London watch were often carried out by "meaner" persons for low wages. Constables pocketed "dead pay" by understaffing the watch, neglected their hours and stations, rarely enforced curfews, and often failed to police from ward to ward (Lindley 1983, 119). Proclamations, decrees, and orders from all levels of government point to hesitant policing and confirm the prevalence of street disorder, vagrancy, riot, crime, inconstant prosecution, and law punishment of such matters (Rumbelow 1971, chap. 3; Critchley 1972, 18–20).

By 1663, less than one-half of the allotted 747 watchmen (21 of 26 wards) were actually hired and on duty, and by 1700 "the night watch in the streets of the metropolis was not a very effective force" at all (Rumbelow 1971, app. I; Tobias 1979, 35).

Surveillance was thus irregular and reluctant. Occasionally law enforcers refused to obey the official summons to police, especially where riots were violent. Lindley (1983, 118) provides some examples:

> A constable of St. Sepulchre was overwhelmed by the size and disposition of the crowd that surrounded him in 1604; a constable of St. Botalph by Aldgate was fined £2 for refusing to help the sheriff's officers arrest the rescuers of their prisoner in 1628....; and, in the same year, constables and other officers in Southwark were criticized for not making arrests among the sailors threatening the White Lion prison.

Local loyalties could take precedence over policing responsibilities. For example, an apprentice threatened: "If I be forced to watch, I will turn Rebel with the rest of my fellow apprentices" (Lindley 1983, 119). At other times the practical weaknesses of law enforcement was compounded by an official local tolerance of disorder. In 1675, when weavers destroyed engine looms because they said that they caused unemployment, they won popular support for their actions. Local constables and the trained bands refused to act against them (Shoemaker 1987, 297–298). Nor was it uncommon for private citizens to fashion their own informal brand of policing. Pickpockets, thieves, and prostitutes were often apprehended and vilified by Londoners. Quick "justice" was administered by crowds without the sanction of the courts: criminals where dunked in mud ponds, and offenders were attacked with stones and dirt or shamed loudly with clamorous shouting, handclapping, and "rough music" (Ingram 1984; Fletcher and Stevenson 1985; Underdown 1985; Emsley 1991; Shoemaker 1991).

Popular convictions and street justice, however, could provide the precedents and justifications for disorder itself. Groups of Londoners regularly slandered brothel keepers, broke their windows, pulled down their houses, and punished sexual misdeeds, which, while not illegal, violated accepted norms of conduct. Popular definitions of illegal behavior in London did not always coincide with the neat definitions of the courts. Riots sometimes resulted. During the bawdy house riots in 1668 properties were damaged and owners were assaulted and injured. During religious conflicts churches and meetinghouses were entered, looted, and burned by avenging crowds (Harris 1986; Shoemaker 1987; Holmes 1976). These and other displays for law and order often appropriated the symbols of legal authority: official proclamations, the beating of drums, military metaphors and organization, and ceremonial colors (Rude 1959; Rogers 1978; Ingram 1984; Shoemaker 1987, 1991).

The difficulties surrounding communal self-policing forced the state to bolster its social control apparatus directly and formally through the offices of the Privy Council and through the creation of city marshals. The Privy Council was not itself a domestic policing institution. It was a political council primarily concerned with problems of government, social unrest, and rebellion. It was instrumental in raising fighting troops, dispensing coercive forces to trouble spots, and coordinating militias against foreign invasions. On occasion, however, the Privy Council did monitor and manage internal domestic problems, and so it evolved a series of "special" policing strategies.

The system of swearing in provost marshals and the use of secret organized searches and roundups were two such strategies designed to increase accessibility to and information about disorderly, disreputable, and dissenting populations. Typically, provost marshals were paid by the Privy Council or by the Corporation of London. Their mandates were short-term and usually included an entitlement to hire armed assistants with wide powers to search, arrest, and punish. Their scope of action was sweeping and their mandates frequently included territorial searches of adjoining counties. Yet the office of the provost marshal was organizationally ill-equipped to perform work other than the suppression of periodic unrest, and even that work created friction (Brindenbaugh 1968; Shoemaker 1987, 296). As Lindley notes, "provost marshals do not appear to have had much of a role in subduing rioters in early Stuart London" (1983, 121).

The Privy Council also developed a system of mass searches and arrests. Some privy searches lasted for 24 hours, others went on for weeks. They were usually performed under cover of darkness, and coordinated to take place throughout the entire city and the surrounding counties in order to prevent escape to nearby sanctuaries (Beier 1985, 155). Communal legal institutions were short-circuited. In the case of vagrants, special bands of watchers and searchers (some numbering over 100 men) were organized to scour each ward or parish. Vagrants outside the realm were to be summarily deported. Those of the realm were to be taken before a justice of the peace and immediately prosecuted. Constables were armed with increased powers of summary justice and examination, and were enjoined to judge suspects "without tarrying for any delay of sessions at the Guildhall, which to the governors should be troublesome and to the house very chargeable" (Beier 1985, 157).

These extraordinary state strategies temporarily alleviated street disorders, closed down some of the haunts and institutions, apprehended and punished a number of the outcasts and dispersed the rest. London marshals, for example, did play an important role in checking and monitoring vagrants because, unlike constables and justices of the peace, they were salaried, better equipped, and more able to cover larger areas than local constables. Yet their battle was by and large a losing one, for the pattern was one of return and reoccurrence (Beier 1985, 153; Brindenbaugh 1968; Kamen 1976).

Constables and the watch had little liking for many of these state-initiated secret searches. They were required to assist in dangerous pursuit and arrest campaigns, to take custody of and responsibility for the many prisoners, and to inflict the harsh punishments of pillorying and whipping. They were not averse to developing covert tactics of noncooperation. Some minimized appearances in public, others evaded recognition by removing identifiable clothing and badges, still others concealed their station and residence by removing their white staff of office from their doorways (Rumbelow 1971).

A second tier of practical centralized policing was the city marshalcy. The model for this position was the office of provost marshal. The Court of Aldermen regularized these duties and powers into a permanent, centralized office and in 1603 appointed a marshalcy for the city of London charged with numerous tasks: carrying off rogues and vagrants to Bridewell; seeing that due punishments were inflicted according to the law; supervising the constables and the watch; maintaining supervision over ward officials to ensure plague regulations were obeyed; and attending to miscellaneous street activities such as licensing traders, fruiterers, hucksters, and other unlicensed itinerants. Their numbers increased from two in 1603 to four in 1617 and to six by 1626 (Rumbelow 1971).

Almost from their inception they faced serious difficulties. Numerically, they were too weak to be effective in riot and crime control. They were easily overpowered by sizeable groupings. James I was said to be furious with the city marshals after they failed to prevent the rescue of apprentices who had attacked the Spanish ambassador in 1621. He harangued city authorities and threatened "to station a garrison in their midst and revoke their charter if they did not maintain better order" (Lindley 1983, 121). Seventy years later, Edward Chamberlayne noted that law officials needed "great courage and virtue" to control rioters, and he lamented that law and order was so dependent on "kind words, pitiable harangues, condescensions, or some such resigning methods" (1694, 458).

Policing was most problematic at the crucial level of detection and prosecution. The task of apprehending rioters was left largely to the victims of riots. Fear for safety, lack of detecting and reporting skills, the threat of counterprosecutions, the practical difficulties and costs of framing and carrying out private prosecutions, and a lack of confidence in the judicial system may explain why few victims prosecuted more than one or two misdemeanours at all (Samaha 1974; Weisser 1979; Shoemaker 1991; Rumbelow 1971). As Shoemaker notes, "only a small proportion of [London] rioters was ever arrested, fewer prosecuted and still fewer [20 percent] convicted" (1987, 294).

As communal duty waned, the contemporary alternative based on fees strengthened. Many state officeholders routinely bought positions and sought personal returns on their investment by means of influence peddling or office farming (Hurstfield 1967, 16-34; Swart 1949). This was particularly so for the city marshalcy. From 1627 to 1637, the city was effectively without its appointed official. The officeholder, Davis, rented out his position for profit. He continued to draw the marshal's salary, however, and paid his hireling a percentage of his wage. In 1632, the nominee marshal and the under-marshal were investigated. Prisoners, thieves, and felons were being released from prison without reason. The deputy was dismissed from office and imprisoned, and Davis was enjoined to resume his office. He refused and rented a replacement, who from 1632 to 1637 served as a deputized city marshal. Eventually, after ten years of nonperformance of office,

Davis was coerced into being reinstated. He served six years before finally being dismissed for abuse of power and incompetence (Rumbelow 1971, 50–51).

Succeeding marshals appear to have been more stable in holding office, although their ability to coordinate and supervize constables, beadles, and the watch remained fragile and fragmented. A proclamation in 1655 criticized justices of the peace, constables, and "other officers" for "want of zeal, care and diligence" in executing the law, and a proclamation by the lord mayor six months later complained of poor policing supervision, poor detection and apprehension, and lax cooperation. Constables were enjoined to make themselves "better known and more readily found," and were further ordered to have their signs of office "set or fixed at their street doors" so all may "detect their dwelling place" (Rumbelow 1971). The city marshalcy could not act as an authoritative agent of social order. It lacked the numbers, coordination, and institutional coherence to coordinate local communal policing and manage even specific problems of social disorder and crime control.

The fragmentation and fragility of social control in the London metropolis was paralleled by equally doubtful military forces. The army and militia were primarily involved in fighting foreign campaigns and in serving as reserve units against alien invasion (Stearn 1973; Hill 1972; Boynton 1967). Loyalties seldom flowed to a central organization core and were instead tied to local patrons who had enlisted the bands of fighting men (Hale 1962, 19–33; Roberts 1956). The English army was an *ad hoc* and loose agglomeration of professional mercenaries and of locally sponsored and trained troops that were formed in time of war and disbanded in peace time (Stone 1965, 199–270; Stater 1986, 280–282; Cruickshank 1966; Western 1965, 70–73).

As a domestic coercive institution, the army lacked administrative uniformity. While it was an effective repressive weapon in curbing territorial revolts, and in dispersing and curtailing riotous crowds, it was cumbersome and slow to mobilize, and virtually incapable of monitoring the everyday world of vagrancy and lawlessness. Nor were the trained bands any more effective. They and the militias were plagued with recruitment problems, poor training, desertion, inadequate financing, and an incoherent system of military logistics, supply, and billeting (Boynton 1967, 271; Emsley 1991, 13; Stater 1986, 292–293). In London, the trained bands consisted of 6,000 men divided into four regiments commanded by colonels under the stewardship of the lord mayor. They were usually deployed as preventative guards or mounted watches, supporting the local watches in the daily round of securing the capital (Allen 1972, 300–302). But the frequency of riots and disorder and the pressing seriousness of vagrancy and crime within the city suburbs raised serious doubts about the efficacy of the trained bands' assistance to the civil powers (Pearl 1972, 104–105, 119–120; Lindley 1983, 124; Harris 1986; Beloff 1938; Rogers 1978). They faced continued, chronic shortages of arms, equipment, training, and personnel, and on numerous occasions they went into action without ammunition (Boynton 1967, 210, 216–217). Absenteeism frequently marred efficiency, and the expenses of mustering and mobilizing men sparked much local resentment. Reliability and loyalty were not always certain. Mutinies and internal revolts at times made the trained militias themselves a problem of social order (Beloff 1938; Lindley 1983; Western 1965). In discussing their role in the Sacheverill Riots, Holmes concludes, "it was a mercy that the City Trained Bands were not called out until the situation was under complete control" (1976, 56).

THE RISE OF PRIVATE POLICING AND THE COMMERCIAL COMPROMISE OF THE STATE

By the later seventeenth century, the English state lacked the coercive capacity to exact a uniform compliance through its social control apparatus. It possessed neither the methods of direct supervision, nor the ability to muster control through the manipulation of traditional sub-élites. So the strategy of social ordering in London came to rest more and more on expanding the punitive net by increasing the offences punishable by death, stimulating public involvement by developing a system of rewards and pardons, and cultivating a private market in police services (Radzinowicz 1948; Rock 1977; McIntosh 1976; Spitzer 1981). The new appeal was to ask "private individuals for no higher motive than self-interest" and to form a system of incentives and deterrents "to exploit human greed and fear so that there would be no need to look for anything so nebulous and unrealistic as public spirit" (Pringle 1958, 1).

Citizens were exhorted and paid to transform themselves into agents of control. The management of social unrest, vagrancy, and crime was organized according to a system of payment by results. Successful information for some offences might bring a profit of 200 pounds, a strong incentive for "common informers to earn their living as private policemen" (Pringle 1958, 16). Informers usually made much less, between three and five pounds a case, and profit was more a matter of volume than value (Babington 1969, 193; Tobias 1979, 119). Proclamations and orders from king and Parliament offered sums of money or commodities in kind to enterprising searchers, and spying, informing for profit, impeachment, and the use of reprieves and pardons grew to the point that "informers were encouraged to inform against informers until it became a national profession (Hill 1969, 97). By the late Stuart period, informing for profit represented an important method of economic regulation, tax collection, excise and customs control, and privateering administration (Andrews 1964; Beresford 1957–1958; Elton 1958; Davies 1956; Thompson 1971). It quickly expanded to cover many minor infringements of the law, including "blasphemy, gambling, shopkeepers' offences like selling short weight, dumping rubbish, throwing fireworks, defrauding the revenue, obstructing the traffic, stealing dogs, and sheltering vagabonds" (Pringle 1958, 16).

When sanctioned by the state, informers generally were entitled to a share of the fine or a portion of the forfeited property. Thus, in the case of counterfeiters of gold or silver objects they could earn a pardon and as well were entitled "to such part of the [seized] forfeiture of the said party to the same offence, as amply as any other informer or relator, not having offended, might have done..." (Davies 1956, 47). Informers also capitalized on another market: the personal rewards offered by "the victims of the crime, insurance companies and prosecution societies, property-owners' associations and bodies of residents, and municipal and parochial authorities" (Pringle 1958, 17). Those who informed soon became known as the "voluntary police" and they were "always on the alert to discover any infringement of the law which prove a source of profit to themselves" (Radzinowicz 1956, 146).

Information leading to the arrest and conviction of offenders, however, was often a matter for private specialists who played both sides against the middle. Undercover guardians of the state sometimes "dissolved into first class members of the criminal classes" (Beresford 1957–1958, 231). The legal context encouraged this drift. The prolonged expenses of taking prosecution through to trial, and the risk of costly upset thereafter "strongly tempted informers to make illegal use of the first entry of an information and the writ issued thereupon" (Davies 1956, 58). Settlements out of court could be more profitable. Expenses could be reduced and more money could be squeezed from the accused. Illegal charges took several forms: licensed compositions but at inflated rates, unlicensed charges on actual evidence, money extorted by forged or pretended information, and fees from defendants for false information to prevent the entering of valid prosecutions (58–76). Legal profiteers exploited the amateur and voluntarist aspects of the legal system, either taking office for its profits or bringing prosecutions for their financial reward. As Brewer notes, "they exploited both the absence of *salaried* officials and the incentives for private action" (1980, 25).

In London, informing, betraying, and thief-taking developed into specialized trades. As Emsley (1987, 175) notes, "if a victim could not follow up an offence in person, with friends, or by advertisement, the only other recourse...was to a thief-taker." Thief-taking came to prominence with the development of government rewards, inducements, and pardons for checking crime and social unrest. Warrants authorized arrest on *suspicion* of wrongdoing and served initially to force apprehended persons to confess, inform, return stolen articles, or face a far more expensive and unpleasant stay in prison. Prison keepers, it seems, benefited enormously. They both controlled the prisoners within jails, and went outside armed with warrants to search and arrest. They emerged as policing entrepreneurs, and relied on fees and extra remunerations to earn a living (Greene 1930, 165; Aydelotte 1913; Hutton 1930, 265–291; Fennor 1930, 423–484; Dobb 1953, 151; Salgado 1977).

Thief-takers were also regularly receivers of stolen property. As brokers, between thieves and victims, they acquired strategic importance by virtue of their merchandiser's role in the world of crime. Profits were gained privately from rewards and forfeitures, and publicly an *imperium in imperio* was established whereby thief-takers became the informal, state-condoned, local elite of crime as well as policing agents par excellence (Rock 1977; McMullan 1984, 1987b; McLynn 1991; Sharpe 1984; Parks 1970; McIntosh 1976). Cliques of thief-catchers, with an intimate knowledge of deviant ways, thus trafficked in crime (Babington 1969, 39; Howson 1970).

As early as the 1630s, Mary Frith, alias Moll Cutpurse, had developed an innovative private policing strategy. She established a "lock" for managing crime and especially stolen property. Her subordinates were paid well and worked mainly for her; she in turn returned goods to their former owners. Her influence as a thief-taker was institutionalized. She had informers and accomplices who kept her advised about robbers and pickpockets and who advertised her reputation. She cultivated a specific brokery in high-value items such as personal jewels, rings, and watches. Her influence in the organization of crime reflected an accumulation of power attributable to her intermediary function as private police officer and defender of the public interest. Her role as an insurance broker was tacitly acknowledged by state officials, commercial interests, and the public at large (*The Life and Times of Mary Frith* 1663; McIntosh 1976; Rock 1977; McMullan 1982, 1984).

Much like the "putting-out" system in manufacturing, those who supplied policing services asserted considerable discretion over how much public work was done and the methods for achieving results (Dobb 1963, 123–124; Linebaugh 1991, 61–65; Beier and Findlay 1986, 161). Buyers and sellers met in the marketplace as autonomous agents, but thief-takers controlled the intelligence networks, profited from finders fees and intermediary payoffs, settled grievances, and delivered the finished products — felons, stolen goods, security of property — to those who contracted their services (Spitzer and Scull 1977, 20; Babington 1969, 40; McIntosh 1976; Spitzer 1981). Their trade grew enormously so that by the end of the seventeenth century, there were hundreds of warehouses and repositories in London where thieves sold their booty and where thief-takers did their business (Howson 1970, 36).

The spread of policing for profit also altered the customary character of the watch and ward system, and of the administration of justice. Constables, watchmen, and beadles were tempted to work for piece rates. They commercialized their unpaid office by accepting private rewards and forfeitures, by extracting profits for routine public duties and obligations, by fraud and by extortion (Radzinowicz 1956, 278). Constables and beadles also exploited watch-duty rules and funds, pocketing public monies as a recompense for other work (Tobias 1979, 35). Justices of the peace negotiated fines for imprisonment in order to profit from their sentencing work (Radzinowicz 1956, 242). They organized strategies to bully the poor, to sell alehouse licences and warrants on the side, to stimulate illegal infractions if it was economically lucrative, to protect lawbreakers in exchange for bribes, and to avoid suppressing illegality if it was not profitable (Babington 1969, 36; Brewer 1980, 25; Emsley 1983, 25; Tobias 1979, 29–30). As Ascoli notes, "all parties were treated alike as sources of personal profit...the catalogue of judicial crime was as varied as the nature of crime itself; and both constable and watchmen were quick to initiate, however modestly, the example of their superiors" (1979, 27–28). Thief-takers and "trading justices" were providing a service that people wanted, and some were dedicated and hardworking, but they were never above suspicion.

By the end of the seventeenth century, law enforcement in London had undergone a major transformation. Accountability for social control in London was no longer mostly communal but rather quasi-legal (civic groups, thief-takers, private informers, monied agents). Action was no longer mostly collective — a matter of neighbours, kin, tithing group or village parish — but rather semiprivatized and commercially organized, predicated on the ability to pay or hire policing services. Payment was no longer mostly by custom or kind but more likely to be by cash or market-means (Manning 1977, 60–61). The contemporary alternative to communal law enforcement, based on venality of office, patronage, and fees for services had turned aspects of policing into a business enterprise (Sharpe 1984, 40; McLynn 1991; Spitzer 1981). Government by the informal mechanism of voluntary consent was challenged by the principle of self-interest at the king's command.

CONCLUSION

In this chapter I have argued that the lineage of policing and social control is erratic, that forms of communal policing and private policing have long, complex, and rich histories, and that being mindful of this allows us to broaden our view of those who qualify as police agents. In studying the early forms of policing that predate the nineteenth-century "new police," we discover that organizations not immediately recognizable as the police nevertheless functioned and practised policing. This suggests that researchers should not assume that they "know" tout court what the police, as an institution, really is. As Cain (1979, 158) points out, "organizations and individuals do not have to call themselves police in order for the sociologist to consider them as such." Indeed, it may be the case that public state policing in its modern variant is out of step with the historical lineage of policing forms. Certainly modern agencies within the private security sector have very long genealogical antecedents in private prosecution societies, informing, spying, thief-taking, private militias, and private protection organizations (South 1984, 171–198).

Adopting a perspective that defines police by virtue of their activities and historical function also reduces the sense of novelty attached to current policing practices. We can identify common, recurrent themes in practice and function as well as in the needs, principles and directives of those who employ and sustain forms of police work. Ignoring past communal, private, and state initiatives narrows our purchase on understanding and explaining the scope and power of policing. The early history of English policing suggests then that we need to avoid the presentist fallacy of studying only the military, the traditional constabulary, and the organized bodies of watchmen "on the mistaken assumption that they alone embodied all the functions later vested in the new police" (Hay and Snyder 1989, 9). Broadening the study of policing, however, allows us to appreciate the influence of commercial policing in the emergence and development of public policing, because private rewards were common in public policing and because much state-based police work arose in what were "the private fiefs of powerful commercial companies" (Brogden 1987, 8–9).

Finally, the history of policing is limited and limiting when viewed from the stance of traditional historiography. Policing has been too often analyzed as a separate and discrete phenomenon and this has led to a truncated institutional mode of research. Realistically, the communal, private, and state provision of services of order maintenance and social control, of intelligence gathering, of apprehension, and of prosecution are part of the fundamental features of social and political life. Specific conditions within political economy, law, politics, and customs all shaped the nature of policing responses to the absence of any centrally organized social control system. This suggests that neighbours, private agents, semipublic, and public officials all played out their parts against a grander backdrop. As the nature and very dimensions of markets and production changed over time, so too did the nature of the social order and the basis of policing legitimacy. The genealogy of police, then and now, cannot be separated from the genealogy of capital (Pasquino 1991, 105–118).

REFERENCES

Abrams, P. 1982. *Historical Sociology*. Shepton Mallet: Open Books.

Allen, D.F. 1972. "The Political Role of the London Trained Bands in the Exclusion Crisis, 1968–81," *English Historical Review*, 87: 291–304.

Andrews, K.R. 1964. *Elizabethan Privateering: English Privateering During the Spanish War; 1585–1603*. Cambridge: Cambridge University Press.

Ascoli, D. 1979. *The Queen's Peace: The Origin and Development of the Metropolitan Police*. London: Hamish Hamilton.

Ashton, R. 1983. "Popular Entertainment and Social Control in Later Elizabethan and Early Stuart London," *London Journal*, 9(1):3–20.

Aydelotte, F. 1913. *Elizabethan Rogues and Vagabonds*. Oxford: Clarendon Press.

Babington, A. 1969. *A House in Bow Street: Crime and the Magistracy in London, 1740–1881*. London: MacDonald.

Beattie, J. 1986. *Crime and the Courts in England, 1660–1800*. Oxford: Clarendon Press.

Beier, A.L. 1985. *Masterless Men The Vagrancy Problem in England, 1560–1640*. London: Methuen.

———. 1978. "Social Problems in Elizabethan London," *Journal of Interdisciplinary History*, 9(2) (1978): 203–221.

———, and **R. Findlay.** 1986. "The Significance of the Metropolis." In *The Making of the Metropolis London, 1500–1700*, edited by A.L. Beier and B. Shearer. London: Longmans.

Beloff, M. 1938. *Public Order and Popular Disturbances, 1660–1714*. Oxford: Oxford University Press.

Beresford, M.W. 1957–58. "The Common Informer, the Penal Statutes and Economic Regulation," *Economic History Review*, 2d ser, 10 (1957–1958): 221–237.

Boynton, L. 1967. *The Elizabethan Militia*. London: Routledge and Kegan Paul.

Brett-James, N.G. 1935. *The Growth of Stuart London*. London: Allen and Unwin.

Brewer, J. 1989. *The Sinews of Power: War, Money and the English State, 1688–1783*. London: Unwin Hyman.

———. 1980. "Law and Disorder in Stuart and Hanoverian England," *History Today* (January): 18–27.

Brewer, J., and **J. Styles,** eds. 1980. *An Ungovernable People: The English and Their Law in the Seventeenth and Eighteenth Centuries*. London: Hutchison.

Brindenbaugh, C. 1968. *Vexed and Troubled Englishmen, 1590–1642*. Oxford: University Press.

Brogden, M. 1987. "The Emergence of the Police — The Colonial Dimension," *British Journal of Criminology*, 27:1.

———. 1982. *The Police: Autonomy and Consent*. London: Academic Press.

Burke, P. 1985. "Popular Culture in Seventeenth Century London." In *Popular Culture in Seventeenth Century England*, edited by B. Reay. London: Routledge.

Cain, M. 1979. "Trends in the Sociology of Police Work," *International Journal of the Sociology of Law*, 7(1): 143–167.

Carson, K., and **H. Idzikowska.** 1989. "The Social Production of Scottish Polishing 1795–1900." In *Policing and Prosecution in Britain, 1750–1850*, edited by D. Hay and F. Snyder. Oxford: Clarendon Press.

Chamberlayne, E. 1694. *Angliae Notitia*. London: John Martyn.

Chartres, J.A. 1986. "Food Consumption and Internal Trade." In *The Making of the Metropolis London, 1500–1700*, edited by A.L. Beier and R. Findlay. London: Longmans.

Clark, P. 1976. "Popular Protest and Disturbance in Kent, 1558–1640," *Economic History Review*, 29.

Cockburn, J.S. 1977. "The Nature and Incidence of Crime in England, 1559–1625: A Preliminary Survey." In *Crime in England, 1550–1800*, edited by J.S. Cockburn. London: Methuen and Co.

Corrigan, P., and **D. Sayer.** 1985. *The Great Arch: English State Formation as Cultural Revolution.* Oxford: Basil Blackwell.

Cressey, D. 1970. "Occupations, Migration and Literacy in East London, 1580–1640," *Local Population Studies,* no. 5 (1970): 53–60.

Critchley, T.A. 1972. *A History of Police in England and Wales, 900–1966.* Montclair, N.J.: Patterson Smith.

Cruickshank, C.G. 1966. *Elizabeth's Army.* Oxford: Oxford University Press.

Curtis, T.C., and **F.M. Hale.** 1981. "English Thinking About Crime, 1530–1620." In *Crime and Criminal Justice in Europe and Canada,* edited by L.A. Knafla. Waterloo: Wilfred Laurier University Press.

Davies, M.G. 1956. *The Enforcement of English Apprenticeship, 1563–1642.* Cambridge, Mass.: Harvard University Press.

Dobb, C. 1953. "Life and Conditions in London Prisons, 1553–1643 With Special Reference to Contemporary Literature." B. Litt. diss., Oxford University.

Dobb, M. 1963. *Studies in the Development of Capitalism.* New York: International Publishers.

Dugdale, W. 1658. *The History of St. Paul's Cathedral.* London.

Dunn, R.M. 1973. "The London Weavers Riot of 1675," *Guildhall Studies in London History,* (1):1, 3–21.

Dunton, J. 1696. *The Night Walker or Evening Rambles in Search After Lewd Women, etc.* Vol. 1, nos. 1–4; vol. 2, nos. 1, 3. London.

Elton, G.R. 1958. "Informing for Profit." In *Star Chamber Stories,* edited by G.R. Elton. London: Methuen.

Emsley, C. 1987. *Crime and Society in England, 1750–1900.* London: Longmans.

———. 1983. *Policing and its Context, 1750–1870.* London: MacMillan.

Fennor, W. 1930. "The Counter's Commonwealth." Reprinted in *The Elizabethan Underworld,* edited by A.V. Judges. London: Routledge and Sons.

Findlay, R., and **B. Shearer.** 1986. "Population Growth and Suburban Expansion." In *The Making of the Metropolis London, 1500–1700,* edited by A.L. Beier and R. Findlay. London: Longmans.

Fisher, F.J. 1976. "London as an Engine of Economic Growth." In *The Early Modern Town,* edited by P. Clark. London: Longmans.

———. 1961. *Essays in the Economic and Social History of Tudor and Stuart England.* Cambridge: University Press.

———. 1950–1951. "London's Export Trade in the Early Seventeenth Century," *Economic History Review,* 2d ser, 3, (1950–1951): 151–161.

Fletcher, A., and **J. Stevenson,** eds.   1985. *Order and Disorder in Early Modern England.* Cambridge: University of Cambridge.

Foucault, M.   1991. "Politics and the Study of Disorder." In *The Foucault Effect: Studies in Governmentality,* edited by G. Burchell, C. Gordon and P. Miller. London: Harvester Wheatsheaf.

———.   1980. "Power and Strategies." In *Power/Knowledge: Selected Interviews and Other Writings, 1972–1977,* edited by C. Gordon. Brighton: Harvester Press.

———.   1977. *Discipline and Punish.* New York: Vintage.

———.   1967. *Madness and Civilization.* New York: Vintage.

George, M.D.   1925. *London Life in the Eighteenth Century.* New York: Alfred Knapf.

Giddens, A.   1987. *The Nation-State and Violence.* Los Angeles: University of California Press.

Gleason, J.H.   1969. *The Justices of the Peace in England, 1558 to 1640.* Oxford: Clarendon Press.

Greene, R.   1930. "A Notable Discovery of Cozenage." Reprinted in *The Elizabethan Underworld,* edited by A.V. Judges. London: Routledge and Sons.

Hale, J.   1962. "War and Public Opinion in the Fifteenth and Sixteenth Centuries," *Past and Present,* no. 22 (1962): 19–33.

Harris, T.I.G.   1986. "The Bawdy House Riots of 1668," *Historical Journal,* 29: 537–556.

Hart, J.M.   1951. *The British Police.* London: Allen and Unwin.

Hay, D.   1980. "Crime and Justice in Eighteenth and Nineteenth Century England." In *Crime and Justice: An Annual Review of Research,* edited by N. Morris and M. Tonry, 2:45–84. Chicago: University of Chicago Press.

———, and **F. Snyder.**   1989. "Using the Criminal Law, 1750–1850 Policing, Private Prosecution, and the State." In *Policing and Prosecution in Britain 1750–1850.* Oxford: Clarendon Press.

Herrup, C.B.   1989. *The Common Peace Participation and the Criminal Law in Seventeenth-Century England.* Cambridge: Cambridge University Press.

———.   1985. "Law and Morality in Seventeenth Century England," *Past and Present,* no. 106:102–123.

Hewitt, W.A.   1965. *British Police Administration.* Springfield: Charles C. Thomas.

Hill, C.   1972. *The World Turned Upside Down Radical Ideas During the English Revolution.* Middlesex: Penguin Books.

———.   1969. *Reformation to Industrial Revolution.* Middlesex: Pelican Books.

Hobsbawm, E.J.   1967. "The Crisis of the Seventeenth Century." In *Crises in Europe 1560–1660,* edited by Trevor Ashton. New York: Doubleday & Co.

Holmes, G. 1976. "The Sacheverell Riots: The Crowd and the Church in Early Eighteenth Century London," *Past and Present*, 72: 55–85.

Howson, G. 1970. *Thief-Taker General: The Rise and Fall of Jonathan Wild*. London: Hutchison.

Hunt, W. 1983. *The Puritan Movement: The Coming of Revolution in an English County*. Cambridge, Mass: Harvard University Press.

Hurstfield, J. 1973. *Freedom, Corruption and Government in Elizabethan England*. London: Jonathan Cape.

———. 1967. "Political Corruption in Early Modern England: The Historian's Problem," *History*, 52 (1967): 16–34.

Hutton, L. 1930. "The Black Dog of Newgate." Reprinted in *The Elizabethan Underworld*, edited by A.V. Judges. London: Routledge and Sons.

Ingram, M.J. 1984. "Ridings, Rough Music and the 'Reform of Popular Culture' in Early Modern England," *Past and Present*, no. 105: 79–113.

Innes, J. 1987. "Prisons for the Poor: English Bridewells, 1555–1800." In *Labour, Law and Crime in Historical Perspective*, edited by F. Snyder and D. Hay. London: Tavistock Publications.

———. and **J. Styles.** 1986. "The Crime Wave: Recent Writing on Crime and Criminal Justice in Eighteenth Century England," *Journal of British Studies*, 25: 4, 380–435.

James, M. 1967. *Social Problems and Policy During the Puritan Revolution, 1640–1660*. London: Routledge and Sons.

Johnston, L. 1992. *The Rebirth of Private Policing*. London: Routledge.

Judges, A.V., ed. 1930. *The Elizabethan Underworld*. London: Routledge and Sons.

Kamen, H. 1976. *The Iron Century: Social Change in Europe 1550–1660*. London: Cardinal.

Kellett, J.R. 1958. "The Breakdown of Guild and Corporate Control Over the Handcraft and Retail Trade in London," *Economic and History Review* 2(10):381–394.

Kempe, A.J. 1825. *Historical Notices of the Collegiate Church or Royal Free Chapel and Sanctuary of St. Martin-Le-Grand*. London: Longmans.

Kent, J. 1986. *The English Village Constable, 1580–1642: A Social and Administrative Study*. Oxford: Clarendon Press.

———. 1983. "Folk Justice and Royal Justice in Early Seventeenth Century England," *Midland History*, 8:78–81.

———. 1981. "The English Village Constable, 1580–1642: The Nature and Dilemmas of the Office," *Journal of British Studies*, 20:2, 26–49.

King, P. 1984. "Decision Makers and Decision-Making in the English Criminal Law, 1750–1800," *Historical Journal*, 27: 25–58.

Kitch, M.J.   1986. "Capital and Kingdom: Migration to Later Stuart London." In *The Making of the Metropolis London, 1500–1700,* edited by A.L. Beier and R. Findlay. London: Longmans.

Knafla, L.A.   1983. "'Sin of All Sorts Swarmeth': Criminal Litigation in an English County in the Early Seventeenth Century." In *Law Litigants and the Legal Profession,* edited by E.W. Ives and A.H. Manchester. London: Royal Historical Society.

Lee, W.L. Melville.   1901. *A History of Police in England.* London: Methuen.

Life and Times of Mary Frith Otherwise Moll Cutpurse, The. 1663. London.

Lindley, K.J.   1983. "Riot Prevention and Control in Early Stuart London," *Translations of the Royal Historical Society,* 5th ser., 109–126.

———.   1982. *Fenland Riots and the English Revolution.*

Linebaugh, P.   1991. *The London Hanged Crime and Civil Society in the Eighteenth Century.* London: Allen Lane.

MacCaffrey, W.T.   1969. "Place and Patronage in Elizabethan Politics." In *Elizabethan Government and Society: Essays Presented to Sir John Neal,* edited by Stanley T. Bindoff, Joel Hurstfield, and Charles Williams. London: Athlone Press.

MacFarlane, S.   1986. "Social Policy and the Poor in the Later Seventeenth Century." In *The Making of the Metropolis London, 1500–1700,* edited by A.L. Beier and R. Findlay. London: Longmans.

McIntosh, M.   1976. "Thieves and Fences: Markets and Power in Professional Crime," *British Journal of Criminology,* 16 (July): 257–266.

McLynn, F.   1991. *Crime and Punishment in Eighteenth Century England.* Oxford: Oxford University Press.

McMullan, J.L.   1987a. "Crime, Law and Order in Early Modern England," *British Journal of Criminology,* 27:3.

———.   1987b. "Policing the Criminal Underworld: State Power and Decentralized Social Control in London, 1550–1700." In *Transcarceration: Essays in the Sociology of Social Control,* edited by J. Lowman, R.J. Menzies, and T.S. Palys. Aldershot, U.K.: Gower.

———.   1984. *The Canting Crew: London's Criminal Underworld, 1550–1700.* New Brunswick, N.J.: Rutgers University Press.

———.   1982. "Criminal Organization in Sixteenth and Seventeenth Century London," *Social Problems,* 29 (February): 311–323.

Malcolmson, R.W.   1980. "A Set of Ungovernable People: The Kingswood Colliers in the Eighteenth Century." In *An Ungovernable People: The English and Their Law in the Seventeenth and Eighteenth Centuries,* edited by J. Brewer and J. Styles. London: Hutchison.

Manning, B.   1976. *The English People and the English Revolution, 1646–1649.* London: Heinemann.

Manning, P.K. 1977. *Police Work: The Social Organization of Policing.* Cambridge, Mass: MIT Press.

Moir, E. 1968. *The Justice of the Peace.* Middlesex: Penguin Books.

Moore, B. 1967. *Social Origins of Dictatorship and Democracy.* Boston: Beacon Press.

Paley, R. 1989. "Thief-Takers in London in the Age of the McDaniel Gang, 1745–1754." In *Policing and Prosecution in Britain, 1750–1850,* edited by D. Hay and F. Snyder. Oxford: Clarendon Press.

Palmer, S.H. 1988. *Police and Protest in England and Ireland, 1780–1850.* Cambridge: Cambridge University Press.

Parks, E. 1970. "From Constabulary to Police Society: Implications for Social Control," *Catalyst* (summer): 76–97.

Pasquino, P. 1991. "Theatrum Politicum: The Genealogy of Capital — Police and the State of Prosperity." In *The Foucault Effect Studies in Governmentality,* edited by G. Burchell, C. Gordon, and P. Miller. Chicago: University of Chicago Press.

Pearl, V.L. 1981. "Social Policy in Early Modern London." In *History and Imagination: Essays in Honour of H.R. Trevor Roper,* edited by H. Lloyd–Jones, V. Pearl and B. Warden. London: Duckworth.

———. 1972. 2d ed. *London and the Outbreak of the Puritan Revolution.* London: Oxford University Press.

———. 1961. *London and the Outbreak of the Puritan Revolution.* London: Oxford University Press.

Plumb, J. 1967. *The Growth of Political Stability in England.* London: Macmillan.

Pound, J.F. 1971. *Poverty and Vagrancy in Tudor England.* London: Longmans.

Power, M.J. 1986. "The Social Topography of Restoration London." In *The Making of the Metropolis London, 1500–1700,* edited by A.L. Beier and R. Findlay. London: Longmans.

———. 1972. "East London Housing in the Seventeenth Century." In *Crisis and Order in English Towns, 1500–1700,* edited by Peter Clark and Paul Slack. London: Routledge and Kegan Paul.

Prestwich, M. 1966. *Cranfield: Politics and Profits Under the Early Stuarts, the Career of Lionel Cranfield, Earl of Middlesex.* Oxford: Clarendon Press.

Pringle, P. 1958. *The Thief-Takers.* London: Museum Press.

Radzinowicz, L. 1956. *A History of English Criminal Law and Its Administration from 1750.* (Vol. 2). London: Stevens.

———. 1948. *A History of English Criminal Law and Its Administration from 1750* (Vol. 1). London: Stevens.

Reiner, R. 1985. *The Politics of the Police.* Sussex: Wheatsheaf.

Roberts, M. 1956. *The Military Revolutions, 1560–1660.* Belfast: University of Belfast Press.

Rock, P. 1977. "Law, Order and Power in Late Seventeenth and Early Eighteenth Century England," *Annals of Criminology,* 16(1, 2): 233–265.

Rogers, N. 1978. "Popular Protest in Early Hanoverian London," *Past and Present,* 79: 70–100.

Rude, G. 1959. "The London 'Mob' in the Eighteenth Century," *Historical Journal,* 2(1): 2–19.

Rumbelow, D. 1971. *I Spy Blue: The Police and Crime in the City of London From Elizabeth I to Victoria.* London: Macmillan Press.

Salgado, G. 1977. *The Elizabethan Underworld.* London: Methuen.

Samaha, J. 1981. "The Recognizance in Elizabethan Law Enforcement," *The American Journal of Legal History,* 25: 189–204.

———. 1974. *Law and Order in Historical Perspective: The Case of Elizabethan Essex.* London: Academic Press.

Sharp, B. 1988. "Popular Protest in Seventeenth-Century England." In *Popular Culture in Seventeenth Century England,* edited by B. Reay. London: Routledge.

Sharpe, J.A. 1988. "The People and the Law." In *Popular Culture in Seventeenth Century England,* edited by B. Reay. London: Routledge.

———. 1985. "Last Dying Speeches: Religion, Ideology, and Public Execution in Seventeenth Century England," *Past and Present,* 107: 144–167.

———. 1984. *Crime in Early Modern England, 1550–1750.* London: Longmans.

———. 1980. "Enforcing the Law in the Seventeenth Century English Village." In *Crime and the Law: The Social History of Crime in Western Europe Since 1500,* edited by V.A.C. Gatrell, Bruce Lenman, and Geoffrey Parker. London: Europa Publications.

Shoemaker, R.B. 1991. *Prosecution and Punishment Petty Crime and the Law in London and Rural Middlesex, c1660–1725.* Cambridge: Cambridge University Press.

———. 1987. "The London 'Mob' in the Early Eighteenth Century," *Journal of British Studies,* 26: 273–304.

Slack, Paul. 1986. "Metropolitan Government in Crisis: The response to plague." In *The Making of the Metropolis London, 1500–1700,* edited by A.L. Beier and B. Shearer. London: Longmans.

———. 1984. "Poverty and Social Regulation in Elizabethan England." In *The Reign of Elizabeth I,* edited by C. Haigh. London: Macmillan.

South, N. 1987. "Law, Profit and 'Private Persons': Private and Public Policing in English History." In *Private Policing,* edited by C.D. Shearing and P.L. Stenning. London: Sage.

————. 1984. "Private Security, the Division of Policing Labor and the Commercial Compromise of the State." In *Research in Law, Deviance and Social Control,* Vol. 6, edited by S. Spitzer and A. Scull 171–198. Greenwich, Ct.: JAI.

Spitzer, S. 1987. "Security and Control in Capitalist Societies: The Fetishism of Security and the Secret Thereof." In *Transcarceration: Essays in the Sociology of Social Control,* edited by J. Lowman, R.J. Menzies, and T.S. Palys. Aldershot, U.K.: Gower.

————. 1981. "The Political Economy of Policing." In *Crime and Capitalism,* edited by David Greenberg. New York: Mayfield Co.

———— and **A. Scull.** 1977. "Social Control in Historical Perspective: From Private to Public Responses to Crime." In *Corrections and Punishment,* edited by David Greenberg, Beverly Hills: Sage.

Stater, V.L. 1986. "The Lord Lieutenancy on the Eve of the Civil Wars: The Impressment of George Plowright," *The Historical Journal,* 29: 2, 279–296.

Stearn, S. 1973. "Conscription and English Society in the 1620's," *Journal of British Studies,* 11, 1–23.

Stone, L. 1965. *The Crisis of the Aristocracy, 1553–1641.* Oxford: Clarendon Press.

Styles, J. 1987. "The Emergence of the Police — Explaining Police Reform in Eighteenth and Nineteenth Century England," *British Journal of Criminology,* 27(1) (winter): 15–22.

Swart, K. 1949. *The Sale of Offices in the Seventeenth Century.* The Hague: Martinus Nijhoff.

Swift, R. 1988. "Urban Policing in Early Victorian England, 1835–86: A Reappraisal," *History,* 73 (238): 211–37.

Tawney, R.H. 1941. "The Rise of the Gentry, 1558–1640," *Economic History Review,* 11: 1–38.

Thomas, K.V. 1976. "Age and Authority in Early Modern England," *Proceedings of the British Academy.* 63.

Thompson, E.P. 1971. "The Moral Economy of the English Crowd in the Eighteenth Century," *Past and Present,* no. 50 (1971): 76–136.

Thornley, I.D. 1924. "The Destruction of Sanctuary." In *Tudor Studies Presented to A.F. Pollard,* edited by R.W. Seton-Watson. London: Longmans.

Thurmond-Smith, P. 1985. *Policing Victorian London, Political Policing, Public Order, and the London Metropolitan Police.* Westport: Greenwood Press.

Tobias, J.J. 1979. *Crime and Police in England, 1700–1900.* London: St. Martins Press.

Underdown, D. 1985. *Revel, Riot and Rebellion: Popular Politics and Culture in England, 1603–1660.* Oxford: Oxford University Press.

Walter, J. 1980. "Grain Riots and Popular Attitudes to the Law: Maldon and the Crisis of 1629." In *An Ungovernable People,* edited by J. Brewer and J. Styles. London: Hutchison.

Weisser, M. 1979. *Crime and Punishment in Early Modern Europe*. Sussex: Harvester Press.

Western, J. 1965. *The English Militia in the Eighteenth Century*. London: Routledge and Kegan Paul.

Williams, P. 1979. *The Tudor Regime*. Oxford: Oxford University Press.

Wrightson, K. 1982. *English Society, 1580–1680*. London: Hutchison.

———. 1980. "Two Concepts of Order: Justices, Constables and Jurymen in Seventeenth Century England." In *An Ungovernable People: The English and Their Law in the Seventeenth and Eighteenth Centuries*, edited by John Brewer and John Styles. London: Hutchison.

Wrigley, E.A. 1967. "A Simple Model of London's Importance in Changing English Society and Economy, 1650–1750," *Past and Present*, no. 37 (1967): 44–70.

POST-CRITICAL PEDAGOGIES: FROM LIBERAL TALK TO AUTHENTIC LIBERATION

Robynne Neugebauer-Visano

INTRODUCTION

Throughout the 1990s, critical pedagogies have suffered several setbacks as a result of a continued accommodation to banal liberalism. Despite the proliferation of progressive publications, informed by the contributions of radical criminology in the 1980s, (Taylor, 1983; West, 1984; Fleming, 1985; MacLean, 1986; Brickey and Comack, 1986; Ratner and McMullan, 1987; Caputo et al., 1989) struggles for social justice in the 1990s are experiencing even greater challenges, both inside and outside criminological circles. Although the formidable liberal orthodoxy cited in contemporary scholarship and teaching is replete with a ritual deference to equality, expressions of cultural exclusion (such as homophobia, antilesbianism, racism, class elitism, misogyny, ageism, and ableism), still escape systematic scrutiny. Instead, a plethora of convenient approaches to criminogenic social conditions exist that run the risk of making Canadian criminology both divisive and sociologically unimaginative. The narrative, or more appropriately the prevailing discourse within mainstream criminology, has cemented itself within the logic of hegemonic imperatives of the state and capital. In addition, liberalism seeks to transform critical pedagogy from a set of meaningfully progressive strategies of social justice to a more vulgar convenience and a manipulation of resources that readily accommodates institutions that reward privileged white, male, or heterosexual individuals.

This paper highlights the intellectual contradictions in criminology, and the dubious benefits of liberal democracy attendant with state-sponsored funding of scholarship, research centres, and teaching. It is argued that post-critical pedagogies must respond more aggressively to the challenges of capital and to the fundamental betrayal of critical directions. The call to action by critical criminology still requires a movement beyond the liberal talk of equality toward a more authentic liberation from oppressive structures, cultural trends, and historical forces. It is argued that liberalism succeeds by appropriating the voices of those individuals and communities traditionally relegated to the periphery and then reconstructs their experiences.

Critical criminologies of the 1980s have certainly been devoted to theoretical and methodological questions that confront wider sociological concerns. Criminology was reconstituted in terms of wider configurations of power that affect an appreciation of crime. A number of issues have been studied: historical materialism; the relationship between micro and macro levels of analysis; the limits of possessive individualism. Additionally, the relationship between structure and agency, the social significance of racism, misogyny, and class elitism, and the limitations of conventional paradigms have been analyzed. Critical criminology courses have confronted contradictions inherent in liberal democratic (capitalist) states, especially in the official treatment of race, gender and class, and concomitant issues of fundamental equality. Courses provided students with a critical reading of privilege as a site of inquiry within comparative and historical contexts of political economy, cultural reproductions, and hegemonic state practices. Also, these courses interrogated accommodative and challenging discourses that discipline the constitution and contributions of extant practices and policies. Accommodations, resistance, and struggle as generic features of survival have also been examined in different sites. Liberal tinkerings within these configurations serve as resources for maintaining the "margins" or the "other," contagious mythologies and compliance with social injustices. Critical-criminology courses have focused on contemporary texts that highlight the struggles over identity and power — linking the dominant culture and attendant values to forms of oppression. This perspective explores the everyday intersections of race, class, and gender within various levels of analytic, theoretical, substantive and methodological inquiry. Major theoretical and methodological trajectories in the study of mainstream criminology have been investigated (Ratner, 1985; Snider, 1991).

Additionally, the prospects and challenges of differing designs ranging from semiology, textual and content analyses, postmodernist articulations, neo-Marxist orientations, orthodox participant observations to an appreciation of "praxis" and ethics of interventionist measures have also been incorporated. Critical criminology concerns the levels of state institutional practices, notably the behaviour of law, notions of subjectivity and common sense, and the array of agencies that articulate structures of power and historical trends. Additionally, in the 1990s critical criminology has broadened the foci by examining a host of fundamental institutions ranging from education, pop culture, work, immigration, media, and international (global) relations. For example, the role of education in exacerbating the experience of marginality by populations officially designated as "different" or criminal need to be elucidated. Interestingly, convenient coping strategies like negotiations, in addition to more direct forms of compliance, are analyzed. Local community initiatives are also discussed in terms of expanding the panoptic surveillance of social advocacy.

OVERVIEW: THE CONTEXTS OF CONTROL AND OPPOSITIONAL PEDAGOGIES

Consistent with the above claims of critical criminologies, critical pedagogies confront the foundations of knowledge. The praxis of critical pedagogies not only demands a genuine commitment to social change but also ongoing critiques of truth claims. The authenticity of these oppositional struggles (resistance) enjoys a rich history — from the contributions of Gramsci (1957, 1971, 1985, 1988), DuBois (1977), Freire (1974), Davis (1983, 1989), hooks (1984, 1990), and Lorde (1984) — from which conventional criminology has remained distant and disinterested.

Critical criminology in Canada has realized, however, perhaps more than its American counterpart, that analyses must move beyond the ethnocentric biases of English-speaking countries. For instance, much effort is needed in incorporating comparative analyses and the contributions of practitioners, scholars, and activists from Africa, South America, Asia, and Mediterranean Europe.

The canons of Canadian criminology remain consistent with official conceptions of constitutive elements of social order. Within the "business of criminology" and the "crime control industry," critical thinking has never been a premium. Indeed, in advanced capitalism only certain forms of knowledge are used to legitimate and secure the interests of the powerful. To what extent has criminology abandoned its conservative moorings in reproducing control? How different is Canadian criminology in the 1990s from the 1970s, or the 1940s? One notices that in the early 1990s there has been considerable talk about colour and crime regarding the appropriateness of collecting crime statistics based on race; the controversy surrounding "eugenics" and crime; the linking of immigration and crime; and continued injustices against aboriginal peoples. Similarly, there has been an inordinate amount of discourse regarding ineffective legislation regarding sexual violence (the dismantling of the rape shield law, and the allowance of drunkenness as a defence), punitive responses toward young offenders (changes to the *Young Offenders Act*), and lax sanctions against corporate crime. Crime spectacles still distract, stupify, and paralyze public participation, as with the sensational Paul Bernardo and OJ Simpson trials and the crusades against crime, drugs, and guns.

Against this background, critical pedagogies strive to liberate social thought from the peculiar incubation of cultural controls. Juxtaposed against a reactionary morality, critical pedagogies encode and decode the production and consumption of discipline. Methods are available, however, in critical cultural theory that assist in deconstructing illusions and critically elaborating on the conditions and consequences of crime.

Critical pedagogies accept, as Habermas (1974, 1976) has indicated, that meanings and symbols of the dominant ideology prevent critical thinking. Social processes, language, and individual consciousness transform the self into a subordinated subject mediated by sophisticated ideological control. In turn, the actor represses, deprives, and denies self-autonomy by projecting normative images of self. Vulnerability and credulity of the individual ensure cultural enslavement. Masked behind dominant liberal ideologies which forever speak the language of individuality, ideologies control the means of mental production. Processes of meaning deconstruction and reconstruction are lost as deference to discipline become commonsensical.

How homogenized are criminology textbooks and curricula? What is considered "essential" and how do we avoid closure that accompanies efforts to "totalize" differences. According to his review of criminology textbooks from 1918 to 1993, Wright notes the influential character (1994, 251) of the textbook. His impressive bibliography evidences the preponderance of conventional liberal writings, with only a few exceptions, such as works by Beirne and Messerschmidt (1991), Chambliss (1988), Michalowski (1985), Pepinsky (1980), and Quinney and Wildeman (1991).

The study of criminology is not only about crime control, but also about the control of a culture that banters in liberalism, ignores differences, and denies authenticity. Moreover, the maturation of Canadian critical criminology, especially critical pedagogies, must equally safeguard against the arrogance of possessive intellectual property rights, self-serving institutional interests, and careerist aspirations. In the following discussion we will explore several general areas of criminological complicity: commissions of inquiry, lucrative state-funded consultative research, and the contrived concept of community and curricular reform.

Commissions and Consultants: At What Costs?

The currency of conventional criminology is politically soothing to the decision-makers whenever social-justice concerns are ignored by well-paid consultants or internal bureaucrats. For the latter, scholarship is defined according to fixed timetables, continued research contracts, artificial claims of objectivity, a deference to extant practices and bureaucratic traditions, and limited or "manageable" reform.

Regrettably, the social organization of scholarship has been subjected to enormous manipulations. From the funding of research to the dissemination of ideas in published form, there is incredible pressure to engage in legitimation performances. So-called objective frames of reference exist that justify professional practices and protect privilege. On the one hand, academicians are expected to respond to the protocol of journal submissions, cater to marketplace conditions created by the competitive publishing industry, and cope with the stress of professional standing (the "publish or perish" syndrome). On the other hand, there are provisions that reward industry either through lucrative contracts or appointments to government panels and agencies. Accordingly, these exercises of patronage (reciprocal obligations) or of patronizing of dissent (co-optation) are socially accepted and historically rooted phenomena.

In a pluralist and highly stratified society, mechanisms are required that encourage a sense of generalized participation. In Canada, royal commissions have been used for a number of different reasons. Specifically in reference to lawmaking, the Canadian state seeks to "incorporate" others, especially minorities, into the decision-making process by claiming to celebrate the "equal" contributions of ethnic, racial, and cultural groupings in the Canadian mosaic. Diverse views are perceived as strengths in this contrived process of consultation.

The state manipulates by "depoliticizing" and "cooling-out." As a mask, commissions are calculable devices used to demystify by dignifying differences, at least on paper. Moreover, the legalistic orientation of royal commissions — the appearance of witnesses, the taking of oaths/affirmations, the illusory legal language, convoluted logic, ambiguous style of legal procedures — succeeds in creating confidence only among individuals who "know" the law, and in mystifying notions of representation. Procedures for legal redress simply target individual villains. This pathological orientation directs attention away from the more oppressive structural inequalities toward criminalized subjects.

Case studies of commissions are highly instructive of the nature of state-sponsored "crime" research. Commissions tend to silence oppositional currents, valorize white male supremacy, exclude feminist and antielitist discourses, maintain the unrepresentativeness and misrepresentations of women, people of colour, the disadvantaged, etc. and demonstrate the behaviour of the untouchable centre and the invisibility of the margins.

Throughout the last few decades there has been considerable time, money, and energy spent on socio-legal bantering, evinced by the proliferation of government commissions and reports. Throughout commissions of inquiry, the law is always projected as neutral, innocent, and too limited in responding to social injustices, thereby escaping its complicities (Fitzpatrick, 1990, 259). The liberal legal appeal of "equality" and the cultural talk of freedom are powerful ideological tools. For instance, Canadians have recently observed an impressive generation of public inquiries, media accounts, and research attention on equality (Visano, 1995). In Canada, however, there is a tendency to opt for the costly proliferation of state-sponsored commissions of inquiries, token gestures by ill-informed politicians. Notice, for example, the following reports for the province of Ontario in dealing with the issue of police discretion: the Morand Report (Ontario, Lieutenant Governor, 1976), the Pitman Report (Metro Toronto, 1977), the Carter Report (Carter, 1979), *Policing in Ontario for the Eighties* (Ontario, 1980), the Bellemare Report (Quebec, Human Rights Commission, 1988), the Lewis Report (Ontario, Task Force on Race Relations, 1989), the Andrews Report (Andrews, 1992), the investigation by Stephen Lewis (Ontario, *Report on Race Relations*, 1992), and the Commission of Inquiry Into Systemic

Racism in the Ontario Criminal Justice System (Ontario, 1993). Millions of public tax dollars have been spent making the same recommendations: increase race awareness training (RAT) and public education, provide more effective outreach, improve public relations and promotion.

Who benefits from these costly enterprises? Who heeds the admonitions of the recommendations? For example, irrespective of the many state-sponsored commissions and studies in sentencing, guidelines continue to falter as judges act with impunity in enforcing the culture of white male superiority. According to the long-awaited inquiry into the treatment of black and other racial minority prisoners in Ontario prisons, *Racism Behind Bars* (Commission of Inquiry Into Systemic Racism in the Ontario Criminal Justice System, 1993, ii–iii), racist language and attitudes plague the environments of many Ontario prisons; the disregard, silence, and the failure of managers to take preventive action contribute to the maintenance of racially poisoned environments. According to this inquiry, racism is tolerated as an assumed price that must be paid in order to maintain peace and order. Moreover, some prisons tolerate and encourage racial segregation in the allocation of prisoners among living units; the rehabilitation services available to black and other racial minority prisoners are inadequate. Finally, the Ontario prison system principally caters to white, Euro-Canadian norms, and many of the service needs of black and other racial minority prisoners remain unacknowledged or dismissed. Many institutions fail to recognize the "inherent dignity and worth" of prisoners or to "treat prisoners as individuals." The commission was reminded repeatedly that some correctional officers in women's and men's prisons are particularly insulting to prisoners whom they believed to be of Jamaican or Vietnamese heritage. The establishment of yet another inquiry, the Commission of Inquiry Into Systemic Racism in the Ontario Criminal Justice System, was a recommendation of the report submitted by Stephen Lewis. The Terms of Reference provided an overview:

> And whereas the government recognizes that throughout society and its institutions patterns and practices develop which, although they may not be intended to disadvantage any group, can have the effect of disadvantaging or permitting discrimination against some segments of society (such patterns and practices as they affect racial minorities being known as systemic racism).

The commission's cochairs, Judge David Cole and Margaret Gittens, and four other commissioners set out in 1992 to probe the extent to which the exercise of discretion at important decision points in the criminal justice system has adverse effects on racial minorities, the treatment of racial minorities in both adult and youth correctional facilities, community policing, justice system officials, policy-making practices of government officials, and legal aid studies. The success of yet another costly inquiry needs to be contextualized in light of the government's past initiatives that were essentially concerned with politicizing race relations within the divisive and bureaucratic priorities. During a recessionary period and at a time when disadvantaged youths were hard hit, the government spent millions of dollars on a commission probing racism in the criminal justice system. The commission held public hearings throughout the province. It is interesting to note that in Metro Toronto only three people showed up at one of the commission's public meetings (*The Toronto Star*, November 4, 1993; Visano, 1994). Various communities were outraged with the callous disregard and stereotypic liberal response of creating more dialogue with royal commissions when the problems were identified by far more perceptive community leaders decades ago. Again, who benefits from these inquiries? Where have the millions of dollars gone? Why was it so necessary to reward the already lucrative businesses of consultants? None of the solutions — situational or strategic — recommended were new. What can we expect from a commission that based its inquiry on a definition of "systemic racism" that is exceedingly limited. Commissioner Cole defined this concept as

> values, practices and procedures that result in black and other racial minority people receiving worse treatment than white people. Even if there is no intention, however, the rules, values, and policies that shape institutions and processes may have discriminatory consequences. (Gittens and Cole, 1994, 6)

Moreover, very few structural changes will be imposed, let alone recommended. The commission has been far too deferential to authorities in the criminal justice system. One could argue that this type of complicity in glossing over fundamental inequalities perpetuated by all actors in the criminal justice system serves only to appease a handful of the more superficially politically correct who refuse to confront their own respective, racist practices. This commission was obviously oriented toward a public relations campaign at a time when support for the provincial NDP government was waning.

Government commissions at all levels have been generous to consultants and self-proclaimed race relations or crime "experts." Also, these inquiries tend to "contain" oppositional currents. Historically, governments manipulate commissions to buy time — to create the impression that something is being done to ameliorate problems and distract the discontent and focus on well-orchestrated public relations campaigns. In other words, government commissions, government-sponsored conferences, and government-funded research institutes are methods of "policing the crisis." The government screens the participation of Canadians and invites proposals ("by request" only) at these events to filter the level of tolerable criticisms, to minimize creativity, and to protect the hegemonic shield.

The cultural representations of subjects in terms of race, gender, and class not only code processes of being and becoming (Bannerji, 1993), but also order power. The creation of the dangerous "other" is extremely apparent in Canada's treatment of its aboriginal peoples. In his report on race relations in Ontario, Lewis says, "The absence of Aboriginal Peoples in this report is glaring. But in truth, their representatives did not come forward" (Ontario, Report on Race Relations, 1992, 36). Why not? Did any government official show any interest, let alone ask, why Canada's Native people were excluded? In addition, why should aboriginal peoples come forward and appear before a white mandated and white controlled commission? Even if they were to submit grievances, why should the white power structure be trusted, given the lessons of history and current exclusionary legal practices? The Royal Commission on the Donald Marshall Jr. Prosecution (1989), appointed by the Nova Scotia government in October 1986, concluded, after recording 16,390 pages of transcript evidence given by 112 witnesses during 93 days of public hearings, that a miscarriage of justice had occurred. The seven-volume report, released in January 1990 by the Commission of Inquiry, found that institutional and structural racism played a part in Marshall's wrongful conviction and imprisonment. The Manitoba Aboriginal Justice Inquiry (Manitoba, 1991) — headed by the Honourable Mr. Justice Alvin Hamilton of the Court of Queen's Bench and Provincial Court Associate Chief Justice, the Honourable Murray Sinclair — was established in 1988 and completed in 1991 at a cost of three million dollars. The inquiry investigated the deaths of Helen Betty Osborne and John Joseph Harper. For example, the federal government created a Royal Commission on Aboriginal Peoples also to inquire into aboriginal justice in April 1991. On the commission's final day of public hearings, the Native Women's Association of Canada delivered a critique denouncing the government's failure to provide "intervenor funding" to the Inuit, promised by the commission to enable Native groups to prepare detailed submissions. Rosemarie Kuptana of the Inuit Tapirisat of Canada noted:

> We are aware that you have for many months now solicited the views of academics with respect to research and the operation of the commission....You have yet to solicit our views on research, operation or priorities...Without a funding commitment, we can't even begin to undertake our research and our community work. (*The Globe and Mail*, July 4, 1992)

The numerous announcements by governments, however, refuse to recognize that Natives have lost respect for non-Native governments. Instead of more lofty words buried in government reports and bureaucratic lexicon, dramatic changes are seriously warranted. Notwithstanding the findings of different and separate commissions of inquiry in Nova Scotia, Manitoba, Saskatchewan, and Ontario, many questions still need to be raised, let alone answered, about the proclivities of governments to launch costly public inquiries (Visano, 1994). At the expense of public funds, and more importantly at the expense of aboriginal peoples, government agencies and departments have (mis)appropriated once again the language of dependency. Rather than finance local, committed, and democratically accountable community initiatives based on a firm grounding and sincere articulation of the issues, governments are determined to create jobs and award lucrative enterprises not to Natives but to well-connected consulting firms mandated to "research," "identify," and develop strategies for improving the situation as perceived by white established authority structures. And, according to Ovide Mercredi, chief of the Assembly of First Nations, the Department of

Indian Affairs is part of the problem — a bureaucratic maze that consumes Native moneys. He noted: "The royal commission can be used to examine how much money comes from Parliament and how much gets to the Indian people" (Gillmor, 1992, 59). For instance, why are public inquiries established especially since the most fundamental causes of inequality remain ignored? Are there mechanisms for looking more broadly into the operation and history of the legal system? Do public hearings exonerate, scapegoat, or disguise the machinations of the criminal justice system? Are these initiatives solely designed to restore confidence in the status quo? By permitting what appears to be public dialogue, do these commissions, studies, and committees on racism enhance the legitimacy of the state by implicating a greater community? Or are they not cheap distractions designed to placate only for the turbulent moment the curiosity of a general public that is periodically aroused and continually manipulated by the press, politicians, and privileged? As University of Lethbridge Professor Hall compares the treatment of Natives to apartheid, he comments on the number of inquiries and commissions:

> One could be asking, is this just more of the same. Is this royal commission creating the appearance of some kind of progress being made, or some kind of process in motion, that really is going to buy government more time, and give it a basis to say "we're studying it", for the umpteenth time. ("Native Justice Reports Gather Dust While Canada Builds New Jails," *The Toronto Star*, February 16, 1993.)

The Royal Commission on Aboriginal Affairs, the most expensive inquiry in Canadian history, is costing fifty million dollars. Appointed by former Prime Minister Brian Mulroney in 1991, the inquiry released 20,000 pages and contacted 1,400 witnesses. Ovide Mercredi, National Chief of First Nations, noted with surprise how little the inquiry has done.

Women too have been overinvestigated by state-sponsored research strategies. In April 1989, Mulroney announced the creation of a two-year, 28.2-million-dollar Royal Commission on New Reproductive Technologies to investigate the causes and prevention of infertility, current and potential developments in reproductive technologies, and the legal, health, and economic implications. In 1993, the commission issued its 1,275-page report and concluded with a number of recommendations. In addition to legislative changes, the report called for the creation of a permanent 12-member National Reproductive Technologies Commission to ensure that new technologies are provided in a safe, ethical, and accountable way that are in the public interest. This commission would regulate services (which would be licensed and reviewed) such as sperm collection, storage, and distribution; assisted conception, including egg retrieval and use; prenatal diagnosis; research involving embryos; and the provision of human fetal tissue for research.

Canada's only federal penitentiary for women was built in 1934 and has been the subject of considerable attention. Four years after this facility was built in Kingston, the 1938 Archambault Committee recommended that it be shut down. Located across the street from the Kingston (male) Penitentiary, thick 16-foot walls without towers segregate women from the outside world. Since 1968, no less than 13 commissions and committees have echoed the need to close this prison. For years, women have been promised newer facilities.

By unraveling the contradictions, exposing the myths, and by moving beyond the acknowledgment of women's oppression, men are also required to speak loudly and act openly against the tyrannical treatment of women. Simply, men can contribute by recognizing their own privilege and limited consciousness in supporting feminist perspectives. Former Supreme Court Justice Bertha Wilson argued that gender bias is not a woman's problem, it's a man's problem: "it's they who must solve it" (*The Toronto Star*, November 1, 1992). In this ongoing understanding, however, women and men must safeguard against men "taking over feminist research the way they do everything else" (Harding, 1987, 12; Visano, Forthcoming). Far too often the interests of men have been motivated by an insidious accommodation to paternalism and conveniently instrumental fixations on material rewards. Rather than struggle in addressing the solutions — immediate and long-term — far too many male researchers continue to be satiated with recycled inquiries that define the problem over and over again. Women know all too well what the problems are without the gratuitous consultation of men. Given that feminists have clearly articulated the systemic problems, cultural obstacles, and institutional barriers, one can only question the constant proliferation of state-sponsored research, especially by men. Beverly Bain, national coordinator for the National Action Committee on the Status of Women says, "We can stop studying this [violence] now... What we want is action to start dealing with the problem" (*The Toronto Star*, November 19, 1993). The task here for male researchers is to return to their respective constituencies and develop strategies for power sharing, consciousness raising, and critical interrogation. Conscience not convenience, the lived commitment not the pursuit of lucrative research projects, and "local action" not more uncontested claims that speak on behalf of women's experiences should prompt men to respond more sensitively. In other words, men need to learn to move over and step aside when releasing the results of their well-funded research. Perhaps some serious thought should be given by both male researchers and their respective funding agencies to ensure that a proportion of their exorbitant budgets be set aside to assist shelters, mother-support groups, day care, and community-based organizations. Undoubtedly, these suggestions will invite vituperative criticisms from male researchers who have invested considerably in investigating the oppression of women. However, the text of male inquiries must be contextualized within wider ideological constructions, the coherent meanings of masculinity, and the presence of simultaneous discourses that inevitably fragment the fundamental agenda of empowering women. As Valverde instructs, feminist political, social, and legal thought seeks to challenge the organization of basic social categories (1991, 241).

Research as a social activity is no exception. The entrepreneurial spirit of the 1990s primarily seeks to generate dividends accompanied by increased circulation of knowledge and enhanced revenues from promoters. Research and class competition for funding are insidious ways in which hegemony serves to control the individual without overt force. Materialism, not authenticity, roots the reality of criminological consultation.

Colonialism looms large in contemporary practices of institutionalized consultation. Financial compensation is not only an integral index signifying the prominence of certain actors, institutes, or centres, but is also a normative guide of professional standing. Money articulates an investment in the dominant culture. Experts have misappropriated commonsense, legalized moral language, and celebrated possessive individualism, leaving behind only mirrors and windows through which knowledge is framed. Seldom is there a call for a moratorium on state-sponsored research centres and studies.

In analyzing the role of commissions, one notices constant references to the community. Just as the concept of a commission legitimates state activity, the concept of "community" is equally appropriated as a mechanism through which the dominant culture maintains its hegemony. The community is refashioned as a set of shared meanings, expectations, and understanding, as a symbolic communication.

THE COMMUNITY AS A CONVENIENCE

Post-critical pedagogies have become yet another post from which to reinvest and rethink strategies. Within this orientation, the culture of corporate corruption and collegial complicity has diverted attention away from authentic voices and action. The pedagogies of local mercenaries, protected professionalism, and lucrative consultation have ushered in a new "banking" system. The rhetorical "talk" of liberal pedagogies fails to respond to the rage, the resistance, and the riots. Liberal talk of consent, commonsense, and community also fails to liberate from the disciplinary cadence of corporate capital.

The concept of community in criminal justice is continually reconstructed according to euphemistic canons of liberal orthodox ideas regarding public participation. The community has become transformed into an attractive instrument of crime control. For several decades, the study of criminology has witnessed a proliferation of activities, strategies, and policies designed to enhance community participation. This vacant discussion of community has attained a heightened significance, especially within the convenient "chatter" of liberal democracy. Community involvement from "community watch" and block-parent programs to the participation of the community in the parole process is a product of structure and manipulation. The concept of the community as envisioned by the state is an illusion that masks differences and struggles. The community concept provides more than ideological legitimacy. As currently manipulated by sophisticated cadres of well-intentioned state bureaucrats committed to public relations campaigns, the community concept is designed to discipline "outside" participation, preempt criticism, and discourage much-needed critical dialogue (Visano, 1994). Relatively little information exists documenting the extent to which the community actually participates in its own right, *sui generis*, independent of government initiatives. State-sponsored community participation reflects discourses of privilege. Discordance, differences of opinions and varying levels of involvement are filtered and sanitized. The "community" concept is too easily appropriated by entrepreneurs to engineer support for limited initiatives that fail to grapple with fundamental inequalities. The community is a complex configuration of values and economies. The community is also a problematic discourse that defies simplistic interpretations. The community, as an exercise in control, is reduced to a juridic and analgesic chatter of crime. This convenient obsession with danger/risks by the contrived community is attributable to community police — the new social philosophers, engineers, and theologians who allude to customary meanings of morality.

How do we explore the conceptual intersections of criminology and community? Dominant social injustices of cultural reproductions are related to wider origins. Underlying societal determinants include structural and historical trends. By studying how moral entrepreneurs, like state agencies, maintain and reproduce social order by securing and protecting the legitimacy of prevailing images such as commissions and community, we are asked to locate the authentic space for criminology in the culture of criminal constructions. We are also asked to move beyond traditional texts of conceptual stagnations toward more challenging critical catalyses. Criminologists, as educators, need to engage in an examination of advocacy and community-based empowerment. This appeal provides a conceptually more comprehensive appreciation of community action. Clearly, consciousness-raising is essential in safeguarding against the currents of assimilation. Without reference to the contexts of visioning, images of the past of our community become but a pretext for ignorance and arrogance.

CRIMINOLOGY AS A COURSE OF ACTION

As noted earlier, pedagogic practices do not exist in a vacuum. Economic as well as bureaucratic convenience often shape the delivery of "knowledge." Despite the gaze of liberalism with its mimetic gestures of benevolence, there are inherent problems located in the learning process. To fully appreciate what criminology delivers in terms of teaching and research, it is also imperative that criminology locate itself within historical and cultural specificities. To what extent has criminology become institutionalized? What are the limitations of criminology? How much can be covered while maintaining a degree of integrity to the discipline, to the teaching enterprise, the community of scholars, the community of the studied, or to the "general" public?

Traditional criminological curricula systematically reproduce inequality by devaluing or pathologizing differences. How is inequity and oppression reproduced by the manner in which courses and readings are organized? Again, with some discomfort, critical pedagogues ask to what degree is criminology a pathology? To elaborate, the text and narration of criminology are based on beliefs that reinforce individual and institutional exclusion. Discrimination is commonplace in criminology in terms of what constitutes crime. Crime is a socially constructed and reproduced historical phenomenon whose form changes in response to transformations occurring within society's socioeconomic base. In other words, crime incorporates a set of economic, political, legal, and ideological practices through which a dominant group exercises hegemony over subordinate groups.

Critical pedagogies, in essence, teach and learn about the exercises of power on the basis of difference, the denial of fundamental human rights. Access to resources for survival in society manifests itself within organizational and institutional structures and programs, as well as within individuals thought or behaviour patterns. The transformation of criminology practice through the ongoing collaborative creation of social relations that foster social justice is a move toward a public political stance against exclusionary trends. Notwithstanding the efforts of such accomplishments as the Journal of Human Justice, social justice in criminology has yet to become an acceptable commitment. Ideologically, critical pedagogies are about the removal of oppressive conditions despite the obvious charge by well-positioned liberal criminologists that these suggestions are not neutral. Critical consciousness and accountability are standards inherent in the praxis reflection and action.

Courses dealing with the criminalization of colour, class, and gender and their corresponding oppressions are desperately lacking. Current teaching and learning practices do not encourage effective resource sharing with "those others" who are typically excluded by the state. It is also important that as educators we do not totalize the subjects by assuming that course content, class discussions, and the delivery of ideas will be similarly received without attention to unique experiences. Therefore, the conceptual framework must include the interconnectedness of racism, sexism, homophobia, classism, etc. In transforming the criminological curriculum, we stand to gain a richness, depth, and creativity in knowledge itself. But we lose the comfort of foundationalism — a comfort that secures the knowledge and expertise of the traditional teacher.

Learning and teaching are not conceived as a coherent exercises that exist outside of situated discoursal practices. Education is constructed within material conditions of existence that legitimize co-optation or loyalty through cultural shields of the fictive promises of law. Critical criminologists have engaged in the project of "normalization," a project that rescues "belongingness" by specifying differences and accepting one's "otherness" — by deconstructing the past and remaining in the margins. Once decentred and de-essentialized, it can be pointed out that the subject of criminology is constructed in contradictions. That is, authenticity is surrendered to authorities. The subject is fractured and complexly articulated within a plurality of discourses that are never stable, static, or fixed. We must then view foundational categories such as crime not as existing "out there" as objective things, but as radically constructed through historical and cultural practices at the everyday level. Accordingly, it is incumbent on teachers and students alike to interrogate the subtext of their own credulity and appreciate the fragmented nature of their own subjectivity. It is certainly an onerous task to move beyond cultural roles and expectations incubated within resources like law, bureaucratic rationality, media, manufactured commonsense, education, employment, etc. Not only are we compelled to probe various battlegrounds of race/ethnicity, gender, heterosexuality, ableism, and class ethnicity, but we must also focus on the cultural reworkings of larger discourses that criminalize the "other." Educators are asked to situate themselves in these struggles that characterize criminology, to ground their perceptions, to avoid closures, to empower themselves conceptually and to engage in open dialogue. By challenging the conceptual closures of the criminological canons of traditional texts, education is oppositional, a political project that invites everyone to position themselves ideologically and historically.

Nonetheless, confining discussions of crime to a legal narrative is a meaningless exercise that forecloses any possibility of social justice discourses — discourses that presumably must implicate such dynamic features as history and political economy. These relations are determined by the evolutionary phase of the forces of production. The totality of these relations forms the economic structure of society. The manner in which people relate to one another in the process of producing their material means of life support shapes consciousness.

According to Marx, through the bourgeois culture, workers are educated in limited ways, which prevent the realization of class interests. Workers are taught to accept subordination. The prevailing culture of capitalism hinders the development of class consciousness. This dominant culture is replete with illusions that enhance alienation. As Marx notes: "Your very ideas are but the outgrowth of your bourgeois production and bourgeois property" (Tucker, 1978, 487). The conditions of the material environment deny creativity and restrict choices.

CONCLUSION: POSTS AND SIGNS

Criminology as a discourse is a major device for interpreting the culture of capital. Criminology is a constructed knowledge that pathologizes and devalues differences. Juridic chatter has attained an exaggerated social significance. Our knowledge of crime and our community ought not to be solely packaged to satisfy market and state conditions, but should also respond to our critical faculties, and document our experiences, consciousness, intention, and their relational contexts.

To the politically naive these arguments will be easily dismissed as rhetoric. Thus, it is incumbent on us as feminists, antiracist educators, and social commentators to investigate the foundations of ideology and practice, and to interpenetrate immediately, to complement with counter discourses through advocacy and a commitment to reform. In this way tensions are explored, and alternatives (informed by a critical perspective) are advanced that go beyond styles of reasoning that are derivative of the dominant ideologies.

Likewise, criminology is a multitiered subject, enjoying a plurality of meanings that are displaced and reconstructed in concert with other hegemonic reproductions of discipline. Crime and law, therefore, are depicted as expressions of political processes and consequences of politicized structures. In other words, the study of crime involves the examination of a multiplicity of struggles. In this paper it is argued that criminology runs the risk of being a barrier to communication if institutionalized within absolutist and corporate interpretive frameworks. Additionally, it was also argued that for-profit research consultation reproduces a repressive site of power relations. Moreover, critical pedagogies strike the very core of political, cultural, and economic conditions. Just as criminology moved away from the realm of the exotic in the 1970s, so too in the 1990s crime subjects such as victims of gendered or racist violence must no longer be colonized for economic gain.

REFERENCES

Bannerji, H. 1993. *The Writing on the Wall: Essays on Culture and Politics*. Toronto: TSAR.

Beirne, P. and **J. Messerschmidt.** 1991. *Criminology*. New York: Harcourt, Brace and Jovanovich.

Brickey, S., and **E. Comack,** eds. 1986. *The Social Basis of Law*. Toronto: Garamond.

Caputo, T. et al., eds. 1989. *Law and Society: A Critical Perspective*. Toronto: HBJ Holt.

Chambliss, W. 1988. *Exploring Criminology*. New York: Macmillan.

Davis, A. 1989. *Women, Culture, Politics*. New York: Vintage Books.

———. 1983. *Women, Race & Class*. New York: Vintage.

Du Bois, W.E.B. [1935] 1977. *Black Reconstruction in the United States, 1860–1880*. Reprint, New York: Russell & Russell.

Fitzpatrick, P. 1990. "Racism and the Innocence of Law." In *Anatomy of Racism*, edited by D. Goldberg. Minneapolis: University of Minnesota.

Fleming, T., ed. 1985. *New Criminologies in Canada*. Toronto: Oxford University Press.

Freire, P. 1974. *Pedagogy of the Oppressed*. New York: Seabury.

Gillmor, D. 1992. "Recoil," *Saturday Night*, (May): 51–77.

Gittens, M. and **D. Cole.** 1994. "Speaking Notes," *Release of the Commission's Interim Report, Racism Behind Bars*. Toronto: Commission on Systemic Racism. February 1.

Gramsci, A.   1988. *Antonio Gramsci: Selected Writings, 1916–1935.* Edited by D. Forgacs. New York: Schocker.

————.   1985. *Antonio Gramsci: Selections From Cultural Writings.* Edited by D. Nowell-Smith and G. Nowell-Smith. Translated by W. Melhower. Cambridge: Harvard University Press.

————.   1971. *Prison Notebooks: Selections.* Translated by Q. Hoare and G. Smith. New York: International Publishers.

————.   1957. *The Modern Prince and Other Writings.* Edited by L. Marks. New York: International Publishers.

Habermas, J.   1976. *Legitimation Crisis.* London: Heinemann Educational Books.

————.   1974. *Theory and Practice.* London: Heinemann Educational Books.

Harding, S.   1987. *Feminism and Methodology.* Bloomington: Indiana University Press.

hooks, b.   1990. *Yearning.* Toronto: Between the Lines.

————.   1984. *Feminist Theory: From Margin to Center.* Boston: South End Press.

Lorde, A. 1984. *Sister Outsider.* Freedom, Calif.: The Crossing Press Freedom Series.

MacLean, B.   1986. "Alienation, Reification and Beyond: The Political Economy of Crime." In *Political Economy of Crime,* edited by B. MacLean. Scarborough: Prentice Hall.

Michalowski, R.   1985. *Order, Law and Crime.* New York: Random House.

Pepinsky, H.   1980. *Crime Control Strategies.* New York: Oxford University Press.

Quinney, R. and **J. Wildeman.**   1991. *The Problem of Crime.* Mountain View, Calif.: Mayfield.

Ratner, R.   1985. "Inside the Liberal Boot: The Criminological Enterprise in Canada." In *The New Criminologies in Canada,* edited by T. Fleming. Toronto: Oxford University Press.

Ratner, R., and **J. McMullan,** eds.   1987. *State Control.* Vancouver: University of British Columbia.

Snider, L.   1991. "Critical Criminology in Canada: Past, Present and Future." In *Crime in Canadian Society,* edited by R. Silverman, J. Teevan and V. Sacco. Toronto: Butterworth.

Taylor, I.   1983. *Crime, Capitalism and Community.* Toronto: Butterworth.

Toronto. *See* Metro Toronto.

Tucker, R., ed.   1978. *The Marx-Engels Reader.* 2d ed. New York: W. W. Norton and Company.

Valverde, M.   1991. "The Rhetoric of Reform: Tropes and the Moral Subject," *International Journal of the Sociology of Law,* 18.

Visano, L.   Forthcoming. *Beyond the Text.*

———. 1994. "The Culture of Capital as Carceral: Conditions and Contradictions." In *Carceral Contexts*, edited by K. McCormick. Toronto: Scholars Press.

West, W.G. 1984. *Young Offenders and the State*. Toronto: Butterworth.

Wright, R. 1994. "Criminology Textbooks, 1918 to 1993: A Comprehensive Bibliography," *Journal of Criminal Justice Education*, 5(Fall):2.

REPORTS

Andrews, A.G. 1992. *Report*. Review of Race Relations Practices of Metro Toronto Police. Metropolitan Toronto Council.

Canada. Parliamentary Committee on Equality Rights. 1985. *Equality for All*. Ottawa: House of Commons.

Canada. Public Commission of Inquiry on War Criminals. 1986. *Report: Part 1*. Ottawa: Canadian Government Publishing Centre.

Canada. Royal Commission on Equality in Employment. 1985. *Report*. R.S. Abella. Ottawa: Government of Canada.

Canada. Royal Commission on Equality in Employment. 1984. *Equity in Employment*. Ottawa: Supply and Services.

Canada. Special Committee on Visible Minorities in Canadian Society. 1984. *Equality Now!* Hull: Supply and Services.

Canada. Standing Committee on Justice and the Solicitor General. 1993. *Crime Prevention in Canada: Toward a National Strategy*. February. Ottawa: Supply and Services.

Canada. Standing Committee on Multiculturalism. 1987. *Multiculturalism: Building the Canadian Mosaic*. Ottawa: Queen's Printer.

Canada. Task Force on Aboriginal Peoples in Federal Corrections Solicitor General. 1988. *Final Report*. Ottawa: Supply and Services.

Carter, G.E. 1979. *Report to the Civic Authorities of Metropolitan Toronto and its Citizens*. Toronto.

Manitoba. Aboriginal Justice Inquiry. 1991. Report. Winnipeg: Government Services.

Metro Toronto. Community Forum. 1993. *Combatting Hate Group Activity and Racist Attacks: Report of the Proceedings of Community Forum*. November 4.

Metro Toronto. Task Force on Human Relations. 1977. *Now Is Not Too Late*. Vols. 1 and 2. W. Pitman. Toronto: Council of Metro Toronto.

Nova Scotia. Provincial Royal Commission on the Donald Marshall Jr. Prosecution. 1989. *Digest of Findings and Recommendations*. Halifax.

Ontario. Commission of Inquiry into Systemic Racism in the Ontario Criminal Justice System. 1993. *Racism Behind Bars, Interim Report*. Toronto: Queen's Printer.

Ontario. Lieutenant Governor's Office. 1976. *Royal Commission Into Metropolitan Toronto Police Practices*. The Hon. Mr. Justice Donald. R. Morand, Commissioner. Toronto.

Ontario. Ministry of the Attorney General. 1987. *Task Force on the Law Concerning Trespass to Publicly-Used Property as It Affects Youth and Minorities*. Raj Anand, Chair. Toronto.

Ontario. Task Force on Race Relations and Policing. 1989. *Report*. Clare Lewis. Toronto: Queen's Park.

Ontario. Task Force on the Racial and Ethnic Implications of Police Hirings, Training, Promotions, and Career Development. 1980. *Policing in Ontario for the Eighties: Perceptions and Reflections*. Reva Gerstein, chair. Toronto: Ministry of the Solicitor General.

Ontario. 1992. *Report on Race Relations in Ontario*. S. Lewis. June. Toronto: Queen's Park.

Quebec. Human Rights Commission. 1988. *Investigation Into Relations Between Police Forces, Visible and Other Ethnic Minorities*. Jacques Bellemare, chair. Montreal: Commission des droits de la personne du Québec.

"GETTING BAIL": IDEOLOGY IN ACTION

Gail Kellough

INTRODUCTION

The criminal justice system has been described as a "morality play" (Ericson and Baranek 1982) and, to carry the analogy further, it is a play to which all members of society have season tickets. There is no sociological subject to which we have been more exposed: we are bombarded daily with news reports of police activities and court cases. A majority of our entertainment features the commission of crime, its detection, and prosecution. The very prevalence of the topic as the subject of news and entertainment establishes a common set of definitions for public discussion about crime, criminals, and punishment.

Behind the scenes of the sensational dramas depicted in our daily newspapers and on our television screens is another series of plays taking place daily on thousands of courtroom stages. Despite a lack of admission charge, these productions do not attract a general audience. Largely unattended and depicting a more mundane and less exciting reality, they are nevertheless inextricably linked to the larger morality play. The statistical and conceptual background, which gives meaning to such terms as "crime," "criminals," or "legal rights," originates in the finales of the mini-dramas that take place at court.

Although there is a connection between public and private crime dramas, to become a member of the courtroom audience is to venture into a venue where generally accepted meanings of fundamental legal precepts do not seem to apply. Although each of these small courtroom productions claims to be a rendering of the same legal script, what occurs in the courtroom often appears to be guided by an alien and alienating assortment of set directions. Occasionally newspaper reports of controversial courtroom judgments reveal a deviation from legal orthodoxy, but more frequently it is academic research that reports a systematic gap between the theory of law and its practice.

The courtrooms that create the largest number of outcomes on a daily basis are those with the mandate to decide the immediate fate of individuals who have been arrested for a criminal offence but who have not yet been tried. The "show cause" hearing, as it has come to be called, is commenced before a justice of the peace without the same formality and attention to legal procedure that is observed at other stages of the criminal justice process.[1] Both the layout of the courtroom and the process that is observed suggest the starring role has been reserved for the justice of the peace. It is the responsibility of this person to decide the winner and loser of each legal contest and to sign the court order that will officially release or detain the accused. In acknowledgment of the stature of the justice of the peace role, he or she sits in an elevated position in the courtroom. All the other actors acknowledge his/her comings and goings with deference, and they will accede to his/her dictates concerning the process to be observed. What is less obvious to the casual courtroom observer is the degree to which this judicial role is a more or less symbolic one: the instrumentality of the role will depend on the information that is presented or withheld by other courtroom actors. The availability of decision-making information is, in turn, dependent on decisions that take place behind the scenes.

Other members of the regular cast include Crown attorneys (always a provincial Crown and sometimes a federal Crown), defence attorneys (always a duty counsel and frequently lawyers from the private bar), and a variety of clerks, court reporters, and other officials employed by the Toronto Police Department and the Ministry of the Attorney General. The bulk of the characters who will appear in this courtroom are irregular performers, some appearing for the first time and some making a repeat performance. Most will not have speaking parts but the various acts presented on any given day will take shape around their appearance. Although the accused are hardly distinguishable from one another, this group of men (and occasionally women) are the reason for the proceedings. For the most part, their role is a passive one and they are moved in and out of the prisoner's box, four or five at a time, frequently making repeat appearances over the course of the day. Periodically their identity is confused, and once in a while they will spark moments of unscripted mirth among the rest of the cast. To complete the cast complement, a few members of the audience will usually be asked to take part in the proceedings, testifying either for or against a particular accused.

In this chapter, I begin with an abridged description of a day in the life of a Toronto bail court, a day that provided the impetus for my research into pretrial decision-making. This depiction has elements that I later came to understand to be typical of an average day at bail court and others that are not so typical. To understand the decisions that were made in this courtroom and the manner in which they can be justified in law, it is necessary to comprehend both the major themes of the legal script and the behind-the-scenes decisions that have gone into producing and directing the activity of the formal proceedings. Thus, this chapter will also describe the fundamentals of Canadian law concerning pretrial release, relate some research findings concerning the "gap" between law and its administration, and from my own research elaborate on the procedural context in which the deviation is constructed.

A DAY IN THE LIFE OF COURTROOM 101

During the summer of 1992, I attended and observed proceedings in Courtroom 101, a bail court at Old City Hall in the city of Toronto. This courtroom houses one of the busiest, if not the busiest, bail courts in Canada. The approximately 50 individuals whose names appear on the day's court docket have been charged and arrested by the police, and a variety of legal actors are now authorized to distinguish between those accused who should be detained in custody until their trial and those who might be released, with or without conditions. What is being depicted on this day, as on past and future days, is a series of decisions concerning the immediate fate of individuals who are charged with the commission of an offence but who have yet to stand trial. Whether the ensuing drama can be described as a farce or a tragedy depends on the perspective of the viewer.

The formal events in this particular court begin at 9:00 a.m. when the justice arrives. However, to a neophyte observer, as I was on this morning, it appears that the real business of the day is never going to begin. Although the police immediately escort four or five accused into the prisoner's box, all are "held down" — a term denoting that they are to be brought back to the prisoner's box at a later time during the day. Some individuals are held down because private counsel has not yet made an appearance, while for others the necessary paperwork has not yet been received. This coming and going of individuals in the prisoner's dock continues for about an hour with intermittent messages from private lawyers requesting that their clients be "held over" until the next day's proceedings. During this first hour, a number of prisoners indicate they have no lawyer or have been unsuccessful in contacting one, and they are spoken to by the duty counsel. This consultation takes place in one corner of the prisoner's box while other individuals are brought in, held down, and taken out.

Following the "private" conversation between prisoner and duty counsel, several accused agree to her representation. A few are held down so further enquiries can be made but the duty counsel is able to assist finally in the disposal of several cases on the docket. One accused asks to be traversed to another courtroom to enter a guilty plea, several are held over until the following day so private counsel can be contacted, and one achieves an agreement for his release following a further private conference between the Crown and duty counsel. The Crown stipulates the terms of this bail will include a requirement for one or more sureties in the amount of one thousand dollars, and conditions that compel the accused to report once a week to the police station and to refrain from having contact with the alleged victim. The justice repeats the terms of the agreement for the court record but does not ask about the offence or the reasons for these particular conditions. At 10:00 a.m., when all of the prisoners have appeared at least once, the justice calls for a short recess. By this time the only knowledge I have gained about the prisoners or the allegations against them is the information that appears on the day's printed docket.

Following the morning recess, lawyers for a number of the accused have arrived and a few others have relayed messages requesting that their clients be held over. Before proceedings begin again, however, the justice of the peace informs the court that one of the hearings is expected to be abnormally lengthy. Because it is expected that this bail hearing will require two or three hours of the court's time, it is to be held immediately following an early noon break. The justice announces that prior to this break the court will handle as many cases as possible; the rest will either be held down until the conclusion of the atypical bail hearing or will be held over until the next day.

Prior to the beginning of the lengthy bail hearing a further number of accused are released on consent of the Crown. For the majority of these "consent releases," the court orders a release requirement of a surety bail coupled with a variety of court-ordered conditions. Although little information is given about these cases, the Crown does inform the court that in one instance release is not being contested because the charge of "fail to appear" has been dropped; the accused had been unable to raise the surety stipulated by his bail release order so he was still in custody at the time he was required to report.

Although most of the activity in and out of the prisoner box resulted in hold-downs, hold-overs, traversals, and consent releases, a number of contested hearings were conducted.[2] A description of two of these is illustrative of a typical contested hearing and one that was decidedly untypical, at least in its length and the attention given to it. The two cases make an interesting contrast for considering bail practices and bail law.

Joseph J. (46 years of age) was no stranger to the courtroom. His criminal record stretched over 20 years and all registered convictions against him were for minor crimes against property. His current charge was of a similar nature: the theft of a pair of socks from a Toronto department store. At the time of his arrest, the accused was living in a rooming house where he had resided for just under one year. He had worked only sporadically during the past number of years, subsisting on welfare and, the Crown argued, on the wages of petty crime. His only family living in the city was a brother with whom he no longer had any contact. Although he apparently had a number of friends living in the same rooming house, there was no possible surety and no one appeared at court on his behalf.

Because Joseph J. had no possible surety, defence counsel informed the court that representatives from the Toronto Bail Program had been asked to interview him and were willing to undertake his supervision during the remand period. Although the defence agreed that the record for minor property offences was lengthy, he pointed out that there were no convictions for failure to appear or for failure to comply with a court order. The Crown agreed that this, coupled with his stable address, was assurance enough that Mr. J. would appear at trial to face his charges. However, the Crown maintained that the bail program was unable to provide the supervision necessary to prevent the commission of further offences. Because detention was being requested on the basis of a risk to community safety and because bail program staff were not available on a 24-hour basis, it was the opinion of the Crown that program staff could not adequately address the concerns of the court. Moreover, the Crown argued that, with no person willing to take a financial risk on behalf of the accused, a substantial likelihood existed that the accused would indeed be inclined to add to his already lengthy record.

The hearing for Joseph J. took between 10 and 15 minutes with the justice concurring that the Crown had shown cause for keeping the accused in custody. He dismissed the defence's suggestion that the accused could be given a condition banning him from the victimized business, stating that the accused had never been selective in his choice of victims and a court order banning him from all business establishments would simply invite a breach.

John A. (35 years of age) was represented by an associate from one of Toronto's top law firms. He was charged with uttering death threats and with failure to comply with the conditions of a previous release order. Awaiting trial on previous charges of assaulting his ex-partner, he was now alleged to have violated the bail condition that prohibited contact with the victim. The current allegations resulted from an alleged stalking of his ex-partner and her parents on an afternoon two days prior to the court hearing. It came out in testimony that although the police had been contacted on the evening of the alleged offence they were unable to arrest the accused because he had unexpectedly (and uncharacteristically) been out of town on business on the previous day. Upon advice of his counsel, he had turned himself in early on the morning of the hearing. John A. was dressed in a suit and tie, and unlike his fellow accused he would have looked perfectly at home sitting with his lawyers.

Because John A. was already on release pending trial for assault, the onus for showing cause shifted from the Crown to the accused. As in the case of Joseph J., the concern of the court was not the risk of a failure to appear: John A. was employed, had a stable residence, and had no previous charges for failing to appear at court. As for the secondary grounds of community security, John A. had no previous convictions for criminal activity so the risk of release was confined to a danger to the current victim. On one other occasion he had been charged with assaulting the same victim but the charges had been withdrawn. The information about previous allegations of assault were submitted to illustrate an ongoing pattern of violence that placed the victim at risk. The Crown called several witnesses: the parents of the victim each gave testimony (with the use of an interpreter) about their daughter's fear of the accused, and a police officer testified concerning evidence that the Crown would present at trial. Allegedly, the accused had continued to follow and torment the victim ever since he had been released on the original charges. Because witnesses were available to testify to this pattern of harassment, the Crown argued that the case was strong enough to justify detaining the accused in order to protect the victim.

Although the accused could not be interrogated about any allegations before the court, he did volunteer the information that he was in the same area as the victim and her parents only to visit his sister who lived in the vicinity. His lawyer also noted that his law firm was located in the same area as the victim's place of employment and the accused's continued presence in this locality was necessary for purposes of legal consultation. Stressing that the accused would plead "not guilty" to the charges, the defence lawyer then focused the presentation of evidence on demonstrating that the accused could safely be released in the interim through a prudent use of bail conditions and the supervision of a surety. The accused's father and sister testified as potential sureties. The father owned a home outside Toronto valued at half-a-million dollars, and his sister owned a condominium in Toronto valued at a quarter-of-a-million dollars. Both were willing to put their property at risk if the court would order a surety release for the accused. The father was willing to have his son move in with him until the completion of a trial and to supervise him accordingly. To further ensure the safety of the victim an area prohibition could be placed on his movements by placing the entire city of Toronto off-limits. The father further stated his willingness to accompany the accused to the lawyer's office whenever a consultation was necessary.

The justice of the peace accepted the alternatives posed by the defence as reasonable, naming the father and sister as sureties on a fifteen-thousand-dollar bail with conditions that prohibited any contact with the victim and any entry into Toronto unless accompanied by the father. The hearing for John A. was most untypical in its length, taking approximately three hours (including an afternoon recess) of the court's time.

The two defendants had only two things in common: the Crown opposed their release on bail and both were white. In the waiting room, however, where family and friends waited to testify as potential witnesses or sureties for other individuals on the day's docket, most were not white. By the time the unusually lengthy bail hearing had concluded most of the lawyers who would have called them to testify had come and gone. I spoke with some of the members of this group and heard their distress about the necessity or impossibility of returning to court on the following day. For the few accused who had managed to secure bail before court was adjourned for the day the court did not name any particular individuals as sureties acceptable to the court. When the surety is not named at court a decision that the good character and personal wealth of the potential surety are acceptable has to be made by another justice, usually with the Crown's consent (Trotter 1987–1988). If any of these prospective sureties should be found unacceptable, the accused's consent release order will translate into further detention.[3] There was, therefore, no guarantee that those who waited to testify on behalf of an accused or who chose to return the following day would actually serve in a surety capacity.

THE SCRIPT: PRECEPTS OF INNOCENCE, EQUALITY, AND SOCIAL DEFENCE

The mandate of the bail court is to determine whether persons accused of a crime and arrested by the police should be detained in jail, released with some specific supervisory conditions, or released on their own agreement to appear for trial. What makes this decision problematic is that any limitation on the liberty of accused persons prior to trial "does great damage to a most fundamental principle of criminal law — *innocent until proven guilty*" (Boyd 1983, 260; emphasis added).

Canadian law clearly specifies that persons accused of crimes are to be considered "innocent until proven guilty in a court of law." The 1982 *Canadian Charter of Rights and Freedoms* entrenches this ethical principle in its statement that any person charged with an offence is "to be presumed innocent until proven guilty according to law in a fair and public hearing by an independent and impartial tribunal" (s. 11(*d*)). In the same vein a presumption of innocence until guilt is proven is implied in the Charter's guarantees of individual liberty: "Everyone has the right to life, liberty and security of the person and the right not to be deprived thereof except in accordance with the principles of fundamental justice" (s. 7) and "everyone has the right not to be arbitrarily detained or imprisoned (s. 9).

The Charter is not the only legislation that pertains to bail practices. More than a decade prior to its enactment, Parliament had considered the problem of bail in relation to another fundamental legal principle: that of *equality before the law*. Historically the function of bail was to ensure that an alleged offender would attend future court dates in order to answer the criminal allegations, and the provision of a sum of cash was the means of providing this assurance. This practice undermined equality of treatment because only those with financial resources could claim their legal right to a presumption of innocence. With the passing of the *Bail Reform Act* in 1970, monetary resources were no longer to be the major determinant of detention or release. The Act stipulated a presumption that *release would be the norm*, and (in most instances) the onus would be placed on the Crown to demonstrate "just cause" for any form of liberty restriction. The Charter reinforced this presumption in its stipulation that an accused is "not to be denied reasonable bail without just cause" (s. 11(*e*)). The provisions in Section 15 further address the equality issues of bail decision-making in the statement that "every individual ... has the right to the equal protection and equal benefit of the law without discrimination...."

Common law traditions emphasize the fundamental nature of the principles of innocence and equality, but Canadian law enforcement is also grounded in another basic principle: social defence (Cragg 1992, 184). Reflecting this concern, the *Criminal Code* stipulates that in the event that detention is not justified on the primary grounds of ensuring attendance at trial, the court may still consider whether

> his detention is necessary in the public interest or for the protection or safety of the public, having regard to all the circumstances including any substantial likelihood that the accused will, if he is released from custody, commit a criminal offence involving serious harm or an interference with the administration of justice. (*Criminal Code*, s. 457(7))

According to current Canadian law full release can only be denied if there is a risk the accused might not appear for trial, or if there is a risk the accused will commit further offences. Unlike American law, Canadian law does not specify the categories of offences for which preventive detention may be considered. Because the presumption of release applies to all accused with few exceptions the allegations are not the major determinant for considering the need for detention, although such allegations may be considered within the totality of the court's consideration.

The *Charter of Rights and Freedoms* guarantees Canadians rights of liberty and equality "subject only to such reasonable limits prescribed by law as can be demonstrably justified in a free and democratic society." The limits that the law considers justifiable are the risk that an accused will fail to appear or the risk posed to societal security. The *Bail Reform Act* and the *Criminal Code* provide a legal framework for professionals to decide whether these risks are sufficiently serious to justify limiting an individual's liberty rights by custodial detention prior to trial or whether other measures will accomplish the same objectives without unduly restricting liberty. The spirit of bail legislation also dictates that status considerations are to be considered relevant only to the extent that they are shown to be pertinent to the allowable exceptions.

THE "GAP" BETWEEN LEGAL PRINCIPLE AND LEGAL PRACTICE

The literature on pretrial detention in countries with an adversarial model of justice illustrates that "the 'innocent until proven guilty' principle has never seemed to deter the holding of individuals who have yet to be found guilty of a crime" (Eskridge 1983, 11). "While laws governing release practices typically state a presumption of release, actual release practices do not embody such a presumption" (Toborg 1981, 61). On any day in Ontario, one-third of the total number of persons confined in institutions are held in pretrial custody. Clearly the norm of unconditional release operates differently in practice than in theory. The majority of individuals imprisoned as remand prisoners are detained on secondary grounds. Moreover, like Joseph J., a large number of persons being detained by the courts "are not accused of violent or strongly anti-social offenses and thus do not pose a true danger to the community" (Brockett 1971, 21). When a nonviolent property crime of an accused is considered within the purview of secondary grounds, his detention would not appear to be "in keeping with the spirit of the reforms of the Bail Reform Act; that it was in fact detaining him because of his previous convictions and assuming that he was guilty now as charged, before his trial" (Watt 1973–1974, 46).

To meet the social defence objective by means of pretrial custody is a costly endeavour, for both society and the accused. A "defendant who is detained on a petty theft involving a few dollars may cost the government thousands of dollars" (Schlesinger 1989, 178). Moreover, there are also secondary impacts of such court decisions. "Those subjected to any protracted period of pretrial detention will likely lose their jobs, which will result in their families joining the welfare rolls" (Eskridge 1983, 12). The costs of pretrial detention might be considered legitimate providing that a measure of reliability is demonstrated for the risk-assessment process. Yet study after study has shown that "predicting a defendant's propensity to commit crime while on pretrial release is at present nearly impossible" (Goldkamp 1979). As Boyd argues, "the great majority of the persons predicted to be dangerous turn out to be 'false positives' (persons predicted as likely to be dangerous but who in fact will not display such behavior)" (1983, 254). One study that examined overprediction errors concluded that "nineteen defendants would have to be inappropriately detained in order to prevent a single pretrial arrest" (Eskridge 1983, 124). Others have demonstrated that there would have to be a substantial increase in detention, with its attendant costs, to achieve even a very modest decline in pretrial crime. On the other hand, "available evidence strongly suggests that more defendants could be released pending trial and that rates of failure to appear and pretrial criminality would not increase substantially, if at all" (Toborg 1981, 52, cf. Friedland 1965; Bottomley 1970; Angel et al. 1971; Flemming 1982; Thomas 1976).

Although the assessment of dangerousness has been said to be "less accurate than the flip of a coin" (Boyd 1983, 249), a short-term loss of liberty could arguably be a reasonable exchange for even a minimal degree of social defence, except for one disturbing correlation: pretrial detention, for whatever reason, is consistently correlated with a more severe disposition (Beeley [1927, 1966; Morse and Beattie 1932; Foote et al. 1954; Alexender et al. 1958; Ares, Rankin, and Sturz 1963; Rankin 1964; Wald 1964; Friedland 1965; Single 1972; Brockett 1971; Landes 1974; Koza and Doob 1974–1975; Doob and Cavoukian 1977; Goldkamp 1985, 1977, 1979; Wheeler 1981; Eskridge 1983). Even when prior record and type of offence are held constant, differential treatment remains. The probability of a prison sentence has been found to be as much as four times higher for individuals detained prior to trial than for those who were released. Surprisingly, pretrial detainees with no prior record are still more likely to receive prison sentences than pretrial releasees without one (Rankin 1964). This research suggests there is a direct "causal connection between denial of bail on the one hand and conviction, frequency of incarceration, and length of incarceration on the other" (Schlesinger 1989, 177), a fact that belies any rational connection between the law and a preservation of the principles of legal innocence and social defence.

The available empirical evidence suggests that neither presumption of innocence nor preservation of societal security are advanced by decisions that currently result in pretrial detention. The integrity and effectiveness of the risk-assessment process is open to the greatest challenge where there are differential consequences for minority or disadvantaged groups. When there is a direct and unwarranted connection between trial outcome and group affiliation, "the right to liberty" and "the right to be presumed innocent until guilt is proven" become privileges that are more easily claimed by advantaged groups. When pretrial detention is correlated with sentence outcome, the additional correlation between group affiliation and sentence outcome undermines any guarantees of *equality before the law*. Particularly disturbing for civil-rights activists are statistics that indicate women, aboriginal, black, and immigrant groups are disproportionately more likely to be detained prior to their trial and/or more likely to be adversely affected by the process (Brockett 1971; Feeley and McNaughton 1974; Mahaffy 1981; Kellough 1982; Eaton 1987; Steury and Frank 1990; Manitoba 1991).

What is also interesting about those who are incarcerated during the interim between arrest and bail is that the decision-making that results in such detention does not reflect even the most general community consensus concerning the threat to safety. Even a cursory examination of actual patterns of pretrial release and detention reveals a discrepancy between the forms of restrictions that are placed on pretrial liberty and the exaggerated fears and concerns Canadian citizens have about violent crime (Doob 1985). As the previous bail hearings illustrate, detainees are more likely to be drawn from groups with few social resources or more likely to be those with morally questionable lifestyles than those who have been charged with an act of violence. It is these groups who are more likely to be found guilty or plead guilty, sentenced to imprisonment, and given lengthy sentences. In turn, it is these groups who will be represented in the statistics that provide the background for our conceptual understanding of crime and criminals.

DISCRETIONARY DECISION-MAKING BEHIND THE SCENES

To study the criminal justice system is, in its most basic sense, a study of decision-making. Laws can never be specific enough to cover the variety of circumstances that are encompassed by their general intent. At the day-to-day level of justice administration, practitioners are called on to interpret what following "the letter of the law" means. The manner in which such discretion is exercised by authorities at different stages of the criminal justice process has been the subject of a great deal of academic research and theorizing. This work has particular import for policy-makers and social activists because discretionary authority does carry with it the possibility of selective law enforcement against certain groups, or, more simply put, of legal discrimination.

Those who examine discrimination resulting from the exercise of police, Crown, or judicial discretion claim on the one hand that there is a "gap" between legal precept and legal practice, while on the other hand there is an essential connection between the formal dictates of law and the informal "recipe rules" used by decision-makers. These conclusions are not necessarily mutually exclusive. They may both be part of a broader problematic concerning the intersection of social and legal discourses in the creation and maintenance of hegemony. Or, as Boyle argues, the legal code has hegemonic power precisely because it interlocks with the social code at critical junctures (1985, 728). Many of these critical junctures are not visible in the formal process of law. Rather, the decisive events are relegated to a back stage where details relevant to the formal balancing of contradictory legal principles are selected from an array of facts about the life situation of the person who is to appear on the main stage. The information available to make this selection will already have been circumscribed by the particular role the person is expected to play on the legal stage: different social facts will be available according to the needs of the legal script. At each stage of the criminal justice process, the decision-makers who select the information to be presented are helping to recreate a legal mind-set that will act "as the bridge between indefinite words and closure of a finite, albeit fuzzy, social world" (Boyle 1985, 728).

Selecting Information to Justify the Social Order

The majority of decisions concerning the release of an accused person prior to trial are either not made in the courtroom or are shaped by factors that occur prior to a bail hearing. The most obvious instance of nonjudicial decision-making concerns consent releases.[4] Usually, judges follow the prosecutor's recommendation without comment or enquiry. Frequently, "this is because the recommendation is not contested by the defendant's attorney" (Brockett 1971, 15). It is not that defence lawyers never contest the requested surety amount or the imposition of a particular condition, but in most instances the provision of additional information occurs outside the formal process. Of relevance for a defence counsel in deciding to oppose the recommendation of the Crown is the availability of a surety: any accused who does not have a potential surety at court will risk a detention order at a contested hearing.

Despite the prevalence of precourt agreements between defence and Crown attorneys, such negotiations do not always appear to be legally mandated. More than one interpreter of release provisions have stated that where the Crown does not show cause the primary duty of the court is to release the accused upon his giving an undertaking without conditions ... where the prosecutor cannot show cause... the justice has no discretion to release the accused in any way other than by an undertaking without conditions... *The prosecutor may not wish to show cause in which case the accused must be released upon his undertaking without conditions.* (Watt 1973–1974, 17,33; emphasis added; Canada 1988)

A literal interpretation of the law is that unless the accused is being released on his/her own undertaking, without conditions, the Crown must demonstrate the necessity for a greater infringement on liberty. However, most of the release orders arrived at by consent of the Crown do include stipulations concerning the provision of one or more sureties and conditions designed to restrict or compel particular kinds of behaviour. What appears to be occurring in these prehearing negotiations is that the Crown is demonstrating necessity for restrictions of liberty only to the defence attorney. Such informal practices "places in the hands of the prosecutorial authorities what would intuitively appear to be a judicial function" (Trotter 1987–1988, 239), but they also illustrate the frequency with which defence counsel accept the "recipe rules" for handling particular kinds of populations (Ericson and Baranek 1982).

Despite the law that exists to define pretrial liberty, prosecutorial powers at this stage are exceedingly vague. In Ontario there is an informal practice whereby Crown attorneys, after the bail hearing and prior to the accused being released, decide on the sufficiency of a proposed surety put forward by the accused, and make predictions without procedural safeguards designed to protect individuals accused of criminal offences (Trotter 1987–1988). Since justices of the peace are not required to specify their reasons for reaching a particular conclusion, it is not surprising that Crown attorneys do not have to do so. Although there is no formal accountability for the majority of discretionary decisions made by the Crown, presumably the accountability is encompassed within the "Minister of Justice" role they are expected to play. In this capacity, a Crown is expected to seek justice rather than simply perform the adversarial task of seeking imprisonment for all those who have been charged. However, where no formal measures of accountability are present, evidence would suggest that the Minister of Justice role is breached more frequently than it is observed (Grosman 1980).

Information is the fodder that permits decisions to be made. Observation at bail court does not provide details about the variety of information available for Crown decision-making concerning any particular accused. Neither does it permit conclusions about the degree to which police are able to influence these decisions. The major piece of information in the Crown's arsenal is a confidential document, termed the "show cause" statement, or "dope sheet." This information is prepared by the arresting officer, and while it contains the police opinion about the character of the accused and a recommendation concerning his/her pretrial fate, the document is not made available for refutation by defence counsel. It is not unreasonable to hypothesize that given the time available for the

Crown to scrutinize the files that police may be exercising undue judicial discretion for reasons that are not prescribed by law. The following excerpts from show cause statements about (1) a woman charged with "communicating for the purpose of prostitution" and (2) a man charged with domestic assault are illustrative of police information on "show cause" documents:

[1] The accused should be held in custody until she can answer to her present charges, for the following reasons:

- in her short career as a criminal she has amassed 3 fail to appear courts. Will she go for 4 if she is released?
- she is a Crack addict who openly refuses treatment.
- she has no respect for the justice system of the public. she demonstrated this to the arresting officers, whom she berated with obscenities and other foulnesses.
- in the process of fulfilling her crack addiction, she disrupts the lives of the normal citizens who are forced to live nearby. Her lewd acts confront children on their way to school or church.
- it is time the Courts, Police and the Community work together to show the accused that her disregard, and contempt for all, will not be tolerated.
- she is uncooperative with police and also has convictions on her record for Attempt obstruct Justice and Obstructing police officer.
- the investigating officer is not prepared to suggest any conditions for her release and is of the opinion that should the accused be released she will only continue to commit further offences of a similar nature.

Detention Order a Must.

[2] The accused is on a probation for a dissimilar offence. The accused appears to have an alcohol problem but he has only one conviction on his record. Since the accused's wife is in great fear of his release, it is the opinion of this officer that should the court see fit to release him, the following conditions should apply:

1. not to associate or communicate with Mrs. [...]
2. not to be within 500 metres of [victim's address]
3. abstain from the consumption of alcohol
4. seek treatment for alcohol abuse
5. carry bail papers on his person at all times

These differences in moral tone characterize police recommendations for different types of offences and for different types of offenders.[5] The police do not always recommend detention but are particularly heavy-handed with regard to the conditions they wish to see imposed, even where there is no apparent relation to the offence now before the court. The variety of conditions that prohibit alcohol or drug use and that impose various kinds of treatment rest on common assumptions about the correlation between lifestyle and a proclivity to commit crime. Those that impose curfews and require the carrying of bail papers equip police officers with an additional power resource in their future interactions with the accused.

Although the stated purpose for limiting pretrial freedom is not to promote the traditional aims of punishment, the justifications of retribution, deterrence, and rehabilitation are as much a part of pretrial decision-making as they are at the sentencing stage after a finding of guilt. The police provide information about accused persons and suggest conditions designed to rectify problems of lifestyle as frequently as they do for conditions related to the current charge. The following recommendation for detention in one police brief concerns a woman charged only with mischief for breaking a window:

> The accused has an addiction to cocaine and also alcohol. The accused should not only remain in custody to expidite proceedings against her but also to provide her with a period to "dry out" and possibly maintain a more productive life style.

Although the Crown may not accept this recommendation for detention, it is also likely that a condition prohibiting alcohol and drug use will be part of any release order that is made. It is not unreasonable to suggest that in the absence of other information Crown attorneys will be influenced by uncorroborated police information. If the information is correct, the release of this woman will mean she risks further punishment on the basis of addiction alone. Where unrelated release conditions become part of the release order, the accused will still be subject to further arrest "for an actual or anticipated violation of these conditions ... and the violation is itself an offence ... which offence may be prosecuted summarily or by indictment" (Watt 1973–1974, 40).

Many of the conditions placed on accused persons both increase the power of the police to control problematic populations and invite future charges of failure to comply. This is particularly true in the case of area prohibitions placed on prostitutes, drug or alcohol prohibitions placed on addicts, and curfews or the carrying of bail papers placed on any who are viewed as requiring control of movement. Should such breaches occur, however, they are frequently a secondary charge that buttress the police's primary reason for arrest, and such charges are more likely to be dropped in return for a plea of guilty on the main charge. Other kinds of breaches that serve the same purpose relate to the accused's failure to appear at court. Before a trial date is actually set, the accused will have been required to attend at set-date court on many occasions over a period of months even though the typical outcome of these court appearances is a further adjournment. Like the breach of another condition, a failure to appear charge results in the onus for showing cause being reversed.[6] For such cases, even where detention is not ordered, the surety amount is typically increased. One accused interviewed in custody[7] gave the following account of his detention following a fail to appear on an original charge of drug possession:

> Duty counsel agreed with the Crown for a $2000 surety, double my last bail which they said I failed to appear on. Duty counsel did not tell the court that this wasn't intentional. I told her I couldn't raise that but the Crown said otherwise

he would go for D.O. So I agreed but no-one tried for Bail Program. I've been in here a week now, [s]o, I will plead guilty to get the time served and get out.

The law that permits a wide discretionary scope for the placing of bail conditions also creates new opportunities for rearrest of individuals who have been released on bail. Such opportunities, however, are not distributed equally. For those who are originally charged with certain kinds of offences certain conditions are the norm (for example, area conditions for prostitutes or drug addicts) and there is a high risk that those who commit these offences will breach the condition. As these groups accumulate these breaches on their record, they become more likely to be subjected to a detention order on future charges. Indeed, many prostitutes serve more time in pretrial custody than the sentence they receive at trial. For many, it therefore makes sense to plead guilty immediately regardless of the evidence against them. One prostitute explained this decision as follows:

> The Crown was seeking my detention, probably because of the number of convictions I have for prostitution. I didn't want to wait for my lawyer and do dead time, so I instructed the duty counsel to traverse my case. I pleaded the next day and got fifteen days.

At contested hearings, the legal grounds for which a detention order is sought are frequently obscure. Particular lifestyle factors about the accused are presented in ways that might support detention on either primary or secondary grounds. Yet, according to Watt "the applicability of the secondary ground should be determined only in the event that and after it is determined that the accused's detention is *not* justified on the primary ground" (1973–74, 47). In other words, the reasons for limiting freedom should be confined to one or the other of the allowable grounds, but not both. In practice, most of the factors considered relevant for showing cause on the primary grounds are used to illustrate the dangerousness of a particular accused. Primary ground factors such as

> the accused's ties in the community, his job status, his assets or lack of same, his marital status, the seriousness of the charge he faces, whether he has ever failed to appear in court on previous occasions or has a record for escaping lawful custody, any difficulties encountered in arresting or apprehending the accused, the strength or weakness of the Crown's case....(Watt 1973–1974, 47)

are also the factors that are used to illustrate secondary ground concerns. This collapsing of evidence and grounds for limiting freedom provides a greater amount of flexibility in the showing of cause and allows any social factor about a particular accused to be selected. Because the Crown is not required to document the relevant grounds, it is not always possible to determine which ground is being argued or the ground upon which the court's judgment is based.[8] In instances where the grounds are stated in court, both are frequently cited.

From the perspective of an accused who is detained or given a surety requirement that cannot be met, the omission of positive factors about their personal background is the greatest source of their discontent with the court's judgment. Interviews with inmates in remand custody in Toronto elicited the following types of comments:

> My lawyer sent an associate and he did not know anything about my case or my situation. He could have mentioned that I turned myself in on the only "fail to appear" on my record. I have medical problems and have to see a doctor every day; sometimes this makes me too weak to walk. This lawyer did not know about this reason nor that I turned myself in. He also could have brought up the large number of times I have NOT failed to appear at court. He just swore me in and asked me questions about whether I support my children, where I live, what is my work history, nothing that would show I always appear. Because I had a failure to appear, the J.P. said D.O.

> The Crown said I was a danger but I don't see how I am a danger. There has never been any violence in my record but this wasn't stated as a reason why I am not dangerous. All the convictions are property offences so how is this a danger to others? I am more of a harm to myself than to society, so if they had detained me to protect myself, maybe I could see it ... to protect others, no I don't think so.

> The last three and a half years didn't mean a damn thing to the court. During that time, I had no charges, I got a job, completed my upgrading from grade 9 to grade 11 and have been attempting to provide support for my children. They don't consider the positives — no matter what good things you have going for you.

The lack of guidelines in the law as to what factors should be considered as evidence of risk and the merging of primary and secondary grounds in practice allows the Crown, in contested hearings, to select negative information from reports supplied by the police. One assumes that in consent releases a similar process of selecting positive factors from police reports is at work.

Another way in which police decision-making can affect the likelihood of detention, and subsequently the plea of the accused, relates to the number and type of charges each accused faces at the initial bail hearing. Although this is another piece of information for the Crown to take into consideration, a majority of the charges that appear on the bail-court docket will eventually be withdrawn or reduced prior to trial. Many of these may be inflated charges that would not be provable at trial, but the strength of the case for a particular charge is difficult to determine at a bail hearing. It is difficult to determine because a defence of the charge is not allowable during procedures that have been specifically designed for deciding about pretrial release.

The *Criminal Code* states that an "accused shall not be examined or cross-examined by the justice or any other person as to the offence with which he is charged, and no inquiry shall be made of him as to that offence" (s. 457.3(1)(*b*)). No such examination is allowed because guilt or innocence is not a relevant factor for bail decision-making. In practice, this means a Crown who elects to show cause on the secondary grounds will implicitly imply guilt that the accused cannot defend against. Because the assessment of secondary reason rests on the assumption that charges are validly laid, the defence counsel is prevented from examining his or her own client as to the facts or circumstances concerning a charge that is suspect and will never hold up at trial. What has been legislated to protect accused people winds up suppressing what they may say in their own defence. As one inmate put it, "you're really assumed to be guilty because you can't use anything at your hearing to show you are innocent."

While the accused cannot provide a defence of the charge at a bail hearing, evidence that would not be admissible at trial is considered relevant for making the release decision. The courts have "held that the strict rules of evidence applicable to criminal trials were not applicable on judicial interim release hearings" (Watt 1973–1974, 35). What is allowable to show danger goes beyond what is allowable at a trial. For example, allegations of crimes made against an accused for which a formal conviction is not obtained are not admissible at trial but such allegations are a factor that will help the court to predict dangerousness during the pretrial period. At trial personal characteristics and lifestyle circumstances of the accused are only relevant at the sentencing stage when guilt has been proven, but at the bail hearing these factors are considered necessary information because they determine the kinds of conditions that will reduce the risks associated with release. Moreover, to reach a conclusion about the magnitude of the court's concerns does not require a criminal burden of proof: "the burden is the civil burden of satisfying the tribunal on a balance of probabilities" (Watt 1973–1974, 42; also see Cohen 1988)

Based on a balance of probabilities, the bail court predicts risks in order to address and prevent them. The favoured method for doing so is the provision of a surety release order. The theory behind the use of surety bail "is that an accused will be deterred from absconding and thus inflicting a loss on his sureties who will normally be friends or relatives" (Canada 1969). Despite this historical relation between primary concerns and surety release, the amount of the surety condition has become the main method for dealing with secondary concerns. Where the potential for surety bail is nonexistent, the existence of the Toronto Bail Program presumably prevents surety release from becoming another form of cash bail. However, the Crown usually argues at contested hearings that the program is not a viable alternative for addressing secondary concerns. Because individuals frequently are placed under the program's supervision where the primary grounds are not an issue, what is apparently meant is that the court believes the bail program cannot address secondary concerns for individuals with certain kinds of backgrounds. To presume that surety release is a more effective safeguard against dangerousness than supervision without monetary considerations ultimately results in detention according to class, a decided contravention of the spirit of the *Bail Reform Act*.

According to the Law Reform Commission of Canada (Canada 1988), rules of criminal procedure are to be carried out with no more interference with liberty than is necessary. If financial resources are not to be a main determinant of release, then sureties would have to be set in accordance with the ability of an accused to raise them. Otherwise they simply become another form of detention order for those who do not pose a risk, or a means of avoiding detention for those who do constitute a danger: low bails may not be met by some detainees and high bails intended as a deterrent may have no effect at all.

Despite the prevalence of surety release, there does not appear to be even an informally agreed upon standard for how the amount of the surety will be determined. An error made by a Crown attorney presenting the terms of a release agreement inadvertently demonstrated the arbitrary nature by which surety amounts are set. Initially, the Crown stated that a surety in the amount of $200 had been agreed upon, but she quickly amended this once she discovered that she had incorrectly read the amount she had written on the accused's file. The original amount she thought adequate was $2,000, but since the prehearing discussion with the defence attorney had resulted in an agreement for a surety in the amount of $200, she proposed that the justice might split the difference and make an order in the amount of $750. While mathematically the defence would appear to be achieving a bargain, in reality the higher bail amount may very well have meant the difference between release or detention. To be detained, for whatever reason, in turn reduces the capacity of an accused to plead not guilty.

Detention: Justifying Discretion by "Encouraging" Guilty Pleas

Legally, there is a distinction between the rights of accused persons and those who have been convicted of a charge. The law is clear that where there is legitimate cause for detention, those who are detained in custody are not to be punished. In practice, however, persons detained in jail prior to sentencing are subjected to worse living conditions than are sentenced prisoners. "The individual who awaits trial behind bars... suffers the worst of two worlds: he suffers the loss of freedom that is enjoyed by those who are able to make bail and he is denied many of the benefits and privileges that are granted to sentenced persons in the inmate community" (Brockett 1971, 18). Overcrowding is the norm, communication with the outside community is restricted by formal and informal procedures, and security is more intense than at the institutions to which some of these detainees will eventually be sentenced. Remanded inmates do not have access to correctional programs that are available to sentenced prisoners because the imposition of treatment or work inside the institution is a limitation of personal freedom that is reserved for the guilty. This lack of meaningful activity not only makes the waiting time a period of incessant monotony but it also prevents an accused from presenting a positive account of his reform intentions at trial or at sentence. As the rules of evidence at bail hearings end up suppressing what an accused may say in his own defence, rules for treating accused persons in detention centres use the principle of innocence to suppress what he can *do* on his own behalf.

It is not difficult to understand the reason behind the higher rates of conviction and lengthier sentences experienced by remanded inmates. They are not free to assist their attorneys in preparing their defences. They cannot hold a job to pay for counsel's fees and to prove their reliability at trial. The likelihood of a guilty plea is enhanced by the intense psychological stress to which they are subjected. Yet, unlike correctional law statutes, the *Criminal Code* provides no protections that address the right of a person in pretrial custody to make full answer or defence or to substantiate allegations of abuse occurring while in custody (Canada 1988). While specifying that the intent of pretrial detention is not one of punishment, Canadian courts have been generally silent about the rights of the individual detained in jail before trial. The result is that more concern has been legally expressed for "the liberty of a parolee who has already been convicted of a crime than it was about a presumptively innocent person who has not been convicted of the charged crime, may not in fact have committed the crime, and may never commit a crime if released pending trial" (Cohen 1988, 327).

Plea bargaining is encouraged by both the process of deciding on detention and the actual conditions of that detention. This is particularly true for those who have been charged with a minor offence. To reject a plea frequently means serving more time in custody prior to sentence. Suspects who are not granted release or cannot meet the surety requirement of their release order quickly realize the wisdom of making a bargain. The reversal of onus where the original charge is weak is particularly troublesome because it not only increases their chances of detention but can lead to a plea of guilty where such guilt could not be proven.

When asked to describe how a failure to receive bail might affect their cases, remanded inmates gave the following accounts for why they would choose to plead guilty:

> You only get your clothes changed once a week in here; that's ridiculous. They just sprayed the other day for cockroaches and you get bugs in your food. I'll plead guilty to get out of here. This is my first time in jail. I feel sick about being here, sometimes I can't eat. I'll plead because I want to go home really badly.

> Dead time counts double against you because it not only does not have to be considered in sentencing but you don't get your "good time" taken off (as when you are sentenced). I am forced to make a deal but it's not really a deal. You would get the same kind of deal if you were out of custody because you could maintain your work and all those other things that count with judges.

> Who wants to sit around and do dead time. If I could spend the 8 or 9 months period until my trial outside of custody and if I don't screw up, then my "clean time" (with no convictions) will go from 4 1/2 years to 5. This will make a good showing in court if I am convicted so it's not just the problem of coping with jail conditions.

> Doing the dead time is the worst. I hate dead time because you're just sitting and waiting all day, every day, and it means nothing. Lack of activity is a real

problem. This might sound trivial to other people but you go squirrely sitting around. You don't know how to do your time so it is usually better to plead. Now I have to crack a deal and they know it.

I know that I did not do anything but they will come to make a deal and you take the deal because you have a record and you are fed up with it. There are 5 police officers who will say that they found drugs on me; They don't care how it affects me but because of dead time, you can't really plead not guilty. So when they come with a plea bargain, you just want to get out.

Because of the Detention Order, I'll plead to simple possession if they drop the other charges. This will reduce my dead time and a trial would be months away. If I were on the street, I would fight these charges all the way.

For first-timers in the system, conditions of the jail and anxiety about circumstances on the outside are potent inducements to plea; for those who have experienced detention for previous charges, the impetus is the greater amount of jail time they will accumulate if they do not plead guilty. In either case, the factors that push individuals to this choice have less to do with their guilt or innocence than with the reality of pretrial detention.

"Reasonable Limits": The Intersection of Legal and Social Codes

The presumption of innocence for all accused, regardless of allegation, means that categories of offences do not form the basis for limiting liberty during the pretrial period. In the absence of guidelines for predicting risk, decisions are made on whatever information is made available by legal actors. The dependence of the judiciary on information supplied by the Crown and the dependence of the Crown on police information coupled with the lack of formal accountability for decision-making about bail makes it difficult to see who is providing the judicial function. Positive information about an accused is most readily available when it is provided by the police in their confidential recommendations, or by a defence lawyer prepared to spend an untypical amount of time contesting the Crown's decisions. The reality of police work and the amount of money defence lawyers earn by defending clients at bail court ensures a class bias, but it is the law that provides the means by which this bias can be justified on any individual case.

The *Charter of Rights and Freedoms* guarantees Canadians rights of liberty and equality, "subject only to such reasonable limits prescribed by law as can be demonstrably justified in a free and democratic society." The Supreme Court of Canada, under Oakes, has specified that "the constitutionality of a state limit rests on a balancing analysis of whether the good of the legislative objective outweighs the negative effect of the restriction" (Kiselbach 1988–1989, 184). The reasonable limits that are specified in Canada's bail law are the risk that an accused person will not appear at trial or will undermine the safety of citizens. The good of the legislative objective can be said to outweigh the negative so long as the legislation is in practice accomplishing its intent (rationally connected), and with a minimal effect on fundamental rights (liberty and equality). At issue, however, is whether the practices associated with bail courts are rationally connected and whether they are affecting fundamental rights as little as possible. Evidence would suggest that, collectively, they are neither. The public interest is hardly served because the process picks up and detains habitual shoplifters, prostitutes, and substance users but releases the potentially violent. For any particular decision, however, they can reasonably be justified within the terms of the law. The law permits an informal negotiation of information about personal characteristics and social background because legal innocence has rendered legal facts and legal protections irrelevant to the bail decision. Once detained, innocent and guilty are punished alike, and since punishment can best be mitigated through the provision of a plea of guilty, social factors then become the foundation upon which criminal statistics are constructed.

The bail process is a mechanism for systematizing inequality, but this process does not stand on its own outside of an institutional structure. The governmental structure that allocates ministerial responsibility for accused persons is fragmented and has a built-in conservative bias (Eskridge 1983). Although remand detention is extremely costly for provincial governments, these costs are not distributed equally between the budgets of different ministries: lower remand populations reduce correctional expenses but increase the risk of appearance failure or increased crime, meaning greater costs in policing and maintaining courts. Thus, measures that would reduce pretrial custody carry immediate economic risks for the ministries of the Attorney General and Solicitor General, while the offsetting savings of undertaking the release risk are more immediately realized by the Ministry of Corrective and Rehabilitative Services. Because the discretionary power that influences the size of the remand population does not rest with correctional personnel, the only way this ministry can cut costs is by reducing services to the populations under its control. Because the policy emphasis of the ministries at the front end of the system highlights social control (ensuring an individual's appearance at trial) and social defence (preventing crime during the remand period), the actual decision-making "authorities have a strong incentive to err on the side of public security where there is any doubt about the risk posed by an offender. And since risk prediction is notoriously unreliable, the possibility of erring on the side of severity...is substantial" (Cragg 1992, 191). Implanting the bail process into this fragmented institutional structure results in conservative decisions about where criminality lies, but this combination of process and structure exacts extravagant costs in both monetary and social terms.

ENDNOTES

1   The description of bail court and its actors that is provided here relates to the process generally followed in the Province of Ontario. Because the administration of justice is a provincial responsibility, bail practices and the roles of various actors will vary somewhat from province to province.

2   In my future observation of bail courts, I discovered that contested hearings constitute the untypical events of the day, the majority of cases being disposed by way of consent releases or hold-overs. On this day, my first exposure to Toronto's bail courts, the time available for hearing Crown arguments was reduced by the inclusion of a lengthy bail hearing, but an average number of contested hearings still took place.

3   The procedures required to demonstrate personal worth may take some time to document. If the potential surety is using real estate to determine worth, he/she must produce a number of documents (title, deed, insurance, mortgage, etc.; if using a bank acount, a letter from the financial institution is often required. In some instances, the financial institution may freeze the amount of cash, making the terms of release similar to a cash bail (Trotter 1987–1988, 240).

4   During a four-month period of research during 1993–1994 in two Toronto bail courts, more than 68 percent of outcomes of bail hearings were reached by consent release.

5   These excerpts from show cause statements were obtained as part of a research project undertaken in Toronto during 1993–1994.

6   The onus is reversed when an indictable offence is committed while an accused is on bail, when a breach of bail conditions has occurred, where the trafficking or exporting/importing of drugs is involved, or where the accused is not ordinarily a resident of the area.

7   Statements from accused persons remanded in custody or unable to raise the required surety were obtained in my 1993–1994 research project.

8   The "warrant of committal, is specifically designed to allow the justice or magistrate to indicate why the accused is being detained in custody. Another form is provided for the justice to indicate his reasons therefor, as is required by s.457(5). This latter form is not mandatory and is not universally used" (Watt 1973–1974, 47).

BIBLIOGRAPHY

Alexander, George, et al.   1958. "A Study of the Administration on Bail in New York City," *University of Pennsylvania Law Review,* 106.

Angel, Arthur R., et al.   1971. "Preventive Detention: An Empirical Analysis," *Harvard Civil Rights–Civil Liberties Law Review,* no. 6.

Ares, Charles E., Anne Rankin, and **G. Sturz.**   1963. "Manhattan Bail Project," *New York University Law Review,* 38:67.

Beeley, Arthur L.   [1927] 1966. *The Bail System in Chicago.* Reprint, Chicago: University of Chicago Press.

Bottomley, Allan K. 1970. *Prison Before Trial.* Occasional Papers on Social Administration, no. 39. London: G. Bell & Sons.

Boyd, Neil. 1983. "Ontario's Treatment of the 'Criminally Insane' and the Potentially Dangerous: The Questionable Wisdom of Procedural Reform." In *Contemporary Moral Issues,* edited by Wesley Cragg. Toronto: McGraw Hill Ryerson.

Boyle, James. 1985. "The Politics of Reason: Critical Legal Theory and Local Social Thought," *University of Pennsylvania Law Review,* vol. 133 (April).

Brockett, William A. 1971. "Presumed Guilty: The Pre-Trial Detainee," *Yale Review of Law and Social Action.* 1(4): 10–26.

Canada. Canadian Committee on Corrections. 1969. "Chapter Seven" in *Towards Unity: Criminal Justice and Corrections.* (Ouimet Report.) Ottawa. Information Canada.

Canada. Law Reform Commission of Canada. 1988. *Compelling Appearance, Interim Release and Pre-Trial Detention.* Working paper 57. Ottawa: Law Reform Commission of Canada.

Cohen, Shari J. 1988. "Circumventing Due Process: A Judicial Response to Criminal Recidivism Under the Bail Reform Act," *Hastings Constitutional Law Quarterly,* vol. 15.

Cragg, Wesley. 1992. *The Practice of Punishment.* London and New York: Routledge.

Doob, Anthony N. 1985. "The Many Realities of Crime." In *Perspectives in Criminal Law: Essays in Honour of John L. Edwards,* edited by Anthony N. Doob and Edward L. Greenspan. Aurora, Ontario: Canada Law Book.

———, and **A. Cavoukian.** 1977. "The Effect of the Revoking of Bail: *R. v. Demeter,*" *Criminal Law Quarterly,* 19:196–202.

Eaton, Mary. 1987. "The Question of Bail: Magistrates' Responses to Applications for Bail on Behalf of Men and Women Defendants." In *Gender, Crime and Justice,* edited by Pat Carlen and Anne Worrall. Philadelphia: Open University.

Ericson, R.V., and **P.M. Baranek.** 1982. *The Ordering of Justice: A Study of Accused Persons as Dependants in the Criminal Process.* Toronto: University of Toronto Press.

Eskridge, Chris W. 1983. *Pretrial Release Programming: Issues and Trends.* New York: Clark Boardman Company, Ltd.

Feeley, Malcolm and **John McNaughton.** 1974. *A Pre-Trial Process in the Sixth Circuit: A Quantitative and Legal Analysis.* New Haven: Yale University.

Flemming, Roy B. 1982. *Punishment Before Trial.* New York and London: Longman.

Foote, Caleb, et al. 1954. "Compelling Appearance in Court: Administration of Bail in Philadelphia," *University of Pennsylvania Law Review,* 102.

Friedland, Martin L. 1988–1989. "Controlling the Administrators of Criminal Justice," *Criminal Law Quarterly,* vol. 31.

———, 1965. *Detention Before Trial: A Study of Criminal Cases Tried in the Toronto Magistrate's Court.* Toronto: University of Toronto Press.

Goldkamp, John S.   1985. "Danger and Detention: A Second Generation of Bail Reform," *The Journal of Criminal Law & Criminology*, 76(1).

———.   1983. "Questioning the Practice of Pretrial Detention: Some Empirical Evidence from Philadelphia," *The Journal of Criminal Law and Criminology*, 74(4).

———.   1979. *Two Classes of Accused: A Study of Bail and Detention in American Justice.* Cambridge, Mass.: Ballinger.

———.   1977. *Two Classes of Accused: A Study of Bail and Detention of American Justice.* Cambridge, Mass: Ballinger.

——— and **Michael R. Gottfredson.**   1985. *Policy Guidelines for Bail: An Experiment in Court Reform.* Philadelphia: Temple University Press.

Grosman, B.   1980. *New Directions in Sentencing.* Toronto: Butterworths.

Kellough, D.G.   1982. *Presumed Innocent? A Report on Pre-trial Detention.* Winnipeg: John Howard and Elizabeth Fry Society of Manitoba.

Kiselbach, Daniel.   1988–1989. "Pretrial Criminal Procedure: Preventive Detention and the Presumption of Innocence," *Criminal Law Quarterly*, 31, 168–196.

Koza, Pamela, and **Anthony N. Doob.**   1974–1975a. "The Relationship of Pre-trial Custody to the Outcome of a Trial," *Criminal Law Quarterly*, 17:391–400.

———.   1974–1975b. "Some Empirical Evidence on Judicial Interim Release Proceedings," *Criminal Law Quarterly*, 17:258–272.

Landes, William M.   1974. "Legality and Reality: Some Evidence on Criminal Procedure," *The Journal of Legal Studies*, 3(2).

Mahaffy, Connie.   1981. "The Discriminatory Application of the Canadian Bail System in Ontario," *Pretrial Services Annual Journal*, 4(July).

Manitoba. Aboriginal Justice Inquiry of Manitoba.   1991. *The Justice System and Aboriginal People*, Vol. 1. Winnipeg: Queen's Printer.

Mewett, A. W.   1972. "Editorial: Pre-Trial Release," *The Criminal Law Quarterly*, 14(2): 121–122.

Morse, Wayne L., and **Ronald H. Beattie.**   1932. "Survey of the Administration of Criminal Justice in Oregon, Report No. 1: Final Report of 1,771 Felony Cases in Multnomah County," *Oregon Law Review*, no. 2.

Rankin, Anne.   1964. "The Effect of Pretrial Detention," *New York University Law Review*, 39: 641.

Schlesinger, Steven R.   1989. "Bail Reform: Protecting the Community and the Accused," *Harvard Journal of Law & Public Policy*, vol. 9.

Single, Eric.   1972. "The Unconstitutional Administration of Bail: *Bellamy* v. *The Judges of New York City*," *Criminal Law Bulletin*, 8:459.

Steury, Ellen Hochstedler, and **Nancy Frank.**   1990. "Gender Bias and Pre-trial Release: More Pieces of the Puzzle," *Journal of Criminal Justice*, 18: 417–432.

Thomas, Wayne H., Jr. 1976. *Bail Reform in America.* Berkeley, Los Angeles, London: University of California Press.

Toborg, Mary A. 1981. *Pretrial Release: A National Evaluation of Practices and Outcomes.* Washington, DC: US Department of Justice, National Institute of Justice.

Trotter, Gary T. 1987–1988. "Fundamental Justice and the Approval of Sureties by the Crown," *Criminal Law Quarterly*, vol. 30.

Wald, Patricia. 1964. "Pretrial Detention and Ultimate Freedom: A Statistical Study," *New York University Law Review*, vol. 39 (June).

Watt, David. 1973–1974. "Judicial Interim Release," *The Criminal Law Quarterly*, vol. 16.

Wheeler, Gerald. 1981. "Two Faces of Bail Reform: An Analysis of the Impact of Pretrial Status on Disposition, Pretrial Flight and Crime in Houston," *Policy Studies Review*, (August).

CHAPTER 9

RECONSTRUCTING CANADIAN MORAL PANIC: YOUTH AND SCHOOL VIOLENCE

W. Gordon West

Rick Collins, a secondary school superintendent in charge of violence issues for the Toronto school board, says there's no question that there is an increase of violence in the schools.

("Back to School With Pen, Paper—and Knives,"
The Toronto Star, September 2, 1994)

"Those are just reported offences," said Det. Sgt. J. Muise of Metropolitan Toronto Police. "There is a huge underbelly of stuff we don't hear about but we feel is happening."

("Schools Turning Into Danger Zones," The Globe and Mail, May 19, 1994)

Minister of Women's Issues [and Attorney General] Marion Boyd said..."Grade school boys must be stopped from sexually harassing girls in playgrounds and corridors."

("Boyd Argues End to Sex Harassment at School," The Toronto Star, May 3, 1994)

INTRODUCTION

In Canada, a lively debate continues on crime, its causes, and its "solution." More specifically, the public, press, police, and professionals have been debating a range of "hot topics" including what to do about the rise in crime rates, the presumed causes in faulty immigration laws and procedures, the devastating effects of sexual offences, and the seeming increase in youth violence—especially in schools. Fueled by victims' outrage, the debate has centred on what changes in the law would stem the tide. To facilitate discussion, this chapter will narrow its concern by focusing on only one of these topics: the debate about youth and violence, particularly in schools.

In this debate, a major issue to be examined is the apparent discrepancy between the ostensible "facts" about crime and delinquency, and the claims made by various actors ("the public," victims' rights groups, police, professionals, criminologists, etc.) While we will examine whether the data indicate an increase in youth violence or not, our central concern will be on how the presumed increase is being understood, conceptualized, and discussed politically. This chapter will examine how this debate regarding counteracting trends and unclear data has generated a "moral panic" in the general public.

Crucially, there would seem to be an increasing manipulation of mass media signifiers with increasingly unclear reference to identifiable phenomena signified—precisely one of the major hallmarks cited by theorists as a hallmark of post-critical society! Statements such as "Rising crime threatens society!" and "Youth violence rampage!" are repeated claims that are becoming increasingly meaningless because they have no identifiable referent, or at least are decreasingly likely to refer to some agreed upon phenomenon. When public actors no longer agree on language use (or, even worse, distort and obfuscate language for their own interests), sustaining the meaningful public debate fundamental to democracy becomes impossible (Crick, 1955). There is a danger that any wrongdoing by those in power increasingly avoids critique and correction, since vastly unequal resources are available for the manipulation of public opinion. Such a post-critical society threatens to undercut a key raison d'être of criminology: social critique. This chapter will focus on the contemporary "youth and violence" debate in Canada as one topic of criminological interest that cannot be comprehended without such a post-critical perspective.

THE LEGAL AND HISTORICAL BACKGROUND

Some specifically Canadian legal and historical background sets the stage for this debate. Our legal framework has some unique qualities, in that criminal justice legislation is a federal (central government) concern, while enforcement of criminal justice, welfare and education are provincial and municipal matters. Thus, the *Juvenile Delinquents Act* (JDA)and its successor, the *Young Offenders Act* (YOA), have been federally legislated, but are administered provincially and municipally. Such divisions provide ample opportunity for different interpretations, divergent administration of the same legislation, and conflict over "turf."

Much of the impetus for the passage of the *Juvenile Delinquents Act* in 1908 lay in its promise to "cure" our society of crime by ensuring the proper socialization of our young (see West, 1984, especially chap. 2.) The "solution" adopted through the Act was to remove civil liberties guarantees for those between 7 and 16 years of age, whereby the state and "psychological" professionals would be more unrestricted regarding socializing any errant youth. The ironic net result was a considerable growth in the removal of youngsters from their parents, families, homes, and communities—a growth in official juvenile delinquency and more institutionalization!

By the middle of this century there was general recognition that the increased incarceration of juveniles had not helped such youngsters individually, nor resocialized them to avoid lives as adult criminals (see, among others, Canada, 1965; Canada, 1971). Juvenile corrections have been as abysmally ineffective in realizing their espoused goals as adult ones: they are expensive, unjust, immoral, and a failure (Morris, 1992). More specifically, the system is expensive in that incarceration of youngsters costs far more than either group home or home "treatment" (e.g., probationary counseling). It has been unjust in that Natives, working-class youngsters, etc. are disproportionately singled out for repressive treatment compared with their actual behaviour. The system is immoral in that such youngsters are more victims of abusive conditions than vile assailants. The system is a failure in that "training schools" and juvenile jails have graphically failed to "rehabilitate" errant youth or to prevent crime in consistently failing to deter each new generation.

After the 1965 Committee on Juvenile Delinquency report (Canada, 1965), some 4 bills were introduced before final passage of the revised *Young Offenders Act* in 1984. The delays came from orchestrated political opposition to legally progressive aspects of the various bills, which granted civil libertarian rights enjoyed by adults to juveniles, raised the age of criminal responsibility (*mens rea*) from 7–15 to 12–17 years, removed the admissibility of hearsay evidence, enshrined the right to legal counsel and the right to refuse psychological/psychiatric treatment/interference, and instituted a maximum sentence of 3 years (then raised to 5, and now being raised to 10). During the debate around the revisions of the JDA, the Canadian Mental Health Association (representing social workers and psychologists), the Ontario government (representing established bureaucracies), and various police (especially the Metropolitan Toronto Police force, the largest in the country) actively opposed any restrictions on their powers, discretionary options, and empires.

As legislation seldom has a direct impact on such complicated behaviour, it is extremely difficult to assess the impact on delinquent behaviour of the *Young Offenders Act* over the last decade. Precise assessment is even more difficult given the splitting of powers between the levels of governments, the change of ages, elimination of some offences, changed administration, etc. in the Act. Additionally, parts of this disjointed system were moving in somewhat different directions, and were not centrally coordinated. For instance, by the late 1970s, before the passage of the YOA, most provinces (in particular Ontario and Quebec) had already moved toward some reduction in placement of youngsters in closed settings, while often expanding their services in "open custody" and "community treatment." With the passage of the YOA, sentences generally have become "harsher" (i.e., longer), there has been an "expansion of the net" (i.e., more rather than fewer youngsters have become caught in the system), costs have skyrocketed, and delinquent behaviour remains as much a public concern and behavioural reality as ever. Simply put, the *Young Offenders Act* does not seem to have solved either the problem of juvenile delinquency or crime in general.

At best, one could characterize these changes as counteracting trends. Nonetheless, there is a public perception of increasingly lax and ineffective responses to juvenile crime (inspired in part by increased legal rights for juveniles). Thus, the Act has been under vigorous attack by "conservatives," including some major police forces, some psychologists (e.g., Leschied, et al. 1991), and some educators (see West, 1993a, b, c, and d). There is a mobilized public outcry for tougher legislation, fewer civil liberties, harsher punishment and longer terms, and compulsory therapy. At its 1994 conference, the Reform Party even debated abolishing the YOA, which would mean having our young tried in adult court.

Partly contrarily, the latest major statement on crime prevention from the federal Standing Committee on Justice and the Solicitor General (Canada, 1993) recommends a "liberal" policy of eliminating the "causes" of criminal behaviour, rather than repressive measures.

> The House of Commons Standing Committee on Justice and the Solicitor General believes that the time has come for Canadians to get serious about crime prevention and community safety. It has studied crime and its prevention and has concluded that our collective response to crime must shift to efforts that reduce opportunities for crime and focus on at risk young people and on the underlying social and economic factors associated with criminal behaviour. (Canada, 1993)

Yet—amazingly—their list of factors could have been written in 1880 by the Booths:

> The witnesses stressed in the submissions that crime cannot be prevented solely by the criminal law and criminal justice services because it is a social problem, and above all a problem of poverty, that requires all sectors of society to work together for safer communities. They note that there is no single root cause of crime. Rather it is the outcome of the interaction of a constellation of factors that include: physical and sexual abuse, illiteracy, low self-esteem, inadequate housing, school failure, unemployment, inequality and dysfunctional families. (Canada, 1993)

The only addition to this litany not heard a century ago concerns sexual abuse of youngsters; the basic statement is that poverty causes crime! The conceptions of crime as centrally involving traditional street crime remains unquestioned. Meanwhile, the major policies of our governments focus on increasing production, which has resulted in constant social/economic disparities over the past few decades rather than a change in poverty levels.

Canadians have been as anxious about youth crime as any society. Besides the bureaucratic division of powers, it is not at all unusual for the three levels of government to have elected political parties of three (or more!) ideological directions. In regard to juvenile delinquency, over the last three decades the federal bureaucracy can be characterized as relatively "progressive," while the two largest provinces' bureaucracies (governing two thirds of the country's population) have been in conflict (Quebec progressive and Ontario intransigently conservative and punitive), and the largest city governments have been relatively progressive, while their police forces have been repressive. (These generalizations, of course, are just such, and invite extensive debate and refutation!) Such divergent trends and ideologies across jurisdictions, however, are revealing in openly demonstrating how radically different interpretations and policy implications can be drawn by different governments while seemingly referring to the same body of "facts."

To clarify some aspects of this discursive practice, we will now focus specifically on the discussions around youth and violence, especially in regard to violence in schools. Examinations of violence—the most serious type of offence—will shed light on how public discussion is elaborated to draw legislative implications in evaluating the YOA. This will entail examining public opinion, newspaper presentations, statements by interest groups and professionals (such as the Ontario Secondary School Teachers Federation, Victims Against Violence and the Metro Toronto Police), all against a backdrop of educational concerns, demographic changes, and political economy. Some more general theoretical concepts will be developed as well as policy and practice suggestions for educators.

VIOLENCE AMONG THE YOUNG IN SCHOOLS

Definitions

An initial difficulty arises from our varying definitions of violence. A typical dictionary entry defines "violence" as "the unlawful exercise of physical force" (*Concise Oxford*, 1990, 8th ed.).

Criminological research favours a relatively narrow, legalistic definition: violence consists of the proven commission of acts against persons involving the unlawful exercise of physical force as prohibited in the *Criminal Code* (usually referring to murder, assault, sexual assault, arson, and robbery). Others advocate a wider definition to include psychological and emotional intimidation (without assault), pornographic depictions of women, etc.

Others suggest shifting the focus from acts committed by individuals to structural violence, examining how social organization systematically harms large groups of people (e.g., ethnic and racial minorities, women, working-class persons, the young, etc.).

We need to note that legal approaches are somewhat irrelevant to some of humanity's most dramatically violent acts, such as warfare. The narrowest definitions are most precise, but can also be excessively limiting for discussion; for instance, by a legal fiction, children under 12 cannot commit any crime. On the other hand the broader the definition, the vaguer the discussion. In the debate over youth and violence, different definitions are frequently used, with resultant confusion.

Some Data

An examination of data using the more narrow but relatively precise legal defin-ition is somewhat clarifying but reveals other difficulties.

Official Statistics

First, the official statistics demonstrate that we need to keep the problem of youth violence in perspective: of more than 3 million incidents of crime reported to Canadian police in 1990, only 9 percent of the total involved some type of violence, and almost all of this was simple assault (i.e, without a weapon being used and without serious physical injury). Some 300,000 total incidents of vio-lence per year do cause concern, but we need to recognize that serious vio-lence is relatively rare, although the mass media focus on reporting such atypical crime.

Over time, since the early 1960s, official violent crime rates have slowly increased; the rate per capita is now three-and-a-half times greater. There is considerable unevenness in the trend, however, with a stabilizing period in the mid-1970s, and more dramatic increases especially in the late 1980s. The last couple of years, however, have seen drops, but the overall crime rate is 13 per-cent higher than a decade ago—an increase, but not particularly dramatic (*The Globe and Mail*, August 24, 1994).

To complicate the picture, different crimes increase differently over time. Sexual assaults constituted only 1 percent of the total crimes in 1990 (about a tenth of all reported violent crimes). The 144-percent increase in the sexual assault reports during the 1980s suggests increased reporting and recording may be responsible for the rise (rather than any changes in actual behaviour) during a period of changing legislative definitions and public encouragement to report, especially because, in contrast, robbery rates and property offences remained almost exactly the same in the same period (*Juristat*, March 1992).

However, these statistically documented trends in officially recorded inci-dents of violent behaviour must also be seen in a longer-term context. Across longer time periods, the trends are much more ambiguous: over the last century, the total officially recorded violent acts per capita have declined, not increased (see Gurr, 1976).

Criminological research almost unanimously identifies certain individual characteristics as more likely to be found in persons committing acts of street violence: they are likely to be young (12–25 years of age), male, working class, a member of certain subcultural groups, and living in less-developed countries. "Property crime and, to a lesser extent, violent crime was found to increase as the proportion of persons looking for work increased" (*Juristat*, March 1992). Such attempts to identify some patterns, however, describe statistical probabili-ties only; the occurrence of violence by persons less likely to offend reminds us to exercise caution in making generalizations.

Even on their own terms, these statistical patterns are complicated and, hence, easily distorted. For instance, while recognizing males as the perpetrators of most individual violent street crimes (murder, assault, rape, arson, robbery), and in particular some of the most violent acts of greatest concern suffered by females (e.g. murder, rape, wife assault, and sexual assault), we must acknowledge that in general the victims of such bodily assaults are also significantly more likely to be males than females. Males are more likely to suffer assault and three times more likely to be murdered (Miles, 1991, 8). Trevethan indicates "for ... children and young teens, the proportion of male victims was substantially higher" (Trevethan, 1992). Ignoring such data, however, feminism has successfully influenced popular opinion into thinking females are most at risk, exploiting the reality that females are more fearful for their own safety. Admitting such a prominent role for sex/gender, of course, is not to leave the field to biological determinism: social and psychological factors still have a major impact (see Hart, 1993 and Thornton, 1993), which opens the debate still further.

Rather than fitting the popular image of violence committed by unknown strangers, in the majority of assault cases in recent Canadian reports victims knew the accused at least casually, in contrast to less than 20 percent in robbery. As with most crime, violent behaviour tends to occur among members of the same groups.

In spite of the recent media concern about violence in schools, "[b]y far the largest numbers of violent crimes committed against child and adult victims occurred in a residence. For teenage victims, however, similar proportions of offences occurred in residences and outdoors." For teens between 12 and 15 years of age, only 15 percent of assaults occurred in school.

In official criminal justice statistics, youth in particular are disproportionately recorded, and some 80 percent of the accused are males. There has been a slow but steady overall increase in juvenile crimes reported (15 percent in 1991–1992 over 1990–1991, and 35 percent over 1986–1987, 10 percent being attributable directly to administrative changes: a 25 percent increase is indicated.) Similar to the overall population, traditionally 12 percent of the total offences involved violence, mostly minor assault (Conway, 1992); this proportion has increased to 17 percent of the overall youth crime, as recorded youth violent crime has increased unusually since 1986. Notably, teenagers are less likely to murder than adults.

But similarly to being disproportionately victimized by crime in general, teens are also disproportionately victims of violent crime, about double their representation in the population (Trevethan, 1992). But most of this again is intragroup violence: "23% of those accused of crimes against younger teen victims were 12-15 themselves, and a further 23% were 16-19." Juristat data also indicate a disproportion of sexual offences officially recorded against teens: of every 10 sexual-assault victims, 4 were teens (and 4 more were under 12.) In contrast to 8 ordinary assault victims among every 10 adult victims of violence, only 7 of 10 older teens, 6 of 10 younger teens, and 3 of 10 children victims of violence were ordinary assault victims (the majority of the rest being victims of sexual assault). This is probably the result of the considerable recent zeal to prosecute child sexual-assault cases with "zero tolerance" (i.e., no exercise of discretion). Nonetheless, the Metropolitan Toronto Police figures in Table 1 show considerable increases in school violence:

Table 1 Offences Reported in Metro Toronto Schools

Offence:	1990	1991	1992	1993
Attempted murder	1	1	1	4
Sexual assault	105	143	105	131
Assault	529	572	666	810
Assault with weapon	156	164	192	221
Armed robbery	46	38	54	73
Possession of a weapon	65	94	112	141
Extortion	24	35	22	62
Threats	135	160	196	253

The Globe and Mail, May 19, 1994.

These data, however, need to be interpreted with great caution. The police themselves recognize that many criminal events take place without their being informed: "Those are just reported offences," said Det. Sgt. John Muise of Metropolitan Toronto Police. "There is a huge underbelly of stuff we don't hear about but we feel is happening" (*The Globe and Mail,* May 19, 1994). While Muise doubtlessly meant to be understood to mean the situation is even more serious than it appears, his statement also indicates that finding and processing more of such "unknown" crime could easily cause the official statistics to rise dramatically *without any change in actual behaviour*! During this time period, the numbers of officers on the street-crime unit has increased, and so has their active interest in encouraging all schools to report illegal behaviour. Most crucially, newspapers in 1993 carried headlines that youth crime had increased 30 percent, as claimed in a report by Metro Toronto Police Chief William McCormack (McCormack, 1993). Closer examination revealed that the charges had increased 30 percent—but the incidents known to the police had increased only by 2 percent (*The Toronto Star,* March 8, 1993). Bluntly put, the Metropolitan Toronto Police would appear to be manipulating data quite wildly for their own political ends, blatantly creating an impression that youth violence is rapidly rising, an impression they either realize is false, or that indicates their incompetence at interpreting such data.

The above summarizations of officially recorded police data should give some indication of the complications of understanding violence among youth. Taking a narrow short-term view, there has been an increase in recorded/reported acts of violence by young people over the last three decades, although most of these are relatively minor, and in particular youth are less likely than adults to murder. Much of the increase in officially recorded violence concerns sexual offences, and would seem to result from changed legislation and administrative procedures. Most violence is perpetrated by males on males, among those known to each other; only a very small proportion of such violence occurs at school.

Self-Report Data

Besides being limited to narrow, legal-code definitions, these official statistics perhaps indicate what people report and changes in such reporting, not what is "actually happening." Increased official crime rates would be expected, for instance, with increasing public belief that any violence is an issue to be dealt with officially; whether there is any change in real behaviour is more difficult to determine. (For instance, the much touted *Juristat* report (vol 12, no 21) that women are equally victimized in many categories of violence probably reflects the imposition of non-discretionary policies for violence against women!) Such statistics might better represent what the crime controllers do than what the criminals do! Hackler and Don (1990) have done extensive research comparing similar cities and finding remarkably large differences in their official rates at different parts of the justice funnel. This suggests that local, informal, historical arrangements, different resources, and different ideologies fundamentally shape the official picture of crime and delinquency, and that local officials have wide discretion in creating these.

To overcome these problems, methods other than those using official statistics provide us with different types of information. First-hand participant observation is useful in showing us the social dynamics involved in actual incidents of violence, and the collective understanding of them by actors (e.g., Short and Strodtbeck, 1965; Willis, 1978; McLaren, 1986.) Unfortunately, such studies are rare and are difficult to generalize.

Self-report studies attempt to avoid these problems by asking randomly selected persons to report on their antisocial acts or victimization. Unfortunately, we have very few such self-report studies of school violence, and no good data on changes over time. The few such studies available suggest that the alarm expressed by many is not warranted.

For instance, Marilyn Kassian and the Ottawa Roman Catholic Separate School Board (Kassian, 1992) have provided some interesting self-report data from an Ontario board that needs replication and improvement. (The definitions are very loose, including "verbal abuse" as violence, and linking violence with lateness, truancy, and homework problems. The scoring is biased in that no incidents could be scored as less than "serious." Most importantly conceptually, there was no opportunity for indicating violence by the school or teachers against students.) "Teachers indicated that approximately 5 percent of the student population were responsible for most of the problems identified," and "the majority of the teachers experienced some form of student-initiated violence," but only 20 percent of these were rated as very or extremely serious (Kassian, 1992, 24). Furthermore, "no significant differences were apparent" over the last five years, with the notable exception of weapons carrying. As in the official statistics, male students reported being more victimized than females, suffering from verbal abuse to assault with weapons, with the notable exception of sexual harassment (Kassian, 16). Interestingly, grade 8 students (average age 13) reported the highest victimization rates, except for sexual and racial harassment, and the few reports of physical assaults with weapons, which were highest in grade 11 (average age 16). Retrospectively, these students reported more experience of verbal abuse in elementary school; interestingly, only on this category did girls self-report having committed more acts of violence.

A recent federal government study on school violence (using data from police records!) has found remarkably similar conclusions: the vast majority of violent incidents in schools are minor, although there seems to be a recent increase in the relatively small numbers of weapons (*The Globe and Mail*, August 24, 1994.)

Similarly, the Statistics Canada survey of crime victims has indicated that Canadians are no more likely to be victims of crime than they were five years ago (*The Toronto Star*, June 14, 1994).

The Orchestration of Data in Competing Discourses

The above presentation of data and analyses should have raised some strong doubts about whether there is much, if any, increase in violent behaviour by the young, with the possible important exception of weapons use. It would be useful to have more and better data. What is clear is that we cannot (with much certainty) sensibly claim that the data demand any particular legal changes. The rest of this chapter will focus on how such ambiguities in the data are nonetheless used to make such demands for legislative change, and will concentrate on the social process of the debate about "youth violence" itself.

The issue of violence in the schools has assumed the magnitude of a "moral panic," a generalized fear that the social order is disintegrating. Cohen (1972) has defined the stages of such panics: a group of people becomes defined as a threat to the social order; mass media stereotypes the behaviour and the perpetrators; "right-thinking" moral entrepreneurs and interest groups defend the moral order; experts pronounce solutions; ways of coping evolve.

Teenagers have been seen as a threat throughout much of this century, especially male, working-class, ethnic-minority ones. Unquestionably, many of us (adults, professors, teachers, teacher organizations, police, etc.) increasingly perceive youth violence as a problem. Those of us who are parents, understandably, are concerned and fear for our children. And some kids express fears of each other (but others do not; see West, 1993a, b, c, and d). There is doubtlessly some reality to these expressions of concern and fear: almost none of us have not felt some fear of being beaten up, either at home, in the play-ground, or on the street. We can all empathize with violence as a threat to our lives. Yet the Statistics Canada survey of victims indicates no change in our experience over the last five years. How, then, have we collectively perceived such a change?

The media (overwhelmingly American) have fed our fears and reinforced them by portraying (recognizably more violent) American realities into Canadian homes and minds. Violence in Canadian schools is relatively low-key, and we need to beware of simply assuming our schools are going the way of American ones. The media thirst for spectacular stories, and are more likely to pick the more vicious incidents, even though these are very rare. To continue to fill pages and air time, the media prefer steady, reliable sources for news items.

Organizations conscious of public relations are best able to provide such news stories. Those most concerned about youth violence in schools are most motivated to provide such material: women's groups, the Ontario Directorate on Women, teachers' unions, school trustee associations, the government ministry, the police, and some community groups offer documentation (understandably presenting material best suited to their own ends). "Students" or "teenagers" do not have comparable organizations or resources to offer regular material to media outlets. It is unfortunate that some concerned discussants of the issue of school violence use the widest possible definitions to augment the number of incidents (including, for instance, verbal abuse, substance abuse, truancy, and neglect of homework!), then cite the worst individual incidents (which are the least frequent), inflaming distorted perceptions of the situation.

These groups are joined by various experts (often professionals) to propose various solutions. These are very often solutions that only the professionals can provide: teachers teach, police police, and psychologists psychologize. In the case of youth violence in the schools, "moral entrepreneurs" among these groups are presently advocating "zero tolerance" policies, harsher responses (e.g. expulsion, etc.), and a toughening of the *Young Offenders Act* to include, for instance, com-pulsory therapy.

More objective, dispassionate, and less self-interested observers offer coun-tering analyses. Kassian states "it could be hypothesized that the increased attention directed at the issue of violence in the schools has led to the percep-tion that violence incidents have increased when in fact, rates have remained stable" (1992, 5). Media reports have pointed out that the alarm about the number of young people injured is seriously overstated, a product of political winds ("A Walk on Vancouver's Wild Side," *The Globe and Mail*, November 28, 1992). Carrington and Moyer (1994) found that there was little evidence to support the popular myth that the 10-year-old *Young Offenders Act* has caused higher crime rates or more serious offences. As Rosemary Gartner has stated,"The last couple of years in Canada there have been, for a variety of rea-sons, different politicians or interest groups that have a stake in conveying to the public that Canada's becoming a more violent place" (*The Globe and Mail*,

August 24, 1994). Without coinciding with the mass-media portrayals, and without vested organizational interests successfully marketing them, these countering analyses are easily dismissed.

SOME IMPLICATIONS

This chapter has analyzed one "hot topic" of criminology currently being debated by the Canadian public—youth violence in schools—in order to better understand how such debates are socially organized. In this debate, claims are frequently made that the facts ("data") support the claim that youth violence in schools is increasing, in part because of moral laxity, and that the legislation should be toughened. We have spent some time examining what data are available, only to find that they are difficult to interpret, and that they would seem to indicate little or no increase in youth violence in school. We then suggested how the use of such data in this debate has fueled a moral panic along the lines suggested by Cohen (1972).

The generation of a moral panic on this issue would seem to rely on a number of structural factors. First, the definitions of the phenomena should be vague, loose, or unclear, preventing refutation of any argument by data or logic; alternatively, loose definitions allow sloppy marshaling of any data. The "dark figure" of unreported criminal acts unknown to the police provide a concrete example of such a loose definition, as we alternate between referring to criminal acts, crimes reported, and crimes charged. As noted earlier, Hackler and Don's (1990) provincial comparisons have shown that local officials and discretionary practices can greatly influence the very delinquency statistics that are presented as "objective," data upon which these officials base politically controversial policies that affect their organizations directly!

Second, selecting a topic with strong moral reference allows the mixing of logics between "is" and "ought" discourses. "Violence" is inevitably a moral concept, identified and understood through our language and discourse within a political context rich in unquestioned background assumptions. For instance, while advocacy of zero tolerance for violence by the young in schools is very popular, three quarters of Toronto respondents in a recent survey believed that physical disciplining of youngsters is appropriate in some circumstances (Currant, 1993.) While many object to "violence," we somewhat contradictorily call for the use of repressive force in the politically correct slogan of "zero tolerance," ignoring the inevitably political aspect of the distinction. Moral absolutes (e.g., "all violence is bad") set unacknowledged, impossible goals: the Canadian public continues to hold the idealistic notion of the complete abolition of violence in Canada through improved social measures, especially regarding the socialization of youth and the elimination of poverty (see Canada, 1993). Addressing unsolvable issues provides one with an inexhaustible demand for one's services.

Third, panics would seem more easily orchestrated when coded words can refer to vague or politically unspeakable emotions: "rising youth violence" and "different kinds of youth" in some contexts refer to West Indian black immigrants without being explicitly racist. These code words can gather inchoate and vague anxieties about any social change. Mass media portrayal is particularly useful in such encoding since visual and visceral connections can be made without specific statements: repeated photos of young, black males being handcuffed convey the message without requiring words. The juxtaposition of newspaper stories and pictures have a similar effect over time.

Fourth, such coded messages around violence successfully deflect attention from the consideration of the various social changes that may lie behind the present moral panic over school violence: the increasing attention paid to feminist expressions of women's concerns; the increasing heterogeneous nature of our schools (racially, ethnically, and culturally), in terms of sexuality and sexual orientation and across social classes; anxieties over economic recession, plant closings, and international competitiveness. Urban sprawl, demographic changes, architecture, and government budgets are sources of other changes impacting on the school.

And finally, moral panics are more likely to be stimulated when the traditional power holders in the bureaucracies and professions sense a threat. As new students challenge schools run by narrow interest groups, schools are challenged as no longer effective or adequate. Maintaining a focus on individual student perpetrators of particular acts allows us to avoid addressing any structural violence by schools against students (such as institutionalized racist practices).

Indeed, such a narrow focus lacking in self-critique tries to channel the debate. It amounts to a symbolic violence upon young people by adults, whether teachers, police officers, social workers, or researchers. We need to seriously reconsider Curtis's claims that "the public school system in Ontario and public school systems in capitalist societies in general are institutions of social violence. ... it is idle to debate which means of violence we would best like to apply to students" (1987, 7).

It is rather sadly revealing that so many of the measures proposed recently involve such approaches as "target hardening," increased surveillance and communication, and co-optation of students rather than addressing any structural, background causes. Such reactive, conservative measures basically ask for more of the same—more technology, more control—the same measures that have led to *increased* official crime rates over the last decades (especially in the United States).

It is unfortunate that the adult participants in a recent dialogue (West, et al. 1993a) seemed to be politically unwilling to address the issue of such social patterns: If we cannot identify any patterns, we are left with no social solutions! Such evasiveness leaves us only with an individualistic conception of violence, an individualism supported by psychological perspectives dominant in education that have not only been argued to be inadequate but partially responsible for various educational ills and blindnesses.

The denial of social patterns with political implications is ironically and threateningly combined with hidden (and, hence, unexamined) political agendas. Thus, there is a denial of clear referents for terms while a series of vague, politically charged referents are subtly substituted. Critique becomes blunted, and there is a danger that the lack of analysis will lead to despair as rational debate becomes impossible. Criminology is in danger of losing its function as rational critique.

As schools become sites of contestation, reclaimed as a part of various communities, various disputes offer the opportunity for positive changes, making schools truly public institutions. For our schools to work better, we may need a new sense of community and school. The "Peacemakers" programme adopted in many Toronto schools, for instance, seeks in part to develop a shared new vocabulary and actions in working with elementary kids. Whatever our solutions, the resolution of the problem of violence will not come about if the issues are defined by traditional power holders alone.

We need to ponder how it is that many similar European societies (France, Sweden, Holland, etc.) have incarceration rates 20 percent to 50 percent lower than Canada's, while the United States' rate has risen from twice to quadruple Canada's, without any noticeable improvement in safety, rehabilitation, crime rates, etc. Nils Christie, a Norwegian survivor of Nazi justice, has remarked that since we have all committed some offence (confirmed overwhelmingly by self-report studies of adolescents) we could legally and rationally arrest ourselves, and interrogate ourselves until we confess what we have done, and could then deal ourselves the appropriate punishment (1992). Following this logic, we would all be inmates in our collectively constructed prison—a crime-free, totalitarian, utopian nightmare!—which could only sustain itself by officially producing more crime!

Alternatively, we could begin to question whether the past two centuries of criminology, penology, and police and school repression are sensible responses to issues of the realities of human degradation, dispute, and despair, or the legalities of guilt, justice, and tolerance, or the humanity of faith, hope, and charity!

ENDNOTES

* This paper is a substantial revision of "Abolitionism in Canadian Juvenile Justice" presented by W.G. West at the International Conference on Penal Abolition, San Jose, Costa Rica, 1993; the latter drew upon some material used in West, 1993a, b, c, and d. The Social Science and Humanities Research Council, the Solicitor General of Canada, ILANUD, and Bath Institution have all financially supported the basic research drawn upon in this paper, although none of the analyses expressed herein should necessarily be attributed to them. My gratitude to various colleagues, including Bernd Frohmann, Heather Berkeley, Elias Carranza, Ruth Morris, Stan Cohen, and especially to Elizabeth, Rosemary, Martin, and Matthew Flanagan, for support and inspiration through this project. Of course, none of the above can be held responsible for any of my errors in this text.

REFERENCES

Alschuler, A.   1980. *School Discipline: A Socially Literate Solution.* New York: McGraw-Hill.

Baker, R.   1989. "Association of Age, Gender, and Ethnicity with Juvenile Victimization In and Out of School," *Youth and Society,* 20 (March): 320–41.

Canada. Committee on Juvenile Delinquency.   1965. *Juvenile Delinquency in Canada.* Ottawa: Committee on Juvenile Delinquency.

Canada. Committee on Youth.   1971. *It's Your Turn....* Ottawa: Queen's Printer.

Canada. Standing Committee on Justice and the Solicitor General.   1993. *Crime Prevention in Canada: Toward a National Strategy.* Twelfth Report. Ottawa.

Carrington, P. and **S. Moyer.**   1994. *Canadian Journal of Criminology.*

Challenger, D.   1987. *Crime at School.* Paper presented at a seminar held 2–4 June, 1987 in Canberra. Canberra, Australia: Australian Institute of Criminology.

Cheater, G.   1993. "Crime Reporting Blamed for Climate of Fear," *The Toronto Star,* April 3.

Christie, Nils.   1992. *Crime Control as Industry.* London: Routledge.

Cohen, Stanley.   1982, "Western Crime Control Models in the Third World: Benign or Malignant?" In *Research in Law, Deviance and Social Control,* Vol. 4, 85–199. New York: JAI Press.

———.   1972. *Folk Devils and Moral Panics.* London: MacGibbon and Kee.

Conway, J.   1992. "Youth Court Statistics, 1991–92 Highlights," *Juristat Service Bulletin,* 12 (16).

Crick, B.   1955. *In Defence of Democracy.* Harmondsworth, Middlesex: Penguin.

Curtis, B.   1987. "On School Violence," *Orbit,* 18 (2): 6–8.

Currant, J.   1993. "Spare the Rod and Spoil the Child? The Physical Discipline of Children and Child Abuse," *Institute for Social Research Newsletter,* 8 (1).

Frank, J.   1992. "Violent Youth Crime." In *Canadian Social Trends,* ed. C. McKie and K. Thompson. Toronto: Thompson Educational Publishing.

3/M.   1991. "Violent Offence Cases Heard in Youth Courts, 1990–91," *Juristat Service Bulletin,* 11(16).

Gottfredson, G.D.   1985. *Victimization in Schools.* New York: Plenum.

Greenberg, P.   1992. "Youth Property Crime in Canada," *Juristat Service Bulletin,* 12 (14).

Gurr, T.R.   1976. *Rogues, Rebels and Reformers.* Beverly Hills: Sage.

Hackler, J.C., and **K. Don.**   1990. "Estimating System Biases: Crime Indices That Permit Comparisons Across Provinces," *Canadian Journal of Criminology,* 32 (2): 243–264.

Hart, F. 1993. "Gender and Violence in the Schoolyard." In "Violence in the Schools/Schooling in Violence," *Orbit*, edited by W.G. West and H. Berkeley. Toronto: OISE Press.

Juristat. 1992 "Crime Trends in Canada, 1962–1990," *Juristat Service Bulletin*, 12 (7).

Kassian, M. 1992. *Report and Recommendations: Safe Schools Survey*. Ottawa: Ottawa Roman Catholic Separate School Board.

Leschied, A., et al., eds. 1991. *The Young Offenders Act: A Revolution in Canadian Juvenile Justice*. Toronto: University of Toronto Press.

Loader, I. and **R. Sparks,** 1993. "Ask the Experts," *The Times Higher Education Supplement*. April 9.

Maran, M. 1993. "Mean Streets," *The UTNE Reader*. April.

McLaren, P. 1986. *Schooling as a Ritual Performance*. Toronto: Oxford.

McCormack, W., Chief of Police, 1993. *Report to Metropolitan Toronto Police Services Board*, March 23.

Miles, M. 1991. *The Rites of Man: Love, Sex, and Death in the Making of the Male*. London: Grafton/Harper Collins.

Morris, R. 1992. *A Practical Path to Transformative Justice*. Toronto: Society of Friends.

Ontario. Ministry of Correctional Services. 1991. *Report*. Toronto: Ministry of Correctional Services.

Pearce, F. 1974. *Crimes of the Powerful*. London: Pluto Press.

Short, J.F. 1990. "Schools and Communities as Behavior Settings for Juvenile Delinquency." In *Delinquency and Society*, edited by J. F. Short. Englewood Cliffs, NJ: Prentice Hall.

——— and **F.L. Strodtbeck.** 1965. *Group Process and Gang Delinquency*. Chicago: University of Chicago Press.

Schmidt, Y., J. Paulette, and **G. Dickenson.** 1990. "Violence in the Schools: A Neglected Research Agenda," *Education and Law Journal*, 3(1): 49–89.

Thornton, A.D. 1993. "Re-Thinking the Links: Sports, Schools, and Violence," *Orbit*, March.

Toronto Star, The. May 7, 1993, "Youth Arrests Rise"

Trevethan, S. 1992. "Teenage Victims of Violent Crime," *Juristat Service Bulletin*. 12(6).

Urban, L. 1987. "Violence and School: A Teacher's Point of View," *Western European Education*, 18(3): 63–73.

West, W.G., et al. 1993a. "A Dialogue on the Nature and Extent of the Problem," *Orbit*, March.

———. 1993b. Introduction to "Violence in the Schools/Schooling in Violence," *Orbit*. March.

———— et al.   1993c. "The Kids' Perspective," *Orbit*, March.

————.   1984. *Young Offenders and the State*. Toronto: Butterworths.

————. and **H. Berkeley,** eds.   1993d. "Violence in the Schools/Schooling in Violence," *Orbit*, March.

Willis, P.   1978. *Learning to Labour: How Working Class Kids Get Working Class Jobs.* Farnborough, Hants.: Saxon House.

A FEMINIST CONTRIBUTION TO ETHICS IN CRIMINAL JUSTICE INTERVENTION

Colette Parent and Françoise Digneffe
Translated by M. Crow, University of Ottawa

INTRODUCTION

In the 1960s, contemporary Western feminism set forth as its objective the liberation of women.[1] At that time, feminist political thought was rooted in the concept of oppression, evoking the submission of one group, women, at the hands of another, men. By establishing a context at the outset in terms of two groups with opposed interests, political struggle became defined as the means by which to ensure liberation of the oppressed group (Jaggar, 1983, 5–6).

Defining the problem in terms of a relationship of oppression, which initially overshadowed other dimensions of gender interrelationships, had an impact on the production of knowledge within the feminist perspective and on proposed solutions toward ending women's oppression. This impact is apparent in feminist analyses of law and criminal justice intervention. Here, as in other cases, while significant improvements for women were facilitated a number of problems were also created.

In the first place, this problem definition tends to universalize the category "woman" and obscure differences in experience and interest among different groups of women. It suggests no potential avenues to facilitate understanding of the different forms of oppression that confront different groups of women, nor for taking such differences into account in the analysis.[2] Second, such a problem definition crystallizes gender opposition and obscures the common interests that some women share with men who also may be subject to some forms of oppression. Locked within these parameters, most feminist analyses of criminal justice do not take into account the complexity of the interplay related to the question of women's oppression. It is not surprising, therefore, to find feminist analyses taking opposing viewpoints concerning criminal justice intervention, or to note the absence of a value framework to guide feminist analysis in this area.

This effect becomes apparent from an overview of feminist analysis, which shows that positions toward criminal justice adopted by feminist authors vary according to the author's theoretical perspective. It also shows a marked gap between analyses concerning women as defendants and as victims. Few analyses in the area of law or penal intervention address both dimensions together. Most feminist authors either address only one dimension, or address them separately without any attempt at integration. Furthermore, while both types of analysis target the sexist bias prevalent within law and the application of justice, they do not draw common conclusions about the law, nor share views about policies to be adopted. Readers might at times feel they are introduced to two different patriarchal institutions, according to whether criminalized or victimized women are the topic of the analysis.

This chapter will examine different feminist positions concerning criminal justice interventions and will present the factors indicative of their opposition, their interests, and their most apparent limitations. Next, attention will be directed toward ethical concerns, and suggestions presented in the form of a procedural definition. To conclude, reference will be made to these reflections and to those concerning "comprehensive ethics" as outlined by Pires (1991), in order to propose potential guidelines for feminist ethics with respect to criminal justice intervention.

FEMINIST POSITIONS CONCERNING CRIMINAL JUSTICE INTERVENTION WITH WOMEN AS DEFENDANTS

Feminist analyses of criminal justice from the viewpoint of criminalized women borrows from two major perspectives. The first adopts the position of critical criminology, which proposes an overall reduction in criminal justice or even abolition of the existing system and its replacement with forms of conflict resolution. The second arises from feminist reflections concerning moral judgment, with the aim of constructing a new, feminized justice system.

Socialist feminist analysis, such as works by Currie (1991), Gregory (1986), and Messerschmidt (1986) belongs to the first group. These authors present a criminal justice system that acts to prolong the oppression of women and of other disenfranchised groups within the framework of a patriarchal capitalist society. Their projected solutions require fundamental social change. With respect to criminal justice intervention, decriminalization and decarceration are the favoured routes toward change. According to Gregory (1986), however, such measures would not facilitate changed, comprehensive, criminal justice policies or aid; the development of more humane forms of treatment and detention that may be required when neither decriminalization nor decarceration are appropriate solutions.

Critical criminological perspectives and radical feminism particularly inspired the reflections of Bertrand (1983), which challenge the morality and legitimacy of criminal law from the standpoint that notions of crime are relative. She challenges the response of criminalization for behaviour for which no consensus exists or survives concerning its importance with respect to basic values. Her work also exposes the harmful nature of some criminal justice practices involving women, contending that the foundation of defined infractions for which women are commonly accused may be even more fragile than that of infractions traditionally associated with men. She states:

> Such interventions result in increased dependency, submission, inequitable relationships between genders, between legislators and defendants, and between marginalized and marginalizing; such interventions can only be defined as criminal. (85)[3]

Bertrand (1983) equally challenges the vindictive attitude of some women's groups toward issues such as pornography and sexual assault. She underlines, appropriately, that incoherence taints their discourse. Can one demand the decriminalization of prostitution while demanding the criminalization of pornography? In short, if the principle of minimal criminalization is appropriate for women, is it not logical to struggle equally against immoderate sentencing for men's unlawful behaviour, even that which has an immediate impact on women?

It is recognized within the framework of this model that criminal justice primarily affects disenfranchised groups: socioeconomically disadvantaged persons, members of ethnicized and racialized groups, and women. The foregoing analyses thus indicate similarities between groups oppressed on the basis of class and/or race, and distance themselves from an unequivocal focus on gender opposition. Conversely, and to the extent that analysis only embraces a de-escalation or nonintervention policy without introducing concrete solutions to end women's oppression within the criminal justice system—whether as criminals or victims—it appears insufficient to rally wider feminist support or even to provide a framework from which to elaborate a body of feminist ethics with respect to criminal justice.

Examining the second category of feminist analyses, particularly radical feminist analysis of criminal justice intervention with women defendants, work is found that both challenges the intrinsically masculine nature of law, and proposes new criminal justice models. This type of analysis is inspired by Gilligan (1982; 1987) who establishes that, contrary to "discoveries" by Kohlberg (1984), women's moral judgment is not underdeveloped compared to men's but rather expresses a different viewpoint (Gilligan, 1987, 22–23). Men's moral judgment develops from the foundation of preoccupation with justice, equality, and individual rights; when moral problems arise, the operative question is, "What is just?" Such a judgment seeks solutions that ensure recognition of an individual's rights. By contrast, women's moral judgment develops from the foundation of relationships, interdependency, and mutual personal responsibility; when moral problems arise the operative question becomes, "How to respond?" Solutions are sought that ensure the maintenance of ties and demand attention to one another's viewpoints. Feminine conceptions of morality are therefore rooted in the search for solutions to conflicts that focus on responsibilities for the consequences of actions rather than on individual rights. A person with a conflict is by definition in a "relationship" with another. What matters is not the application of principles, but the attempt to resolve problems with reference to the actual person involved rather than to the "rights" of each one.

According to Gilligan (1987, 22), the moral voices of justice and responsibility are not opposed. She does not imply that the voice of justice ignores mutual responsibility, or that the voice of responsibility is blind to the imperatives of justice. Essential differences between the two viewpoints are found in the way basic elements of moral judgment are organized: oneself, others, and the relationship between the two. Argument therefore gravitates around either the concept of equality or that of mutual responsibility (attachment).

Inspired by Gilligan's identification of this difference in orientation, Heidensohn (1986) proposes a distinct and specific model of feminine justice, founded on an ethic of responsibility and supported by its validation or revalidation of women's own experiences. This model is labeled "the justice of Persephone".[4] It involves cooperation and responsibility, and promotes an informal, contextual justice based on relationships between individuals: it is personalized and empathic. Some similarities can be identified between this model and the perspectives of both abolitionists, such as Hulsman and Bernat de Celis (1982) and Hees (1986), and authors supporting alternate forms of criminal justice. Harris (1987), in turn, projects a new model of justice, borrowing both from Heidensohn's model and from abolitionist thought, but she associates justice with the abolition of the criminal justice system.

Analyses from this perspective add strength as well as create difficulties for the articulation of feminist ethics in criminal justice intervention. Among its advantages a new model of justice based on an ethic of responsibility finally gives women a voice, allowing for description in women's own voices and through women's own experiences. This model also facilitates an understanding of the viewpoint of others. It focuses on the consideration of problems in relation to situations and the need to examine those situations, and determine responsibility not only for action but for each other—both individually and socially.

This ethical feminist model was not introduced, however, without arousing anxiety and inspiring criticism. First, such a model is questioned for its essentialist dimension: it appears to assume inherent differences between men and women's views of morality. To adopt a dualistic vision of morality within current patriarchal society can have worrisome consequences. Smart (1989) underlines, for example, that to revalidate the feminine viewpoint within a framework of patriarchy means to accept the attribution of traditional female characteristics.

While it acknowledges power relations between men and women, it does so at the risk of reproducing that *status quo*. The issue of violence against women provides an example: does a model that accents greater responsibility not run the risk of penalizing the woman who already feels responsible for her partner, and even for his behaviour?[5]

Heidensohn (1986, 296) also demonstrates that the "justice of Persephone" is incompatible with the masculine voice of traditional justice. As long as women live with a patriarchal justice system, where men control power and resources, the masculine concept of justice will prevail. The "Persephone" model, therefore, could only be implemented if women control the justice system. Within the framework of our current criminal justice system, only the prison system isolates women from men, and thus provides an arena where an ethic of responsibility may be developed. Heidensohn (1986, 297) does in fact envision a separate prison system for women that would meet their specific needs, in private homes or hostels, and which would provide access to community connections and supports. For the rest, Heidensohn (1986, 297) only credits the "Persephone" model with providing tools to formulate criticisms and explore new routes.

In summary, projections of a separate feminine justice prolongs male-female distinctions, and does not provide tools for extending empathy to other oppressed groups.

Whatever its foundation, however, feminist analysis of criminal justice intervention involving women defendants introduces a fundamental criticism of criminal justice. This is true of analyses not progressing beyond male-female opposition, as well as of those limited by the critical criminology framework.

FEMINIST POSITIONS CONCERNING CRIMINAL JUSTICE INTERVENTIONS WITH WOMEN AS VICTIMS

An examination of analyses concerning women victims, generally rooted in the contemporary women's movement, demonstrates that such models contribute to defining or redefining problems as primarily based on male-female opposition. It must be acknowledged, however, especially where issues of spousal violence and sexual assault are concerned, that the situation itself appears related to this opposition, leading the way and giving more credibility to models based on oppression and struggle.

It is not surprising, therefore, to find in the framework of these analyses a very different relation to law and criminal justice. Certainly, few feminists fall into the trap of considering law the only and ultimate solution to the problem of violence against women. But because law figures so strongly in individual lives, and because law may—at least in theory—be so readily mobilized, changes in criminal law are from the outset perceived as a necessary element of the problem's solution. In any case, how else may one respond to an immediately violent situation than by turning to the police, and from there to the courts? Perceiving legal intervention as a necessary solution, however, leaves no room to question the values or limits of criminal justice, and none for the emergence of ethical concerns. Furthermore, the work of many feminist authors writing at the end of the 1970s shows little familiarity with criminal justice systems, and therefore little knowledge of their limits and social costs. The overall feminist initiative on the topic of women victims joins the women's movement in calling for legal recourse to eliminate discriminatory content from particular laws, and to ensure male-female equality before the law. Most adopt uncritical attitudes toward the potential of law to meet the needs and protect the interests of women.

With respect to sexual assault, for example, one of the primary demands made by Canadian women during the late 1970s and early 1980s was for the elimination of the discriminatory dimension of law that permits cruel treatment of female victims by police and before the courts. The second was for a more efficient application of the law with the aim of increasing prosecution and convictions of offenders. The third was for a clear message that sexual assault is a crime of violence and domination, not a crime of passion (Los, 1994). Although feminists projected a required change in public opinion as well as in law, changes that would affect all levels and all sectors, priority was given to changing criminal justice (Clark and Lewis, 1983, 165).

To address the inertia of criminal justice systems, as manifested in the issue of spousal violence, various measures were proposed.[6] These included the elimination of marital immunity from rape charges; zero-tolerance policies toward spouse battering; increased sentence severity to reflect the seriousness with which society views such behaviour, etc. The aim, in a nutshell, was to ensure women's protection through effective application of the law and to raise awareness symbolically that spousal assault is a crime like any other form of assault. Other initiatives—shelters for battered women, sensitization or education campaigns addressing the question of violence toward women—were certainly identified as necessary elements in the struggle. However, many such analyses present increased, more punitive, and better coordinated criminal justice interventions as essential.

Despite the many reservations expressed, including those by feminists themselves, the affirmation that women have the same right to justice as any other victim of criminal actions justifies recourse to criminal justice. Furthermore, some will argue that feminists are not responsible for our patriarchal system of justice; they simply ask for the regular and efficient application of the law toward all, including men (Currie, 1991, 85). Overall, feminist analyses concerning women's victimization show little critical analysis of law or criminal justice intervention, offer few elements to develop ethics in law beyond the boundaries of its framework of interests, and are not broad enough to apply to women or other oppressed groups as defendants.

Criticism of the view that law and criminal justice have the potential to meet the needs and interests of women will, in time, increase and arise from different sources.

In the early 1980s, a discordant voice in feminist production points to the negative effect of the earlier initiative. Currie (1991), Davis (1988), Klein (1981), Pitch (1985, 255–256), and Snider (1985; 1992) are inspired by socialist feminist thought, which views criminal justice as a means of reproducing existing social relations of class, gender, and "race." The authors demonstrate that by mobilizing criminal justice intervention, women's fate will be decided by middle-class, patriarchal justice. Not only does it seem utopian to expect a positive outcome, but feminists also risk aligning themselves with conservative views that demand more severe reactions from justice, and the protection of traditional values. This creates a contradiction that is difficult to maintain or endorse. Smart (1989), following more than a decade of reflection on feminist engagement with law, denounces the power of law to define social reality and to disqualify, or at least to resist, alternate definitions. She views law as resistant to feminist discourse and dismissive of women's experience and knowledge. Rather than looking for solutions to women's needs or interests in judicial reforms, Smart (1989, 4–25) proposes developing feminist theory as a means to remove law from centre stage, to challenge judicial discourse and its pretexts of truth.

Analyses of outcomes of judicial and criminal justice reforms also challenge recourse to criminal law as a strategy, particularly in the cases of sexual assault and spousal violence. According to Los (1994, 43–47), Canadian feminist initiatives leading to the 1983 rape law reforms were unsuccessful at redefining the social representation of rape so as to address the interests and experiences of women. Evaluation also demonstrates some mitigating effects of these reforms. A new, tripartite, infraction structure, for example, poses serious symbolic difficulties. And while police statistics do indicate increased incident reporting, they also demonstrate a growing tendency to classify infractions at the least serious level of sexual assault. Maximum penalties are severe and permit a severe reaction from the court, but the minimal classification tendency communicates a message that only minor sexual assaults are committed or reported.[7] Moreover, available data concerning sentencing practices have demonstrated that reforms have not changed the individual attitudes and perceptions that shape judges' decisions (Mohr, 1994, 182).

Results also fall short of expectations with respect to spousal violence. A variety of research shows that arresting an assailant is not a more effective way of preventing recidivism than other, less or nonpunitive means (Snider, 1992; Buzawa and Buzawa, 1993). Numerous studies show that most female victims do not perceive police or criminal justice involvement as a priority in the battle to end spousal violence (Smith, 1984). There have even been cases where victims refused to testify against their partners, and found themselves in contempt of court.[8]

The emergence of opposition from victims themselves to various feminist policies aimed at assisting victims can particularly be foreshadowed by outcomes in spousal assault cases, as more women describe the stigma attached to the "victim" label, and the subsequent loss of control over their lives (McLeod, 1989, 7).

Other women present evidence that police intervention involves a dispropor-tionate representation of persons from identified ethnicized or racialized groups, and that it aggravates their oppression.[9] Such accounts expose the experience of other, hidden forms of oppression and submission to oppression as a woman's lot because of her gender.

Such analyses, outcomes, and protests have inspired more feminist col-leagues[10] to reexamine criminal justice more closely. Current analyses that pro-pose ethical models of criminal justice interventions, however, cannot be relied on to reach beyond concepts of essential male-female opposition, nor to inte-grate the viewpoints of women as both victim and accused.

To propose a means of bypassing this contradiction first requires some reflec-tion on the question of ethics itself, as seen from a feminist perspective. Within the framework of the current debate concerning ethics, such reflection intro-duces important elements to this analysis. At least a brief (and therefore superfi-cial) overview of the significant aspects of this rich and varied production is required. Using the ideas already presented in this text, and drawing from the work of Pires (1991) concerning "comprehensive ethics," some guidelines will be proposed to define feminist ethics in criminal justice intervention.

THE CONCEPT OF ETHICS

Mainstream production in the field of criminal justice all too often obscures par-ticular aspects of feminist production concerning ethics. Contributions from Gilligan and subsequent feminist analyses concerning ethics and morals provide examples (Gilligan, 1982; 1987; Benhabib, 1987; Walker, 1989).[11]

First, as correctly emphasized by Benhabib (1987), theoretical debate con-cerning the ethics developed in Western patriarchal society is essentially rooted in the principle of universality. General rules must be developed, applicable to all (and therefore abstract), and constructed independently of the contextual dimension within which moral choices are made. Morals are therefore con-ceived as universal, disembodied, and outside of social context.[12] Implicit in ref-erence to the moral subject as man and not as woman, however, and because of the eighteenth-century notion of the "social contract," public life and politics has become the domain appropriate to moral definitions. Morality is associated with reason, excluding the sphere of private life or intimate relations that are associ-ated with sentiment. Resulting ethical concepts are only concerned with reason-ing individuals who make abstract choices, who see justice based on individual rights, equality, and reciprocity. Mainstream concepts of ethics, therefore, do not touch questions of what she refers to as the "good life," that is, areas of daily life interactions that encompass relationships of family, romance, friendship, sexual-ity, or even public relations involving notions of accomplishment.[13] Questioning those areas is considered of lesser importance, principally dependent on senti-ment, and entirely confined to a domain of personal morals. As the social group that did not participate in public life, for the most part, women were therefore excluded from resulting ethical concepts.

Feminist analyses brought this exclusion to light, along with its overall implication for ethical concepts. As already noted, Gilligan's work draws attention to the fact that in making moral choices, women do not emphasize the same aspects as men. Faced with moral dilemmas, women do not respond by abstract reasoning with a view to individual rights, or seek justice based on equality. Women take the concrete and contextual aspects of a given situation into account, and tend to evaluate actions according to their consequences for others as well as for themselves. Apparent in women's response to problems is concern for the well-being of others, not as abstract individuals with certain rights, but as real persons operating within systems of relationships. Such a response is based on assumptions of responsibility for one another. It conceives of justice as the attempt to achieve equity and complementary reciprocity, not as a means of determining rights and achieving equality (Digneffe, 1989, 57–98). A view of ethics that stresses well-being resembles some of the fundamental concepts of Aristotle and the early Christians, who insisted that solicitude, concern, and responsibility for the well-being of others—rather than for the rights of others—must regulate questions of ethics.[14]

Judging by how women are integrated into society, their aim when making ethical decisions cannot be an impersonal search for justice applied to abstract beings endowed with individual rights. It must instead be concerned with the good life, with individuals responsible for one another and the maintenance of relationships marked by equity and complementary reciprocity.

By shedding light on the shortcomings of dominant conceptions of morality, feminists were also able to pinpoint incongruence among some concepts. If morality represents reciprocity, it in fact makes it imperative to take one another's viewpoints into account. But the conception of "another" as only a rational being, thus devoid of social context and physical substance, obscures such consideration and allows a "general other" rather than a "concrete other" to emerge. How can a moral decision be evaluated without knowing the history of the persons concerned? How can we judge whether the proposed moral solution is appropriate for another if contextual data is not taken into account?[15]

To consider possible positions that may be adopted toward criminal justice intervention, useful reference may be made to Benhabib's (1990) proposals on how to consider the ethical debate. This work can be placed at the heart of the trend toward "communicative ethics," ethics based on the notion that ethical models are constructed progressively through discussions rather than a search for *a priori* rules (Habermas, 1986). Benhabib's work supports original feminist positions, and resembles that of some neo-Aristotelians. It considers that ethical debate must not only discuss questions relative to research aimed at a degree of generalization, but must also question implications for the good life. "A model of communicative ethics, which views moral theory as a theory of argumentation, need not restrict itself to questions of justice" (Benhabib, 1990, 349). It maintains that universal, unanimously acceptable conceptions of the good life should not be the expected outcome of such discussions. An *a priori* decision that a number of questions are relevant to conceptions of the good life (and therefore not subject to discussion), differs greatly from the assertion that "moral communication will establish a line between individual conceptions of the good life to be pursued freely, and shared norms and values to be cultivated collectively" (Benhabib, 1990, 350). Benhabib (1990) also affirms a fundamental need that conceptions of a good life be considered a topic for debate, even without universality in this area as a goal.

This chapter demonstrates that feminist ethics, conceived along these lines, must be elaborated progressively. Serious discussion is required in which each must participate freely. Each affirmation must be open to challenge, regardless of its content, and without subjecting the challenger to authoritarian pressure, whether internal or external (Habermas, 1986). The ethical position must equally integrate the need to debate which questions are relevant to conceptions of the good life in order to establish and respect individual choices and preferences. The ethical position in justice research must be described as the position concerned with showing solicitude and demonstrating concern for the individual as a unique person, rather than as an abstract individual with rights to be treated according to principles of equality with one's fellows (Digneffe, 1992).

Pires (1991) adopts an (in some ways) analogous viewpoint to feminist work, suggesting that reflection be directed toward a criminal justice system founded on "comprehensive ethics" rather than "total ethics." He describes "comprehensive ethics" as "constructed progressively." "Development of this paradigm will flow from a renewal of the problematic of human rights, and the reexamination of its relationships to criminal justice" (Pires, 1991). Such affirmations resemble those made by feminist authors who demand more willingness to reexamine the rationale and functions of an institution that has developed from, and functions in accord with, a punitive rationale, analogous in several ways to dominant moral reasoning. Such a reexamination would allow more equitable solutions to be developed that take into account concrete situations, and the context within which the actors of a criminal justice intervention have evolved.

To conclude this dual consideration of ethics and criminal justice a number of guidelines for feminist ethics in criminal justice intervention will be proposed. These guidelines, of course, represent only halting steps toward the definition of a model. They are suggested with the intention of inspiring critical commentary, addition, and revision.

The following seem essential components of a feminist ethic in criminal justice intervention:

1. The male-female opposition approach must be overcome; ethics constructed through communication cannot be founded on such reductions. Male-female conflicts and male-female power relationships must remain a concern, however. Women cannot be said to participate in an ethical deliberation without guarantees for personal security, and the freedom to participate fully and

autonomously in such an effort. Prudence is particularly important in examining issues of sexual assault and violence between partners.

2. The existence of other oppressed groups, whether male or female, must be acknowledged and the question of power must be examined comprehensively. In this sense, women of identifiable minorities within women's groups have demanded that their oppression not be confused with that of women of a dominant culture. They demand acknowledgment that their problems differ from those of other women and are more likely to be shared with men of their cultural community. They demand articulation of solutions, appropriate to their concerns.

To meet both these conditions is not a simple task. Women's groups that support women as victims and/or as defendants could ensure cultural and experiential diversity in their own ranks, and thus provide their members with better exposure to the complexity of the effort to find solutions. Such women would come to understand the varied shared experiences of oppression (including the oppression experienced by men of their own and other cultural inheritances), and the different situations with which their fellow members live. Projected solutions will then reflect specific needs and interests of individuals more closely and better account for the complex nature of their problems.

3. An ethical model must acknowledge that the criminal justice system is an institution that engenders significant negative social consequences, and that it is fundamentally ineffective at regulating human social problems. A model with a firm basis in the many articles of research and critical analysis that have been produced during the last few decades is presupposed. Not only the needs of women, both as victims and as criminals, must be considered, but also the needs of all other persons affected by criminal justice.

4. Feminist ethics require acceptance that responsibility for actions does not necessarily imply the need for punishment, but only gives authority to punish. This would reduce the perceived need for predetermined responses that do not consider specific contexts, and would open the way to appropriate solutions that acknowledge differences.

5. To resolve conflicts or problem situations requires escaping from enclosure within the narrow rhetoric of sentencing theories. This definition ignores research on the effectiveness of criminal justice intervention and requires bowing to the demands of an institution based on complete polarization and on condemnation rather than communication.

6. Approaching justice as the attempt to repair rather than to punish opens the route to different measures, according to particular problem situations. Reparation requires consultations with victims, whether male or female, concerning their needs. It requires the introduction of appropriate options to meet social needs identified by both male and female defendants wherever the security of others, or of society in general, is not threatened.

These guidelines may help to determine an overall ethical model, not only for criminal justice intervention but also for the eventual reform of our criminal justice system. This is a very complex question, however, and the debate will likely not be settled in the near future.

ENDNOTES

1   Prior to the 1960s, feminists advocated a search for equality rather than liberation.

2   See, for example, Caroline Ramanazoglu, 1989. *Feminism and the Contradictions of Oppression*. New York: Routledge.

3   Our translation.

4   Persephone in Greek mythology is the daughter of Demeter; their legend concerns cycles of fertility, planting, and harvesting, from conception to birth.

5   For concerns about adopting this concept of morality within a social reality of women's oppression, see Barbara Houston, 1987. "Rescuing Womanly Virtues: Some Dangers of Moral Reclamation." In *Science, Morality & Feminist Theory*, edited by M. Hanen and K. Nielsen, 237–262. Calgary: University of Calgary Press.

6   See for example the provincial policies concerning wife battering adopted in Ontario and Quebec; see also Currie 1991, 84–85 and Zoë Hilton, 1989. "One in Ten: The Struggle and Disempowerment of the Battered Women's Movement," *Canadian Journal of Family Law*, 7: 328–329.

7   For a discussion concerning the impact of a tripartite structure for classifying or reporting sexual assault, see Alvaro Pires, and Julian V. Roberts. 1992. "Le renvoi et le classification des infractions sexuelles," *Criminologie*, 25(1): 27–64.

8   The January 4, 1984 edition of the daily *Le Droit* presented an article entitled, "Seconde femme en prison. Refus de témoigner contre son mari" [Second woman jailed for refusal to testify against her husband]. A 22-year-old woman, six-months pregnant, refused to testify against her husband charged with assaulting her. She was sentenced to three-months for contempt of court.

9   For example see Amina, Mama, 1989. "Violence Against Black Women: Gender, Race and State Responses," *Feminist Review*, 32: 41–42.

10 For example see the evolution in Linda McLeod's work, from her first publication in 1980 to the present.

11 The following collections also address the issue of feminist ethics: E.B. Cole, and S. Coultrap-McQuinn, eds. 1992. *Explorations in Feminist Ethics*. Bloomington: Indiana University Press; M. Hanen, and K. Neilson, eds. 1987. *Science, Morality and Feminist Theory*. Calgary: University of Calgary Press; E.F. Kittay, and D.T. Meyers, eds. 1987. *Women and Moral Theory*. Totowa, NJ: Rowman and Littlefield; M.J. Larrabee, ed. 1993. *An Ethic of Care: Feminist and Interdisciplinary Perspectives*. New York: Routledge.

12 Seyla Benhabib uses the expression "disembedded and disembodied" (Benhabib, 1987, 81).

13 While it is not possible to define the parameters of the "good life" precisely, Ricoeur (Paul Ricoeur, 1990. *Soi-même comme un autre*. Paris: Seuil) states that a concept of

good life, for each individual, is the nebulous collection of ideals and dreams of accomplishment by which we judge our lives as more or less successful (210) (our translation). Ethical debates therefore concern what is "preferable," rather than what is "desirable."

14 This way of framing questions concerning ethics is also connected to particular (by no means dominant) elements of current ethical debate, such as described in Ricoeur, 1990.

15 To voice this question is not to reply to debates concerning whether or not ethics are universal, nor to decide the levels at which such debates should be situated. See, to this effect, Seyla Benhabib, and Fred Dallmayr. 1990. *The Communicative Ethics Controversy*. Cambridge, Mass: MIT Press. This work is cited in order to highlight the viewpoints and contributions of feminists on the question of ethics. It is not the implications and viewpoints in themselves (and in all their complexity) that are the concern of this article, but rather their use as a basis from which to articulate a precise problematic.

REFERENCES

Benhabib, Seyla. 1990. "Afterword: Communicative Ethics and the Contemporary Controversies in Practical Philosophy." In *The Communicative Ethics Controversy*, by S. Benhabib and F. Dallmayr, 330–369. Cambridge, Mass: MIT Press.

———. 1987. "The Generalized and the Concrete Other: The Kohlberg-Gilligan Controversy and Feminist Theory." In *Feminism as Critique*, edited by S. Benhabib and D. Cornell, 77–95. Minneapolis: University Press.

Bertrand, Marie-Andrée. 1983. "Femmes et justice: Problèmes de l'intervention," *Criminologie*, 16(2): 77–88.

Buzawa, Eve S., and **Carl G. Buzawa.** 1993. "The Scientific Evidence Is Not Conclusive: Arrest Is No Panacea." In *Current Controversies on Family Violence*, edited by R. Gelles and D.R. Loseke, 337–356. Newbury Park: Sage.

Clark, Lorenne and **Debra Lewis.** 1983. *Viol et Pouvoir*. Montreal: Les éditions coopératives Albert Saint-Martin.

Currie, Dawn H. 1991. "Battered Women and the State: From the Failure of Theory to a Theory of Failure," *The Journal of Human Justice*, 1(2): 77–96.

Davis, Nanette J. 1988. "Battered Women: Implications for Social Control," *Contemporary Crises*, 12: 345–372.

Digneffe, Françoise. 1992. "La reconnaissance de droits spécifiques pour les femmes: Une question de justice ou de responsabilité," *Déviance et Société*, 16(3): 279–286.

———. 1989. "*Éthique et délinquance: La délinquance comme gestion de sa vie.*" *Médecine et Hygiène*, 57–98. Geneva/Paris: Meridiens-Klienksieck.

Gilligan, Carol. 1987. "Moral Orientation and Moral Development." In *Women and Moral Theory*, edited by E.V. Kittay and D.T. Meyers. Totowa, NJ: Rowman & Littlefield.

————— 1982. *A Different Voice: Psychological Theory and Women's Development*. Cambridge, Mass.: Harvard University Press.

Gregory, Jeanne.   1986. "Sex, Class and Crime: Towards a Non-sexist Criminology," in *Confronting Crime*, 53–71. Beverly Hills: Sage.

Habermas, Jurgen.   1986. *Morale et communication: Conscience morale et activité communicationnelle*. Paris: Cerf. Originally published as *Moralbewusstein und kommunikatives Handeln* (Frankfurt: Suhrkamp, 1983).

Harris, M. Kay.   1987. "Moving into the New Millenium: Toward a Feminist Vision of Justice," *The Prison Journal*, 67: 27–38.

Hees, Joyce.   1986. "The Patchwork of Reality: Exploring Non-Criminal Means of Intervention." In *Abolitionism: Towards a Non-Repressive Approach to Crime*, edited by R. Van Swaaningen and H. Bianchi, 219–227. Amsterdam: Free University Press.

Heidensohn, Frances.   1986. "Models of Justice: Portia or Persephone? Some Thoughts on Equality, Fairness, and Gender in the Field of Criminal Justice," *International Journal of Sociology of Law*, 14: 287–298.

Hulsman, Louk and **Jacqueline Bernat de Celis.**   1982. *Peines perdues: Le système pénal en question*. Paris: Éditions du Centurion.

Jaggar, Alison M.   1983. *Feminist Politics and Human Nature*. Totowa, NJ: Rowman & Allanheld.

Klein, Dorie.   1981. "Violence Against Women: Some Contradictions Regarding its Causes and Its Elimination," *Crime and Delinquency*, 7(11): 64–80.

Kohlberg, Lawrence.   1984. *The Psychology of Moral Development*. San Francisco: Harper & Row. Quoted in Carol Gilligan, "Moral Orientation and Moral Development." In *Women and Moral Theory* (Totowa, NJ: Rowman and Littlefield, 1987).

Los, Maria.   1994. "The Struggle to Redefine Rape in the Early 1980s." In *Confronting Sexual Assault: A Decade of Legal and Social Change*, edited by J.V. Roberts and R. Mohr, 20–56. Toronto: University of Toronto Press.

McLeod, Linda.   1989. *La violence conjugale: Comprendre pour prévenir*. Ottawa: Conseil consultatif Canadien sur la situation de la femme.

Messerschmidt, James W.   1986. *Capitalism, Patriarchy and Crime: Toward a Socialist Feminist Criminology*. Totowa, NJ: Rowman & Littlefield.

Mohr, Renate.   1994. "Sexual Assault Sentencing: Leaving Justice to Individual Conscience." In *Confronting Sexual Assault: A Decade of Legal and Social Change*, edited by J.V. Roberts and R. Mohr. Toronto: University of Toronto Press.

Pires, Alvaro.   1991. "Ethiques et réforme du droit criminel: Au delà des philosophies de la peine," *Ethica*, 3(2): 47–78.

Pitch, Tamar.   1985. "Violence sexuelle, mouvement féministe et criminologie critique" *Déviance et Société*, 9(3): 255–256.

Smart, Carol.   1989. *Feminism and the Power of Law*. New York: Routledge.

Smith, Pamela. 1984. *Breaking the Silence: Descriptive Report of a Follow-Up Study of Abused Women Using a Shelter*. Regina: University of Regina. Quoted in Linda McLeod, 1989.

Snider, Laureen 1992. "Effets pervers de certaines luttes féministes sur le contrôle social," *Criminologie*, 25(1): 5–26.

———. 1985. "Legal Reform and Social Control: The Danger of Abolishing Rape," *International Journal of Sociology of Law*, 13: 337–356.

Walker, Margaret Urban. 1989. "Moral Understandings: Alternative 'Epistemology' for a Feminist Ethics," *Hypatia*, 4(2): 15–28.

MEN, MASCULINITIES, AND CRIME

Kathleen Burke and Brian Burtch

INTRODUCTION

The generic area of critical criminology embraces a wide range of theoretical frameworks for understanding crime, law, and formal and informal mechanisms to transform social and economic relations. In this chapter, we consider how the growing area of masculinities might be useful in reconsidering the nature of criminal victimization, especially as this is connected to men. Just as there has been a movement within criminology to take seriously the experiences of victims of crime (Fattah 1991; Lowman and MacLean 1992) and to explore women's experiences of criminal activity (Faith 1993), some criminologists are beginning to take more seriously ways in which masculinity promotes criminal activity and possibilities for new masculinities to counteract both criminal and noncriminal forms of violence and domination by men over men and women (Messerschmidt 1993; Stanko and Hobdell 1993). The connections between masculinities and crime, victimization, and possible strategies for reversing dominance and violence in society will be discussed later in this chapter. For now, we turn to the contributions of some key writers in the growing field of masculinities.

CONTRADICTIONS IN MASCULINITIES

The concept of masculinity is contradictory, and becomes more so as we examine what it means to be a man. Masculinity is associated with adulthood (becoming a man as opposed to remaining a boy), and with vigour, power, and determination. People may think of muscularity, intelligence, practicality, and inventiveness. Others may associate masculinity with companionability, friendship, fatherhood, and mentoring. Even where desirable aspects of masculinity are lacking, such as indifference among fathers or lack of male intimacy, several books offer concrete advice for men seeking to move beyond confining roles, to close the distance between themselves and others (see Seel, 1987; Hass 1994). These positive, attractive qualities of masculinity are often contrasted with other masculine "traits": bullying, injuring, physically dominating, and aggressiveness through to warlike qualities (militarism) and homicide. Some modern writers such as Stoltenberg (1989) enumerate a wide range of "manly" behaviours, often placing conventional masculinity in a negative light, as a force that interferes with social justice for men *and* women. It is also clear that between these opposing views of what it means to be masculine there are a number of contradictory views of masculinity. Hence, we use the term "masculinities" to refer to these competing images of what it means to be masculine.

One of the earliest books that both explored various dimensions of what it means to be a man and highlighted the pitfalls of masculine ideology was Andrew Tolson's *The Limits of Masculinity* (1977). Tolson explored contradictions in masculinity, including experiences of humiliation and alienation for workers in capitalist societies, especially for blue-collar ("manual") workers (1977, 58). And yet, these often deep feelings of inferiority and desperation are often unvoiced, hidden: "The working-class idea of 'being a man' thus demands a certain inarticulacy, or distance towards the complexity of personal experience ... beneath its formal structure, the 'masculine front' conceals the disillusionment of its emotional interior" (71). Tolson cautions that even for men seeking to move out of the masculine front, there are barriers to this, including men's tendency to "theorize about themselves" from a distance, rather than blending personal and theoretical elements in their understanding (19).

There are of course dissenting voices here. More radical groups of men move away from the notion of masculine fragility, and instead emphasize and challenge male privilege. Canada's White Ribbon Campaign is one example of men organizing against men's violence. Strategies to reduce men's violence and male power have received less attention from media, but these strategies still challenge male privilege. Other groups explore economic aspects of being a man, including discriminatory salary practices against women, and more widely a critique of capitalist relationships. A common understanding is that men must change their behaviour and become more critical of entrenched patriarchal relationships in various societies.

There are also subsets of men who may face special stigmatization and victimization. Recent work on masculinity, while alluding to men's power over women, allows for a closer examination of ways in which gender is mediated through sexual orientation, social class, and race (Mercer and Julien 1988). This means that men's power is leavened to some extent by social forces such as homophobia or racism: "Men who are gay, for example, have a sense of how their gayness places them in many situations of vulnerability in homophobic societies. Non-white men must negotiate their physical vulnerability because of white racism" (Stanko and Hobdell 1993, 401; see also Mercer and Julien 1988, 139).

Following the considerable interest in film, literature, and theatre in repre-senting women's experiences in society, there is now a growing literature and scholarship often referred to as "men's studies" or the "men's movement." Titles such as *The Hazards of Being Male, The Myth of Male Power: Why Men Are the Disposable Sex,* and *Absent Fathers, Lost Sons* have become more prominent, as vari-ous psychological, cultural, and political frameworks are used to reassess mas-culinity and men's power. Much of this work is humanistic, exploring men's challenges as they become spouses and fathers, encounter health problems and the ways in which work (and unemployment) structure and often distort men's experiences of themselves. In addition, there is a growing body of literature by intellectuals such as Robert Connell (1987), Arthur Brittan (1989), and Jeff Hearn (1992). Much of this literature concerns intimate relationships, sexuality, violence, parenting, and law. But there is little interest in an area that is almost quintessentially male: criminal involvement and incarceration. We now turn to this omission in the context of recent work by Stanko and Hobdell (1993) and Messerschmidt (1993).

Engendering Men

The current concern with men and masculinity owes much to the activism and scholarship of feminists over the past 20 years. Although feminism is not a uni-form theoretical or practical approach (Boyd and Sheehy 1989; Menzies and Chunn 1991), feminist discourses have common ground in respect to concerns over the seeming "naturalness" of power imbalances between men and women, and how these imbalances are translated daily into sexist ideologies and practices in society. The devaluation of women's work—whether in domestic situations or in waged work (Oakley 1988; Hessing 1991; Luxton 1993)—is one example of sexism at play. So also is the pervasive fear women experience in public places, particularly settings where women are alone, out after dark, or in enclosed set-tings such as underground parking lots (see Stanko 1990). Ongoing work on violence experienced by women has generated considerable critiques of men's exercise of power over women, through battering, sexual assaults, and other violent acts (Kelly 1988; DeKeseredy and Kelly 1993). Thus, feminists have chal-lenged the argument that men and women are essentially equals, and have explored how men and women are gendered beings. More recent research has treated men's exposure to violence as problematic, as researchers trace nearly "continuous" exposure to violence among some boys and young men. Violence can take the form of inter- or intraracial violence, political violence (including along religious lines, such as in Ireland), and daily threats and assaults (see Stanko and Hobdell 1993, 404).

A common theme that has emerged out of the various men's groups and writings on men is the fragility of masculine identity (Seidler 1991). Having to prove one's masculinity is seen as generating insecurity for men, leads to men's isolation from other men, as well as competitiveness and defensiveness. Within this framework, men have written about emotional distance between sons and fathers, and explored various aspects of fathering within marriages, and after separation and divorce (Kruk 1992).

The theme of men in crisis and in need of liberation has become commonplace in media representations of the modern men's movement. Newspapers, magazines, talk-radio shows, and television programmes draw on many representatives of the men's movement, and the theme that "men are hurting too." Key figures within this movement are Robert Bly and Sam Keen, who aspire to help men obtain a secure, "authentic" manhood while implicitly or explicitly downplaying the extent of men's power and privilege. These American writers explore the importance of men becoming more authentic, and thus not acting out various roles that weaken men and leave them less open to life.

Both the US-based National Organization for Men Against Sexism (NOMAS), the National Organization for Changing Men (NOCM), and local collectives of men that identify themselves as antisexist have been largely ignored by the mainstream media. The views and actions of these groups, for the most part, emerged in direct response to "the complacency and egocentricity of much of the 'men's movement,' its failure to confront patriarchy, its blindness to race and class" (Carrigan, Connell, and Lee, 1985, 574). There are also men involved in acting against violence against women. For instance, following the killing of 14 female engineering students at the University of Montreal in 1989, debate intensified over violence by men against women. The dismissal of this mass murder as an insane act was challenged by other interpretations that highlighted widespread fears and victimization of women (see *After the Montreal Massacre* 1990; Burtch 1992, 71). Collectives of men organized against sexism and male violence. Both the White Ribbon Campaign and Men Marching Against Violence Against Women are efforts that "asked men to [publicly] acknowledge their part in sexism" (Luxton 1993, 364).

The writing of antisexist men also contradicts many themes of the early men's liberation movement. Stoltenberg, in *Refusing to Be a Man* (1989), dismisses the notion that men are incapable of expressing their feelings: "men as a class have always expressed their feelings, eloquently, and extensively ... Men have expressed their feelings about women, wealth, possession, and territory and turned those feelings into laws and nation-states. Men have expressed their feelings about women, murder, and the masculinity of other men and from those feelings forged battalions and detonable devices ... Men have *institutionalized* their feelings" (1989, 92). However, Stoltenberg has attracted criticism for moralizing, and insisting that men must abandon their masculine identities in order to identify with and further feminist struggles (Seidler 1990, 1991). Instead, men must redefine masculinity, rather than "refusing to be a man." Other criticisms include marginalizing gay men and men of colour, since the antisexist movement by men continues to be led by white males.

In attempting to avoid the sexist—and especially heterosexist—pitfalls of various men's movements, Schein (1977) outlined four dangers that need to be considered in developing antisexist men's groups:

1. Guard against the groups becoming arenas for denouncing women.

2. Ensure that anger is directed at appropriate sources, such as larger structures that reinforce patriarchal relations, instead of individual women.

3. Preserve the importance of critiquing men's individual and collective sexism, so that group members avoid unconditional acceptance of occasional regression toward sexism by some men.

4. Challenge the sexism of coworkers, friends, and family members (Schein 1977, 132–134). Other men's groups (e.g., the White Ribbon Campaign, and Men Marching Against Violence Against Women) work closely with feminists in working to screen known abusers from participation, and deciding where to concentrate financial and political support (Luxton 1993).

The men's movement, then, is not a monolith. It is not confined to Bly's mythopoetic approach, Jungian insights, or Keen's spiritual journey toward a manhood of fierceness and passion (*Fire in the Belly*). But how does this movement coincide with the interests of men of colour? A commonly criticized feature of the men's movement is that they appeal widely to white, middle-class, middle-aged, heterosexual men, rather than a wider cross-section of men. Identifying himself as a black, feminist, and bisexual man, Michael-David Gordon confronts the whiteness of the contemporary men's movement: "I challenge you to make us people of color a part of your daily lives and work. I challenge you white men to not behave as if you were the centre of the universe" (Luxton 1993, 17).

In the preface to his book *Iron John*, Robert Bly admits he does not directly address the lives and experiences of homosexual men because "mythology as I see it does not make a big distinction between homosexual and heterosexual men" (Bly 1990, x). Margaret Randall, however, disagrees: "[m]ythology is the reproduction of values, and our culture certainly places a different, inferior, value on that which is homoerotic" (Randall 1992, 145). Gay activists continue to emphasize the centrality of sexuality to discussions of gender, particularly masculinity. Kinsman argues that "the 'naturalness' of heterosexuality so permeates 'common sense' that ... unless we view heterosexuality as socially made we cannot see how gender and sexual relations are accomplished in everyday life" (1993, 6).

An exception to the near-invisibility of masculinity is what some refer to as a "new sociology of masculinity" (Carrigan, Connell, and Lee 1985). This approach is exemplified in the work of Robert Connell (1987), who explores gender with respect to wider structural forces. He argues that gender relations can best be understood by analyzing the impact of structures of labour, power, and cathexis. His research focuses on how these structures—and men's responses to them—accomplish masculinity. A central theme throughout Connell's work is what he views as the *relational* character of masculinity, defined in opposition to both femininity and homosexuality. Connell gives several examples of masculine representations that contradict or reinforce the hegemonic form of masculinity.[1]

CRIME

"It is now often noted not only that males commit more crimes than females do, but that they also commit crimes that are more serious than those committed by females. Moreover, it is also well-established that males are more likely than females to recidivate, and to become professional criminals" (Liddle 1994, 71). Recent research has highlighted the pervasiveness of male violence, especially directed against women. A study of male violence in Canadian homes found that 9.9 percent of men in their sample exhibited physical and psychological acts of violence against their wives (Lupri, Grandin, and Brinkerhoff 1994). DeKeseredy and Kelly (1993) noted the pervasive character of serious physical and psychological abuse of females by males in their study of the role of violence in Canadian university and college dating relationships.[2] The point remains that there is little literature that focuses on male criminals as gendered beings, using a critique of masculinity as an analytical point of departure.

Some argue that there is considerable overlap between masculine and feminine qualities, such that these contours of masculinity are impossible to draw out. But in criminology, and post-critical theory more generally,[3] we are faced with a considerable correlation between men's involvement in crime (Hartnagel 1992, 97–106) , not only as perpetrators but also as victims, and often as decisive actors in such roles as police, prosecutors, judges, and prison officials. Work that explores gender and crime in a more dynamic, multidimensional way is imperative to a post-critical perspective on crime and victimization.

James Messerschmidt's *Masculinities and Crime* (1993) is a comprehensive approach to ways in which masculinities are associated with criminal activities. He begins by noting that gender is the single most explanatory variable for criminal involvement: men, and especially young men, are at the heart of much criminal activity in Western societies (1, 87). Drawing on Connell's theoretical framework, Messerschmidt explores how "oppositional masculinity" is a widespread feature of young men's behaviour, and specifically how white, middle-class males demonstrate their manliness by opposition outside of school activities, while largely conforming to the relatively authoritarian framework of formal schooling. Arguably, most of these males have a stake in completing school, and tend to not confront school authority directly. In contrast, Messerschmidt (1993, 117) sees many African-American or Hispanic-American men as acting more directly against authority, both inside and outside school settings. He suggests that even grotesque, violent crimes—such as gang rape involving killing or particularly violent beatings—are not simply atavistic. Rather, "such group rape helps maintain and reinforce an alliance among the boys by humiliating and devaluing women, thereby strengthening the fiction of masculine power" (114). Thus, Messerschmidt reinforces Connell's notion of the relational character of masculinity, demonstrating how abuse of women is for some males a way to accomplish a dominant representation of masculinity. Violence toward other men may sometimes reinforce a sense of dominant masculinity for bullies, and self-hatred and fear for their victims.[4]

Messerschmidt (1993) also provides a detailed critique of some writings by radical feminists. While sympathetic to the reality of patriarchal power, not least of all the myriad expressions of violence against women by men (Stanko 1985), he criticizes sweeping approaches that damn all heterosexual involvement as essentially coercive and exploitative. Such views "were similar in the sense that they saw masculine dominance, power, and violence as social (not as biological) phenomena reproduced through cultural practices and processes, and the emphasis was on the similarities among men and between men and the institutions of patriarchal society; namely, masculine ideals" (36). Messerschmidt (1993, 48–49) treats this approach as hyperbolic. He notes that, on the one hand, rather than using sex as a proverbial weapon, for some men "it is precisely through sex that many men experience their greatest uncertainties, dependence and deference in relation to women—in stark contrast, quite often, with their experience of authority and independence in the public world" (Lynn Segal, cited in Messerschmidt, 1993, 48). On the other hand, it is misleading to treat heterosexual women's experiences of sex as oppressive through and through. Rather, sexuality for many women is neither passive nor demeaning, and reflects women as active in deciding how and when they will be sexual (see also Kitzinger 1985).

Messerschmidt's work contests the stereotyping of men as a monolithic group sharing a hegemonic power over women. Instead, the archetypical male must be broken into substantially different experiences of male power. He notes: "not only does the exercise of power over women differ among men, but also among men themselves. Heterosexual men exercise greater power than gay men, upper-class men greater power than working-class men, and white men greater power than men of color" (Messerschmidt 1993, 72). And even this kind of stratification among men could be more searching; for example, that not all homosexual men are less powerful than heterosexual men, or that expressions of power vary among men of different races.

Research exploring victimization of men within a framework of gender is rare. As Stanko and Hobdell (1993, 413) lament: "what is never questioned in the literature on crime, victimization, and fear of crime is masculinity." Nevertheless, both masculinity and an emphasis on experiences of victims have been important in theorizing sexual abuse of boys and young men. In the past several years there has been a marked increase in academic and popular interest in men's experiences of molestation during childhood. Unfortunately much of this work reveals a singular and static image of masculinity. The ways in which men *resist* such representations and instead reconstruct what it means to be a man is rarely evident in this literature (Burke 1994). Moreover, this literature often uncritically reinforces the equation of masculinity with heterosexuality, noting that the same-sex character of abuse of boys violates both their bodies and their masculinity.

EMBODYING RESISTANCE: GAY MEN AND SEXUALITY

The emergence of a visible and vocal gay movement during the 1970s has had a significant impact on current discourses about men and masculinities. Gay activists treat assumptions of masculinity as *inherently* heterosexual as problematic (see Carrigan, Connell, and Lee 1985). Theoretical work linked the social construction of a homosexual identity in the late nineteenth century with the need to promote heterosexual masculinity as normal. Gay men were thus able to challenge psychiatric models of homosexuality as a sickness, a form of gender inversion. This included the removal of homosexuality from the American Psychiatric Association's Diagnostic and Statistical Manual in 1973 (Salamon 1988).

Victimization of gay men has been highlighted by some work within gay studies. Many studies have addressed discrimination against gay men, including covert and overt obstacles for gay men who are working in such traditionally masculine occupations as policing (M. Burke 1993). There is also ongoing interest in "gay bashing" as manifested in seemingly random, public attacks on homosexuals (Kinsman 1987a, 1987b; Messerschmidt 1993, 183–184). There is much more to this movement than reduction of violence. Despite some evidence of greater tolerance of same-sex relationships, there remain concerns over disparities in age of consent (to sex) between heterosexuals and homosexuals, and pervasive stigmas facing gay and lesbian youth. For example, a recent Canadian film—*Out* (1993)—documents the experiences of some high-school youth considering whether or not to come out. Salamon (1988, 106–107) contends that negative stereotyping of homosexuals is "tenacious" in the United States and in Canada. Nevertheless, the gay liberation movement challenges the equation of masculinity with heterosexuality, and also seeks to break down stereotypes of gays or lesbians as effeminate or masculine, respectively. Instead, sexuality is seen as far more complex than these archetypes allow. Thus, the gay liberation movement, including its more recent manifestation of "queer politics" poses a direct challenge to homophobia in its celebration of sexualities (see Liddle 1994, 58–59). And while there are serious concerns about legal struggles being co-opted into greater control of personal behaviour by government, some writers credit gay and lesbian liberation as helping to "destabilize" such concepts as the traditional family (see Herman 1994, 147).

CONCLUSION

An appreciation of masculine socialization and the influence of gender in all aspects of social relations is long overdue within criminological research. It is well-known that men are more likely to be involved in criminal activities than women, and some expressions of machismo such as battery of women are wide-spread and have far-reaching effects on women so victimized (Stoltenberg 1989, 203–204). Criminological inquiry is connected with concrete efforts to promote social justice, including public safety and removal of obstacles facing women, people of colour, and other groups who to some degree or another face covert and overt barriers in the modern world (Young 1990). We agree with Messerschmidt (1993, 1–2) that there is a paradox between the well-known association of men with criminal involvement and the tendency among crimi-nologists to not delve into the motivations and experiences of men who become criminals. Furthermore, the current movement to treat masculinity seriously, as neither an idealized expression of strength, achievement, and fair-mindedness, nor as hell incarnate for those under the boot of masculine powers, must take into account the seriousness of men's violence toward girls and women, and toward men as well (see Stanko and Hobdell 1993).

At the same time, many writers are concerned not only with mapping the nature of masculinities, but moving beyond current roles and powers played by men and women. Hearn (1992) sees "public men" as a creation of a wide variety of historical and social forces, manifested in law, family relations, the military, media, work, and sexuality, to name only several. Today, he sees men's actions as both destructive and potentially affirmative: "Men, individually and collec-tively, now exist in definite, recognizable relations both to the increasingly inter-national capabilities of men (both possible and actual) in economic exploitation, in militarism, in methods of domination and destruction … in ecological, nuclear, biological, and chemical capabilities and disasters, and also to peaceful organization and resistance" (Hearn 1992, 229). Hearn calls for the "deconstruc-tion of public men," involving the breaking down of traditional patriarchal forms, yet he is also skeptical about some "new" men's formations within an essentially patriarchal culture. "The notion of 'public men' needs to be decon-structed: the authority of men in public has to be undermined as much as the authority of men in private … while we need to critique men, we need also to look with doubt upon reorganizations of men, new solidarities of men, and new identities of men; all of these may have to go if men are to be de-centred. We need to fully recognize and change men's powers, and to support women's liber-ation, and yet at the same time undermine 'our' identities as men" (Hearn 1992, 231). Hearn's work underscores a point feminists have long been making: for men to change their behaviour, and in the interests of social justice, men must bring themselves into account if sexual stratification is to be altered.

Work in this area also needs to be more refined and rigorous. Some of the excesses of earlier writings by men about masculinity, as well as sweeping cri-tiques of men as power blocs, are being corrected by research that highlights how race, for example, intersects with gender. There are also studies that uncover contexts in which women exercise power, despite often deeply embed-ded sexism in many societies. Carrigan, Connell, and Lee (1985) assert that mas-culine and feminine power intersects with class and race relations. And yet the authors allow that the majority of men "benefit from the subordination of women" (592).

Emerging work on masculinities marks a significant break from the deterministic approaches of the positive school of criminology, with its emphasis on biological factors in criminality (Caputo and Linden 1992, 172–176). And there are new connections being made to work with men (both inside and outside prison) to reduce men's violence (see Light 1994; Murphy and Joels 1994). In addition, new programmes and services are being developed to help men cope with their sexual victimization (K. Burke 1993). The movement is also pressured to become more inclusive with its focus on men of colour, gay men, prisoners, among others. Post-critical criminology is thus bringing into focus men's primary contributions to violence in society, and developing new ideas and resources to better support men. In this, the movement continues to attract derision from many quarters, whether from the viewpoint that men are privileged vis-à-vis women or the premise that such work is unmanly. These efforts to deconstruct what it means to be a man and to promote alternative ways to stark or slick male oppression of others have been slow to seep into criminological discourse and practices. Just as there are many perspectives within what has been dubbed the men's movement, there is also diversity among men in terms of how they define and accomplish masculinity. Unfortunately, this diversity is often not captured when we speak abstractly of men, as amorphous representations of humanity, citizens, criminals, or victims. As we emphasized in this chapter, there are dangers in painting men and men's actions with a broad brush. In the context of criminology, engendering crime means exploring what it means to be a man, and how this shapes not only men's criminality, but also criminal victimization.

ENDNOTES

1   The concept of hegemonic masculinity has become central to critical analyses of masculinity. In Connell's work it refers to the historically specific and idealized representations of masculinity that achieve social dominance (through a complex series of ideological, social, political, and economic transformations). While not all men practice "hegemonic masculinity," the point is that it is institutionalized such that most men benefit from it. Since a detailed discussion of this concept is beyond the scope of this chapter, we recommend the following: Carrigan, Connell, and Lee (1985); Connell (1987); and Donaldson (1993).

2   Violence against girls and women is vividly portrayed in literature as well. For two recent Canadian examples, see Svendsen (1992) and Roberts (1993).

3   Post-critical theory aims to subvert notions of male omnipotence. Instead, it encourages the examination of how gender is fractured. It explores "the inherent instability of seemingly hegemonic structures, that power is diffused throughout society, and that there are multiple possibilities for resistance" (Handler 1992, 697). Post-critical theory highlights heterogeneity among men, and how masculinities can be reconstructed along lines of social class, disabilities, race, and ethnicity, for example.

4   "Vinnie made a hawking sound and spit a glob of phlegm on the brick beside Austin's face. 'Come on, homo—lick that off.' Austin whimpered and tried to pull back ... One of the brute lieutenants pushed Austin's face along the brick, scraping it raw. And now Austin, broken, surrendered whatever dignity was left. His tongue lolled out, and he licked up the phlegm while the bullies cheered. 'Swallow it!' Vinnie commanded. From where I stood, by my locker, I saw in a daze of horror, the self-disgust in Austin's face as he got it down without retching ... neither I nor anyone else made a move toward Austin—slumping in the corner as if it would have been easier to die than survive this thing. We all went hurrying away to eat our waxed-paper lunches. I never, never talked to Austin again ... The cold truth I took from the scene of Austin Singer's humiliation was this: *At least I could still pass.* I never even gave a thought to the evil of what Vinnie had done, how sick with confused desire, the carnal thrill of degradation. The only reality lesson in it for me was not to be recognizably Other" (Monette 1992, 35–36).

REFERENCES AND BIBLIOGRAPHY

After The Montreal Massacre [documentary]. 1990. National Film Board of Canada (Studio D) and Canadian Broadcasting Corporation. Directed by Gerry Rogers and produced by Nicole Hubert, Ginny Stikeman, and Louise Lore. Ottawa. 30 minutes.

Bly, Robert.   1990. *Iron John: A Book About Men.* Reading, MA: Addison-Wesley.

Boyd, S. and **E. Sheehy.**   1989. "Overview: Feminism and the Law in Canada." In *Law and Society: A Critical Perspective,* edited by T. Caputo, M. Kennedy, C. Reasons, and A. Brannigan, 255–270. Toronto: Harcourt Brace Jovanovich.

Brittan, A.   1989. *Masculinity and Power.* Oxford: Basil Blackwell.

Burke, K.   1994. "Masculinities and Male Child Sexual Abuse." Paper presented at the Feminist Institute for Studies on Law and Society Symposium, Simon Fraser University, Vancouver, British Columbia.

——.   1993. "Getting Through: Selected Professional Perspectives on Male Survivors of Child Sexual Abuse in the Lower Mainland [of B.C.]." Paper presented at the Western Association of Sociology and Anthropology Meetings, Vancouver, British Columbia.

Burke, M.   1993. *Coming Out of the Blue: British Police Officers Talk About Their Lives in 'The Job' as Lesbians, Gays and Bisexuals.* London: Cassell Books.

Burtch, B.   1992. *The Sociology of Law: Critical Approaches to Social Control.* Toronto: Harcourt Brace Jovanovich, Canada.

Caputo, T. and **R. Linden.**   1992. "Early Theories of Criminology." In *Criminology: A Canadian Perspective,* 2d ed., edited by R. Linden, 165–183. Toronto: Harcourt Brace.

Carrigan, T., B. Connell, and **J. Lee.**   1985. "Toward a New Sociology of Masculinity," *Theory and Society,* 14: 551–603

Connell, R.   1987. *Gender and Power.* Cambridge: Polity Press.

DeKeseredy, W. and **K. Kelly.** 1993. "The Incidence and Prevalence of Woman Abuse in Canadian University and College Dating Relationships" *Canadian Journal of Sociology,* 18: 137–159.

Donaldson, M. 1993. "What is Hegemonic Masculinity?" *Theory and Society,* 22: 643–657.

Faith, K. 1993. *Unruly Women: Theories of Confinement and Resistance.* Vancouver: Press Gang.

Fattah, E. 1991. *Understanding Criminal Victimization: An Introduction to Theoretical Criminology.* Scarborough: Prentice Hall Canada.

Handler, J. 1992. "Postmodernism, Protest, and the New Social Movements," *Law and Society Review* 26: 697–731.

Hartnagel, T. 1992. "Correlates of Criminal Behaviour. In *Criminology: A Canadian Perspective,* edited by R. Linden, 91–126. Toronto: Harcourt Brace Jovanovich Canada.

Hass, A. 1994. *The Gift of Fatherhood: How Men's Lives Are Transformed by Their Children.* New York: Fireside/Simon and Schuster.

Hearn, Jeff. 1992. *Men in the Public Eye: The Construction and Deconstruction of Public Men and Public Patriarchies.* London: Routledge.

Herman, D. 1994. *Rights of Passage: Struggles for Lesbian and Gay Legal Equality.* Toronto: University of Toronto Press.

Hessing, M. 1991. "Talking shop(ping): Office Conversations and Women's Dual Labour," *Canadian Journal of Sociology,* 16: 23–50.

hooks, bell. 1992. "Men in Feminist Struggle—The Necessary Movement." In *Women Respond to the Men's Movement,* edited by K. Hagan, 111–117. San Francisco: Pandora.

Keen, Sam. 1991. *Fire in the Belly: On Being a Man.* New York: Bantam Books.

Kelly, L. 1988. *Surviving Sexual Violence.* Minneapolis: University of Minnesota.

Kinsman, G. 1993. "'Inverts,' 'Psychopaths,' and 'Normal' Men: Historical Sociological Perspectives on Gay and Heterosexual Masculinities." In *Men and Masculinities: A Critical Anthology,* edited by T. Haddad, 3–35. Toronto: Canadian Scholars' Press.

———. 1987a. "Men Loving Men: The Challenge of Gay Liberation." In *Beyond Patriarchy: Essays on Men, Pleasure, Power, and Change,* ed. M. Kaufman, 103-119. Toronto: Oxford University Press.

———. 1987b. *The Regulation of Desire: Sexuality in Canada.* Montreal: Black Rose Books.

Kitzinger, S. 1985. *Women's Experience of Sex.* Harmondsworth: Penguin.

Kruk, E. 1992. *Divorce and Disengagement: The Patterns of Fatherhood Within and Beyond Marriage.* Halifax: Fernwood Books.

Liddle, A.M. 1994. "Masculinity, 'Male Behaviour' and Crime: A Theoretical Investigation of Sex-Differences in Delinquency and Deviant Behaviour." In *Masculinity and Crime: Issues of Theory and Practice—Conference Report,* 55–94. London: Centre for Criminal Justice Research, (Brunel University).

Light, P.W.   1994. "The Everyman Centre." In *Masculinity and Crime: Issues of Theory and Practice—Conference Report,* 139–142. London: Centre for Criminal Justice Research, (Brunel University).

Lowman, J. and **B. MacLean,** eds.   1992. *Realist Criminology: Crime Control and Policing in the 1990s.* Toronto: University of Toronto Press.

Lupri, E., E. Grandin, and **M. Brinkerhoff.**   1994. "Socioeconomic Status and Male Violence in the Canadian Home: A Reexamination," *Canadian Journal of Sociology,* 19: 47–73.

Luxton, M.   1993. "Dreams and Dilemmas: Feminist Musings on 'The Man Question.'" In *Women Respond to the Men's Movement,* edited by K. Hagan, 347–374. San Francisco: Pandora.

Menzies, R. and **D. Chunn.**   1991. "'Kicking Against the Pricks:' The Dilemma of Feminist Teaching in Criminology." In *New Directions in Critical Criminology,* edited by B. MacLean and D. Milovanovic, 97–164. Vancouver: The Collective Press.

Mercer, K. and **I. Julien.**   1988. "Race, Sexual Politics and Black Masculinity: A Dossier." In *Male Order: Unwrapping Masculinity,* edited by R. Chapman and J. Rutherford, 97–164. London: Lawrence and Wishart.

Messerschmidt, J.   1993. *Masculinities and Crime: Critique and Reconceptualization of Theory.* Lanham, Maryland: Rowman and Littlefield Publishers.

Monette, P.   1992. *Becoming a Man: Half a Life Story.* London: Abacus Books.

Murphy, K. and **J. Joels,**   1994. "Groupwork on Men and Offending." In *Masculinity and Crime: Issues of Theory and Practice—Conference Report,* 99–103. London: Centre for Criminal Justice Research (Brunel University).

Oakley, A.   1988. *The Sociology of Housework.* Oxford: Basil Blackwell.

Out: Stories of Lesbian and Gay Youth. 1993. National Film Board of Canada. Directed by David Adkin and produced by Silva Basmajian. Executive Producer: Dennis Murphy. Ottawa. 79 minutes.

Randall, M.   1992. "'And so She Walked Over and Kissed Him ...': Robert Bly's Men's Movement." In *Women Respond to the Men's Movement,* edited by K. Hagan, 141–148. San Francisco: Pandora.

Roberts, A.   1993. *The Last Chance Cafe and Other Stories.* Vancouver: Polestar Press.

Salamon, E.   1988. "Homosexuality: Sexual Stigma." In *Deviance: Conformity and Control in Canadian Society,* edited by V. Sacco, Toronto: Prentice Hall.

Schein, L.   1977. "Dangers With Men's Consciousness-Raising Groups." In *For Men Against Sexism,* edited by J. Snodgrass. Albion, CA: Times Change.

Seel, R.   1987. *The Uncertain Father: Exploring Modern Fatherhood.* Bath: Gateway Books.

Seidler, V.   1991. *Recreating Sexual Politics: Men, Feminism and Politics.* London: Routledge.

————. 1990. "Men, Feminism, and Power." In *Men, Masculinities & Social Theory,* edited by A. Metcalf and D. Morgan, London: Unwin Hyman.

————. 1988. "Fathering, Authority and Masculinity." In *Male Order: Unwrapping Masculinity,* edited by R. Chapman and J. Rutherford. London: Lawrence & Wishart.

Stanko, E. 1990. *Everyday Violence: How Women and Men Experience Sexual and Physical Danger.* London: Pandora Books.

————. 1985. *Intimate Intrusions: Women's Experience of Male Violence.* London: RKP.

———— and K. Hobdell. 1993. "Assault on Men: Masculinity and Male Victimization," *British Journal of Criminology,* 33: 400–415.

Stoltenberg, J. 1989. *Refusing to Be a Man: Essays on Sex and Justice.* Harmondsworth: Penguin/Meridian Books.

Svendsen, L. 1992. *Marine Life.* Toronto: HarperCollins.

Tolson, A. 1977. *The Limits of Masculinity.* London: Tavistock.

Young, I. 1990. *Justice and the Politics of Difference.* Princeton: Princeton University Press.

THE DIALECTICS OF MANDATORY ARREST POLICIES

Jacqueline Faubert
and
Ronald Hinch

INTRODUCTION

Considerable attention has been focused on the criminal justice system's response to spousal assault. The most controversial response has been the creation of so-called *mandatory arrest* policies. There are those who argue that these policies have achieved what was intended: they have reduced both incident and recidivism rates (Berk, et al., 1992, Jaffe, et al., 1986, Ursel and Farough, 1986). But there are also those who argue that there is no clear evidence that these policies have achieved these goals (Buzawa and Buzawa, 1993b, Sheptycki, 1991). There has even been some concern that the policies may actually increase recidivism rates in certain situations (Sherman, 1992a).

The intent of this chapter, however, is not to argue *for* or *against* mandatory arrest. Rather, our purpose is to argue that policies, such as the mandatory arrest policy, are created within a specific context, a context within which the state is asked to do something about a particular social problem without necessarily eliminating the cause of the problem (Chambliss, 1986; Chambliss and Seidman, 1982). Thus, reforming arrest policies may resolve certain issues with regard to how wife assault is policed, but it does not resolve the conditions that lead to wife assault. Further, even though the reform measures may provide solutions to some conflicts in policing wife assault, they produce new conflicts in need of resolution. It is our intent to illustrate this argument by reviewing the circumstances leading to the creation of the policy, assessing the ways in which the policy fulfilled those initial objectives, and by showing how the policy has produced results requiring further policy changes.

FACTORS INFLUENCING THE DEVELOPMENT OF THE MANDATORY ARREST POLICY

There are several factors that led to the creation of mandatory arrest policies. One of the most significant of these was the perception that the criminal justice system's response to wife assault was inadequate. This section examines the impact of sociopolitical factors, as well as the impact of social science research on the creation and development of mandatory arrest policies. The focus is primarily but not exclusively Canadian.

The Impact of the Sociopolitical Factors

The women's movement, the desire of various state agencies to be seen to be doing something about the problem, and a general trend toward a more punitive criminal justice system were all influential in the creation and evolution of mandatory arrest policies. This section summarizes the role played by each of these factors.

It can be argued that the movement to do something about wife assault emerged out of the antirape movement. Certainly, by the end of the 1970s, the antirape movement had already begun to widen its focus. The movement became concerned that the issue of violence against women could not be resolved by focusing on rape issues alone. There were other types of violence against women that needed to be addressed. The antirape movement had already exposed the fact that the criminal justice system treated rape victims in a negligent manner (Clark and Lewis, 1977; Kasinski, 1978). The transfer of energy to a focus on the criminal justice system's treatment of wife assault was a logical extension of the concern that female victims of violent crime be taken seriously.

While no single event can be said to represent the only factor leading to a change in legal policy, it is obvious that one widely publicized incident in Canada brought the issue out of the "private troubles" closet. In 1980 it was reported in the House of Commons that a recent study had estimated that one out of every ten women was assaulted by her husband. The members of the House, in obvious disbelief, erupted into laughter.

The study that elicited the laughter had been prepared for the Canadian Advisory Council on the Status of Women (Canada, 1980). The report surveyed what was known about wife assault at that time, and helped initiate an intensive investigation of the criminal justice system's response to the problem. It also began a consultation process that brought together women from different regions of Canada to discuss the issues (Walker, 1990). As a result of this consultation process, the term "wife assault" began to be used to refer to the problem. Adoption of the new label placed the issue of wife abuse within a legal/criminal framework, and helped forge the commitment of feminist activists to reform the justice system's law-enforcement role (Walker, 1990).

The definition of men's violence against their wives as assault and the resulting search for a vehicle of change within the criminal justice system was also the focus of many other reports. For example, the 1982 report of the federal legislature's Standing Committee on Health, Welfare, and Social Affairs focused on the legal protection of battered women. Protection was defined as having two elements: the enforcement of assault legislation and legislation for keeping the peace (Canada, Standing Committee on Health, Welfare, and Social Affairs, 1982). Recommendations for a uniform police charging policy that stressed arrest grew out of this focus on protection. After a rather intense House of Commons debate in 1982, the House adopted a resolution calling for police to lay charges in all instances where there was reasonable and probable grounds that an offence had occurred. Consequently, on July 15 of that year, the federal solicitor general sent a letter to the executive of the Canadian Association of Chiefs of Police encouraging all police to lay charges in cases of wife battering. There were, of course, some individual police departments who were willing to devise their own version of a mandatory arrest policy. For example, in 1981 the London, Ontario police department devised its own policy, in cooperation with community groups. Their policy was subsequently used as the model for other police departments across Canada. In the wake of the solicitor general's letter, and the model provided by the London police department, most provinces and most police forces in Canada developed their own version of the directive.

The policy, however, was not simply a product of pressure tactics from the women's movement. It was also an extension of a trend toward increased punitiveness, and the criminalization of behaviour previously treated as private troubles. For example, the *Young Offenders Act,* which replaced the *Juvenile Delinquents Act* in 1984, was clearly a move toward more punitive treatment of juvenile offenders (Havemann, 1986; 1992). Similarly, there was also a determined effort to be more punitive toward drunk drivers and child abusers (Binder and Meeker, 1988). Demands from a "new right" faction in Canada and the United States encouraged a law and order campaign with a distinctly conservative character. It demanded increased powers for the state, including broader powers of surveillance and arrest (Burtch, 1992, 3).

Other researchers have suggested an additional factor may have also contributed to the creation of mandatory arrest policies. Frisch argues that the most compelling reason for the policy change came in the form of police fear of civil liability (1992, 212). For example, in New York and Oakland battered women began challenging the police departments' policy of nonarrest in the early 1980s. In 1984, in *Thurman* v. *Thorrington Police Department,* a battered woman was permitted to sue the police for their failure to protect her from an abusive partner. The victim was awarded $1.9 million in damages. In addition, by March 1988 at least 30 Thurman-type cases were pending in courts within the United States (Pennsylvania, 1984, 17–18).

The Influence of Social Science Research

There has been no shortage of research supporting the emphasis on law and order and the effectiveness of a punitive orientation toward wife assault. The common threads in this research are the impact that mandatory arrest has on victim safety and the reduction in recidivism rates.

The main impetus behind advocating mandatory arrest is to communicate to abusive men that assaulting their wives is a crime. The intended effect of such a policy is to deter individuals on both a specific and general level (see for example Burris and Jaffe, 1983; Sherman and Berk, 1984). Specific deterrence is the ability to deter an individual who has been previously arrested from committing a new criminal act based on known consequences. The criminological research refers to this phenomenon as one that lowers recidivism rates. On a general level, deterrence operates to prevent other prospective offenders in the general population from offending due to the threat of probable punishment. Both of these arguments are explicit in perhaps the most influential research encouraging mandatory arrest in Canada and the United States.

Because the London, Ontario police department's policy on wife assault was the first in Canada, it was also the first to be subjected to academic scrutiny. This scrutiny not only provided support for the policy, it led to specific recommendations that other police departments adopt similar policies (Burris and Jaffe, 1983; Ontario, 1985). Using both police records and victim survey data from the London area, Burris and Jaffe (1983), and Jaffe, Wolfe, and Telford (Ontario, 1985) found that charges laid by police increased while victim-laid charges decreased under the policy. They also found that the proportion of cases where there was a finding of guilt resulting in a substantial court sentence was significantly higher in cases where the police laid the charges. Fewer of the charges were withdrawn or dismissed when they were police initiated. Therefore, the proportion of cases heard in criminal courts rose dramatically. Furthermore, Jaffe, Wolfe, and Telford claimed that police charges produced the most radical reduction in recidivism rates, as well as a reduction in the degree of verbal and physical aggression reported by the victim. Thus, these research findings provided support for those favouring a mandatory arrest policy. Indeed, Jaffe, Wolfe, and Telford (Ontario, 1985, 44) recommended continuance of the policy.

In the United States, the Minneapolis experiments conducted by Sherman and Berk (United States, Police Foundation, 1984) provided similar support for the policy. Like the Jaffe, Wolfe, and Telford study (Ontario, 1985), the Minneapolis experiment employed two key measures of repeat violence: official police records and victim interviews. The findings from these sources initially supported the deterrence argument. Police records showed that arrest was clearly an improvement over temporary separation of victim and offender. Temporary separation resulted in two-and-a-half times the number of repeat incidents compared to arrest. Victim interviews also indicated that fewer repeat incidents occurred after arrest than after the use of any other police intervention strategy (Sherman and Berk, 1984; United States, Police Foundation, 1984). The researchers concluded, "on the basis of this study alone, police should probably employ arrest in most cases of minor domestic violence" (Sherman and Berk, 1984, 270). The United States Attorney General Family Violence Task Force (Pennsylvania, 1984) took the initiative and recommended mandatory arrest as the preferred police strategy.

EFFECTIVENESS OF THE MANDATORY ARREST POLICY

The debate on the effectiveness of the mandatory arrest policy focuses on several issues. First, there are concerns about the methodology used to assess the effectiveness of the policy. Second, there are concerns about the theory of deterrence upon which the effect is said to exist. Third, can it be shown that the policy has increased the perception by the victims that the policy has helped them? Finally, can it be shown that the police have changed their attitudes and practices when it comes to enforcing the law?

Problems in Research Methods

Mandatory arrest policies are based, in part, on the deterrent value of arrest. In this regard, the Sherman and Berk (1984, also, United States, Police Foundation, 1984) and Burris and Jaffe (1983) studies have played a significant role in confirming this aspect of the policy. However, a number of studies have debated both the validity of these findings, and more specifically, the evidence that deterrence is the specific mechanism that links arrest to reducing recidivism (see for example Buzawa and Buzawa, 1993b and Sheptycki, 1991).

Criticisms of the Sherman and Berk (1984) study, as well as the replication studies that followed, range from a general attack on the ethical and methodological approach to the specific problems inherent in the initial research design. The overriding criticism aimed at these experiments concerns their seemingly unethical design. The design specified that police response to reported incidents of spousal assault be randomized. Thus, rather than basing their decisions on the characteristics of the incident and using their discretion, police were required to use one of three options: they could make an arrest, remove the perpetrator from the scene for eight hours, or attempt to act as mediators. The choice of options was made by the researchers using a random selection process.

One problem with this study is that it has the potential to put victims at risk. Since the researchers begin with the assumption that some responses might be preferred over others, but are presumably uncertain as to which response is best, there is the potential that the randomly selected outcome in individual cases may not be appropriate for that case. For example, in some situations where the offender was not arrested but did commit a second offence, it could be argued that the second offence might not have happened had he been arrested for the first offence.

With regard to validity, Sherman and Berk's (1984; United States, Police Foundation, 1984) work ignores other relevant factors within the arrest-violence equation. Their experiments isolate arrest from other criminal justice factors, including prosecution and sentencing. Lerman (1992) notes that the experiments reflected a test-tube attitude toward solving a social problem. She advocates the need to "take a peek outside the test tube" in order to identify other relevant variables that might have affected the design of the study (220).

The reliability of the experiments is questioned when considering the virtually impossible task of comparing persons of the same relevant characteristics. As one of the original researchers commented, "people are far too complex...it is very difficult to compare arrested offenders to nonarrested offenders" (Berk, 1993, 325). Other researchers go beyond the task of whether or not comparison is possible, and point out that the experiments conducted did not compare persons with the same sociodemographic characteristics. Sherman (1992b) himself notes the diversity in the sample populations utilized across replication studies regarding employment status, prior arrest, and prior domestic assaults.

Another threat to internal validity and reliability must include examining the wide variation in the duration of time that the offenders were held after arrest. The question arises as to whether or not the chance of recidivism is increased in cases where offenders were held for only three hours compared to those who were held for a longer period of time. If the length of time that offenders were detained could have been controlled, a better indication of the deterrence value of the duration of arrest could have been realized.

The possibility that the police officers involved in these studies could have violated assumptions of the random assignment of prearranged responses by upgrading a particular call, or by not responding to a particular call at all, also affects the reliability of these studies. Sheptycki (1991) notes that, in one experiment, only three police officers responded to 28 percent of the cases in the study sample. Sheptycki (1991) also cautions that these experiments also failed to standardize other forms of intervention. For example, each responding officer has his or her own divergent form of mediation. This inherent difference in mediation techniques between officers seriously threatens the construct validity of these experiments.

Given these criticisms, many academics question the role of social research in the creation of social policy (see for example Binder and Meeker, 1988; Bowman, 1992; Sheptycki, 1991; Frisch, 1992). They argue that there are inherent dangers in utilizing these studies for the purpose of advocating or supporting specific policy changes. In many instances these studies have not been adequately scrutinized: they may use unreliable and/or invalid measures and may lack controls for extraneous factors. The fact that these studies are frequently conducted in isolation from consideration of other components of the criminal justice system also casts doubts on their ability to assess the deterrent value of arrest, which is the key assumption underlying the policy.

Assessing Recidivism Rates

In addition to the methodological and design problems of these studies, there is a fundamental question of whether or not arrest deters offenders. Gelles (1993) claims that arrest, in and of itself, does not appear to have the deterrent value espoused. However, when arrest is considered along with particular attributes of the offender it may serve as a deterrent (Gelles, 1993, 583–584). In connection with this acknowledgment, Sherman's replication studies in Milwaukee, Charlotte, and Omaha showed that, in the long term, arrest actually increased violence or had a criminogenic effect on the unemployed, unmarried, and racial minority perpetrators in cases of wife assault (1992a, 29). Conversely, in two out of the five replication sites, arrest did have a crime-reduction effect for those perpetrators who were employed, married and had earned a secondary-school diploma. These studies present the dilemma that arrest may help some victims at the expense of others. This dilemma has led Sherman to call for the movement to repeal mandatory arrest laws especially within areas comprised primarily of ghetto poverty populations and areas with high unemployment rates (1992b).

The incidence of recidivism after arrest could be explained by numerous factors. First, in light of the finding that victims often do not report violence to police due to the fear of revenge by the offender, arrest can be seen as a direct cause of retaliation by the abusive partner.[1] However, this reasoning assumes that arrest is the prime motivator in subsequent violence. It should not be assumed that if the batterer beats his wife after having been arrested that the arrest itself—isolated from other factors—was the sole cause of his behaviour. Further, some of these subsequent arrests may be attributed to the difficulties associated with marriage breakdown, separation, and divorce. It is well-known that this is a particularly traumatic period, and that women face increased risk of physical abuse during this period.

Recidivism after arrest could also be explained by the process of victim empowerment through the use of arrest by police. A victim may threaten to leave an abusive relationship or may threaten to have the offender arrested again. These threats, if perceived by the abuser to be a form of power, may lead him to abuse the victim in order to regain control of the relationship.

Sherman cites several other possible theoretical explanations for recidivism after arrest, including social control theory (1992b). This theory posits that the inclination to commit crime is universal and thereby inhibited only by the development of strong bonds to conventional society. If these bonds are weak or missing and social conformity is not desired by the abuser then he may reoffend (1992b, 158). In addition to offering this interpretation, Sherman explains that sanctions are more likely to deter individuals when they have more to lose (159). In other words, maintaining a stake in conformity is a factor that inhibits people from committing more crime (159). Therefore, an employed, married person would have more to lose with regard to societal conformity than one who is unemployed and unmarried. This theory is supported by the evidence presented in the replication studies (Sherman, 1992a, 32–33).

Another possible explanation for recidivism after arrest lies in the growing lack of shame at the individual level as a result of each individual's relative independence within society. If people are less dependent on others they are less likely to be affected by the informal control of shame and stigma, and as a result are more likely to reoffend (Sherman, 1992b, 162). Sherman concludes that an expanded theory of deterrence must include informal and formal controls as two necessary conditions for the control of crime (1992b).

The relationship between arrest, deterrence, and violence is more complex than initially hypothesized. Manning (1993) argues that there is a "black box" problem inherent in the reasoning behind deterrence objectives: the connection between arrest and violence is interrupted by unknown factors that constitute a black box of uncertainty. Events that occur between arrest and future violence, or a lack of future violence, are not known and have not been adequately examined, which results in a flawed theory of causation.

This uncertainty is problematic with regard to the assumed general and specific deterrent value of the mandatory arrest policy. It is not clear whether the aim of mandatory arrest is to deter individual criminal acts or to reduce the crime rate by deterring the general population from committing an initial act of violence. The latter aim involves the assumption of general deterrence. However, it is clear that the experiments conducted in both London, Ontario and Minneapolis attempted to test the assumption of specific deterrence. Little research, if any, has been conducted to test the possible general deterrent value of the mandatory arrest policy.

The difficulties associated with testing deterrence theory are endless. For example, how would a target population be defined? Is there any way that a potential abuser could be identified in order to determine if knowledge of the policy would deter him? If this were the case then the researcher would be waiting in the wings, so to speak, to see if any individuals within the sample committed the crime of wife assault. The ethical dilemma posed by this situation is not easily resolved.

The focus on the deterrent value of arrest also assumes that the potential abuser is aware of the policy and has an understanding of the certainty of punishment. The importance of this knowledge is crucial in both general and specific deterrent objectives. With regard to specific deterrence, if the abuser has been arrested and the case is dropped at the court level, or if he receives a lenient sentence, such as a peace bond, then the question arises as to the strength of the deterrent. In a case such as this, the abuser is not substantially held accountable for his actions, and therefore the probability that he will reoffend increases. Utilizing exchange theory (Blau, 1964), this process could be explained as an event that involved low costs to the abuser. Perhaps the rewards as perceived by the abuser outweighed the experienced costs of his criminal behaviour. Sirles, Lipchik, and Kowalski found that 62 percent of arrested men (*N*=22) indicated that the proarrest strategy would deter them from future violence (1993, 273). Yet this study is limited due to its small sample size and its lack of control for extraneous factors. For example, only 20 percent of the men in this study were prosecuted. This characteristic might have had an impact on the perceptions of the abusers. The need to conduct further research utilizing arrested men and their perceptions of the policy and its deterrent value is apparent.

General deterrence also assumes that the potential abuser is aware of the existence of the policy and perceives the costs of his action to outweigh the rewards. Given Jaffe, Wolfe, and Telford's findings that only 25 percent of cases where police laid charges of simple assault and 45 percent of cases where police laid charges of assault causing bodily harm resulted in fines or imprisonment, it is incorrect to assume certainty of punishment (Ontario, 1985, 27). However, this also assumes that potential abusers know of this uncertainty. With regard to knowledge of the policy by a potential abuser, only one third of the men arrested in the Sirles, Lipchik, and Kowalski study knew of the policy prior to being abusive (1993, 273).

More recently a number of studies have called for an examination of the influence of other criminal justice interventions on the deterrent value of arrest in cases of wife assault (see for example Stark, 1993; Bowman, 1992). Researchers have advocated that the proarrest strategy is most effective when it is coupled with consistent intervention from other criminal justice and social service systems. Unfortunately, more research needs to be conducted—especially in Canada—on what might be defined as consistent intervention and whether this type of intervention is in fact being carried out. The impact of a jail sentence, the effectiveness of counselling and the availability and effectiveness of victim follow-up on reducing recidivism rates are just some of the research issues in need of examination.

The Victim's Point of View

Preoccupation with the deterrence question focuses attention on the offender and his actions and motives. Emphasis on the victim ensures a balanced perspective on the possible role of arrest in cases of spousal assault. The benefits of the mandatory arrest strategy are more obvious from the point of view of the victim. First, as revealed by the Jaffe, Wolfe, and Telford (Ontario, 1985) study, the policy has resulted in an increase in police intervention and arrest rates. Arrest ensures the victim's right to be free from violence in the short term. The policy also takes the onus away from the victim to press charges. The arrest of an abusive partner could allow a victim time to think about the options that she has at her disposal, or to plan for alternative living arrangements. Arrest of the abuser often precludes a visit by the victim to a shelter. Research has shown that just one day in a shelter, where victims encounter support, encouragement, and counselling is beneficial in aiding the victim in her decision to leave an abusive relationship (Berk, Newton, and Fenstermaker Berk, 1986, 489).

The mandatory arrest policy could also have an impact on the perceptions of victims regarding the police. For example, Jaffe, Wolfe, and Telford (Ontario, 1985) report that a comparison of abused women's perceptions before and after the implementation of the mandatory arrest policy indicates that victim satisfaction with the police improved. Overall, in 1979 (prior to the policy) 47 percent of victims were dissatisfied with the police response. In 1983 (after the policy) this figure dropped to 5.5 percent (Ontario, 1985, 31). It is interesting to note that 31 percent of the victims in 1979 felt that the officer should be more understanding. This figure dropped to approximately 13.5 percent in 1983 (31). In comparison, the National Survey on Violence Against Women discovered that of the women who reported abuse to police, 39 percent said there was nothing else that the police should have done, 24 percent felt the police should have been more supportive, and 20 percent felt the police should have laid a charge against the perpetrator (Statistics Canada, 1994, 16).

These perceptions are significant findings for two reasons. First, it has been reported elsewhere that victims of wife assault are more likely to call police for assistance if they have a positive image of the police (Statistics Canada, 1994). Second, if we use victim perceptions to gauge the awareness and helpfulness of the police, then it appears that the policy has contributed to these elements of police practice in cases of wife assault. However, as evidenced by the findings of the most current National Survey on Violence Against Women, between 20 percent and 25 percent of those women who report abuse to police are still dissatisfied with police response (1994).

It is necessary to consider whether the police are equipped to handle an influx of calls in the event that reports of wife assault increase in expectation of more effective police assistance. A cost-effective analysis may reveal that an increase in attention to domestic disputes could require a larger slice of the police-resource pie. In the event that calls requiring assistance in handling domestic disputes increase substantially, would calls have to be screened? Would women that require immediate assistance be in jeopardy due to delays in response time or because there was no response at all? Future research on this possibility is warranted.

The mandatory arrest policy also assumes that the victim will be satisfied with the outcome of the police response and as a result have no objections to the arrest and potential prosecution of the abuser. It has been found that in some cases of abuse, women are reluctant to call the police because they do not want the abuser arrested and/or they do not want to engage in the court process (Statistics Canada, 1994, 17). For example, 71 percent of the victims interviewed in the Sirles, Lipchick, and Kowalski study did not want their arrested abuser prosecuted (1993, 273). In this regard, mandatory arrest has the potential to disempower the victim. With charges laid by the police, the victim does not have a choice. Their requests may be silenced by a procedural policy. In addition, economic and emotional dependence on the abuser may make this process extremely painful and financially devastating to the victim. Finally, Buzawa and

Buzawa (1990, 1993a, 1993b) claim that the policy deprives women of control over their lives, presumably reinforcing the sense of powerlessness already inflicted on the victim by the batterer.

These potentially negative outcomes of mandatory arrest policies may deter some victims from calling the police. Again, this assumes that the victim is aware of the mandatory arrest policy. Both the Burris and Jaffe study in London (1983) and the Lacey study in eastern Canada (Newfoundland, 1993) reveal that women were not deterred from calling the police as a result of the presence of the policy. However, research on the possible reluctance of victims to call the police due to a known outcome of arrest has been limited. Similarly, there is a lack of research on those victims who are unaware of the policy and call police for assistance but not to invoke an arrest. One possible outcome of a lack of victim cooperation with an arrest response might be the failure of the victim to testify in court. For example, in Canada, a woman was sentenced to three months in jail (later reduced to one week) for refusing to testify against her assailant ("Jailed One Week for Not Testifying," *The Globe and Mail*, March 20, 1984).

It is also important to consider that women who have resorted to physical violence in order to defend themselves or in order to engage in mutual assault may fear their own arrest. Brinkerhoff and Lupri (1992) argue that men should also be examined as victims. Similarly, Straus (1993) suggests that husbands are victimized by their spouses at higher rates than previously perceived. DeKeseredy's (1992a, 1992b) response to this assertion is that these studies attempt to negate the self-defence explanation for female violence. Other researchers have pointed out that even if female violence is used, male violence is more frequent and involves higher rates of assault that result in greater injury (for example see Saunders, 1988, 1986). Despite these findings, research has shown that in some regions of the United States, the implementation of mandatory arrest has resulted in higher rates of dual arrest in cases of domestic disputes (Pennsylvania, 1984).

In sum, mandatory arrest policies produce mixed results for both offenders and victims. These mixed results result from such factors as offender characteristics, offender and victim knowledge of the policy and its implications, as well as support from other criminal justice and social service interventions. In light of these findings, the deterrent value of such a policy is seriously questioned. The evidence also suggests that mandatory arrest policies may solve some problems, but may also create new problems. Further research directed toward examining and empirically testing the unintended consequences of the policy, whether they be positive or negative, is warranted.

Police Decision Making

As previously mentioned, the police response to spousal assault has traditionally been one of nonarrest. Past research has shown that the police response to wife assault relies heavily on extra-legal factors such as victim and offender disposition toward the police, the use of alcohol by the victim and the offender, marital status, etc. (see for example Berk and Loseke, 1980–1981; Smith and Klein, 1984; Waaland and Keeley, 1985). One intended function, therefore, of mandatory arrest policies is to reduce police discretion in cases of wife assault. Determination of patterns in police discretion based on both extra-legal and legal factors becomes necessary to assess whether or not the policy encouraging arrest is being utilized, and if so, the extent of its use.

Because there is an extensive literature dealing with police decision making in cases of wife abuse, it is useful to divide the discussion into four parts. In part one, the focus is on assessing influence of sociodemographic variables on police practices. Part two focuses on situational factors, such as victim and offender characteristics. Part three focuses on the influence of organizational factors. Part four focuses on police perceptions of mandatory arrest policies.

Sociodemographic Factors

Age, education, and rank appear to have an impact on police decision making, but the association between these characteristics and compliance with the policy are not direct. For example, studies have revealed that younger officers are more likely to view their role in wife-assault calls as important and functional (Levens and Dutton, 1980). Breci and Simons (1987) found that the more education an officer has, the more likely he or she will value police intervention in wife-assault cases. It is important to note here that younger officers tend to have higher levels of education (Campbell and Reingold, 1994) and as a result, the relationship between age and positive role perceptions regarding wife-assault cases appears to be a function of education. Younger, highly educated officers tend to value training more than senior officers. Perception of the value of training has also been found to be a prominent factor in positive role perception when dealing with wife assault (Breci and Simons, 1987).

With regard to gender, Homant and Kennedy (1985) found that female police officers are generally more helpful and are more concerned about the welfare of the victim. Other studies on the effect of gender on police response have been inconclusive (see for example Breci and Simons, 1987). Similarly, officers' marital status appears to have no significant impact on police practices. However, marital stress, approval of marital violence, and the use of violence in officers' marriages have been shown by Stith (1990) to be significantly associated with a decreased likelihood of arrest in cases of wife assault. To date, this is the only study that empirically tests these associations.

Role perceptions and ultimately the propensity to arrest are also affected by an officer's attitudes toward victims and offenders. These attitudes may take the form of stereotypes that guide intervention tactics. For example, Stith (1990) found that officers who hold more stereotypical sex-role attitudes will be less likely to arrest perpetrators and more likely to mediate.

To illustrate this association, Hatty (1989) argues that the police conceptualize any departure from traditional gender-based behaviours as a contributing factor to the violence, and as a result assign a degree of responsibility for the assault to the abused woman. Police officers who are influenced by these conceptualizations are less likely to arrest (Hatty, 1989:80). Police may also conform to the stereotype of masculinity. This conception of masculinity involves allowing men to "get away with" some degree of aggressive behaviour toward others. It has also been demonstrated that police often rationalize abuse as a reaction to a social stress such as unemployment (80). This rationalization is consistent with the misaligned sociopsychological theories that feminists have criticized for ignoring the constructs of power and control in the context of gender inequality.

Police officers' adherence to these constructions may ultimately minimize the criminal nature of assault, reduce responsibility for the abuser, and result in minimal action in response to domestic violence. These documented attitudes of officers may actually compromise female victims' rights to police protection as well as the successful implementation of a policy that emphasizes the criminality of wife assault.

Contrary to these arguments, Sherman (1992b) suggests that the fundamental police attitude toward domestic violence is not one of sympathy for the male, but rather frustration at feeling unable to do anything about the "kinds of people" chronically involved in such incidents. These people, according to Sherman (1992b), are of low socioeconomic status. Evidence of social-class stereotyping, implicit in Sherman's (1992b) argument, has been a factor identified in influencing police practices. Ferraro (1989a, 1989b) indicates that police tend to dichotomize the community into normal and deviant citizens. A normal citizen maintains employment, sobriety, and a clean home. A deviant citizen is characterized as a "normal" wife beater and his behaviour is usually perceived as a product of a particular social or economic strain. This stereotype removes responsibility from the abuser and minimizes the criminal nature of his actions.

Several researchers hypothesize that the possible danger associated with domestic-dispute calls is one reason why police are reluctant to intervene. Other researchers point out that this danger is overstated. For example, Ellis, Choi, and Blaus (1993, 162) discovered that danger rates for policing domestic disputes are far lower than for robbery and for arresting/transporting suspects and prisoners. If police are in less danger when attending domestic disputes, but in more danger when arresting suspects, then what happens when the domestic call results in the arrest of the perpetrator? Could the higher danger rate during an arrest be an explanation for traditionally low arrest rates and a historical practice of mediation in cases of wife assault? Attitudinal surveys have found that police believe that the potential risk involved in cases of wife assault is not a decisive factor for arrest or nonarrest (see for example Dolon, Hendrick, and Meagler 1986; Waaland and Keeley, 1985). Loving (United States, Police Executive Research Forum, 1980, 116) found that 97 percent of the officers surveyed felt very well-prepared to take self-protective measures and arrest assailants in cases of spousal assault, whereas only 88 percent of the officers felt prepared to mediate and negotiate. These studies suggest low arrest rates and the reluctance of police to intervene in cases of wife assault are not the result of danger, either real or perceived.

Situational Factors

Situational factors refer to the characteristics of a particular wife-assault incident and include such elements as the relationship between the victim and offender, use of a weapon, and seriousness of injury. The overwhelming bulk of the academic literature that examines these factors is based on interviews, observations, record analyses and personal assessments (see for example United States, Police Executive Research Forum, 1980; Waaland and Keeley, 1985).

Police officers assign importance to factors consistent with a criminal investigation that reveal the presence of reasonable and probable grounds that an assault has taken place. For example, the seriousness of injuries to the victim has been a consistent influencing factor. An Alberta Family and Social Services study revealed that in situations where women required medical attention the arrest rate was 30.7 percent (1990, 32). This was 5.5 percent higher than the average rate of arrest. The use of violence against a police officer, the commission of an indictable offence, a hostile and antagonistic perpetrator, and the use of a weapon in cases of wife assault are factors that influence police officers to arrest (United States, Police Executive Research Forum, 1980; Dolon, Hendrick, and Meagler, 1986; Buzawa and Austin, 1993; Smith and Klein, 1984; Alberta, Family and Social Services, 1990). The Alberta study (1990, 32) revealed that arrest rates were higher (31 percent) when a weapon was used compared to when an offender used a hand or fist (25 percent).

It has also been suggested that the marital status of the couple and the use of alcohol by one or both parties are also influential factors in police response. However, the weight of these influences is currently a source of debate. The findings regarding the influence of the relationship between the victim and the offender are inconsistent. Bell (1987) argues that the victim-offender relationship is the primary determinant in the decision to arrest or not arrest. His study reveals that the police are far less likely to arrest in cases where the victim is married and living with the offender (1987). Conversely, Worden and Pollitz (1984) found that police are less likely to make an arrest if the offender and victim are not married. However, Buzawa and Austin (1993, 616) failed to confirm that marital status was a major predictor of police action.

Several studies claim that arrests are more common in cases in which the abuser is intoxicated (Dolon, Hendrick, and Meagler, 1986; Berk and Loseke, 1980–1981; Smith and Klein, 1984). Other studies show that police focus more on the victim's drinking behaviour. For instance, the Alberta Family and Social Services study revealed a higher arrest rate for abusive partners of victims who were intoxicated (1990, 32). Perhaps, the decision to arrest in these cases stems from a perceived inability of the victim to defend herself during an intoxicated state.

Frequent calls from the household for police help has also been identified as an influencing factor (United States, Police Executive Research Forum, 1980; Dolon, Hendrick, and Meagler, 1986; Smith and Klein, 1984). However, contrary to these findings, Waaland and Keeley (1985) found that over one half of the officers that they interviewed gave no consideration to past assault or incident information.

A comparable level of insight into police decision making can be deduced by examining factors that influence a police decision to not make an arrest. The decision not to arrest may be more consequential than the decision to arrest. The data on this element of police decision making reveal two main themes. First, the most influential factors relating to nonarrest appear to be centred around the perception that the victim will either refuse to testify in court or will drop the charges (see for example Dolon, Hendrick, and Meagler, 1986; Berk and Loseke, 1980–1981; United States, Police Executive Research Forum, 1980).

These studies also reveal that a lack of serious injury and the absence of a weapon are the second most influential factors relating to nonarrest. An officer may be reluctant to arrest an abuser if there are not sufficient grounds to prove that an assault occurred. This leads to an exploration of the role of the court system that ultimately judges the validity of the evidence of assault.

Organizational Factors

Far less research has been conducted on the role of intraorganizational and interorganizational factors in influencing police practice with regard to domestic violence. It is known that police peers and the police subculture exert a direct influence on an officer's conception of the police role and the way that they respond (Breci and Simons, 1987, 101). It is also known that officers conform to what they expect their departmental role to be. Therefore, officers are more likely to arrest when departmental priorities reinforce arrest as the appropriate strategy (1987). In addition, an overall lack of professional incentives within the agency to perform well in accordance with the dictates of the mandatory arrest policy also contribute to variations in an individual officer's use of arrest (United States, Police Executive Research Forum, 1980).

A lack of training and lack of support from other criminal justice agencies appear to have an influence on police officers' inaction in wife-assault cases. The lack of support for the mandatory arrest policy from other criminal justice agencies, such as the courts, has been shown to affect the deterrent value of arrest. It seems reasonable to conclude that this lack of support also affects the way in which police implement and follow the mandatory arrest policy.

Police Perceptions of the Policy

To date, only two Canadian studies have explored police officers' perceptions of the mandatory arrest policy. The first study was conducted in London, Ontario by Jaffe, Wolfe, and Telford (Ontario, 1985). The second study, conducted by the

Women's Policy Office (under the direction of Beth Lacey) in Newfoundland and Labrador (Newfoundland, 1993), interviewed officers from the Royal Canadian Mounted Police (RCMP) and Royal Newfoundland Constabulary (RNC).

Jaffe, Wolfe, and Telford found that officers had mixed opinions about the effectiveness of the policy: 33 percent felt the policy was not at all effective, and 33 percent felt it was definitely effective (Ontario, 1985, 34). Lacey found that 50 percent of the RCMP and 25 percent of the RNC felt that the laying-of-charges policy was an effective policy and needed no improvements (Newfoundland, 1993, 13).

The Jaffe study revealed that 42 percent of the officers thought that the policy helped women (Ontario, 1985, 34). However, approximately 30 percent of the police interviewed in both studies thought that the directive made the lives of the women more difficult (Newfoundland, 1993, 10; Ontario, 1985, 34). Further, only 10 percent of the officers surveyed in Eastern Canada perceived that the policy had deterrence value (Newfoundland, 1993, 11). Similarly, only a small number of officers (20.5 percent) in the London study felt that the policy would put an end to family violence (Ontario, 1985, 34).

The opinion of the London officers as to whether or not there are any negative side effects resulting from the policy was again somewhat divided. When asked if the policy would make women hesitant to call police, police responded as follows: 27.9 percent said not at all; 40.4 percent said they were uncertain; and 31.6 percent said definitely (Ontario, 1985, 34). The London study also asked if the policy and its resultant arrests could contribute to an increase in offender violence, and 16 percent of the officers felt that it would definitely contribute to future violence (1985, 34). A question pertaining to the possible criminogenic effect of the policy was not asked in the Newfoundland study.

Suggestions for improving the policy were not aimed at the policy itself, but instead at the placement of other programs in collaboration with the policy. For example, Lacey's study of the police in Newfoundland and Labrador indicates that the police believe that increased training, follow-up programs for victims of wife assault, an increase in the number of cases proceeding to court, and tougher sentences would help make the policy more effective (Newfoundland, 1993, 13). The police officers also felt that the policy was not taken seriously by the courts and that this undermined the work that they were trying to do (13). It is interesting to note that a sizable majority of the officers (56 percent) in the London study also felt that the courts do not support the present police policy (Ontario, 1985, 35).

At best, the research on factors that influence police practices and perceptions discerns possible sources of variation in the application of the mandatory arrest policy. It appears that police use legal factors, such as availability of evidence, or quasi-legal factors, such as victim cooperation, to determine if an arrest is warranted. The relative weight of these factors and the definition of what may constitute a "good" legal factor is less clear. The possibility that the interpretation of legal factors may be influenced by individual officer perceptions, the use of stereotypes, and conceptualization of gender roles is in dire need of investigation. In addition, the connection between quasi-legal factors such as victim cooperation in testifying against the assailant and general support for the policy from other criminal justice apparatuses have been inadequately studied. Similarly, the lack of research on police perceptions of the policy of mandatory arrest points to the inconclusiveness of this body of research.

CONCLUSION

Feminists and the women's movement were quick to point out the lack of governmental initiative, particularly the lack of cooperation from the criminal justice system, in addressing wife assault. The conflict between feminist demands and the inaction of governmental agencies in responding to wife assault became increasingly salient and soon represented a dilemma for the state to address. The feminist demand that men's violence against women be defined as a crime of assault was accommodated by the state's emphasis on the criminality of wife battering. The resulting focus on the criminal justice system was seen as an avenue for change and progressive reform by both feminists and the state. Gradually, the focus on the criminal justice system's response to wife assault led to a focus on police policy regarding spousal assault.

Some have argued that this focus was intentional and signified a course of action that the state could easily accommodate. In other words, the state apparatus gave voice to outside reformers only to the extent that their demands could be accommodated by the reform policy it chose. As Currie and MacLean (1992) note, the issue of wife assault was transformed into a technical matter for policing wife assault that could be safely met within the current system without significant changes in the relations of power.

The development and implementation of the mandatory arrest policies were offered by the state as resolutions to certain conflicts between men and women. However, it can be said that the change signified by the policy did not address the fundamental contradiction of uneven power differentials between men and women and its resulting gender inequality. Instrumentally, the state has provided a mechanism by which women could redress some of the power inequities inherent in the patriarchal structure. However, on another level the state's response increases women's dependency on the state and state agencies.

Thus, the mandatory arrest policy gives the appearance of change, and the appearance of redressing the inequities that create the conditions leading to wife assault, but does nothing to alter these conditions. If in the resolution of particular conflicts the basic contradictions are not resolved, the seeds for further conflicts are planted.

ENDNOTES

1   The National Survey on Violence Against Women discovered that women do not report violence to police for a variety of reasons: a fear of the partner; a perception that the incident is too minor; they don't want to get involved with the police; they

don't want their partners arrested; shame; and belief that the incident should remain private (Statistics Canada, 1994, 17).

BIBLIOGRAPHY

Alberta. Family and Social Services, Women's Shelter Program. 1990. *Police Intervention in Wife Abuse.* Edmonton: Office for the Prevention of Family Violence.

Bell, Daniel. 1987. "The Victim-Offender Relationship: A Determinant Factor in Police Domestic Dispute Dispositions, *"Marriage and Family Review*, 12(1–2): 87–102.

Berk, Richard A. 1993. "What the Scientific Evidence Shows: On the Average, We Can Do No Better Than Arrest." In *Current Controversies on Family Violence*, edited by R.J. Gelles and Donileen R. Loseke, 323–336. Newbury Park: Sage Publications.

———., **A. Campbell, R. Klap,** and **B. Western.** 1992. "The Deterrent Effect of Arrest in Incidents of Domestic Violence: A Bayesian Analysis of Four Field Experiments," *American Sociological Review*, 57: 698–708.

———., **P. Newton,** and **S. Fenstermaker Berk.** 1986. "What a difference a Day Makes: An Empirical Study of the Impact of Shelters for Battered Women," *Journal of Marriage and the Family*, 48: 481–490.

———., and **P. Newton.** 1985. "Does Arrest Really Deter Wife Battery? An Effort to Replicate the Findings of the Minneapolis Spouse Abuse Experiment," *American Sociological Review*, 50 (April): 253–262.

Berk, Sarah Fenstermaker, and **Donileen R. Loseke.** 1980–1981. "Handling Family Violence: Situational Determinants of Police Arrest in Domestic Disturbance," *Law and Society Review*, 15: 317–346.

Binder, Arnold and **James Meeker.** 1988. "Experiments as Reforms," *Journal of Criminal Justice*, 16: 347–358.

Blau, Peter. 1964. *Exchange and Power in Social Life.* New York: Wiley.

Bowman, C. G. 1992. "The Arrest Experiments: A Feminist Critique," *The Journal of Criminal Law and Criminology.* 83(1): 201–208.

Breci, M.C. and **R.L. Simons.** 1987. "An Examination of Organizational and Individual Factors that Influence Police Response to Domestic Disturbances," *Journal of Police Science and Administration.* 15(2): 93–104.

Brinkerhoff, M. and **E. Lupri.** 1992. "Interspousal Violence." In *Debates in Canadian Society*, edited by Ron Hinch, 225–244. Scarborough, Ont.: Nelson Canada.

Burris, Carole Anne, and **Peter Jaffe.** 1983. "Wife Abuse as a Crime: The Impact of Police Laying Charges," *Canadian Journal of Criminology*, 25(3): 309–318.

Burtch, B. 1992. *The Sociology of Law: Critical Approaches to Social Control.* Toronto: Harcourt Brace Jovanovich Canada.

Buzawa, Eve S. and **Thomas Austin.** 1993. "Determining Police Response to Domestic Violence Victims: The Role of Victim Preference," *American Behavioral Scientist*, 36(5): 610–623.

————., and **Carl G. Buzawa.** 1993a. "The Scientific Evidence Is Not Conclusive: Arrest Is No Panacea." In *Current Controversies on Family Violence,* edited by R.J. Gelles and Donileen R. Loseke, 337–356. Newbury Park: Sage Publications.

————. 1993b. "The Impact of Arrest on Domestic Violence: Introduction," *American Behavioral Scientist,* 36(5): 558–574.

————. 1990. *Domestic Violence: The Criminal Justice Response.* Newbury, Calif.: Sage.

Campbell, G., and **B. Reingold.** 1994. "Private Security and Policing in Canada," *Juristat Service Bulletin,* 14(10)

Canada. Canadian Advisory Council on the Status of Women. 1983. *A Brief on Wife Battering with Proposals for Federal Action.* Debra J. Lewis. Ottawa.

Canada. Canadian Advisory Council on the Status of Women. 1980. *Wife Battering in Canada: The Vicious Circle.* Linda MacLeod. Ottawa.

Canada. Canadian Federal-Provincial Task Force on Justice for Victims. 1983. *Report.* Ottawa: Ministry of Supply and Services.

Canada. Canadian Panel on Violence Against Women. 1993. *Changing the Landscape: Ending the Violence, Achieving Equality.* Ottawa: Ministry of Supply and Services.

Canada. Parliament. 1982. House of Commons. *Debates.* Official Report. 32nd Parliament, 1st sess. Vol. 15. Ottawa: Canadian Government Publishing Centre.

Canada. Standing Committee on Health, Welfare and Social Affairs. 1982. *Report on Violence in the Family: Wife Battering.* Ottawa.

Canada. Standing Committee on Health and Welfare, Social Affairs, Seniors and the Status of Women. 1991. *The War Against Women.* Ottawa.

Canada. Statistics Canada. 1994. "Wife Assault: The Findings of a National Survey," *Juristat Service Bulletin,* 14(9).

————. 1990. "Conjugal Violence Against Women," *Juristat Service Bulletin,* 10(7): 1–7.

Canada. Supply and Services. 1980. *The Social Service Role of the Police—Domestic Crisis Intervention.* Bruce R. Levens and Donald Dutton. Ottawa: Minister of Supply and Services.

Chambliss, William. 1986. "On Lawmaking." In *The Social Basis of Law: Critical Reading in the Sociology of Law,* edited by S. Brickey and E. Comack, 26–51. Toronto: Garamond Press.

————, and **Robert Seidman.** 1982. *Law, Order and Power.* 2d ed. Reading, Mass.: Addison-Wesley Publishing Company.

Clark, Lorenne, and **Debra Lewis.** 1977. *Rape: The Price of Coercive Sexuality.* Toronto: The Women's Press.

Currie, Dawn, and **B.D. MacLean.** 1992. "Women, Men and Police: Losing the Fight Against Wife Battery in Canada." In *Rethinking the Administration of Justice,* edited by Dawn H. Currie and Brian D. MacLean, 251–275. Halifax: Fernwood Publishing.

DeKeseredy, Walter. 1992a. "Confronting Woman Abuse in Canada: A Left-Realist Approach." In *Realist Criminology: Crime Control and Policing in the 1990s*, edited by J. Lowman and B.D. MacLean, 264–285. Toronto: University of Toronto Press.

———. 1992b. "In Defence: Demystifying Female Violence Against Male Intimates." In *Debates in Canadian Society*, ed. Ron Hinch, 245–252. Scarborough, Ont.: Nelson Canada.

Dolon, R., J. Hendrick, and **S. Meagler.** 1986. "Police Practices and Attitudes Toward Domestic Violence," *Journal of Police Science and Administration*, 14(3): 187–192.

Ellis, Desmond, Alfred Choi, and **Chris Blaus.** 1993. "Injuries to Police Officers Attending Domestic Disturbances: An Empirical Study," *Canadian Journal of Criminology*, April, 149–168.

Ferraro, Kathleen J. 1989a. "Legal Responses to Woman Battering in the United States." In *Women, Policing and Male Violence: International Perspectives*, edited by J. Hanmer, D. Radford and E. Stanko, 155–184. London: Routledge.

———. 1989b. "Policing Woman Battering," *Social Problems*, 36: 61–74.

Frisch, Lisa A. 1992. "Research That Succeeds, Policies That Fail," *The Journal of Criminal Law and Criminology*, 83(1): 209–216.

Gelles, R.J. 1993. "Constraints Against Family Violence: How Well Do They Work?" *American Behavioral Scientist*, 36: 575–586.

———., and **Claire P. Cornell.** 1985. *Intimate Violence in Families*. Beverly Hills: Sage.

Hatty, Suzanne. 1989. "Policing and Male Violence in Australia." In *Women, Policing and Male Violence: International Perspectives*. London: Routledge.

Havemann, Paul. 1992. "Crisis Justice for Youth: Making the *Young Offenders Act* and the Discourse of Penalty." In *Rethinking the Administration of Justice*, edited by Dawn H. Currie and Brian D. MacLean, 86–112. Halifax: Fernwood Publishing.

———. 1986. "From Child Saving to Child Blaming: The Political Economy of the *Young Offenders Act*, 1908–84." In *The Social Basis of Law*, edited by S. Brickey and E. Comack, 225–41. Toronto: Garamond Press.

Homant, R.J., and **D. B. Kennedy.** 1985. "Police Perceptions of Spouse Abuse: A Comparison of Male and Female Officers," *Journal of Criminal Justice*, 13: 29–47.

Jaffe, Peter, et al. 1986. "The Impact of Police Charges in Incidents of Wife Abuse," *Journal of Family Violence*, 1: 37–49.

Kasinski, R. G. 1978. "The Rise and Institutionalization of the Anti-Rape Movement in Canada." In *Violence in Canada*, edited by M. A. B. Gammon, 151–67. Toronto: Methuen Publications.

Lerman, Lisa G. 1992. "The Decontextualization of Domestic Violence," *The Journal of Criminal Law and Criminology*, 83(1): 217–240.

Manning, Peter. 1993. "The Preventative Conceit: The Black Box in Market Context," *American Behavioral Scientist*, 35(5): 639–650.

Newfoundland. Women's Policy Office. 1993. *Police Response to Wife Assault: An Examination of the Charge Laying Policies in Newfoundland and Labrador.* Beth Lacey. St. John's.

Ontario. Provincial Secretariat for Justice. 1985. *A Research Study to Evaluate the Impact and Effectiveness of the Policy Directive that Police Lay Charges in All Domestic Violence Incidents where Reasonable and Probable Grounds Exist.* Peter Jaffe, D. Wolfe, and A. Telford. Toronto.

Pennsylvania. Attorney General Family Violence Task Force. 1984. *Domestic Violence: A Model Protocol for Police Response.* Harrisburg.

Saunders, D.G. 1988. "Wife Abuse, Husband Abuse, or Mutual Combat?" In *Feminist Perspectives on Wife Abuse,* edited by K. Yllo and M. Bograd, 90–113. Newbury, Calif.: Sage.

———. 1986. "When Battered Women Use Violence: Husband Abuse or Self Defence?" *Victims and Violence,* 1: 47–60.

Sheptycki, J.W.E. 1991. "Using the State to Change Society: The Example of 'Domestic Violence,'" *Journal of Human Justice.* Vol.3: 47–66.

Sherman, Lawrence W. 1992a. "The Influence of Criminology on Criminal Law: Evaluating Arrests for Misdemeanour Domestic Violence," *The Journal of Criminal Law and Criminology,* 83(1): 1–45.

———. 1992b. *Policing Domestic Violence, Experiments and Dilemmas.* New York: Free Press.

———. 1991. "From Initial Deterrence to Long Term Escalation: Short Custody Arrest for Poverty Ghetto Domestic Violence," *Criminology,* 29: 821–849.

———. 1989. "Repeat Calls for Service: Policing the `Hot Spots.'" In *Police and Policing: Contemporary Issues,* edited by Dennis J. Kennedy, 150–165. New York: Praeger.

———. 1984. "Experiments in Police Discretion: Scientific Boom or Dangerous Knowledge?" *Law and Contemporary Problems,* 47(4): 61–81.

———., and **Richard A. Berk.** 1984. "The Specific Deterrent Effects of Arrest for Domestic Assault," *American Sociological Review,* 49(2): 261–272.

Sirles, Elizabeth, Eve Lipchik, and **Kate Kowalski.** 1993. "A Consumer's Perspective on Domestic Violence Interventions," *Journal of Family Violence,* 8(3): 267–276.

Smart, Carol. 1989. *Feminism and the Power of the Law.* London: Routledge and Kegan Paul.

Smith, Douglas A. 1987. "Police Response to Interpersonal Violence: Defining the Parameters of Legal Control," *Social Forces,* 65: 767–82.

Smith, D. and J. Klein. 1984. "Police Control of Interpersonal Disputes," *Social Problems,* 31(4): 463–481.

Smith, M. 1987. "The Incidence and Prevalence of Woman Abuse in Toronto," *Violence and Victims,* 2(3): 173–187.

Stark, Evan. 1993. "Mandatory Arrest of Batterers: A Reply to Its Critics," *American Behavioral Scientist*, 35(5): 651–680.

Stith, Sandra M. 1990. "Police Response to Domestic Violence: The Influence of Individual and Familial Factors," *Violence and Victims*, 5(1): 37–49.

Straus, Murray A. 1993. "Physical Assaults by Wives: A Major Social Problem." In *Current Controversies on Family Violence*, edited by R.J. Gelles & Donileen R. Loseke, 67–88. Newbury Park: Sage Publications.

Thomas, David R. and **Nevill R. Robertson.** 1990. "A Conceptual Framework for the Analysis of Social Policies," *Journal of Community Psychology*, 18 (July): 194–209.

United States. Police Executive Research Forum. 1980. *Responding to Spouse Abuse and Wife Beating.* Nancy Loving. Washington, DC.

United States. Police Foundation. 1984. *The Minneapolis Domestic Violence Experiment.* (Police Foundation Reports, no. 1). Lawrence W. Sherman and Richard A. Berk. Washington, DC.

Ursel, Jane. 1991. "Considering the Impact of the Battered Women's Movement on the State: The Example in Manitoba." In *The Social Basis of Law: Critical Readings in the Sociology of Law*, 2d. ed., edited by E. Comack and S. Brickey 238–260. Toronto: Garamond.

————. 1989. "The State and the Maintenance of Patriarchy: A Case Study of Family, Labour, and Welfare Legislation in Canada." In *Gender and Society: Creating a Canadian Women's Sociology*, edited by A. Tigar McLaren, 108–145. Toronto: Copp Clark Pitman.

———— and **Dawn Farough.** 1986. "The Legal and Public Response to the New Wife Abuse Directive in Manitoba," *Canadian Journal of Criminology*, 28(2): 171–183.

Waaland, Pam, and **S. Keeley.** 1985. "Police Decision-Making in Wife Abuse: The Impact of Legal and Extra-Legal Factors," *Law and Human Behaviour*, 9(4): 355–366.

Walker, Gillian. 1990. *Family Violence and the Women's Movement: The Conceptual Politics of Struggle.* Toronto: University of Toronto Press.

Walker, Lenore. 1979. *The Battered Woman.* New York: Harper and Row.

Worden, R.E., and **A.A. Pollitz.** 1984. "Police Arrests in Domestic Disturbances: A Further Look," *Law and Society Review,* 18(1): 105–119.

THE DIALECTICS OF CONSTITUTIONAL REPRESSION

Michael Mandel

There is hardly a law on the books that does not affect some people differently from others.[1]

EQUAL IN LAW, UNEQUAL IN LIFE

Inequality in Canada

Canada is a country of great social inequality. Statistics on income distribution give us only the barest glimpse of this. They tell us, for example, that the annual income of the top 20% of income receivers is eight times that of the bottom 20% (Vaillancourt 1985, 11–12). But quintile averages exclude the great extremes we encounter in everyday life. The $700,000 annual salary reported by senior partners in large Toronto law firms in 1988 was over *seventy-five times* the salary of a worker earning Ontario's minimum wage of $4.55 per hour (Watson 1988, 7). At the same time, chief executive salaries paid by Canada's major corporations were regularly topping $1 million per year and reaching as high, as far as the public record was concerned, as $3.8 million (Vancouver *Sun*, April 12, 1988: D1). However, even income figures exclude those factors associated with the greatest wealth, such as capital gains, and those associated with the greatest poverty, such as income on Indian reserves and among Canada's increasing prison population (Vaillancourt 1985, 58–59). And they give no indication of the way differences in income turn into much larger differences in wealth. In terms of actual wealth, estimates for 1980 showed the richest 1% of Canadians owning about 19% of Canada's total personal wealth, for an average of about $900,000, the richest 10% owning 57%, an average of $270,000, while the 40% occupying the large area at the bottom had to divide less than 1% of the total wealth among themselves for an average of $1,000 each (Osberg 1981, 35–40). In 1986, the richest 1% of corporations controlled about 80% of all

Canada's corporate assets and the top .01% owned 44.9% of them (CALURA 1988, 56; Glasbeek 1988). Not surprisingly, at the very top of Canada's personal wealth list are some of the richest people in the world. The Reichmann brothers of Toronto, with $9 billion from real estate, were ranked third in the world in 1988 by *Forbes* magazine, K.C. Irving of Saint John, with $8 billion in oil, paper, and land, was ranked fifth, and Kenneth Thomson of *The Globe and Mail*, with $5 billion, was ranked eleventh (*The Globe and Mail*, July 8, 1988: A10). *Fortune* magazine placed the same three in the top ten in 1987, though in a different order and all trailing the fifth-ranked Queen Elizabeth of England (and Canada) (*Fortune*, October 12, 1987: 120).[2]

If anything, inequality seems to have worsened in the era of the Charter. Inequality in income distribution has been creeping up decade by decade since World War II and the 1980s seem to have been the worst decade yet, with the rich taking a bigger slice of the diminishing pie (Ross 1980, 13, 51; Armstrong and Armstrong 1994, 198; Statistics Canada 1991, 1993a, 1993c, 1993d). Wealth distribution at the end of the Charter's first decade appeared to be considerably worse than at the beginning, with an Ontario survey estimating on the conservative side that in 1989 the richest 1% of Ontario households owned 23% of all the net wealth, the richest 5% owned 46%, and the richest 20% owned 74% (Ontario 1993: A15). The Charter's first decade was also a bad one for merely being able to hang on to a decent job. Unemployment averaged 9.3%, up from 6.7% for the 1970s and 5.0% for the 1960s. A growing proportion of those employed were holding only low-paying, insecure, part-time jobs (Leacy 1983, D491–497; Statistics Canada, 1993b; Kitchen et al. 1991, 44), while others were working overtime to compensate for stagnating wages. In Ontario, the minimum wage declined in real terms from $6.35 per hour in 1973 to $5.40 in 1991, or from 120% of poverty line to 85% (Kitchen et al. 1991, 35). Welfare rolls in Toronto quadrupled during the decade to reach over one hundred thousand people being assisted monthly (*The Toronto Star*, November 14, 1991: A1).

In fact, as we noted earlier, the Charter came on stream at the same time as a neo-conservative ideology that re-structured the state's relations with the economy and the tax system to "accommodate the rich" (Brooks 1993). This included cuts in income support programs and a shift in the tax burden from the rich to the average income earner (Brooks 1993; Kitchen et al. 1991, 39–40; *The Globe and Mail*, November 5, 1992: B3). These developments followed powerful international trends found not only in the United States, where inequality and repression shot up during the decade, but also in a global concentration of power that saw the formation, through mergers and takeovers, of gigantic transnational corporations and financial conglomerates that dictated one-sided terms to formally independent states ever more helplessly in their debt (Baily, Burtless, and Litan 1993; Davis 1987; Ontario 1993; *The Globe and Mail*, December 30, 1989: E11; March 6, 1992: B5). By the end of the decade, the market, the great unequalizer (Ross and Shillington 1989, 63–64; Armstrong and Armstrong 1994, 198) had come to dominate the world.[3]

In a market economy differences in wealth are not just differences in standards of living—though they are certainly that.[4] They are *relations of power*, the power, among other things, to claim other people's labour and not vice-versa, and to determine what is made with that labour. In a market economy the democratic principle of the private sphere is "one dollar, one vote."

These huge inequalities in social power and living standards have nothing to do with differences in natural endowment, talent, hard work and so on. We are all born into a vast and complicated hierarchy that distributes economic and social power and life chances in anything but an evenhanded fashion, according to such uncontrollable factors as one's sex, ethnicity, region and social class of origin. The greatly rich and the greatly poor in this country almost all started out that way (Hunter 1981, 146–150; Forcese 1975, 80–81).[5] As for the rest of us, the narrow band set by sex, ethnicity, and region is further circumscribed by the occupational and educational attainment of our parents (Hunter 1981, 143–146; Forcese 1975, 57–81).

Yet section 15 of the Charter proclaims with disarming simplicity:

> Every individual is equal before and under the law and has the right to the equal protection and benefit of the law without discrimination and, in particular, without discrimination based on race, national or ethnic origin, colour, religion, sex, age or mental or physical disability.

It is no accident that the Charter's list of the items according to which we must be equal in law are the very things according to which we are unequal in life. Could the Charter actually achieve this miracle?

Section 15 and the Status Quo

So fearsome were the implications of section 15 that it was not given immediate effect on entrenchment of the Charter. Governments were given three years (until April 17, 1985) to clean up their laws and to prepare to defend the ones they were not willing to change. Taken literally, section 15 threw everything up for grabs. "It is an all-encompassing right governing all legislative action" (*Re Education Act* 1986, 42). Taken literally, it was capable of engulfing the entire Charter, section 1 included. In fact, one of the technical problems plaguing the legal profession was how to reconcile section 15 and section 1, and indeed the rest of the Charter, without rendering any of them redundant:

> No one section should be regarded as paramount or as encompassing all of the other sections. That, however, may be what will become of s. 15 if it is interpreted as being violated by any distinction or unequal treatment. (Justice MacLachlin of the British Columbia Court of Appeal in *Andrews*, 1986, 607)[6]

Many of the issues of social power that we have already encountered were replayed once again with the coming into force of section 15. The anti-nuclear movement invoked section 15 in Charter litigation aimed at making the nuclear power industry more responsible (*Energy Probe* 1987). French speakers outside of Québec tried to overcome the limits of the explicit language provisions of the Charter by using the equality section to expand the use of French in the courts (*Re Use of French in Criminal Proceedings in Saskatchewan* 1987; *Paquette* 1987; *McDonnell* 1986) and to improve the quality of French language education (*Mahé* 1987). Workers tried to use it to expand collective bargaining rights (*Canadian Union of Postal Workers* 1987; *Hutton,* 1987). Business tried to use it to fight union rights (*The Globe and Mail,* October 13, 1986: A9), indeed all forms of regulation (*Smith, Kline & French Laboratories* 1986; *Aluminum Co. of Canada* 1986) including the Sunday closing laws. Sunday opening made a second weary trek through the court system, this time on equality grounds, courtesy of Toronto furrier Paul Magder and his lawyer Timothy Danson, among others (*London Drugs Ltd.* 1987). The Ontario doctors also brandished section 15 in their fight against the ban on extra-billing.

It comes as no surprise that the courts have not allowed themselves to be swept away in the vast literal expanse of section 15. They have not used it to dismantle Canada's hierarchical structure nor even to make a dent in our basic social inequalities. Nor is there any chance that they will. Legalized politics does not allow for that sort of thing. In fact, it comes equipped with many devices meant to prevent it. Important among these is the preoccupation of the Charter with "government" power. As Professor Hogg has pointed out in his constitutional law text:

> The real threat to egalitarian civil liberties in Canada comes not from legislative and official action, but from discrimination by private persons—employers, trade unions, landlords, realtors, restaurateurs and other suppliers of goods or services. The economic liberties of freedom of property and contract, which imply a power to deal with whomever one pleases, come into direct conflict with egalitarian values ... (Hogg 1985, 786)[7]

Those who conceived and drafted the Charter did their best to ensure that this system of private power remained well beyond the reach of the Charter and the courts have applied it accordingly. The common law rules of private property and "freedom" of contract, the basic building blocks of private power, were, as we have seen, declared out of bounds in *Dolphin Delivery*. Other courts have held that it does not render a body subject to the Charter merely to be the creature of statute (like all corporations) or to receive funding from the government (like most corporations, indeed all, if we take into account the biases of the tax system in favour of business vis-à-vis wage earners: McQuaig, 1987) (*Blainey* 1986; *McKinney* 1987).[8] This neatly avoids the embarrassment of having to reconcile the immense powers wielded in the corporate sphere with the requirements of section 15, since there is no question of these powers being in any way limited. In fact, the Charter implicitly removes questions of economic power from the scope of judicial review by consigning them to a purely hortatory part of the constitution. Part III, entitled "Equalization and Regional Disparities," claims that Canadian governments "are committed to" the following egalitarian ideals:

(a) promoting equal opportunities for the well-being of Canadians;

(b) furthering economic development to reduce disparity in opportunities; and

(c) providing essential public services of reasonable quality to all Canadians.

But these commitments are prefaced by the disclaimer that they do not in any way alter the legislative authority or powers of any government, which ensures that no court will take any government to task for failing to live up to them.[9]

Even in the absence of such cues the courts have had no difficulty reading into the equality provision other fundamental assumptions and political necessities of the Canadian social status quo. A most vivid example of this was Ontario's Catholic school funding controversy. Opponents of the extension of full public funding to Catholic high schools argued that it contravened section 15 in singling out one religion for government largesse ($80 million per year). Opponents went so far as to call the program a form of "apartheid" (*The Globe and Mail*, March 15, 1988: A1). But the courts rejected the challenge, holding that section 15 had to take second place to what was variously called "the basic compact of Confederation" and "the original confederation bargain." (*Re Education Act* 1987, 43, 61). Original compromise apart, the majority of the Ontario Court of Appeal placed the separate school controversy in the *contemporary* context of Ontario-Québec relations, for which it was originally and to some extent was still a proxy:

> [T]he purpose of Bill 30 has to be seen as an attempt to redress a historical grievance in Ontario and to remove a continuing irritant in relations with Québec when comparing the treatment of the beneficiaries of Section 93 with their counterparts in this province. (*Re Education Act* 1986, 57)

Section 15 could not be allowed to undo the main political goals of the Charter as a whole. It would have to take a back seat:

> These educational rights, granted specifically to the Protestants in Québec and the Roman Catholics in Ontario, make it impossible to treat all Canadians equally. The country was founded upon the recognition of special or unequal educational rights for specific religious groups in Ontario and Québec. The incorporation of the Charter into the *Constitution Act, 1982*, does not change the original Confederation bargain. (*Re Education Act* 1986, 64)

This passage was quoted with approval by a majority of the Supreme Court of Canada, who helped matters out by stretching the "original bargain" somewhat and holding that the Constitution not only permitted but actually *required* full funding. Bill 30, they decided, "returns rights constitutionally guaranteed to separate schools by s. 93(1) of the *Constitution Act, 1867* " (*Re Education Act* 1987, 59). To reach this conclusion the Court had to overrule a decision from the 1920s in which four levels of courts had upheld Ontario legislation that had deprived the French minority of rights which the Court now said had always been guaranteed (*Tiny Separate School Trustees* 1928)—yet another example of how the Constitution expands and contracts, at least in language matters, according to the political climate. Indeed, the majority recognized the inconsistency of this holding with their new conservative line on language, but they had little difficulty minimizing it: "it must still be open to a court to breathe life into a compromise that is clearly expressed" (*Re Education Act* 1987, 44). For the minority this historical revisionism went too far:

> It would be most inappropriate and indeed dangerous for this court over a half century later to review and then reverse or revise findings of fact made at trial by Rose J., confirmed by a unanimous Court of Appeal and undisturbed by the even division of this court ... [I]t would be imprudent for an appellate court sitting almost 60 years distant from the scene to reassess a factual situation peculiarly within the experience of the members of the other courts who were called upon to make their judgment of then recent history. (Justice Estey in *Re Education Act* 1987, 22)

Nevertheless the minority found its own reasons for acquiescing in the result.[10]

The Ontario Catholic School Funding case is just one illustration of the determination of the courts not to allow a free interpretation of equality rights to upset the Canadian political balance of power.[11] Another example, on a much lower judicial level, is a tax case in which the Ontario Public Service Employees Union challenged the right of business to deduct donations to political lobbyists such as the National Citizens' Coalition. The union pointed out that workers were not allowed such deductions except in limited circumstances (registered charities or registered political parties) and claimed discrimination. The judge was totally unsympathetic. Like the Supreme Court of Canada in the Right to Strike cases, he relied on a version of the principle/policy distinction to avoid doing anything so radical. The Charter, he said, would be "trivialized" if courts "get into the weighing and balancing of the nuts and bolts of taxing statutes" (*OPSEU* 1987, 452).[12]

Section 15 and Judicial Power

Reading section 15 so as not to upset the fundamental aspects of the Canadian system of power is not the same thing as reading it narrowly. Once section 15 came into force, the courts showed no hesitation in going beyond even the listed categories of prohibited discrimination to carry out pet law reform projects. These always seemed to have the effect of expanding judicial power.

For example, in criminal law some appeal courts introduced the notion of "geographic discrimination." The Ontario Court of Appeal ruled it a violation of equality rights that an exception to the minimum prison term for drunken driving available in some provinces had not been made applicable to Ontario. The federal government had let the provinces decide whether they wanted the exception and the most populous provinces, Ontario, Québec, and British Columbia, as well as Nova Scotia, had declined. The Government of Ontario argued that the exception weakened the deterrent effect. The Court of Appeal, however, held that it was unfair to Ontario residents not to have this right and, in effect, proclaimed it in force for Ontario (*Hamilton* 1986). But the effect of the exception was not to guarantee anyone the right to be excused from prison (the alternative was probation with a treatment order), merely to give the sentencing court the *discretion* to order it in an appropriate case.[13] And what is an appropriate case will always involve a question of the status of the convict. Indeed, the characteristic tenderness of courts to drunken drivers, despite popular objection, is closely related to the fact that drunken driving cuts across class boundaries more than any other offence (Mandel 1984).

When it was not a question of judicial rights but only of the accused person's rights, this argument about geographic discrimination was less likely to be successful. The Ontario Court of Appeal held in a subsequent case that it was *not* a denial of equality rights that persons accused of murder in Ontario could not choose the mode of trial the way one could if one lived in Alberta. Where it was a question of the *accused's* rights and not the *judge's*, the Court was able to find plenty of justification for discrimination (*Turpin* 1987).

Equality rights were also seen by some lawyers as a golden opportunity to subvert legislative schemes that bypassed the courts in favour of more rational forms of administration. They solemnly invoked the Charter in their hardly disinterested attempts to prevent the introduction of new schemes such as "no fault" motor vehicle accident compensation, as well as in attempts to roll back such venerable institutions as the workers' compensation system.

In the nineteenth century, common law judges devised many rules to prevent the increasing number of victims of industrial accidents from suing their employers. The "fellow servant" doctrine meant that if, as usual, a co-worker was responsible for an injury, the injured worker was barred from suing the company even though it was the company that made the profits and that had the money to pay; instead, the injured worker had to sue the co-worker and wind up with nothing. "*Volenti non fit injuria*" meant that injured workers were refused compensation when they "voluntarily" took jobs known to be dangerous (Tucker 1984, 260). And then there was the "fault" doctrine itself, which focussed on the narrow, immediate, individual cause of the accident and ignored its social, economic, or systemic cause. Litigation was a lottery with most of the prize money going to the legal profession (Glasbeek and Hasson 1977). Workers fought for a compensation scheme to circumvent the courts, and workers' compensation schemes began to appear in Canadian provinces around the time of the First World War (an era of great working-class militancy and the expansion of the suffrage to working people). Under these new schemes, workers injured on the job would be compensated with no question of fault, *volenti*, or "fellow servant" involved. The schemes would be administered by boards and not courts. They would be paid for by premiums from the companies.

Workers' compensation schemes have long been in place in all of the provinces. Compensation rates are far from adequate, and injured workers' groups have constantly campaigned for increases in amounts and for extensions to injuries not yet covered. In a serious accident, the amount one is likely to receive is certainly less than what a sympathetic jury might award a successful litigant. But successful litigants were rare in the common law courts and they are rare today in those American jurisdictions that allow suits alongside the compensation scheme (one out of a hundred according to one estimate: *The Toronto Star*, January 2, 1988: D1, D6). And the size of any award is greatly diminished by the lawyer's fee. In Canada, every scheme includes the barring of any civil suit against employers. This was the price extracted by employers for their consent to the scheme, but it also suits employees. A "two-tiered" system such as exists in most of the United States inevitably results in a deterioration of the no-fault scheme: "If you don't like it, sue." Naturally, lawyers claim the system is an outrage. With the advent of the Charter they started to hammer away at it. This is another case where assailants could be found on the left as well as on the right.[14]

Some initial success was achieved when two trial courts found that the schemes discriminated against industrial accident victims by depriving them of their hallowed access to the courts. The case that attracted the most attention was *Piercey*, in which the Chief Justice of Newfoundland granted a woman the right to sue for the industrial death of her husband despite the prohibition in the workers' compensation scheme.[15] Nobody could accuse Chief Justice Hickman of having a low opinion of courts:

> Of all the institutions to ensure the well-being of a democratic society, the Courts alone stand free and totally independent of Parliament, the Crown and any individual or group of individuals. The Courts acting through their inherent jurisdiction, strengthened by the clear intention of the framers of the Charter, stand between the would-be oppressor and the intended victim ... [S]tatutory tribunals, such as the Workers' Compensation Commission, created for the purpose of carrying out the will of the Legislature, do not have the same unimpaired independence or knowledge of the law and the skill to interpret same which the judiciary and courts have and must continue to enjoy. No substitute has been devised, to date, to replace the Courts as the guardian of liberty and freedom of all Canadians and to deprive a class of citizens of access to the Courts is at variance with the intent of the Charter and in particular, section 15 thereof. (*Piercey* 1986, 384)

This decision struck panic in the hearts of governments, large employers and unions alike. Workers' Compensation Boards from across the country, the Canadian Manufacturers Association, the Canadian National Railway and the Canadian Labour Congress all appeared in force at the appeal in St. John's to support the legislation. Despite the fact that Mrs. Piercey (and the legal profession) had the expert assistance of Charter enthusiast Professor David Beatty, imported from Toronto to do the necessary "conversing," the forces were simply too uneven.[16] When the legal profession opposes powerful interests, we know who is going to win. The Newfoundland Court of Appeal was unanimous in overturning the decision of the trial judge and upholding the legislation. There was no discrimination because what workers got in exchange for their right to sue left them in no way worse off:

> The workers' compensation scheme provides a stable system of compensation free of the uncertainties that would otherwise prevail. While there may be those who would receive less under the Act than otherwise, when the structure is viewed in total, this is but a negative feature of an otherwise positive plan and does not warrant the condemnation of the legislation that makes it possible. Judicial deference to the legislative will is required here. (Chief Justice Goodridge in *Re Workers' Compensation Act (Nfld.)* 1987, 524)

> In my view any economic loss that may be sustained by taking away the "right of action" for work-related injuries is more than offset by the overall benefit of the Act and is a necessary incident to the implementation of a valid legislative scheme. (Justice Morgan in *Re Workers' Compensation Act (Nfld.)* 1987, 532)

Of course, lawyers could be expected to fight to their last breath in defence of the sacred right to litigate. Workers compensation was a long shot over territory they had lost almost a century earlier. They fought harder and with more success in defence of their longstanding turf in the car accident compensation business, against the menace of "no-fault" auto insurance. But in this case they had the insurance industry on their side, at least as long as what was contemplated was a *public* auto insurance scheme. Appearing before the Ontario Inquiry into Motor Vehicle Accident Compensation, the Canadian Bar Association declared any such scheme unconstitutional and vowed to fight it in the courts should the government have the temerity to try to end the car accident lottery in favour of universal compensation (Schmitz 1987). Though the Ontario Supreme Court Judge conducting the inquiry did not buy the lawyers' Charter arguments (Ontario 1988, 619–641), he did accept their points about the "moral values" inherent in the fault system (Ontario 1988, 543) and recommended that the right to sue in tort remain, thus rendering a Charter test unnecessary for the time being.

Recent Developments in Equality Jurisprudence

The Ontario no-fault automobile insurance saga continued to a farcical conclusion not very different from what occurred with Sunday shopping. In the face of rising car insurance premiums the Liberal government reached a deal with the insurance companies and in 1990 introduced what amounted to a private no-fault system for most accidents (*Insurance Act* 1990, s. 267ff). The lawyers were left out in the cold except for a provision allowing litigation for "permanent serious" disfigurement. Though they achieved some success in getting the courts to interpret the threshold in a way congenial to litigation, they lost on a frontal Charter challenge to the legislation in the case of a motorcycle accident victim whose legal costs were paid by members of the personal injury bar (what sweet guys!) (*Hernandez* 1992; *The Law Times*, December 14–20, 1992: 5). In the meantime, the NDP had formed a majority government on a campaign promise to introduce a *public* no-fault system. Now the insurance business re-joined forces with the lawyers and hammered away at the NDP's socialist idealism in the face of a deepening recession and growing deficits. The NDP capitulated in stages. In 1991 they officially abandoned the idea of taking over the auto insurance business but promised to strengthen the no-fault element of the system by improving benefits and removing the right to sue for economic loss or any claim under $15,000 (Morton 1991, A21). In 1993 they weakened the no-fault system by lowering the threshold to $10,000, removing the word "permanent" and allowing litigation through the back door by the ingenious device of permitting insurance companies to sell a litigation option for economic loss beyond what the law allowed automatically. In effect, the insurance companies would be able to sell the right to sue that was supposed to have been removed by the law: those buying the endorsement would "buy their way back into the tort system" (*The Lawyers Weekly*, December 10, 1993: 1; *The Toronto Star*, December 23, 1993: E1; S.O. 1993, c. 10; Ont. Reg. 823/93). This made nobody happier than the lawyers who, despite their lack of success with constitutional arguments, had landed us pretty near right back where we started from.

The Ontario Court's rejection of the lawyers' constitutional claim against the no-fault system in *Hernandez* (1992) was based on recent Supreme Court of Canada jurisprudence that had placed some controversial limits on the vast literal scope of section 15. The Supreme Court finally got its chance to talk about the meaning of the clause in February 1989 in the case of *Andrews*. It was fitting that the first case in which the Charter's equality guarantees were considered would have to do with lawyers, and as the Free Trade Agreement kicked in, the fact that one of them was an American citizen claiming that citizenship should not be a bar to plying her trade in Canada made it too ironic for words. The legislation governing admission to the practice of law in British Columbia required Canadian citizenship. Andrews was a British subject and his co-plaintiff Kinersly an American. Both were permanent residents of Canada and the big discrimination was that they would have to wait three years for citizenship before being admitted to the Bar, which, given the length of time it took to become a lawyer, would not even have to have delayed their licence to practise law by one minute. Though the Court struck down the prohibition by a 4-2 margin, the judges seemed most anxious to lower the expectations that had been raised over the clause. Judge McIntyre reminded us that section 15, like the whole Charter, only applied to the government sphere:

> This is not a general guarantee of equality; it does not provide for equality between individuals or groups within society in a general or abstract sense, nor

does it impose on individuals or groups an obligation to accord equal treatment to others. It is concerned with the application of the law. (*Andrews* 1989, 10)

And Judge La Forest added that the courts would tread warily:

I am convinced that it was never intended in enacting s. 15 that it become a tool for the wholesale subjection to judicial scrutiny of variegated legislative choices in no way infringing on values fundamental to a free and democratic society ... Much economic and social policy-making is simply beyond the institutional competence of the courts: their role is to protect against incursions on fundamental values, not to second-guess policy decisions. (*Andrews* 1989, 38)

Apart from this, the majority of the judges gave a rather pedestrian reading to section 15, repudiating some pre-Charter jurisprudence that had denied there could be unequal treatment when parties were not "similarly situated" (*Bliss* 1978, discussed below) and laying down some non-controversial ground rules that limited the apparently vast scope of section 15 so as not to "trivialize" it and yet leave some potential work for section 1. It was not enough to violate the section that there was unequal treatment; there had to be "discrimination" based on "personal characteristics" as opposed to "merits or capacities." The suspect characteristics were either those set out in the section or "analogous" ones. Denying admission to the Bar on a citizenship basis was "discriminatory" and citizenship "analogous" because citizenship did not involve "educational and professional qualifications or the other attributes or merits of individuals in the group."

The issue that officially divided the Court was whether the restriction was a "reasonable limit" under section 1. The majority felt that citizenship was irrelevant to a lawyer's duties, while the minority (Judges McIntyre and Lamer) felt that citizenship symbolized "commitment to Canada" (*Andrews* 1989, 29) and that the burden was not great. However, there were some differences of more general importance between the judges, mostly having to do with the relevance of social power. Judge McIntyre studiously avoided the question while Judge Wilson (speaking as well for Judges Dickson and L'Heureux-Dubé), though claiming to agree with McIntyre, made an important and controversial addition to his definition, which suggested that power and disadvantage would play an important role in determining whether a group could rely on section 15:

I emphasize, moreover, that this is a determination which is not to be made only in the context of the law which is subject to challenge but rather in the context of the place of the group in the entire social, political and legal fabric of our society. While legislatures must inevitably draw distinctions among the governed, such distinctions should not bring about or reinforce the disadvantage of certain groups and individuals by denying them their rights freely accorded to others. (*Andrews* 1989, 32–33)

This was, of course, a subtle version of the "vulnerable group" doctrine seen in the business cases mentioned earlier; it suggested that access to the protection of section 15 would be restricted to disadvantaged groups. Some form of such a doctrine was absolutely essential if the Charter were not to be used by powerful groups to roll back legislated protections for the less powerful by the device of a tight judicial blindfold.

On the other hand, the formula was sufficiently vague to make everything depend on its application. In *Andrews*, for instance, lack of citizenship was abstractly equated with lack of power:

> Relative to citizens, non-citizens are a group lacking in political power and as such vulnerable to having their interests overlooked and their rights to equal concern and respect violated ... Non-citizens, to take only the most obvious example, do not have the right to vote. (Justice Wilson in *Andrews* 1989, 32)

> [N]on-citizens are an example without parallel of a group of persons who are relatively powerless politically, and whose interests are likely to be compromised by legislative decisions. (Justice La Forest in *Andrews* 1989, 39)

Justice La Forest even invoked the racist anti-Chinese laws of the turn of the century, but he must have had a very tight blindfold on not to see the difference between those laws and these mild, almost non-existent, limits on citizens of the United Kingdom and the *United States of America*, the world's only remaining superpower. We are talking about a class of non-citizens whose collective and individual economic power over Canada determines almost every aspect of our lives from the toothpaste we use to what our elected majority governments are required to do to ensure American "business confidence." In the neo-conservative nineties, dollars, especially US dollars, are far more powerful than ballots.

Though they left plenty to argue about, the limits imposed by *Andrews* allowed the Court to get rid of some of the (politically) easy equality cases on its docket. For example, the Workers' Compensation Act action could be dismissed in one sentence: "The situation of the workers and dependents here is in no way analogous to those listed in s. 15(1)." (*Re Workers' Compensation Act (Nfld.)* 1989). On the other hand, a major rhetorical turning point seemed to occur later in the year in the case of *Turpin*, where the Court endorsed a full "disadvantage" inter-pretation of section 15 (*Turpin* 1989). This was the case of "geographical discrim-ination" mentioned above in the text. In an opinion written by Judge Wilson, the court unanimously held that a statute denying Ontario residents the right to choose a non-jury trial in a murder case did not violate their right to "the benefit of trial by jury." This uncharacteristically narrow reading by Judge Wilson of a Charter guarantee for accused persons left little doubt that she was after bigger fish, namely section 15, which she then proceeded to bar to the accused on the ground that people charged with murder outside of Alberta were not an other-wise "disadvantaged" group:

> Persons resident outside of Alberta and charged with s. 427 offences outside Alberta do not constitute a disadvantaged group in Canadian society within the contemplation of s. 15. (*Turpin* 1989, 36)

This holding, on behalf of a unanimous court of six judges (Wilson, Dickson, Beetz, Lamer, La Forest and L'Heureux-Dubé) did the jurisprudential trick of establishing disadvantage as a condition precedent to the use of section 15:

> A finding that there is discrimination will, I think, in most but perhaps not all cases, necessarily entail a search for disadvantage that exists apart from and independent of the particular legal distinction being challenged. (*Turpin* 1989, 34)

According to Judge Wilson, the purpose of section 15 was "remedying or preventing discrimination against groups suffering social, political and legal disadvantage in our society" and the "*indicia*" of discrimination included "stereotyping, historical disadvantage or vulnerability to political and social prejudice" (*Turpin* 989, 35).

The *Turpin* view of section 15 was re-iterated in *Swain* (1991), a decision on the insanity defence where, however, the equality question was very peripheral. The Court had fashioned a new rule for determining when the Crown could adduce evidence of insanity over the accused person's objection and asked itself whether this new rule violated equality rights. Naturally, the answer was no, but it was not because the mentally disordered offender was not "disadvantaged," so the issue of advantage and disadvantage did not really arise. Nevertheless, Chief Justice Lamer (with the apparent though disinterested assent of the others) formulated the rule as follows:

> Furthermore, in determining whether the claimant's s. 15(1) rights have been infringed, the court must consider whether the personal characteristic in question falls within the grounds enumerated in the section or within an analogous ground, so as to ensure that the claim fits with the over-all purpose of s. 15; namely to remedy or prevent discrimination against groups subject to stereotyping, historical disadvantage and political and social prejudice in Canadian society. (*Swain* 1991, 520–1)

Though the issues in *Turpin* and *Swain* were rather low profile, the matter broke out into the open when the Federal Court of Appeal applied the disadvantage doctrine to the higher visibility questions of marriage and taxes. In *Schachtschneider* (1993), a married couple complained of discrimination by the *Income Tax Act* because through an anomaly (eliminated by the time the case came to court) the law gave certain common-law spouses with children a tax advantage over marrieds (though other provisions did the reverse). The claimants claimed discrimination by religion—they had married out of religious obligation—and marital status. The Court of Appeal dismissed the claim on the explicit ground of lack of disadvantage according to the *Turpin-Swain* doctrine. The majority put it simply:

> [M]arried persons with a child of the marriage, living together and not supporting each other ... [are] not a group that can be described as being disadvantaged in the context of its place in the entire social, political and legal fabric of our society. (*Schachtschneider* 1993, 174)

Judge Linden tried to soften it somewhat, but the basic message was the same:

> For historically disadvantaged groups, evidence that a law further disadvantages them will normally support a claim almost automatically under s. 15(1), whereas, for an advantaged group to succeed, a clear indication of prejudice will be necessary. In other words, in order to establish the *indicia* of discrimination, a member of an advantaged group would have to show direct or immediate prejudice stereotyping, although not necessarily intentional discrimination. The prejudice or stereotyping against an advantaged group cannot be assumed. Mere disadvantage under the legislation in question is not sufficient for advantaged groups, although it may be for disadvantaged groups. (*Schachtschneider* 1993, 188)

It wasn't long before conservative columnists were howling that the courts had re-written the constitution (*The Toronto Star*, July 16, 1993: A25) and editorialists were warning that group rights, indeed "group *histories* [are] determining individual rights" (*The Globe and Mail*, July 14, 1993: A16). Reform Party Leader Preston Manning quickly chimed in his agreement with these condemnations and promised to make it an election issue (*The Globe and Mail*, July 30, 1993: A18).

But even before these journalistic pronouncements had been made, the more conservative members of the Court under the leadership of the newly arrived Judge McLachlin (who took no part in either *Turpin* or *Swain*) were thinking along exactly the same lines. In *Nguyen* (1990) the Court pronounced against a law (typically, already repealed by the time the case was decided) that had created the absolute liability offence of sexual intercourse by a male with a person under 14 years of age. Judge McLachlin, on behalf of herself and Judges Sopinka and Gonthier, wrote an opinion expressly repudiating the "disadvantage" condition of *Turpin*:

> Some of the words used in *Turpin*, on the other hand, may be read as suggesting that discrimination is not established merely by a distinction within s.15 which imposes a greater burden or confers a greater benefit. Rather one should look for a disadvantage peculiar to the "discrete and insular minority" discriminated against, to determine if it suffers disadvantage apart from and independent of the particular legal distinction being challenged ...

> In my view, these arguments take the interpretation of the language in *Turpin* further than is justified. There is not suggestion in that language that men should be excluded from protection under s.15 because they do not constitute a "discrete and insular minority" disadvantaged independently of the legislation under consideration. The court must be taken to have had in mind s.28 of the Charter, which provides that notwithstanding any other provisions, the rights and freedoms referred to in the Charter are guaranteed equally to male and female persons ... Moreover, the qualified language used in *Turpin* suggest that the court viewed the so-called requirement of independent disadvantage not as an absolute requirement for a finding of discrimination, but rather as an

element which would be found in many of the cases where discrimination is found ... In my view, the essential requirements for discrimination under s.15 remain as set forth in *Andrews*.

Applying that test, I find that s.146(1) constitutes discrimination under s.15 of the Charter. It makes distinctions on the enumerated ground of sex. It burdens men as it does not burden women. It offers protection to young females which it does not offer to young males. It is discriminatory. (*Nguyen* 1990, 189–191)

This was a minority opinion, but even the majority opinion written by Judge Wilson herself seemed ready to water down *Turpin*. Suddenly, disadvantage was no longer a condition precedent; one merely was to "look" at the "larger social, political and legal context." Wilson agreed that even men might be able to use section 15 in an appropriate case:

Thus, were the legislature suddenly to decide that first degree murder would only be an offence when committed by a man, one would face an illegitimate dictinction that would trigger s.15(1). (*Nguyen* 1990, 179)

Wilson did her best to avoid confronting the question by advancing an incomprehensible argument that women could not commit the factual offence of having sexual intercourse with a minor. Once again the question remained at the level of rhetoric: even the minority was willing to uphold the law under section 1 because older males preying on younger females were "the gravamen of the problem" (*Nguyen* 1990, 200) and it was the majority that held that the (ex-)law violated the fundamental principles of criminal law.

Similarly, in a recent equality case, the Court, while not holding social power to be a bar to access to section 15, nevertheless used the question of power to deny that *different* treatment of male and female prisoners was *unequal* treatment because of the "reality of the relationship between the sexes" (*Conway* 1993, 5, discussed below), which sounded a lot like the "similarly situated" test that everybody loved to hate after *Bliss* (1978). In the child-care tax deduction case of *Symes* (1993, also discussed below), a majority of the Court invoked the *Turpin-Swain* position in rejecting a business-woman's claim, but emphasized that it was not an "exhaustive definition" or a "test." The Court appears to have retreated from *Turpin* to its preferred position of leaving all possible options open, which is perfectly understandable but hardly consistent with the image of a disinterested oracle of constitutional justice.

Charter equality jurisprudence is limitless and there is no hope of dealing adequately with all of the important subjects that come under its heading. We will have to restrict further discussion to two important and revealing examples of what the Charter has meant for those on the bottom end of Canada's structure of inequality. However, the experience of the aboriginal peoples and of women with legal politics demonstrates plainly enough that none of Canada's many equality struggles can be understood in isolation from one another.

ABORIGINAL PEOPLES AND THE CHARTER

In the Parliamentary debate on the Charter, Ian Waddell of the NDP claimed he was voting for the Resolution because it embodied, if imperfectly, his picture of Canada "as two founding societies, the English and the French, built on the foundation of the aboriginal people" (*House of Commons Debates*, November 27, 1981, 13429). On another occasion he used the metaphor of the Charter as a layer cake with the most important layer being "the bottommost layer of the cake—recognition of the rights of Canada's original people" (Sheppard and Valpy 1982, 122). Rights apart, Canada's aboriginal peoples are certainly at the bottommost level of the social power structure. The descendants of those who first peopled Canada and flourished for thousands of years before any European set foot here are by every material measure the least equal in the society declared equal by section 15. As the Charter was being entrenched, status Indians were living twice as many persons to a room as other Canadians, less than half as many households had a bath and toilet, two-thirds as many had a sewage system and about 20 times as many had no running water. Infant mortality rates were more than twice those of the Canadian population, and for those who survived life expectancy was about ten years shorter for both men and women. Status Indians were about one-sixth as likely to have some post-secondary education and four to five times as likely to be unemployed as other Canadians. They were three to four times as likely to be victims of violent crime and just as disproportionately represented in the prison population (Valentine 1980, 81–90; Zimmerman 1992, 413–414). These are all relative measures, but aboriginal poverty is no less "relational" than other forms of poverty. It is a product of centuries-old antagonistic relations between the aboriginal peoples and Canadian governments and businesses, characterized to this day by the relentless destruction, expropriation, colonization, and exploitation of both lands and peoples, the ruination of the natural bases of traditional aboriginal economies and the undermining of anything capable of replacing them (Valentine 1980, 71–77; Frideres 1983; McCullum and McCullum 1975; Nova Scotia 1989, 19–24).

Nobody is pretending that these depressingly familiar facts get close to the realities of aboriginal life, either to the depths of its adversity, or the determination with which that adversity has been confronted, or the strength and richness of aboriginal cultures, traditions and institutions. But they do point unmistakably to a lack of *power*—power of the one-dollar-one-vote variety—and thus provide a good test of the Charter's ability to even political odds. Furthermore, since the aboriginal peoples are also a classic "minority group" (at about 4% of the Canadian population) and lack one-person-one-vote power as well, their experience also provides a good test of the Charter's ability to "trump" majoritarian politics with principle.

The experience of the aboriginal peoples confirms the utter uselessness of legalized politics in the face of massive social inequality and, indeed, the many dangers lurking within this political form for those on the receiving end of it. In fact, the legalization of politics was one of the mechanisms with which the Canadian government tried to implement its postwar policy of ending Indian "special status," abolishing the reserves and assimilating aboriginal peoples "into the mainstream of Canadian life" (Sanders 1985, 536). Indians were given the vote for the first time when the *Canadian Bill of Rights* was enacted, and the first law declared by the Supreme Court of Canada to be inoperative under it was a provision of the *Indian Act* that treated Indians differently from non-Indians (*Drybones* 1969). At about the same time, the new government of Pierre Trudeau was proposing that Indian special status be done away with altogether, applying to Indians the logic of his solution to the problem of Québec (Sanders 1983, 319). Trudeau soon backed away from his plans in the face of massive aboriginal opposition, and the same thing seems to have contributed to the Supreme Court of Canada's rather clumsy about-face in *Lavell* (1973) on the relationship between the *Canadian Bill of Rights* and the *Indian Act* (Sanders 1985, 539–547). The early seventies saw aboriginal peoples increasingly emphasizing land claims, treaty rights and self-government, all oriented towards sovereignty and away from the notions of equal juridical status that the Charter movement was trying to establish as the guiding principle of Canadian political life.

Aboriginal Rights in the Charter

This is probably why the aboriginal peoples were barely mentioned in the first draft of the Charter (October, 1980). They figured only in the purely negative clause that is now section 26, which originally provided that the guarantees in the Charter

> shall not be construed as denying the existence of any other rights or freedoms that exist in Canada, *including any rights or freedoms that pertain to the native peoples of Canada.* (Hogg 1985, 703; emphasis added)

In other words, aboriginal peoples' issues were to be put on hold while the new constitutional arrangements were put in place. The major Native organizations were not about to let this happen. They saw the constitutional turmoil as an opportunity to advance their claims to land and self-government and launched a massive public relations attack on the whole Charter enterprise. Like the PQ, the National Indian Brotherhood (NIB) opened an office in London to lobby British MPs against passage of the federal resolution. The Native Council of Canada appeared before the Bertrand Russell Peace Foundation in Amsterdam and had Canada found guilty of "ethnocide." The Union of British Columbia Indian Chiefs chartered a train ("the Constitution Express") to take Indians from across the country to Ottawa and then on to the United Nations (Sheppard and Valpy 1982, 167).

Only after much soul-searching did the NIB agree to appear at the Charter hearings in late 1980. There they put forward a detailed plan of constitutional amendments that would put aboriginal rights, treaties, and lands not only beyond the reach of the Charter but beyond the reach of Parliament and the Legislatures as well, with clauses providing no diminution in aboriginal rights, even by constitutional amendment, "without the consent of those aboriginal peoples so affected" (Canada 1980–81, Issue No. 27: 87–89). In addition, they called for explicit declarations that "within the Canadian federation, the aboriginal peoples of Canada shall have the right to their self-determination" and that the various Canadian governments "are committed to negotiate with the aboriginal peoples of Canada mutually satisfactory constitutional rights and protections" including, among a long list, "rights of self-government," representation in Parliament and the Legislatures, "the right to adequate land and resource base and adequate revenues ... so as to ensure distinct cultural, economic and linguistic identities of the aboriginal peoples of Canada" (Canada 1980–81, Issue No. 27: 87). In other words, like the PQ they were after national, not individual rights. They wanted to deal with Canada as sovereign peoples, not as equal citizens. In fact, they expressed fears—which would prove not at all unfounded—about the potential of section 15 to *interfere* with their special status, and called for amendments to provide explicit protection for aboriginal and treaty rights from its operation. In short, they refused to be submitted to the biased discipline of Justice's Blindfold.

How the aboriginal leadership was persuaded to relent from this uncompromising position we may never know. But somehow the representatives of the major aboriginal groups, the National Indian Brotherhood, the Inuit Tapirisat of Canada and the Native Council of Canada, came to accept the federal government's offer of some modest amendments that were nowhere near what the NIB had called for. In a maudlin session of the Joint Committee, Jean Chrétien called the three Native leaders forward to sit beside him ("Now, they are my advisers!"), described the new amendments as representing "agreement among the aboriginal people themselves," and had portions of the amendments read out by various honourees as if it were a religious ceremony (Canada 1980–81, Issue No. 49: 88–89). The amendments amounted to two distinct clauses. The first was what is now section 25 of the Charter, a non-derogation clause providing that the Charter "shall not be construed so as to abrogate or derogate from any aboriginal, treaty or other rights or freedoms that pertain to the aboriginal peoples of Canada," including those "recognized" or those that "may be acquired ... by way of land claims settlement." Though also purely negative, the clause was a definite advance on the previous formulation, which had provided merely that lack of mention in the Charter did not necessarily preclude the existence of aboriginal rights, but neither recognized nor protected them. The new provision at least protected aboriginal rights from the Charter itself. To this was added a completely new clause:

> The aboriginal and treaty rights of the aboriginal peoples of Canada are hereby recognized and affirmed.

This clause was to be situated just outside the Charter, which had the advantage of making it subject neither to the override of section 33 nor to the "reasonable limits" of section 1. Though the clause was, in fact, rather ambiguous, most constitutional scholars and at least one court (*Sparrow* 1987) have taken "recognized and affirmed" to mean constitutionally guaranteed, that is to say beyond the reach of Parliament or the Legislatures except by constitutional amendment or by voluntary extinguishment (Hogg 1985, 566).

The agreement was immediately regarded as a betrayal by Indian leaders across the country. It was formally repudiated by the major Indian and Métis organizations within three months, with claims of a misunderstanding about whether the rights were to be subject to the amending formula (*The Globe and Mail*, April 17, 1981: 10; April 21, 1981: 8; Sheppard and Valpy 1982, 169; Romanow et al. 1984, 122). The aboriginal groups increased their London lobbying activities and even went to the English courts claiming that the British government continued to have responsibility for protecting their rights (Sheppard and Valpy 1982, 169). When the "kitchen deal"[17] was reached in November between the federal government and the English Canadian provinces, the aboriginal rights clause had been dropped. Defending this in the House of Commons, Jean Chrétien blamed the Premiers and the aboriginal people themselves:

> The cause of the constitutional recognition of aboriginal rights was not helped by the fact that leaders of the native peoples have spent a great deal of time and energy lobbying against the section in the previous resolution which they now seem to like. (*House of Commons Debates*, November 20, 1981: 13045)

The NDP, who had been crowing incessantly about their role in the formulation of the original clause but whose sincerity in the whole affair has been doubted (Sheppard and Valpy 1982, 170), now said they would not support the Resolution without the aboriginal rights clause back in. A compromise, apparently proposed by Alberta, watered down the clause by restricting it to "existing rights," and it was quickly restored. Though the NDP protested the dilution and unsuccessfully tried to have "existing" deleted, they nevertheless supported the final package (Sheppard and Valpy 1982, 170; House of Commons Debates, November 24, 1981: 13219 ff.). Canada's aboriginal peoples were not impressed. They pursued their vain legal and political struggles in England to the bitter end, but the most they could achieve was a few weeks postponement of the day when the Queen would sign the Constitution on Parliament Hill. Perhaps they can take credit for her having to do it in the midst of an April shower. The event was protested by status Indians all over the country, who flew flags at half-mast, kept their children home from school, and wore black arm bands (The Globe and Mail, April 3, 1982; A3; April 17, 1982: A8).

As a consolation prize for failing to entrench anything of meaning to aboriginal peoples the federal government inaugurated a curious constitutional ritual, that of (temporarily) entrenching constitutional conferences and their agenda items. In the era of the Charter one has to entrench *something*, and if it cannot be a right it will have to be the right to *talk* about entrenching a right. Section 37 of the Constitution provided that a constitutional conference would be called within one year and would

> have included in its agenda an item respecting constitutional matters that directly affect the aboriginal peoples of Canada, including the identification and defini- tion of the rights of those peoples to be included in the Constitution of Canada, and the Prime Minister of Canada shall invite representatives of those peoples to participate in the discussion on that item.

The conference was held as promised, and the results were the first amend- ments to Canada's new constitution: a clause clarifying the status of land-claims agreements as "treaty rights" (now section 35(3)); a clause guaranteeing aborigi- nal rights "equally to male and female persons" (section 35(4)), reversing *Lavell*, by then substantially reversed in practice anyway (Sanders 1985, 549); a (consti- tutional!) promise by the governments—but only "in principle"[18]—to consult aboriginal representatives before diminishing the federal constitutional jurisdic- tion over Indians and lands reserved for Indians (section 35.1); and finally— more conferences. At least two would be held, one before April 17, 1985 and one before April 17, 1987 (section 37.1).

This charade came to an end in March 1987 as the last of the entrenched constitutional talks closed with no agreement. At the final conference the irrec- oncilability of the respective positions was finally admitted. The aboriginal groups' minimum condition was the "explicit constitutional recognition of the right to self-government":

> Any amendment to the Constitution at this time must contain certain key ele- ments. It must recognize our right to self-government, lands and resources, an historic right inherent in our unsurrendered sovereignty ... Either bilaterally with the federal government or trilaterally including provincial governments, there must be an obligation to negotiate agreements or treaties at the request of each first nation or tribal group, or collectively, on jurisdictional matters, includ- ing self-government, lands, resources and fiscal relations ... These agreements must be constitutionally protected ... We must be guaranteed of the enforceability of our rights and jurisdictions ... We intend to engage in a dynamic and living intergovernmental relationship on the same nation-to-nation basis that was rec- ognized in the Royal Proclamation of 1763. (Erasmus 1987a, 1–4)

The federal government was miles away from this. Its "compromise" posi- tion was to recognize the right to self-government "in principle," or what the Assembly of First Nations (formerly the NIB) characterized as a "contingent" right to self-government: contingent upon further agreements with the govern- ments, not enforceable in the courts until any such agreement was reached, and then only to the extent contemplated by the agreement (Assembly of First Nations 1987, 2). Even this was opposed by the western provinces and Newfoundland. And, of course, it was unacceptable to the four organizations representing the aboriginal groups. No government, federal or provincial, was willing to leave this one to the courts. The meeting broke up with the aboriginal group leaders calling the Premiers "racist," and no further meetings were scheduled (*The Toronto Star*, March 28, 1987: A1, A4). The amendment referring to aboriginal rights' conferences neatly self-destructed, leaving no trace of the issue in Canada's constitution.[19]

When the Meech Lake Accord came, just one month later, it added insult to inaction. The sole reference to aboriginal peoples was the oblique one in Clause 16, which provided only that nothing in section 2 (the "distinct society" clause) "affects" section 25, 27, or 35 of the Constitution (aboriginal rights and multiculturalism). This was described by Georges Erasmus for the Assembly of First Nations as "the bare minimum":

> For five years we were engaged in constitutional discussions and it's this *"Bare Minimum"* attitude that prevailed throughout the process.

As far as the Assembly of First Nations was concerned, aboriginal interests were threatened by almost every clause of the Meech Lake Accord. What galled them the most, though, was the "distinct society" clause.

> It perpetuates the idea of a duality in Canada and strengthens the myth that the French and the English peoples are the foundation of Canada. It neglects the original inhabitants and distorts history. It is as if the peoples of the first nations never existed. It suggests that historically and presently as well the French peoples in Québec form the *only* distinct society in Canada. The amendment fails to give explicit constitutional recognition to the existence of first nations as distinct societies that also form a fundamental characteristic of Canada ... We were told for five years that governments are reluctant to entrench undefined self-government of aboriginal peoples in the constitution. Yet, here is an equally vague idea of a "distinct society" unanimously agreed to and allowed to be left to the courts for interpretation. (Erasmus 1987b)

The experience of Canada's aboriginal peoples is another refutation of any pretensions legalized politics might have to being a means of redressing major Canadian injustices. In effect, the aboriginal peoples tried to "hijack" the Charter enterprise to address their claims to the economic and political wherewithal for communal survival. But the Charter is highly resistant to hijacking. Its offer of formal equal citizenship is meant not to redress the balance of power but to legitimate it. It is most at home treating people as abstract equal individuals (no matter how unequal they are) and is most uncomfortable accommodating real flesh-and-blood communities. Canada's aboriginal peoples are too far and too thoroughly removed from the material and cultural presuppositions of this deal ever to be more than fleetingly attracted to it; it is, rather, something they have consistently tried to oppose. Not that opposing the legalization of politics is an easy matter. The aboriginal peoples were not allowed to opt out of the Charter any more than Québec was—even less, because they had no section 33 to turn to. From the way the courts have been behaving, they could have used one.

Charter Decisions on Aboriginal Rights

Section 15(2) of the Charter was inserted because American experience had shown how much an obstacle *constitutional* equality could be to the achievement of *real* equality. In the notorious *Bakke* decision of the United States Supreme Court, an affirmative action program instituted at a California medical school that gave preferential admission to certain historically disadvantaged groups, including black people, was held to violate the Fourteenth Amendment guarantee of "equal protection of the law" (*Bakke* 1978). In other words, a post-Civil War amendment enacted to turn the country's back on slavery was used to cut back on the gains black people were finally achieving after 100 years through political means. Since *Bakke*, successive drafts of the Canadian Charter attempted to allay fears of a Canadian version of the decision by inserting clauses more or less to the effect of the current section 15(2):

> (2) Subsection (1) does not preclude any law, program or activity that has as its object the amelioration of conditions of disadvantaged individuals or groups including those that are disadvantaged because of race, national or ethnic origin, colour, religion, sex, age or mental or physical disability.

The aboriginal groups appearing before the Joint Committee were not content to trust the courts with this and tried to have added to this list laws that had as their object "the recognition of the aboriginal and treaty rights of the aboriginal peoples of Canada" (Canada 1980–81, Issue No. 27: 88). But even this would not have protected them from the judicial ingenuity shown by Manitoba's Justice Simonsen in the first application of this provision to aboriginal peoples. He read into the exception a limit closer to the typically legal "fault" requirement used by the majority in *Bakke* than anything in the words of section 15(2). In fact, the case was really an application of the *Bakke* principle *despite* 15(2). According to the judge, affirmative action programs had to "demonstrate a reasonable relationship between the cause of the disadvantage and the form of ameliorative action" to be permitted under the Charter (*Apsit* 1987, 643). That is, they had to address the *cause* of the disadvantage. The Manitoba government had adopted an "affirmative action" program "to encourage native people to take a leading role in the wild rice industry" and had embarked upon a program of granting new licences exclusively to Indians in most of the areas of the province.[20] The government received approval from the provincial human rights commission for the scheme. But, as in *Bakke*, some non-Indians claimed discrimination. An association of wild rice growers applied to court, and the Court struck down the policy as violating the equality guarantees of the Charter. Because poverty and not discriminatory licensing was found to be the cause of the Indian inability to compete successfully in the industry, discriminatory licensing was not a permitted cure:

> The disadvantage of the target group did not arise from an inability to obtain wild rice licences, but rather the disadvantage lay in the target group's lack of

> resources to take advantage of the opportunities available in the industry ... I conclude that the target group needed capital and management assistance in order to achieve its objective to have a leading role in the industry. In my view the respondent has failed to demonstrate a reasonable relationship between the cause of the disadvantage and the form of ameliorative action. (*Apsit* 1987, 643)

This is but another example of some of the key elements of Charter politics: the Charter is not self-enforcing, so claims under it have to be put through the judicial filter, and the judiciary is most uncomfortable righting social wrongs at the expense of formal legal equality even when given the clearest of mandates. It is almost fitting that it should be a judge to remind aboriginal peoples that they have nothing to hope for from purely legal remedies. The trick is how to get "capital and management assistance" when only purely legal remedies are available on the menu.

Nor have the bare equality rights of the Charter proved of any value to Native people. Their limits have been as evident here as they are elsewhere. In *Sinclair* (1986), a Manitoba status Indian convicted of murdering a prison guard claimed his equality rights were violated when the panel from which his jury was to be selected had only two Indians (out of 148), only one of whom was actually chosen. Sinclair wanted half the jury to be Indian, preferably fluent in Cree, his native language. The Court of Appeal rejected the claim on the grounds of multiculturalism and the rights of *jurors*:

> To so interpret the Charter would run counter to Canada's multicultural and multiracial heritage and the right of every person to serve as a juror (unless otherwise disqualified). It would mean the imposition of inequality. (*Sinclair* 1986, 421)

When reminded of the new rights of English and French Canadians to a jury composed entirely of jurors who speak their language (*Criminal Code* s. 462.1), the Court reminded Sinclair of the structure of the Canadian layer cake, anticipating the approach that would be taken in *Re Education Act* (1987):

> Language, because of its special place in the constitutional history of Canada, is given a special categorization in the Charter consistent with our constitutional history. Indians are treated the same as all other races. (*Sinclair* 1986, 422)

Even in the non-formal realm of "aboriginal rights," the fundamentals of legalized politics are fully in evidence. Once again, we have a parallel to the case of Québec. The aboriginal claim for self-government through negotiated agreements was a claim for *self*-administration. But "aboriginal rights" in the context of a Charter of Rights—even when generously interpreted—mean *judicial* administration, a different thing entirely. The case of *Sparrow* (1987) is an example. The accused, a member of the Musqueam Indian band residing near Vancouver, was convicted of taking salmon with a net much bigger than allowed by federal regulation. This was in no sense an individual aberration but part of a century-old conflict between the Canadian government and West Coast Indians over control of the fishery (Shaffer 1988). The British Columbia Court of

Appeal took a generous view of the phrase "existing aboriginal and treaty rights" in the Charter and decided, over the Crown's objection and the trial judge's decision, that the Constitution protected rights even where there were no treaties and even when they were subject to federal regulation at the time of the Charter's entrenchment. But that did not mean, as the defence claimed, that the aboriginal rights should be *self*-regulated by the right holders:

> The aboriginal right which the Musqueam had was, subject to conservation measures, the right to take fish for food and for the ceremonial purposes of the band. It was in the beginning a regulated, albeit self-regulated, right. It continued to be a regulated right, and on April 17, 1982 it was a regulated right. It has never been a fixed right, and it has always taken its form from the circumstances in which it has existed. If the interests of the Indians and other Canadians in the fishery are to be protected, then reasonable regulations to ensure the proper management and conservation of the resource must be continued ... The general power to regulate the time, place and manner of all fishing, including fishing under an aboriginal right, remains. (*Sparrow* 1987, 608–609)

Sparrow was sent back for a new trial to see if the limits were reasonably related to conservation purposes. The Court had, in effect, introduced the notion of a "reasonable limit" into a section of the Charter formally immune from it.[21] And this was a *generous* reading of the aboriginal rights clause.

Recent Developments in Aboriginal Rights under the Charter

> Lawyers are like cockroaches who feed off the misery of native people.[22]

The early 1990s saw a frenzy of activity over aboriginal rights. It was to be an aboriginal parliamentarian—Manitoba's only one despite constituting 80% of the province's population—to deliver the *coup de grâce* to Meech Lake, and the aboriginal leadership was very much a protagonist in the subsequent run for the money that was the Charlottetown Accord. However, the Charlottetown Accord was rejected not only by Canadians in general but also by aboriginal communities in particular. The most convincing explanation for that rejection remains that the strategy of the negotiators was felt by the community they represented to be too timid, selling the First Nations' signature on the Canadian Constitution at too cheap a price (e.g., Doxtater 1993). As if to vindicate this view, supporters of aboriginal rights have been arguing that the centrepiece of the Accord, the "inherent right of self-government," was *already* a feature of the Canadian Constitution (Slattery 1992). The Royal Commission on Aboriginal Peoples released a report in August 1993 endorsing this position (*The Toronto Star*, August 19, 1993: A3). Co-Chair René Dussault, trying his best to reconcile the big claims of Charlottetown with this new position, was able only to say that "the Charlottetown Accord would have made that fact explicit, but it would not have created the right; it would only have confirmed it" (*The Globe and Mail*, September 7, 1993: A17). Indeed, the Liberal Party came into federal office with a platform plank that promised that it's government, too, would act on the basis that the inherent right was already in the Constitution (*The Globe and Mail*, October 12, 1993: A10).

On the other hand, this academic and political consensus has not been shared by the Courts. A major post-Charlottetown set-back occurred in British Columbia where a huge land claim had been thrown out of court in March of 1991 (*Delgamuukw* 1993). The Gitskan and Wet'suwet'en peoples did not only claim "ownership" of 58,000 square kilometres of central B.C., they also claimed "jurisdiction," that is "the right to govern" the territory (*Delgamuukw* 1993, 116). After four years of hearings the Chief Justice ruled that all aboriginal rights in the area had been "extinguished" and that all that remained was "a continuing legal right to use unoccupied or vacant Crown land in the territory for aboriginal sustenance purposes." Moreover, the Province had the absolute authority to extinguish these rights should it want to devote the land to another use (*Delgamuukw* 1993, 113). In its 1993 decision on the appeal from the judgment, the Court of Appeal modified this position somewhat but still rejected the aboriginal claim by a margin of 3-2. The difference in approach by the Appeal Court no doubt had something to do with the fact that when the appeal was argued a new provincial NDP government was in office and it repudiated the position taken by its predecessor Social Credit government at trial. The NDP's new line reflected the more conciliatory approach of the Charlottetown Accord that was being concluded just as the appeal was being argued, an approach that emphasized constitutionally mandated negotiations. The Appeal Court was asked to proclaim limited self-government and aboriginal rights but to leave the details up to bargaining between the parties:

> Both [parties] asked for declarations that the plaintiffs have certain aboriginal rights which have not been extinguished, but asked that the particular location, scope, content and consequences of those rights be permitted, following the making of the declarations requested, to be negotiated by the parties. Neither party asked for an order that the parties be compelled to negotiate. They asked only that declarations in general terms about the existence and nature of the plaintiffs' aboriginal rights be made by formal orders now, and that the remaining issues in the appeal be adjourned to permit the parties to use the general declarations that have been made as a framework for their negotiations. (*Delgamuukw* 1993, 251)

In other words, each party was arguing for a kind of judicial Charlottetown Accord that would presumably give extra sanctimony or at least legitimacy to the ongoing negotiations, which could be expected to continue with or without Charlottetown. The majority of the Court was not so compliant, however, and rejected any notion of constitutional rights to self-government:

> With respect, I think that the trial judge was correct in his view that when the Crown imposed English law on all the inhabitants of the colony and, in particu-

lar, when British Columbia entered Confederation, the Indians became subject to the legislative authorities in Canada and their laws. In 1871, two levels of government were established in British Columbia. The division of governmental powers between Canada and the Provinces left no room for a third order of government (*Delgamuukw* 1993, 152)

The majority was willing to recognize the theoretical existence of lesser aboriginal rights, but only so long as any details and implications were left to another day:

> ... The Gitskan and Wet'suwet'en people have aboriginal rights in a large area of land ... These rights, along with land already in reserves, may provide a foundation for the preservation and development of an Indian community. Self-regulation and new economic opportunities for Indian communities may be secured in ways yet to be negotiated ...

> Legal questions will arise as to the extent to which aboriginal rights may have been diminished by provincial grants, leases, permits or licences and the extent to which they may compete or co-exist with other interests. They were not raised in this case.

> Aboriginal rights need to be considered on the facts pertinent to specific people and specific land. Aboriginal rights can never be determined in a vacuum ... It is necessary to consider whether they are in conflict or can co-exist with other activities ...

> The parties have expressed willingness to negotiate their differences. I would encourage such consultation and reconciliation, a process which may provide the only real hope of an early and satisfactory agreement which not only gives effect to the aspirations of the aboriginal peoples but recognizes there are many diverse cultures, communities and interests which must co-exist in Canada. A proper balancing of those interests is a delicate and crucial matter. (*Delgamuukw* 1993, 179–80)

Even Judge Lambert, the most pro-claimant of the two dissenters, re-interpreted the claim for "ownership" as a weaker claim for "aboriginal title" and he left the meaning of that entirely up to negotiations. The same went for "self-government and self-regulation," although Judge Lambert further limited the latter by claiming for the Court a supervisory jurisdiction to ensure that this did not include

> any of those rights which related to Sovereignty and so were inconsistent with British Sovereignty over the territory; any of those rights which would at the time have been repugnant to natural justice, equity, and good conscience, and have not since then so modified themselves as to overcome that repugnancy; and any of those rights which were contrary to the part of the common law that was not from local circumstances inapplicable. (*Delgamuukw* 1993, 373)

To this extensive list of exemptions Lambert added that "aboriginal title" rights to harvest, manage and conserve the lands and their resources were to be subject to environmental restrictions and "consultation and cooperation with ministries and agencies of the Crown and with the private sector who may be affected by the exercise of the plaintiffs' rights" (*Delgamuukw* 1993, 374). Indeed, the Court had granted intervenor status to Alcan Aluminum Limited and a business coalition of mining, lumber, fishing, agricultural and commercial interests (*Delgamuukw* 1993, 109–110).

So the most the claimants could get out of even the friendliest of these judges was a mini-Charlottetown Accord—lots of rhetoric, but no substance—complete with a "peace order and good government" clause that kept the whole thing under judicial control in case powerful private interests should ever be threatened.

R. v. Sparrow

In early 1994 *Delgamuukw* was bound for the Supreme Court of Canada and the prognosis was for even more non-committal rhetoric with no action. This, in any event, was what could be predicted from the Supreme Court's decision in the fishing rights case of *Sparrow*, an appeal from the decision discussed above in the text. The Supreme Court, too, rejected the Crown argument that the aboriginal right in question had been extinguished, holding that for this to occur there had to be a clear intention on the part of the government to do so. So, like the Court of Appeal, the Supreme Court was generous on the existence of the right. However, the Court could afford to be generous on the *existence* of the right because it was going to keep the *nature* of the right firmly under control by subjecting it to "reasonable limits" even though this required a re-writing of the Constitution no less brazen than the one in *Québec Protestant School Boards*. In the Québec case, the Court had read *out* section 1 where it literally applied; in *Sparrow*, it read *in* the equivalent of section 1 where it literally did not apply. Even though the Charter, and therefore section 1, technically stopped at section 34 (the section on aboriginal rights being number 35), the Court invented its own section 1 for aboriginal rights:

> In response to the appellant's submission that s. 35(1) rights are more securely protected than the rights guaranteed by the Charter, it is true that s. 35(1) is not subject to s. 1 of the Charter.

That is, the words of the Charter did not subject aboriginal rights to "reasonable limits" or any limits at all. Nevertheless:

> In our opinion, this does not mean that any law or regulation affecting aboriginal rights will automatically be of no force or effect by the operation of s. 52 of the *Constitution Act, 1982*.

How come?

> There is no explicit language in the provision that authorizes this court or any court to assess the legitimacy of any government legislation that restricts aboriginal rights.

What about the words "recognized and affirmed" in section 35? What about the words in section 52 that "any law that is inconsistent with the Constitution is, to the extent of the inconsistency, of no force or effect?" Granted, the terms are ambiguous, but no more so than any other words in the Charter. That never prevented the Court from feeling itself explicitly authorized to assess the legitimacy of legislation before.

> Yet, we find that the words "recognition and affirmation" incorporate the fiduciary relationship referred to earlier and so import some restraint on the exercise of sovereign power.

Here the Court seemed to be saying that "recognition and affirmation" of a right was something less than its "guarantee," and that the much-celebrated "fiduciary obligation" (Slattery 1992, 263) was something less than other constitutional obligations. Remember that the Court called this a "generous" interpretation (*Sparrow* 1990, 286).

The Court continued:

> Rights that are recognized and affirmed are not absolute.

Well, that depends, doesn't it, on how they are interpreted by the Court. For example, in *Québec Protestant School Boards* the right to an education was held to be absolute in the sense that it could not be overridden by recourse to section 1.

> Federal legislative powers continue, including, of course, the right to legislate with respect to Indians pursuant to s. 91(24) of the *Constitution Act, 1867*.

And so did the provincial powers of education continue in *Québec*. And so do all the powers under section 91 and 92 that are now subject to the Charter.

> These powers must, however, now be read together with s. 35(1). In other words, federal power must be reconciled with federal duty and the best way to achieve that reconciliation is to demand the justification of any government regulation that infringes upon or denies aboriginal rights. (*Sparrow* 1990, 288)

Q.E.D. Maybe this is what Holmes meant when he said that "the life of the law is not logic."

Thus, the Supreme Court arbitrarily wrote a "reasonable limits" clause into aboriginal rights:

> To determine whether the fishing rights have been interfered with such as to constitute a *prima facie* infringement of s. 35(1), certain questions must be asked. First, is the limitation unreasonable? (*Sparrow* 1990, 290)

According to the Court, a government regulation of aboriginal rights would be reasonable if it had its priorities right. The first priority was conservation; aboriginal rights would have to take second place to this, though there was a hint that some form of "fair compensation" might be required "in a situation of expropriation" of an aboriginal interest and that the aboriginal peoples had a right to "consultation" on conservation measures (*Sparrow* 1990, 295). Then came the major concession to aboriginal rights which, in fact, involved a major dodge by the Court: constitutional protection of aboriginal rights, said the Court, meant that, after conservation, "top priority" had to be given to "Indian *food* fishing" (*Sparrow* 1990, 293; emphasis added) which would rank before all commercial and sport fishing. I emphasize "*food*" fishing because the Court took pains not to decide whether aboriginal *commercial* fishing had any constitutional priority at all, even though there was plenty of evidence that the Musqueam had bartered fish in pre-contact times. The Supreme Court, having granted intervenor status on the appeal to commercial fishing companies, held itself to affirming the aboriginal right to consumption for subsistence, ceremonial and social reasons. On the other hand, the Supreme Court showed other courts the way to reject claims to commercial rights by turning aboriginal conceptions of property against the claimants:

> Fishing rights are not traditional property rights. They are rights held by a collective and are in keeping with the culture and existence of that group. Courts must be careful, then, to avoid the application of traditional common law concepts of property .... (*Sparrow* 1990, 290)

So despite its generosity in the rhetoric department, *Sparrow* was really a decision about how to bring aboriginal rights under constitutional *control*, not constitutional protection.

The impact of *Sparrow* was immediately disputed, with both Native and non-Native fishing groups claiming victory (*The Globe and Mail*, June 2, 1990: A3). A raft of litigation followed the case, intricately interwoven with the negotiations for the Charlottetown Accord. In British Columbia, where a major dispute was brewing between the aboriginal and non-aboriginal fishery (*The Globe and Mail*, January 29, 1993: A15), the Court of Appeal—in a series of decisions issued at the same time as the land-claims judgment in *Delgamuukw* (1993)—took a narrow view of *Sparrow* and held it inapplicable to commercial fishing (*Vanderpeet* 1993; *Gladstone* 1993; *N.T.C. Smokehouse Ltd.* 1993) or anything that smacked of a sovereignty claim (*Nikal* 1993). Though the Court was willing to extend *Sparrow* from subsistence fishing to subsistence hunting (*Alphonse* 1993; *Dick* 1993), even this was done on a concession by the NDP government.[23] According to a majority of the Court, commercial fishing was ruled out even though there was trade, gift and barter in surplus fish in pre-contact times because the aboriginal peoples did not fish in order to supply a market, "there being no regularized trading system" (*Vanderpeet* 1993, 470). Consequently, they could participate in the commercial fishery "[b]ut they must be subject to the same rules as other Canadians who seek a livelihood from that resource" (*Vanderpeet* 1993, 473).

What all this means is that the Court would not give the aboriginal peoples the constitutional right to trade in their traditional forms of economy for their modern equivalents, even though it must have been obvious to the judges that forms of economy that provided a dignified existence before the conquest could no longer do so once their material and cultural bases had been destroyed and they had been confined to the narrow margins of a vast, dominant market system. In effect, Justice's Blindfold had struck again. Aboriginal peoples were not to be allowed to use the Charter to go beyond equal individual rights, no matter how unequal the circumstances; even the Charter's explicit and apparently unlimited aboriginal rights clauses would be narrowly confined to purely historical significance and thus rendered irrelevant to the modern struggle for equal dignity. They would be frozen in history.

Even the friendlier judges seemed anxious to ensure that aboriginal rights were historically limited. In his dissent in the *Vanderpeet* case, Judge Lambert said he would recognize aboriginal commercial fishing rights only to the extent of guaranteeing pre-contact subsistence levels. According to him, aboriginal peoples were entitled by the constitution to sell only as much salmon as would enable them to *eat* as much salmon as they did in 1800:

> [A]n aboriginal right... to catch and, if they wish, sell... sufficient salmon to provide all the people who wish to be personally engaged in the fishery, and their dependent families, when coupled with their other financial resources, with a moderate livelihood, and in any event, not less than the quantity of salmon needed to provide everyone of the collective holders of the aboriginal right with the same amount of salmon per person per year as would have been consumed or otherwise utilized by each of the collective holders of the right, on average, from a comparable year salmon run, in, say, 1800. (*Vanderpeet* 1993, 499–500)

Just before the Charlottetown Accord fiasco, Professor Peter Russell wrote:

> Canada's aboriginal peoples may turn out to be among the few beneficiaries of Canada's protracted constitutional struggle. Opening up both the substance and the process of constitutional politics would eventually provide an opportunity for aboriginal peoples to be part of the Canadian community. It is unlikely that such an opportunity would have occurred had Canada's constitutional debate not addressed fundamental questions about the nature of the country and kept those questions open so long. (Russell 1992, 94–95)

The idea seems to be that the Charter provided participation rights—and here, I suppose, we would have to credit Pierre Trudeau's constitutionally entrenched constitutional conferences—which allowed aboriginal peoples to get a better hearing for their claims. Unfortunately, as we know from our examination of procedural rights, better hearings do not necessarily provide better results. Except for their presence at the constitutional table, aboriginal peoples have precious little in the way of equality to show for their decades of legal politics.

It is true that a massive influx of federal money into aboriginal communities ($26 billion in the 1970s and 1980s) changed some of the statistics cited at the beginning of this section: most houses on reserves now have furnaces, toilets and running water. On the other hand, despite being newly built, reserve housing is more than three times as likely to be in need of major repair and about sixteen times as likely to be overcrowded (by official definitions) than non-reserve housing (Elliott 1992, 2–3). More importantly, with respect to health, the infant mortality gap between aboriginal and non-aboriginal communities appears not to have changed at all (Zimmerman 1992, 412), and aboriginal adult life expectancy has apparently shaved only one year off of the decade difference that existed thirty years ago (Elliott 1992, 4; *The Globe and Mail*, June 27, 1990: A9). Aboriginal people are also twice as likely to suffer from physical disabilities (*The Globe and Mail*, March 26, 1994: A7). Similarly, the unemployment gap appears not to have varied in the decade of the Charter from two-and-a-half times the national average (*The Toronto Star*, September 21, 1993: A12; Elliott 1992, 2; Nova Scotia 1989, 26), and the apparent decrease in the gap from the 1970s was in all probability due more to recessionary increases in non-aboriginal unemployment than to increases in aboriginal employment (Valentine 1980, 90). The education gap has remained the same, with about half as many aboriginal adults having a grade 9 education as the Canadian average and only about one tenth as many having a university degree (Elliott 1992, 4; Zimmerman 1992, 412). And the most telling social indicators point if anything to a worsening situation. In the late 1980s, aboriginal people were four times as likely (one out of every three) to die accidentally or by violence, and males 15 to 24 years of age had six times the Canadian suicide rate (*The Globe and Mail*, June 27, 1990: A9). There is also evidence that aboriginal over-representation in jail populations was worse in the late eighties than in the late sixties (Elliott 1992, 4; Zimmerman 1992, 413–414).

All in all, it is more realistic to view the Charter as having operated to *manage* aboriginal claims than as having operated to *promote* them. As long as you could get the aboriginal peoples to stay in court or at the constitutional bargaining table nothing radical could possibly happen; and when the long drawn-out legal processes had exhausted themselves you could generally count on being back where you started, with those who had dared to challenge the status quo a lot worse for wear. Emblematic of this was the Ontario land claim by the Teme-Augama Anishnabai started in 1973 with a legal caution on property rights. No doubt back in 1973 the claimants thought they were using the legal system to "trump" politics. The Court case dragged on for two decades. So did the negotiations. The Supreme Court of Canada threw out the case in 1991, holding that the aboriginal rights had been surrendered but that the government was still bound by its famous "fiduciary obligation" (*Bear Island Foundation* 1991, 575). It was as if everything had to wait for the legal proceedings to conclude (and the Charlottetown Accord to fail) before anything could be accomplished, because negotiations finally came to a conclusion with a settlement in 1993 (*The Globe and Mail*, August 19, 1993: A4). The Band rejected the deal as inadequate within six months (*The Globe and Mail*, March 4, 1994: A11). The constitutional bargaining chip turned out to be a twenty-year bust.

Then there are the instances where the Charter is used not only to co-opt aboriginal aspirations but to directly thwart them, as when Toronto lawyers argued against aboriginal governments' access to the override clause during the

Charlottetown debate (Ruby 1992) or when a British Columbia judge invoked the Charter to limit an aboriginal community's right to use traditional forms of discipline (*Globe and Mail*, February 8, 1992: A6). An instructive saga of politics and law along these lines came from Davis Inlet in Labrador, where a small Innu community with 6000 years of history behind it had been reduced to total government dependence in 26. It became world-famous for the suicidal substance abuse of its youth in 1993 (*The Globe and Mail*, February 13, 1993: D5). When, a year later, the Chief ordered a Provincial Court judge out of the community for using jail sentences too freely, the judge's first reflex was to get tough and invoke the Charter:

> Now, my response to this at first blush, and I'll seek the assistance of counsel, is to advise anyone who is here trying to interfere with the operation of an independent court under the Canadian *Charter of Rights and Freedoms* to cite you for contempt in the face of the court and to order you all in custody.

To which a voice in the crowd responded: "You're not big enough." In the ensuing melee, the judge and the RCMP beat a hasty retreat from the community (*The Globe and Mail*, January 29, 1994: D5).

The Charter and Racism: R. v. Zundel

Though not specifically related to aboriginal peoples, my candidate for the most shameful Supreme Court decision under the Charter is also a case about racism.

Ernst Zundel, a German immigrant of strong neo-Nazi convictions (one of his early publications bore the catchy title "The Hitler We Loved and Why") was charged in Toronto in 1983 with the little-used offence of "publishing false news" or more precisely "publishing a statement that he knows is false and that causes injury to a public interest" contrary to section 181 of the *Criminal Code*. The publication in question was Holocaust denial literature, a pamphlet entitled "Did Six Million Really Die?" mostly authored by a British neo-Nazi named Verral with additions by Zundel, which alleged that the slaughter of European Jewry during the Second World War was a myth—a "vast imaginary slaughter, marking with eternal shame a great European nation, as well as wringing fraudulent monetary compensation from them"—perpetrated by a worldwide Jewish conspiracy (would that it were!). The pamphlet's stated purpose was to clear racism of its bad name by clearing Nazism of this charge so that the "countries of the Anglo-Saxon world" were not weakened in the face of "the gravest danger in their history, the danger posed by alien races in their midst" (*Zundel* 1992, 455). The "false news" provision was an odd law to charge a racist with, and indeed the way the prosecution came about was very odd. The major Jewish organizations in the city of Toronto would have preferred Zundel to be charged under another *Criminal Code* provision that prohibited the "wilful promotion of hatred" (s. 319), but this offence, enacted after much debate in the 1960s, compromised by requiring the attorney general's consent, unlike almost every other section of the *Criminal Code*. Ontario Attorney General Roy McMurtry refused, claiming that he thought the law might violate the Charter (*The Globe and Mail*, August 29, 1992: A9). As it turns out he was only wrong by one vote in the Supreme Court of Canada, which narrowly upheld the law in 1990 in the cases of *Keegstra* and *Andrews*.

Keegstra was a high school teacher in Alberta who taught his students that Jews were "treacherous," "sadistic" "child killers" who "created the Holocaust to gain sympathy." Andrews was leader of the Nationalist Party of Canada, which published racist literature that was both anti-black and anti-semitic (the sticker cards it issued included "Nigger go home," "Hoax on the Holocaust," "Hitler was right. Communism is Jewish"). Having taken such an extreme view of freedom of expression in the advertising cases, the Supreme Court of Canada felt bound to extend the constitutional guarantee to even the "wilful," i.e., intentional, promotion of hatred. The offence provided accused persons with a defence of "truth" for their hateful statements (s. 319(3)(a)), but shifted the burden of proof to the defence, thus offending against the judicial definition of the "presumption of innocence." The four judges in the majority argued that the victims of hate propaganda deserved the added protection of a slight shift in the burden of proof and upheld the law as a reasonable limit. The three judges in the minority argued that hate propaganda laws were of little value anyway: "Any questionable benefit of the legislation is outweighed by the significant infringement on the constitutional guarantee of free expression effected by s. 319(2) of the *Criminal Code*" (*Keegstra* 1990, 124).

Given the refusal of the attorney general to authorize a prosecution under the hate literature provisions, a small break-away group of Toronto Jews decided to prosecute Zundel under the other *Criminal Code* section prohibiting injurious false statements. Though it did not refer explicitly to racism, it seemed literally to cover the case and did not require the attorney general's consent. A heart-rending trial took place in 1985 with Nazi death camp survivors having to withstand the degrading cross-examination of defence counsel Douglas Christie, who just happened to be Keegstra's lawyer as well.[24] Christie tried to discredit their eye-witness testimony to the slaughter of Jews with the usual bag of preposterous defence counsel tricks, but the jury didn't buy it and convicted Zundel of writing the false and harmful pamphlet with "no belief in its truth." He was sentenced to 15 months imprisonment and three years probation. The Ontario Court of Appeal threw out the conviction on the ground that the standard of "knowledge had been too low." Zundel could only be convicted, they held, if he "knew" that his pamphlet was false, not merely if he was reckless. Furthermore, they felt the trial judge should have gone out of his way to help Zundel choose his jury, even though the racist questions he had proposed to ask were improper.

So there was another trial, much more low-keyed because the prosecution was not based on the global question of the Holocaust but on more than two dozen specific claims from Zundel's pamphlet that could be shown to be false. For example, the pamphlet claimed that:

[T]he Nazi concentration camps were only work camps; that gas chambers were built by the Russians after the War; that the millions who disappeared through the chimneys of the crematoria at Auschwitz, Sobibor, Masjdanek and elsewhere actually moved to the United States and changed their names ... *The Diary of Anne Frank* is a work of fiction ... the films and photographs [of the camps] are clever forgeries ... there are no witnesses to or survivors of the slaughter and every perpetrator who later revealed his complicity was coerced ...

The pamphlet alleged that a memorandum from Joseph Goebbels revealed that the "Final Solution" was never more than a plan to evacuate Jews to Madagascar. It was shown [at Zundel's trial] that there was no such memorandum but that the reference was to Goebbels' diary entry of March 7, 1942. This diary extract was adduced and shown to state nothing of the kind. The Crown went on to point out that the entry for March 27, 1942, made clear that the "Final Solution" was, in fact, genocide:

> "Not much will remain of the Jews. On the whole, it can be said that about 60 per cent of them will have to be liquidated, whereas only about 40 per cent can be used for forced labour ..."

The pamphlet alleges that no documentary evidence exists of the Nazi plan to exterminate Jews. The Crown adduced speeches by Heinrich Himmler, head of the SS, made on October 4, 1943, to his troops in Posen in which he refers to the program of extermination of the Jews. Himmler stated:

> "I also want to talk to you, quite frankly, on a very grave matter, among ourselves it should be mentioned quite frankly, and yet we will never speak of it publicly ...

> "I mean the clearing out of the Jews, the extermination of the Jewish race ..."

The appellant argued that the term "exterminate" used in this passage really meant "deport." It was left to the jury to consider whether they accepted that this was a possible interpretation. (Justices Cory and Iacobucci dissenting in *Zundel* 1992, 455, 458–459)

In the second trial Christie had more freedom to choose his jury but they, too, convicted his client. Zundel was sentenced to nine months in jail and the Court of Appeal upheld the conviction and sentence. It was at this point that the Supreme Court of Canada gave him leave to appeal on the constitutionality of the law. And in August 1992, after seven years of trials, the Supreme Court definitively freed Zundel of the charges, holding that the law under which he was twice convicted was an unconstitutional violation of the Charter guarantee of freedom of expression.

One of the most astounding things about the Supreme Court's judgment is the fact that the entire court considered *deliberate lies* (so found by a jury, unanimously and "beyond a reasonable doubt") to be entitled to the protection of the Charter. In the words of the dissenting judges:

> The activities of Zundel involved the deliberate and wilful publication of lies which were extremely damaging to members of the Jewish community, misleading to all who read his words and antithetical to the core values of a multicultural democracy. (Justices Cory and Iacobucci dissenting in *Zundel* 1992, 469–470)

But on the basis of *Keegstra*

> constitutional protection under s. 2(b) must ... be extended to the deliberate publication of statements known to be false which convey meaning in a nonviolent form. Freedom of expression is so important to democracy in Canada that even those statements on the extreme periphery of the protected right must be brought within the protective ambit of s. 2(b). (Justices Cory and Iacobucci dissenting in *Zundel* 1992, 470)

Remember that this was the Court that found no room in the Charter for the right to strike.

While the dissenting judges found the fact that Zundel's case involved deliberate lying relevant to their conclusion that the limit imposed by the law was "reasonable," the majority held that the distinction between lying and telling the truth was irrelevant. The argument for the majority, written by Justice Beverley McLachlin, had two main strands, both of which deserve the Kafka prize for legal reasoning. The first was the idea that lying had a social value worth constitutionally protecting:

> Exaggeration—even clear falsification—may arguably serve useful social purposes linked to the values underlying freedom of expression. A person fighting cruelty against animals may knowingly cite false statistics in pursuit of his or her beliefs and with the purpose of communicating a more fundamental message, eg., "cruelty to animals is increasing and must be stopped." A doctor, in order to persuade people to be inoculated against a burgeoning epidemic, may exaggerate the number or geographical location of persons potentially infected with the virus. An artist, for artistic purposes, may make a statement that a particular society considers both an assertion of fact and a manifestly deliberate lie; consider the case of Salman Rushdie's *Satanic Verses* viewed by many Muslim societies as perpetrating deliberate lies against the Prophet. (*Zundel* 1992, 508–509)

What a shameful insult to Rushdie to put him in the same category with Zundel! Rushdie wrote a sensitive work of fiction and was condemned to death for its *attitude*, as much to the Iranian leadership as to the Prophet Muhammad, not for the accuracy of any factual claims made in it (of which there are none) and certainly not for its sincerity or lack of it. Zundel wrote a deliberate falsification of one of the great crimes of history in order to advance the cause of racism, and got nine months in jail. Not only that, the notion that proponents of progressive causes or health professionals might routinely lie to promote their causes, and that there are no important differences between lying and attempting to tell the truth, indeed between good causes and bad causes, is the kind of thing that could only come out of the mouth of a lawyer.

McLachlin's refusal to distinguish between a novel on the one hand and a deliberate falsification of history on the other, or between lying and attempting to tell the truth, was part and parcel of the second element of her judgment, really its most chilling aspect, a radical historical relativism that makes the judgment read like, and indeed for a part of, Holocaust-denial literature itself. In fact, the entire judgment rests on the supposed impossibility—not just difficulty—of distinguishing historical truth from historical falsehood. According to Judge McLachlin, we can never be even moderately certain about historical events, which is precisely what the modern racists want us to believe, because in that way they can clear modern racism of the bad name it has acquired on the basis of the historical record. They want to condemn us to repeat our history by saying we cannot know it. In many places in her judgment McLachlin put words like "false," "truths," and "fact" in quotation marks (eg., *Zundel* 1992, 503, 504, 505, 507) and she seemed to think it an accident that after trials in which Zundel could adduce all the evidence he wanted, two juries selected for their impartiality were unanimously convinced beyond a reasonable doubt that his claims were false; at least one of these juries was unanimously convinced beyond a reasonable doubt that he *knew* they were false (the other being at a minimum convinced that he had "no belief in their truth"):

> All it takes is one judge and twelve jurors who believe that certain 'falsehoods' compromise a particular "public" interest, and that such falsehoods 'must have been' known to the accused, in order to convict. (*Zundel* 1992, 522)

Elsewhere McLachlin's judgment speaks of "the imprisonment of people ... on the ground that they have made a statement which 12 of their co-citizens deem to be false and mischievous to some undefined public interest" (*Zundel* 1992, 500), but, of course, the jurors are selected for their impartiality and do not merely have to believe or "deem" the statement to be false but have to be convinced beyond a reasonable doubt of its falsity. Besides, all it takes to send someone away to prison for life is that one judge and twelve jurors believe that person pulled the trigger and "must have known" the gun was loaded. As for "mischief to some undefined public interest," listen to what Judges Iacobucci, Gonthier and Cory said in dissent:

> To deliberately lie about the indescribable suffering and death inflicted upon the Jews by Hitler is the foulest of falsehoods and the essence of cruelty ... Section 181 provides protection, by criminal sanction, not only to Jewish Canadians but to all vulnerable minority groups and individuals ... It achieves this goal by expressing the repugnance of Canadian society for the wilful publication of statements known to be false that are likely to cause serious injury or mischief to the public interest .... (*Zundel* 1992, 475)

However, McLachlin was not blaming the jury system itself:

> The fault lies rather in concepts as vague as fact versus opinion or truth versus falsity in the context of history .... (*Zundel* 1992, 505)

As vague as the concept of truth versus falsity? This is a vague concept? If you were a Nazi Holocaust denier, is there anything more you could have asked for from the Supreme Court of Canada than this?

In addition to her assault on the truth-falsity distinction, Judge McLachlin offered some more legalistic reasons for her judgment. Because of the vagueness of the law and the unusual nature of the questions to be determined she did not feel that "as a practical matter the Court can be certain, even in this instance, that the defendant was accorded procedural justice" (*Zundel* 1992, 504). From the mouth of another judge you might consider such objections plausible, but Judge McLachlin cavalierly rejected this very sort of claim (and the right to freedom of expression) when the Alberta Nurses were in the prisoners' dock convicted of criminal contempt of court (*United Nurses of Alberta* 1992). And even though leave to appeal had not been granted on the point, Judge McLachlin did not like the fact that the trial judge did not require the prosecution to prove the Holocaust all over again:

> By applying the doctrine of judicial notice and telling the jury that the "mass murder and extermination of Jews in Europe by the Nazi regime" was an (historical) fact no "reasonable person" could dispute, the judge effectively settled the issue for them ... The logic is ineluctable: everyone knows this is false; therefore the defendant must have known it was false ... The verdict flowed inevitably from the indisputable fact of the publication of the pamphlet, its contents' divergence from the accepted [!] history of the Holocaust, and the public interest in maintaining racial and religious tolerance. There was little practical possibility of showing that the publication was an expression of opinion, nor of showing that the accused did not know it to be false, nor of showing it would not cause injury or mischief to a public interest. (*Zundel* 1992, 504–506)

McLachlin did not, of course, have the nerve to suggest that a trial on the issue of the Holocaust could have had any other outcome. She just seemed to think it was unfair to Zundel that he decided to lie about something that nobody could plausibly dispute. As if it were unfair to someone charged with murder that they did it in front of a dozen independent witnesses and the judge said, "You are entitled to take into account the fact that twelve independent witnesses are unlikely all to have lied."

At several places Judge McLachlin also compared the false news law unfavourably with the hate-literature law used against *Keegstra* and *Andrews*:

> Like my colleagues, I readily acknowledge the pernicious effects of the propagation of hate; such effects are indeed of relevance to a s. 1 analysis of s. 319, as was evident in this court's decision in *Keegstra, supra* ... [T]he restriction on expression effected by s. 181 of the *Criminal Code*, unlike that imposed by the

hate propaganda provision at issue in *Keegstra*, cannot be justified under s. 1 of the *Charter*. (*Zundel* 1992, 516)

You would never dream from what she said in *Zundel* that Judge McLachlin dissented with all of her might in *Keegstra* and *Andrews*, too (along with Judges La Forest and Sopinka for whom she spoke, though not Judge L'Heureux-Dubé, the only judge to vote against Keegstra and for Zundel); in other words, if she had it her way there would be neither a false news law *nor* a hate literature law.

The majority in *Zundel* could also claim the support of Alan Borovoy's Canadian Civil Liberties Association, which gave the whole thing legitimacy by intervening on the side of Zundel, as it did with the rapists in *Seaboyer*, the tobacco companies in *RJR-MacDonald Inc.*, and against pay equity in the Ontario legislature (*The Toronto Star*, September 2, 1993: A11). If anything, this demonstrates how conservative the notion of "civil liberties" has become. One is reminded of Catherine MacKinnon's designation of the American Civil Liberties Union as the "house counsel for the American Nazi Party".[25]

The *Zundel* case also shows the essential malleability of the Supreme Court's "vulnerable group" doctrine, because vulnerability is in the eye of the beholder. For the minority the vulnerable ones were, naturally enough, the victims of racism, whose numbers are growing world-wide as the managers of collapsing economic systems seek new scapegoats. In Germany, Nazism is the standard borne by those who attack, burn and kill non-Aryans, and their daily bread is imported Holocaust-denial literature of which Zundel is said to be among the world's largest purveyors (*The Toronto Star*, June 8, 1993: A21, *The Globe and Mail*, May 21, 1994: D2). But to Judge McLachlin, the vulnerable side was represented by Zundel himself, no matter how powerful the interests that backed him up and stood to benefit from his historical denial and her historical agnosticism.

> I concur, as well, with the *dicta* in *R. v. Wholesale Travel Group Inc.*, [1991] 3 S.C.R. 154, that the *Charter* should not be used "as a weapon to attack measures intended to protect the disadvantaged," but I find the principle's application in this context ironic. Section 2(b) of the *Charter* has as one of its fundamental purposes the protection of the freedom of expression of the minority or disadvantaged, a freedom essential to their full participation in a democracy and to the assurance that their basic rights are respected. (*Zundel* 1992, 516)

Naturally, Judge McLachlin neglected to point out that she also dissented in *Wholesale Travel* and sided with the corporation trying to "attack measures intended to protect the disadvantaged."

There has been a lot of talk of the false news law being a "bad law." Naturally, the press has been fighting a campaign for the total deregulation of information and congratulated the majority of the Court for its decision (*The Globe and Mail*, August 28, 1992: A16; August 31, 1992: A10). As Judge McLachlin pointed out, a Working Paper commissioned by the Law Reform Commission of Canada recommended repeal of the law in 1986 (Law Reform

Commission of Canada 1986, 30), though, as she neglected to point out, even this was tied to a recommendation that the requirement of the attorney general's consent for promotion of hatred prosecutions be abolished to give access to what the commissioners thought the more appropriate charge (Law Reform Commission of Canada 1990, 68). Of course, just because the press and some lawyers (not to mention most racists) do not like a law does not mean it should be repealed. That's why the rest of us are allowed to vote. But even conceding for the sake of argument that it was a bad law, it was not the only bad law. If it was a bad law it should have been repealed before Holocaust survivors had to go through two trials and two convictions only to have four smug judges of the Supreme Court of Canada wade in with a judgment that was both stupid and harmful. The prosecution was indeed ill-advised, but it was ill-advised precisely because courts can be expected to behave this way, which doesn't let the courts off the hook one bit. The Charter has allowed the Canadian judicial system to give the racists of the world a nice present.

WOMEN AND THE CHARTER

> The decisions of the Supreme Court and other courts, the courts generally, have been very bad.
>
> *Lynn McDonald* (1980)[26]

> Long live the Supreme Court of Canada.
>
> *Michelle Landsberg* (1988)[27]

The Charter Hearings

The women's advocates who appeared before the Joint Parliamentary Committee in 1980-81 were not nearly as apprehensive about the Charter as the aboriginal peoples' groups; their position was more one of ambivalence. They mostly liked the general idea of an entrenched Charter, but they were very skeptical about the precise document being offered. The major independent women's umbrella group, the National Action Committee on the Status of Women, started its submission to the Joint Committee with this:

> Women could be worse off if the proposed charter or rights and freedoms is entrenched in Canada's constitution. (Canada 1980-81, Issue No. 9: 57)

The group's major fear was what unrestrained judicial power might mean for women, and the frame of reference was the experience with the *Canadian Bill of Rights*, under which, as NAC President Lynn McDonald said, decisions had been "very bad." Two of the Supreme Court's *Bill of Rights* decisions were infamous among women. The first was *Lavell* (1973), in which the Supreme Court held that the double standard in the *Indian Act* that deprived Indian women, but not Indian men, of Indian status for marrying non-Indians did not deprive them of equality before the law. To reach this conclusion, the Court had to go back on its decision in *Drybones* (1969) and distinguish between inequality *in the law itself* and inequality in its *administration*. With no particular justification, the *Bill of Rights* was held only to prohibit the latter. Of course, the context of the decision was massive opposition by male-dominated Indian organizations who saw in the litigation a threat to the *Indian Act* in general: a piecemeal destruction of the special status they were just then trying to assert and the imposition of non-Indian definitions of band membership (Sanders 1985, 539–547). But to women, especially the non-Indian women who led the Charter movement, *Lavell* had nothing to do with that and everything to do with judicial biases against women in general. The other decision in the women lawyers' rogues gallery was *Bliss* (1978), in which discrimination in unemployment insurance benefits to women who were laid off because of pregnancy was held by a unanimous Supreme Court of Canada not to discriminate on the basis of sex because—believe it or not—not all women were pregnant:

> If section 46 treats unemployed women differently from other unemployed persons, be they male or female, it is, it seems to me, because they are pregnant and not because they are women. (*Bliss* 1978, 191)

Then there was the divorce case of *Murdoch* (1973), in which a wife's years of contribution to ranchwork were held by the Supreme Court (over the dissent of about-to-be Chief Justice Laskin) not to entitle her to any share of the ranch when the marriage broke up.

The strategy employed by the women's groups who appeared before the Joint Committee was to get the Charter tightened up in order to make such decisions less likely. "Given the sorry record of the courts on women's rights cases, this is not a matter to be left to judicial discretion" (Canada 1980–81, Issue No. 9: 59). NAC's main focus was the equality rights clause. They wanted marital status and sexual orientation included in the prohibited grounds of discrimination. They opposed the delayed action of the equality clause. They wanted women specifically mentioned in section 15(2). They felt the original general term "disadvantaged persons" would allow judges to defeat affirmative action programs designed to help women with arguments that women were not "disadvantaged." They wanted the aboriginal rights clause to be applied "equally to native men and to native women" (Canada 1980–81, Issue No. 9: 60). They wanted a representative number of women on the courts, conceding that it "would take some time for women to be appointed and to work up to that 50 per cent." (Canada 1980–81, Issue No. 9: 71). They favoured, though the idea did not originate with them, a clause saying that the Charter applied equally to men and women.[28] NAC argued for the deletion of the "reasonable limits" clause altogether (Canada 1980–81, Issue No. 9: 58). Many of these ideas were echoed by the Canadian Advisory Council on the Status of Women ("a federal government-established organization": Sheppard and Valpy 1982, 307) and the National Association of Women and the Law, a group composed mainly of women lawyers (Canada 1980–81, Issue No. 9: 123ff; Issue No. 22), though both groups, for their own reasons, were rather more sanguine about the Charter than NAC.

Although far from completely successful the women's groups did not come away empty-handed. They got most of the changes they wanted to section 15(1), and sex was specifically mentioned in the "affirmative action" clause, section 15(2). The "reasonable limits" clause was considerably tightened up. The moratorium clause was left in and there was nothing included about the representation of women on the courts, but the next appointment to the Supreme Court of Canada was, in fact, a woman, and it was not long before she was joined by a second, bringing the representation of women on the Supreme Court (slightly) above representation in the legal profession altogether.[29] The general equality clause (section 28) went in, was dropped out as part of the deal of November 5, and then quickly put back in—and not made subject to the new section 33 override—after intense pressure was applied in a national lobbying campaign (Pal and Morton 1986, 156–7; Sheppard and Valpy 1982, 307–309). The Native women's clause only had to wait two years (*Constitutional Amendment Proclamation 1983*, s. 2). All in all, pretty successful:

> [Feminist and civil liberties groups'] objectives coincided fortuitously with the nation-building agenda of then Prime Minister Trudeau and the Liberal Party ... Feminist groups proved to be crucial allies in Trudeau's constitutional quest. They effectively bargained their support for a rewording of the equality rights clause that would preclude any future decisions like *Bliss* ... No lobby fared better than the feminists. (Pal and Morton 1986, 153–156)

During the three-year waiting period feminist lawyers honed their weapons. They undertook their own "legislative audits" that went far beyond anything that the governments were willing to undertake. While governments adopted "a minimalist methodology," limiting equality to the excision of sexist terms from legislation, feminists argued for an "equality of result" approach to section 15 to end "systemic" discrimination. They wrote articles and prepared arguments to use "systematic litigation" as a "vehicle for social change" (Pal and Morton 1986, 157–158). When April 17, 1985 finally came, they were not discouraged by the lack of substantive action on the part of the governments; they celebrated a "Feminist Fantasy of the Future."[30]

Women on the Defensive

But women soon discovered that they did not have a monopoly on the equality clause, at least as far as the courts were concerned. Not long into the life of section 15, organizations started sprouting up with the express aim of using the Charter to oppose laws giving advantages to women. A coalition called "Men and Women for a Fair Market Wage" said Ontario's proposed pay equity law violated the holy constitutional principles of supply and demand; prominent among the group's members were the National Citizens' Coalition and the anti-feminist group REAL Women of Canada (*The Globe and Mail*, May 17, 1986: A15). Another group called "In Search of Justice" was founded to oppose all forms of affirmative action (including pay equity), to win fathers a say in abortion, and to win more rights for those accused of sexual assault (*The Globe and Mail*, March 11, 1988: A1, A8; March 15, 1988: A6). Though NAC vice-president Marjorie Cohen expressed confidence in the Charter's ability to withstand these claims ("we have very good provisions in our Constitution calling for equality": *The Globe and Mail*, May 17, 1986: A15), all over the country men set out to prove her wrong.

Crimes Against Women

Some decisions made it seem as if section 15 was going to turn out to be a Frankenstein's monster. One of these was *Howell* (1986), in which a Newfoundland District Court Judge invoked not only section 15 but also section 28 of the Charter to strike down the *Criminal Code* prohibition against incest because it only applied to incest committed by men and not by women. Thus, a man who had sexual intercourse with his 11-year-old stepdaughter was acquitted because the section did not apply to stepmothers who had intercourse with their stepsons:

> For better or for worse [the Charter] may sweep away legislation which heretofore granted special status and protection to women ... The Charter grants no special status to either males or females. (*Howell* 1986, 110)

This decision even had the *defence* lawyer who made the argument worrying about its effect on children's safety (*Canadian Lawyer*, June, 1986, 10.5: 26). Another such decision was *Neely* (1985), in which an Ontario District Court Judge found that the offence in section 146 of the *Criminal Code* of statutory rape (sexual intercourse with a female under the age of fourteen) was of no force and effect because the prohibition only applied to men.[31] Of course, there were decisions going both ways in these and similar matters, but the outcome was very uncertain until the Courts of Appeal started to exercise a restraining effect with some reassuring rulings.

The British Columbia Court of Appeal won praise for its "feminist approach" (Noonan 1985) to pornography in *Red Hot Video* (1985). The obscenity prohibitions of the *Criminal Code* had been challenged as interferences with freedom of expression and, in their vagueness, fundamental justice. Given the control exercised by the judges over the "community standards" test in obscenity, it is not surprising that the standard was held not to be unduly vague.[32] More noteworthy was the court's defence of the law as necessary to advance the equality of women. One of the judges even invoked section 28 of the Charter and wrote:

> If true equality between male and female persons is to be achieved it would be quite wrong in my opinion to ignore the threat to equality resulting from the

exposure to male audiences of the violent and degrading material described above ... The materials in question ... have no literary or artistic merit and in a revolting and excessive way create an attitude of indifference to violence insofar as women are concerned and tend to dehumanize both men and women. They approve the domination of women by men as an acceptable social philosophy. (Justice Anderson in *Red Hot Video* 1985, 59–61)[33]

In *Le Gallant* (1986), the same court also came through and upheld the *Criminal Code* limitations on defences and defence strategies available in sexual assault cases. The case involved a 37-year-old man charged with sexually assaulting a 13-year-old boy. Where the victim was under 14, the *Criminal Code* provided that consent was no defence unless the accused was less than three years older than the victim. The trial judge held this to be age discrimination, but the Court of Appeal ruled that the "distinction does not amount to discrimination" because "it is neither unreasonable nor unfair" (*Le Gallant* 1986, 300).[34]

Another important question in *Le Gallant* was the constitutionality of the special *Criminal Code* provisions designed to make life easier for complainants in sexual assault cases and more difficult for those who assault them. In 1983, responding to an intense lobbying campaign by women's organizations, the federal government enacted severe restrictions on the rights of defence lawyers to turn rape trials into trials of the complainant's sexual reputation. These replaced the common law rules under which (1) the complainant could be cross-examined about any prior sexual behaviour on her part on the theory that a woman who was "unchaste" was probably a liar, too, and (2) evidence of the complainant's prior sexual conduct was admissible on the theory that if she had consented before with someone else she had probably consented this time with the accused, consent being a major issue in sexual assault cases. The only protection complainants had from this abuse was the trial judge's discretion to exclude irrelevant matters, but it appears that "the discretion was never resorted to" (*Seaboyer* 1987, 60). The general effect of such questioning and such evidence, besides discouraging complaints, was to encourage juries to acquit even those they felt to be guilty if they felt that it wasn't really a crime if the woman was not the classic virginal victim. The history of the law and certain principles within it (spousal immunity, the importance of penetration) show quite convincingly that its primary concern was with patriarchal notions of sexual proprietorship and not with the autonomous bodily integrity of women. A half-hearted reform in 1976 gave trial judges the discretion to reject such evidence, but set out a procedure for doing so, which, when turned to advantage by defence lawyers (with the endorsement of the Supreme Court of Canada in *Forsythe*, 1980), actually made matters *worse* for complainants. The general sexual assault law reform of 1983 made the exclusion of such questions and evidence automatic except in very limited, very specific circumstances.[35] In no case could these be used to impugn credibility.

With the enactment of the Charter these restrictions came under heavy judicial pressure. In *Le Gallant*, the trial judge agreed that the restrictions prejudiced the accused's section 7 Charter rights but the Court of Appeal held that the provisions achieved "a balance of fairness between the complainant and the accused" (*Le Gallant* 1986, 304). However, this was not the universal appellate approach. The Ontario Court of Appeal took quite a different view in *Seaboyer*, 1987, a case with far more important implications for women than *Le Gallant*. Where *Le Gallant* involved a homosexual assault, *Seaboyer* involved heterosexual assaults. Where *Le Gallant* heard argument only from the parties themselves, *Seaboyer* pitted the women's Charter litigation group, LEAF, arguing in defence of the law on the side of the government, against the Canadian Civil Liberties Association, arguing against the law on the side of those accused of sexual assault. To complicate matters further, LEAF's lawyer was a man and the Civil Liberties Association lawyer was a woman, Toronto law professor Louise Arbour, soon to be Justice Louise Arbour of the Supreme Court of Ontario. The law survived, but barely (3-2) and in a somewhat mutilated form. The minority would have just shot it down as interfering with the judge's unfettered power to ensure a fair trial (for the accused) by permitting any evidence thought relevant and not too prejudicial, essentially the position of the 1976 reforms. The majority thought the law generally worked well but that the judge should retain a discretion to admit evidence:

> In my view, while s. 246.6 will be applicable in most cases, there may be occasions when conformity with s. 7 of the Charter will require the court to consider the defence and the evidence proffered in support of that defence. If that defence is a legitimate one and the evidence has real probative force on a fact in issue, it will be admitted. (Justice Grange in *Seaboyer* 1987, 64)

The majority thought the instances in which these defences would arise would be "rare," but the dissenting judges disagreed, which is why they dissented:

> It is quite apparent that there will be cases where this question will arise. This is certain. But, unlike my brother Grange, I doubt that such cases will be rare ... Certainly there is no evidence before us which would justify saying that such cases will be rare or attempting to determine their number and frequency. Whatever the number, no one should be placed in a position that he does not have the same right to make his defence as any other person charged with a crime ... In my view, the answer is simply to treat an accused charged with a sexual offence as an accused charged with any other crime, by applying the general rules with respect to the relevancy and the admissibility of the evidence, and make certain that the jury is properly instructed as to the use they can make of it .... (Justice Brooke in *Seaboyer* 1987, 74, 79)

In the end, there was not much difference between majority and minority. The judge would decide whether the defence was "legitimate" and whether the evidence had "real probative force," and the judge would instruct the jury what to do with it. The fact that that judge might be Justice Louise Arbour would not give women much comfort.[36]

The Ontario Court of Appeal has generally shown much more confidence in the exercise of judicial discretion than Parliament. In *Canadian Newspapers* (1985), it modified the absolute right of a complainant in a sexual assault case to have her identity protected under section 442(3) (another 1983 reform) into a question for the discretion of the trial judge, invoking "freedom of the press" under the Charter:

> The administration of justice is dependent on public confidence in the judiciary. The discretion given to the trial judge ... is a sufficient safeguard for the protection of the identity of the complainant. (*Canadian Newspapers* 1985, 402)

Three years later, the Supreme Court of Canada would overrule this decision on the ground that the protection of the complainant's identity justified the minimal infringement on freedom of the press. However, the Court emphasized that the case involved an application by a *newspaper*, not by someone accused of sexual assault. It sidestepped and expressly left open the question of what the result would be if an accused person's interests in a "fair trial" were in the balance (*Canadian Newspapers* 1988). In such cases, the general tendency of the Supreme Court of Canada, too, is to rely heavily on judicial discretion to reconcile the conflicting interests (*Corbett* 1988).

Still, notwithstanding the initial jitters, the overall success rate for attacks on the protections of the criminal law for women in the 1980s was fairly low. On the whole, it appeared that the damage control of groups such as LEAF had been successful despite the sanctity of the criminal trial and the importance of appearing to give accused persons every chance. On the other hand, this basically defensive posture had its costs in squandered resources that could have been used for other purposes had there been no Charter in the first place:

> Cases such as *Seaboyer* and *Canadian Newspapers* have increasingly demanded the attention and resources of groups like LEAF which were originally formed to use the Charter to further feminist struggles for equality. As a result of the Charter, feminist organizations are having to spend precious time, energy and money in the courts defending legislation that it took many women many years to achieve. (Fudge 1988, 48)[37]

Recent Developments in Crimes against Women

Worst came to worst in the appeal from *Seaboyer*, when by the lopsided margin of 7-2 the Supreme Court of Canada endorsed the minority position in the Court of Appeal and struck out section 276 of the *Criminal Code*, a key element of the "rape-shield" law (*Seaboyer* 1991). The majority opinion was written by Justice Beverley McLachlin (concurred in by six of the seven men on the Court) and the basic argument was that nothing could ever justify interfering with the traditional judicial discretion to admit any evidence felt relevant and not unduly prejudicial. Otherwise, argued Judge McLachlin, there was a possibility that innocent persons might be convicted, and no value was higher than "the fundamental tenet of our judicial system that an innocent person must not be convicted" (*Seaboyer* 1991, 391):

> In exchange for the elimination of the possibility that the judge and jury may draw illegitimate inferences from the evidence, [the rape-shield law] exacts as a price the real risk that an innocent person may be convicted. The price is too great in relation to the benefit secured, and cannot be tolerated in a society that does not countenance in any form the conviction of the innocent. (*Seaboyer* 1991, 402)

Judge McLachlin conjured up all sorts of hypothetical examples of relevant evidence being excluded under the law's restrictions, though as the dissent pointed out (written by the other women on the court, Justice L'Heureux-Dubé and concurred in by Justice Gonthier), the examples McLachlin gave were of evidence that could either be admitted on any intelligent reading of the law as it stood (*Seaboyer* 1991, 358–60) or that depended for its presumed relevance on the very stereotypes that the majority conceded the law was right in trying to eliminate:

> Moreover, much of this evidence depends for its relevance on certain stereotypical visions of women; that they lie about sexual assault and that women who allege sexual assault often do so in order to get back in the good graces of those who may have their sexual conduct under scrutiny. (Judge L'Heureux-Dubé dissenting in *Seaboyer* 1991, 364)

Indeed, McLachlin's only concrete example of relevant evidence that would be excluded (an example that had absolutely nothing to do with either of the cases at hand in *Seaboyer*) was of this very sort, an Oregon decision from fifteen years prior where a man accused of intercourse and sodomy with a ten-year-old child wanted to introduce evidence that the child was lying to protect herself because the accused had caught her engaged in sexual activities with others. Even this case was really only a hypothetical example because it never actually proceeded to a verdict; the accused was discharged and never re-tried solely because the evidence had been "unconstitutionally" excluded (*Jalo* 1976). Another case relied on as an instance of relevant evidence being excluded by the rape-shield law (this time without any supporting examples) was the defence of "mistaken belief in consent." Because the Supreme Court of Canada had previously defined this defence to include even "unreasonable" mistakes, any prejudices the assaulter claimed to hold about the relation between the victim's prior sexual behaviour and her consent could be relied on by him to support his mistaken belief. This was, in fact, the argument that one of the accused parties in *Seaboyer* had been relying on; when a new trial was ordered as a result of the Supreme Court decision—six years after the trial had originally started—the victim decided she did not want to go ahead with it and dropped the charges altogether (Shaffer 1992, 209). Of course, once evidence was admitted for its tenuous relevance to consent, the judge or jury would be free to use it to feed their prejudices about sexual assault victims, no matter what the judge or the law might instruct them about permitted and prohibited uses.

The central question in the case was once again the central question of legalized politics: should women be forced to put their trust in judicial discretion or could they use their democratic power to formulate the ground rules beforehand and insist that they be binding on police, lawyers *and judges*? According to dissenting Judge L'Heureux-Dubé, "[h]istory demonstrates that it was discretion in trial judges that saturated the law in this area with stereotype."

> In the face of a previous legislative provision that was emasculated by the courts and on the heels of this, the continued application of stereotype, Parliament's measured and considered response was to codify those situations wherein sexual history evidence may be both relevant and sufficiently probative such that its admission was warranted. Parliament exhibited a marked, and justifiably so, distrust of the ability of the courts to promote and achieve a non-discriminatory application of the law in this area. In view of the history of government attempts, the harm done when discretion is posited in trial judges and the demonstrated inability of the judiciary to change its discriminatory ways, Parliament was justified in so choosing. (Judge L'Heureux-Dubé dissenting in *Seaboyer* 1991, 376, 377)

Actually Parliament's "choice" was encouraged by a terrific lobbying effort on the part of women growing out of feminism's revolt in the 1970s against violence against women (Canada 1982; Allison 1991). The fact that 98% of sexual assaults are committed by men and 84% of the victims are women (*Juristat* 1994, 7) is enough to demonstrate that we are talking about a crime that is a central part of patriarchal relations of power. Evening up the odds in Court required extraordinary measures, given that the assaulter already had the advantage of the many other procedural protections of the Charter including the reasonable doubt standard, the requirement of jury unanimity and, last but not least, the exclusionary rule—which, as Judge L'Heureux-Dubé pointed out in dissent (*Seaboyer* 1991, 365), also showed that the Court had no qualms about excluding relevant evidence when values close to its heart were at stake. While the evidence of the effect of rape-shield laws on rates of sexual assault, or even rates of reporting, is equivocal, proof of their effect on the conviction rate is strong; and they certainly deprive the accused of a potent weapon in the courtroom battle of the sexes (*Seaboyer* 1991: 342–345).[38] But according to the majority, it was the *assaulter* who was the weak party in need of constitutional assistance. While the minority invoked *Irwin Toy* to apply the "vulnerable group" doctrine to victims of sexual assault, the majority tightened its blindfold and imagined only potential Donald Marshalls (*Seaboyer* 1991, 387).

Once again, a majority of the Supreme Court identified human rights with their judicial administration and interpreted the Charter as a declaration of judicial independence from the binding rules laid down by representative government. Once again, the Court insisted that the acquittal of the "innocent" (whom the Court seemed to equate with anybody who might beat the charge for whatever reason) would have to take precedence over, and not merely be equal to, the conviction of the guilty. "Innocence at any price," it was called by one commentator (Houle 1992), meaning, in effect, that the protection of victims had to take a back seat to the purity of the judicial process.

Seaboyer was the first unequivocal defeat for women at the hands of the Supreme Court, and women's groups involved with violence against women were very vocal in their criticism, calling it "devastating," "terrible," and "a step backward for women" (*The Toronto Star*, August 22, 1991: A24; August 23, 1991: A11; *The Globe and Mail*, December 21, 1991: D7). Some called for the invocation of section 33 (*The Law Times*, September 23–29, 1991: 10), but the Mulroney Tories were not about to invoke that demon clause, especially when they were using its existence to discredit Liberal commitment to constitutional rights. Before too long, women's law groups gave up on trying to restore the old law and decided to go on the offensive. Since the law would have to be repaired to recognize judicial discretion, why not take this "truly historic opportunity" (*The Globe and Mail*, December 21, 1991: D7) to strengthen other aspects of the law that had not been questioned in *Seaboyer*? By year's end there was a new sexual assault law on the table and by the anniversary of *Seaboyer* it had been enacted (*Criminal Code*, s. 276). The new law gave the required ground on evidence admissibility but made substantial changes to the definition of consent. Where before it had been defined only negatively (the absence of threats, fraud and the exercise of authority), it was now defined positively as "voluntary agreement." The negative definitions were also strengthened by adding "abusing a position of trust, power or authority" and whenever the victim "expresses, by words or conduct, a lack of agreement" as situations where there could be no consent. Of course, these requirements could be vitiated by the mistake of fact defence—an assaulter could claim he believed there was consent even where the law said there could be none—but this, too, was tightened by excluding the defence where the accused "did not take reasonable steps to ascertain that the complainant was consenting."

These changes led at least one commentator to claim that *Seaboyer* might have been "a blessing in disguise" and that the Supreme Court "may unwittingly have done women a service" (Shaffer 1992, 211). A supporter of Charter politics could argue from this, along the lines laid down by the American Robert Dahl in the 1950s (Dahl 1956), that even the worst defeats in the courts are at most only temporary setbacks for progressive movements. The problem with this thesis is that it cuts several ways. If losses in the courts for progressive movements can be overcome so effectively in Parliament, why should not the same apply to successes? The American legislative assault on the abortion law decision *Roe v. Wade* (1973) is the most obvious example of this phenomenon (see below). Secondly, if the democratic power of progressive movements is so irresistible, this is hardly an argument for Charter politics. The Charter is meant to *trump* representative politics not to enhance their effectiveness. Who needs a Charter when you hold up 52% of the sky?

Most importantly, it would be rash to celebrate the legislation coming out of *Seaboyer* as any sort of victory. All those vague phrases ("voluntary," "abuse," "power" etc.) amount to a Charter of Rights for the judiciary to use their famous discretion to introduce the prejudices of the month right back into the law.[39] This is precisely what happened when the Supreme Court turned its attention to pornography. Within a year of *Seaboyer*, the Supreme Court unanimously upheld the *Criminal Code* prohibitions against obscenity (defined as the "undue exploitation of sex") as a justifiable infringement of freedom of expression, using the explicitly feminist line of argument that pornography was degrading and dehumanizing and therefore harmful to women.[40] This then became the constitutional definition of obscenity: "Explicit sex which is degrading or dehumanizing ... if the risk of harm is substantial." (*Butler* 1992, 151). The Court stayed out of specifics and endorsed the hoary old "community standards" test ("The courts must determine as best they can what the community would tolerate others being exposed to on the basis of the degree of harm that may flow from such exposure.": *Butler* 1992, 150). That this just amounted to judicial prejudice became clear in *Tremblay* (1993), a criminal charge of keeping a common bawdy house "for the purpose of the practice of indecent acts."

Tremblay concerned a club in Montréal where for $40 a woman would dance nude for a customer in a private cubicle, using a vibrator on herself while he undressed and masturbated. The Supreme Court upheld the trial judge's acquittal on the ground that this was not "indecent" behaviour. The majority judgment, written by Judge Cory on behalf of himself and Judges L'Heureux-Dubé and McLachlin, can only be described as juvenile for its utter lack of either common sense or sense of propriety. According to Cory, since masturbation was common, indeed "one of the principal themes of the well accepted novel, *Portnoy's Complaint*, by the outstanding author Philip Roth" (*Tremblay* 1993, 59), and since the club's prohibition against touching reduced the likelihood of physical harm, "it would be tolerated by the majority of the community":

> In these times when so many sexual activities can have a truly fatal attraction, these acts provided an opportunity for safe sex with no risk of infection. (*Tremblay* 1993, 59)

The fact that it was women doing the dancing and men doing the paying, and that the reasons why young working-class women have to put up with being bought by strangers as sexual playthings have nothing to do with "voluntary agreement" and everything to do with social class and patriarchy, did not, according to the Court, make this "degrading" or anything other than a matter of "consenting adults."[41] The Court further revealed how anchored in everyday prejudice it was by citing in favour of its conclusion and without a hint of disapproval the "expert" testimony that Canadians would be more likely to tolerate this behaviour because it was heterosexual and not homosexual.[42] That is probably why the *Butler* decision did not change the practices of the police, who continued to target gay and lesbian publications while leaving the big business of degrading hetero-porn untouched (*The Globe and Mail*, March 26, 1993: A13; Wollaston 1993). As for the dancers now "free" to "voluntarily" become virtual prostitutes or find another job, they greeted *Tremblay* and its progeny with pure contempt (*The Toronto Star*, September 3, 1993: A7; *The Globe and Mail*, March 14, 1994: A11).

The point is that the Court has a very limited repertoire of alternatives in the field of sex crime: either repression or, in Marcuse's phrase, "repressive tolerance" (Marcuse 1965), that is to say the abandonment of the field to the free play of market forces. The option of democratizing social relations between men and women is not available in this forum, and as this forum tends to replace all the others the democratic option tends to become invisible. The same slim pickings—repression or privatization—could be seen between majority and dissent in the Court's decision upholding the prostitution laws (*Re ss. 193 and 195.1(1)(c)* 1990).[43]

All this means that when it comes to drawing the line between the repressed and the tolerated in applying the new open-ended definitions of sexual assault that came out of *Seaboyer*, there is no likelihood that the Courts will use them to challenge as oppose to merely legitimate current prejudices. As for the rest of the new law, the result of the inevitable Charter attack on the negligence standard in the defence of mistake is anything but given. Supreme Court jurisprudence makes any tinkering with traditional *mens rea* a very risky business.[44] Nor should it be thought that *Seaboyer* was the only case in which women victims have been sacrificed to the purity of the criminal process. To give just a few examples, the case of *Brydges* (1990), where the Supreme Court threw out an incriminating statement and upheld the acquittal of an accused because he had not been advised of his right to legal aid, was not just a "Charter case"; it was an otherwise unsolved murder case in which the victim was a woman. In *Broyles* (1991), a 16-year-old charged with murdering his grandmother was let off because his confession was obtained through the stratagem of getting a friend to talk to him when he wouldn't talk to police on the advice of his lawyer. In *Evans* (1991), the accused was acquitted of the first-degree murder of two women because, being of borderline intelligence (but not so as to affect his criminal responsibility), it was not clear that he understood his Charter rights. In the British Columbia Court of Appeal Madame Justice Southlin said this:

> If there be anything more likely, by every rational community standard, to bring the administration of justice into disrepute than letting the accused, a self-confessed killer, go free to kill again on the basis of such infringements, I do not know what it is. (*Evans* 1991, 308)

It is true that a purely repressive solution to crimes against women is doomed to failure the way it is with any crime of power. But cases like *Seaboyer* offer victims only the yet worse alternative of "repressive tolerance." Indeed, the whole philosophy of the Charter cases on criminal law—the philosophy of "denunciation," a version of classic abstract "principled" reasoning—is to detach crime from its social conditions by the device of Justice's Blindfold, with the evident intention that we take for granted the fundamental inequalities at the base of these crimes and feel helpless to do anything about them except build more jails.

ENDNOTES

1. Justice Stewart of the United States Supreme Court in *San Antonio School District* (1973: 60) quoted by the Ontario Court of Appeal in *Blainey* (1986: 740).

2. Alas, Canada appears to have come down in the world of personal wealth in the 1990s. Not one of our capitalists made it into the top ten in the 1993 *Fortune* survey. Even Her Majesty barely hung on at the number nine spot with $7.8 billion (US). However, Canadians were far from complete slouches, holding down places number 17 (Ken Thomson with $5.7 billion), 22 (the Bronfmans with $4.9 billion), 36 (the Westons with $3.9 billion) and 40 (the Irvings with $3.7 billion) in the list of the richest 101 families in the world (*Fortune*, June 28, 1993).

3. In the 1990s neo-conservatism tightened its grip even more. Welfare rolls climbed while governments attacked public sector employees and weakened the so-called "social safety net" available to those made redundant to profit-making. Toronto's monthly welfare rolls, which grew at a rate of 11,000 a year during the eighties, grew three times as fast in the early nineties, surpassing 200,000 by 1993 (*The Toronto Star*, November 14, 1991: A1; November 24, 1993: A6). In 1989 Parliament vowed to eliminate child poverty by the end of the century; instead, child poverty increased by 30% by 1993 to comprehend one out of every five children in Canada (*The Toronto Star*, November 24, 1993: A12). Statistical income inequality edged past the already historic highs of the eighties (Statistics Canada 1993d, 147) but it was in the extremes that things became really obscene. As Canadian food banks reached the record number of 372, serving a regular clientele of 2 million (*The Globe and Mail*, September 25, 1992: A1), Canadian CEOs were drawing record salaries. In 1992 Seagrams Corporation paid President Edgar Bronfman $3.7 million, an increase of 173% over 1991. Vice President Stephen Banner was paid $11.4 million for only six months on the job. Placer Dome paid President Anthony Petrina $2.6 million and Northern Telecom paid Desmond Hudson $2.3 million (*The Globe and Mail*, April 3, 1993: B1). When the banks disclosed their top salaries for the first time in 1993, we learned that these fiscal tight-wads where government deficits were concerned were paying their CEOs salaries of between $1.3 and $2.6 million annually (*The Toronto Star*, December 15, 1993: C3; *The Globe and Mail*, December 18, 1993: B1). Also in 1993, the year business demanded restraint in public sector compensation in the form of Ontario's "Social Contract" and Premier Bob Rae told Ontario Housing Corporation staff who asked for a 5% raise to "wake up and smell the coffee," First Marathon Inc. investment dealers paid CEO Lawrence Bloomberg $6.9 million, a raise of 138% (*The Globe and Mail*, April 13, 1994: B1). Meanwhile, though Ontario's minimum wage had risen to $6.70 per hour ($13,400 per year)—in real terms about

equal to the 1973 rate—according to the Coalition for Fair Wages and Working Conditions for Homeworkers the majority of thousands of home garment workers in Ontario were working on a piecework basis at *less* than, sometimes as little as half of, the minimum wage (*The Globe and Mail*, February 15, 1993: A16).

4. The rich don't just have more money than the poor. A study of child poverty in Canada shows poor children with a 56% higher death rate than rich children and with twice the chronic health problems, twice the school drop-out rate and five times the level of child abuse of non-poor children (Kitchen et al. 1991, 6–10).

5. One couldn't agree more with "young buck of the new right" David Frum, heir to the minor Murray-Barbara Frum fortune, when he intoned "You cannot run a country by saying that we're going to redistribute income from people who earn it to people who don't." (*The Globe and Mail*, February, 1994: D5). Apart altogether from how the wealthy "earn" their money when they earn it, about half of the great wealth in America is accounted for by inheritance, while most people inherit nothing at all (Inhaber and Carroll 1992, 73, 138).

6. See also *Blainey* (1986) and *McKinney* (1987) in the Ontario Court of Appeal.

7. Hogg suggests that this power is adequately neutralized by provincial human rights legislation: "and in all Canadian jurisdictions the former have now been subordinated to the latter by the enactment of human rights legislation, which forbids various discriminatory practices on pain of a penalty, and establishes a commission to administer the legislation" (Hogg 1985, 786). However, human rights legislation has its own limitations when it comes to private power.

8. As with *Dolphin Delivery* itself, these Charter limits are entirely self-imposed. The courts have little difficulty in intervening in the private sphere when it suits them. See *Blainey* below for one example.

9. Amendments to this provision featured importantly in the failed Charlottetown Accord of 1992.

10. They found an implied *power*—as opposed to a duty—in the Province to expand separate school rights if it wished and said that the Charter could not destroy powers found elsewhere in the Constitution.

11. Indeed *Re Education Act* (1987) was soon extended to a case of sex discrimination when an Alberta court used it to uphold the right of a Catholic school to fire a woman teacher for pre-marital sex despite section 15 (*Casagrande* 1987).

12. Affirmed by the Ontario Court of Appeal (*OPSEU* 1990).

13. In the cases raising the constitutional issue nobody qualified for the exemption, but it was applied at least once to save a woman from a 28-day jail sentence. She was sentenced to a two-year alcohol treatment program instead (*The Globe and Mail*, June 20, 1987: A11).

14. See the spirited exchange between my colleague Harry Glasbeek and lawyer Harry Kopyto in *The Law Union News*, Vol. 2 November, 1985: 6-8. To Glasbeek's impressive list of reasons why injured workers groups themselves oppose the re-invention of the old system Kopyto responds with the dilemma of the individual who just possibly stands to gain at everybody else's expense: "Do we tell the present victims of the system that there are no immediate solutions to their problems except engaging

in long-term political activity?" Kopyto took this same approach when he challenged the collective bargaining arbitration system under section 15 of the Charter for denying access to the courts to a worker whose union would not proceed with his grievance. The court of first instance rejected the claim (*Bartello* 1987).

15. The other success occurred in Alberta, but the circumstances made the import of the decision much narrower. The law banned all suits against third parties whether or not they were contributors to the plan. In this case it was a municipality. The Court did not seem to disapprove of the bar against employers under the plan or against employees, but held the bar against the municipality unreasonable (*Budge* 1987). A similar challenge failed in Ontario (*The Toronto Star*, January 23, 1988: A15).

16. The government had given her, or rather her lawyers, $10,000 towards the costs of conversation (*The Globe and Mail*, June 8, 1987: B13).

17. So called because the original compromise was scribbled down by Roy Romanow for the government of Saskatchewan and Jean Chrétien for the federal government in a kitchen pantry at the Conference Centre in Ottawa (Sheppard and Valpy, 1982: 288).

18. "The government of Canada and the provincial governments are committed to the principle ..."

19. The Constitutional amendment of 1983 contained this clause: "54.1 Part IV.1 and this section are repealed on April 18, 1987" (*Constitutional Amendment Proclamation* 1983, s. 5).

20. All expired licences that had not been allowed to lapse were renewed whether or not the holders were Indians.

21. The Ontario Court of Appeal reached the same conclusion in a case where federal regulations contradicted express treaty rights (*The Globe and Mail*, August 4, 1988: A16).

22. Bill Wilson, Chairman of the First Nations Congress of British Columbia speaking in 1990 (Mucalov 1991, 19).

23. The importance of a government's position to the effective nature of constitutional rights was underlined in Ontario where a sympathetic NDP government declined to appeal lower court decisions that struck down pre-*Sparrow* regulations restricting commercial fishing rights even though the government claimed to disagree with the decisions. Instead, the government seized the opportunity to negotiate new conservation agreements (*The Globe and Mail*, May 21, 1993: A4; *Star*, June 3, 1993: A8). On the question of fishing licences, the Québec Court of Appeal, like the BC Court in *Nikal*, held licences and access fees to be "reasonable limits" on aboriginal fishing rights under treaty (*Côté* 1993).

24. Christie also found his way to Malcolm Ross, the Moncton teacher removed from the classroom by the New Brunswick Human Rights Commission for publishing anti-semitic pamphlets and letters to the editor claiming the Holocaust was a hoax and that a Jewish conspiracy was trying to destroy Christian civilization. Because Ross' views were stated only outside the classroom, the New Brunswick Court of Appeal (in a 2-1 decision) agreed with Christie that the removal violated the Charter guarantee of "freedom of expression" (*Ross* 1993). Christie's winning

streak on behalf of Nazism continued when he persuaded the Supreme Court of Canada (in a 4-3 decision) to approve an absurdly narrow interpretation of the war crimes law which helped his client Imre Finta escape conviction for his part in rounding up and deporting 8,617 Hungarian Jews to Nazi death camps in 1944 (*Finta* 1994).

25. Despite my best efforts I have been unable to locate the source of this quotation, but for the general idea see MacKinnon (1987: 209–210).

26. As President of the National Action Committee on the Status of Women appearing before the Joint Parliamentary Committee on the Charter on November 20, 1980 (Canada 1980–81, Issue No. 9: 66).

27. Writing in *The Globe and Mail* (January 29, 1988: A2) the day after the Supreme Court of Canada struck down the abortion law in *Morgentaler*.

28. This clause was actually a result of a recommendation by Gordon Fairweather, Chief Commissioner of the Canadian Human Rights Commission, who also recommended what was to be the ultimate specific wording of section 1 (Canada 1980–81, Issue No. 5: 5A: 3–4).

29. At the time about 20% of lawyers were women. By 1993, the percentage of lawyers had risen to 27%, with the percentage of law students reaching parity (*The Globe and Mail*, August 23, 1993: A2). The number of women on the Supreme Court remained constant at two.

30. A handbill for a "Dinner and Cabaret $20.00" in Toronto hosted by the "Charter of Rights Coalition," with "Proceeds to Legal Defense Fund, LEAF" read: "Feminist Fantasy of the Future / COME / Celebrate the complete Charter of Rights! / Celebrate Clause Fifteen! / Celebrate Our Future!"

31. *Neely* was reversed by the Ontario Court of Appeal on the ground that the trial judge had wrongly given section 15 retroactive effect (*Lucas* 1986).

32. "[T]he judge must, in the final analysis, endeavour to apply what he, in the light of his experience, regards as contemporary standards of the Canadian community" (*Red Hot Video* 1985, 42).

33. *Red Hot Video* was followed in *Mood Video*, 1987 (Newfoundland Supreme Court, Trial Division).

34. This reasoning was adopted by the Newfoundland Court of Appeal in *Halleran*, 1987.

35. Where the prosecution made it an issue first, where prior sexual activity might establish somebody other than the accused as the offender, or where the activity was with the accused on the same occasion and might thereby show consent.

36. Despite Judge Wilson's claims that women judges would "make a difference" (Wilson 1990), evidence of a feminist impact on the bench has yet to be found (McCormick and Job 1993). The trial judge whose expansive reading of the Charter led to a sexual assault acquittal in *Halleran* was a woman and she was overruled by an all-male appeal court. Then there is Judge Beverley McLachlin of the Supreme Court of Canada who has authored the most anti-women Charter decisions yet to come out of the Court, including the appeal in *Seaboyer* (see below). "If women judges do make a difference, not *all* women judges will make a difference.

When women enter male-dominated professions, many adopt the male perspective—or in the case of women judges, a male perspective may be an initial criterion for appointment to the bench" (Brockman 1993, 161). In fact, it may be that the feminist impact of some, even many, women judges is completely outweighed by the legitimacy and encouragement given their anti-feminist male colleagues by the presence of a few women judges who are just as hostile to feminism as the men are. This is arguably what happened in the Supreme Court in *Seaboyer*. While the women on the Court were proportionately more supportive of the protections for sexual assault victims than the men (50% as opposed to 14%), the fact that the majority opinion was authored by one of the two women no doubt made the six men who voted with her feel more comfortable about their position.

37. Therefore, judges are required to weigh questions of protection versus freedom of the press.

38. Only 6% of sexual assaults were reported in 1993; the reason most often given for not reporting (44%) was that it was "too minor." On the other hand, 9% said they "didn't want involvement with the police or courts," another 9% said "shame and embarrassment" and 6% said they "wouldn't be believed." There has been no apparent drop off in sexual assault reports after *Seaboyer*, though this could be due to any number of reasons (*Juristat 1994, 6–8*).

39. In fact, even before *Seaboyer*, appeal courts had already subverted the intention of the sexual assault reforms, which were clearly designed to emphasize the violent as opposed to the sexual nature of sexual assault, by re-introducing a sexual focus to sentencing (Allison 1991).

40. Of course, there is a vigorous debate among feminists over the censorship of pornography and it would be foolhardy of me to wade into it here. See, for example, Segal, 1993.

41. "Many Canadian observers (such as the Fraser Committee) have argued that prostitution is, at least partly, a reflection of the structural economic disadvantage of women, a disadvantage accentuated by the on-going feminization of poverty in contemporary western societies." (Lowman 1991b, 160). "That prostitution is the consequence of economic disadvantage is abundantly clear" (Edwards 1987, 53).

42. "In the opinion of Dr. Campbell the acts performed in the Pussy Cat were nonpathological acts of voyeurism and exhibitionism which did not cause harm to anyone ... Furthermore, the fact that the activities in question involved consensual and heterosexual adults increased the likelihood that they would be tolerated ... I am of the view that it was entirely appropriate for the trial judge to take into account the expert testimony of Dr. Campbell in determining the community standard of tolerance." (Justice Cory for the majority in *Tremblay* 1993, 53)

43. Indeed, it seems that the police are more democratic than either the courts, the users or the pimps, because although about an equal number of men and women are charged with "communicating for the purpose of engaging in prostitution or of obtaining the sexual services of a prostitute" (*Criminal Code*, s. 213), women are about eight times likely to be sentenced to jail for it, while women prostitutes outnumber their customers as murder victims five to one, accounting for 5% of all women murder victims in 1991 and 1992 (*Juristat* 1993, 8–13). Police charging prac-

tices, however, appear to vary in this regard according to region and social class of neighbourhood (Lowman 1991a).

44. See *Creighton* (1993), for example, where a negligence *mens rea* was held constitutionally permissible for the offence of manslaughter, but the fact that this was the traditional *mens rea* for that crime was said to be an important consideration.

REFERENCES

Allison, Marni D. 1991. "Judicious Judgements? Examining the Impact of Sexual Assault Legislation on Judicial Definitions of Sexual Violence." In *Criminal Justice: Sentencing Issues and Reforms,* ed. by Les Samuelson and Bernard Schissel. Toronto: Garamond Press.

Alphonse. 1993. *R.* v. *Alphonse,* [1993] 5 W.W.R. 401.

Aluminum Co. of Canada. 1986. *Re Aluminum Co. of Canada, Ltd. and The Queen in Right of Ontario; Dofasco Inc., Intervenor* (1986), 29 D.L.R. (4th) 583.

Andrews. 1990. *R.* v. *Andrews* (1990), 61 C.C.C. (3d) 490.

———. 1989. *Andrews* v. *Law Society of B.C.* (1989), 56 D.L.R. (4th) 3 (Supreme Court of Canada).

———. 1986. *Andrews* v. *Law Society of British Columbia et al.* (1986), 27 D.L.R. (4th) 600 (British Columbia Court of Appeal).

Apsit. 1987. *Apsit* v. *Manitoba Human Rights Commission,* [1988] 1 W.W.R. 629.

Armstrong, Pat, and **Hugh Armstrong.** 1994. *The Double Ghetto: Canadian Women and Their Segregated Work.* 3rd ed. Toronto: McClelland and Stewart.

Assembly of First Nations. 1987. *Brief Analysis of Federal Constitutional Proposals,* (February 19–20). Toronto: Assembly of First Nations (National Indian Brotherhood).

Baily, Martin Neil, Gary Burtless, and **Robert E. Litan,** 1993. *Growth with Equity: Economic Policy-making for the Next Century.* Washington, DC: The Brookings Institute.

Bakke. 1978. *Regents of the University of California* v. *Bakke,* 438 U.S. 265 (1978).

Bartello. 1987. *Bartello* v. *Canada Post Corp.* (1987), 46 D.L.R. (4th) 129.

Blainey. 1986. *Re Blainey and Ontario Hockey Association et al.* (1986), 26 D.L.R. (4th) 728 (Ontario Court of Appeal).

Bliss. 1978. *Bliss* v. *A.G. Canada,* [1979] 1 S.C.R. 183.

Brockman, Joan. 1993. "A Difference Without a Distinction?" *Canadian Journal of Law and Society,* 8: 149, 161.

Brooks, Neil. 1993. "The Changing Structure of the Canadian Tax System: Accommodating the Rich," *Osgoode Hall Law Journal,* 31: 137.

Broyles. 1991. *R.* v. *Broyles* (1991), 68 C.C.C. (3d) 308.

Brydges. 1990. *R. v. Brydges* (1990), 53 C.C.C. (3d) 330.

Budge. 1987. *Re Budge et al. and Workers' Compensation Board* (1987), 42 D.L.R. (4th) 649 (Alberta Queen's Bench).

Butler. 1992. *R. v. Butler* (1992), 70 C.C.C. (3d) 129.

CALURA. 1988. *Annual Report of the Minister of Supply and Services Canada Under the Corporations and Labour Unions Returns Act.* (Part I—Corporations 1986).

Canada. 1982. House of Commons, *Minutes of Proceedings and Evidence of the Standing Committee on Justice and Legal Affairs,* Nos. 78-80, 91, 97, and 107, April 27 to July 28, 1982.

————. 1980–81. *Minutes of Proceedings and Evidence of the Special Committee of the Senate and of the House of Commons on the Constitution.*

Canadian Newspapers. 1988. *Canadian Newspapers* v. *Canada (A.G.)* (1988), 43 C.C.C. (3d) 24 (Supreme Court of Canada).

————. 1985. *Canadian Newspapers Co. Ltd.* v. *A.G. Can.* (1985), 17 C.C.C. (3d) 385 (Ontario Court of Appeal).

Canadian Union of Postal Workers. 1987. *Canadian Union of Postal Workers* v. *Attorney General of Canada and Canada Post Corporation,* Statement of Claim filed in Québec Superior Court, November 3. 1987.

Casagrande. 1987. *Re Casagrande and Hinton Roman Catholic Separate School* (1987), 38 D.L.R. (4th) 382.

Corbett. 1988. *R. v. Corbett,* [1988] 1 S.C.R. 670.

Côté. 1993. *R. v. Côté* (1993), 107 D.L.R. (4th) 28.

Creighton. 1993. *R. v. Creighton* (September 9, 1993—Supreme Court of Canada).

Dahl, Robert. 1956. *A Preface to Democratic Theory.* Chicago: University of Chicago Press.

Davis, L.J. 1987. "The Next Panic: Fear and Trembling on Wall Street," *Harper's Magazine,* 274: 35 (May).

Delgamuukw. 1993. *Delgamuukw* v. *British Columbia,* [1993] 5 W.W.R. 97.

Dick. 1993. *R. v. Dick,* [1993] 5 W.W.R. 446.

Doxtater, Michael. 1993. "Wampum Wisdom: Why Many Natives Viewed the Charlottetown Agreement as a Con," *This Magazine,* 26(6): 24.

Drybones. 1969. *R. v. Drybones,* [1970] S.C.R. 282.

Edwards, Susan S. M. 1987. "Prostitutes: Victims of Law, Social Policy and Organised Crime." In *Gender, Crime and Justice,* ed. by Pat Carlen and Anne Worrall. Milton Keynes: Open University.

Elliott, D. W. 1992. *Law and Aboriginal Peoples of Canada.* Toronto: Captus Press Inc.

Energy Probe. 1987. *Re Energy Probe and Attorney General of Canada* (1987), 42 D.L.R. (4th) 349 (Ontario High Court of Justice).

Erasmus, Georges. 1987a. *Opening Remarks to the First Ministers Conference on Aboriginal Constitutional Affairs,* March 26, 1987. Ottawa: Assembly of First Nations (National Indian Brotherhood).

————. 1987b. *Presentation to the Special Joint Committee on the 1987 Constitutional Accord,* August 19, 1987. Ottawa: Assembly of First Nations (National Indian Brotherhood).

Evans. 1991. *R.* v. *Evans* (1991), 63 C.C.C. (3d) 289.

Finta. 1994. *R.* v. *Finta* (Supreme Court of Canada, March 24, 1994 - unreported).

Forcese, Dennis. 1975. *The Canadian Class Structure.* 2nd ed. Toronto: McGraw-Hill Ryerson.

Forsythe. 1980. *R.* v. *Forsythe* (1980), 53 C.C.C. (2d) 225.

Frideres, James S. 1983. *Native People in Canada: Contemporary Conflicts.* Toronto: Prentice Hall Canada.

Fudge, Judy. 1988. "The Public/Private Distinction: The Possibilities of and the Limits to the Use of Charter Litigation to Further Feminist Struggles," *Osgoode Hall Law Journal,* 25: 485.

Gladstone. 1993. *R.* v. *Gladstone,* [1993] 5 W.W.R. 517.

Glasbeek, Harry J. 1988. "The Corporate Social Responsibility Movement—The Latest in Maginot Lines to Save Capitalism," *Dalhousie Law Journal,* 11: 363.

————, and **R. A. Hasson.** 1977. "Fault—The Great Hoax." In *Studies in Canadian Tort Law,* ed. by Lewis Klar. Toronto: Butterworths.

Halleran. 1987. *R.* v. *Halleran* (1987), 39 C.C.C. (3d) 177.

Hamilton. 1986. *R.* v. *Hamilton* (1986), 54 C.R. (3d) 193.

Hernandez. 1992. *Hernandez* v. *Palmer,* [1993] I.L.R. 1–2905.

Hogg, Peter W. 1985. *Constitutional Law of Canada.* 2nd ed. Toronto: Carswell.

Houle, France. 1992. *L'innocence à tout prix! L'affaire Seaboyer à la cour Suprême du Canada.* Unpublished paper.

Howell. 1986. *R.* v. *Howell* (1986), 26 C.C.C. (3d) 104.

Hunter, Alfred A. 1981. *Class Tells. On Social Inequality in Canada.* Toronto: Butterworths.

Hutton. 1987. *Hutton* v. *Ontario (Attorney General)* (1987), 46 D.L.R. (4th) 112.

Inhaber, Herbert, and **Sidney Carroll.** 1992. *How Rich Is Too Rich? Income and Wealth in America.* New York: Praeger.

Jalo. 1976. *State* v. *Jalo,* 557 P.2d 1359 (Court of Appeals of Oregon).

Keegstra.   1990. *R.* v. *Keegstra* (1990), 61 C.C.C. (3d) 1.

Kitchen, Brigitte, et al.   1991. *Unequal Futures: The Legacies of Child Poverty in Canada.* Toronto: The Child Poverty Action Group and the Social Planning Council of Metropolitan Toronto.

Lavell.   1973. *Attorney General of Canada* v. *Lavell; Isaac et al.* v. *Bedard,* [1974] S.C.R. 1349.

Law Reform Commission of Canada.   1990. *Working Paper Number 62: Controlling Criminal Prosecutions: The Attorney General and the Crown Prosecutor.* Ottawa.

———.   1986. *Working Paper 50: Hate Propaganda.* Ottawa.

Leacy, F.H., ed.   1983. *Historical Statistics of Canada.* 2nd ed. Ottawa: Minister of Supply and Services Canada.

Le Gallant.   1986. *R.* v. *Le Gallant* (1986), 29 C.C.C. (3d) 291.

London Drugs Ltd.   1987. *London Drugs Ltd.* v. *Red Deer (City)* (1987), 44 D.L.R. (4th) 264.

Lowman, John.   1991a. "Punishing Prostitutes and Their Customers: The Legacy of the Badgley Committee, The Fraser Committee and Bill C-49." In *Criminal Justice: Sentencing Issues and Reforms,* ed. by Les Samuelson and Bernard Schissel. Toronto: Garamond Press.

———.   1991b. "Street Prostitutes in Canada: An Evaluation of the Brannigan-Fleischman Opportunity Model," *Canadian Journal of Law and Society,* 6: 137, 160.

Lucas.   1986. *R.* v. *Lucas, R.* v. *Neely* (1986), 27 C.C.C. (3d) 229.

MacKinnon, Catherine A.   1987. *Feminism Unmodified: Discourse on Life and Law.* Cambridge: Harvard University Press.

Mahé.   1987. *Mahé et al.* v. *The Queen in Right of Alberta* (1987), 42 D.L.R. (4th) 514 (Alberta Court of Appeal).

Mandel, Michael.   1984. "Democracy, Class and Canadian Sentencing Law," *Crime and Social Justice,* 21–22: 163.

Marcuse, Herbert.   1965. "Repressive Tolerance." In Robert Paul Wolff, Barrington Moore Jr., and Herbert Marcuse, *A Critique of Pure Tolerance.* Boston: Beacon Press.

McCormick, Peter, and **Twyla Job.**   1993. "Do Women Judges Make a Difference? An Analysis by Appeal Court Data," *Canadian Journal of Law and Society,* 8: 135.

McCullum, Hugh, and **Karmel McCullum.**   1975. *This Land Is Not for Sale: Canada's Original People and Their Land: A Saga of Neglect, Exploitation and Conflict.* Toronto: Anglican Book Centre.

McDonnell.   1986. *McDonnell* v. *Fédération des Franco-Colombiens* (1986), 31 D.L.R. (4th) 296.

McKinney.   1987. *McKinney* v. *University of Guelph et al.* (1987), 24 O.A.C. 241.

McQuaig, Linda.   1987. *Behind Closed Doors: How the Rich Won Control of Canada's Tax System...and Ended Up Richer.* Toronto: Penguin Books Canada.

Mood Video.   1987. *R.* v. *Mood Video* (1987), 33 C.C.C. (3d) 221.

Morton, Desmond.   1991. "How NDP Blew Chance for No-Fault Auto Plan," *The Toronto Star*, September 20, 1991: A21.

Mucalov, Janice.   1991. "Indian Warriors," *Canadian Lawyer*, 15(4):19.

Neely.   1985. *R.* v. *Neely* (1985), 22 C.C.C. (3d) 73.

Nguyen.   1990. *R.* v. *Nguyen* (1990), 59 C.C.C. (3d) 161.

Nikal.   1993. *R.* v. *Nikal*, [1993] 5 W.W.R. 629.

Noonan, Sheila.   1985. "Pornography: Preferring the Feminist Approach of the British Columbia Court of Appeal to That of the Fraser Committee," *Criminal Reports* (3d), 45: 61.

Nova Scotia.   1989. *Royal Commission on the Donald Marshall Jr. Prosecution.* Halifax.

N.T.C. Smokehouse Ltd.   1993. *R.* v. *N.T.C. Smokehouse Ltd.*, [1993] 542.

Ontario. Fair Tax Commission.   1993. *Working Group Report: Wealth Tax.* Toronto.

———.   1988. *Report of the Inquiry Into Motor Vehicle Accident Compensation in Ontario.* Vol. 1. Toronto: Queen's Printer for Ontario.

OPSEU.   1990. *OPSEU* v. *National Citizens' Coalition* (1990), 69 D.L.R. (4th) 550 (Ontario Court of Appeal).

———.   1987. *Ontario Public Service Employees Union et al.* v. *National Citizens' Coalition et al.* (1987), 39 D.L.R. (4th) 449 (Ontario High Court of Justice).

Osberg, Lars.   1981. *Economic Inequality in Canada.* Toronto: Butterworths.

Pal, Leslie A., and **F. L. Morton.**   1986. "*Bliss* v. *Attorney General of Canada*: From Legal Defeat to Political Victory," *Osgoode Hall Law Journal*, 24: 141.

Paquette.   1987. *R.* v. *Paquette (No.2)*(1987), 46 D.L.R. (4th) 81.

Piercey.   1986. *Piercey* v. *General Bakeries Ltd.* (1986), 31 D.L.R. (4th) 373.

Re Education Act.   1987. *Reference Re An Act to Amend the Education Act (Ontario)* (1987), 40 D.L.R. (4th) 18 (Supreme Court of Canada).

———.   1986. *Reference re an Act to Amend the Education Act* (1986), 25 D.L.R. (4th) 1 (Ontario Court of Appeal).

Re ss. 193 and 195.1 (1)(c).   1990. *Ref. Re ss. 193 and 195.1 (1)(c) of Criminal Code*, (1990), 56 C.C.C. (3d) 65.

Re Use of French in Criminal Proceedings in Saskatchewan.   1987. *Reference re: Use of French in Criminal Proceedings in Saskatchewan* (1987), 44 D.L.R. (4th) 16.

Re Workers' Compensation Act (Nfld.).   1989. *Reference re: Workers' Compensation Act, 1983 (Nfld.)* (1989), 56 D.L.R. (4th) 765 (Supreme Court of Canada).

————. 1987. *Re ss. 32, 34, Workers' Compensation Act, 1983* (1987), 44 D.L.R. (4th) 501 (Newfoundland Court of Appeal).

Red Hot Video.   1985. *R. v. Red Hot Video Ltd.* (1985), 45 C.R. (3d) 36.

Roe.   1973. *Roe* v. *Wade* 410 U.S. 113 (1973).

Romanov, Roy, John Whyte, and **Howard Leeson.**   1984. *Canada...Notwithstanding: The Making of the Constitution, 1976–1982.* Toronto: Carswell/Methuen.

Ross.   1993. *Ross* v. *Board of School Trustees* (New Brunswick Court of Appeal, December 20, 1993 – unreported).

Ross, David P.   1980. *The Canadian Fact Book on Income Distribution.* Ottawa: The Canadian Council on Social Development.

————, and **E. Richard Shillington.**   1989. *The Canadian Fact Book on Poverty—1989.* Ottawa: The Canadian Council on Social Development.

Ruby, Clayton C.   1992. "Law and Society." *The Globe and Mail*, October 20: A32.

Russell, Peter.   1992. *Constitutional Odyssey: Can Canadians Become a Sovereign People?* Toronto: University of Toronto Press.

San Antonio School District.   1973. *San Antonio School District* v. *Rodriguez 411 U.S. 1 (1973).*

Sanders, Douglas.   1985. "The Renewal of Indian Special Status." In *Equality Rights and the Canadian Charter of Rights and Freedoms,* ed. by Anne F. Bayefsky and Mary Eberts. Toronto: Carswell.

————. 1983. "The Rights of the Aboriginal Peoples of Canada." *Canadian Bar Review,* 61: 314.

Schachtschneider.   1993. *Schachtschneider* v. *Canada* (1993), 105 D.L.R. (4th) 162.

Schmitz, Cristin.   1987. "No-Fault Insurance Offends Charter: CBAO," *The Lawyers Weekly,* 27 (March): 1.

Seaboyer.   1991. *R.* v. *Seaboyer. R.* v. *Gayme* (1991), 66 C.C.C. (3d) 321 (Supreme Court of Canada).

————. 1987. Re Seaboyer and the Queen; Re Gayme and the Queen (1987), 37 C.C.C. (3d) 53 (Ontario Court of Appeal).

Segal, Lynn.   1993. False Promises—Anti-Pornography Feminism. *The Socialist Register 1993*: 92.

Shaffer, Martha.   1992. "*Seaboyer* v. *R.*: A Case Comment," *Canadian Journal of Women and the Law,* 5: 202.

Shaffer, Marvin.   1988. "It's Time to Make Advances on Indians' Fishing Rights." *The Globe and Mail*, August 19: A7.

Sheppard, Robert, and **Michael Valpy.**   1982. *The National Deal: The Fight for a Canadian Constitution.* Toronto: Fleet Books.

Sinclair. 1986. *R.* v. *Kent, Sinclair and Gode* (1986), 27 C.C.C. (3d) 405.

Slattery, Brian. 1992. "First Nations and the Constitution." *Canadian Bar Review,* 71: 261

Smith, Kline & French Laboratories. 1986. *Smith, Kline & French Laboratories Ltd. et al.* v. *Attorney General of Canada* (1986), 34 D.L.R. (4th) 584 (Federal Court of Appeal).

Sparrow. 1990. *R.* v. *Sparrow* (1990), 56 C.C.C. (3d) 263 (Supreme Court of Canada).

———. 1987. *Sparrow* v. *R. et al.,* [1987] 2 W.W.R. 577 (British Columbia Court of Appeal).

Statistics Canada. 1993a. *Family Incomes: Census Families, 1991.* Ottawa: Minister of Industry, Science and Technology.

———. 1993b. *Historical Labour Force Statistics, 1992.* Ottawa: Minister of Industry, Science and Technology.

———. 1993c. *Income After Tax, Distributions by Size in Canada, 1991.* Ottawa: Minister of Industry, Science and Technology.

———. 1993d. *Income Distributions by Size in Canada, 1992.* Ottawa: Minister of Industry, Science and Technology.

———. 1991. *Income After Tax, Distributions by Size in Canada, 1989.* Ottawa: Minister of Industry, Science and Technology.

Swain. 1991. *R.* v. *Swain* (1991) 63 C.C.C. (3d) 481.

Tiny Separate School Trustees. 1928. *Tiny Separate School Trustees* v. *The King,* [1928] A.C. 363.

Tremblay. 1993. *R.* v. *Tremblay* (1993), 156 N.R. 30.

Tucker , Eric. 1984. "The Determination of Occupational Health and Safety Standards in Ontario, 1867–1982: From the Market to Politics to...?" *McGill Law Journal,* 29: 260.

Turpin. 1989. *R.* v. *Turpin* (1989), 48 C.C.C. (3d) 8 (Supreme Court of Canada).

———. 1987. *R.* v. *Turpin, Siddiqui and Clauzel* (1987), 60 C.R. (3d) 63 (Ontario Court of Appeal).

United Nurses of Alberta. 1992. *United Nurses of Alberta* v. *Alberta (Attorney-General)* (1992), 89 D.L.R. (4th) 609.

Vaillancourt, François. 1985. "Income Distribution and Economic Security in Canada: An Overview." In *Income Distribution and Economic Security in Canada.* Vol. 1 of studies commissioned as part of the research program of the Royal Commission on the Economic Union and Development Prospects for Canada (François Vaillancourt, Research Coordinator). Toronto: University of Toronto Press.

Valentine, Victor F. 1980. "Native Peoples and Canadian Society: A Profile of Issues and Trends." In *Cultural Boundaries and the Cohesion of Canada,* ed. by Raymond Breton, Jeffrey G. Reitz, and Victor R. Valentine. Montreal: The Institute for Research on Public Policy.

Vanderpeet.   1993. *R.* v. *Vanderpeet,* [1993] 5 W.W.R. 459.

Watson, Debbie.   1988. "1988 National Compensation Survey." *Canadian Lawyer,* 12 (5): 6.

Wholesale Travel.   1991. *R.* v. *Wholesale Travel Group Inc.* (1991), 67 C.C.C. (3d) 193.

Wilson, Madam Justice Bertha.   1990. "Will Women Judges Really Make a Difference?" *Osgoode Hall Law Journal,* 28: 507.

Wollaston, Paul.   1993. "When Will They Ever Get It Right? A Gay Analysis of *R.* v. *Butler,*" *Dalhousie Journal of Legal Studies,* 2: 251.

Zimmerman, Susan.   1992. "The Revolving Door of Despair: Aboriginal Involvement in the Criminal Justice System," *University of British Columbia Law Review,* 26: 367.

Zundel.   1992. *R.* v. *Zundel* (1992), 75 C.C.C. (3d) 449 (Supreme Court of Canada).

CRIME PREVENTION AND CRIMINAL JUSTICE

Ross Hastings

INTRODUCTION

One of the major trends in criminal justice policy and practice in recent years has been the increasing priority given to the importance of the prevention of crime and victimization. At the heart of this trend is the conviction that our reliance on punitive or rehabilitative strategies targeted at individual offenders has failed to increase individual or community safety, and does little or nothing to compensate victims of crime for their losses. Instead, we need a more comprehensive and integrated strategy that targets the factors associated with crime and victimization in a proactive and preventive manner.

Certainly, prevention is a response to crime that holds enormous promise. The basis of its popularity is threefold. To begin, the commitment to prevention serves as a rallying point for otherwise diverse approaches to criminological theory and criminal justice practice. Next, preventive strategies provide an alternative to the current overreliance on reactive and repressive responses to crime. Finally, the concept of prevention has the potential for being the basis for reorganizing and unifying the multitude of groups, agencies, and levels of governments involved in dealing with crime and disorder.

Yet, for all the commitment to the strategy of prevention, and for all the energy and resources that have been invested in prevention initiatives, the rates of crime and victimization have stubbornly refused to fall. At first glance it might seem that prevention has failed to deliver on its promise. This suggests that prevention promises more than it can deliver, and that it may not be the best path for us to follow.

We are left with the question of what we should do next. One option would be to give up: we could simply give in to the increasing clamour from both politicians and the public for more repression and more punishment of offenders. However, there is little or no scientific evidence that such a strategy will bear fruit. For that matter, the recent experience in the United States provides a lesson in the limitations of this approach. Our American neighbours have more than tripled the number of people in federal prisons over the last 15 to 20 years, and yet there has not been any significant impact on crime rates. Another option is simply to soldier on as best we can. This is the approach that is most popular in the political arena. It allows politicians to give the impression of action, and to reap the ideological benefits of the rhetoric of prevention without investing significant levels of resources in new programs or initiatives, and without having to take on the vested interests of those groups or organizations who are already active in the criminal justice field.

The final possibility is to try a new approach to the conceptualization and implementation of the strategy of prevention. I will argue that this is the route we must take. This is based on my conviction that the failure of prevention to deliver on its promise can be explained in two ways:

1. We have failed to resolve many of the underlying theoretical and political debates that underlie the apparent consensus over the strategy of crime prevention—much of what has happened so far under the guise of crime prevention is based on a very weak and contradictory theoretical foundation. In too many cases the rhetoric of prevention has simply provided an excuse for both academics and policy-makers to avoid having to make hard choices between competing perspectives or interest groups.

2. We have only tried a very limited range of the programs and initiatives that are conceivable under the umbrella of prevention. Everyone talks about prevention, but too often this is little more than an ideological overlay that helps to mask the ongoing extension of control and punishment, which thus serves the interests of the beneficiaries of the current criminal justice system (Cohen, 1985). We have not given the strategy of prevention a fair chance to prove what it can deliver.

The objective of this chapter is to attempt to take on these issues. It will be organized in three sections. The first will briefly describe the apparent consensus that underlies the current popularity of crime prevention in an attempt to identify the basic minimum agreement shared by all who support this approach. The second will attempt to flesh out the notion of prevention in more detail, and to suggest a conceptual framework that will assist us in the task of describing the range of strategic options that are conceivable under the banner of crime prevention. The third will address the question of the implications of this framework for the planning and implementation of prevention policies and programs.

My basic theme is that we must extend prevention initiatives beyond our current tendency to be satisfied with new ways of delivering old kinds of services and programs: only a limited range of crime prevention options has been tried, and there is little evidence of consistent successes in either the communities that most suffer from crime or among the vulnerable sectors of our population that most need our help.

THE CONSENSUS OVER PREVENTION

There is general agreement that any serious attempt to respond to the problems of crime and victimization will require a comprehensive and integrated strategy that balances proactive (preventive) and reactive (repressive or rehabilitative) approaches (Canada, Standing Committee on Justice and the Solicitor General, 1993; Canada, Ad Hoc Advisory Committee to the Minister of Justice on a National Strategy for Community Safety and Crime Prevention, 1993). Clearly, this requires a commitment to exploring and implementing a full range of prevention options. The problem is that there is little or no agreement as to what exactly this range of options might be! A discussion of this issue requires that we identify what the various approaches to prevention have in common, and a description of the various options that are possible within the basic framework or consensus. The next two sections of this chapter will deal with these two issues.

The cornerstones of the crime prevention movement are to be found in the trinity of acts of faith made by almost all its adherents and advocates. The consensus over prevention usually involves a commitment to three basic tenets.

First, there is an insistence on recognizing that crime is a significant problem and a refusal to dismiss people's concerns as being based merely on unwarranted fears. Moreover, this general concern with the problem of crime is usually balanced with a recognition that the most significant and harmful consequences of crime are not born by society as a whole but by the victims of crime and by the communities that are undermined and threatened by victimization and the fear of crime. The recognition of the extent of the problem, however, is accompanied by a conviction that progress in the fight against crime is possible if we balance our commitment to the reactive practices of detection and correction with a *proactive approach* to prevention, one that attempts to deal with the factors associated with crime before harm occurs.

Second, there is a growing realization that there are limits to the ability of the criminal justice system to reduce crime or to deal with the factors associated with crime and victimization. As a result, there is a tendency to shift the focus away from an exclusive reliance on the criminal justice system and toward an attempt to mobilize the *community*. There is, however, considerable debate over the role the community should play. Some would argue that the community must be given the *right to participate* in the definition of the problems and priorities in the fight against crime; in practice, this requires significantly more sharing of power on the part of the justice system and other levels of government than is easily imaginable at the present. A more popular variant of the reliance on community is the notion that the community has a *responsibility to participate* in the implementation and delivery of crime prevention programs. In this view, the basic notion is that the participation of the community, usually in some form of volunteer participation, is necessary to compensate for the increasingly limited resources available to deal with the problems associated with crime and victimization.

Finally, the current fiscal context makes it unlikely that any significant level of new resources will be allocated to criminal justice initiatives. This is especially true of initiatives that go beyond the traditional focus on repression, or that create new responsibilities for the state or new entitlements for certain categories of citizens. There is, however, a sense that we can overcome this situation through *cooperative partnerships*, especially in the form of interagency programs and initiatives. This would allow for greater efficiency in the use of available resources, and thus maximize our ability to influence a broader range of the factors associated with crime and victimization.

Unfortunately, these acts of faith are so taken for granted that many of the preventive efforts that ensue tend to skip over some of the difficult theoretical and political issues that must be resolved in any attempt to design a comprehensive crime prevention policy. For example, in spite of the recognition of the need for a proactive response to the factors associated with crime, there is little agreement as to what exactly these causes are. Advocates of different theoretical positions will identify different causes, and different strategic responses for dealing with these causes (Hastings, 1993). The same is true in the case of the community. While there is enormous support for including the community in prevention and justice initiatives, there is little agreement on exactly which role the community should play, or on how much power or control it should have. In addition, there is no clear sense of who or what the community is, nor much agreement on how governments can best consult the community. This is especially true in cases of heterogeneous communities, or in situations characterized by greater levels of conflict. Finally, there are limitations on the ability of partnerships and interagency cooperation to deliver more. In many cases, partnerships are actually labour and cost intensive, and thus represent a significant challenge for small groups or agencies who already tend to operate on shoestring budgets. Moreover, there is little indication that most groups or agencies are willing to give up significant degrees of their control over their clientele or constituency on behalf of a commitment to a partnership initiative.

As a result, it is probably fair to say that the consensus on prevention is shallow, and perhaps even somewhat illusory (Hastings, 1991, 1993). There is no doubt that there is agreement for the need to orient the system to more preventive approaches and initiatives, but there is still a lot of difficult theoretical and policy work to be done before we can achieve a common sense of what a comprehensive prevention strategy might look like, and over what role different theoretical approaches or different groups or organizations might play in this strategy.

CRIME PREVENTION: A CONCEPTUAL FRAMEWORK

The first task in attempting to develop a blueprint for prevention is to describe the range of possible policy and program options, and to develop a set of priorities to guide decision making. This involves three specific tasks:

1. Defining the "problem" of crime,
2. Deciding on the appropriate level of intervention, and
3. Deciding on the appropriate point of intervention.

Our decisions on these three levels will provide the basis for a framework or typology of crime prevention options. Hopefully, this will improve our ability to select appropriate targets for intervention, and contribute to a more efficient and effective use of the limited human and financial resources available for prevention initiatives.

The "Problem" of Crime

It will be difficult to design and implement a viable crime prevention strategy unless we take on more seriously the issue of just what exactly it is we wish to prevent (which types of crime or victims most deserve our attention?), and just what our priorities will be in this area (who is most deserving of the help we can provide with the limited resources at our disposal?).

This requires that we abandon an exclusively legalistic approach to the definition of crime and its consequences. Instead, the political and scientific debate must attempt to balance a concern with three levels of the consequences of crime:

1. **Society:** At this level, the concern is with the impact of crime on fundamental social values, and with the harm it causes to society. The threat of crime, at this level, is to the sense of trust and of mutual responsibility, which is essential for the preservation of social organizations.

2. **Victims:** At this level, the concern is with the loss or damage suffered by different kinds of victims of crime (physical, financial, emotional, or secondary injuries), and with our ability to repair this damage or compensate this loss.

3. **Community:** At this level, the concern is with the impact of crime and disorder on our ability to create and maintain viable and healthy communities. At this level, the prevention of crime and victimization should be considered an important component of a wider community development strategy.

The notions of the "harm" or "costs" of crime are anything but simple and straightforward. As a result it is incumbent on us to be more self-conscious about what crime prevention policies are designed to accomplish. In this context, it is worth repeating that, at present, the vast majority of the efforts and resources of the justice system are directed at arresting, convicting, and sentencing criminal offenders—evidence indicates that this has only limited impact on the safety and security of society in general, or of particular communities, and does almost nothing to repair the damage caused to victims by crime. A failure to engage in the types of policy work and strategic planning necessary to identify and prioritize our needs will make it almost impossible to actually create a systematic and integrated set of prevention programs and initiatives.

Levels of Intervention

The next issue is to decide the appropriate level of intervention for crime prevention policies and initiatives. In general, crime prevention can be targeted at one of three levels of intervention (Brantingham and Faust, 1976; Lab, 1988).

The most general level of policy and intervention is called *primary prevention*. Activities at this level are generally targeted at a broad range of problems or issues, and usually focus on crime only in an indirect manner. Activities and initiatives at the primary level are based on the recognition of the link of a broad range of social factors to criminal offending, opportunities for crime, and the vulnerability to victimization. Universal medical insurance and unemployment insurance are two examples of such activities: their goals are much broader than crime, but they nevertheless operate to alleviate some of the conditions that are correlates or causes of criminal activity. In the realm of criminal justice, broadly targeted public education programs against drugs or drinking while driving would fall into the category of primary prevention.

Secondary prevention is targeted more specifically at individuals or situations considered to be "at risk." The basic assumption at this level is that neither crime nor victimization are random. We know a great deal about the types of characteristics or factors associated with offending or victimization—the idea is to apply this information to the identification of risk, and to the design of programs that intervene *before* a crime occurs, rather than waiting until after the offence to take action. At this level, the strategy might focus on the desirability of targeting the factors associated with persistent offenders (as identified through longitudinal studies), and on the need to address these "underlying causes" of crime before they "erupt." Alternatively, it may focus on those situations that are most conducive to the commission of a criminal act, and on the need to redesign the environment in order to make crime more difficult or less likely.

Tertiary prevention programs focus on individuals who have actually been involved in an offence; the aim is to deter any further criminal activity (recidivism), or at least to minimize the consequences of the offence for the victim. This is the traditional realm of the criminal justice system, and involves the vast majority of the activities that we can subsume under the heading of "police, courts, and corrections." At present most of the activity at this level is concerned with the detection, conviction, and punishment or treatment of offenders. There is relatively little attention paid to the needs of victims.

The Elements of a Crime Event

The decision as to the appropriate level of intervention is only the first step in the process of formulating a conceptual framework for crime prevention. The next step is to decide on the actual target of a crime prevention initiative. This requires an attempt to identify the elements or components of a criminal event. For researchers who adopt what is called the routine-activity approach to prevention (for example, Cohen and Felson, 1979), a criminal event involves the interplay of three elements: a motivated offender, a vulnerable victim, and a situation that provides the context or opportunity for these individuals to come together.

The focus on the *offender* raises the questions of the *motivation* of a criminal act (intention), and of the types of control that can be exercised over an individual. The basic issue to be addressed at this level is whether or not the individual has a choice in the matter. There are age-old debates in criminology between proponents of the notions of responsibility and authenticity favoured by the various forms of classical theory, and the notions of determinism and differentiation favoured by the different forms of positivist approaches. Those who focus on the notions of the choices or responsibility of the individual are more likely to argue in favour of punishment as a deterrent to criminal action, while those who argue that individuals are formed or influenced by the circumstances that surround them are more likely to favour interventions aimed at treating individual defects or shortcomings, or at reforming social arrangements.

The thrust of a crime prevention strategy at this level is on those individuals who have either committed a criminal act, or who are more or less likely to consider and commit such an act in the future. The available options for intervention range from biological, psychological, or social correctionalism to programs of social reform aimed at reducing or eliminating criminogenic structural and situational elements.

The focus on the *victim* raises the question of the *vulnerability* of certain individuals or groups to victimization. The basic issue at this level concerns the degree of control or responsibility an individual or group bears for their victimization: how much can (or should) people do to protect themselves from victimization? Attempts to answer this question range from a concentration on victim precipitation (suggesting at least some degree of responsibility) to a focus on the personal, situational, or structural factors that conspire to place an individual in a higher risk category, and over which the individual may have little or no control (suggesting at least a degree of determinism or differentiation). The thrust of crime prevention strategies at this level is on the attempt to decrease vulnerability, usually through programs aimed at educating individuals to reduce or manage their risk of victimization, or at providing vulnerable individuals with at least some of the resources they need to reduce or eliminate their vulnerability.

The focus on the *situation* raises the issue of the *opportunity* to commit a criminal act. Not all individuals who consider the possibility of committing a criminal act—that is, who are at what David Matza has called the "invitational edge" (1969, 110–111)—actually carry out their fantasy or intention. The focus here is on the issue of the extent to which crime is a function of situational factors that deliver a vulnerable victim to a motivated offender under circumstances that facilitate the commission of the act or that make the detection or punishment of the act unlikely. The thrust of crime prevention strategies at this level is either on making it more difficult for the offender to commit a certain type of criminal act (target hardening), more likely that he or she will be observed and punished (deterrence), or less likely that a criminal act will be rewarding to the offender (Clarke, 1992).

Mapping Crime Prevention: A Conceptual Framework

So far, I have attempted to lay out a description of the decisions that underlie the formulation of a crime prevention policy. In summary, my argument is that one must define the problem more thoroughly and identify more clearly the theoretically and politically appropriate levels of intervention and targets at which policy and programs will be directed.

All of this is designed to provide the basis for the development of a conceptual framework of crime prevention options and alternatives (see Fig. 14.1). In essence, this typology simply attempts to sort out the various points at which different theoretical orientations are likely to clash, or at which point different political strategies and programs are likely to come into conflict.

FIGURE 14.1:   A Crime Prevention Typology

	Offender	Situation	Victim
Primary	7.	8.	9.
Secondary	4.	5.	6.
Tertiary	1.	2.	3.

Levels of Intervention (vertical axis)

Elements of Crime Event (horizontal axis)

The typology allows us to identify the basic strategic options for criminal justice policy and programs.

Traditional Law Enforcement (Box #1)   Activities at this level involve the full range of deterrence, control and treatment activities that the criminal justice system ("police, courts, and corrections") has traditionally directed against criminal offenders. The major theoretical debate at this level is between positivists, who argue that the offender is an individual in need of treatment, and neoclassicists, who argue that punishment has a deterrent effect on individual decision making.

Crisis Intervention (Box #2) Activities at this level focus more narrowly on the issue of the most appropriate way for justice officials to respond to incidents-in-progress, such as hostage takings or domestic assaults. The focus of the debates in this area are on the identification of the most effective tactics and strategies for preventing an incident (or at least the escalation of the incident), or for reducing the impact or consequences of the incident for the victim.

Victim Services (Box #3) Activities in this sector involve attempts to repair the harm experienced as a result of a criminal victimization. The debates at this level range from a humanist commitment to helping the victim to a more prosaic concern with increasing the efficiency of the traditional system, usually through ensuring greater cooperation on the part of victims and witnesses in the process of identifying, arresting, and prosecuting offenders.

Community Crime Prevention (Box #5) Activities in this sector are designed to deter crime through improvements in the capacity of a community to supervize and control potential offenders. The emphasis here is on the impact of informal social control, usually through programs such as Neighbourhood Watch or Crimestoppers. These types of programs involve interventions in the social rather than the physical arrangements in a community. The basic strategy usually involves attempting to involve the members of the community on a volunteer basis as the "eyes and ears" of the justice system. The underlying assumption is that this will provide more information to the police and the courts, thus allowing them to improve their rate of arrests and convictions. The theory is that this will deter offenders, and thus improve community safety. Unfortunately, the research on this type of programs is not very supportive of this approach: there is little indication that crime rates are reduced, and it appears that these programs are extremely difficult to set up in the communities that need them the most (see Rosenbaum, 1988; Skogan, 1990).

Situational Crime Prevention (Box #5) As in the case of community crime prevention, activities in this sector are targeted on risky situations. The difference is that these activities focus more on the physical environment. In general, they are designed to eliminate targets, or at least make them less accessible or attractive. Examples of this approach include a broad range of target hardening or environmental design activities. These strategies are based on the assumption that there is relatively little social policy intervention can do to influence the motivation of offenders, or the structural factors linked to the vulnerability of certain individuals or groups. The strategy is thus to focus on the "limited rationality" of the potential offender (Clarke, 1992). The notion is that potential offenders must make a series of decisions at the point of temptation, and thus, that the most feasible and effective intervention strategies will be those that successfully influence this decision-making process.

Victim Risk Management (Box #6)   Activities in this sector focus on the responsibility of potential victims to reduce or manage the risk of being victimized by crime. The focus can range from an individual's responsibility not to contribute to or precipitate) a criminal event, to a wide range of educational activities designed to inform victims how to protect themselves from potential criminals or to encourage them to modify their lifestyle in a manner that increases their personal safety.

Crime Prevention Through Social Development—The Developmental Approach (Box #4)   Activities in this sector focus on the underlying causes associated with the development of persistent offenders. This approach reflects a commitment to the findings of positivist longitudinal (cohort) studies of persistent offenders. The main theoretical focus of this approach is on the early identification or diagnosis of the factors associated with criminal offending It usually targets problems in the family or the school, and insists on an interagency approach to the delivery of the services and resources necessary to eliminate or alleviate the situation.

Crime Prevention Through Social Development—The Social Approach (Boxes 7,8 and 9)   Activities in this sector focus on the broad economic, political, and ideological factors associated with the rate of crime in our society. There are two very different variants of this approach. Radical criminologists work within to a left-oriented notion of class and social inequality, and a recognition that changes in policy at this level can have a significant impact on the likelihood of developing significant rates of motivated offenders or vulnerable victims among different sectors of society, or of having situations that are more or less conducive to crime (see for example Currie, 1985). Criminologists who work within a more conservative or right-wing perspective tend to focus more on the impact of cultural changes on key social norms and values, and place special importance on the negative social impact of increased permissiveness on individual behaviour and community development (see for example Wilson, 1975).

There is no doubt that this schematic representation oversimplifies the distinction between different theoretical approaches to the explanation of crime, and different strategic orientations to crime prevention. Moreover, it underestimates the degree of overlap among actual practices: there are a few crime prevention initiatives (or organizations) in the "real world" that fit neatly and exclusively into one (and only one) box. This framework, however, does help to illustrate the range of decisions that are at the basis of the development of a balanced and comprehensive crime prevention strategy. We must resist the temptation to reduce the debate over crime to a simple distinction between the punishment or the treatment of offenders. This deals only with the offender and focuses only on the tertiary level of intervention; it is a debate that focuses only on box #1 of the typology. It ignores most of the factors that play an important role at the secondary and primary levels of intervention, and almost completely ignores criminogenic situations and the victims, or potential victims, of crime. Surely an informed debate over prevention strategies must do more.

PRIORITIES FOR PREVENTION

Two basic questions remain: what do we know about crime prevention in Canada at this point in time, and where do we go from here?

To begin, there is some indication that much of the crime prevention activity in Canada in recent years would fall under the rubric of either situational crime prevention, community crime prevention or victim risk management (Hastings and Melchers, 1990). The available evaluation research (see for example Rosenbaum, 1988) suggests that these are actually the very strategies least likely to have a significant impact on crime or the fear of crime. Moreover, they are also strategies that are easiest to implement in the communities that need them least, and almost impossible to implement in the communities that need them most (Skogan, 1990). This does not make for the most effective targeting of the limited resources of the criminal justice system, and it is hard to argue that we are getting the best possible return on our investment in prevention.

Second, the programs and activities in question rarely go beyond the ideologically tried and true (Hastings and Melchers, 1990; Hastings, 1991). In general, it seems to be less a question of new services or approaches, and more a question of new ways of delivering the same old thing. The community is mostly involved as an extension of the police—their eyes and ears in the community. There is little indication of a "revolution" in our collective thinking about or responses to crime.

Finally, there is the question of the reform potential of the developmental approach (box #4) to crime prevention. This approach tends to be dominated by a commitment to the findings of longitudinal studies of youth cohorts. The result of this focus on differentiated individuals is an emerging tendency to justify new and preemptive forms of social control. The idea is that we should now be able to predict the type of young person who is at risk of becoming an habitual offender, and that we should also be able to intervene in a corrective manner "before it is too late" (this means that the "at risk" individual must be considered guilty of having a potential for crime). The end result is likely to be an extension of the intrusion of the criminal justice system ever deeper into the lives of the members of certain social classes or groups.

This leaves us with the problem of what to do next. For the moment, I would argue that the immediate priorities for any attempt to develop a comprehensive crime prevention strategy fall into two broad categories: the first deals with social policy considerations, and the second with research needs.

Let us begin with the policy level. One of the obvious implications of the typology I have proposed is that an overreliance on a traditional law enforcement or correctionalist approach to crime will only have a limited impact on many of the factors related to crime. At the very least, little will be done at the secondary or primary level, and little attention will be directed to situations or victims. This suggests that justice institutions will have to take on a wider range of targets or objectives, and consider a broader spectrum of strategies.

This is hardly news. As evidenced by the current popularity of mission statements and strategic planning, most criminal justice institutions and professionals are well aware of the need to broaden their concept of what it is they do, and how they should go about doing it.

However, the design and implementation of such programs or initiatives requires *policy guidance* in a number of crucial areas. I will mention two examples. First, criminal justice organizations need more direction in deciding when to rely on law enforcement as the optimum strategy and when to shift to alternatives. For example, community policy strategies can be set up in an attempt to increase law enforcement capacities (for instance, by giving the police access to more and better information), or they can be imagined as an attempt by the police to be a catalyst to community development (in which case, the prosecution of community members might be inimical to the accomplishment of objectives). The same types of debates characterize areas such as diversion, alternative sentencing, and the classification and treatment of convicted (or potential) offenders.

Similar guidance is necessary in striking a balance between the rights and responsibilities and individuals, and the needs of communities. In the realm of law enforcement, it is clear that our Constitution gives priority to the rights of the individual (for example, the right to be considered innocent until proven guilty). The problem is that the logic of a prevention strategy requires intervention before an offence can even occur—there is considerable work to be done on the issue of the relative rights of individuals and the state in this area. When, for instance, can we offer—or require—a young child treatment for a supposed "pre-criminogenic" condition?

A concern with victims will require guidance as to how to balance the rights of "competing" individuals; we will need to make difficult political decisions about the circumstances under which the needs or rights of a victim may take priority over those of an offender. Moreover, the focus on situations and communities will require direction on the issue of whether community rights can supersede those of a victim or an offender.

In both these cases, some insight can no doubt be found from well-conducted research. In the end, though, a great deal depends on our collective willingness to make political and ideological decisions about the relative priority that ought to be accorded to certain values or goals, or to certain types of persons.

Our research needs can be stated very simply: we need to know more about what works (and why) in the field of crime prevention. What are the "success stories" in this area, and can these initiatives be replicated in other areas or against other types of crime problems.

I would argue that we have two main types of research needs. On the one hand, we need to know a great deal more about the *substance of crime prevention*. It is important that this research not focus narrowly on the impact of a program on traditional law enforcement capacities. Rather, it should attempt to identify the programs or initiatives that (at a given level of human and social resources) have had a measurable impact on reducing crime and the fear of crime, and on improving individual and community safety and security.

On the other hand, we also need to know a great deal more about the infrastructural and resource requirements of the *successful implementation of crime prevention*. The fact that prevention initiatives are often most difficult to implement where they are the most needed, and the consequent class bias in the distribution of the benefits of crime prevention should alert us to the need to learn more about when and how prevention works. This requires knowledge about what motivates individuals to participate in crime prevention (or any other form of community action), and about the characteristics of successful community development.

The point is that many of the failures of prevention initiatives can be readily explained. In some cases, the failure is the result of poor implementation of a good idea or theory, and in other cases it is the result of investing time and money in an organization that is working from a weak or deficient theory and policy base (in other words, it has nothing useful to do!). In either case, valuable time, energy and resources have been wasted.

CONCLUSION

The thrust of my argument is that, at this point in time, our political and emotional commitment to crime prevention surpasses our knowledge of how exactly we can have the maximum impact on rates of crime and victimization, and provide the maximum benefits to victims and communities.

Our traditional overreliance on law enforcement responses to the problem of crime has led us down a path to a one-dimensional response to a complex and multidimensional problem. We need to avoid the seduction of efficiency arguments (the need for more resources to traditional approaches) in favour of an exploration of alternative and more effective responses to the problem of crime. The strategy of crime prevention will be a major part of any such exercise.

However, prevention should and must mean a great deal more than better law enforcement. This is not a case of finding new tactics designed to provide for a more efficient implementation of an old idea. Rather, we need to rethink our commitment to law enforcement in the context of a wider and more balanced set of policies and strategies targeted at the needs of victims, communities, and society as a whole. This is the promise of prevention.

REFERENCES

Brantingham, Paul J., and **Frederic L. Faust.** 1976. "A Conceptual Model of Crime Prevention," *Crime and Delinquency,* 22: 284–296.

Canada. Ad Hoc Advisory Committee for a National Strategy for Community Safety and Crime Prevention. 1993. *Community Safety Through Crime Prevention.* Ottawa: Department of Justice.

Canada. Standing Committee on Justice and the Solicitor General. 1993. *Report of the Standing Committee on Justice and the Solicitor General* (The Horner Report). Ottawa: House of Commons.

Canadian Criminal Justice Association. 1989. "Safer Communities: A Social Strategy for Crime Prevention in Canada," *Canadian Journal of Criminology,* 31(4): 359–401.

Clarke, Ronald V., ed. 1992. *Situational Crime Prevention: Successful Case Studies.* New York: Harrow and Heston.

Cohen, Lawrence E., and **Marcus Felson.** 1979. "Social Change and Crime Rate Trends: A Routine Activity Approach," *American Sociological Review,* 44: 588–608.

Cohen, Stan. 1985. *Visions of Social Control.* Cambridge: Polity.

Currie, Elliot. 1985. *Confronting Crime: An American Challenge.* New York: Pantheon.

Hastings, Ross. 1993. "La prévention du crime: L'illusion d'un consensus," *Problèmes actuels de Science criminelle,* 6: 49–69.

———. 1991. "An Ounce of Prevention...," *Journal of Human Justice,* 3(1): 85–95.

———, and **Ronald Melchers.** 1990. "Municipal Government Involvement in Crime Prevention in Canada," *Canadian Journal of Criminology,* 32(1): 107–123.

Lab, Steven. 1988. *Crime Prevention: Approaches, Practices and Evaluations.* Cincinnati: Anderson.

Matza, David. 1969. *Becoming Deviant.* Toronto: Prentice Hall.

Rosenbaum, Dennis. 1994. *The Challenge of Community Policing: Testing the Promises.* London: Sage.

———. 1988. "Community Crime Prevention: A Review and Synthesis of the Literature," *Justice Quarterly,* 5: 323–395.

Skogan, Wesley. 1990. *Disorder and Decline: Crime and the Spiral of Decline in American Neighborhoods.* New York: Free Press.

Wilson, James Q. 1975. *Thinking About Crime.* New York: Bodic Books.

PANOPTICON OF IMPULSES: PUNISHMENT AND THE ELECTRIFIED PRISON

Kevin R. E. McCormick

We have seen that in penal justice, the prison transformed the punitive procedure into a penitentiary technique; the carceral archipelago transported this technique from the penal institution to the entire social body. With several important results. (Foucault, 1977, 298)

ELECTRIFYING THE PENAL TECHNIQUE: AN INTRODUCTION

Currently, the Canadian penal system is being shaped by an all-consuming infatuation with the emancipatory possibilities of each new technological innovation. The introduction of devices such as electronic inmate monitors and offender management computer systems serves to designate linguistic, mechanical, and conceptual contours that electronically translate traditional penal techniques. Technological implementations in carceral contexts electrify the correctional process. In so doing, technology transforms the penal agenda. The purpose of this chapter is to facilitate a more critical appreciation of the role of electronic technology within various contexts of the correctional system: prisons, parole/probation, and "rehabilitative" programs. This penal-technological investigation will detail clearly the extent to which the correctional process has become electrified. The attendant techniques of control are evermore reliant on devices as instruments of imprisonment and rehabilitation. A careful examination of these interventive processes demonstrates that technology is per se an exercise in control despite the universal celebration of its liberating potential and participation of a consensually oriented technocratic society. As a cultural marker, technology mirrors a generic deference to authority, electronically translating care/control practices and management principles throughout all sectors of the penal system.

TECHNOLOGY AND THE PRISON: ELECTRIFYING THE CARCERAL

Historically, the administration of punishment has been profoundly affected by a myriad of technological advancements, which have scripted carceral actors according to a highly coercive and technically alienating penal agenda. While the fundamental precepts of "law" and "order" remain, techniques of punishment expand the traditional notions of the omniscient power of the penal system. These penal techniques establish disciplinary powers that readily transcend traditional mandates of the prison and rehabilitative programmes. From the advent of the Panopticon (Bentham, 1843) to the implementation of prison monitors and computer systems (McCormick, 1994), the panoptic gaze of the state continues to demand that all carceral actors become fully subjectified within the infinite scope of the penal system.

The power of various methods of penal persuasion expand infinitely when cloaked in the pallium of invisibility. Indeed, those within the system are at times unaware of their surveillance and techniques of control enacted upon them daily by the state:

> Disciplinary power is exercised through its invisibility; at the same time it imposes upon those whom it subjects a principle of visibility. In discipline, it is the subjects who have to be seen. Their visibility assures the hold of the power that is exercised over them. It is the fact of being constantly seen, that maintains the disciplined individual in his subjection. (Foucault, 1977, 187)

Thus, as techniques of control and punishment become even more accessible to the agents of the correctional system, punishment will become increasingly dependent on these innovations as the convenient and effective techniques by which to administer the penal agenda.

Traditionally, the prison as an apparatus of social control and mechanism of moral regulation establishes the "carceral network" (Foucault, 1977) through various techniques of penal persuasion. Whether through the utilization of intensive institutional based programmes or the physical isolation of the offender, the method of control has become as crucial as the legal or moral foundations upon which the rationale of rules rest. Servitude to religious doctrine as a method of rehabilitation as practised in the penal structure centuries ago has been expanded to include secular notions of obedience, namely to the state and its functionaries. Replete with contradictions, the penal system has become a complex constellation of state-run institutions and private agencies each offering a slightly different technique of penal persuasion. While the methods of control may differ, and to a lesser extent the ideological assumptions under which the control is exercised, each clog in the penal machine is driven by a desire to find a technique of control that will expedite the mandate of the justice system. It is thus the case that the correctional system today continues the search for that which is convenient and cost effective in the administration of punishment, including in its arsenal of techniques, penal apparatuses that have increasingly become technologically grounded and electronically powerful.

Interestingly, while the penal system has become enamoured by the new and highly obtrusive technologies of control and surveillance, the fundamental effect that these devices have had on the entire correctional system remains under–investigated. Rather than merely celebrating within the euphoria of convenience and novelty of each new technology introduced into the prison system, researchers, care and control agents, and (x)offenders must critically examine how these apparatuses will impact on the very trajectory of the penal structure for years to come. While many criminologists and agents of the criminal justice system systematically lament the ease at which justice will be administered electronically in the future, they ignore through somnambulistic rationalizations the dramatic alteration that is ongoing as a result of the electrification of the correctional system. Further, mechanisms of resistance and challenge required to offset the panoptic power of the technologicalization of the penal system remain on the level of theoretical chatter, rather than in the arena of practice and policy. Therefore the focus of criminological discourse must take into account the role of technology in the penal system and its ability to shape and direct the techniques of punishment and surveillance routinely enacted on individuals and groups in the name of "law" and "order."

TECHNOLOGICAL APPLICATIONS AND CARCERAL CONTEXTS

The social introduction and technical application of computers into the formal sphere of social control has translated technology into a formidable resource in the arsenal of state coercive exercises (Ackroyd, et al., 1977). In all facets of society, both formal and informal, control mechanisms have been expanded as a result of various technological innovations. Heise (1981) forecasted that technological implementation would dramatically impact on the very nature of social existence:

> By the end of the decade, microcomputers will have changed the way social scientists do research, the way they teach courses and the way they work in applied settings. Further, computers will also create new topics for social analysis as the microcomputer revolution reaches diverse sectors of society. (1981, 395)

Physical computer systems and their concomitant operating systems have become the centre point of most social interactions in society. These activities range from leisure (entertaining) pursuits to medicine, education, and the criminal justice system. Technological innovations designate for the users lexicons and electrified norms of etiquette, electrified parameters in which the user must develop and execute strategies of social interaction and articulation. As a result of this imposed "techno-contract" between the apparatus and the user, a disproportionate power dynamic is initiated. Both the experiences and methods of social presentation utilized by the user are imprisoned in a technologically mediated environment. While the user felt that this agreement was a small expense considering the benefits promised by the device, the influence must not be merely considered causally utilitarian, but observed that "repressive technologies were developed to help suppress the revolt of a partially subjugated caste" (Ackroyd, et al., 1977).

In submitting to these lexicons, conceptions, and definitions, human experiences are organized according to the state agenda and translated through a socially articulated and highly coercive technological script (Pfaffenberger, 1988; Meyrowitz, 1985). This agenda is not readily manipulated by the user, but rather causes users to articulate and thereby position themselves socially and exclusively through the techniques prescribed by the apparatus. Users of any technology must avoid becoming hypnotized by the convenience afforded them by the device, and must realize that the relationship between the user and apparatus is not utilitarian but rather insidious in its carceral impact. Emancipatory assurances of the computer in correctional settings are hollow cliches, couched in the rhetoric of convenience and firmly entrenched in the inequality of the political.

THE CONVENIENCE MYTH: ELECTRONICALLY ERECTED STAGES OF SOCIAL PERFORMANCE

Technology is manifested according to functions that facilitate an economy of convenience in the performance of tasks. Further, the implementation of technologies into the correctional system establishes a "culture of compliance" (Franklin, 1990). It is this culture that establishes a mortgage between the device and the user:

> the mortgage means that we live in a culture of compliance, that we are ever more conditioned to accept orthodoxy as normal, and to accept that there is only one way of doing 'it'. (24)

Regrettably, the latent repercussions attendant with the social introduction of technology, like the imprisonment of the user within imposed definitions of the specific situation, are far too frequently overlooked. This techno–carceral process limits social interaction "configuring the user—defining the identity of putative users and setting constraints upon their likely future actions" (Woolgar, 1991, 58). Thus, the relationship between technology and the user is inherently carceral given the ubiquitous nature of conflict within power imbalances. Asymmetry establishes dynamic stages of social interaction upon which a myriad of "technological dramas" are enacted routinely (Pfaffenberger, 1988; Manning, 1992; Meyrowitz, 1985).

Beyond mere enhanced levels of convenience in the control industry, the computer is transforming the nature of social interaction. This specific technology used by state functionaries, for example, is not a separate entity from the individual, used and then placed down, but rather in its utilization becomes part of the person, "a dynamic by which the technology becomes an extension of the users central nervous system" (McLuhan, 1964, 64). By extending the scope of their senses, the proclivity to perceive a greater spectrum of opportunities also increases. These sites of interaction are not physical settings, but constitute "virtual communities," cultures comprised of electronic impulses housed in technical casings. Agents of formal control present themselves electronically through the medium of the computer; they perform before an electronically constructed and politically constituted audience with well-defined organizational expectations. What is generated is not merely a rearticulation of techniques of performance used when depicting self in an intimate social circumstance, but rather a societal presentation contained within and constrained by the specific vocabularies, protocols, and precepts attendant with the technology.

While extant technological power differentials are evident in all aspects of life, the negative impact is more fully appreciated whenever the device fails to emancipate and succeeds as a method of social and technological incarceration. The processes by which individuals first become imprisoned in "technological barriers" and subsequently internalize the apparatus's unique lexicons as methods of social articulation and definition are not temporally nor spatially restricted. Conceptually, control is not situation–specific, but rather a social context that characterizes the relationship of the device and the user. While assisting the user in certain tasks, technologies readily transcend the "convenience function" by imposing on the user an electronically defined and mediated framework that comprehends and traverses immediate social environments presented by technology. Traditionally, users of devices have disregarded the carceral implications inherent in technologicalization. Rationalizing technology as a mere cost–saving programme blatantly ignores "technology as a system of exploitation" (Buchanan, 1962, 535). In order to be "convenienced" by the device, the user suspends and brackets his/her personal experiences and modes of social presentation. The seductive powers of the technology unconditionally submits the unsuspecting and at times euphoric user to a foreign dogma replete with rituals, a catechism of lexicons, and a set of reconstructed societal values and beliefs (McCormick and Visano, 1992).

Hysteria and hypnotic effects have accompanied the social introduction and implementation of every technical device. For example, the computer continues to be heralded in popular culture as the "greatest invention since the wheel." This infatuation with the role of computers in enhancing everyday life tends to overshadow current theoretical debates regarding the appropriate role of this device within the wider social order. Levin (1986, 116) argues for a critical appreciation of the technology's introduction, noting that "social scientists still wonder whether the computer, rather than people, has dictated the trajectory of sociological theory in recent decades." Instead of blindly embracing the ease by which certain mundane tasks can now be accomplished by the computer, social analyses of this technology must look beyond the "liberation" thesis. A critical evaluation of the ways in which the computer captures the user in a prison defined and mediated by "the technological order" (Ellul, 1976) is warranted.

TECHNO–CONTROL: COMPUTERS AS FORMAL CONTROL AGENTS

The carceral aspects of technological implementation is most clearly illustrated when examining the introduction of electronic devices into the criminal justice system. From the advent of radio communications, mainframe computer systems, to the use of personal computers, the penal system has undergone a dramatic period of change over the last decade. The proliferation of various electronic devices has transformed agents of the correctional system into technocrats, concerned with the expedition of justice through the most convenient and accessible apparatus. This all-consuming relationship that the penal system has with technology alienates both the care/control agents and the offenders from the process and imprisons them within a carnival of illusions that conveniently masks the true agenda of the state.

As a direct result of computer implementation, the penal process has ushered in a new dimension of social control in which expectational structures and performance techniques become technologically defined and articulated. This technological revolution was celebrated within the liberal rubric of convenience, subscribing to a humanist techno–orientation. The time saved on paperwork will result in greater time spent on the direct service side of the penal industry (Campbell, 1989; Gooderham, 1986). Within the physical prison the individual's movements are observed within the parameters established by the prevailing political and economic sentiments of the state. The introduction of electronic devices as penal techniques of punishment translates directly the physical manipulation and isolation of inmates into a technological sphere.

For years, electronic surveillance (Whitehead, 1992; Clear and Hardyman, 1990; Marx, 1991) has retarded the actual nature of traditional work itself by injecting different and "more improved" neutralizations and interesting vocabularies and controversial practices in the penal system. From the cumbersome ankle bracelets to powerful and miniature devices, "modern" penal administration has ushered in each new innovation with unchallenged obedience. Most officials in the system celebrate the use of electronic devices as contributing immeasurably to cost-saving and efficiency-enhancing initiatives. Interestingly, electronic monitors, while physically limiting the offender, also act as an ongoing visible reminder to the offender of their responsibility to an omnipresent process of social control. These apparatuses of penal servitude are technologically restricting and physically oppressive. We are witnessing the technological translation of carceral conditions in the physical institution to the widespread generation of "electronic jails" (Berry, 1985).

Technological implementation within the Canadian penal system seemingly "liberates" authorities as they welcome a commitment to convenience. For the (x)offender, technology serves to render rules, pervasive conditions, and overall patterns of accountability of anonymous state officials even more invisible. On the other hand, the authority of policing agencies is calibrated according to resources (Manning, 1992; Colton, 1979; Colton and Herbert, 1979). Technology as an empowering resource structures discretionary practices. In turn, those within the carceral culture are subordinated by the normative contours of the techno-culture, cast into an environment of their design but beyond their control. This process of techno–incarceration is witnessed in every facet of the Canadian penal structure, including prisonization, decarceration, rehabilitation, and educational programmes for both inmates and care/control agents. Any sacrifice offered to this electronic guard by those seeking electronic liberation only further incarcerates the user within a technologically invisible panopticon of impulses far more carceral than any physical mode of surveillance and control.

THE ELECTRONIC CELL: PENOLOGICAL IMPLICATIONS OF TECHNOLOGICAL INNOVATION

The introduction of electronic devices such as computers into the penal system has erected an invisible electronic cell of imprisonment that constricts the actions of both the offender and those agents charged with their monitoring. Rather than serving as a visible reminder to the offender of their relationship to the penal system, the computer's implementation into the process of parole and probation has established an invisible electronic system of technological "decarceration" (Chan and Ericson, 1981; Scull, 1977) where the all-seeing eye of the state becomes directly internalized by the offender and consequently present in all aspects of his existence. Interestingly, the carceral contexts that the computer constructs are systemically overlooked, while the "liberating" capabilities attendant with the apparatus are focused on:

> there is a general tendency for scholars and researchers, to ignore or even deny the effects of invisible environments and the latent effects of technologies, simply because they are invisible. (Meyrowitz, 1985, 20)

Computerization entraps the (x)inmate within an electronic cage of social articulation, a stage of presentation that, ambiguous in intent, causes the offender to rely upon formal organizations (Clegg and Wilson, 1991) to define the social parameters of their social interactions. The role confusion established by the disproportionate power relationship incarcerates all social performances within an electronic file, not merely the actions that transgressed from the specific conditions of release, but every aspect of their human existence. Infusing itself directly into all actions of the inmate, the computer rearticulates the carceral experiences. Clearly, the constitution of electronic control perpetuates the cultural values of penal institutions, including compliance with authority and a liberal sprinkling of participation in activities exposing the accredited values of the system. The computer has electronically extended the traditional model of the "panopticon." The daily lives of offenders both inside and outside the institution are under the constant scrutiny of penal agendas, dictated and enforced by an all-encompassing "technological eye."

PANOPTICON OF IMPULSES: ELECTRIFYING THE CARCERAL

Far more detrimental in its impact on the entire penal system is the introduction of electronic devices into the very nature of correctional control/care. The transformation of the carceral culture into the computer age constricts the actions of both the offender and their agents within electronically scripted and politically contextualized agendas. The computer readily transcends the physical reminder of penal servitude afforded by electronic monitoring devices attached to the body of the offender. Rather, the individual's body becomes extended electronically through interaction with the computer, erecting a technological stage of performance upon which new forms of penal negotiation are constituted.

Implementation of computers in the penal system imprisons the (x)offender in a technological prison, electronically extending the all-seeing eye of the criminal justice system through the omniscient power of various computer networks, including Offender Management Systems. Imposing itself directly in the daily lives of offenders, the computer serves as a constant reminder of carceral servitude. Obedience and complete subjugation to the rules and agents of the prison structure demanded within the confines of the physical institution are electronically replicated by the computer. This electrification of the formal correctional structure technologically extends conditions and practices consistent with the carceral culture. As a repercussion of the computer's social introduction and technical implementation into the penal system, the daily, routine lives of offenders both inside and outside of the institution become captured, adjudicated, and sanctioned by the omniscient power afforded the structure by the technologically magnified panoptic eye of the computer.

COMPUTERS AND THE CORRECTIONAL SYSTEM: ELECTRIFYING THE PENAL AGENDA

While both the applied (direct services) and conceptual (policy development and implementation) sides of the penal system have celebrated the benefits of various computer devices and software programs, few actors have paused from their electronic pace to reflect on the long-term effects that the introduction of these apparatuses will have on the intricate process of correctional care/control. While the computer and various software packages may alleviate the individual from certain tasks, the more insidious effects of its technological intrusion on the overall correctional process must not be disregarded. What is required is a critical examination of computers and the entire penal enterprise noting the impact that the device has on all institutional structures (Meyrowitz, 1985; Ackroyd et al., 1977) including care/control officers and (x)offenders (Gomme, 1992; Whitehead, 1992). It is this call for a critical examination that comes out of the hypnotic and game-like effect that computers have had on the penal system.

The correctional system itself has adopted the fundamental precepts of computer emancipation and in doing so has ushered in a new and far more panoptic system of control and coercion. Further, both the physical devices and associated software programs are implemented into the very core of the correctional system as management principles, systematically ignoring the impacts that these devices will have on the lives of all those within the carceral culture. During a conference of the Canadian Correctional Service (CSC) entitled, *Control: Neither Too Much nor Too Little* (1982), a senior official noted:

> Wardens and other managers were mainly concerned with their number one mandate—the control of inmates.'Today that's no longer sufficient.' C.S.C.'s managers are facing a challenging new world where a variety of management controls are essential to administer budgets and staff, as well as inmates. (CSC Publication, 1982)

Attitudes such as these raise crucial questions regarding the ethical ramifications of technological applications in the penal system. The introduction of electronic devices into practices associated with community corrections has radically impacted on the very nature of the personal relationship between care/control agents, clients, and the community. Whitehead notes:

> The contemporary community corrections worker may be conducting curfew checks or collecting urine samples, whereas yesterday's officer was leading group counselling sessions or referring a troubled probationer to a community counselling agency. Today's officer possibly thinks of the job of community corrections as a job of surveillance whereas yesterday's officer often saw the job as one of service. (1992, 155; Studt, 1973)

All sectors of the correctional system, including prisons, detention centres, and parole and probation programs, have fully embraced the merger of the computer and effective penal management objectives, urging its employees to learn the ease with which impulses can be manipulated. The computer prioritizes the actions of control agents, organizing the penal enterprise according to the technical abilities of the device as contextualized within specific political agendas. The success of computer implementation is premised on the ability of those designing the systems to distance the user from the personal ramifications of each program executed.

Originally, when computers were first implemented as a directly accessible apparatus in the penal system, managers and wardens were lured to the technology with carnival–like promises. A senior correctional official

> urged wardens, parole directors and superintendents attending the National Administrator's Conference to zap space invaders, play electronic blackjack and other computer games to get the feel and scope of the computer terminal. (CSC Publication, 1982)

While educational practices would dictate establishing a level of comfort with the computer, this process must not occur to the exclusion of those most dramatically affected by the device; namely inmates and other intimates in the process. Correctional attitudes such as those mentioned fail to adopt a critical appreciation of the technological innovation, which notes that

> new tools and the skills to use them raise significant methodological questions, as much as they encourage new kinds of questions and new answers to old ones, the real challenge will be to shape the technology and use it well. (Gerson, 1987, 407)

Clearly, the liberation thesis inherent in correctional computing demonstrates a blind technological infatuation that requires submission to the device's language and definition in order to reap its electronic benefits. What is required is that those charged with care/control responsibilities remain vigilant, consciously attributing a life behind each touch of the computer keyboard. While the new computing care/control officer may feel detached from the process when using the technology, he/she must never lose sight of the effects of the electrified carceral process on the future of those (x)offenders not as technologically empowered.

COMPUTERS AND THE CARCERAL CONTEXTS: ELECTRONIC REFLECTIONS

In conclusion, this inquiry has illustrated technology as a carceral culture and incarceration as increasingly technological. Technology shapes and is shaped by the nature of the cultural definitions. The subject of technology is a problematic discourse that defies simplistic interpretations. It was argued that the convenience of technology reproduces compliance. Seasoned users or technocrats have become the new philosophers, theologians concerned with the hegemonic moralities of convenience. But the phenomenon of technology is about exclusion and resistance, not just about accommodations contextualized within the normative culture of convenience. Technology is an extension of traditional modes of social control designed to mirror a generic deference to authority. The dominant order, with its emphasis on convenience, scripts technology as a commodity that is marketable and profitable for those who have a stake in the penal structure. What warrants further investigation is the extent to which technology itself is contextualized culturally, mediated politically and articulated economically. The user must challenge the myths, monologues, and recipes that mediate knowledge and encourage electronic colonialism. Users are not well-informed citizens; knowledge is not available but filtered through self-serving organizations demanding deference to technology. A carnival of illusions and images make the user a vulnerable target of manipulation. Lamentably, the user readily consents to his/her own incarceration and in turn reproduces forms of incarceration in encounters with less privileged and technologically empowered populations.

BIBLIOGRAPHY

Ackroyd, C., et al.   1977. *The Technology of Political Control.* Britain: Pluto Press.

Bentham, Jeremy.   [1843] 1977. *La Panoptique.* Reprint, Paris: Pierre Belfond.

Berry, B.   1985. "Electronic Jails: A New Criminal Justice Concern," *Justice Quarterly,* 2: 1–24.

Buchanan, R.A.   1965. *Technology and Social Progress.* Oxford: Pergamon.

Buchanan, Scott.   "Technology as a System of Exploitation," *Technology and Culture,* 3(4): 535–543.

Campbell, Colin.   1989. "Laptop Computers for Parole Officers," *Let's Talk,* vol. 14, no. 2.

Chan, J., and **R.V. Ericson.**   1981. *Decarceration and the Economy of Penal Reform.* Toronto: Centre of Criminology, University of Toronto.

Clear, T., and **L. Hardyman.**   1990. "The New Intensive Supervision Movement," *Crime And Delinquency,* 36(January): 42–60.

Clegg, Stewart, and **Fiona Wilson.**   1991. "Power, Technology and Flexibility in Organizations." In *A Sociology of Monsters,* edited by John Law. London: Routledge.

Colton, Kenneth W.   1979. *Police Computer Technology.* Lexington, Mass.: D.C. Heath.

———, and **Stephen Herbert.**   1979. "Police Use and Acceptance of Advanced Development Techniques: Findings From Three Case Studies." In *Police Computer Technology,* ed. by Kenneth W. Colton. Lexington, Mass.: D.C. Heath

Correctional Service Canada.   1982. "C.S.C.'s Computer Revolution: Greater Management Controls the Watchword for 1982 Says Commissioner," *Let's Talk,* vol. 7, no. 2.

Ellul, J.   1976. "The Technological Order." In *Technology as a Social and Political Phenomenon.* USA.: John Wiley & Sons, Inc.

Foucault, M.   1986. *Power/Knowledge.* Edited by C. Gordon. New York: Pantheon.

———.   1977. *Discipline and Punish.* London: Allen Lane.

Franklin, Ursula.   1990. *The Real World of Technology*. Ontario: House of Anansi Press.

Gerson, Elihu M.   1987. "Do We Sincerely Want To Be Programmers?" *Qualitative Sociology*, vol. 10, no. 4.

Gomme, Ian M.   1992. "From Big House to Big Brother: Confinement in the Future." In *Canadian Penology: Advanced Perspectives and Research*, ed. K. McCormick and L. Visano. Toronto: Canadian Scholars Press.

Gooderham, Helen.   1986. "Staff Microcomputers Revolutionize CSC's Way of Handling Information," *Let's Talk*, vol. 11, no. 13.

Heise, David R.   1981. "Microcomputers and Social Research," *Sociological Methods And Research*, vol. 9: 395–536.

Levin, M. L.   1986. "Technological Determinism in Social Data Analysis," *Computers and Social Sciences*, vol. 2.

Manning, P. K.   1992. "Technological Dramas and the Police: Statement and Counterstatement in Organizational Analysis," *Criminology*, vol. 30, no. 3.

Marx, Gary.   1991. "The New Surveillance," *National Forum*, 71(3): 32–36.

McCormick, Kevin, ed.   1994. "Prisoners of Their Own Device: Computer Applications in the Correctional System." In *Carceral Contexts: Readings in Control*. Toronto: Canadian Scholars Press.

———, and **Livy Visano,** eds.   1992. "Technology and Control: Generic Trends." In *Canadian Penology: Advanced Perspectives and Research*. Toronto: Canadian Scholars Press.

McLuhan, Marshall.   1967. *The Medium Is the Message*. New York: Random House.

———.   1964. *Understanding Media: The Extensions of Man*. New York: Mentor Books.

Meyrowitz, Joshua.   1985. *No Sense of Place*. New York: Oxford University Press.

Pfaffenberger, Bryan.   1988. *Microcomputer Applications in Qualitative Research*. USA.: Sage Publications Inc..

Scull, A.   1977. *Decarceration*. Englewood Cliffs, NJ: Prentice Hall.

Studt, E.   1973. *Surveillance and Service in Parole*. Washington, DC: US Department of Justice.

Whitehead, John.   1992. "Control and the Use of Technology in Community Supervision." In *Corrections: Dilemmas and Directions*, edited by P. Benekos and A. Merlo. USA: Anderson Publishing Co.

Woolgar, Steve.   1991. "Configuring the User: The Case of Usability Trials." In *A Sociology of Monsters*, edited by John Law. London: Routledge.

PENAL SATURATION

Jean-Paul Brodeur

INTRODUCTION

On March 1 of this year, the new French penal code was finally declared in force. It replaced the old *Code Pénal* enacted in 1810 under Napoleon. Except for a few innovations, this legislation, 21 years in the making, can be described as an attempt on the part of its legislators to escape nineteenth-century Napoleonic managerialism—an attempt that landed them with one foot in eighteenth-century liberalism, with its emphasis on human rights and penal restraint, and the other foot in early twentieth-century correctionalism. The most striking feature of this code is its abolition of all the minimum terms of imprisonment previously specified for any offence punishable by incarceration. This abolition, nearly one century after the work of Saleilles (1898), was consequent upon the legal recognition of the principle of the individualization of sanctions.

In the United States, the recently enacted *Crime Bill*, aptly described as an ounce of prevention for a pound of repression, could be listed with little doubt among Radzinowicz's "penal regressions" (Radzinowicz, 1990). In Canada, any significant penal reform is stalled, despite the 1987 report of the Canadian Sentencing Commission (Canada, 1987) and a flurry of subsequent government papers (Doob, 1994). The research and policy-making departments of the solicitor general, the Canadian ministry responsible for corrections, is still staffed by true believers in rehabilitation.

We could pursue this review of recent legal developments in penology and discuss other legislation such as England's *Criminal Justice Act 1991* without finding any conclusive evidence for a change of paradigm in penology. The penal infrastructure and practices remain to a large extent the same except for the increasing dependence on imprisonment. The most perceptible changes are those made to the superstructure of objectives, discourses, and symbols that coat this harsh reality.

Yet the sun is never so bright as when it is setting, and it is difficult to deny the pervasiveness throughout the criminal justice system of what Robert Reiner

341

called "fin-de-siècle blues" with regard to policing (Reiner, 1992a; 1992b, 250; see also Reiner, 1994). Albeit belatedly, references to the postmodern and its derivatives—postmodernism and postmodernity—are cropping up with growing frequency in the criminological literature. In their article on postmodern thought and criminology, Schwartz and Friedrichs (1994) review more than 50 articles and books, most published after 1990, that hint at a new criminology or a new penology.[1]

The issue of postmodernism in penology raises two different questions. The first question is *historical* and it relates to fact: is the situation now (or that shortly will be) prevailing in the field of penal practice discontinuous with what we have been experiencing for the last two centuries, or is it the consolidation of a program that was expressed over the last two centuries and is now becoming self-conscious and self-critical?[2] The second question is *theoretical:* is the sociology of modernity an adequate framework in which to consider the present developments in penology? These questions are so intrinsically related that an answer to the first one seems to determine the answer to the second one. If we believe with Giddens (1990, 51) that we live in an age of radicalized modernity, it immediately follows that the sociology of modernity is an appropriate tool to understand our current predicament (with the important provision that it also should be radicalized). This is the position taken by David Garland in his paper entitled "Penal Modernism and Postmodernism" (Garland, forthcoming). If, on the other hand, we have moved beyond modernity we need a new perspective to grasp the meaning of what is presently happening in the field of criminal justice. There is however at least one other position. We may for a variety of reasons suspend judgment on the historical question and argue instead that we need to transform in a radical way our conceptual apparatus in order to throw light on an increasingly complex sociological reality. This is the position that I will attempt to defend.

What do I mean by a suspension of judgment with regard to the historical question? One of the meanings given in the *Oxford English Dictionary* for the word "saturation" is "the action of charging or the state of being charged up to the limit of capacity." I would like to suggest that the correct but provisory answer to the historical question is that we are in a period of transition or pretransition that can best be described as penal saturation. I find this notion of saturation useful because it can be applied to the situation presently existing, while reaching at the same time back toward the past and forward to the future. With regard to etymology, saturation derives from a Latin verb meaning to fulfill or to satiate, which is an action undertaken in relation to a previous state or appetite, or using a more abstract word, a previous program. Saturation is then organically linked to the past. However, if the process of saturation is allowed to continue, it results in transformation. To take two examples from the natural world: adding an undissolved solute to a saturated solution results in the production of crystals; when the air is saturated with water vapour, clouds and eventually precipitation are generated. By analogy, penal saturation can be expected to result in penal transformation: the penal process is presently saturated but we continue to increase our recourse to it. Describing present reality as a state of penal saturation is tantamount to suspending judgment on whether we are modern or postmodern precisely for the reason that this notion of penal saturation encompasses both the assertion of modernity and the presumption of its metamorphosis.

The crucial difference between saturation as a physical state and saturation as a social phenomenon is that we are knowledgeable about the former and can predict its effects, whereas we know very little about the latter. This is why I believe that we should develop a theoretical framework that would allow us to identify the signs of a possible transformation in penology, a framework that would help us understand the meaning of these signs, and that would assist us in drawing an outline of what that transformation might be. In this chapter, I intend to build upon themes developed by postmodern theory and use them as a rough chart to conduct theoretical explorations that may (or may not) lead to useful insights in penology.

The chapter is divided into four parts. I begin by briefly reviewing some of the main themes of postmodern theory. I then propose a series of sketches or sightings of the landscape of a postmodern penology, which I divide into penal discourses, penal practices, and penal systems. In my conclusion, I revisit the notion of penal saturation in light of the preceding explorations.

THE POSTMODERN: SOME FEATURES

I shall avoid using the term "postmodernism" in this chapter. It refers to a development in aesthetics, which is mostly relevant to the visual arts and more particularly to architecture (Jencks, 1987). Since expressions such as "postmodernity" and "postmodern" explicitly refer to time, specifying which period corresponds to postmodernity may help to avoid misunderstandings.

Rose (1991) traces the use of "postmodern" and its derivatives back to 1870 in the written work of the painter John Watkins Chapman. However, the first use of this terminology in a sense akin to its present meaning is to be found in the work of Pannwitz (1917), where it refers to a crisis in European culture. Closer to us, Wright Mills (1959) uses the adjective "postmodern" as the descriptive of a "Fourth Age," which breaks with the ideals of the Enlightenment. Although Wright Mills is somewhat ambiguous about when this Fourth Age actually began, the end of the Second World War would serve. Indeed, there seems to be a general agreement among theorists of postmodernity that the latter began at the end of this war. Lyotard, for example, one of the principal reference points for the definition of postmodern, dates it from the period that followed 1945:

> My argument is that the program of modernity (the realization of universality) was not relinquished, forgotten, but destroyed—"liquidated". There are many modes of destruction, and many names are its symbols. Auschwitz can be taken as a paradigm name of the tragic uncompletedness of modernity. (1988, 36; my translation)

What Lyotard has to say is not only pertinent for situating postmodernity in time, it also contains an important clue to theories of postmodernity. These theories are usually highly normative in their content: postmodernity is not so much posited as fact as it is norm. Because of the magnitude of the Holocaust, there is a moral imperative that dictates that the period following this genocide *cannot* be conceived as continuous with anything that preceded it. Many important theorists of postmodernity, such as Bauman, not only view the Holocaust as a watershed in history, but are under the spell of Adorno's gloom in *Negative Dialectics*. Like Primo Levi and other Jewish survivors of the Holocaust, Adorno seems to believe that the genocide perpetrated by the Nazis has permanently affected the meaning of human life and that life after the Holocaust is transformed by guilt into the shadow of an existence.[3] Although few sociologists are ready to adopt this extreme attitude, there is little doubt that the Holocaust is viewed as a permanent trauma and is shown as such in Bauman's book on modernity and the Holocaust (Bauman, 1989). This trauma has a particular significance for penology, which is precisely the area where the state exercises its power to segregate, to inflict pain, and eventually to kill. Nils Christie's latest book—*Crime Control as Industry* (1992)—which makes extensive use of Bauman's research on the Holocaust, bears witness that penal practices are vulnerable to accusations of genocide. Christie suspects the US criminal justice system of perpetrating genocide against the African-American minority.

The definition of the postmodern condition most frequently quoted is Lyotard's (1979, 7). It is also cited in Garland (forthcoming): "Simplifying to the extreme, I define *postmodern* as incredulity towards metanarratives". We are tempted to substitute "grand narratives" for Lyotard's more opaque "metanarratives." There is no harm in this as long as we remember that "metanarrative" is used by Lyotard in its proper technical sense. The object of a *meta*narrative is not extralinguistic reality but another language. In Lyotard (1979), subtitled "A Report on Knowledge," this other language is the language of science. The purpose of the metanarratives he criticizes is essentially to justify scientific knowledge. Hence the problem Lyotard addressed is a problem of legitimation (1979), the second section of the book being precisely subtitled "The Problem: Legitimation." The object of postmodern incredulity is not just any grand narrative, then, although all such narratives are under suspicion, but legitimating narratives. Indeed, a systematic concern with the issue of legitimation is a conspicuous feature—although not a *distinctive* feature—of postmodern theory. *Legitimation Crisis*, probably the most widely referred to book on this feature, was written by Habermas, one of the best-known proponents of the enduring relevance of the ideals of the Enlightenment and of modernity. It is not the focus on the legitimation crisis that makes postmodern theory distinctive, but rather how it proposes to resolve this crisis. This will be examined in the second part of this chapter.

The use of the expression "metanarrative" in Lyotard's simplified definition of the postmodern perspective also reveals what is perhaps its most general trait. With few exceptions—Simon (1993a, b) being one of the most notable—there is agreement that the most immediate object of postmodern thought is discourse, to which it applies methods developed in semiotics or more idiosyncratic methodologies such as Foucault's archaeology of knowledge (Foucault, 1969) or Derrida's deconstruction (Derrida, 1972). However, postmodern theorists do not limit the validity of their conclusions to the discourses that are analyzed. On the contrary, they tend to derive the properties of extralinguistic reality from the results of discourse analysis. Actually, the more radical proponents of postmodern theory would argue that my last assertion is meaningless since the whole of *structured* reality is identified with "text." There is consequently no stuff beyond text on which it would be necessary to project what is discovered through the analysis of discourse. Discourse is self-contained: it contains within itself worlds and what Wittgenstein (1953) has called forms of life.

The key feature of the postmodern theory of language and text is its radical opposition to any form of *instrumentalism*, the idea that language is merely a passive tool that can be completely controlled by whoever is using it. Most postmodern theorists have developed their version of linguistic anti-instrumentalism. It was given a seminal expression by such towering figures as the philosophers Heidegger and Wittgenstein. The former declared that human beings are spoken through by language rather than speaking it themselves. The latter's notion of language as families of interfacing language games making a giant puzzle that no single player can resolve has now been widely adopted. A corollary of the adoption of Wittgenstein's view of language was the rejection of structuralism in favour of *system theory*. Wittgenstein's rejection of linguistic essentialism, according to which all propositions shared the same features, did not entail the relinquishing of all structure, as the notion of family resemblance reminds us. Postmodern theorists had then to find a conception of structure that dispensed with structuralism's rigidity while retaining the all-important notion of connection. The system theory allowed both for interconnecting patterns and for paradox, viewed as a pathology of system, and the *systemic approach* came to be influential among the postmoderns (Lyotard, 1979, 11–12; Watzlawick, Helmick-Beavin, and Jackson, 1967; Von Bertalanffy, 1975; Dillon, 1983).

The critique of linguistic instrumentalism had very far-reaching consequences. What was language reputed to be the instrument of? The most obvious answer is rational thought. Thus a rejection of linguistic instrumentalism was pregnant with a crisis that in its mildest form implied at least the collapse of rationalism and in its more extreme manifestations undermined rationality itself. Any crisis affecting rationality, one of the fundamental features of thought, ripples through our whole conceptual structure and can generate significant changes in the ways in which we conceive reality. Perhaps the most economical way of describing these changes would be to define postmodern thought as both the exploration and the exploitation of all themes that can be expressed with the use of the Latin prefix "*dis.*" This prefix signifies an inversion of the state or process to which it is joined (e.g., disunity, disorder, discontinuity, dissemblance).

There is one last trait that is difficult to pin down, because it consists of a shifting movement. Self-reflection is an essential component of consciousness, hailed by the seventeenth-century creators of modern epistemology as one of the basic tools for the pursuit of theoretical truth. But self-reflection is also a tricky exercise, and it can lead to paradox and dead ends. Solipsism affords an example: the thinking subjects cannot be certain of anything except their own existence. Hence, there is a powerful drift that threatens to carry conscience from self-reflection to self-reference. The shifting threshold where self-reflection becomes self-reference and where all external reality is dissolved inward has been a focus of interest for postmodern theory. Moreover, it also became obvious that postmodern theory was itself not immune from the perversion that it sought to identify. Its inclination to pile up layers upon layers of metalanguage, as in "the critical sociology of reflexive sociology," occasionally results in conceptual explorations that are journeys into the autistic. This tendency of retreating inward complements the features that we previously described. Postmodern theory seems at times to swing between two converse worlds—the world of the prefix "dis" and the world of "self"—without being grounded in a centre encompassing both inner and external reality.

The features of the postmodern that we have been describing so far are so general that they raise the issue of whether they determine any specificity. This issue is crucial but should be left open for the present. Harvey (1990, 43) and Rose (1991, 49–50) make use of Hassan's list in their inquiry into the origins of the postmodern. Although Hassan succeeds in creating an appearance of specificity for the postmodern, his characterization is fraught by an essential weakness, which can be revealed by asking the following question. Would it be possible to generate the physics of Copernicus and Galileo by merely pairing the descriptors of Greek physics with their antonyms? Such an operation might at best provide the general *background* of modern physics but it would never in itself yield the formulation of the scientific laws that effected the transition from one paradigm to another one. To put it in another way, when Marx said that he put Hegel's philosophy back on its feet claiming that it had been walking on its head, he neglected to point out, analogically, that whether an acrobat is walking on his head or his feet, he remains the same person. While it is far from clear that establishing contrasts is tantamount to inventing a new paradigm, the exercise may prepare the ground for such an invention. Thus, in spite of their weakness, claims that we have entered a new era, be it in penology or whatever, deserve careful attention.

POSTMODERN PENOLOGY: THE LEVEL OF DISCOURSE

I will discuss what I consider to be new developments in penology and penal practice. Whether these developments are continuous or discontinuous with modernity is not determined. Whether the question of their continuity or discontinuity can be answered without forcing the facts into a particular mold is debatable. Although novelty may not be as subjective as aesthetic concepts, it rests at least in part in the eyes of the beholder. A good case could be made that there is not a single goal of punishment not anticipated by Plato in *The Laws* (IX, 862 a–d).

Crime Statistics as Conflict

There is general agreement that one of the defining traits of penal modernity is the reliance of penal practice on expert knowledge. Authors only disagree on the kind of knowledge that should be used. Feeley and Simon (1992, 452), for example, stress the consequences of replacing the clinical assessment of individual offenders with actuarial calculations that allow the development of prediction tables applicable to whole populations of delinquents. Garland (forthcoming) disputes the notion that criminology has relinquished all etiology, thus breaking with the modern endeavour to search for the truth of crime outside of the criminal occurrence itself.

According to official statistics the rates of criminal assaults rose sharply between 1973 and 1987, whereas victim survey data present a picture exactly opposite.[4] I believe that such conflicting statistics are now proliferating in crime statistics, and that three major developments in the collection and processing of quantitative data account for these conflicts. First, they stem from the multiplication of sources for criminal statistics. They also are generated by the fact that we have been adding to our knowledge over time and can produce statistics that deal with longitudinal analysis of homicides committed by young offenders, such as those regularly published by the Canadian Centre for Justice Statistics.

As Tonry (1993) showed in this regard, depending on which segments of different statistical curves you choose to correlate with other irregular curves (e.g., rates of offending with rates of incarceration), you can make opposite claims. Finally, in the third place, statistical pictures may depict very different situations depending on the level of aggregation at which a statistician is operating.

Such conflicting uses of statistics have led decision-makers to rely increasingly on public opinion rather than on experts in the development of penal policy. When Philip Heymann, who was, until his recent resignation, undersecretary at the US Department of Justice, lectured in Toronto on the *Senate Crime Bill*, I asked him what part research had played in the writing of this legislation. He unhesitatingly answered that it had played no part at all. A second effect of the undermining of statistical expertise is that policy is increasingly made on the basis of a few instances—in some cases a single instance—that have a high profile in the media. For example, in Canada we have had several widely publicized failures by parole board authorities to predict correctly the dangerousness of released offenders. These cases led to the resignation of the chairman of the Canadian National Parole Board, a reform of the process of appointing commissioners to the Parole Board, and more importantly to a curtailment of early-release programs for whole categories of offenders.

In one of the most seminal essays in the sociology of postmodernism, Bauman (1987) argued that intellectuals have been forced to exchange the role of legislator, bestowed upon them by modernity, for the much more ambiguous role of interpreter of reality in conformity with the vision of the powerful. We also should ask whether a similar fate is not awaiting experts in criminology and penology.

An Excess of Goals

Rationalization and the search for consistency is also a hallmark feature of modernity. Discussions that address changes in penology generally account for the substitution of one penal rationale for another. Garland (1985) describes the transition from a juridical penology, which focused on the offence or conviction, to a criminological penology, which focused on the individual offender. Simon (1993a, b) describes how the ideals of rehabilitation and reintegration of individual offenders were superseded by a brand of managerialism geared to the protection of society.

After more than ten years of research and consultation, the Canadian Department of Justice finally tabled in 1994 an *Act to Amend the Criminal Code* before Parliament. This Act contains a statement on the *Purpose and Principles of Sentencing* that reads:

> **718.** The fundamental purpose of sentencing is to contribute, along with crime prevention initiatives, to respect for the law and the maintenance of a just, peaceful and safe society by imposing just sanctions that have one of the following objectives:
>
> (a) to denounce unlawful conduct;
>
> (b) to deter the offender and other persons from committing offenses;
>
> (c) to separate offenders from society, where necessary;
>
> (d) to assist in rehabilitating offenders;
>
> (e) to provide for reparations for harm done to victims or to the community; and
>
> (f) to promote a sense of responsibility in offenders, and acknowledgement of the harm done to victims and to the community.

The Act would be more in accord with judicial parsimony if it limited itself to asserting that a Canadian judge may sentence an offender for any reason found in Western and colonial jurisprudence. This Act does not effect the substitution of one rationale for another; it marks the transition from one *form* of penology, which valued consistency and gave priority to one sentencing rationale over others, to a different form that can only be characterized as *laissez-faire* sentencing. The statement of purpose and principles exemplifies not merely eclecticism but an extreme form of syncretism that may become a characteristic of the postmodern. In the US, the federal Sentencing Commission also declared for penal syncretism, to which the commissioners tried to attach a new respectability (Doob, forthcoming). The main effect of such syncretism is that it defines disparity—usually understood to mean *unwarranted* variation in sentencing decisions—out of existence by making it the system's rule. With regard to the current proliferation of sentencing purposes, goals, and principles for which we have provided a Canadian example, *any* variation can be justified on the basis of some sentencing principle.

Beyond Legitimation

Shortly after the original publication in French of *Discipline and Punish* (*Surveiller et Punir*, 1975), Foucault was invited by an organization committed to the defence of prisoners' rights to lecture in Montreal. He was given a list of questions that focused on alternatives to incarceration, which he was asked to address in his lecture. Foucault proceeded to reject the idea of alternatives to incarceration altogether. He claimed that talk of alternatives only reinforced what was at the core of the penal system and should above all else be questioned: the very notion of punishment.[5] In so doing he was displaying his own incredulity about metanarrative in the sense that the word would be used by Lyotard more than ten years later. Foucault and many others, such as Christie (1982), Hulsman (1986), Hulsman and Bernat de Celis (1982), Mathiesen (1974) and Melossi and Pavarini (1981) did not question just any grand narrative, which like rehabilitation partially justified a kind of punishment, but they assailed the notion of punishment from which all lower levels of justifying narratives derive. In other words, these thinkers questioned the legitimation of punishment itself.

As I previously noted, the concept of a legitimation crisis is not postmodern as such. It is the way such crises are resolved that may be described as modern or postmodern with all the caution that the use of such imprecise terms warrants. It cannot be doubted, for instance, that Habermas's partiality for reason and for a reactivation of the *Aufklarung*'s ideals for resolving crisis puts him with the modernists (see the last section of Habermas, 1973, which is subtitled "Being Partial to Reason").

The greatest challenge to Habermas's ideas is Luhman's notion of *autopoiesis*, that is, the conception of the legal system as a self-referential entity that legitimizes itself through internal legal procedure (Luhman, 1983; Teubner, 1987, 1988, 1989; Deflem, 1994). As noted by Deflem (1994, 102), legal self-legitimation suspends any external reference to a nonlegal standard such as morality or social utility. It really amounts to a relinquishment of the systemic need for legitimation, as defined by Max Weber. Whether legal, rational, traditional, or charismatic, legitimation signified for Weber the necessity for a system of domination to *reach beyond itself to be accepted* (Weber, 1954, 334–337). Luhman's theory implies that the question of legitimation in Weber's sense is now obsolete. Luhman's abolition of external legitimation is, we believe, much more germane to the present reality than Habermas's attempts to revitalize the search for such legitimation. Society presently functions (or malfunctions) with thoroughly discredited systems and organizations—e.g., certain police forces, the courts, prison systems, and parole boards—which prevail simply because they endure and there is no known alternative to them.

It might be objected to this dispirited view that the legitimacy of the most repressive practices is constantly reconstructed by public opinion, as we are in a position to verify. This objection could be handled with the help of Baudrillard's concept of simulation or parody (1981). Weber's definition of legitimacy provides a reason for *everyone* to submit to a form of domination (Weber, 1954, 335–36). What is presently being reconstructed as legitimation is not a justification for a *general* obedience to law but a circumstantial reason for exercising control over that part of civil society that is felt to be particularly threatening (the nonwhite underclass) (Simon, 1993a, b). Isn't this reconstruction really a simulation, if not a caricature, of legitimacy, fabricated by politicians and the media in a TV studio where there are too many lights to see who is manipulating whom?

POSTMODERN PENOLOGY: THE LEVEL OF PRACTICE

When we move from the level of discourse to the level of practice we cannot eschew relying on quantitative analyses. Texts may be variably interpreted but they remain the same in time whereas quantitative data are constantly evolving, making conclusions based on them tentative. I will have to confront this problem throughout this section of the chapter.

System Overload

Generally speaking, postmodern penological theorists attempt to determine the consequences of a massive influx of persons coming under the yoke of the penal system at a time when the financial resources to deal with this influx are perceived as increasingly limited. Concepts such as the widening of the penal net (Chan and Ericson, 1981; Cohen, 1984; Pease, 1985; McDonald, 1986; Canada, 1987, c. 12; Morris and Tonry, 1990), managerialism (Bottoms, 1983), the shift from reintegrating individual offenders into society to segregating from society whole populations once again stigmatized as dangerous classes (Feeley and Simon, 1992; Simon 1993a, b) reflect the growth of penalized populations and more particularly the increase in prison population.

Because of the volatility of penal and crime statistics, concepts like these are highly vulnerable to criticism. McMahon's critique of the widening of the net theory seemed, for instance, particularly devastating (1992). A striking example of the shifting statistical ground can be shown by Morgan's conclusion to his article on imprisonment in the recently published *Oxford Handbook of Criminology*. Morgan begins by quoting evidence given to the Woolf Inquiry in the UK to the effect that the work of the Prison Service has been plagued by overcrowding and that the elimination of overcrowding is an indispensable pre-condition for improving prison conditions. He then writes:

> At the time of writing (early 1993) the prison system is for the first time in almost half a century not overcrowded: there are approximately 2,000 more places than prisoners. (Morgan, 1994a, 935)

Yet Morgan cautions us against believing that prison overcrowding has been eliminated. Readers of the *Handbook* should indeed heed his advice, for in the June 1994 issue of the *Overcrowded Times*, he writes that given the punitive policies and politics in the UK:

> system overcrowding seems destined, all else equal, to return to the 10–15 percent levels that prevailed in the early 1980s and to continue at that level into the 21st century. (Morgan, 1994b, 9)

Based on her examination of Ontario statistics on imprisonment and probation between 1951 and 1984, McMahon found that the rates of imprisonment fell from 168 prisoners per 100,000 adults in 1951 to a low of 134 in 1984, thus accounting for a 20 percent decrease (McMahon, 1992, 96). Furthermore, judging from Ontario statistics for the period 1961–1984, McMahon was able to show that probation may have served as an alternative to incarceration, since decreased admissions to prison accompanied the increased use of probation (McMahon, 1992,105–106). These analyses deal a serious blow to the widening of the net theory. McMahon's research is much more thorough in its review of two Canadian studies (Chan and Ericson, 1981; Hylton, 1981) than in her review of the evidence from the UK and the US, a review incomplete and somewhat perfunctory.[6] Second, she mostly uses *admission* data, which measure the flow of persons through a system rather than the average daily size of its population, thus overestimating the impact of a decrease in admissions on system overcrowding.[7] Finally, an examination of the most recent Canadian statistics shows that over the five-year period from 1987 to 1988 to 1991 to 1992 the average physical count of prisoners serving a sentence of incarceration of more than two years increased by 12 percent; the average offender caseload in Canadian Corrections (custodial and noncustodial, federal and provincial) increased by 29 percent; the average count at the federal and provincial levels for noncustodial populations (federal parole/mandatory supervision and provincial parole and probation) increased by 33 percent. Although there was a substantial rise in noncustodial dispositions, the size of the prison population also increased, albeit at a slower pace. In neighbouring US, the prison population increased by 115 percent from 1980 to 1989 (US Department of Justice, 1989).

These remarks cannot be interpreted as a reinstatement of the widening of the net theory, although they suggest that it should not be hastily dismissed. Certainly, an increase in prison populations has not everywhere proceeded at the same pace that it has in the United States. However, with few exceptions in

Western democracies, it does appear that overcrowding has been a persistent feature of imprisonment since 1945, and that, barring some unlikely development such as the abolition of drug offences, it will continue to be a persistent feature well into the next century.

Overcrowded prisons are just one manifestation of a general phenomenon of overload that affects all components of the criminal justice system. Emergency calls to the police typically double every ten years, although the number of public police has generally stagnated, if not decreased.[8] The Supreme Court of Canada in the 1990 *Askov* ruling determined that delaying the proceeding of a criminal case beyond two years violated the Charter provision for trial within a reasonable time. Pursuant to this judgment, charges against at least seventy thousand defendants were dropped by several Canadian provinces.[9] In an unusually strongly worded declaration, the chief justice of Canada compared the overburden of the courts and the delays this generates to the AIDS epidemic.

Such overloading has several effects. When the resources of the penal system are stretched beyond their capacity, deterioration of the conditions of imprisonment and a move to privatize different penal agencies result. The penal process is also affected. It was observed by the 1967 Katzenbach commission that "speed is the watch word" in courts and that trials for misdemeanors were over within a matter of a few minutes. Actually, the number of cases that judges had to dispose of (e.g., twenty thousand cases a year per judge in lower courts in Detroit or Atlanta) resulted in sentencing hearings lasting less than 30 seconds (United States, 1967, 30). During my work in British Columbia, I discovered that defence lawyers were strongly opposed to the use of computerized sentencing data to prepare for their argument in a sentencing hearing because the short amount of time they spent before the judge did not justify the cost and energy of using a sentencing data bank (Brodeur, 1990). As was argued by the Canadian Sentencing Commission (Canada, 1987, 281–283), these time constraints are absolute anathema to the individualization of sentences at the judicial level and make the use of guidelines geared to categories of offenders rather than individuals almost inevitable. This is a point that is repeatedly missed by critics of the sentencing guideline systems.

This transition from the treatment of the individual to the penal handling of sets of offenders and its attendant managerialism has been emphasized by several of the authors I have mentioned. But I wish to add to their description by noting that the intense pressures created by system overload have transformed this managerialism into permanent *crisis management*. Inconsistent policies of incapacitation have sprouted on an *ad hoc* basis, as the consequence both of external political pressure for more severity and of the massive releases of inmates who cannot serve custodial sentences because of internal constraints like overcrowded prisons. In numerous US jurisdictions (Minnesota being one), the presumptive durations determined by the sentencing grid are reshuffled if their application overloads the available prison resources. The contradictions resulting from such crisis management have hastened the drift of penology into *aimlessness*. Penologists and politicians attempt to cover up this aimlessness with noise about the protection of society being the primary aim of the criminal justice system. And all the traditional goals—specific and general deterrence, incarceration, rehabilitation, denunciation, reconciliation—that the system failed to meet are then simultaneously reactivated as "means" or "subgoals" to attain that fundamental purpose: protecting the public.

It is easy to lay bare the emptiness of this "protecting the public" rationale. Research has shown that the extent of the physical and sexual abuse of women and children is considerable. Judging from the number of persons serving sentences for such offences, the amount of protection afforded to these vulnerable populations is so small as to be much beneath what could be considered minimal.[10] Penal practice is truly caught in a hapless cycle. As the inconsistencies stemming from penal crisis management become more blatant, the need to appeal to the blanket justification of public protection in order to cover up those inconsistencies becomes more pronounced. The emphasis on the system's mandate to protect the public then generates increasing public demand for protection. More failure adds ever more cosmetic promises, bound to be unfulfilled, to the cycle.

Intermediate Punishments

The most general solutions to the problem of penal overload are community sanctions and intermediate punishments (Canada, 1987; Petersilia, 1987; Morris and Tonry, 1990). Community sanctions are defined as any sanction, including fines, that does not involve segregating the offender from the community; intermediate punishments involve a degree of deprivation of freedom falling between incarceration and probation (intensive supervision/probation programs, house arrest under electronic monitoring, shock incarceration, boot camps, and under certain conditions community service orders).

Gordon (1991, 130) acknowledges that intermediate punishments are, numerically, still a marginal practice in the US. She quotes Petersilia to the effect that in 1988 approximately fifty thousand convicted offenders were in intensive supervision programs, as compared to 3.7 million persons incarcerated, on probation or parole (United States, 1989). There were 386 participants in a community control program in New Jersey as compared with 53,000 on felony probation. Yet Gordon's section of her book where she gives these figures is entitled "The Tip of the Iceberg." She actually states that *"intermediate punishments and probation have the potential for the greatest growth, if only because they are so much cheaper than prisons"* (emphasis added). Although MacKenzie (1994) is cautious in her assessment of boot-camp programs in the US, she notes that support for boot camps is growing: there are already 65 programs for adult and juvenile offenders in state and local jails and in federal prison systems. Nowhere in her survey does one get the impression that these programs are the product of penal nostalgia as it is claimed by critics of the notion of a new penology. Influential thinkers such as Morris and Tonry (1990) advocate intermediate punishment as the way to solve the crisis created by prison overcrowding.

Of course, what reformers are pushing for and what actual penal practices result may be altogether different things. The history of penal reform bears this out. Rothman (1980, 134) tells us that in 1926, when rehabilitation was the dominant correctional ideology, there were only 29 full-time psychiatrists on the prison staff of 13 US states; five of these were in one state, New York. The Canadian Sentencing Commission reviewed 16 reports on incarceration written between 1831 and 1983 only to discover that they all came to the same dispiriting conclusion:

> Gaols managed as most of ours are...are seminaries at the public expense for the purpose of instructing Her Majesty's subjects in vice and immorality, and for the propagation and increase of crime. (Committee of the House of Assembly [1831], reported in the *Journal of the House of Assembly*, Appendix 211–212. Quoted in Canadian Sentencing Commission, Canada, 1987, 40–41)

> Growing evidence exists that, as educational centres, our prisons have been most effective in educating less experienced, less hardened offenders to be more difficult and professional criminals. (Solicitor General of Canada [1977], *A Summary and Analysis of Some Major Inquiries on Corrections, 1938–1977*. Quoted in Canadian Sentencing Commission, Canada, 1987, 44)

Depending on the criteria used to acknowledge change, confrontation between theory and practice can either lead to the conclusion that everything is always in flux or that nothing ever changes. Granting that there is now a disproportion between the discourse on intermediate punishment and that on penal practice, we could still justifiably conclude that intermediate punishment may play a significant role in a postmodern penology.

Sex and Ethnicity

Although not all authors working in those fields would agree, cultural and gender studies make an important part of postmodern thought. Both kinds of studies focus on various expressions of discrimination such as sexism and racism and on abuses of power, which may take extreme forms, like genocide, violence against women, and colonialism (e.g., Marcus, 1993).

Cultural and gender studies raise difficult questions for penology. It might be claimed on the first hand that legal principles such as equality before the law, equity, and impartiality are enshrined in the constitution of many Western democracies, and thus that gender and ethnicity ought only to have a negative role in penal law and penal practice and be referred to only in order to strengthen our commitment against sexism and racism. In its formative years, roughly from the end of the French monarchy to the end of the First World War, modern penal practice was almost completely oblivious to gender, ethnicity, and race. The important debate over the respective merits of the Pennsylvanian and the Auburn systems of imprisonment, for example, took place in the US before the Civil War, while slavery was still practised in many states of the union.

However, such blindness to the issues of gender, ethnicity or race would seem unproblematic today as long as the ideals of universality and impartiality, largely articulated during the years of the Enlightenment, could provide a solution to these issues. Penal modernity, as it were, could be claimed to hold solutions to problems that it never even considered and that would arise much later.

Such a claim can also be disputed. While we may not question the ideals of penal modernity with regard to their substance, we can believe they are too far removed from contemporary reality to provide concrete answers to problems they were not meant to solve. A case in point: the US federal sentencing guidelines require that the amount of crack cocaine possessed by an offender be multiplied by a factor of 100 in order to determine a sentence, making every gram of crack cocaine the equivalent of 100 grams of powdered cocaine for the purposes of sentencing. It might be argued that for all its harshness such a rule does not violate the principle of equality of treatment, as long as it is applied impartially to all offenders.

This first kind of position, in line with the ideals of classical penal modernity, immediately runs into trouble. Since most users and providers of crack cocaine belong to minorities and particularly to African-American minorities, whereas most users and providers of powdered cocaine are whites, such penal policies have the result of significantly increasing racial disparities in US prisons, particularly in the federal system (Doob, forthcoming; Tonry, 1994). In 1991, the percentage of African-Americans admitted to state prisons had reached 54 percent—up from 42 percent in 1980—although this minority represented only 11 percent of the US population. The 1993 US mean rate of incarceration was 351 offenders per 100,000 (United States, 1994); it had two years earlier reached a staggering 3,000 per 100,000 for African-Americans in some states (Wicker, 1991; *Wall Street Journal*, 1991). Although the US Sentencing Commission was not deliberately targeting African-Americans, US legislators were fully aware that its 100-to-1 rule in relation to crack cocaine would increase the proportion of African-Americans in federal prisons.[11]

In view of these facts, one might adopt a second kind of position. Regarding the issues related to ethnicity, it would then be argued that no penal policy that will clearly have the effect of increasing racial disparities should be enacted, and that when such a policy is unintentionally developed and adopted it should be amended as soon as the bias of its effects are noted (Hudson, 1993 quoted by Smith, 1994, 1043).

The point that we wish to make is not that this second position is preferable.[12] Rather, the important point is that resolving the debate between the two courses that we have just outlined is very likely to take us *beyond penal modernity*. Even when penal modernity presents itself as self-conscious, it is doubtful that it is elaborate enough to confront issues of gender, ethnicity, and race without unduly reducing their complexity. If we put the emphasis on the *self* component of the *self*-consciousness of penal modernity, it is difficult to see how it can find within it*self* elements that were never part of it.

Issues of gender, ethnicity and race do more than raise difficult questions about the conceptual framework of penal modernity. They have also modified penal practices in varying degrees, although it is largely premature to decide whether these changes provide some of the basis for a new penology. I will now briefly review some of these changes. They tend to vary significantly from one country to another, depending on the size of the ethno-racial minorities and also depending on the presence or absence of aboriginal communities (like those in Australia, Canada, New Zealand, and the United States).

Guidelines

Despite the example of the 100-to-1 rule that is used in applying the US Sentencing Commission guidelines, it cannot be doubted that reducing disparity based on sex, status of employment, ethnicity, and race was a prominent concern among those who developed sentencing guidelines (Von Hirsch, 1982; Von Hirsch, Knapp, and Tonry, 1987). Feeley and Simon (1992, 461) and Simon (1993b, 232) believe that the impetus for such guidelines came from the legislative budget process. One feature of presumptive guidelines that is systematically neglected by their critics bears that reducing discrimination was indeed an important goal in developing sentencing guidelines. Judges have the option of departing from the guidelines and using a list of aggravating and mitigating factors that permits more individualization of sentences. At the same time, however, most sentencing guidelines packages provide explicit instructions disallowing any individualization based on sex, race, ethnicity, schooling, and status of employment. Several jurisdictions, following the example of Minnesota, closely monitor the contribution of the guidelines to the elimination of ethnoracial disparity. Unless one suspects that such costly monitoring is done mainly to save appearances, it must be conceded that in this one instance at least the elimination of unwarranted sentencing variation is indeed a goal of sentencing guidelines. It is however not the only one.

Community

There is no idea like "community" to encapsulate present movements in the field of criminal justice, or depending on the way one looks at it, the present dead end. Whether the idea originated in the context of policing or in the context of penal practice is beside the point. It is generally admitted that one of the major catalysts behind the rediscovery of the community was the necessity of reducing the costs of isolating offenders. One other force that accelerated the trend toward the use of the community as a substitute for or adjunct to incarceration is the growing political clout of ethnoracial minorities. They generally push for a softer exercise of social control, be it in policing or in corrections (Skogan, forthcoming; Williams and Murphy, 1990).

Accountability

A third feature attributed to high or postmoderm penology is its emphasis on self-monitoring and a rigorous auditing of the exercise of penal power (Simon, 1993b, 248). In this case, as in the previous one, a penal trend is generated by two factors. Self-monitoring and audits are expressions of a more general concern for accountability. Accountability can be understood in a budgetary sense in that it fosters strict self-monitoring and auditing. It also refers to externally generated requests for transparency and external review (Goldstein, 1990, 47–49). The protection of the civil rights of minorities played a decisive role in this quest for normative accountability. It might even be hypothesized that the enthusiasm with which penal agencies embraced self-monitoring was an attempt to fend off external—and potentially more threatening—review.

Inertia

The attempt by penal agencies to avoid external review by willingly submitting to internal monitoring and auditing was only partially successful. External review bodies such as oversight and complaint committees actually multiplied (Goldsmith, 1991; Lustgarten, 1986). In Canada, there were numerous commissions of inquiries appointed to investigate police shootings of members of minorities and other serious violations of their rights (e.g., Quebec, 1994b; Quebec, 1988; Ontario, 1989). In every Western country there were official inquiries into race riots and prison riots. The multiplication of *ad hoc* inquiries and permanent oversight bodies is having a chilling effect on a number of penal agencies: accordingly they have opted for laissez-faire and noninterventionism. In some cases, penal noninterventionism should be understood in its strict sense. For example, aboriginal reservations are increasingly left to themselves: police choose not to interfere, sentencing judges refuse to sit, and sanctions are to a large extent not applied. Penal agents are, with increasing urgency, recasting the question "who is going to guard us from our guardians," which resonates since Roman antiquity into "who is going to protect us, the protectors." In some Canadian jurisdictions, police and judges refuse to go to aboriginal reservations, because of a lack of army protection.

What other forms might noninterventionism take? One general expression of it is the confusion into which penal practitioners and penologists are thrown when they face cases that involve cultural diversity. This was starkly illustrated by a recent *cause célèbre* in the province of Quebec. On January 14, 1994, Judge Raymonde Verrault of the Quebec provincial court (the court that rules in the overwhelming majority of criminal cases in the province) sentenced an Islamic offender to 23 months in a provincial jail for having regularly sodomized the female child of his common-law wife during a period of three years. On the basis of her evaluation of the importance of virginity in Islamic religion and Arab culture, the judge viewed as a mitigating factor the fact that the sexual aggressor had preserved the virginity of the child victim. Although this example is admittedly excessive and shocking, we would be wrong to dismiss it as a freak incident without significance. It is just an extreme form of the crisis of confidence in Western middle-class values that is apparently undermining the will to even attempt rehabilitating persons through the imposition of these values (Allen, 1981). This value crisis has also diminished our capacity for denouncing such behaviour. In my field work, I have frequently talked with police and judges involved in the control of domestic violence. They were genuinely confused about the appropriate action to take when intervening in families whose culture greatly differed from their own. The current penchant for political correctness has helped to stimulate such confusion, and we would be ill-advised to dismiss it.

Another general expression of noninterventionism is the routinization of police and penal practice and the spread of a cynical "cover your ass" mentality. The multiplication of controls over the operation of penal agencies and the attention of the media to errors—particularly those involving an alleged abuse of power against members of ethnic or racial minorities—have a chilling effect on the motivation of those who work in such agencies. The system's continuing expansion seems to be the product of its own unstoppable momentum. The only goal it can apparently achieve through its own demoralization is the strident reassertion of its own nature as one gigantic machine for physical segregation.

High Politicization

A general characteristic of penology is that it has become highly politicized, especially since 1993 when violent crime became a major concern for American citizens, according to public opinion pollsters. In its current sense, the politicization of an issue means that enlisting for or against it becomes a major lever in getting votes in an election. Since the drug crusades of the Reagan and Bush administration, the politics of law and order have been an issue in elections at almost every level in the US.

Penology may become a political issue in a much more fundamental way. The linkage between crime and penal issues and the state are much more fundamental than electoral rhetoric when criminal organizations challenge the state's monopoly on the running of a country's public affairs. Misguided penal practices can trigger events that burgeon into national crises, which in turn take the appearance of the beginning of civil war (Simon, 1993b, 266–67). Such was the case in Canada when in 1990 members of the Mohawk community resisted a court order to dismantle a barricade and started a summer-long confrontation with the Canadian state that shook it to its foundations. Mohawk dealing in cigarette contraband forced the provincial governments to reform their cigarette taxation policies. In the US, the acquittal of the police aggressors of Rodney King was followed by riots that transformed parts of American cities into so many Beiruts. I believe that we should make a distinction between the entwinement of penal policies and the survival of the state on the one hand, and of penal policies and electoral politics on the other.

High politicization is more likely to take place when the issues involved engender interracial or interethnic conflict. This is true with regard to penal practice. It is also true with regard to issues of crime. Criminal organizations pose a threat to the state in countries like Italy and Russia. It is not coincidental that the criminal organizations involved are all composed of and led by ethnic minorities (the Sicilian Mafia, the Calabrese N'Drangheta, and the Neapolitan Camorra; in Russia the most powerful criminal organizations are based in Georgia, Azerbaijan, and Tchetchenia). Even if we limit the discussion to police and penal practices, it is not obvious that modernity offers the conceptual tools to deal with high politicization and its relationship to issues of gender, race, ethnicity, and the underclass.

Postmodern Penology: The Level of Systems

Privatization

In the preceding analyses, I have occasionally allowed myself to range over the three components of the criminal justice system—the police, the courts, and corrections—while staying within the bounds of corrections whenever possible. As I stated earlier, systems analysis is a hallmark of postmodern thought. I will now explicitly discuss different features of criminal justice as they exist within the context of the whole system. I believe that Garland's point about the prison being a complex institution (Garland, 1990, 290) also applies to punishment as a whole. Punishment is a process carried out by a complex system of interconnected parts: the police, the criminal courts, and corrections. As it is readily acknowledged in Garland (forthcoming), the monopoly exercised by the state over criminal justice is one of the defining traits of penal modernity. Extended privatization in any part of the system would imply a move beyond penal modernity, if not a rupture with it.

Private correctional facilities have been utilized only on a small scale. France has launched a limited program of private incarceration (Robert, 1989). In the US, private detention has been used mainly with illegal immigrants. The number of secure adult correctional facilities in the US operated by private firms had in 1991 a total capacity of 16,573 beds, a negligible number considering the 1.2 million offenders held in public facilities (McDonald, 1992, Table 5, 386–390). The most significant growth in private facilities has been in the institutionalization of juvenile offenders. According to McDonald (1992, Table 1, 370), the creation of private juvenile correctional facilities in the US has outpaced the development of public facilities by a proportion of two to one (2,167 private facilities in 1989 as compared to 1,100 public facilities). In 1950, 80 percent of juveniles in correctional facilities were in the public sector; in 1989, 58 percent of juveniles in correctional facilities are in public institutions and 42 percent are in private facilities (McDonald, 1992,Table 2, 371). Interestingly, the growth of juvenile incarceration may represent a case of the widening of the net: the rate of juveniles in private facilities more than trebled from 1950 to 1989, growing from 45 per 100,000 juveniles in the US population to 154 per 100,000 (McDonald, 1992, Table 4, 378). Yet, the rate of juveniles in public facilities also increased from 188 per 100,000 in 1950 to 221 per 100,000 in 1989, thus prompting McDonald to conclude that "the emergence of private facilities consequently afforded a greater reliance on incarceration throughout this period, without a concomitant reduction of juveniles placed in public facilities" (McDonald, 1992, 379). In Canada, nongovernmental organizations such as the John Howard Society are now involved in the supervision of offenders on probation or on parole. Premier Ralph Klein of Alberta has just announced a program for privatizing all provincial prisons.

The limited character of these ventures does not yet permit any general conclusion to the effect that the state is relinquishing its traditional monopoly over corrections. Nevertheless, it can hardly be denied that we are witnessing at least the beginning of a trend toward correctional privatization.

There is however one component of the criminal justice system where privatization has made very significant and permanent inroads, namely, policing. This is documented by exhaustive reports from researchers like Kakalik and Wildhorn (United States, 1972), Cunningham and Taylor (1985) and Cunningham, Strauchs, and Van Meter (1990) for the US. In the UK, Johnstone's recent book (1992) bears witness to the growth of private and hybrid forms of policing. I have reviewed important developments in the other countries of Europe (Brodeur, forthcoming).

It could of course be said that the move toward privatization mainly affects policing and that penology itself remains, as we have seen, relatively untouched. Even granting this point, it must be stressed that from a systems analysis perspective, a criminal justice system with a highly privatized policing component is with regard to its *systemic features* a significantly different *system* than one, which in all of its components is the expression of a state monopoly. In other words, penal practices do not have to be themselves privatized to feel the impact of the privatization that is becoming a prominent feature of the entry component of the system.

The Shape of the System

In its present state, the criminal justice system can be represented as a straight arrow oriented from left to right, composed of three segments sequentially arranged. The first of these segments is the police, the second is the court system, and the third is corrections or penology understood in its narrow sense. The functions of these three components differ; the first involves surveillance, and when necessary intervention; the second consists of a decision procedure that adjudicates guilt or innocence and determines a sanction in the case of a conviction; the third component carries out the sentence imposed at the previous step, the most onerous of these sanctions being the complete loss of liberty. There are few feedback loops in this linear system.

If intermediate punishments are developed as some theorists and practitioners predict and hope, they may transform the orientation of the criminal justice system. Intermediate sanctions have this in common with policing: they entail a large degree of surveillance. Hence, the two extremities of the system may be inclined by their common function of surveillance one toward the other—an inclination that might first be represented by a horseshoe but then by a ring in which the two extremities meet. The whole system then would be turned in on itself as one huge feedback loop. Its reshaping could result in the restricting encirclement of targeted populations such as the underclass. Alternatively, the system could expand and circumscribe a whole society or large segments of it. Needless to say, such a description is highly speculative, but then so is the whole debate on the possibility of a postmodern penology.

CONCLUSION: PENAL SATURATION

In the course of this chapter, we presented a series of sightings that we believe take us beyond modern penology, as a theory of penal practices and as a program for reforming them. With regard to modernity as a program of reform, we would tend to agree with Bauman more than with Habermas. In *Modernity and the Holocaust*, Bauman attempted to show that the Nazi program of genocide was not a demented aberration for which there were no sources in modern thought, but rather a program that carried to their extreme consequence ideas that were developed during the Enlightenment. In some sense the Nazi regime not only implemented certain aspects of modern penology but carried them out to a monstrous degree of saturation. Of course, this is not to imply that the Enlightenment's ideals provided the program for genocide—that would be absurd. It does mean that there is a darker side to eighteenth-century rationalism and that reactivating it should not be attempted without a careful consideration of which features of the paradigm can appropriately be kept and reactivated. I shall not pursue this examination, since normative questions are not the object of this chapter.

My sightings were made from three perspectives: discourse, practice, and system. I believe that most of these sightings can be brought together under the concept of penal saturation.

We saw that in its literal sense saturation meant the action of charging or of being charged beyond capacity. Most of my observations on the chronic overload that affects all components of the criminal justice system, but most noticeably its correctional facilities, lead me to think that penal saturation characterizes our present situation. However incipient they may appear to be, the search for intermediate punishments and the steps toward privatization are indications that this situation is perceived as the dead end that it really is and that there are attempts to break out of it. The growth of the private sector in the provision of policing and security services has been sufficiently extensive to change the balance between the pre and post sentencing components of this system and may have a serious effect upon our conceptions of justice and the exercise of social control.

There is a second feature of penal saturation that is more speculative. Saturation is a natural phenomenon, neither intended nor unintended. It merely happens. In human affairs, however, we may raise the question of intention and ask ourselves what would be the purpose of maintaining a situation of penal saturation. Is there any example of saturation in the field of penology that is not morally and socially offensive?[13] Surely such saturation in a field of human endeavour can only be conceived as a manifestation of aimlessness, the aimlessness that results from a lack of purpose, or as we have seen from a glut of contradictory objectives. I believe that the aimlessness reflected in the prevailing permanent crisis management mode is the correlate at the policy level of the penal saturation predicament.

To conclude, I shall extend the metaphor of saturation. One of the attractive features of this concept was, as I stressed before, its capacity for characterizing a situation that, having reached its limits, was compelled to go through metamorphosis. There are two very different ways to conceive this transformation. Chemistry teaches us that if a saturated solution remains in contact with an undissolved form of the solute, the number of molecules going into solution will be exactly balanced by the number crystallizing out. In the same way, clouds saturated by water vapor break out into rain. Like rain, crystallization is a change into what was; it brings back the past in its solidified, less flexible form. Therein lies the risk of penal saturation. It may preserve itself, permanently—as it were—crystallizing imprisonment.

However, crystallization is not the only way out of saturation. We may try to escape altogether from this depressing cycle. Indeed, we may be breaking out of it already unawares, and thus unprepared, without any plan for the shape of the criminal justice system that is evolving. It seems to me that developing a new theoretical penology could be a modest contribution toward avoiding both the crystallization of current penal practices and their transformation into something still less desirable than what we have now.

ENDNOTES

1   The article reviews more than a hundred titles related in varying degrees to criminology and penology. For instance, Feeley and Simon (1992), Simon (1993a; 1993b), Milovanovic and Henry (1992) and Henry and Milovanovic (1993) explicitly bear on a postmodern penology, whereas Rosenau (1992) are relevant to this field only tangentially. Ericson and Carriere (forthcoming) also address the issue of the fragmentation of recent criminological research and they review more than a 120 publications, many of which could be said to be groping with "postmodern" issues.

2   Garland (1985, 5) argues that there is a discontinuity—but no radical break—
    between the Victorian penology preceding the Gladstone Report of 1895 and the present-
    day pattern established between 1895 and 1914. In one of his more recent papers,
    "Penal Modernism and Postmodernism," Garland argues that the present culture of
    penal modernity is a "legitimate child" of the Enlightenment and in many ways "the
    highest expression of that tradition's rationalist and utilitarian ambitions" (Garland,
    forthcoming). In this paper, we will follow Garland (forthcoming) and adopt the
    broader perspective that sees an essential continuity between the Enlightenment and
    the present predicament as a working hypothesis. This hypothesis will be critically
    evaluated.

3   In a section of *Negative Dialectics* entitled "After Auschwitz," Adorno writes: "...it may
    have been wrong to say that after Auschwitz you could no longer write poems. But it
    is not wrong to raise the less cultural question whether after Auschwitz you can go
    on living..." (Adorno, 1973, 362–363). He who was spared "will be plagued by
    dreams such as that he is no longer living at all, that he was sent to the ovens in
    1944 and his whole existence since has been imaginary, an emanation of the insane
    wish of a man killed twenty years earlier." (Adorno, 1973, 363)

4   Examples of conflicting figures could be multiplied. When in June 1994 the
    Canadian federal government released its 1988–1993 victimization survey showing
    that there was no overall increase in crime, many police chiefs issued their own local
    crime statistics, which they claimed showed the contrary. In Toronto, Chief
    McCormack released his figures to *The Toronto Sun* (June 14, 1994) and the paper
    printed them in a first-page article under the title "It's Criminal! Cops Blast Fed
    Study That Claims Crime's Not Getting Worse." The remarks of Mr. Scott Newark,
    the general counsel for the Canadian Police Association, epitomize all the inconsis-
    tencies. Speaking on behalf of the Association, which supports the reinstatement of
    the death penalty, he declared that "murder rates have doubled since the death
    penalty was last used in 1962 and the number of murders have quadrupled" (*The
    Toronto Sun*, May 2, 1994). In one of many skirmishes with academics claiming that
    crime statistics showed that there was no reason to make the *Young Offenders Act*
    more punitive, Mr. Newark said that "statistics in many ways are the last refuge of
    socialists and losers" (*The Edmonton Journal*, June 18, 1994).

5   After formulating the question of alternatives to incarceration, Foucault immediately
    declared: "So I believe that with regard to this question of alternatives to prison, we
    must react with a first scruple, a first doubt or with a first laugh, as you may wish;
    what if we did not want to be punished by those people? Or for the reasons that they
    claim...what if we didn't want to be punished at all? What if, after all, we were not
    able to really know what punishing meant? Is this thing called punishment and
    which appeared obvious to Western civilization for centuries and perhaps for millen-
    niums, is this very notion of punishment now appearing to us as obvious as all that?
    What does it mean to be punished? Must we really be punished?" (Foucault, 1993,
    14; my translation).

6   For example, the important studies by Pease (1985) and McDonald (1986) are not
    mentioned. Also, McMahon concludes her review of the US research: "In sum,
    knowledge of prison and penal trends in the United States continues to be rudimen-
    tary" (McMahon, 1992, 71). I know of no country about which such an assertion
    could not be made.

7   Landreville (1994) has shown that the use of compensatory work programs in lieu of imprisonment for defaulting on a fine has succeeded in reducing by 45 percent the number of prison admissions for fine default in the province of Quebec. Yet, since incarceration for fine defaults does not account for more than 5 percent of the Quebec provincial prison population, this 45-percent decrease in admissions only translates into a less than 3-percent decrease in the size of the prison population.

8   The Clinton administration *Crime Bill* of 1994 has a provision for the recruitment of one hundred thousand police. However, the money to pay for this increase in police personnel is only provided for five years. Numerous critics of this legislation have pointed out that it might be overwhelmingly difficult to find the necessary funds after this initial period.

9   After it was publicly revealed that the province of Ontario had dropped the charges against forty thousand defendants, there was such an uproar that provincial governments stopped publishing the figures. Needless to say, most of these defendants were accused of minor violations. Yet there was a significant number of felony charges that went into the wash. The figure of seventy thousand that we have given is a low approximation of the number of charges dropped across Canada.

10   This is not an argument in favour of jailing more sex offenders. What is claimed is that the idea of using incarceration to protect women and children from sex abuse is absurd with regard to the capacity of the prison system.

11   In his 1994 lecture at the University of Toronto Law faculty, Heyman confirmed that point in answer to my question.

12   Such a position seems on first examination arguable with regard to race, ethnicity, and even social class. However, it is far from obvious with regard to gender. Should we amend our criminal legislation on the basis that it massively applies to men in a particular age group rather than to women, and how should we amend it in order to avoid this disparity?

13   The only practice we know of is what is called "saturation patrol," which is effected in high-crime-density zones and particularly in ethnic ghettos. These urban areas are swamped for periods of time by police cruisers. This tactic usually produces short-term crime displacement. Its generalization would be unpalatable to a democratic society.

REFERENCES

Adorno, Th. W.   1973. *Negative Dialectics*. Translated by E. B. Ashton. New York: The Seabury Press.

Allen, F.   1981. *The Decline of the Rehabilitative Idea*. New Haven: Yale University Press.

Baudrillard, J.   1981. *Simulacres et Simulation*. Paris: Galilée.

Bauman, Z.   1989. *Modernity and the Holocaust*. Ithaca, NY: Cornell University Press.

———.   1987. *Legislators and Interpreters: On Modernity, Post-Modernity and Intellectuals*. Ithaca, NY: Cornell University Press.

Bottoms, A. E. 1983. "Some Neglected Features of Contemporary Penal Systems." In *The Power to Punish,* ed. by D. Garland and P. Young, 166–216. London: Heinemann.

Brodeur, J.-P. Forthcoming. "Contrôle social et dispersion," *Dévian et Société* .

———. 1990. *Computers and the Law: UBC Sentencing Database, Final Report.* Ottawa: Department of Justice.

Canada. Canadian Sentencing Commission. 1987. *Sentencing Reform: A Canadian Approach.* Ottawa: Minister of Supply and Services.

Chan J., and **R. V. Ericson.** 1981. *Decarceration and the Economy of Penal Reform.* Toronto: Centre of Criminology, University of Toronto.

Christie, Nils. 1992. *Crime Control as Industry.* Oxford: Oxford University Press.

———. 1982. *Limits to Pain.* Oxford: Martin Robinson.

Cohen, S. 1984. *Visions of Social Control.* Cambridge: Polity.

Cunningham, W. C. and **T. Taylor.** 1985. *Private Security and Police in America*: *The Hallcrest Report.* Portland: Chancellor Press.

———**, J. J. Strauchs,** and **P. Van Meter.** 1990. *Private Security Trends, 1970 to 2,000: The Hallcrest Report II.* Toronto: Butterworth.

Deflem, M. 1994. "La notion de droit dans la théorie de l'agir communicationnel de Jürgen Habermas," *Déviance et Société,* 18(1): 95–120.

Derrida, J. 1972. *La dissémination.* Paris: Seuil.

Dillon, J. A. 1983. *Foundations of General Systems Theory.* Seaside, Calif.: Intersystems Pub.

Doob, A. N. Forthcoming. "The United States Sentencing Guidelines: If You Don't Know Where You Are Going, You May Not Get There." *In Sentencing Reform Across National Boundaries,* ed. by R. Morgan and C. Clarkson.

———. 1994. "Sentencing Reform in Canada," *The Overcrowded Times,* 4(5): 1, 11–13.

Ericson, R. V., and **K. D. Carriere.** Forthcoming. "The Fragmentation of Criminology." In *The Futures of Criminology,* ed. by D. Nelken.

Feeley, M. M., and **J. Simon.** 1992. "The New Penology: Notes on the Emerging of Corrections and Its Implications," *Criminology,* 30(4): 449–474.

Foucault, M. 1975. *Surveiller et Punir.* Paris: Gallimard.

3/M. 1969. *L'archéologie du savoir.* Paris: Gallimard.

Garland, D. Forthcoming. "Penal Modernism and Postmodernism." In *Law, Punishment and Social Control,* ed. by T. Blomberg and S. Cohen.

———. 1990. *Punishment and Welfare: A Study in Social Theory.* Chicago: The University of Chicago Press.

———. 1985. *Punishment and Welfare.* Croft Road, Aldershot: Gower.

Giddens, A.   1990. *The Consequences of Modernity*. Cambridge: Polity Press.

Goldsmith, A., ed.   1991. *Complaints Against the Police: The Trend to External Review.* Oxford: Oxford University Press.

Goldstein, H.   1990. *Problem-Oriented Policing*. Philadelphia: Temple University Press.

Gordon, D. R.   1991. *The Justice Juggernaut: Fighting Street Crime, Controlling Citizens*. New Brunswick, N.J.: Rutgers University Press.

Habermas, J.   1973. *Legitimation Crisis*. Boston: Beacon Press.

Harvey, D.   1990. *The Condition of Postmodernity: An Inquiry Into the Origins of Cultural Change*. Oxford: Blackwell.

Henry, S., and **D. Milovanovic.**   1993. "Back to Basics: A Postmodern Redefinition of Crime," *The Critical Criminologist*, 5(1–2): 12.

Hudson, B.   1993. "Penal Policy and Racial Justice." In *Minority Ethnic Groups and the Criminal Justice System*, ed. by L. Gelsthorpe and W. McWilliam. Cambridge: Cambridge University Institute of Criminology.

Hulsman, L. H. S.   1986. "Critical Criminology and the Concept of Crime," *Contemporary Crises*, 10(1): 63–80.

———, et **J. Bernat de Celis.**   1982. *Peines perdues*. Paris: Éditions Le Centurion.

Hylton, J.   1981. *Reintegrating the Offender: Assessing the Impact of Community Corrections*. Lanham, MD: University Press of America.

Jencks, C.   1987. *Post-Modernism: The New Classicism in Art and Architecture*. New York: Rizzoii International Pub.

Johnstone, L.   1992. *The Rebirth of Private Policing*. New York: Routledge.

Landreville, P.   1994. "Compensatory Work Programme: A Way of Limiting Prison Use? The Québec Experience," *The Howard Journal of Criminal Justice*, 33(3): 236–246.

Luhman, N.   1988. "The Unity of the Legal System." In *Autopoietic Law: A New Approach to Law and Society*, ed. by G. Teubner, 12–35. Berlin: Walter de Gruyter.

———.   1983. *Legitimation durch Verfahren*. Frankfurt: Suhrkamp.

Lustgarten, L.   1986. *The Governance of the Police*. London: Sweet and Maxwell.

Lyotard, J.-F.   1988. *Le Postmoderne expliqué aux enfants*. Paris: Galilée.

———.   1979. *La condition Post-Moderne: Rapport sur le Savoir*. Paris: Les Éditions de Minuit.

MacKenzie, D. L.   1994. "Boot Camps: A National Assessment," *Overcrowded Times*, 5(4): 1, 14–18.

Marcus, G. E., ed.   1993. *Perilous States*. Chicago: University of Chicago Press.

Mathiesen, T.   1974. *The Politics of Abolition*. London: Martin Robinson.

McDonald, D.C.   1992. "Private Penal Institutions." In *Crime and Justice: An Annual Review of Research*, ed. by M. Tonry, 16: 361–419. Chicago: University of Chicago Press.

————. 1986. *Punishment Without Walls.* New Brunswick, NJ: Rutgers University Press.

McMahon, M. W. 1992. *The Persistent Prison: Rethinking Decarceration and Penal Reform.* Toronto: University of Toronto Press.

Melossi, D., and M. Pavarini. 1981. *The Prison and the Factory: Origins of the Penitentiary System.* London: Macmillan.

Mills, C. Wright. 1959. *The Sociological Imagination.* New York: Oxford University Press.

Milovanovic, D., and S. Henry. 1992. "Toward a New Penology: Constitutive Penology," *Social Justice,* 18(3): 204–224.

Morgan, R. 1994a. "Imprisonment." In *The Oxford Handbook of Criminology,* ed. by M. Maguire, R. Morgan, and R. Reiner, 889–948. Oxford: Clarendon Press.

————. 1994b. "Punitive Policies and Politics Crowding English Prisons," *Overcrowded Times,* 5(3): 1–2, 9–10.

Morris, N., and M. Tonry. 1990. *Between Prison and Probation: Intermediate Punishments in a Rational Sentencing System.* New York: Oxford University Press.

Ontario. Ministry of the Solicitor General. 1989. *The Report of the Race Relations and Policing Task Force.* Toronto.

Pannwitz, R. 1917. *Die Krisis des Europäischen Kultur.* Werke, Band 2, Nürnburg.

Pease, K. 1990. *Criminal Justice Systems in Europe and North America.* Helsinki: Helsinki Inst. for Crime Prevention and Control.

Petersilia, J. 1987. *Expanding Options for Criminal Sentencing.* Santa Monica, Calif.: Rand.

Québec. Commission des droits de la personne. 1988. *Rapport du Comité d'Enquête sur les Relations entre les Corps Policiers et les Minorités Ethniques et Visibles.* Montréal.

3/M. Ministère de la Sécurité publique. 1994a. *Rapport sur l'émeute de la Coupe Stanley, Montréal, 1993,* enquête dirigée par le juge à la retraite Albert F. Malouf. Québec.

————. **Ministère de la Sécurité publique.** 1994b. *Rapport sur l'Inspection du Service de Police de la Communauté Urbaine de Montréal.* Québec.

R. v. Askov (1990) 2 S.C.R. at 1199.

Radzinowicz, Sir L. 1990. "Penal Regressions," *The Cambridge Law Journal,* 50(930): 422–444.

Reiner, R. 1994. "Policing and the Police." In *The Oxford Handbook of Criminology,* ed. by M. Maguire, R. Morgan, and R. Reiner, 705–772. Oxford: Clarendon Press.

————. 1992a. "Policing a Post-Modern Society," *Modern Law Review.* 55(6): 761–781.

————. 1992b. *The Politics of the Police.* 2d ed. Toronto: University of Toronto Press.

Robert, P. 1989. "The Privatization of Social Control." In *Crime and Criminal Policy in Europe: Proceedings of a European Colloquium,* ed. by Roger Hood, 104–120. Oxford: Centre for Criminological Research, University of Oxford.

Rose, M. A. 1991. *The Post-modern and the Post-industrial: A Critical Analysis*. New York: Cambridge University Press.

Rosenau, P. M. 1992. *Post-Modernism and the Social Sciences*. Princeton, NJ: Princeton University Press.

Rothman, D. J. 1980. *Conscience and Convenience: The Asylum and Its Alternatives in Progressive America*. Glenview, Ill.: Scott, Foresman and Co.

Saleilles, R. 1898. *L'individualisation de la peine*. Paris: Librairie Félix Alcan.

Schwartz, M. D. and **D. O. Friedrichs.** 1994. "Postmodern Thought and Criminological Discontent: New Metaphors for Understanding Violence," *Criminology*, 32(2): 221–246.

Simon, J. 1993a. "From Confinement to Waste Management: The Postmodernization of Social Control," *Focus on Law Studies*, 8(4): 6–7.

———. 1993b. *Poor Discipline: Parole and the Social Control of the Underclass, 1890–1990*. Chicago: University of Chicago Press.

Skogan, W. G. Forthcoming. *Comparisons in Policing: An International Perspective.*

———. 1989. "Social Change and the Future of Violent Crime." In *Violence in America, Volume 1: The History of Crime*, ed. by T. R. Gurr, 235–250. Newbury Park, Calif.: Sage.

Smith, D. J. 1994. "Race, Crime and Criminal Justice." In *The Oxford Handbook of Criminology*, ed. by M. Maguire, R. Morgan, and R. Reiner, 1041–1117. Oxford: Clarendon Press.

Teubner, G. 1989. "How the Law Thinks: Toward a Constructivist Epistemology of Law," *Law and Society Review*, 23(5): 727–757.

———, ed. 1988. *Autopoietic Law: A New Approach to Law and Society*. Berlin: Walter de Gruyter.

———, ed. 1987. *Juridification of Social Spheres: A Comparative Analysis in the Areas of Labor, Corporate, Antitrust and Social Welfare Law*. Berlin: Walter de Gruyter.

Tonry, M. 1994. "Drug Policies Increasing Racial Disparities in U.S. Prisons," *Overcrowded Times*, 5(3): 1, 11–14.

———. 1993. "General Barr's Last Stand," *Overcrowded Times*, 4(1): 2–3.

———. 1988. "Structuring Sentencing." In *Crime and Justice: A Review of Research*, Vol. 10, ed. by M. Tonry and N. Morris, 267–337. Chicago: University of Chicago Press.

United States. Department of Justice. 1994. *Prisoners in 1993*. Washington, DC: GPO.

———. 1990. *Prisoners in 1989*. Washington DC: GPO

———. 1989. *Correctional Populations in the United States, 1988*. Washington, DC: GPO.

———. 1972. *Private Police in the United States: The Rand Report*, J. S. Kakalik and S. Wildhorn. Washington.

United States. The President's Commission on Law Enforcement and Administration of Justice. 1967. *Task Force Report: The Courts*. Chairman, Nicholas de B. Katzenbach. Washington, DC: GPO.

Von Bertalanffy, L. 1975. *Perspectives in General Systems Theory: Scientific-philosophical Studies*. Edited by P. Taschdjian. New York: G. Brazilier.

Von Hirsch, A. 1982. "Constructing Guidelines for Sentencing: The Critical Choices for the Minnesota Sentencing Guidelines Commission," *Hamline Law Review*, 5: 164–215.

————, **K. A. Knapp** and **M. Tonry.** 1987. *The Sentencing Commission and Its Guidelines*. Boston: NorthEastern University Press.

Wall Street Journal. 1991. "U.S. Incarceration Rate Highest in the World," January 7, 1991, B5.

Watzlawick, J., J. Helmick-Beavin, and **D. Jackson.** 1967. *Pragmatics of Human Communication: A Study of Interactional Patterns, Pathologies, and Paradoxes*. New York: Northorn.

Weber, Max. 1954. *Max Weber on Law in Economy and Society*. Edited by Max Rheinstein,. Translated by Edward Shils and Max Rheinstein. Cambridge, Mass.: Harvard University Press.

Welsch, W. 1988. "`Postmoderne'. Genealogie und Bedeutung eines umstrittenen Begriffs." In *"Postmoderne" oder Der Kampf um die Zukunft*, ed. by P. Kemper, 9–36. Frankfurt am Main, Fisher Taschenbuch Verlag.

Wicker, T. 1991. "The Iron Medal," *New York Times*, January 9, 1991, A21.

Williams, H. and **P. V. Murphy.** 1990. "The Evolving Strategy of Police: A Minority View," in *Perspectives on Policing*. Washington, DC: National Institute of Justice, US Department of Justice. Cambridge, Mass.: John F. Kennedy School of Government, Harvard University.

Wittgenstein, L. 1953. *Philosophical Investigations*. Translated by G. E. M. Anscombe. New York: Macmillan.

EXPLAINING LAW AND COLONIALISM: TOWARD AN AMERINDIAN AUTOHISTORICAL PERSPECTIVE ON LEGAL CHANGE, COLONIZATION, GENDER, AND RESISTANCE

Russell Smandych and Gloria Lee

INTRODUCTION

This chapter is part of a larger work on the transformation of dominant mechanisms of legal ordering and social control in western Canada from 1670 to 1870.[1] One of the goals of this research is to make use of the wealth of primary historical data on private justice and social control contained in the archives of the Hudson's Bay Company.[2] In 1670, a royal charter granted by the English monarchy gave the Hudson's Bay Company the exclusive right to rule over an area that encompasses most of what is now the western part of Canada. As part of its original charter, the Hudson's Bay Company was given the power to enact any laws and regulations not repugnant to the laws of England that were deemed necessary to govern its relations with its servants and to maintain social order in the territory of Rupertsland.[3] In 1821, the company was granted a licence to extend its trade monopoly and legal authority to encompass the territory referred to as "Indian country," which included all of the land beyond Rupertsland where rivers drained into the Pacific and Arctic oceans (Foster,

1990).[4] In effect, the Charter of 1670, along with later enabling legislation, gave the board of governors of the Hudson's Bay Company the authority to govern a territory that covered approximately 5 percent of the land surface of the earth (Smandych and Linden, 1995).

Although the history of the Hudson's Bay Company is known to many Canadians and the company is recognized for the important role it played in the early postcontact history of western Canada, we know very little about the role played by the company in lawmaking and as an instrument of European colonization. During the early years following 1670, the board of governors of the company based in London established the legal foundation for a self-governing chartered trading company complete with its own private justice system and complex arrangement of related mechanisms of social control. The arrival of the Hudson's Bay Company in western Canada also marked the beginning of European economic and cultural intrusion into a territory that had for many centuries been populated by aboriginal people who had their own complex set of cultural and social institutions, including customary laws and traditional methods of dispute resolution and social control. The early servants of the company, sent to establish the first fur-trade posts along the coast of Hudson's Bay, brought with them orders from the London Committee on how they were to carry out the fur trade and conduct their relations with the different bands of Indians with whom they hoped to do business. Over the next two hundred years, to 1870, the Hudson's Bay Company remained a dominant presence in western Canada. Throughout this period, its employees remained key actors in determining the outcome of the initial contact between European and aboriginal peoples in the Canadian West.

In other papers we have looked in detail at the development of Hudson's Bay Company law and the way it was applied to aboriginal peoples (Smandych and Lee, 1994; Smandych and Linden, 1995), and at the private justice system created by the company to deal with disobedient company servants (Smandych and Linden, 1994). In this chapter, we outline the theoretical perspective that we are using to guide our work on law and colonialism in the Canadian West. Although developed specifically as a heuristic tool for defining the theoretical boundaries of our own research, we believe that the theoretical perspective we have developed may be of general interest to other researchers undertaking research on the history of law and social control in colonial societies. The theoretical perspective that we propose in this chapter is grounded in theoretical and empirical work from a number of different fields, including the history and sociology of social control, the study of legal pluralism, and the study of the process of colonization as it has been approached in recent years by specific feminist scholars and First Nations historians.

The chapter begins with an overview of studies of legal pluralism and social control that have generated the basic theoretical questions that we are addressing in our research. This is followed by a discussion of a number of recent studies that have looked at the impact of European colonization and the fur trade on

North American Amerindians. In particular, we look at the recent work completed in this area by feminist and First Nations historians, which suggests the need for developing a more explicit Amerindian autohistorical perspective for approaching the study of law and colonialism. Drawing critically on work of these authors, we outline what we consider to be the key elements of a more explicit Amerindian autohistorical perspective, and discuss how this new perspective can be used to help generate research on the interconnected issues of legal change, colonization, gender, and resistance.

STUDIES OF LEGAL PLURALISM AND SOCIAL CONTROL

Recent years have seen the development of a growing literature in the field of the sociology of "social control" (cf. Cohen and Scull, 1983; Garland and Young, 1983; Lowman, Menzies, and Palys, 1987). The growth of this new subfield of criminology, which has been mainly the product of the work of sociologists, has occurred during the same years that the study of "legal pluralism" has become an increasing concern to a more diverse collection of academics, including sociologists, anthropologists, legal scholars, and historians (Merry, 1988; 1991). Although on the surface these two fields appear rather isolated and unconnected, one can find a number of studies that display a considerable amount of overlap in the theoretical and empirical questions addressed by sociologists of social control and students of legal pluralism (Black, 1990; Ellickson, 1991; Fitzpatrick, 1983a, 1983b; Henry, 1983, 1987a, 1987b, 1994; Merry, 1990; O'Malley, 1987; Santos, 1987). The following section provides an overview of the studies that have led to the basic theoretical questions raised in this chapter.

Sociologists of social control have raised a number of important theoretical and conceptual questions that have yet to be fully addressed in empirical research: How can "social control" be defined conceptually? What is the precise nature of the relationship between law and other forms of social control? How do different "state" and "nonstate" institutions and agencies of social control work together to create and maintain social order? How can we explain changes in the dominant character of legal punishment and social control? In our research, we pursue this line of questioning by building on the work of authors such as Donald Black (1976, 1984, 1990), Stanley Cohen (1985, 1989), Michel Foucault (1977), David Garland (1985, 1990, 1991), and Stuart Henry (1983, 1987a, 1987b), as well as on the first author's earlier historical work on the changing character of dominant mechanisms of social control in nineteenth-century Upper Canada (Smandych, 1989, 1991a, 1991b, 1995).

A related theoretical point of departure for our research is the growing literature on "legal pluralism." Specifically, our work begins from a combined theoretical interest in traditional studies of "classical legal pluralism," and the more recent theoretically challenging "new legal pluralism" literature (Merry, 1988). As described by Merry (1988), studies that fall under the rubric of classical legal pluralism have for the most part been concerned with describing and explaining how new (usually European) legal systems and laws (brought by colonizers) are superimposed on indigenous customary laws and preexisting methods of dispute settlement and social control. According to Merry (1988, 873), the new legal pluralism, exemplified in the work of such authors as Stuart Henry (1983), Bonaventura De Sousa Santos (1987), and Peter Fitzpatrick (1983b), "moves away from questions about the effect of law on society or even the effect of society on law toward conceptualizing a more complex and interactive relationship between official and unofficial forms of ordering." Some of the key concepts coined by researchers who have led in the development of the new legal pluralism include the notions of "interlegality," "plural legal orders," and "private justice." Collectively, these concepts are now being used by leading proponents of the new legal pluralism to study the many different and complex ways in which state and nonstate forms of legal ordering and social control coexist and interact with one another to produce social order.[5] According to Santos (1987, 297–99), the concept of legal pluralism is "the key concept in a postmodern view of law," because it requires that we shift our priorities from "engaging exclusively in the critique of the existing state legality," to also attempting to "uncover the (more) latent or suppressed forms of legality in which more insidious and damaging forms of social and personal oppression frequently occur."[6]

Although a more detailed discussion of the work of proponents of the new legal pluralism is not required here, it is important to consider the findings of studies that have looked at how law has been used as a tool of colonization. In particular, it is important to look at the general findings that have emerged out of studies that have made an effort to explain how historically and in different geographical settings indigenous peoples have tried to cope with attempts that were made to impose external systems of law.

Over the past twenty years, research on the role of law as an instrument of European colonialism has become more theoretically sophisticated. This increased theoretical awareness has led researchers to give closer attention to nuances in historical data. The direction taken by these developments is reflected in the different themes and new research questions that have surfaced in the law and colonialism literature during the period. As Merry (1988, 1991) and other reviewers (Greenberg, 1980, 139; Snyder and Hay, 1987) have pointed out, one of the focuses of early research concerned imperial domination and its relationship to law. Many of the early studies on the law and colonialism completed in the 1960s and 1970s "demonstrated the power of the state to reshape the social order, suggesting the dominance of this form of law over other normative orders" (Merry, 1988, 879). In addition to showing how externally imposed state law often served as an effective and powerful tool for controlling colonial populations (cf. Kennedy, 1989), some researchers attempted to show how European colonizers sought to exert control over indigenous populations through co-opting local elites and undertaking efforts to formalize preexisting customary methods of dispute settlement and social control (cf. Snyder, 1981;

Gordon, 1989). In particular, a number of researchers carrying out historical research on different colonial settings were able to show that, rather than having existed previously on its own, "the creation of customary law...was an ongoing, collaborative process in which power was clearly unequal, but subordinate groups were hardly passive or powerless" (Merry, 1988, 880).

By the late 1970s, students of classical legal pluralism were more frequently beginning to recognize that indigenous peoples were not simply the passive recipients of externally imposed law (Kidder, 1979). Increasingly in the 1980s, attention shifted from studies of the deceptive and coercive imposition of European law to questions about the manner in which indigenous peoples resisted and accommodated such laws. Since the mid-1980s, the study of "forms of resistance, including both overt and covert resistance" have become a central topic in research on law and colonialism (Snyder and Hay, 1987, 24). Although more recent researchers have not necessarily turned away from looking at how colonizers have attempted to dominate indigenous populations through ideological manipulation and direct coercion (Gordon, 1989; Kennedy, 1989), more attention is now being given to examining "the way nonstate normative orders resist and circumvent penetration or even capture and use the symbolic capital of state law" (Merry, 1988, 881).

Several examples of research that has pursued the theme of resistance to European colonial domination could be elaborated on in this review. The work of Peter Fitzpatrick (1987, 1989) on "Crime as Resistance: The Colonial Situation," and Mike Brogden (1990) on "Law and Criminal Labels: The Case of the French Métis in Western Canada" are two relevant examples. Also, one could look at studies that have pursued this theme in the often richly detailed historical literature that has attempted to assess the impact of European contact on specific indigenous populations in different countries. For example, in her review of the writing of academic historians on the consequences of European contact for the Aborigines of Australia, Attwood (1990) notes a pattern of shifting research themes that parallels those found in the more general classical legal pluralism literature. Themes ranged from studies published in the 1960s and 1970s on "the destructive impact of European capitalism and racism on traditional Aboriginal society" (1990, 121) to more recent studies concerned with providing more historically nuanced accounts of different types of *relations* and *reciprocal obligations* that developed between Europeans and Aborigines, and the various kinds of *creative strategies* used by Aborigines to deal with European colonizers (125–28).[7]

Recent studies of law and colonialism in Africa (Snyder and Hay, 1987), Australia (Attwood, 1990), and elsewhere (Merry, 1991) draw attention to the types of questions that need to be addressed in order to develop an understanding of the complex social processes and specific historical circumstances involved in determining the outcome of the imposition of one type of legal system on another already existing system of dispute settlement and social control. These studies also illustrate how significantly varied the experiences of different groups of indigenous peoples have been in different parts of the world. The findings of this comparative historical research, and the various explanations offered by different authors to account for their findings, highlight further questions that need to be addressed in the study of law and colonialism in the Canadian West. One of the questions that obviously needs to be addressed is the extent to which the indigenous peoples of western Canada resisted being dominated by servants of the Hudson's Bay Company and other early European colonizers.

Another important new theme reflected in the law and colonialism literature is the importance of gender and gender relations in shaping the outcome of the early contacts between European colonizers and indigenous peoples. Significantly, in the same way that several feminist historians have shown was the case in the history of early postcontact western Canada (Brown, 1980; Van Kirk, 1980), Attwood (1990, 126) points out, through her review of the work of Ann McGrath (1987), that "gender played a fundamental role" in affecting the nature and outcome of the early relations that developed between Europeans and Australian Aborigines.[8] Since the early 1980s, feminist scholars, including sociologists, anthropologists, and historians, have begun to develop a much more nuanced picture of both the role played by aboriginal women in the process of European colonization, and of the impact this process had on gender relations among indigenous peoples (Leacock, 1978, 1980; Van Kirk, 1987; Anderson, 1991; Bonvillian, 1989; Bourgeault, 1988, 1989; Devens, 1992; Emberley, 1993; Foster, 1993). In the following section we look at the most important themes and issues that have been raised in recent North American literature on aboriginal women and colonization. As we will see, one of the most significant trends in this literature is the movement reflected among authors toward recognizing the need for adopting an Amerindian autohistorical perspective (cf. Sioui, 1992). We argue that adopting this perspective in a more explicit manner can help us better understand how Amerindian people themselves may have interpreted the historical events of which they were a part.

WOMEN, COLONIZATION, AND RESISTANCE: TOWARD AN AUTOHISTORICAL APPROACH

The attempt to understand how the people of North American First Nations reacted to European colonization has been part of the approach taken in recent decades by sociohistorians and historical anthropologists who have been commonly referred to as "ethnohistorians" (cf. Axtell, 1992; Calloway, 1987, 1991; Delâge, 1993; Jaenen, 1976; Jennings, 1975; Trigger, 1976, 1985). However, thus far, ethnohistorians have avoided the attempt to explicate a specific theoretical approach that can be used as a heuristic device for approaching the study of the ways in which Amerindian people viewed and responded to the process of European colonization. In this chapter, we propose a specific theoretical framework for approaching the study of law and colonialism in the Canadian context.

The essential elements of the autohistorical perspective we propose can be captured in the form of a diagram (see Fig. 17.1).

The approach we illustrate in this diagram builds on the work of a number of authors who have independently drawn attention to the need for abandoning the Eurocentric approach that conventional historians have taken to investigating Amerindian history. In the following brief discussion of their work we try to accurately represent the ideas and insights offered by these authors and show how they contribute elements of this approach. At the outset, however, the reader needs to be aware that in the following discussion we do not make an effort to compartmentalize and discuss separately each of the key concepts included in our illustrative diagram. Nor do we attempt to sketch out an assumed causal order, or a set of postulated cause-and-effect relationships that one might otherwise look for to link these concepts. This explains the absence of arrows or symbols connecting the key concepts in our diagram, as well as the open circle at the centre of our diagram. As we will see shortly, the rationale for these decisions resides in the underlying logic of the Amerindian autohistorical approach. The view of social and spiritual life shared by Amerindian people is one in which all forms of human interaction are necessarily recursive and have reciprocal effects.

FIGURE 17.1: **Essential Elements of an Amerindian Autohistorical Perspective for the Study of Law and Colonialism**

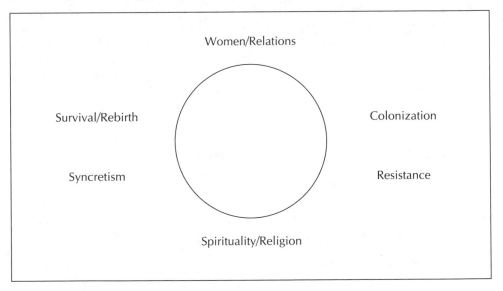

The need for proposing an explicit autohistorical approach was recognized by the authors from our reading of Georges Sioui's recent book, *For an Amerindian Autohistory: An Essay on the Foundations of a Social Ethic* (1992). Sioui calls for an explicit acknowledgment of the fact that the unfolding postcontact history of North America was viewed differently by Amerindian people than it was by European colonizers. Moreover, Sioui argues that regardless of whether historians are of European or aboriginal descent they will never be able to accurately capture the meaning of historical events unless they try to view them as Amerindian people likely tried to interpret them. According to Sioui (1992, 37), "[t]he goal of Amerindian autohistory is to assist history in its duty to repair the damage it has traditionally caused to the integrity of Amerindian cultures."

In his book, Sioui explains "the system of values proper to Native American societies" and attempts to show "the value systems of Amerindians are superior to and more viable than those of Euroamericans." At the centre of this shared set of values of Amerindian people is the idea of the "sacred circle of life" as "opposed to the evolutionist concept of the world" (1992, xi, xxi). Contrary to the depiction of the unfolding of postcontact North American history by Eurocentric historians as a "European takeover," Sioui argues that what occurred in the decades and centuries following first contact was the reverse process of the " `Americanization of the world,' whereby the essence of original American thought [was] communicated to other continents" (1992, xxii–xxiii). In the chapter of his book on "The Sacred Circle of Life," Sioui highlights the pivotal role played by *women* in "gynocentric" Amerindian societies like those of the Iroquois and the Huron. Specifically, Sioui notes:

> deference towards the women reflects the recognition, in matricentric societies, of a human brotherhood vested in the Earth-Mother, source of respect for personal vision in those societies. Non-Native writers still frequently do not perceive this fundamental cultural difference. Instead, they tend to insist on depicting Amerindian societies, especially hunting societies, as being governed by the naturally more imposing men, whereas the reality is quite different...

> The "high status" of Amerindian women is not, as some authors have declared, "the result of their control over the tribe's economic organization." The matricentric thought in these societies springs from the Amerindian's acute awareness of the genius proper to women, which is to instil into man, whom she educates, the social and human virtues he must know to help maintain the relations that are the essence of existence and life. (1992, 17–18)

In another recent work that looks at Amerindian history from a similar perspective, Ronald Wright (1992) uses the term "syncretism" to capture something of the above idea advanced by Sioui. In his study *Stolen Continents: The "New World" Through Indian Eyes*, Wright (1992, 150) defines syncretism as "the growing together of new beliefs and old...[as] a way of encoding the values of a conquered culture within a dominant culture." Used as a heuristic concept, syncretism provides a more explicit way to refer to the many different types of exchange-based reciprocal relations that grew between Europeans and Amerindians in the postcontact period.[9]

In the context of historical research on law and colonialism, the notion of syncretism can be applied to both *gender relations* and the reverse assimilation of ideas about law and justice. First, with regard to ideas about law and justice, Merry (1991), in her critique of law and colonialism literature, points out it is also important to ask questions about how the contact with indigenous peoples affected the thinking and behaviour of the colonizers. Specifically, she (1991, 55) suggests we ask: Who were the people who brought and imposed new conceptions of law and what were their concepts of law?; What effects did their earlier experiences have on the way they treated colonized peoples?; How did their encounter with the legal system of an indigenous people affect their ideas of their own law, their identities, and their sense of entitlement and cultural supremacy?

Any theoretical perspective that attempts to encompass a concern for explaining aspects of the relationship linking law, colonialism, and gender relations in postcontact Amerindian societies must address the issues raised in the recent work of feminist ethnohistorians. One question that has caused much discussion and debate in recent years is the question of the extent to which precontact Amerindian societies were egalitarian societies. In the following discussion, we identify and outline the different views that have been expressed about whether, and to what extent, precontact societies were more egalitarian than the one we live in today. We believe that this reflection on the literature is important because all researchers interested in investigating aspects of the history of law, colonialism, and gender relations in the Canadian historical context must identify the specific model of precontact Amerindian society that they believe existed prior to the colonization process. An understanding of gender relations and the respective roles accorded to women and men in precontact Amerindian societies is an indispensable starting point of any analysis of the later impact of colonialism on Amerindian societies.[10] In turn, we also need to look at the role played by Amerindian women in shaping the character of Amerindian-European relations in the early postcontact period.

There is a great deal of evidence supporting the view that Amerindian women played a central role in shaping the outcome of the early contact between Europeans and Amerindians in what is now the eastern part of Canada and the northeastern United States. In addition, evidence about the way in which Amerindian women influenced and altered the ideas that European male colonizers had about gender and gender relations is contained in several recent studies that have been completed by feminist scholars and First Nations historians. As we will see shortly, the work of these more recent investigators reflects a movement toward recognizing the need for approaching the study of women and colonization from a more explicitly-stated non-Eurocentric Amerindian autohistorical perspective.

In her widely-acclaimed recent work, Olive Dickason (1992) offers a corrective to the traditional Eurocentric approach taken by conventional historians. Although Dickason does not use the term "autohistorical perspective" to summarize the nature of her historical approach, it is clear from her book, *Canada's First Nations,* that she tries to interpret North American history as it was more likely seen through the eyes of Amerindian people. In her discussion of the role of women in the postcontact period, Dickason argues that "women played a pivotal role in both trade and Amerindian society generally" (1992, 43). Significantly, Dickason points out that from the earliest period of French settlement in Quebec, "the official idea was that [the men] would intermarry with the indigenous population, producing a French population overseas" (1992, 165).[11] Referring to the role played by Amerindian women in later years of the fur trade and western Canadian settlement, Dickason notes :

> In short, co-operation with Amerindians was necessary for Europeans to establish a viable colony, and when it came to selecting a mate, an Amerindian or, later, a Metis had obvious advantages over her European counterpart. Despite determined efforts from [the board of governors of the Hudson's Bay Company in] London to prevent it, this pattern of intermarriage was repeated among the English when they established themselves on Hudson Bay. (1992, 168)

Other recent work by feminist and First Nations scholars has added to the knowledge we have about the impact of colonization on gender relations. At the same time, most of these works fall short of providing the kind of Amerindian autohistorical approach we argue is needed as a methodology for reexamining the history of Amerindian responses to European colonization.

Karen Anderson's (1991) study of aboriginal women in New France in the seventeenth century provides one example of this. In her book on the subjugation of Huron and Montagnais women, Anderson uses variants of contemporary Marxist and feminist theory as the starting point for her analysis of how gender relations were transformed by Jesuit priests in the period from 1609 to 1649. In introducing her study, Anderson explains:

> One task will be to discern the basis on which differences between men and women were established in native society and which brought relations of power between women and men into play. This discussion will focus on the points of concern already identified by marxist and by feminist theory—production, reproduction, kinship and the formation of the psyche and emotional life. (1991, 8–9)

Anderson argues that at the time of first contact with Europeans, Amerindian women in general enjoyed greater freedom and power in their societies than did most European women who lived at that time. She maintains that although life was far from easy, women were not subjugated because gender roles were clearly defined and women and men had their own spheres of control.[12] What this meant in practice was that neither men nor women could do without each other, and it was likely the case that, if anything, women were recognized as being more powerful than men.[13]

Anderson acknowledges that her understanding of Huron and Montagnais history has been shaped in part by a critical reading of Eleanor Leacock's (1978, 1980) earlier influential work on the status of women in Amerindian societies. In her influential essay, Leacock (1978) set out to describe how the hierarchical structure we usually accept as given in modern society distorts the analysis of egalitarian social/economic structure and women's status in egalitarian societies.

Leacock's critique of the problems of interpretation created by a Eurocentric perspective has been used by most subsequent researchers as a starting point for examining the impact of colonization on gender relations in Amerindian societies. It has also been important in influencing feminist scholars to move closer toward adopting an Amerindian autohistorical perspective.

The influence of Leacock's (1978) work is also reflected in Carol Devens' (1992) study, *Countering Colonization: Native American Women and the Great Lakes Missions, 1630–1900*. In her study, Devens makes an explicit attempt to combine the themes of *gender* and *resistance*. Devens argues that aboriginal men were relatively easy to convert to Christianity because Christianity presented a way of adapting to the new economic situation they faced following the arrival of the European fur trade and Jesuit missionaries. On the other hand, Devens maintains that aboriginal women actively and persistently resisted the efforts made by missionaries to force the aboriginal peoples of the Great Lakes region to abandon their customary religious and social practices. Devens claims that aboriginal women rejected Christianity for the most part because it did not provide easement for them in society, but rather they saw Christianity as a tool that had the potential to destroy their families. For example, when daughters were taken to a mission school the mothers lost control of child rearing. Devens addresses this issue when she states:

> As men grew more receptive to introduced practices and values that they hoped would allow them to deal successfully with whites, women stood only to lose status and autonomy. Thus, whereas many men favored accommodation, women tended to stress "traditional" ways. (1992, 4)

However, Devens does much more in her book than simply claim that the egalitarian social structure of precontact Amerindian society began to break down under the pressure of Christianizing missionaries. While Devens accepts the premise that precontact Amerindian societies were more egalitarian, she also recognizes that women and men thought and responded differently to events that occurred in the world around them. Devens points out that the purpose of her study "is to consider how native communities perceived colonizers and how those perceptions influenced whether people presented a unified front or split into factions of accommodation and resistance" (1992, 3).[14] In addition to providing a more complex picture of the impact of colonialism on gender relations, Devens implicitly recognizes the need for adopting an Amerindian autohistorical perspective.

According to Devens, if we want to understand the status and role of women in Amerindian societies today, we have to look back at the way in which colonization affected aboriginal women. As males gradually moved from the old ways toward an acceptance of Christianity and education, women increasingly identified themselves, and were so identified by men, with traditional culture. In some ways this change protected women's status and interests, for the very separateness of the female world helped preserve it from the disintegration that often devastated the lives of men. Indeed, this separation became so pervasive that it effectively hid women's lives from observers (Devens, 1992, 119).

A crucial contribution made by Devens (1992) resides in her recognition of the possibility that current gender dichotomies and gender conflict in Amerindian societies may be one of the historical legacies of colonization.[15] Women are also seen as the ones who have had the power to struggle for the *survival* of traditional culture. Perhaps because colonization is male directed and male specific, women are inherently overlooked. In the practice of colonization, it may be the case that men are incorporated into the system while women are largely ignored except when it becomes obvious to the colonizers that they can not survive without the help of women. This might help explain why women are rarely mentioned in the historical records left by colonizers (like the Hudson's Bay Company records), and why, when they are mentioned, they are almost always described in relation to men. Indeed, this could explain why early historians of women and the fur trade, like Sylvia Van Kirk (1980) and Jennifer Brown (1980) focused on fur trade marriages and the families that resulted from these marriages. Thinking this problem through from an autohistorical perspective, the more important question that perhaps should have been asked was why did so *few* aboriginal women marry Europeans, or why did they resist so strongly compared to aboriginal men?[16]

What is important about Devens' (1992) analysis is that it points out that the perceptions and goals of men and women were very distinct from each other. Such a divergence in responses leads one to naturally speculate that men's and women's traditional lives were also very different. This speculation is also supported by our knowledge and use of the Amerindian autohistorical perspective, which reaffirms the view that while women in Amerindian societies possessed a great deal of power and personal freedom (Sioui, 1992, 15–18), they were also constrained by the roles that were assigned to them by their traditional culture. Thought of in Amerindian autohistorical terms, we could say that a culture is a reflection and product of the spiritual life and world views of the people who make up a society. There is nothing inherent in the Amerindian autohistorical perspective that says because precontact men and women were both Amerindian they could not have had their own gendered world views.

No detailed work comparable to Anderson's (1991) and Devens' (1992) work on gender and resistance has been done for western Canada. The closest to it are Ron Bourgeault's (1983, 1988, 1989) essays on issues of race and class in the fur-trade society of the Canadian West and the colonial domination of Indian women. Bourgeault also accepts Leacock's (1978) account of the nature of precontact gender relations, and applies a structurally based Marxist political economy perspective to explain the decline in the status of women after the arrival of the Hudson's Bay Company and the growth of the fur trade. However, in recent years both the validity and generalizability of Leacock's arguments about the egalitarian nature of precontact Amerindian societies have come under question.

One of the first historians to question Leacock's thesis was Sylvia Van Kirk. According to Van Kirk, the "study of the role of women in pre-contact native societies is a vital foundation for any historical study of native peoples' response to European contact" (1987, 1). Van Kirk questions the accuracy of Leacock's claim "that hunting and gathering societies such as the Montagnais-Naskapi were egalitarian because the women made an essential economic contribution to the survival of the band," and because they "had an important voice in the decision making process and enjoyed considerable autonomy in domestic and reproductive concerns" (1987, 2). She also questions Ron Bourgeault's "even more extravagant assessment of Chipewyan society where the idyllic nature of pre-contact sex roles was apparently destroyed by the fur trade" (Van Kirk, 1987). Van Kirk argues that "[a] feminist perspective demands that such statements be examined with caution and that the scholar guard against translating what are really relativistic claims into absolute ones" (1987). Van Kirk maintains that a more realistic feminist perspective on native history would begin with the premise that women were likely more equal to men in precontact societies, but only in relative terms compared to the European societies "which subsequently sought to impose their own patterns of sex roles and values on native societies" (1987, 2).

Most recently, Martha Foster (1993) has looked at the impact of colonization on gender and status among Hidatsa and Crow women. Foster raises the concern that "[v]ery few early observers noted differences in women's roles among tribes, and even fewer attempted to examine Native American society through the women's eyes" (1993, 121). Foster notes that the purpose of her paper is to explore problems inherent in the evaluation of Hidatsa and Crow women's roles and status. In particular, she maintains that "the importance of tradition, of the spiritual world, and of matrilineal kinship are often ignored or misunderstood by Western observers" (1993, 144).

At the most basic level, in her paper Foster sets out to display the shortcomings inherent in work of anthropologists and historians who have argued that the declining status of Hidatsa and Crow women in the nineteenth century resulted mainly from economic factors, including the fur trade and acquisition of the horse and gun. Foster calls this the "Great Plains Model" (or interpretation) of nineteenth-century Amerindian history. Foster notes that according to this "historical materialist framework," the decrease in women's status "manifested itself in an increased workload, increased polygyny, and loss of control over trade" (Foster, 1993, 121). In essence, proponents of the Great Plains Model argue that whereas the status of women was comparable to that of men prior to the integration of the horse and heavier reliance on the buffalo trade, this integration resulted in a relative decline in women's status.

Foster's (1993, 123) analysis indicates that this economic-determinist model does not apply to either Hidatsa or Crow nations and that it distorts the real nature of the roles and status of women in these societies. Foster points out that a major problem with this model is that it lacks supportive empirical evidence. She notes that while many of the early ethnographic accounts that have been used as evidence to support the model were "colorful and dramatic," they "seldom reported important day-to-day activities," and women and their activities were for the most part invisible in them.

Foster argues that many of the dualisms that we take for granted, like the "separation of the religious and the secular," and dichotomies "such as our interpretation of male/female or public/private, are Western creations and are not necessarily applicable to the Hidatsa and Crow" (1993, 126). She maintains that one of the consequences of this was that early "[t]raders and ethnologists misunderstood domestic power in Hidatsa and Crow society and assumed reproductive and domestic work to be demeaning." More specifically, Foster points out that "it is Western, male-dominated thought that views the domestic, nurturing role as restrictive, uncreative, and inferior. This Eurocentric view cannot be projected cross-culturally or assumed to be appropriate when applied to Hidatsa and Crow women" (1993, 140). It is clear from her analysis that Foster (1993) is also trying to work from an autohistorical perspective. This is reflected in particular in the emphasis she places on the need for us to understand the significance of Amerindian cultural values and *spirituality.*

The evidence brought forth by Foster to cast doubt on the Great Plains Model is too detailed to relate here. However, in essence, Foster (1993, 139) shows that when the historical data on Hidatsa and Crow women are examined against any of the four criteria that have been used for evaluating women's status—economic, political, religious, and personal freedom—there is little evidence "to justify the conclusion that `the status of women declined sharply.'" Although Foster does not offer any one explanation for why the status of Hidatsa and Crow women did not decline sharply, she does suggest that "symbolic/cultural theories" may be used to help explain "the ability of women to maintain equality in such societies as the Hidatsa and Crow." Significantly, Foster notes that

> Symbolic/cultural theories, while often used to explain continued male dominance, can explain the maintenance of women's positions in society, even after considerable economic change and cultural stress. When a strong ideology supports women's personal autonomy and their economic and religious positions, as in matrilineal societies such as the Crow, a model based primarily on economic factors is incomplete. Status is a product of a variety of factors. To suggest that one theory, whether it is economically, biologically, or psychologically determined, can answer all questions as to status is to miss the point of this complexity. (1993, 142–143)

The element of importance overlooked by other previous researchers, with the exception of Foster (1993), is the element of spirituality. If one is going to determine the reasons for the observed equality or inequality of women and men in native society, then one needs to understand the importance of native spiritual beliefs. The basic element of all Amerindian culture and societal structure is the spirituality of individuals and the collective spirituality of the society in general. The function of spirituality in Amerindian life was all-encompassing and provided the foundation for understanding. In a very fundamental way it taught relationships and respect. At the same time, spiritual beliefs also provided the basis for the differences found in Amerindian culture and relationships.

We may postulate that power within the culture and in individual relationships was balanced in a way that would help preserve social harmony. However, that is not to say that all things were equal. What we need to understand is that the power balance that existed in Amerindian societies was perceived from the standpoint of a different set of values than those that currently dominate Western society. We can also postulate that the power of women was understood to be very potent and was accepted as common knowledge.

With spirituality as the basis of knowledge the autohistorical perspective leads us to further hypothesize that relations of power between men and women existed along with checks and balances to regulate the distribution of power. In precontact society the balance of power between men and women and power relations were constantly changing and being challenged. It wasn't until the patriarchal side of the scales was tipped by European colonizers that the women were truly subjugated to a level they had never before experienced. This later subjugation was perpetuated because it came to be accepted as a means of survival by native men (cf. Anderson, 1991; Devens, 1992) and because it was enforced by European male colonizers. This understanding of the possible explanations that arise in attempting to explain the nature of gender relations in precontact Amerindian societies is needed as a background to any study we may try to undertake that looks at women, colonization, and resistance.

In any study of law and colonialism in the Canadian context, we must consider the cultural values and beliefs of Amerindian society, which were constant and which provided the basis of strength that sustained Amerindian people during war, famine, disease, and spiritual challenge. Sioui (1992) has argued that there is present in all Amerindian belief systems a fundamental belief that all forms of human, animal, and spiritual life are connected in "the sacred circle." He notes it is commonly recognized that all of these relationships in the physical and spiritual worlds have to be acknowledged and respected. If we accept Sioui's claim, we must conclude that, to a certain degree, precontact Amerindian societies were inherently more egalitarian.

CONCLUSIONS AND DIRECTIONS FOR FUTURE RESEARCH

In our more detailed historical work (Smandych and Lee, 1994; Smandych and Linden, 1994, 1995) we attempt to describe the historical circumstances that led to the imposition of a private justice system created by the Hudson's Bay Company on the preexisting dispute-settlement system of the indigenous peoples of western Canada. In this research, attention is given to pursuing specific themes and questions raised in the recent work of sociologists of social control and students of legal pluralism. In addition, we use the Amerindian autohistorical perspective articulated in this chapter as a starting point for our interpretation of the manner in which the imposition of Hudson's Bay Company law was likely perceived by aboriginal people. This perspective recognizes that when we look at historical topics, such as the nature of traditional methods of dispute settlement and social control used by aboriginal people, or the different roles played by men and women in Amerindian societies prior to European intervention, we are limited to assessing the documents left by the skewed perspective of the European colonizer. In our work, we use this perspective to expose the inadequacy of the theoretical and methodological approaches adopted by conventional historians, and to provide the corrective needed in order to overcome these inadequacies.

We are still at an early stage in our research in which we examine the impact that the Hudson's Bay Company and its private legal system, as an embodiment of European colonization, had on aboriginal peoples living in what is now western Canada. One of the major findings that has emerged from our research so far is that, from a very early date following the arrival of this private justice system in western Canada, aboriginal people began to be dealt with under the system created by the company (Smandych and Lee, 1994; Smandych and Linden, 1995). However, we have also begun to uncover evidence that shows that, rather than being passive victims of a process in which law is used as a tool of colonization, the aboriginal peoples of western Canada actively resisted having the private justice systems of the Hudson's Bay Company and other early European colonizers imposed on them. We are currently involved in carrying out the archival research that is needed to further address important theoretical questions raised in recent years by sociologists of social control and students of legal pluralism, along with feminist and Amerindian historians.

A particularly important feature of our current work is the use we make of the Amerindian autohistorical perspective as a way of approaching the study of the impact of the colonization process on aboriginal women, and their involvement in the process as agents of syncretism and resistance. In addition, we are undertaking work that is aimed at deconstructing the meaning of historical documents in which mention is made of the role and status of women in early post-contact Amerindian societies (Emberley, 1993). We have also begun to address in our research the questions posed by Merry (1991) concerning the impact of the colonizing experience on European colonizers themselves. Canadian fur-trade historians have already found a great deal of evidence that shows that for many years the servants sent out by the Hudson's Bay Company depended on indigenous peoples to provide them with the cultural knowledge and basic material resources they needed to survive (Ray and Freeman, 1978; Russell, 1991; Thistle, 1986). The impact indigenous peoples had on the thinking of Europeans also likely led them to rethink their own preconceived ideas about law and justice. A great deal more remains to be learned about who the people were "who brought and imposed new conceptions of law" and what effect "their earlier experiences [had] on the way they treated colonized peoples" (Merry, 1991, 55). Ultimately, we hope that bringing attention to questions like this will help generate new knowledge about the interconnected issues of legal change, colonization, gender, and resistance.

ENDNOTES

The research carried out for this study was helped by funding received from the Social Sciences and Humanities Research Council of Canada and the Solicitor General of Canada through its contributions grant to the Criminology Research Centre at the University of Manitoba. The authors would also like to acknowledge the excellent research assistance provided by James Muir, Tannis Peikoff, and Ruth Swan.

1   The research for this paper was undertaken as one of several projects we are working on as part of a three-year research program funded by the Social Sciences and Humanities Research Council of Canada. The working title of the research program is "The Transformation of Legal Ordering and Social Control in pre-1870 Manitoba: A Study of the Development and Interaction of Aboriginal, Private, and State-Run Justice Systems." The two principle co-investigators are Rick Linden and Russell Smandych, of the Department of Sociology, University of Manitoba.

2   The Hudson's Bay Company Archives (HBCA) now exist as part of the Provincial Archives of Manitoba in Winnipeg. The HBCA contain a detailed historical record of the operation of the Hudson's Bay Company in western Canada from the 1670s to the end of the nineteenth century.

3   "The Royal Charter Incorporating the Hudson's Bay Company, 1670," reproduced in E. H. Oliver (1914, 135–53). According to the Charter of 1670, the territory of Rupertsland included all of the land drained by rivers flowing into Hudson Bay.

4   This licence was granted in 1821 by way of provisions contained in *An Act for Regulating the Fur Trade, and establishing a Criminal and Civil Jurisdiction within parts of North America*, (1&2 Geo. 4., ch. 66, 1821). The licence was renewed in 1838 for another 21 years. It was not until 1859 that the Hudson's Bay Company gave up its lawmaking role and "law enforcement obligations" in the "Indian Territories" (Foster, 1990, 5).

5   Some of the more recent works of leading representatives of the new legal pluralism include: Santos (1992) and Fitzpatrick (1992a, 1992b).

6   Recently, the use of the concept of legal pluralism by the above noted authors has come under attack from Brian Z. Tamanaha (1993) in an article entitled "The Folly of the `Social Scientific' Concept of Legal Pluralism." In essence, Tamanaha develops a critique of the concept of legal pluralism. He argues that the insights about legal change and nonstate forms of normative ordering provided by these authors "do not depend upon the concept of legal pluralism and may be hindered by it" (1993, 212).

7   For examples of recent work on the effect of law and colonialism on the Maori people of New Zealand, see John Pratt (1991) and Kayleen M. Hazlehurst (1993). For an excellent recent collection of studies on the colonial experience of a number of countries in Africa, Asia, and America, see Dirks (1992). For a number of good accounts of the postcontact experience of indigenous peoples of North and South America see Bourgeault et al. (1992).

8   In another recent work, Attwood (1992, 302) looks at how modern female Aborigine writers have helped to "define or proclaim an Aboriginal consciousness or identity."

9   The work of North American ethnohistorians frequently reflects the implicit, and sometimes more explicit, use of this concept (cf. Axtell, 1992; Calloway, 1987, 1991; Delâge, 1993; Jaenen, 1976; Jennings, 1975; Trigger, 1976, 1985).

10   As Julia Emberley (1993, 101) notes in her recent deconstructionist work on Native women's writings and postcolonial theory, "[t]he necessity for a theory of gender subordination in postcolonial criticism cannot be insisted on too forcefully."

11   Dickason also quotes the words of Champlain, who said to the Huron, "Our young men will marry your daughters, and we shall be one people" (1992).

12   As an example of the relatively equal sexual division of labour, Anderson points out that in Huron society men cleared fields while women planted crops. Men were the traders, hunters, and warriors, while women tended crops, harvested, gathered wild foods, and prepared and controlled the distribution of food and clothing.

13   A similar argument about the status of women in precontact Huron society is advanced by the Quebec sociohistorian Denys Delâge (1993, 66–69). In particular, Delâge argues that "Living in a society where coercive power did not exist, the Hurons, like the Iroquoians or the Algonkians in general, were proud, strongly individualistic, tolerant, and free" and that "This applied to both men and women" (1993, 66).

14   Devens' book is largely concerned with identifying patterns of resistance and accommodation to colonization and how these patterns changed over time. The first two patterns involved united responses. In the first, whole communities expelled missionaries, whom they viewed as threats to tribal security and ways of life. At other times, adverse economic conditions elicited a quiet, if grudging, accommodation to Christianity by the entire group. The third pattern, however, was a split response. When missions or economics affected women and men unevenly, communities divided along gender lines into factions that supported different approaches to dealing with changes disrupting their world. By the late nineteenth century the latter pattern had become the norm. As men grew more receptive to introduced practices and values that they hoped would allow them to deal successfully with whites, women stood only to lose status and autonomy. Thus, whereas many men favoured accommodation, women tended to stress "traditional" ways. As a consequence, friction between men and women eventually prevailed in many communities. Deven (1992, 4) argues that this third pattern clarifies the significance of gender in the colonization process; the friction between men and women in aboriginal communities is in fact the bitter fruit of colonization. Devens maintains that while men viewed education and conversion as an advantage, women saw Christianity, schools, and clergy as a threat, and the mission schoolhouse became a silent battleground. Her examination of nineteenth-century mission schools suggests that they had a great impact on children who were suddenly removed from native lifestyles, and on mothers, who abruptly lost control of their daughters' educations (1992, 108–109).

15   See also Paula Gunn Allen (1986, 224).

16   A comparable body of literature that raises questions more like this is now developing out of the study of gender and resistance to colonization in California, especially during the early period in which California was colonized by the Spanish (cf. Castillo, 1994; Brady, Crome, and Reese, 1984).

REFERENCES

Allen, Paula Gunn. 1986. *The Sacred Hoop: Recovering the Feminine in American Indian Traditions.* Boston: Beacon Press.

Anderson, Karen. 1991. *Chain Her by One Foot: The Subjugation of Women in Seventeenth-Century New France.* London: Routledge.

Attwood, Bain. 1992. "Portrait of an Aboriginal as an Artist: Sally Morgan and the Construction of Aboriginality," *Australian Historical Studies*, 25: 302–318.

———. 1990. "Aborigines and Academic Historians: Some Recent Encounters," *Australian Historical Studies*, 24: 123–135.

Axtell, James. 1992. *Beyond 1492: Encounters in Colonial North America.* New York: Oxford University Press.

Black, Donald. 1990. "Elementary Forms of Conflict Management," in *New Directions in the Study of Justice, Law, and Social Control,* School of Justice Studies, Arizona State University. New York: Plenum Press.

———. 1976. *The Behavior of Law.* New York: Academic Press.

Black, Donald, ed. 1984. *Toward a General Theory of Social Control.* 2 vols. New York: Academic Press.

Bonvillian, Nancy. 1989. "Gender Relations in Native North America," *American Indian Culture and Research Journal*, 13: 1–28.

Bourgeault, Ron. 1989. "Race, Class, and Gender: Colonial Domination of Indian Women. In *Race, Class, Gender: Bonds and Barriers,* ed. by J. Vorst et al. Halifax: Garamond.

———. 1988. "Race and Class Under Mercantilism: Indigenous People in Nineteenth-Century Canada." In *Racial Oppression in Canada,* 2d ed., ed. by S. Bolaria and P. Li. Toronto: Garamond Press.

———. 1983. "The Indian, the Métis, and the Fur Trade: Class, Sexism and Racism in the Transition from "Communism" to Capitalism," *Studies in Political Economy*, 12: 45–79.

Bourgeault, Ron, et al., eds. 1992. *1492–1992—Five Centuries of Imperialism and Resistance.* Toronto: Fernwood.

Brady, Victoria, Sarah Crome, and **Lynn Reese.** 1984. "Resist! Survival Tactics of Indian Women," *California History*, (spring): 141–151.

Brogden, Mike. 1990. "Law and Criminal Labels: The Case of the French Métis in Western Canada," *Journal of Human Justice*, 1: 13–32.

Brown, Jennifer. 1980. *Strangers in Blood: Fur Trade Company Families in the Indian Country.* Vancouver: University of British Columbia Press.

Calloway, Colin G., ed. 1991. *Dawnland Encounters: Indians and Europeans in Northern New England.* Hanover: University Press of New England.

————. 1987. *Crown and Calumet: British-Indian Relations, 1783–1815.* Norman: University of Oklahoma Press.

Castillo, Edward D. 1994. "Gender Status Decline, Resistance, and Accommodation Among Female Neophytes in the Missions of California: A San Gabriel Case Study," *American Indian Culture and Research Journal,* 18: 67–93.

Cohen, Stanley. 1989. "The Critical Discourse on `Social Control': Notes on the Concept as a Hammer," *International Journal of the Sociology of Law,* 17: 339–363.

————. 1985. *Visions of Social Control: Crime, Punishment and Classification.* Cambridge: Polity Press.

————, and **Andrew Scull,** eds. 1983. *Social Control and the State.* New York: St. Martin's Press.

Delâge, Denys. 1993. *Bitter Feast: Amerindians and Europeans in Northeastern North America, 1600–64.* Translated by Jane Brierley. Vancouver: University of British Columbia Press. Originally published as *Le pays renversé* (Paris: Les éditions du Boréal, 1985).

Devens, Carol. 1992. *Countering Colonization: Native American Women and Great Lakes Missions, 1630–1900.* Berkeley: University of California Press.

Dickason, Olive. 1992. *Canada's First Nations.* Toronto: McClelland and Stewart.

Dirks, Nickolas B., ed. 1992. *Colonialism and Culture.* Ann Arbor: University of Michigan Press.

Ellickson, Robert C. 1991. *Order Without Law: How Neighbours Settle Disputes.* Cambridge: Harvard University Press.

Emberley, Julia V. 1993. *Thresholds of Difference: Feminist Critique, Native Women's Writings, Postcolonial Theory.* Toronto: University of Toronto Press.

Fitzpatrick, Peter. 1992a. "The Impossibility of Popular Justice," *Social & Legal Studies,* 1: 199–216.

————. 1992b. *The Mythology of Modern Law.* London: Routledge.

————. 1989. "Crime as Resistance: The Colonial Situation," *The Howard Journal of Criminal Justice,* 28: 272–281.

————. 1987. "Transformations of Law and Labour in Papua New Guinea." In *Labour, Law, and Crime: A Historical Perspective,* ed. by F. Snyder and D. Hay. London: Tavistock.

————. 1983a. "Law, Plurality and Underdevelopment." In *Legality, Ideology and the State,* ed. by D. Sugerman. Toronto: Academic Press.

————. 1983b. "Law and Societies," *Osgoode Hall Law Journal,* 22: 115–138.

Foster, Hamar. 1990. "Long-Distance Justice: The Criminal Jurisdiction of Canadian Courts West of the Canadas, 1763–1859," *The American Journal of Legal History,* 34: 1–48.

Foster, Martha Harroun. 1993. "Of Baggage and Bondage: Gender and Status Among Hidatsa and Crow Women," *American Indian Culture and Research Journal,* 17: 121–152.

Foucault, Michel. 1977. *Discipline and Punish: The Birth of the Prison.* New York: Vintage Books.

Garland, David. 1991. "Punishment and Culture: The Symbolic Dimension of Criminal Justice," *Studies in Law, Politics, and Society,* 11: 191–222.

———. 1990. *Punishment and Modern Society: A Study in Social Theory.* Chicago: University of Chicago Press.

———. 1985. *Punishment and Welfare: A History of Penal Strategies.* Aldershot: Gower.

———, and **Peter Young,** eds. 1983. *The Power to Punish: Contemporary Penality and Social Analysis.* London: Heinemann.

Gordon, Robert. 1989. "The White Man's Burden: Ersatz Customary Law and Internal Pacification in South Africa," *Journal of Historical Sociology,* 2: 41–65.

Greenberg, David F. 1980. "Law and Development in Light of Dependency Theory," *Research in Law and Sociology,* 3: 129–159.

Hazlehurst, Kayleen M. 1993. *Political Expression and Ethnicity: Statecraft and Mobilization in the Maori World.* Westport, Conn.: Greenwood Press.

Henry, Stuart. 1987a. "The Construction and Deconstruction of Social Control: Thoughts on the Discursive Production of State Law and Private Justice." In *Transcarceration: Essays in the Sociology of Social Control,* ed. by J. Lowman, R. Menzies, and T. Palys. Aldershot: Gower.

———. 1987b. "Disciplinary Pluralism: Four Models of Private Justice in the Workplace," *Sociological Review,* 35: 279–319.

———. 1983. *Private Justice: Towards Integrated Theorizing in the Sociology of Law.* London: Routledge & Kegan Paul.

———, ed. 1994. *Social Control: Aspects of Non-State Justice.* Brookfield, Vt.: Dartmouth Publishing.

Hill, Jonathan D. 1994. "Overview: Contemporary Issues Forum: Contested Pasts and the Practice of Anthropology," *American Anthropologist,* 94: 809–815.

Jaenen, Cornelius. 1976. *Friend and Foe: Aspects of French-Amerindian Cultural Contact in the Sixteenth and Seventeenth Centuries.* Toronto: McClelland and Stewart.

Jennings, Francis. 1975. *The Invasion of America: Indians, Colonialism, and the Cant of Conquest.* New York: Norton and Co.

Kennedy, Mark. 1989. "Law and Capitalist Development: The Colonization of Sub-Saharan Africa." In *Law and Society: A Critical Perspective,* ed. by T. Caputo et al. Toronto: Harcourt Brace Jovanovich.

Kidder, Robert L. 1979. "Toward an Integrated Theory of Imposed Law." In *The Imposition of Law,* ed. by S. Burman and B. Harrell-Bond. New York: Academic Press.

Leacock, Eleanor. 1980. "Montagnais Women and the Jesuit Program for Colonization." In *Women and Colonization: Anthropological Perspectives,* ed. by M. Etienne and E. Leacock. New York: Praeger.

———. 1978. "Women's Status in Egalitarian Society: Implications for Social Evolution," *Current Anthropology,* 19: 247–275.

Lowman, J., R. Menzies, and **T. Palys.** 1987. *Transcarceration.* Aldershot: Gower.

McGrath, Ann. 1987. *"Born in the Cattle": Aborigines in Cattle Country.* Sydney: Allen & Unwin.

Merry, Sally. 1991. "Law and Colonialism," *Law and Society Review,* 25: 889–922.

———. 1990. *Getting Justice and Getting Even: Legal Consciousness Among Working Class Americans.* Chicago: University of Chicago Press.

———. 1988. "Legal Pluralism," *Law and Society Review,* 22: 869–896.

Oliver, E. H. 1914. *The Canadian North-West: Its Early Development and Legislative Records.* Vol. 1. Ottawa: Government Printing Bureau.

O'Malley, Pat. 1987. "Regulating Contradictions: The Australian Press Council and the Dispersal of Social Control," *Law and Society Review,* 21: 82–108.

Pratt, John. 1991. "Citizenship, Colonisation and Criminal Justice," *International Journal of the Sociology of Law,* 19: 293–319.

Ray, Arthur, and **Donald Freeman.** 1978. *Give Us Good Measure: An Economic Analysis of Relations Between the Indians and the Hudson's Bay Company Before 1763.* Toronto: University of Toronto Press.

Russell, Dale R. 1991. *Eighteenth-Century Western Cree and Their Neighbours.* Hull, Quebec: Canadian Museum of Civilization.

Santos, Bonaventura De Sousa. 1992. "State, Law and Community in the World System: An Introduction," *Social & Legal Studies,* 1: 131–142.

———. 1987. "Law: A Map of Misreading: Toward a Postmodern Conception of Law," *Journal of Law and Society,* 14: 279–302.

Sioui, Georges E. 1992. *For an Amerindian Autohistory: An Essay on the Foundations of a Social Ethic.* Montreal and Kingston: McGill-Queen's University Press.

Smandych, Russell C. 1995. "William Osgoode, John Graves Simcoe, and the Exclusion of the English Poor Law from Upper Canada." In *Law, State, and Society: Essays in Modern Legal History,* ed. by L. Knafla and S. Binnie. Toronto: University of Toronto Press.

———. 1991a. "Rethinking 'the Master Principle of Administering Relief' in Upper Canada: A Response to Allan Irving," *Canadian Review of Social Policy,* no. 27: 82–86.

———. 1991b. "Tory Paternalism and the Politics of Penal Reform in Upper Canada, 1830–1834: A 'Neo-Revisionist' Account of the Kingston Penitentiary," *Criminal Justice History: An International Annual,* 12: 57–83.

————. 1989. "The Upper Canadian Experience With Pre-Segregative Control," Ph.D dis., University of Toronto.

————, and Gloria Lee. 1994. "Resisting Company Law: Aboriginal Peoples and the Transformation of Legal Ordering and Social Control in the Canadian West to 1850." Paper presented at the annual meeting of the Western Association of Sociology and Anthropology, Saskatoon, March 3–5.

Smandych, Russell, and **Rick Linden.**   1995. "Co-Existing Forms of Native and Private Justice: An Historical Study of the Canadian West." In *Legal Pluralism and the Colonial Legacy: Indigenous Experiences of Justice in Canada, Australia, and New Zealand,* ed. by Kayleen M. Hazlehurst. Cambridge: Cambridge University Press, in press.

————. 1994. "Company Discipline in the Hudson's Bay Company, 1670–1770." Paper prepared for the annual meeting of the Canadian Law and Society Association, Calgary, June 13–15.

Snyder, Francis G.   1981. "Colonialism and Legal Form: The Creation of `Customary Law' in Senegal," *Journal of Legal Pluralism,* 1: 49–92.

————, and **Douglas Hay.**   1987. "Comparisons in the Social History of Law: Labour and Crime." In *Labour, Law and Crime,* ed. by F. Synder and D. Hay. London: Tavistock.

Tamanaha, Brian Z.   1993. "The Folly of the `Social Scientific' Concept of Legal Pluralism," *Journal of Law and Society,* 20: 192–216.

Thistle, Paul.   1986. *Indian-European Trade Relations in the Lower Saskatchewan River Region to 1840.* Winnipeg: University of Manitoba Press.

Trigger, Bruce.   1985. *Natives and Newcomers: Canada's `Heroic Age' Reconsidered.* Kingston and Montreal: McGill-Queen's University Press.

————. 1976. *The Children of Aataentsic: A History of the Huron People to 1660.* Kingston and Montreal: McGill-Queen's University Press.

Van Kirk, Sylvia.   1987. "Toward a Feminist Perspective in Native History." Occasional paper, no. 14, Centre for Women's Studies in Education, Toronto.

————. 1980. *"Many Tender Ties": Women in Fur Trade Society in Western Canada, 1670–1870.* Winnipeg: Watson & Dwyer.

Wright, Ronald.   1992. *Stolen Continents: The "New World" Through Indian Eyes.* Toronto: Penguin.

CHAPTER 18

OMNES ET SINGULATIM IN CRIMINOLOGICAL THEORY

George Pavlich and R. S. Ratner

INTRODUCTION

With the appearance of postmodern challenges to criminological theory, modern traditions of thought are being exposed to fundamental criticism. The assumptions, categories and even legitimacy of modern analyses of crime have been questioned as the quite different approaches, issues and concerns of postmodern discourse are placed on theoretical agendas (C. Smart, 1990; Barak, 1994; Hunt, 1990; Milovanovic, 1989; Henry and Milovanovic, 1993). The following discussion attempts to provide a framework by which to conceptualize the confrontation between various modern and emerging postmodern approaches to criminology. It does this by situating modern criminology as a disciplinary form of knowledge associated with liberal modes of governance (Foucault, 1981, 1991). In contrast to the "law and sovereign" model, such governance operates by carving—through discourse—the areas it seeks to regulate into singular instances (e.g., individuals), which are then located as elements of more general composite dimensions (e.g., society, see Foucault, 1980; also, see Gordon, 1991; Burchell, 1991). The success of liberal governance relies on a capacity to reconcile objects of singular regulation with a wider totality. Following Foucault (1981), we shall refer to this core feature of liberal government as the *omnes et singulatim* (all and each) epistemic theme. It is a theme that has assumed various guises at different historical moments, but it is central to the political rationality of liberal governance (Gordon, 1991) and is an auspice of the modern liberal episteme (Foucault, 1971).

Tracing the genealogy of modern criminology as a discipline, one is able to show a fundamental association with different formulations of the *omnes et singulatim* theme; that is, modern criminology as a discipline is both a product and proponent of the expansion of the liberal governmental logics associated with this epistemic theme. While the various ways in which modern criminology has formulated the theme surely indicate different specific approaches to regulation, it is only with more recent postmodern formulations that the epistemic theme itself has been problematized (Hunt, 1990). And it is in the fundamental difference between assuming the validity of this theme as opposed to challenging it that allows us to conceptualize the clash between modern and postmodern criminological theory in precise terms. Understanding the confrontation in these terms allows one to consider seriously the rise of postmodern thinking in criminology. It is not simply a faddish development that renders the "social" anachronistic, or overthrows the very auspices of criminology (Baudrillard, 1983). Nor is it something to embrace without question, as if it were intrinsically capable of freeing us from the iron cage of technocratic, correctionalist reasoning. Instead, there are both perils and opportunities in problematizing modern assumptions and grand "metanarratives" of universality (Lyotard, 1984).

Such an endeavour is crucial because it seems unlikely that the postmodern controversies that now pervade social thought (B. Smart, 1992, 1993) will permit criminologists, or sociologists, to continue with business as usual (Bauman, 1992; Touraine, 1989). It is, therefore, important to consider postmodern problematizations carefully in order to pursue lines of political reasoning that could yield equitable forms of control. Hence, after showing how modern criminology might be conceptualized as elaborating upon different aspects of the liberal *omnes et singulatim* epistemic theme, our analysis critically examines emerging postmodern attempts that problematize it. We conclude by reconsidering the project of critical criminology in light of the discursive ethos engendered by postmodern challenges.

THE RISE OF LIBERAL GOVERNMENT

During the sixteenth and seventeenth centuries an emerging cameralist discourse (a "science of police") introduced rather different conceptions about the nature of government than was current at the time (Foucault, 1991; Pasquino, 1991b). This discourse did not focus on issues associated with Machiavellian notes to princes, the divine right of kings, or with Hobbes's law and sovereign conception of power. Rather, it viewed the state as a discrete entity with its own reason, whose strength is bolstered when "security" is attained in a given principality (Pasquino, 1991b; Foucault, 1991). Such security was thought to be attainable by developing conditions favourable to the well-being of particular subjects within a principality (Gordon, 1991).

By the eighteenth century this line of political reasoning began to take a particular form. The composite (totalizing) object of government was enunciated as the "population," which was said to comprise a number of constituent individuals (Dean, 1991). What emerged here, as Pasquino points out, were concepts of "population and individuals, where previously, in the old social structure, there were only groups, *stande*, orders or estates inviolable (juridically, at least) in their eternal hierarchy" (1991b, 114).

The condition of populations was articulated through particular kinds of knowledge about its size, strength, density, health, welfare, etc. (e.g., Quetelet, 1984). This notion foreshadowed the rise of such "disciplines" as demography and statistics to provide "reliable" records of the state of a given population (Hacking, 1991). At the same time, the health of a population was said to depend on the welfare and condition of the individual lives that gave the composite its life (Burchell, 1991). In effect, reflecting a particular instance of the *omnes et singulatim* epistemic theme, this ensconced a dichotomous conception of what is to be regulated: the wider population on the one hand, and the individual life on the other.

While the precise formulation of the epistemic theme has assumed different guises over the last two hundred years (e.g., population/individual, state/individual, society/individual), the assumption of a totality constituted by singular elements has been central to (modern) human science thinking.[1] In modern sociology and criminology, for example, the *omnes et singulatim* theme has been sustained through images of a wider "social" domain comprising "individuals" (Pasquino, 1991a; Donzelot, 1979).[2] Moreover, as Foucault (1977) has argued, such human science disciplines have provided fields of knowledge in which disciplinary power relations associated with liberal democracies have been deployed. There is in such power/knowledge arrangements an explicit conjunction of liberty and social security; that is, in liberal political logic social order is maintained not at the expense of individual freedom, but by preserving it. In this political rationality, individual liberty and social security are regarded as mutually sustaining features of good government—the preservation of a particular kind of individual liberty is viewed as a precondition for securing collective order and promoting the strength of the liberal state (Gordon, 1991).

As part of this political rationality, modern criminology has predicated its various analyses of crime upon the elaboration of singular lives within "social" existence. It thus appears, from our vantage point at least, as part of an attempt to extend a liberal governmental logic to the sphere of "criminal" relations (Pasquino, 1991a). More explicitly, modern criminology is concerned with antisocial (mostly individual) behaviour that threatens a presumed social order. Therefore, for much of the last two centuries its quest has been translated into the problem of achieving social order as efficiently as possible without relinquishing the individual voluntarism that Enlightenment thinking had ensconced as a prime value.

Let us now turn to an analysis of how the *omnes et singulatim* theme—and thereby liberal political rationality—has been incorporated into modern variants of criminology. Of course, our narrative of the different theories is extremely limited, since our concern is to explore the ways in which the epistemic theme is assumed by modern criminological theories.[3] To reiterate, our intention here is to show how a particular version of the theme (what we call the individual = society exemplar) is to modern criminological theory, and then to examine how postmodern criminology challenges the very auspices of the theme. By conceptualizing the clash between modern and postmodern criminology in this way, we aim to explore fruitful avenues for future critical enquiries. Table 18.1 provides an overview of the variants of modern criminological theory to be discussed below.

TABLE 18.1   A Summary of Central Formulations of the *Omnes et Singulatim* Theme in Criminological Theory

Grounding Theory	Key Theorists	Logic of Control	Omnes	Singulatim
Classical	Beccaria; Bentham	hedonistic calculus; degree of punishment required to prevent the commission of the criminal act	a consensually agreed upon societal order ("social contract")	free and rational individuals
Positivist	Lombroso; Garafolo	treatment of pathological offenders	"normal" society; criminal vs. noncriminal populations	biological or psychologically determined individuals
Functionalist	Durkheim; Erikson	"normal" deviance enhancing social organization	"functioning" social system	individual units comprising the whole
Ecology	Park; Burgess	restore balanced human ecology through planned social reorganization	social "ecosystem"	individual groups with ecological niches
Anomie	Merton	social reform to alleviate the malintegration of cultural goals and institutional means (auxiliary goals/means structures and increased meritocracy)	anomic society	conformist and deviant modes of adaptation
Cultural Transmission	Sutherland; Cressey	unlearning of deviant behaviour patterns and positive learning of prosocial behaviours	a society composed of various sub-cultures ("ecological pluralism")	individual who is capable of learning/ unlearning
Societal Reaction	Lemert; Becker	curtail secondary deviation by limiting control responses	differential social power	the labeled individual
Critical Criminology	Taylor, Walton and Young	reduce the power to criminalize by democratizing social relations	capitalist mode of production and society	exploited individuals
Postmodernism	Foucault; Smart; Hunt; Sawicki	deconstruct power/ knowledge relations in search of different and contextualized logics of control	contingent emergence of the "social"	decentred subject

OMNES ET SINGULATIM IN MODERN CRIMINOLOGY

The development of dominant patterns in criminological theory reflects various forms of knowledge about the criminal individual and society, which are inextricably related to associated modes of control. The classical perspective, for example, symbolizes a certain Enlightenment optimism, which assumed all individuals to be essentially rational beings with free wills of their own (Beccaria, 1963; Bentham, 1973). Such individuals are therefore necessarily choosing agents, but their choices are governed by a natural drive toward pleasure and away from pain. They come to live in peaceful association with others when they agree to live under certain laws that limit their choices to those that are "rational" and guided by right reason. Conversely stated, a rational society comprises reason-based laws that circumscribe reasonable individual choice. As such

> Laws are the conditions under which independent and isolated men unite to form society. Weary of living in a continual state of war, and enjoying a liberty rendered useless by the uncertainty of preserving it, they sacrificed a part so they might enjoy the rest of it in peace. (Beccaria, 1963, 11)

In order to preserve liberty, that is, individuals are legally obliged to limit their freedom to the choices that render rational, social being possible. If, however, an individual chooses an unlawful course of action, and thereby elects to follow an unreasonable, criminal course of action, a rationally calculated degree of punishment (pain) must be inflicted on him/her to deter this individual (and others who might be tempted to pursue similar courses) from choosing such actions in the future. Correspondingly, the use of punishment was not to demonstrate—as in the public spectacle—the awesome power of the king, nor was it simply a form of public retribution. On the contrary, punishment was here invoked to encourage individuals to embrace a logic that was deemed to be innate. In this version, or exemplar, of the *omnes et singulatim* epistemic theme, the conjunction between individuals and society is achieved through postulating a common thread of "right reason," the preservation of which is seen to be central to the achievement of social order and (parenthetically) the legitimate task of criminology. Yet classical reformers (and their Enlightenment vision) failed to demonstrate that reason was innate to all individuals; hence, the gradual acceptance of neoclassical modifications to the theory (e.g., the insanity plea), which led to various positivist responses.

Fascinated by Darwin's evolutionary theory and how it might be applied to society, Spencer (1874) and Lombroso (1918) incorporated some of this theory's precepts within the domain of criminology. As Pasquino notes, this positivist criminology emerged in a discursive environment saturated with symbols of evolution:

> In the midst of social evolution and by virtue of its progress, archaic residues can be identified comprising those individuals and groups who, outpaced and left behind by the proper rate of evolution, endanger by their very existence the orderly functioning of the whole. (1991b, 242)

Whether the criminal individual is described as a Lombrosian atavist, or a psychological degenerate (Garofalo, 1914), positivist theory entrenched the view that a certain class of (criminal) people were fundamentally different from others because they had not progressed far enough along the evolutionary scale, and could not match the degree to which the rest of society had evolved. One of the most significant effects of this, reflecting the positivist obsession with classification, was its bifurcation of the *singulatim* into pathological "criminal" types versus normal "noncriminal" types. Since the former were thought to pose a direct threat to society, positivist criminology—borrowing heavily from medical imagery—concerned itself with diagnosing criminal types and subjecting these individuals to various rehabilitative treatments.

If positivist criminology tended to focus its attention on individuals in its quest to achieve social control, early twentieth-century theorists—replicating Durkheim's (1982) concern with social facts *sui generis*—increasingly turned their attention to the society side of the individual = society exemplar (e.g., see Lilly, Cullen, and Ball, 1989). No doubt, this emphasis on the social domain coincided with the rising significance of the welfare state and its concern with securing order through a social security network for individuals (Barry, 1990). In the wake of early progressive reformers, the social disorganization theorists of the Chicago School explained rising crime rates, and the attendant threats these posed to a given normative order, as a direct manifestation of rapid social change (Park, Burgess, and McKenzie, 1967; Shaw and MacKay, 1969). The ensuing disorganization of the social domain was thought to produce criminal patterns that could only be contained in a more "evolved," or "reformed," social environment. Similarly, the functionalist (Durkheim, 1982) and anomie theorists (Merton, 1938) suggested that high crime rates should be explained with reference to some dysfunction within the social system, a situation that could only be corrected by reforming that system.

This shift of emphasis to notions of "society" had a number of effects on criminological theory. To begin with, it raised certain questions about the salience of the positivist bifurcation of the individual into criminal versus noncriminal types. For if crime were a function of maladies engendered within a given society, then the notion of criminality as an innate aspect of individuality was thrown into question. Hence, Sutherland (1937, 1947) explicitly attacked the latter assumption by positing that criminal behaviour was learned rather than innate (also, Matza, 1969; Matza and Sykes, 1961). In this move, the logic of control shifted from individual treatment to a broader form of social engineering that would either expunge social conditions favouring the production (learning) of criminal behaviour, or create social spaces designed to entice people away from criminal lives. In effect, this focus on the social aspects of crime moved criminological discourse away from the *singulatim* and raised doubts about the medical model assumptions of the preceding era.

However, in a more radical critique of the positivist bifurcation of individuals into criminal and noncriminal types, and as an attack on the implicit acceptance of some absolute conception of crime in all previous formulations, labeling theorists proposed that deviant behaviour was no more than behaviour to which societal definitions had been successfully applied. The label "criminal" is, in this view, no more than a societally created definition that is imposed on particular individuals in specifiable sets of circumstances (Lemert, 1972; Becker, 1963). By thus relativizing the notions of crime and deviance, this formulation began a process that called into question the "correctionalist" bias of criminology. That is, where previous approaches had implicitly, or explicitly, conceptualized disjunctions between the individual and society as "pathological"—and in need of correction through more effective social controls—the societal reaction perspective offered a (liberal) critique of social control itself. Not unlike Hirschi's (1969) analysis that focused on why people actually conform and emphasized mechanisms of social control, labeling theory proposed that social regulation did not limit individual deviance but rather was the very means by which such deviance was created.

This reformulation of the relationship between the criminal individual, society, and social control nurtured a significant discursive rupture. It opened a space for the emergence of a critical version of criminology that shifted its emphasis away from issues of effective control toward concerns with patterns of domination within given historical formations and their effects on particular classes of people. For instance, conflict theorists explored crime as an important instrument in ruling class domination where certain groups of people (i.e., those who threaten dominant social groups) are treated as criminals in order to ensure their compliance with the existing social order (Quinney, 1970). Criminal individuals were seen to be the terminal effects of a complex power play between a plurality of social groups competing in struggles for dominance within a particular social order. Whilst this version of criminological thought colonized a different object of analysis, its conceptualizations of dominance were vague and abstract as proponents speculated about criminal outcomes in given struggles (Turk, 1969). In response to this lack of specificity, Marxist and neo-Marxist criminologists sought—through materially grounded critiques—to provide a detailed conception of capitalist domination and its effects on processes of criminalization.

More specifically, the "new" criminology developed out of an "immanent critique" of existing traditions in criminological theory, and underscoring its rejection of individualistic theories attempted to formulate a "fully social theory of deviance" (Taylor, Walton and Young, 1973). Stated differently, it was new to the extent that it sought to reformulate the *omnes* side of the epistemic theme by offering Marxist analyses of capitalist society and enunciating the criminal individual as one effect of the class struggle within a capitalist mode of production (Spitzer, 1975). Here, one class of individuals (owners) exploits another (workers) in the ongoing quest to perpetuate a society that preserves the dominant position of the former. Such critical analyses argued that previous versions of the *omnes et singulatim* theme led to construction of a class of criminals that helped to perpetuate capitalist modes of production.

Clearly, for the new criminologists, progressive praxis could not require that criminology seek more effective forms of control to reconcile individuals and society within the existing capitalist order. Rather, the aim was to expose the iniquities of existing forms of control, to combat entrenched patterns of working-class subjugation, and to commence the difficult task of enunciating a "socialist criminology" for a socialist order (Taylor, 1981; Matthews and Young, 1986). For them, a socialist criminology would require a radically different formulation of the individual = society exemplar than that offered by correctionalist criminology, since the autonomous agent in capitalist society was no longer viewed as an individual but as a unified class of labour; that is, the working class (Lea and Young, 1984). But importantly, the emancipatory project of the new criminology did not seek to overthrow the modern exemplar as such, as is evident from the following statement from Taylor, Walton, and Young's concluding chapter:

> sociology must be fully social (unbroken by the assertions of biological or other non-social assumptions) and...it must be able to account (in a historically informed fashion) for men's imprisonment within social structures that constrain his possibilities. (1973, 269)

In other words, they merely reconceptualize the exemplar by advocating that the social dimensions (as enunciated from a neo-Marxist viewpoint) be elevated above the focus on individuals when dealing with crime.

The above analysis indicates that despite significant differences between approaches, the modern criminological theories discussed above have a common link: their conceptions of crime are all predicated on one or other version of the *omnes et singulatim* theme. In each case, different notions of individuals and/or society are emphasized, but in no case is the theme or the elements of the exemplar challenged. As such, a particular exemplar of the epistemic theme provides an important assumptive foundation for both correctionalist and critical versions of modern criminology. In addition, critical criminologists—in our view—reasserted the modern project of their predecessors, albeit in a progressive format, by emphasizing the importance of universal principles (e.g., the contradictions of capitalist society). This time, however, the purpose was not one of heuristic "discovery" but of "emancipation" (Lyotard, 1984). In other words, critical criminologists had accepted that their critique of capitalism was to proceed by clinging to a (Marxist) metanarrative, to universal socialist principles that stand against exploitation and the suffering of social inequities. Emancipation for each individual would come from an emancipation of all; the revolutionary transformation of capitalist forms of the individual and society nexus could yet lead to a reconceptualized vision of the "one" and the collective "all" in a socialist society. While critical criminology does not focus on the precise nature of this socialist society, it clearly acknowledges the historical necessity of maintaining the *omnes et singulatim* epistemic theme.

It is only when specific versions of the theme are fundamentally attacked that the auspices of modern criminology begin to be questioned. And it is here that the clash between modern and emerging postmodern forms of criminology is highlighted.

EMERGING POSTMODERN IMAGES IN CRIMINOLOGY

Although not well-developed, there appears to be an emerging interest in reworking postmodern controversies within the context of critical criminology (see Barak, 1994; Thomas and O'Maolchatha, 1989; Hunt, 1990). In particular, these formulations seem to be concerned with contemporary forms of power, and with problematizing a dominant version of the *omnes et singulatim* theme itself—the individual-society exemplar. For instance, various feminist criminologists have figured prominently in some significant attacks on the "individual" featured in many modern criminological theories. In particular, they point out that modern criminology has either ignored women, or has explained women's involvement with crime by referring to degrading generalizations of a purported "nature" that is assumed to be different from men (e.g., Simon, 1975; Leonard, 1982; Morris, 1987; Heidensohn, 1989). Even critical criminology—as is evident from the previous quotation—had ignored the conspicuous role that gender appears to play in the criminalizing process, and in the creation of criminalized "men" and "women" (Laberge, 1991).

Yet, if most early feminist critiques problematized the *singulatim* by illustrating how patriarchal power formations in criminology had omitted women, more recent formulations attack the epistemic theme directly. Initially, feminists sought to "add" women into the individual side of the theme, showing how feminist theory could be of extreme benefit to criminology (e.g., Simon, 1975; Messerschmidt, 1986). More recently, though, Carol Smart (1989; 1992) has embarked on a line of enquiry that problematizes the political rationality implicated in the *omnes et singulatim* theme itself. Her position dovetails with other attempts to deconstruct flexible and subtle disciplinary modes of control that have enunciated individuals, society, and even crime as true categories in the first place (Henry and Milovanovic, 1993; Milovanovic, 1989; MacLean and Milovanovic, 1991). Thus, the postmodern call to "decentre the subject," "pluralize the social" and avoid foundationalism are attempts at deconstructing the very auspices of the theme and its associated models of power (see Hunt, 1990).

Given these developments we would argue that contemporary criminological theory stands poised on the possible brink of a significant discursive rupture, and it is of a different order from the shift between correctionalist and critical modern theories. Indeed, the transformation that currently stands before us is one that is concerned with the very auspices of modern criminology as a discipline, and that begins to question whether criminology can be anything other than a form of knowledge directly implicated in (liberal) disciplinary modes of power.

In general terms, to get some idea of the switch involved, postmodern theorists reject the value of metanarratives as a means of guiding us in social and political choices. This stance underscores their repudiation of any absolute, fixed, essential qualities to the world (Lyotard, 1984; Agger, 1991; Benhabib, 1984). They see *contingency* where modernists allege necessity, *history* where theorists of modernity assert nature, and *chance* where empiricists suspect the operation of scientific laws (B. Smart, 1992). Postmodern analysis involves an ongoing critique of present limits that cannot appeal to final, universal principles (Lyotard, 1984; B. Smart, 1993; Agger, 1991; Bauman, 1992). The aim of such critique is to examine specific contexts to try to retrieve "knowledges" that have been deliberately silenced by existing power relations (Foucault, 1980). The underlying assumption here is that power and knowledge are inextricably linked and that if one is to rescind existing oppression, it is important to listen to the knowledge that is silenced by dominant power/knowledge relations, and to use these knowledges to commence the difficult task of developing counterpowers (Sawicki, 1991).

Moreover, postmodern criminologists repudiate the individual = society exemplar and its attendant modes of control in three main ways. First, as noted, they seek to decentre the individual subject from its privileged position in human science discourses, arguing that far from serving as vehicles for human liberation the (liberal) individual is a *means* by which contemporary subjects are controlled (e.g., C. Smart, 1990). The individual, in short, is not an agent of emancipation, as liberalism might suggest, but a product of efficient subjection. Agency, if it is to be effective, will have to assume a social identity more capable of resistance than can be mustered from liberal versions of individuality (Laclau and Mouffe, 1985). Second, postmodern approaches in criminology question the value of the "society" side of the exemplar because the (Enlightenment) development of a "social" domain has proved to be an important way in which modern power relations have operated in the guise of "security" (Burchell, 1991; Gordon, 1991). The social security of the welfare state, for instance, has exerted considerable power through the successful development of a social domain with its own "problems" (such as crime), which could be resolved through technocratic means—hence correctionalist criminology (C. Smart, 1990; Hunt, 1990). Finally, postmodern theorists see the importance of deconstructing the binary opposition implicit in notions of individual and society; that is, they see the need to dispose of the linguistic hierarchy set up by these constructs and to begin the process of questioning the discursive edifice (and its power relations) that rests upon this hierarchy (Milovanovic, 1989).[4]

LOOKING AHEAD: CRITICAL CRIMINOLOGY RECONSIDERED

We have offered a discursive framework by which to conceptualize the debate between modern and postmodern criminology; that is, one that revolves around their respective approaches to the *omnes et singulatim* epistemic theme. Let us now scrutinize aspects of both the critical modern and postmodern approaches to criminology to move on to the final task of our discussion: exploring possible directions in which critical criminological enquiry may usefully head in light of significant contributions of both modern and postmodern approaches.

One of the major contributions of the critical modern tradition is it provides justifications for political engagement, and on the basis of this formulates directed strategies of resistance. In other words, because critical modernity situates its critiques on absolute conceptions of value, it has the potential to mobilize political engagement around specific epistemological/analytic ends. In this way it actively seeks to clarify the form of constructive (progressive) political praxis. Second, by defining subordination in broad class terms, critical modernity strives to nurture unification among those who must endure the widely different patterns of exploitation in capitalist society. Its explicit quest is to underscore the common ties between counterhegemonic groups.

However, a glaring weakness of the modernist vision lies in the apparent failure to achieve social justice through its universal principles. The many webs of oppression that characterize the contemporary social landscape have not been substantially reversed by the project of modernity (B. Smart, 1992). Conversely, the assertion of a labour-led path of resistance to such oppression has been unable to capture the sheer complexity of modern forms of domination (gender, race, sexual orientation) in the specific quest for a working-class identity, an omission that has seriously undermined the hopes for rectification once attributed to this perspective (Laclau and Mouffe, 1985; Young, 1990).

By contrast, postmodern theories have sought to describe the complex oppression of given power formations, focusing on various ways of capturing "subjugations" so that they might come to assume the identities of "oppression" (Laclau and Mouffe, 1985). The theoretical strength of this position is bolstered by the postmodern contention that analysts should reflect continuously on the multiple places in a society where power operates, recognizing that resistance must indeed assume diverse forms. By being released from the need to legitimate its enunciations through universal metanarratives, postmodern theory is more open to contingency, subtle definitions of oppression and the formulation of contextually relevant resistance strategies (Lyotard, 1984; Hunt, 1990).

However, this approach is flawed by a lack of direction, which could obviate planned, intercontextual resistance to forms of power that are articulated across given contexts. A politics of diversity may, then, further the isolation of subordinated identities, conceivably maintaining a fragmentation in opposition groups that would play into the liberal democratic state's disingenuous pluralist strategies (Young, 1990; see also Hunt, 1990). In postmodern formulations there is a feature that is likely to be exulted and exploited by adversaries whose power structures thrive on the principle of divide and conquer. There is therefore a double edge to advocating a multiple politics of diversity, for if this allows the expression of subjugated and silenced identities it has the potential to fragment and disorganize resistance, even within local settings.

Such assessments, brief as they are, begin to suggest possible directions a future critical criminology may take. In view of the weaknesses of both the modern and the postmodern approaches, it may be useful to explore a perspective that is not so much a complete reformulation of the modern (i.e., post-modern) as it is a "countermodern" endeavour that recognizes the value of postmodern contributions in the course of reformulating modernist critical criminology and its logics of control. In particular, this countermodern criminology need not jettison the *omnes et singulatim* epistemic theme or deconstruct it without considering the possible effects of such a move, but it would certainly have to rethink the individual/society exemplars (or versions of the theme). The explicit point of such an endeavour would be to rework the discursive foundations of existing social control patterns by continuing the critical search for a regulatory logic that promotes social justice. It would, however, differ from past critical endeavours by directing its criticisms to the hitherto unquestioned individual/society linkage.

To carry out such a task, the *singulatim* object of criminology could be reconstituted not as the liberal individual with a dubious freedom to act within tightly circumscribed behavioural fields; rather, the singular aspect may be construed as an agent of history whose identity is delineated by a subjugated group who seek to define their subjection (oppression) by mobilizing as a unified identity. This concept is certainly not novel and has been the basis of the rise of "new social movements."[5] Reconstructing the *singulatim* thus has the dual effect of remaining sensitive to the oppression of given contexts without disavowing a version of unity to avoid political fragmentation. Of course, the difficult task here is to achieve strategically significant amalgamations between new social movements.

At the same time, the *omnes* side of the formula ought not to be conceptualized through the reified notion of society, but rather left open as that condition that has yet to emerge; i.e., striving toward forms of *association* that yield freedom as a practice (as opposed to as an abstract concept).[6] The plural ("forms of association") is deliberately used here to avoid hypostatizing the *omnes* as an easily identifiable, describable and universal condition in the way that the term "society" has been constituted for uncritical consumption. In combination, this reworked *omnes et singulatim* theme in the context of a newly constituted criminology would emphasize the logics of control that are most appropriate for given circumstances. The aim is to encourage and facilitate the quest for social justice in differentiated contexts.

CONCLUSION

By way of conclusion, the previous analysis posits a way of conceiving the emerging debate between modern and postmodern criminology around the individual = society exemplars. Our conception then offers a way of reconstituting the theme in a critical criminology so as to capitalize on the strengths of modern and postmodern approaches while avoiding certain weaknesses. We have suggested that such a criminology assume neither the primordial existence of natural individuals, nor a fixed conception of society. Moreover, our proposed critical criminology need not conceive of agency through the liberal individual of correctionalist criminology, nor through the working class of critical criminology. Instead, our contention is that at transitional moments in history, it may be of some value to recast epistemic themes with different inflections. So, in a countermodern shift away from either modern or postmodern conceptions, we have argued that agency be developed as contextually-bound, where people coalesce around collective identities that offer resistance to existing patterns of domination.

The *singulatim* of such a countermodern criminology is no longer the individual, but the collective groups whose common subordinations in given contexts provide the impetus for identifying them as the "oppressed," as local issues activists, as new social movements, etc. By contrast, the *omnes* side of the theme is not some hypostatized, essential, or fixed notion of society, but rather an open field of possible association whose ideal state is a practical freedom from oppression.[7] In tandem, the *omnes et singulatim*, thus conceived, implies a different sort of criminology whose logic of control is not geared toward the correction of deviant "individuals," nor even the correction of an unjust society. On the contrary, this is a logic of control whose task is the continuous pursuit of resistance to oppression in specific contexts, and—through this—the positive search for modes of association that have conquered oppression.

ENDNOTES

The authors wish to thank Barry Smart and Mariana Valverde for their helpful suggestions.

1   See Foucault (1972). To take an important example from a range of possible confirming instances, one may note that even when a central protagonist of liberal theory like Mill emphasizes the individual's liberty, he nevertheless reaffirms the epistemic theme by concluding that "the worth of a state, in the long run, is the worth of the individuals composing it..." ([1859] 1956, 140).

2   In other words, disciplinary practices moulded individuals and articulated them to notions of society in fields of knowledge (the disciplines), which claimed a capacity to expose the essential features of individual and/or social existence (Foucault, 1977). This separation, as Smart (1992) argues, is integral to sociology as a discipline.

3   Detailed expositions of specific theories are frequently released in the criminology literature; e.g., Gibbons (1994), Pfohl (1985), Taylor, Walton, and Young (1973), etc.

4   For background to this position see Derrida (1976), Norris (1982), and Sarup (1989); on the deconstructionist position in criminology, see Henry and Milovanovic, 1991 and 1993.

5   Without wishing to range, in this chapter, over the considerable literature regarding the proliferation of "new social movements," we note its resonances to the position

we are trying to construct with regard to criminology. In general, see Plotke (1990) and Epstein (1990).

6   In a similar vein, Young (1990, chap.2) regards the concept of "oppression" as central to the discourse of contemporary emancipatory social movements. Justice, for Young, is based on a "social" rather than a "distributive" notion, one evoked by oppressions in context rather than by a presumptive universal axiom.

7   The struggle of oppressed groups to achieve this ideal state is reflected, for example, in the women's movement through both the development of a feminist jurisprudence (MacKinnon, 1983, 1987), and by the contrary disavowal of law as a discourse that can accommodate feminist concerns (C. Smart, 1989, 1990).

REFERENCES

Agger, Ben.   1991. "Critical Theory, Poststructuralism, Postmodernism: Their Sociological Relevance," *Annual Review of Sociology*, 17: 105–131.

Barak, Gregg.   1993. "Criminological Theory in the Postmodern Era." In *Varieties of Criminology: Readings from a Dynamic Discipline,* ed. by G. Barak. Westport: Praeger.

Barry, Norman.   1990. *Welfare.* Buckingham: Open University Press.

Baudrillard, Jean.   1983. *In the Shadow of Silent Majorities…or the End of the Social and Other Essays.* New York: Semiotext(e).

Bauman, Zygmunt.   1992. *Intimations of Postmodernity.* London: Routledge.

Beccaria, Cesare.   [1764] 1963. *On Crimes and Punishments.* Indianapolis: Bobbs-Merrill.

Becker, Howard S.   1963. *Outsiders: Studies in the Sociology of Deviance.* New York: Free Press.

Benhabib, Seyla.   1984. "Epistemologies of Postmodernism," *New German Critique*, 33: 103–126.

Bentham, Jeremy.   1973. *An Introduction to the Principles of Morals and Legislation.* New York: Hafner Press.

Burchell, Graham.   1991. "Peculiar Interests: Civil Society and Governing the System of Natural Liberty." In *The Foucault Effect,* ed. by Graham Burchell, Colin Gordon, and Peter Millar. New York: Routledge.

Dean, Mitchell.   1991. *The Constitution of Poverty: Towards a Genealogy of Liberal Governance.* London: Routledge.

Derrida, Jacques.   1976. *On Grammatology.* Baltimore: Johns Hopkins University Press.

Donzelot, Jacques.   1979. *The Policing of Families.* New York: Pantheon Books.

Durkheim, Emile.   1982. *The Rules of Sociological Method.* New York: Free Press.

Epstein, Barbara.   1990. "Rethinking Social Movement Theory," *Socialist Review,* 20(1): 35–64.

Foucault, Michel. 1991. "On Governmentality." In *The Foucault Effect*, ed. by Graham Burchell, Colin Gordon, and Peter Millar. New York: Routledge.

———. 1981. "Omnes et Singulatim." In *The Tanner Lectures on Human Values*, Vol. 2, edited by Sterling M. McMurrin. Cambridge: Cambridge University Press.

———. 1980. *Power/Knowledge: Selected Interviews and Other Writings, 1972–1977*. Edited by Colin Gordon. Brighton: Harvester Press.

———. 1977. *Discipline and Punish: The Birth of the Prison*. London: Allen Lane.

———. 1972. *The Order of Things: An Archaeology of the Human Sciences*. New York: Vintage Books.

Garofalo, Raphaele. 1914. *Criminology*. Boston: Little, Brown.

Gibbons, Don C. 1994. *Talking About Crime and Criminals*. Englewood Cliffs, N.J.: Prentice Hall.

Gordon, Colin. 1991. "Government Rationality: An Introduction." In *The Foucault Effect*, ed. by Graham Burchell, Colin Gordon, and Peter Millar. New York: Routledge.

Hacking, Ian. 1991. "How Should We Do the History of Statistics?" In *The Foucault Effect*, ed. by Graham Burchell, Colin Gordon, and Peter Millar. New York: Routledge.

Heidensohn, Frances. 1989. *Crime and Society*. London: Macmillan.

Henry, Stuart, and **Dragan Milovanovic.** 1993. "Back to Basics: A Postmodern Redefinition of Crime," *Critical Criminologist*, 5(2–3): 1–2, 12.

———. 1991. "Constitutive Criminology: The Maturation of Critical Theory," *Criminology*, 29(2): 293–316.

Hirschi, Travis. 1969. *Causes of Delinquency*. Berkeley: University of California Press.

Hunt, Alan. 1990. "Postmodernism and Critical Criminology," *The Critical Criminologist*, 2(1): 5–6, 17–18.

Laberge, Danielle. 1991. "Women's Criminality, Criminal Women, Criminalized Women: Questions in and for a Feminist Perspective," *The Journal of Human Justice*, 2(2): 37–56.

Laclau, Ernesto, and **Chantal Mouffe.** 1985. *Hegemony and Socialist Strategy*. London: Verso.

Lea, John, and **Jock Young.** 1984. *What Is to Be Done About Law and Order?* Harmondsworth: Penguin.

Lemert, Edwin, M. 1972. *Human Deviance, Social Problems and Social Control*. Englewood Cliffs, N.J.: Prentice Hall.

Leonard, Eileen. 1982. *Women, Crime and Society: A Critique of Theoretical Criminology*. New York: Longman.

Lilly, J. Robert, Francis Cullen, and **Richard Ball.** 1989. *Criminological Theory: Context and Consequences*. London: Sage.

Lombroso, Cesare. 1918. *Crime: Its Causes and Remedies*. Boston: Little Brown.

Lyotard, Jean-François. 1984. *The Postmodern Condition: A Report on Knowledge*. Minneapolis: University of Minnesota Press.

MacKinnon, Catherine. 1987. *Feminism Unmodified: Discourses on Life and Law*. London: Harvard University Press.

————. 1983. "Feminism, Marxism, Method, and the State: Toward Feminist Jurisprudence," *Signs*, 8(2): 635–658.

MacLean, Brian, and **Dragan Milovanovic.** 1991. *New Directions in Critical Criminology*. Vancouver: The Collective Press.

Matthews, Roger, and **Jock Young,** eds. 1986. *Confronting Crime*. London: Sage.

Matza, David 1969. *Becoming Deviant*. Englewood Cliffs, N.J.: Prentice Hall.

3/M., and **Gresham, M. Sykes.** 1961. "Juvenile Delinquency and Subterranean Values," *American Sociological Review*, 26(5): 712–719.

Merton, Robert K. 1938. "Social Structure and Anomie," *American Sociological Review*, 3: 672–682.

Messerschmidt, James. 1986. *Capitalism, Patriarchy and Crime: Towards a Socialist Feminist Perspective*. New Jersey: Rowman and Littlefield.

Mill, John S. [1956]. *On Liberty*. Reprint, New York: Bobbs-Merrill Company.

Milovanovic, Dragan. 1989. "Critical Criminology and the Challenge of Postmodernism," *Critical Criminologist*, 1(4).

Morris, Allison. 1987. *Women, Crime and Criminal Justice*. Oxford: Basil Blackwell.

Norris, Christopher. 1982. *Deconstruction: Theory and Practice*. London: Methuen.

Park, Robert E., Ernest V. Burgess, and **Roderick D. McKenzie.** 1967. *The City*. Chicago: University of Chicago Press.

Pasquino, Pasquale. 1991a. "Criminology: The Birth of Special Knowledge." In *The Foucault Effect*, ed. by Graham Burchell, Colin Gordon, and Peter Millar. New York: Routledge.

————. 1991b. "Theatrum Politicum: The Genealogy of Capital: Police and the State of Prosperity." In *The Foucault Effect*, ed. by Graham Burchell, Colin Gordon, and Peter Millar. New York: Routledge.

Pfohl, Stephen. 1985. *Images of Deviance and Social Control*. New York: McGraw-Hill.

Plotke, David. 1990. "What's So New About Social Movements?" *Socialist Review*, 20(1): 81–102.

Quetelet, Adolphe. 1984. *Research on the Propensity for Crime at Different Ages*. Translated by Sawyer Sylvester. Cincinnati: Anderson Publishing Company.

Quinney, Richard. 1970. *The Social Reality of Crime*. Boston: Little, Brown.

Rabinow, Paul, ed. 1994. *The Foucault Reader*. New York: Pantheon Books.

Sarup, Madan. 1989. *An Introductory Guide to Post-Structuralism and Postmodernism*. Athens: University of Georgia Press.

Sawicki, Jana. 1991. *Disciplining Foucault: Feminism, Power and the Body*. New York: Routledge.

Shaw, Clifford R., and **Henry D. McKay.** 1969. *Juvenile Delinquency and Urban Areas*. Chicago: University of Chicago Press.

Simon, Rita. 1975. *Women and Crime*. London: Lexington Books.

Smart, Barry. 1993. *Postmodernity*. London: Routledge.

———. 1992. *Modern Conditions, Postmodern Controversies*. New York: Routledge.

Smart, Carol. 1992. *Feminism and the Power of Law*. London: RKP.

———. 1990. "Feminist Approaches to Criminology or Postmodern Woman Meets Atavistic Man." In *Feminist Perspectives in Criminology*, ed. by Lorraine Gelsthorpe and Allison Morrison. Milton Keynes, Philadelphia: Open University Press.

———. 1989. *Feminism and the Power of Law*. London: Routledge.

Spencer, Herbert. 1874. *Principles of Sociology*. New York: Appelton.

Spitzer, Steven. 1975. "Toward a Marxian Theory of Deviance," *Social Problems*, 22(5): 638–651.

Sutherland, Edwin H. 1947. *Criminology*. Philadelphia: J. B. Lippincott.

———. 1937. *The Professional Thief: By a Professional Thief*. Chicago: University of Chicago Press.

Taylor, Ian. 1981. *Law and Order: Arguments for Socialism*. London: Macmillan.

———, **Paul Walton**, and **Jock Young.** 1973. *The New Criminology*. London: Routledge and Kegan Paul.

Thomas, Jim, and **Aogan O'Maolchatha.** 1989. "Reassessing the Critical Metaphor: An Optimistic Revisionist View," *Justice Quarterly*, 6(2): 143–172.

Touraine, Alain. 1989. "Is Sociology Still the Study of Society?" *Thesis Eleven*, 23: 5–34.

Turk, Austin. 1969. *Criminality and Legal Order*. Chicago: Rand-McNally.

Young, Iris Marion. 1990. *Justice and the Politics of Difference*. Princeton: Princeton University Press.

BEYOND CRITIQUE: TOWARD A POST-CRITICAL CRIMINOLOGY

Tullio Caputo and Ken Hatt

INTRODUCTION: LOOKING FORWARD BY LOOKING BACK

The past decade has been one of fundamental change in many areas of social and political thought. Serious challenges to conventional theorizing have had a considerable impact on disciplines such as sociology, anthropology, political science, and criminology. In this chapter, we trace some of the key theoretical developments in criminology and examine how the discipline is responding to the changes underway in social theory. In particular, we examine the contributions and shortcomings of critical criminology and some of the issues that a post-critical criminology must address.

Our emphasis is on the types of questions raised by criminologists and the theoretical models they have developed to address their concerns.[1] This approach allows us to highlight the differences between the various models developed within the modern paradigm that has informed criminology since its inception. For example, while some criminologists have been primarily concerned with understanding the nature of crime and criminality, others, such as critical criminologists, have focused on the creation and implementation of law and the social control process. Furthermore, our comparative approach also allows us to consider the criticisms of modern criminology raised by theorists struggling to overcome the limitations of the modern paradigm. These include feminist scholars, left realists, Foucauldians, post-modernists, and other social scientists.

We begin by presenting a four-quadrant model that outlines the key elements of modern theorizing in criminology. It addresses the types of questions raised by the different theories, the methodologies employed, the level of analysis, the treatment of temporality and the particular voice different theories use to facilitate their analyses. We discuss how various modern criminological theories fit the four-quadrant model according to these criteria. We also examine how the approach taken by critical criminologists sought to overcome the limitations of earlier modern criminological theories. In this sense, we consider critical criminology to represent the culmination of modern theorizing in criminology.

We review the critiques made of critical criminology and consider both its contributions and limitations as a modern theory. We also examine the way various critical criminologists have responded to the challenges directed at them. Our own theoretical efforts are presented in this context and we review our attempts at developing a model that is uniquely Canadian, historically specific, and holistic. The challenges posed by feminists, left realists and Foucauldians to critical criminology—and to modern criminology more generally—are then considered. We conclude with some thoughts about what a post-critical criminology must take into account and show how these ideas have influenced our own thinking.

A FOUR-QUADRANT MODEL OF MODERN THEORIZING IN CRIMINOLOGY

Two central aspects of the analytical strategy employed by modern criminologists include the level of analysis they use and their treatment of temporality. The first of these has to do with the scope or scale of the analysis. We refer to studies of individuals and their characteristics as representing a microsociological level of analysis. A macrosociological level of analysis focuses on the social structure and includes larger concepts such as class, gender, and race.

The second dimension of the model is more concerned with temporality in theoretical terms. Here we distinguish between research styles that are either synchronic or diachronic in nature. The synchronic style undertakes research or explains its problems through strategies that involve working with a "slice of time"; for example, by employing a sample survey. By contrast, the diachronic style is concerned with analysis "through time" or studying how things change.

These two central aspects of modern theorizing can be represented as axes in a model of modern theorizing in which one axis represents the spatial dimension (macro versus micro levels of analysis) and the other the time dimension (synchronic and diachronic). The intersection of these two axes results in a four-quadrant table in which modern theories can be located according to whether they are microsynchronic, macrosynchronic, microdiachronic or macrodiachronic. The four quadrants of the table reflect the distinctive styles of theorizing characteristics of modern criminology. The theories that occupy each quadrant can be distinguished in terms of the unit of analysis they employ, the type of question that drives the analysis, and the "voice" of the analyst.[2] A description of the types of theories that occupy each of the four quadrants in the model is presented below.

FIGURE 19.1:   Basic Styles of Criminological Reasoning

Synchronic	Macrosociological	Diachronic

Social Organization
Why does criminal
activity persist?
Synechdoche: part/whole
Strain Theory

Social Change
What are the dynamics by
which crime and criminal jus-
tice change?
Irony
Critical Criminology

Acts
Why do some people commit
a crime?
Metaphor-Resemblance
Social Learning Theory

Interaction
What is the process by which
individuals come to be defined
as criminal?
Metonymy-Essence
Labeling Theory

Microsociological

Accounting for Differences in Behaviour: Microsynchronic Theories

Microsynchronic theorists ask, "What causes some people (rather than others) to commit deviant or criminal acts?" The unit of analysis they use is either the person or interpersonal relations. The style of research used by these theorists consists primarily of a multivariate analysis of survey data gathered from respondents, most often at one point in time. The voice in which these analysts speak is that of similarity and difference, or in dramaturgical terms, resemblance. For example, these theorists examine the similarities and differences between the characteristics of "criminals" and "noncriminals." In their quest, some microsynchronic theorists tried to determine whether criminals have different body types than noncriminals. Others have examined genetic factors such as chromosomes, while still others have looked at intelligence as the feature distinguishing criminals from noncriminals.

Classical criminologists developed the first microsynchronic approach in modern criminology (Beccaria, [1764] 1963; Bentham, [1775]; Phillipson, 1970). Classical criminologists celebrated the ideas of individual responsibility, rationality, and free will. The question of why people committed crime posed no mystery to these theorists. They argued that people commit crime for rational reasons. They steal, for example, to acquire the pleasure afforded by the stolen property without paying the costs of acquiring the goods legally. Classical criminologists further argued that in order to curb crime, one need not resort to vicious or extreme punishment. What was needed was to make the cost of getting caught for committing crime slightly greater than the pleasure that could be derived from the criminal activity. Rational human beings had merely to complete the requisite social calculus to come to the realization that they should refrain from crime.

These ideas are more than a historical curiosity. Current thinking about crime and punishment owes a great deal to the Classical School of Criminology. Theories of deterrence based on notions of utility, individual responsibility, and free will echo the thinking of the classical criminologists. For example, current conservative criminal justice policies have been translated into an appeal to "let the punishment fit the crime." This demand reverberates in ongoing calls for stricter sentencing guidelines, tougher laws, and more stringent law-enforcement practices.

The main question asked by microsynchronic criminologists changed with the appearance of positivist criminology in the late nineteenth and early twentieth centuries. The major thrust of the positivists was to explain criminal behaviour by differentiating between the characteristics of criminals and noncriminals (Lombroso, 1876; 1912). They sought the sources of criminal behaviour in the biological, physiological, psychological and social characteristics of individual criminals. Unlike classical criminologists, the positivists rejected notions of free will, favouring a deterministic approach instead. They argued that individuals who commit crime should not be held responsible since crime is due to forces over which they have little or no control. The best that could be done was that experts from the emerging disciplines of psychiatry and psychology could provide the appropriate treatment to these individuals. The faith that the positivist criminologists had in these strategies contributed to a wider belief in the ability and legitimacy of science to solve social problems such as crime.

The question raised by microsynchronic theorists changed once again in the late 1940s with the introduction of Sutherland's theory of differential association. Differential association represented a significant shift away from the focus on personal characteristics and crime. Sutherland (1939) argued that there was little difference in the way we learn conventional and criminal behaviour. His formulation challenged the earlier notion that there was one group in society that was criminal and another group that wasn't. Criminal behaviour, he argued, was learned and not directly produced by the characteristics of either the individuals involved or the neighbourhoods in which they lived. Instead, Sutherland stated that crime is more likely to occur when individuals find themselves in situations in which definitions favourable to crime outweigh definitions favouring law-abiding behaviour. This idea was developed further in "social learning" theory (Bandura, 1979). Social learning theory focuses on the life experiences of individuals through which persons learn to be aggressive. Bandura (1979), a major proponent of social learning theory, argued that criminality was learned through behavioural modeling, which was found in three major areas: the family, experiences in the environment, and the media.[3]

Variations in the Distribution of Crime: Macrosynchronic Theories

The top left-hand quadrant reflects macrosynchronic theories. They address the question, "What causes crime rates or socially organized criminal activity to vary throughout a society?" Macrosynchronic theory examines either group activity (gangs), crime rates, or more generalized deviance and explains it in relation to the social structure. The voice in this mode of thinking is represented by the metaphorical device of synecdoche, where the object of expression is to show how the part fits into the whole. Part/whole analysis is precisely the approach taken by the functionalist theorists who can be located in this quadrant of our model.

The work of Clifford Shaw and Henry McKay (1939; 1942) is an example of a macrodiachronic approach. It was based on the compilation of life histories of delinquents. However, Shaw and McKay are primarily recognized for their use of demographic information to plot crime patterns in various areas in Chicago. They identified different zones in the city according to rates of delinquency, rates of illness, the extent of residential or industrial activity, economic status, and the composition of various neighbourhoods. They argued that normal social relations cannot be maintained in certain zones of the city and criminal or delinquent subcultures emerge as a result. They concluded that higher rates of delinquency were characteristic of areas that are socially disorganized. In this way, their approach moved away from analyses of individual characteristics to include macrostructural factors. The primary question addressed by Shaw and McKay shifted criminology's emphasis from explaining why certain individuals commit crime to understanding higher crime rates in certain areas of the city.

The work of Robert Merton (1938) provides another example of how modern criminology moved away from its earlier emphasis on the characteristics of those involved in crime. Merton was concerned with the impact that broader social structures had on more general expressions of crime. Using Durkheim's notion of "anomie," Merton argued that much criminal activity was induced by cultural and structural pressures generated within society. This was visible in the differential crime rates or patterns of criminal behaviour found in various segments of the population. He argued that the overarching emphasis in America on material success, "the American Dream," resulted in significant pressure for achieving this goal. In the absence of legitimate means, some people turned to illegitimate means to achieve legitimate goals. Essentially, he argued that the strain of anomie could lead to deviant adaptations such as innovation (which includes conventional criminal behaviour), ritualism, retreatism, or rebellion.

Merton's ideas were extended by Cloward and Ohlin (1960) who noted that access to illegitimate means was also restricted. Entry into organized criminal groups, for example, is not automatic but based on access to illegitimate opportunity structures. These illegitimate structures operate in ways similar to their legitimate counterparts. Cloward and Ohlin identified various types of gang adaptations as subcultures that develop in response to the strain produced by modern industrial society.

Interactive Processes and Societal Reaction: Microdiachronic Theories

The bottom right-hand quadrant contains the microdiachronic theories. Theorists using this approach ask, "What is the process by which some persons rather than others come to be defined as criminal (or deviant)?" The work of labeling theorists and other interactionists such as Lemert (1951; 1972), Becker (1963), Goffman (1963), Matza (1969), and Schur (1972) provide examples of this approach. These types of analyses exhibit a voice that speaks of the "essence" of a phenomenon.

The emergence of symbolic interactionism and labeling theory in the 1960s and early 1970s shifted the major preoccupation in modern criminology away from individuals or social structures to emphasize processes of interaction. As such, the labeling theorists provided the first serious challenge to the dominance of earlier, synchronic theorizing in modern criminology. Crime and deviance began to be looked at differently as the importance of societal reaction and labeling became recognized as essential elements in the social control process. Labeling theorists argued that most people are involved, at some time in their lives, in actions that could be called crime. Only a small portion, however, are ever labeled as criminals. Labeling theorists recognized the role that power plays in the labeling process. Their studies revealed that powerful groups and individuals are more able than others to avoid being labeled. The powerful are also more likely to have their values and beliefs incorporated into law. Gusfield's (1955) study of prohibition laws and Becker's (1963) explication of the role of moral entrepreneurs are examples of these types of studies. They were particularly influential in demonstrating the importance of power in defining crime and labeling criminals.

State, Class and Social Control: Macrodiachronic Theories

The top right-hand quadrant identifies the macrodiachronic theories. Critical criminology is the major example of theories in this quadrant. Critical criminologists ask, "What are the dynamics by which criminality and criminal justice change?" Crime and criminal justice are interpreted in the context of the dynamics of late-capitalist social formations (see for example Chambliss and Seidman, 1971; Taylor, Walton, and Young, 1973, and Hall et al., 1978). The voice used is an ironic one, for it characterizes "crime" as epiphenomenal. That is, crime is produced by those in power whose purpose and claim to legitimacy rests on a grander, but unacknowledged, system of exploitation (i.e., capitalism). This ironic voice identifies the tensions inherent in critical criminology.

Critical criminology provided a fundamental challenge to other modern criminological theories. The rise of the new left in the 1960s and the resurgence of Marxist scholarship in the United States during this period gave critical criminology its original impetus. Scholars such as Quinney (1970), Chambliss and Seidman (1971), the Schwendingers (1976), Spitzer (1975), and Scull (1977) conducted class-based, if not expressly Marxist, analyses of crime and social control. Much of this work extended the focus on the exercise of power initiated by the proponents of labeling theory. The class-based nature of power, and its exercise by the state through the creation and enforcement of law, provided fertile ground for analyses.

The neo-Marxist approach gained considerable attention with the publication in 1973 of *The New Criminology* by the British scholars Taylor, Walton, and Young. This book represents a watershed in the development of critical criminology. These authors not only provided a serious critique of other modern criminological theories, they issued an explicitly socialist call to arms.

CRITICAL CRIMINOLOGY AND THE CRITIQUE OF MODERN CRIMINOLOGY

Much of the early work in critical criminology sought to demonstrate the inadequacy of modern criminology's preoccupation with individual motivations for criminal behaviour. Even when the social structure is identified as the source of the problem, as is the case with strain theory, the remedies that are advanced inevitably seek to rehabilitate or reform individuals. In this way, a problem that is essentially structural in nature is transformed by modern criminology into the shortcomings or recalcitrance of individuals. Solutions are based on making up for the "deficits" of these individuals rather than on changing the social structure.

Critical criminologists argued that this preoccupation with individuals, and with street crime more generally, legitimated the use of harsh social-control measures against the working class. At the same time, the more harmful behaviour of white-collar criminals, corporations, and the state received little attention. Critical criminologists pointed out that the continued focus on the behaviour of the powerless represented an important ideological tool that aided in defining certain types of crime (street crime) more dangerous and worthy of social control than other types (white-collar or "suit" crime).

In response to this situation, many early critical criminologists sought to demystify and debunk the pluralistic, egalitarian ideology of the law in liberal democracies such as the United States. They attempted to expose the ruling class bias of the state and the law. The early work of American critical criminologists reflects an instrumental Marxist stance that identifies the state and the law as tools or instruments of ruling class oppression. Critical criminologists in Canada initially followed a similar course, with authors such as Goff and Reasons (1978) and Snider (1979) documenting both the harm done by corporate and white-collar crime, and the lack of state response to this behaviour.

The work of Greenaway and Brickey (1978), and Reasons and Rich (1979) signaled an initial shift away from the study of traditional topics in criminology to an emphasis on issues related to law and social control. The contributions of Ian Taylor (1982; 1983) furthered the movement of Canadian critical criminologists away from modern criminology toward the sociology of law. Taylor's work advanced the debate beyond the realm of crime and its control to encompass a much broader social analysis that considered ideology, political economy, and the role of the state.

As the movement toward the sociology of law gained momentum in Canada, a number of changes took place in the theoretical models that were being employed. To begin with, the earlier instrumental Marxist approach began to be challenged. Empirical evidence indicated that the ruling class is not always able to use the law and the state to its own advantage. At times, workers win considerable victories. Furthermore, a more complex model of the state and the ruling class was required than the simplistic one underlying early instrumental Marxist criminology.

A structural Marxist model, based on the work of Nicos Poulantzas (1973), was promoted to address some of the shortcomings of the instrumental Marxist approach. The structural Marxist model recognized that the ruling class was not a monolithic entity but that there were fractions and strata within it. A histori-cally specific analyses that took into account the competing interests of the vari-ous fractions and strata of the ruling class was advocated. This approach provided a more complex analysis of the ruling class.

The structural Marxist model further noted that the state did not always act in the interest of specific capitalists, but rather exercised "relative autonomy" in pursuit of the long-term interests of capital. The state is defined as a "capitalist state" in this formulation and its actions are best understood as such. Thus, in certain circumstances, it was possible for individual capitalists to be subjected to censure or for the working class to make significant gains as long as the integrity of the capitalist system was ensured.

While the attention of early critical criminologists had been directed toward the coercive functions of the law and the state, subsequent analyses shifted to an examination of the role of ideology and legitimation in the social control process. These analyses showed how social control involves a combination of consent (legitimation) and coercion. The specific nature of this relationship varies accord-ing to how power is distributed and exercised. The strength of the labour move-ment, public support for coercive measures, the role of the media, and other related factors all play a role in establishing the context within which the social control process, that is, the explicit use of consent and coercion, takes place.

The Growth of Critical Criminology and the Sociology of Law in Canada

In an article published in 1985, Bob Ratner examined the state of criminology in Canada and concluded that the prospects for the development of a critical criminology (specifically a political economy of crime) were quite bleak. He delineated the factors that supported the liberal-progressive control of the criminological establishment in Canada. These factors included the continued control by liberal-progressives of institutional positions in criminology, the small size of the criminological community, geographical dispersion, funding scarcity, and the meager resources available to criminologists outside of the establishment. He also noted the difficulties in attracting recruits to critical criminology since both academic and institutional careers are limited. Prospects were unpredictable and chancy, according to Ratner, for those who did not "choose to walk lockstep inside the liberal boot" (1985, 26).

Even as Ratner was writing these words, however, significant changes were taking place in criminology in Canada. A number of new critical criminologists were establishing themselves across the country. Their numbers and influence have grown, so that today a considerable number of criminologists in Canadian academia are sympathetic to a critical approach. This does not mean that critical criminologists are able to exercise much institutional power or influence. However, the situation appears to be far different from that described by Ratner just a decade ago.

After Ratner's assessment of the state of critical criminology in Canada, a number of volumes were published that reflected how active critical criminologists were in Canada. They also showed the extent to which the focus had shifted to issues involving the nature and role of the law and the state. For example, in 1985 Fleming published *The New Criminologies in Canada*, which contains several important contributions in the development of the sociology of law in Canada. In 1986, Brickey and Comack published *The Social Basis of Law: Critical Readings in the Sociology of Law,* which contains a number of empirical examinations of the nature and role of law and the state. Two additional edited volumes appeared in 1986 that contributed to the growing debate by critical criminologists in Canada. These were Boyd's *The Social Dimensions of Law* and MacLean's *The Political Economy of Crime*. Also in 1986, an entire issue of the American journal *Crime and Social Justice* was devoted to the situation in Canada.

Critical Criminology and the Debate Over Neoconservatism in Canada

The publication in 1987 of *State Control* by Ratner and McMullan gave a specific focus and texture to the various debates taking place in Canadian critical criminology at the time. These included discussions about the usefulness of the concept of relative autonomy and a debate about Canada's experience with neocon-servatism in the wake of Thatcherism and Reaganism.[4] Briefly, this debate cen-tred around understanding the nature of the Canadian social formation, and in particular the role of the state in light of the relative absence of neoconservatism in Canada. Some theorists argued that Canada had developed an "exceptional state" similar to that in Britain and the United States. Others suggested that the lack of a well-developed, working-class opposition in Canada reduced the need for the type of ideological and political conflict experienced in Britain and the United States. For these theorists, Canada represented a thoroughly "bourgeois" social formation.

An examination of the various positions expressed in this debate revealed that each had amplified a particular aspect of the Canadian reality but none pro-vided a satisfactory approach. A model was needed that was historically specific and took into account the peculiarities of the Canadian social formation. These include, among others, such unique characteristics as Canada's colonial past, small population, vast geography, regionalism, the federal-provincial split in jurisdiction, its proximity to the United States, and the role it plays in the world economic community. Attempts at responding to these various conditions have resulted in the development of a particular style of governing in Canada that we have called "managing consent."

Our model of managing consent (Hatt, Caputo, and Perry, 1990; 1992) sug-gests that the federal government is limited in its actions by both external and internal constraints. Externally, the need to be in harmony with foreign markets represents a significant constraint on the federal government. Actions such as protectionism, economic nationalism, or generous labour settlements put the country at odds with its international trading partners, most notably the United States. Internally, too strong an attack on unemployment insurance or other social welfare payments that Canadians have come to expect results in signifi-cant domestic political pressure. In this way both external and internal factors severely limit the options available to the Canadian state.

One strategy adopted by the federal government is to pass its fiscal problems on to the provinces. The jurisdictional split between federal and provincial gov-ernments in Canada supports such a strategy. The federal government in Canada is responsible for passing legislation while the provinces are responsible for its implementation. Provinces can also enact their own legislation and have sole jurisdiction over certain areas such as education and health care. The federal government pays for its programmes through an elaborate system of transfer payments. It also provides some funds to provinces to pay for programmes under their jurisdiction. The result is a complex, overlapping jurisdictional web and the development of a series of strategies to take advantage of such a situation, including "pork barreling" and "brokerage politics."

As the fiscal crisis worsened in recent years (O'Connor, 1973), there has been a mounting federal budget deficit. In response, the federal government has passed on part of the problem to the provinces, who in turn have passed the problem on to municipalities. In this context, the federal government subtly manages consent within a politically limited context while it forces provincial governments to "manage crises" in much more open and potentially volatile environments.

The concept of consent we are using here requires some elaboration. We distinguish in the model between policies that are "consented to" and those that reflect a "consensus." We understand consensus to include negotiation and compromise between competing interests. The outcome of such a process is usually an agreement that is acceptable to the parties involved. We distinguish between this type of consensus and our concept of consent, which implies that some groups accept political decisions while not necessarily agreeing with them. We believe that various groups may tolerate specific policies for instrumental reasons or because of a lack of power to oppose them. In this way consent lacks the mutual agreement, which in our view forms the basis of consensus. Moreover, our definition of consent does not portray actors as passive or powerless pawns caught in a political vortex, nor does it resort to the imputation of false consciousness as the basis of hegemony. Consent is understood as dynamic, transitory, and reflecting both the immediate and long-term interests of the participants.

Our model of managing consent outlines a number of strategies developed by the Canadian state to govern such a diverse and varied nation. Elements of Canada's political economy, history, and the way that legitimacy operates in this country are considered. The model represents our initial attempt to come to grips with the Canadian experience by placing the actions of the state, or governance, at the centre of the analysis.

THE LIMITS OF CRITICAL CRIMINOLOGY

The movement by many criminologists in Canada toward critical criminology and the sociology of law reflected their attempt to address various shortcomings of other modern criminological theories. They also sought to build on the contributions of labeling theory and instrumental Marxist formulations while avoiding the limitations of these approaches. Their efforts increasingly diverted attention away from questions of individual motivation to commit crime to analyses of the nature and role of law and the state. Insights derived from political economy and other macro approaches were used to better understand broader processes of social control.

Ironically, the potential of critical criminology to provide a more useful analysis of the law and the state began just as the nature of the state in advanced Western capitalist social formations was undergoing dramatic change. The unraveling of the postwar compromise and the emergence of a world system has resulted in a fundamental restructuring that has had a profound impact on the nature and role of the state. The influence of multinational corporations has been an important part of this restructuring, especially with the development of electronic data transfer technology. The world system is increasingly being dominated by a few transnational corporations who owe no allegiance to particular nation states. This reality places the relevance of the concept of the state in question. As a result, existing theoretical formulations of the state are being reexamined as theorists grapple with the meaning of the changes taking place.

The relevance of critical criminology has been challenged on several other fronts as well. An important internal critique stems from the inability of Marxist-inspired models to escape charges of being determinist or even functionalist in nature. The adoption of the Poulantzian notion of "relative autonomy" was, in part, an attempt to respond to these charges. Critics pointed out, however, that the structural Marxist models are still essentially determinist and functional if "in the last instance" the state acts in the interests of the capitalist system. The difficulties with the earlier instrumental Marxist approach had not been resolved by the more complex structuralist Marxist model. The state could still be defined as a tool in the hands of the ruling class, even though this relationship was somewhat less direct than it had been in instrumental Marxist formulations.

Other criticisms of structural Marxist approaches began to emerge. Some centred on the level of abstraction while others cited the lack of human agency in the model. For example, the move toward analyses of the law and the state provided little opportunity for the struggles of real individuals or groups to be considered. In particular, this approach could not address the contradictions that the consequences of crime had for working-class people. At a more fundamental level, Marxist-inspired models failed to come to grips with the problem of order and what to do if people break the law or harm others. Will there be a means of enforcing laws? What of punishment for those who commit crime and cause harm? Some critical criminologists put forward the concept of community as a response to these questions. This strategy, however, raised more questions than it answered. For example, who is included in the community? What happens if the "community" turns out to be intolerant of the actions of particular members. Several scholars suggested that contrary to an idealized and romanticized notion of community, real communities can be reactionary, racist, and sexist (Cohen, 1985).

Other critics charged that Marxist-inspired models failed to adequately conceptualize the problem of crime and criminals. In rudimentary Marxist formulations, criminals are seen as protorevolutionaries and crime understood as actions against the capitalist system and the oppression it represents. In more sophisticated Marxist formulations, crime is understood as people responding to the alienating and oppressive conditions of a capitalist society. Critics have argued that neither of these formulations is able to deal adequately with the real problem that crime represents in people's lives.

Both instrumental and structuralist Marxist models raised serious questions about the status of crime in Marxist analyses generally. Some scholars suggested that crime is not an appropriate category for Marxist theory since it is essentially a bourgeois concept with no place in a Marxist model (O'Malley, 1983; 1988).

In this critique, crime is understood as a consequence of the operation of the capitalist system. The subjugation of the working class, including the exploitation and domination required for the extraction and appropriation of surplus value and the maintenance of a reserve army of labour, are aspects of the operation of the capitalist system that result in social control measures being implemented against the working class. Crime is a device created by the bourgeoisie to legitimate such a process. Others have taken a more direct approach on this question with some actually calling for an anticriminology stance (Cohen, 1988).

In addition to these theoretical issues, some scholars have questioned critical criminology on methodological grounds. The critique of positivism accepted by many Marxist scholars creates a number of methodological concerns. How, for example, should Marxist criminological analyses be undertaken? What of the nature of evidence and the use of such things as government statistics or survey analysis. Are the techniques of positivist analysis flawed or is the criticism of positivism primarily aimed at its underlying theoretical and philosophical assumptions? With the exception of several well-worn nostrums, little was provided by Marxist scholars that went beyond a critique of positivism. Marxist analyses were to be historically specific and holistic. Detailed techniques for conducting research had to be imported from other disciplines, such as history or literary criticism, or adapted from existing positivist approaches with the requisite claims of ideological purity and superiority to differentiate them from their disavowed positivist roots. Some Marxist scholarship skirted this issue by focusing on theoretical and philosophical matters while avoiding "empirical" questions. In some cases, debates among critical criminologists turned into internal discussions about their own theoretical abstractions, with little reference to the experience of those most affected by crime. The criticisms of positivism and the need for a Marxist methodology were not resolved in these efforts, but avoided.

Finally, critical criminology had to grapple with issues surrounding an appropriate stance for the analyst. Like all modern theories, critical criminology reflected a stance in which the analyst stood apart from the subject of inquiry, treating it as epiphenomenal. Insights derived from cultural studies and studies of postmodernity suggest that such a stance for the analyst is no longer viable. An alternative strategy is required that includes the analyst within the field of study.

These represent some of the major challenges facing critical criminology. It is important to note that many critical criminologists were aware of these shortcomings, including the criticisms that they themselves had raised. Those continuing to work in this area adopted several strategies to address these problems. As Ratner and McMullan (1987) point out, some took their cue from political economy and followed a capital-logic approach. Others adopted a more dynamic class conflict model, turning to the work of Antonio Gramsci for direction. Still others attempted to incorporate the insights they derived from feminism, left realism, or the work of Michel Foucault.

FURTHER CHALLENGES TO CRITICAL CRIMINOLOGY: FEMINISM, LEFT REALISM, AND FOUCAULT

A number of other criticisms of critical criminology emerged beyond the ones discussed above. These include, among others, those raised by feminists, left realists and Foucauldians. Each of these will be discussed briefly.

Critiques based on feminist theory apply to critical criminology as well as to other modern criminological theories. Feminist scholars pointed out that women were invisible in male-stream criminological analyses (Boyd and Sheehy, 1989; Cain, 1990; Currie and Kline, 1991; Daly and Chesney-Lind, 1988; Smart, 1989; and Smith, 1987). When not invisible, female criminals were either misinterpreted by being male-defined or "medicalized" by having their behaviour pathologized. The other common portrayal of women in criminological writings was as victims. Feminist criminologists came to recognize the pitfalls of trying to understand women's behaviour in the context of a male-defined and male-dominated criminal justice system. Their efforts to address issues of female criminality within this context proved unsatisfactory, serving to reproduce the values and categories of the existing system. In response, feminists called for analyses that decentre the male-stream theoretical and analytical models of modern criminology, including critical criminology.

The decentring of male-stream criminology was accomplished, in part, through the use of more reflexive methodologies sensitive to the experiences of women (Smith, 1987). In addition, patriarchy was taken into account, including the ways it conditions both social and gender relations. Patriarchy had not been a major variable in criminological analyses to this point. Its inclusion by feminist scholars challenged the priority given to class by critical criminologists. In fact, a critique of critical criminologists was that they were patriarchal precisely because they did not "see" women in their analyses. In addition to gender, the alternative methodologies developed by feminist scholars emphasized multivocality as a way of including the voices of those not present in the analysis.

Feminist scholars also recognized the importance of the stance of the analyst in conducting criminological research (Cain, 1990). They developed methodological strategies that incorporated this insight. They argued that the analyst has a role to play that goes far beyond that of the detached and "objective" researcher of earlier positivist approaches. The analyst becomes a participant in the research, reflecting both a political stance and a commitment to other participants in the process. In this way, theory and praxis become inexorably fused in the research enterprise.

For their part, the left realists (Kinsey, Lea, and Young, 1986; Lea and Young, 1984; Lowman and MacLean, 1992; Matthews, 1987; Young, 1987) presented a number of serious critiques of critical criminology, or what they call "left idealism." They charged that the left idealists had lost crime as a political issue to the neoconservatives by ignoring the harm crime causes to working-class men, women, and children. The long-term agenda of the left idealists had sacrificed short-term political action such that the working class was turning to Thatcher and Reagan who had made crime a political priority. Left realists argued that the emphasis of a critical criminology had to be shifted away from such macrosociological concerns as the nature and role of law and the state to address the harsh reality that crime represents for working-class people. This strategy would, at a minimum, wrest the issue of crime away from the neoconservatives whose policies exacerbated the situation, often resulting in even greater violence against the working class at the hands of state authorities.

Left realists were also critical of the methodology employed by modern criminologists, including critical criminologists. They rejected the abstract empiricism of sample surveys and official statistics, approaches based on abstractions of individuals and crime that failed to deal with the reality of crime in people's lives. Left realists proposed an alternative to state-sponsored research and government statistics based on their own surveys of working-class men, women, and children. Their approach was to take crime seriously and emphasize the reality of crime. They focused on microsociological explanations of the impact that capitalist exploitation has on the lives of working people. They noted that working-class men beat up other working-class men and working-class women. Class exploitation was made the focus of analysis in this formulation, rather than the macrostructural concerns of the left idealists.

The left realists pointed out that in many Marxist models, crime is treated as an epiphenomenon. That is, it does not exist as an essential category of these models nor does it have a place within the theoretical schema. Crime exists, instead, as a by-product of the operation of the capitalist system. Left realists argued that crime had to be taken much more seriously. They incorporated a "realism" based on the philosophical writing of authors such as Keat and Urry (1975) and Benton (1977). Instead of looking at capitalism as a total movement, they focused on the impact that it has on the lives of real people.

The final criticisms to be examined here are based on the work of Michel Foucault. Critics taking a Foucauldian approach would raise a number of serious challenges for critical criminology (Foucault, 1977, 1980, 1991; Gordon, 1991; O'Malley, 1992; Palmer and Pearce, 1983). They stem from a radically different conceptualization of power. Foucault transformed existing approaches by looking at power in a very different way. Instead of analyzing structures of power, Foucault identified it as a generative phenomenon that tended to be reproduced through discursive practices, especially that of expertise. He pointed out, for example, that the emergence of modern criminology coincided with the development of experts, such as psychiatrists, who dealt with people's souls.

Associated with the rise of experts in the modern era was the notion of subjectivity; that is, the creation of persons or individuals as "subjects." The radical nature of Foucault's critique rests on his argument that without the transformation of persons into subjects, the various forms of discourse or regulation through expertise would not have been possible. The emphasis for Foucault was on regulatory techniques and processes as opposed to hierarchical control. This represents an alternative theoretical conceptualization to the one that informed modern criminology. He also provided an alternative methodology. He traced the genealogy of the discourses of power and the way they operated and spread in the regulation of criminality, sexuality, and mental illness.

CRITICAL CRIMINOLOGY AS THE CULMINATION OF THEORIZING IN MODERN CRIMINOLOGY

Critical criminology can be described as the culmination of modern criminology because it sought to understand crime and criminality as inherent features of the social structure. That is, it rejected the notion that crime could be understood apart from the macrostructural processes that characterize the operation of a particular social formation. In this conceptualization, state, class, and social control processes are key dimensions of the analysis. This contrasts with both microlevel conceptualizations of crime and those macro analyses that attempt to account for differential crime rates apart from the dynamic features of the social structure.

While they sought to overcome the limitations of earlier criminological theories, the critical criminologists were unable to overcome the limitations inherent in the modern paradigm. For example, critics of critical criminology shared a skepticism about the adequacy of a theory that centres on the dynamics of the structure of capitalism. This point was made in a variety of ways. Some feminist scholars, for example, noted that patriarchy had been neglected as a dominant structure manifest in law and other gendered relations. Others called attention to the absence of an adequate conceptualization of the experiences of women. Left realists called for a criminology that could come to terms with the harm faced by the working class. They expressed cynicism about the adequacy of the "ironic" voice of critical criminology in which crime is seen as a by-product of the dynamics of capitalism. For their part, Foucauldians stressed the emptiness of any analysis that relies primarily on structural trends. They called, instead, for studies that deal with power as a complex and dynamic phenomenon. For example, they noted the importance of understanding the manner in which disciplinary and surveillance practices are transformed through techniques of expertise into regimes of regulation.

Each of these critiques calls for a fundamental reformulation of criminology that goes beyond what was accomplished by the critical criminologists. Questions exist about the proper domain for criminological analyses and the manner in which these analyses should be undertaken. However, many of the critics of critical criminology are themselves subject to serious criticisms. For example, despite their attempts to overcome the shortcomings of modern criminological theories, neither the feminists, left realists, nor Foucauldians have dealt satisfactorily with the analysis of social space and the problem of conflation.

The problem of conflation represents a dilemma faced by theorists in dealing with social space. According to Archer (1988, 25–102), conflation involves theorizing in which either the macro- or microsociological level has been neglected or reduced, or where both levels are subsumed in a more general analysis. That is, if an analyst focuses on structure to such an extent that activity at the micro or local level is ignored, concerns about the adequacy of the theory can be raised. This is precisely the charge made of critical criminology by its critics. Recall that feminist scholars correctly pointed out that women's voices were being ignored by critical criminologists. Left realists also showed how critical criminology had failed to take into account the real suffering and harm that crime causes working-class people. In focusing predominantly on local and interpersonal events, however, these critics leave themselves open to similar charges since they ignore the structural constraints that impact on the local interaction. While their criticisms have merit, they do not provide us with viable alternatives.

Archer (1988) points out that the issue is not simply a matter of devising a more general process in which both micro and macro levels are easily contained. Such a fluid way of thinking does not help us specify the nature of structural change or the role that local events play in it.

A second problem can be identified by applying our four-quadrant model. This problem is based on the time dimension of the model and deals with temporality. The criticisms directed at the modern paradigm suggest that it can no longer be assumed that social relations naturally evolve as synchronic theories assume they do. Nor are they automatically reproduced in the manner described by diachronic theorists such as labeling theorists or critical criminologists. In future theorizing, the very nature of change must be problematized and addressed directly.

These dilemmas within the modern paradigm are joined by two other major concerns that arose as a result of the critiques by feminists, left realists, Foucauldians and from other social scientists. The first deals with the stance of the analyst. It is no longer possible to conceptualize criminology as an exercise in which the criminologist is invisibly located at a distance from the object of analysis. We now need to deal with the relation of the analyst to the object of analysis within our theoretical frame. That is, the object of investigation in modern criminology has been conceptualized as being located apart from the analyst, existing separately in time and space. It is precisely this separation that was criticized by feminists, left realists, Foucauldians, and "postmodern" theorists. Each of these critiques, in one way or another, insists that theorizing regarding criminality must include a specific formulation of the relation of the analyst to the subject of analysis.

Another major change follows from this: the very definition of crime and its status in the enterprise of knowing has shifted. The relation between the analyst and the subject of analysis forces a recognition of the interactive and political nature of the research enterprise. This can have a profound effect on what becomes defined as crime, who is defined as criminal, and how processes of social control are created and implemented.

BEYOND CRITIQUE: SOME SUGGESTIONS FOR FUTURE THEORIZING IN CRIMINOLOGY

Based on the analysis above, four key problems must be addressed in any attempt to move beyond critical criminology. These include: (1) the problem of avoiding conflation of micro- and macrosociological levels; (2) the need to develop an approach that assumes neither natural evolution of social relations nor their automatic reproduction; (3) the importance of addressing the relationship between the analyst and the subject of analysis; and (4) the resulting implications that these changes have for rethinking the very nature of criminology and the definition of crime.

A consequence of addressing the problems described above is that rather than focusing primarily on crime and criminals, criminology is better conceived of as the study of governance. By this we mean that crime can no longer be conceptualized apart from the relations of power within which it is defined. These relations include questions of citizenship and rights, and the specific manifestations of power, knowledge, and expertise that reflect regulatory practices and resistance to these practices. The role of the state and the media are central in such a conceptualization since they impact directly on the forms that governance takes in contemporary social formations, including the social control process.

Any attempt to go beyond critical criminology must take seriously both the problems raised within the modern paradigm and those that emerge from the criticisms of feminists, left realists and Foucauldians. Moving beyond critical criminology involves acknowledging the following considerations: crime must be understood as a process that occurs within the context of existing relations of power; power is seen as having structural dimensions (that is, it can have coercive elements to its use); power contains a hegemonic dimension (that is, coercion and consent are variously present in every hegemonic moment and reflect ongoing struggles for power); power needs to be reconceptualized in dynamic rather than static terms, as is reflected in the concept of regulation.

If seen in this way, the historical preoccupation of criminology with crime and criminals is subsumed within the study of criminality. Criminality refers to the process by which those in power exercise this power to define crime and implement various social control practices. In formally organized societies, this is usually associated with having exclusive access to the coercive apparatus of the state, that is, the police and the armed forces. This places criminology squarely within the domain of governance, since it focuses on an important aspect of how hegemony is constituted in specific social formations at particular points in history.

Approaching criminology in terms of governance provides a means of addressing many of the concerns associated with the modern paradigm. To begin with, the concept of hegemony can be used in an analysis of the relationship that exists between leaders and led. The concept of hegemony emphasizes the dynamic nature of this relationship, such that any existing hegemonic arrangement is understood as being inherently transitory and subject to transformation. From the point of view of temporality, the reproduction of any existing hegemonic arrangement cannot be automatically assumed. Rather, hegemony is understood as being constantly reproduced. This provides an opportunity of including in the analysis both the actions of those seeking to maintain hegemony and those resisting or seeking to change it.

Criminology as the study of governance also allows us to better address the problem of conflation. It provides a means of dealing with local or microlevel interactions while recognizing that these take place within an existing structural context. The limiting nature of the social structure is thus noted, including its coercive elements. At the same time, local interactions are not ignored but are given a place within a broader and more textured analysis. Such an analysis might include a focus on the role of ideology or the media in influencing individual behaviour or the actions of the state. It might also examine the way that knowledge as power is generated and applied by different actors in the struggle over maintaining or resisting particular hegemonic arrangements.

If the approach described above were adopted, a "reflexive" voice would be more appropriate than the ironic voice of critical criminology. That is, it must be recognized that criminology is not just a series of statements by an analyst about criminality. Criminology is also a set of messages directed at an audience or audiences. The reflexive voice conveys a stance that reflects the interrelatedness between analyst, subject of analysis, and audience. This acknowledges the important role that expertise plays in the criminological enterprise. It also implies that others are affected by the actions of the analyst and that the analyst, in turn, is affected by the response of the audience.

An additional point follows from this. It is our view that the reflexive voice requires a form of communication that enhances equality, democratic participation, and social responsibility. Adopting a reflexive voice means recognizing that many voices exist and that they have a right to be heard. Moreover, rather than obscuring the political nature of the social control process, the reflexive voice seeks to clarify competing interests and the way power is expressed in any social context. While some modern criminologists have acknowledged the power dimensions of their role as expert, a reflexive voice makes this much more explicit. It highlights the inherent relationship between the criminologist and others who are involved in the research process.

Applying this approach to our own work our model of "managing consent" might be reconceptualized in the Canadian context as "contested governance." For example, governance is reflected in existing jurisdictional frameworks, including both federal-provincial and international relations, and a hegemonic arrangement consisting predominantly of disciplinary and risk-management strategies (O'Malley, 1992). Contested governance becomes a model for understanding the dynamic and competitive framework within which resistance to the existing hegemonic arrangement in Canada is expressed by regions, classes, or individuals. In the process of engaging in resistance, the structures of competition that call out the resistance in the first instance are further elaborated as the struggle over hegemony unfolds. Furthermore, the notion of contested governance allows an analysis of both macro and micro interaction. Thus, it implies that certain groups or individuals are engaged in contesting the existing hegemonic arrangement. This occurs, however, within the broader competitive framework of a late capitalist society. It is both the contesting and the framework within which this occurs that are the focus of our model of contested governance.

SUMMARY

In summary, we have argued in this chapter that critical criminology is the culmination of the modern project, which attempts to locate the origins of crime and harm in persons or social processes. Ironically, by extending this analysis to the broader parameters of structural change, critical criminology reflected the inherent shortcomings of the modern scientific paradigm in which criminology had operated. Critical criminology shared many of the basic assumptions of all modern criminology. The phenomenon it studied was conceptualized as being located in a distinct spatial and temporal location, in which the analyst does not participate. Critical criminology also rejected the more conventional views in which criminality was associated with personal, demographic, or structural pressures. Criminality came to be cast, however, as a residual by-product of the structural dynamics of capitalist society. Critical criminology was unable to cope with both its own internal contradictions and criticisms that change was, indeed, more problematic than a matter of reproduction. It also failed to adequately address the importance of local activity. In the discussion above, we noted how critical criminologists in Canada attempted to modify their analyses to meet many of these challenges and criticisms.

At this juncture, the most basic elements of the criminological enterprise require attention. The legacy of critical criminology has been profound. Its basic agenda has resulted in a consideration of a new series of formulations, which require discipline to be recast. This includes linking our efforts directly to a revised understanding of power, articulating the relation of the analyst to the subject of analysis, and redefining the very nature of crime and criminality. By taking these steps, criminology could be reconceptualized as that set of discourses in which power is generated, mobilized, resisted, and elaborated through expertise concerning harm and governance. The focus on criminology is thus central to and essential for the study of governance and the dynamic processes involved in the creation and maintenance of any particular hegemonic arrangement. This places criminology—and governance more particularly—alongside of class, gender, and ethnicity as central areas of social inquiry.

ENDNOTES

1   There is, however, a peculiarity about theorizing in criminology that must be acknowledged at the outset of this chapter. Much of what passes as criminology does so in the context of the operation of a criminal justice system and includes an emphasis on such "applied" issues as prison administration or forensic science. This work stands in stark contrast to the abstract theorizing about the nature and role of the state characteristic of critical criminology. These two dimensions of the discipline have very little in common beyond a general concern with the same substantive area. There is a consequence to this "dual" nature, however, since a great deal of work in the discipline appears almost atheoretical in its pursuit of descriptive knowledge on particular criminological "topics." The disjuncture between such applied studies and the more abstract and theoretical work in the discipline represents an ongoing concern.

2   Our use of the various voices is an adaptation of an article by White (1973) in which he shows how Foucault's early work is derived, in part, from that of Vico (1968) and Burke (1969). White argues,

> In other words, Foucault does have both a system of explanation and a theory of the transformation of reason, or science, or consciousness, whether he knows it or will admit it or not. Both the system and the theory belong to a tradition of linguistic historicism which goes back to Vico, and beyond him to the linguistic philosophers of the Renaissance, thence to the orators and theoreticians of classical Greece and Rome. What Foucault has done is to rediscover the importance of the projective or generational aspect of language, the extent to which it only "represents" the world of things, but also constitutes the modality of the relationship among things by the very act of assuming a posture before them. It was this aspect of language which got lost when "science" was disengaged from "rhetoric" in the seventeenth century, thereby obscuring to science itself an awareness of its own "poetic" nature (1973, 48–49).

3   Hirschi used the same strategy but shifted the question. He argued that since all people have the potential to violate the law, what needs to be explained is why more people *don't* commit crime. The search for social bonds that lead to conformity formed the basis of his control theory.

4   A note of explanation is required to put this review of Canadian publications in context. The works identified above are not offered as exhaustive or even indicative of the types of Canadian scholarship in criminology and the sociology of law at the time. They do, however, reflect an attempt by a group of Canadian scholars to pull together critical materials and engage with other interested parties in intellectual debate. In the absence of a national forum such as a journal devoted to these topics, these edited volumes represented the only vehicle available for the exchange of ideas and debate in the country. The appearance of the *Canadian Journal of Law and Society* and the *Journal of Human Justice* were attempts to fill this void. The Learned Societies Conference provides an additional if somewhat limited forum for people to discuss and exchange ideas. It is unsatisfactory, however, to the extent that the exchanges must fit a conference format and since the papers are not routinely published. The edited volumes, therefore, played an important role in the development of critical criminology and the sociology of law in Canada.

BIBLIOGRAPHY

Archer, Margaret S. 1988. *Culture and Agency: The Place of Culture in Social Theory.* Cambridge: Cambridge University Press.

Bandura, Albert. 1979. "The Social Learning Perspective: Mechanisms of Aggression." In *Psychology of Crime and Criminal Justice*, ed. by H. Toch. New York: Holt, Rinehart and Winston.

Bartholomew, Amy, and **Susan Boyd.** 1989. "Toward a Political Economy of Law." In *The New Canadian Political Economy*, ed. by W. Clement and G. Williams. Kingston, Montreal, London: McGill-Queen's University Press.

Beccaria, Cesare. [1764] 1963. *On Crimes and Punishment.* Translated by Henry Pablucci. Indianapolis: Bobbs-Merrill.

Becker, Howard S. 1963. *Outsiders: Studies in the Sociology of Deviance.* New York: Free Press.

Bentham, Jeremy. 1775. "Principles of Law." In *The Works of Jeremy Bentham*, Vol. I, ed. by J. Browning. New York: Russell and Russell.

Benton, Ted. 1977. *Philosophical Foundations of the Three Sociologies.* London: Routledge & Kegan Paul.

Boyd, Neil, ed. 1986. *The Social Dimensions of Law.* Scarborough: Prentice Hall.

Boyd, Susan B., and **Elizabeth A. Sheehy.** 1989. "Feminism and the Law in Canada: Overview." In *Law and Society: A Critical Perspective*, ed. by T. Caputo, et al. Toronto: Harcourt Brace Jovanovich.

Brickey, Stephen L., and **Elizabeth Comack,** eds. 1986. *The Social Basis of Law.* Toronto: Garamond Press.

Burke, Kenneth. 1969. *A Grammar of Motives.* Berkeley and Los Angeles: The Free Press.

Cain, Maureen. 1990. "Towards Transgression: New Directions in Feminist Criminology," *The International Journal of the Sociology of Law*, 18: 1–18.

Chambliss, William, and **Robert Seidman.** 1971. *Law, Order and Power.* Reading, Mass.: Addison-Wesley Publishing Company.

Cloward, Richard, and **Lloyd Ohlin.** 1960. *Delinquency and Opportunity.* Glencoe, Ill.: Free Press.

Cohen, Stanley. 1988. *Against Criminology.* New Brunswick, NJ: Transaction Books.

———. 1985. *Visions of Social Control: Crime, Punishment and Classification.* Cambridge: Polity Press.

Comack, Elizabeth. 1987. "Theorizing the Canadian State and Social Formation." In *State Control,* ed. by R. S. Ratner and J. L. McMullan, 225–242. Vancouver: University of British Columbia Press.

————. 1986. "'We'll get some good out of this riot yet': The Canadian State, Drug Legislation and Class Conflict." In *The Social Basis of Law*, ed. by S. Brickey and E. Comack. Toronto: Garamond Press.

Currie, Dawn H., and **M. Kline.** 1991. "Challenging Privilege: Women, Knowledge, and Feminist Struggles," *Journal of Human Justice*, 2(2): 1–37.

Daly, Kathleen, and **Meda Chesney-Lind.** 1988. "Feminism and Criminology," *Justice Quarterly*, 5: 4, 498–538.

Fleming, Thomas, ed. 1985. *The New Criminologies in Canada*. Toronto: Oxford University Press.

Foucault, Michel. 1991. "On Governmentality." In *The Foucault Effect: Studies in Governmental Rationality*, ed. by Colin Gordon. Hemel Hempstead: Harvester Wheatsheaf.

————. 1980. *Power/Knowledge: Selected Interviews and Other Writings, 1972–77*. Ed. Colin Gordon. Trans. Colin Gordon, Leo Marshall, John Mepham, Kate Soper. Hemel Hempstead: The Harvester Press.

————. 1977. *Discipline and Punish: The Birth of the Prison*. Trans. Alan Sheridan. New York: Vintage Books.

Goffman, Erving. 1963. *Stigma*. Englewood Cliffs, NJ: Prentice Hall.

Goff, Colin H., and **Charles Reasons.** 1978. *Corporate Crime in Canada: A Critical Analysis of Anti-Combines Legislation*. Scarborough: Prentice Hall.

Gordon, Colin. 1991. *The Foucault Effect: Studies in Governmental Rationality*. Hemel Hempstead: Harvester Wheatsheaf.

Gramsci, Antonio. 1971. *Selections from the Prison Notebooks of Antonio Gramsci*. Ed., trans. Q. Hoare and G. N. Smith. London: Lawrence and Wishart.

Greenaway, William, and **Stephen Brickey,** eds. 1978. *Law and Social Control in Canada*. Scarborough: Prentice Hall.

Gusfield, Joseph. 1955. *Symbolic Crusade: Status Politics and the American Temperance Movement*. Urbana: University of Illinois.

Hall, Stuart, et al. 1978. *Policing the Crisis: Mugging, the State, and Law and Order*. London: Macmillan.

Hatt, Ken, Tullio Caputo, and **Barbara Perry.** 1992. "Criminal Justice Policy Under Mulroney: Neo-Conservatism, Eh?" *Canadian Public Policy/Analyse de Politiques*, 18(3): 245–260.

————. 1990. "Managing Consent: Canada's Experience with Neo-Conservatism," *Social Justice*, 17(4): 30–48.

Havemann, Paul. 1986. "Marketing the New Establishment Ideology in Canada," *Crime and Social Justice*, 26: 11–37.

Keat, Russell, and **John Urry.**   1975. *Social Theory as Science.* London: Routledge & Kegan Paul.

Kinsey, Roger, John Lea, and **Jock Young.**   1986. *Losing the Fight Against Crime.* Oxford: Basil Blackwell.

Lea, John, and **Jock Young.**   1984. *What Is to Be Done About Law and Order?* Harmondsworth: Penguin.

Lemert, Edwin.   1972. *Human Deviance, Social Problems and Social Control.* Englewood Cliffs, NJ: Prentice Hall.

———.   1951. *Social Pathology.* New York: McGraw-Hill.

Lombroso, Cesare.   1912. *Crime: Its Causes and Remedies.* Boston: Little, Brown and Company.

———.   1876. *L'Uomo delinquente.* Milan.

Lowman, John, and **Brian D. MacLean,** eds.   1992. *Realist Criminology: Crime Control and Policing in the 1990's.* Toronto: University of Toronto Press.

MacLean, Brian D., ed.   1986. *The Political Economy of Crime: Readings for a Critical Criminology.* Scarborough: Prentice Hall.

Martinson, R. M.   1974. "What Works? Questions and Answers About Prison Reform," *Public Interest,* 35: 22–54.

Matthews, Roger.   1987. "Taking Realist Criminology Seriously," *Contemporary Crises,* 11: 371–401.

Matza, David.   1969. *Becoming Delinquent.* Englewood Cliffs, NJ: Prentice Hall.

Merton, Robert K.   1938. "Social Structure and Anomie," *American Sociological Review,* 3(October): 672–682.

O'Connor, James.   1973. *The Fiscal Crisis of the State.* New York: St. Martin's Press.

O'Malley, Pat.   1992. "Risk, Power and Crime Prevention," *Economy and Society,* 21(3): 252–275.

———.   1988. "The Purpose of Knowledge: Pragmatism and the Praxis of Marxist Criminology," *Contemporary Crisis,* 12: 65–79.

———.   1983. "Marxist Theory and Marxist Criminology," *Crime and Social Justice,* 29: 70–87.

Palmer, Jerry, and **Frank Pearce.**   1983. "Legal Discourse and State Power: Foucault and the Juridical Relation," *International Journal of the Sociology of Law,* 11: 361–383.

Phillipson, Coleman.   1970. *Three Criminal Law Reformers.* Montclair, NJ: Patterson Smith Publishers.

Poulantzas, N.   1973. *Political Power and Social Classes.* London: New Left Books.

Quinney, Richard. 1977. *Class, State and Crime: On the Theory and Practice of Criminal Justice*. New York: David McKay.

———. 1973. *Critique of Legal Order*. Boston: Little, Brown.

———. 1970. *The Social Reality of Crime*. Boston: Little, Brown.

Ratner, R. S. 1985. "Inside the Liberal Boot." In *The New Criminologies in Canada*, ed. T. Fleming. Toronto: Oxford University Press.

Ratner, Robert S., and **John L. McMullan.** 1987. *State Control: Criminal Justice Politics in Canada*. Vancouver: University of British Columbia Press.

———. 1985. "Social Control and the Rise of the 'Exceptional' State in Britain, the United States, and Canada." In *The New Criminologies in Canada: State, Crime and Control*, ed. T. Fleming. Toronto: Oxford University Press.

Reasons, Charles, and **Robert Rich.** 1979. *Law and Society*. Toronto: Butterworths.

Schwendinger, Hermann, and **Julia Schwendinger.** 1976. "Social Class and the Definitions of Crime," *Crime and Social Justice, Issues in Criminology*, 7: 4–13.

Schur, Edwin M. 1972. *Labeling Deviant Behavior*. New York: Harper and Row.

Scull, Andrew. 1977. *Decarceration: Community-based Treatment and the Deviant: A Radical Review*. Englewood Cliffs, NJ: Prentice Hall.

Shaw, Clifford, and **Henry McKay.** 1942. *Juvenile Delinquency and Urban Areas*. Chicago: University of Chicago Press.

———. 1939. *Social Factors in Juvenile Delinquency*. Washington: US Government Printing Office.

Smandych, Russell. 1985. "Marxism and the Creation of Law: Re-examining the Origins of Canadian Anti-Combines Legislation, 1890–1910." In *The New Criminologies in Canada: Crime, State and Control*, ed. T. Fleming, 87–99. Toronto: Oxford University Press.

Smart. C. 1989. *Feminism and the Power of Law*. London: Routledge.

Smiley, Donald. 1988. "An Outsider's Observations on Federal-Provincial Relations Among Consenting Adults." In *Perspectives on Canadian Federalism*, ed. R. D. Olling and M. W. Westamacott, 279–284. Scarborough: Prentice Hall.

———. 1987. *The Federal Condition in Canada*. Toronto: McGraw-Hill Ryerson.

Smith, D. 1987. *The Everyday World as Problematic: A Feminist Sociology*. Toronto: University of Toronto Press.

Snider, Laureen. 1979. "Revising the Combines Investigation Act: A Study in Corporate Power." In *Structure, Law, and Power: Essays in the Sociology of Law*, edited by P. Brantingham and J. Kress. Beverly Hills: Sage.

Spitzer, Stephen. 1975. "Toward a Marxian Theory of Deviance," *Social Problems*, 22: 638–651.

Sutherland, Edwin H. 1939. *The Principles of Criminology.* 3d ed. Philadelphia: Lippincott.

Taylor, Ian. 1987. "Theorizing the Crisis in Canada." In *State Control,* ed. R. S. Ratner and J. L. McMullan, 198–224. Vancouver: University of British Columbia Press.

———. 1985. "Criminology, the Unemployment Crisis and the Liberal Tradition in Canada." In *The New Criminology in Canada,* ed. T. Fleming. Toronto: Oxford University Press.

———. 1983. *Crime, Capitalism and Community.* Toronto: Butterworths.

———. 1982. *Law and Order: Arguments For Socialism.* London: Macmillan.

Taylor, Ian, Paul Walton, and **Jock Young.** 1973. *The New Criminology.* London: Routledge and Kegan Paul.

Vico, Giambattista. 1968. *The New Science.* Trans. Thomas A. Bergin and Max H. Fisch. Ithaca.

White, Hayden V. 1973. "Foucault Decoded: Notes From Underground," *History and Theory: Studies in the Philosophy of History,* 12: 23–54.

Young, J. 1987. "The Tasks Facing a Realist Criminology," *Contemporary Crises,* 11: 337–356.